American Folk Gospel

Logoi,
Witness Accounts of the Life of Jesus
and
Fundamental Devotional

THOMAS E. Q. WILLIAMS, EDITOR

Available at

Coiny Publishing Co.,
P.O. Box 585
Greenfield, IN 46140
317-462-7758

To S. S. and D. M. this book is dedicated

American Folk Gospel

Copyright, 1999, Thomas E. Q. Williams
Library of Congress Catalogue No. 97-091856
ISBN: 1-887495-08-8

With Thanks to

The Institute For New Testament Textual Research,
Munster/Westphalia,

and

The United Bible Societies
for *The Greek New Testament* used in Translation

and

The Gladys Hunt collection of Americana Miscelleny

Design and Composition by
Richard Lee Doll

Printed by
Thomson-Shore

iii

Table of Contents

iv

WITNESS ACCOUNTS OF THE LIFE OF JESUS
COINY GREEK TO HUMBLE AMERICAN TRANSLATION

FUNDAMENTAL DEVOTIONAL

Song Of Jesus

Keep this thought about Jesus in you which comes from God:
    He was possessed of the form of God.
    He did not resort to robbery to become equal to God.
    He emptied himself and took the form of a slave,
        Becoming in every likeness as a person.
    We discovered him in this form as a person.
    He humbled himself to become obedient even to death,
        Death on a cross.
Because of this, God raised him to the highest place
And elevated his status more than all others
So that before the presence of Jesus every knee should bow
And every tongue confess that Jesus, God come to earth,
is our Familyhead fully attending God the Parent.

Abraham Lincoln:

The American Patriarch's Creed

(*Compiled from Lincolnalia by William E. Barton*)

I believe in penitential and pious sentiments, in devotional designs and purpose, in homages and confessions, in supplications to the Almighty, solemnly, earnestly, reverently.

I believe in blessings and comfort from the Parent of Mercies to the sick, the wounded, the prisoners, and to the orphans and widows.

I believe it pleases Almighty God to prolong our national life, defending us with guardian care.

I believe in God's eternal truth and justice.

I believe the will of God prevails. Without God all human reliance is vain. Without the assistance of that Divine Being I cannot succeed. With that assistance I cannot fail.

I believe I am a humble instrument in the hands of our Heavenly Parent. I desire all my works and acts may be according to God's will and that it may be so, I give thanks to the Almighty and seek God's aid.

I believe in praise to Almighty God, the beneficent Creator and Ruler of the Universe.

* * * * *

Peter   Paul

Logoi

Stories, Songs, and Miscellany

with

Folklore, History and

Personal Example

* * * * *

(Star Illustration)

Christmas Story

Once God was so tired God couldn't sleep a wink.

Finally, God thought to God's self, I guess I will just read a little bit from the book of life.

But it was late at night, so late they wasn't a single light on.

So God reached into the creation bag God always kept around for emergencies.

Then God pulled out lots of stars to get one for a reading light. There was big ones and little ones, glaring ones and soft ones.

God couldn't decide which one would make the best reading light so God scattered them all over the sky. Then God tried reading under this one and that one.

Only one problem.

Since they was so many of them scattered across the sky, they made God feel even worse, kind of lonely really.

So God thought to God's self.

I guess I will create some to share these reading lights.

And while God was at it, God thought to create some to share the reading of the book of life.

So God created the earth for these "somes" to live on.

Then God created plants, but they wouldn't listen to the story God was reading in the starlight. In fact they wilted until God had to create the sun for them to grow better in.

The sunlight turned out to be better for the earth too.

But God still didn't have any one to like the story God wanted to tell out of the book of life.

Try as they did, the plants just couldn't pay attention to the story God was telling them. All they could do was grow and bloom flowers and smell as good as they could for God.

God was still very very lonely.

God decided to create some with ears.

God pulled animals out of the creation bag.

They had ears and could listen except they couldn't understand nothing. They just wanted to run around on the earth and dance with joy at having God pay attention to them.

Finally, God looked in a mirror.

Maybe I won't be so lonely if I create some that look like me, God thought.

So God reached clear to the bottom of the creation bag and pulled out a heart and a brain and bones and eyes and teeth and fingers and toes and skin and blood and put them all together with other stuff and stuck them on the earth.

The first one was Adam and them came Eve to even out how people were supposed to live, in pairs.

And then God started reading the book of life to them.

And as God read, time went on and on. The sun came up and went down.

People was having children and spreading out on the earth and God was having trouble reading to so many.

God decided to single out one to read to, Abraham.

Abraham listened and asked questions for the first time.

What do you want us people to do? Abraham asked.

God took a break from story reading and thought about it.

God liked having some to listen to the story God was telling, but God never thought what people would do with it other than listen.

So Abraham and God talked person to creator and figured out maybe people should bond more.

God put the book of life down and said, From now on this story of life won't come from any book. It will come from how you and your children and I get along.

So God and people become a living story with characters and interacting plots with God working in the story lines and the like.

Then God really couldn't sleep.

God counted the sun coming up and down like sheep jumping over a fence, and even the stars telling God it's nighttime agin couldn't stop God from staying up and worrying.

After all these people looked like God's baby pictures.

These people was God's self.

The people was worrying themselves. They knew they was going to die.

They knew the next minute could bring disaster.

They didn't know what they was doing was worthwhile.

God figured there was only one thing to do.

Give people a Christmas present.

Only one present would do.

God would give people God's self.

So God got born among people just the way they did.

Shepherds came from the hills to see God coming down to earth like a star falling when the little one was born. Mary was chose to be the little one's mother and she called the little one Jesus.

God brought the book of life down when God come too, so as to be able to remember to tell people everything they needed to know to live right.

God liked being able to tell the stories in person without having to send the stories through the prrophets that come before.

God could just sit beside the sea, or on boats, or on mountains and call people and here they would come to there in big crowds or sometimes in little groups that learned to like being together so much that later they kept wanting to be together enough for churches to start up all over the world. That came after some of the rest of the story I'm telling.

When God was born, like I said, God told people to love each other and especially to care for the ones they was closest to. That way love could spread out like a wave.

The thing was being taken to and people was learning to be called a new breed, Hoosiers.

It turned out some jelling was needed.

And still what was happening wasn't enough.

God needed to show this new bunch of story listeners that what they was going through wasn't the end of the stories they had been listening to.

God wanted people to see for themselves that death wasn't final, that fate wasn't in charge, that meaning comes in relationship to the stories God was telling.

So God let people do their worst. God let people loose to do their laughing, to do their whipping, to hang their only storyteller from a cross.

Now you think what kind of a Christmas present did God give us Hoosiers?

God died, right? God died on a cross centuries ago? right?

Well, did the stars die? Did the sun die? What about the plants, aren't they still agrowing? And don't animals still run around on the face of the earth? And how about these people, don't they still look like God?

Yes, God still lives too.

That's the point of God's story from the book of life.

God has turned all of us into Abrahams to be specially bonded to.

Our lives are God's and to be lived for God and with God too.

And God has even helped us to know the story by coming to earth to make sure we understood it.

It is so we can live in God's life as God's children.

So Hoosiers got a Christmas present that come long ago but still is being given.

It breaks into our lives not just Christmas but every day, streaking across our days like lightning and rolling through our minds like thunder.

It's the fact that God is with us still, telling us this God of ours loves us since we are God's. We even look so good to God that God sees in us a family resemblance no matter what we see in a mirror.

God whispers for us to love each other too, in every silent wind or hurricane that enters our lives.

And God gives us the promise that one day another shooting star will come down to earth, to set things up for an even better story to come some future Christmas, where any tears we've not been able to control, even knowing what we do, will get wiped away.

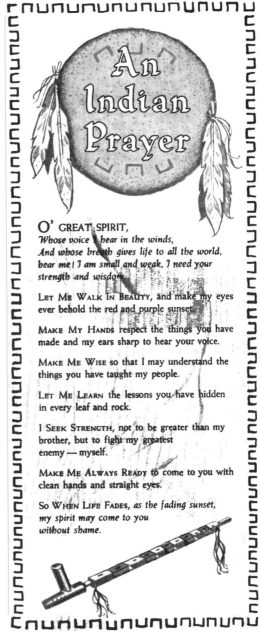

An Indian Prayer

O' GREAT SPIRIT,
Whose voice I hear in the winds,
And whose breath gives life to all the world,
hear me! I am small and weak, I need your
strength and wisdom.

LET ME WALK IN BEAUTY, and make my eyes
ever behold the red and purple sunset.

MAKE MY HANDS respect the things you have
made and my ears sharp to hear your voice.

MAKE ME WISE so that I may understand the
things you have taught my people.

LET ME LEARN the lessons you have hidden
in every leaf and rock.

I SEEK STRENGTH, not to be greater than my
brother, but to fight my greatest
enemy — myself.

MAKE ME ALWAYS READY to come to you with
clean hands and straight eyes.

So WHEN LIFE FADES, *as the fading sunset,*
my spirit may come to you
without shame.

After Josephus and Septuaginta

Moses and the Ten Commandments

For four hundred years the Jews were left in Egypt as slaves. Their lives were lived in great affliction. This causes great sadness to God.

Nevertheless, the slaves grew in numbers in Egypt.

It is not surprising that God come to listen to their cries for an emancipator. This was Moses.

Among their other vices the Egyptians failed to worship God. They did, how-ever, listen to their own religious scribes. One of them was very popular with the rulers. He predicted the future. He said a child would be born to the slaves who, if he was allowed to grow up, would overthrow the Egyptian dominion and would raise the Jews from slavery. He described this slave-child as one who would excel all men in virtue, and obtain a glory that would be remembered through all ages. This frightened the Egyptian king. The king believed this scribe with all his heart.

That's why this ruler commanded that from then on all male slave children should be seized and cast in the river to drown. If any parents should try to save their male children alive, they and their families was to be executed.

If God chooses that a people be emancipated from slavery can any earthly force thwart this result? Does any holocaust against a race work?

No one nor no people can withstand the purposes of God though thousands or millions of plans be conceived to do so. Let some mad person try to figure. God will out-figure.

One of the slaves named Amram feared most the plan of the Egyptian king to destroy the Jews. All the slaves knew without young men, the slaves would die out. Amram was personally afraid too because his wife was pregnant. What if he was to be the father of a son?

Amran believed in God. In a prayer, he asked God to have compassion on the enslaved people for the slaves respected and worshipped God. Their problem was an emanicpator was needed.

God listened to Amram's prayer and was moved to help. God stood by him in his sleep and whispered to him not to despair. God said he would not forget any enslaved people - never - and would always grant comfort. Then God reminded Amram God brought Abraham out of Mesopotamia into Canaan and give Abraham's barren wife not just one but many children there. God also reminded Amram that Israel was given to the Jews for occupation until the end of the world and suggested they return led by his son. This son would be famous while the memory of the world lasts.

When Amram awoke, he told his wife Jochebed about the vision. Both decided to risk the king's orders to kill Jewish male children and the parents who shielded them. They was goin to keep their child no matter what. Although the Egyptians watched all slave women to see if they was close to childbearing - to know to get their male children to kill, none of the Egyptians detected the pregnancy of Jochebed and her child was born so easy and without pain that her delivery was not observed. Her male child was born safe.

And so Moses - though unnamed just then - was born. The father and mother concealed the child at home for three months on fear of their lives. Then Amran grew too fearful of discovery and decided he must leave the future care of his child to the will of God alone.

He made an ark of bulrushes looking like a cradle and sufficient for his child to be laid in without over- restraint. Then he daubed it over with slime to keep out the water from entering between the bulrushes and put the infant into it. The father and mother set the ark of bulrushes afloat upon the river and left its preservation to God alone.

The river received the child and carried him along. The progress of the ark downriver was watched by Miriam, the child's sister. She walked along the bank as the ark floated away, as her mother bid her, to see where the ark got to.

Down the river was Thermuthis, the Egyptian king's daughter. She was having fun with her attendants. When she saw a cradle carried along by the current, she sent one of her attendants who could swim to fetch the ark and bring it to her.

It was love at first sight. Thermuthis picked up the baby and knew at once she would devote all of her love for him. The baby was a large child and very handsome. God provided the child to be physically strong and good looking.

When the baby started crying, Thermuthis tried to find a nurse to feed the child. One by one she commanded nursing women to be brought to offer their breasts to the child. The child turned away from all of them and refused to be breast fed by any of them.

Miriam was close by when these events happened. She pretended to be there accidentally. When the child refused to be nursed, Miriam said, "It won't work, Queen, to try to have these women nourish the child. They are not Jews. This child is a Jew. I am a Jew too. Would you like me to find a Jewish woman to breastfeed this child?" Thermuthis thought her idea was a good one and had her go find a woman to nurse the child. Naturally, Miriam went to find the child's mother although the king's daughter did not know it. This way, the child was nursed by his mother.

Here is how the child was named. His Egyptian adoptive mother give him the name Moses when he was taken from the river. The Egyptians call water by the name of "Mo", and a saved drowning victim is called by the name of "Uses." Thermuthis put these two words together. Thermuthis adopted Moses as her son and had him educated with great care. It did not matter that Thermuthis knew Moses was a Jewish boy. She protected him from her father and everybody else. Moses grew to the age of maturity. Love never belongs only to one folk.

Moses came to great fame in Egypt when he was still young. This happened when Egypt suffered a great invasion by the Ethiopians. These people are next neighbors to the Egyptians up river. At first the Ethiopians made inroads into Egypt and won all of the early battles over the Egyptians. The invaders drove toward Memphis where the rule lived. About then the king consulted his sacred scribes. God told them that Moses must be the general if Egypt was to survive. The king commanded his daughter to bring Moses to him and give him the command of the Egyptian army. Only then did the Egyptian troops taste victory. Eventually, Moses drove the Ethiopians back to their own country. In fact he was on the verge of capturing the Ethiopian capital city when the daughter of the Ethiopian king saw Moses from a wall and fell in love with him. She risked her life to arrange a truce between her people and Moses. The surrender she negotiated saved the Ethiopian city and also permitted her to marry Moses.

The Egyptians began to fear Moses after his victory over the Ethiopians. They forgot how they had turned to him to save their country. Instead they come to fear that Moses would lead an insurrection by the slaves and overthrow the Egyptians so they would have to do their own work.

The Egyptians insisted Moses be killed. The king was convinced to do this.

When Moses learned of his danger, he quickly escaped Egypt and took flight through the deserts and where his enemies could not suspect he would dare travel. He had no food to eat and no water to drink, but he drove on until he came to Midian, a city on the Red Sea. There he set upon a well and rested. The time was around noon.

The land of Midian did not have many wells or water of any kind. The wells were very important to the shepherds of the area. Among those who herded flocks were the seven daughters of a priest, Raguel who was also called Jethro. While Moses rested, the seven daughters come to the well, drew water for their sheep and placed the water in troughs. Before their herds could drink, along came other shepherds who were in the process of appropriating the girls' water when Moses intervened and drove them off. The girls told their father how Moses had helped them. The father rewarded Moses by making him his son and giving him one of his daughters to marry. Then he placed Moses in charge of his cattle which was a great mark of honor since cattle in those days constituted wealth.

Later, Moses fed his flocks at Mount Sinai. Moses was daring to do this since the folk of the place thought God lived on Mount Sinai. Here Moses observed a burning thorn bush that puzzled him full. The green leaves and the flowers was not consumed. Nor were the fruit branches despite the great leap of the flames. Moses was scared and even more so when the bush spoke to him by name. The voice told Moses not to venture too close. Then the voice spoke the most important words. Moses was commanded to return to Egypt to become the commander of the slaves against the rule of the oppressors and to deliver the slaves from the Egyptians. God said the Jews must go to inhabit the land given to Abraham but when he was taking the slaves out, Moses was to stop back at Mount Sinai to offer thanksgivings.

Moses was reluctant but God persuaded him to be courageous because God would be with him. As a sign, God had Moses drop his rod to the ground which become a snake for a time. Then God had Moses put his hand into his shirt and when Moses took it out it was chalky white before looking fleshy again. Then God commanded Moses throw water on the ground which turned into blood. Seeing these signs, Moses went to Egypt to emancipate the Jews from slavery. How could he disbelieve that God was with him?

Moses asked God what his name was and God told him, "YHWH - Jehovah. I am who I am and I will be who I will be." No one knew God's name before this.

Moses picked up the news that the king of Egypt who ordered him killed was dead. After Moses obtained Jethro's assent to go to Egypt to free his slave people, Moses left with his wife Zipporah and children Gersom and Eleazer. At the border, Moses's brother Aaron was waiting for him. Then Jewish leaders come to him and Moses performed the special signs that God gave Moses to have to convince them God was behind him. Moses searched their hearts. Yes, the slaves really wanted freed. Liberty was in their hearts.

Moses went to the new king of Egypt and demanded that the slaves be set free. Moses reminded the king of his service as commander of the Egyptian troops in the Ethiopian War and also told him what God told him at Mount Sinai. Moses warned the king not to disbelieve God nor oppose God's purpose.

The king did not listen. He called Moses a runaway slave so he was there illegal and said his signs was just tricks. The king called his priests in and told Moses his own priests could do the same signs that Moses could. The king's priests threw their rods down and they turned into snakes just as Moses's did. Then Moses threw his rod down on the floor. Moses's rod become a snake which one by one devoured the Egyptian snakes from the priests' rods and then returned to being a rod in Moses's hands. This only made the king more angry yet. He refused to free the Jews from slavery and committed worse atrocities against them. Now, the king ordered the slaves must make bricks with chaff they gathered themselves at night. This meant that the slaves must work both by day to make bricks and by night to gather the chaff for the brick-making. The slaves blamed Moses for their double labor. Moses kept up his courage and did get the king to allow the slave people to go with him to Mount Sinai to sacrifice to God.

When the Egyptian king would not free the slaves, God caused them to suffer great plagues. These plagues was great liberation strokes from the hand of God. They need to be repeated for the good of humanity so that God's power can become known. God's anger can be very great and it is a serious matter to provoke God. God is always on the side of oppressed people and frees all those who are set in bondage.

God turned the river of Egypt into a bloody color. As the Egyptians drank it they suffered pain and torment. But when the slaves drank it, the river water was sweet and fit as usual. When this happened, the king told Moses the slaves could leave Egypt. After the plague ceased, the king took back his word and would not let the slaves go.

This treachery by the king of Egypt caused God to send another plague. This time a multitude of frogs descended on Egypt. They ate everything that grew in the fields and filled the river. The river water was spoiled and killed the animals that drank from it. The country was filled with frog slime and the frogs invaded the homes in the land. They were found in the food of the homes and went in great numbers onto beds. Again, the king called in Moses and told him the slaves could leave Egypt. As soon as the plague stopped, the king changed his mind.

So God sent a plague of lice upon Egypt. Now the bodies of the Egyptians were crawling with lice. Many died. The lice could not be controlled with washing or ointments. Again the king told Moses the slaves could leave. Again the plague stopped.

After the lice plague was over, the king called in Moses to tell him he had another condition to his promise to allow the slaves to go to Mount Sinai. Yes, he would permit Jewish women and children to go, but the slaves must leave behind their cattle as sureties to return. Moses told the king this condition was unjust since the slaves needed their cattle for sacrifices at Mount Sinai. As this stalemate continued God caused a thick darkness to descend on Egypt. This darkness spread itself over the Egyptians obstructing their breathing and killing many from the very thickness of the air.

The sight of all the misery bothered Moses. He went to the king to ask, "How long will you be disobedient to the commands of God? God wants slaves freed! You will continue to suffer calamity until you do so!" Then Moses left the king's presence.

God prepared another liberation stroke against the Egyptians. God told Moses to have the Jews prepare for this one. God ordered the destruction of the oldest child of each family which did not sacrifice as God ordered. The slaves sacrificed as Moses told them to do. The homes of the slaves were marked against this plague with sacrificial blood spread with bunches of hyssop. The meat of the sacrificial animals was burnt. The plague passed over the slaves who Moses gathered together by tribes in preparation for departure.

This event was one still remembered. It is called Pascha or the "Feast of the Passover." It was a time of great sadness in Egypt for during the period from the tenth of the month Xanthicus to the fourteenth, God give the slaves to ready themselves for release from slavery.

Now again, the king told Moses the slaves could leave Egypt. This time the Egyptians were convinced they must permit the slaves to leave without conditions. Many Egyptians hated to see the slaves go out of affectionate ties for them. Some sent departure gifts out of friendship. Others merely wanted them to leave quickly so that nothing else happened.

The slaves left in great haste. Moses led them toward the Red Sea at a place called Baalzephon. It was their third day out of Egypt and the slaves had no food from the land. To prepare for the rest of the trip, they baked loaves of kneaded flour warmed only by the gentle heat of the day and made use of this bread for the next thirty days. In memory of this event, a "Feast of Unleavened Bread" became an annual feast day. The adults in the assembly numbered six hundred thousand.

The time of this event was four hundred thirty years after Abraham was given Canaan as a place of residence. It was in the Egyptian month of Xanthicus on the

The Lamb

Little Lamb, who made thee?
Dost thou know who made thee?
Gave thee life and bade thee feed
By the stream and o'er the mead;
Gave thee clothing of delight,
Softest clothing, woolly, bright;
Gave thee such a tender voice,
Making all the vales rejoice:
   Little Lamb, who made thee?
   Dost thou know who made thee?

Little Lamb, I'll tell thee!
Little Lamb, I'll tell thee.
He is called by thy name,
For He calls Himself a Lamb:—
He is meek, and He is mild;
He became a little child:
I, a child, and thou, a lamb,
We are called by His name.
   Little Lamb, God bless thee;
   Little Lamb, God bless thee.

—WILLIAM BLAKE

fifteenth day of the lunar month. The slaves took with them the bones of Joseph for reburial in the promised land.

The king of Egypt took stock. He feared he had liberated the slaves of his land only because of tricks by Moses. He sent his troops to fetch the slaves back into Egypt. The Egyptian army took up its arms prepared for an easy victory. The slaves were unarmed and thought to be weak from their journey up to that time. So the pursuit of the slaves began. The Egyptians committed six hundred chariots, fifty thousand horsemen and two hundred thousand footmen, all armed, to this enterprise.

The route of the Egyptian army did not prove to be an easy one. Moses led the slaves across deserts and not along the roads travelled by traders with the Philistines. Moses did this not only to avoid conflict with Philistines who hated the slaves but also so that the slaves might go to Mount Sinai as God required.

When the slaves heard this force was soon to come upon them, they were very frightened. Not only were they short of food, but now they expected to be destroyed. They challenged the leadership of Moses. Moses merely continued to trust God. Moses gathered together the slaves and told them they should not distrust him nor God and "Never to despair of the providence of God by whose power all the liberation strokes were performed and who was committed to free them from slavery." He added, "Depend upon God as your Protector since God is able to make small things great and to show that this mighty force against you is nothing but weakness. Do not be frightened of the Egyptian army. You will be preserved. The mountains behind us, if God so chooses, may be made plane ground and the sea become dry land."

After saying this, Moses led the slaves to the shores of the Red Sea while the Egyptian army looked on. Moses raised his rod and prayed to God to give assistance. Moses said, "O Familyhead. It is beyond human strength and human effort to avoid the difficulties we face. It must be your work to deliver us slaves who left Egypt with your help. We have recourse only to the hope we have in you. Let your power come quickly and empower us and give us slaves to overcome depression about our situation. We are helpless. We stand before a sea. Nevertheless this sea is yours and we pray you to open it."

Then Moses touched the sea with his rod. The sea parted into two great watery banks with a dry road in between. Moses was the first to enter this road and then the slaves followed him on into the parted sea.

When the Egyptian army first saw this, they believed the slaves were committing mass suicide. Then they observed the parting of the sea and decided to pursue the slaves down this strange road. The slaves were reaching safety on the other side of the Red Sea when the sea closed on the Egyptian army pursuing them. God made this road only for the slaves and not for those who pursued them. Not only was the pursuit a disaster for the Egyptian army but also those remaining behind were encompassed within a great storm and thunderbolts darted among them so that not one survivor remained to return to tell the Egyptian king of the woe.

Now the slaves were on the other side of the sea in a great desert without much food. There they were - slaves wandering in this state for two years. Water was a terrible problem. During their first days of wandering they came upon a place called Marah. A well was there but its water was so bitter not even the cattle could drink it. It was unfit for people. Moses prayed to God to make the water fit to drink and God answered. Moses directed the slaves to withdraw most of the water and then the rest was so agitated and purified as to be fit.

They next wandered toward a place appearing to have many palm trees, a place called Elim. When the slaves arrived closer, they found the place very parched and the trees were twisted and creeping for lack of water. There were only moist places and no springs. Now the slaves were free thirty days but they were so weary and filled with want that the deliverance seemed like a hated thing. Moses felt the anger of the slaves grow towards him. It was necessary for Moses to address them and remind them of what they had been through to avoid stoning. Moses kept his courage and reminded the slaves that they should not despair of providence. Then Moses went to a high place and prayed. The prayer was answered. God promised Moses God would take care of them.

After Moses came down from the place of prayer, Moses gathered the slaves together and told them the good news. Not much later, a vast number of quails flew overhead hovered over them. These quails then were so weary of light that they fell down upon the slaves who caught them and satisfied their hunger with this great supply.

Almost as quickly a second gift was provided. As Moses lifted his hands in prayer, a dew fell down. The dew stuck to the hands of Moses and Moses immediately concluded it was another blessing. Moses tasted it and the substance tasted like honey. The slaves took to gathering it. They called it manna which signifies "What is it?"

Now the slaves came to Rephidim close to death from thirst. Now again the slaves turned against Moses. After Moses avoided their fury, he went to pray again. God promised the slaves a fountain and God did not long delay. God commanded Moses to strike a rock nearby with his rod and from this rock gushed a mighty stream of water. Now the slaves drank their fills and had renewed faith that Moses was chosen by God.

Soon the news spread that a new multitude of people were in the area. This caused the native peoples to conspire, especially the warlike Amalekites. They decided to crush and destroy the slaves before they took permanent residence somewhere and gained prosperity at the expense of the native peoples. Moses did not anticipate war.

When war was inevitable, Moses sorted out the young men and placed them under Joshua, the son of Nun, of the tribe of Ephraim. Others were detailed to guard the watering places, the women and the children and the camp itself. Then Moses committed the army of the slaves to God and retired in prayer to a high place.

The battle was joined. Moses stretched out his hands towards heaven for help and as he did so the slave army prevailed but when Moses could not hold his hands stretched out to heaven and let his hands down the enemy Amalekites prevailed. Moses noticed this and begged his brother Aaron and another man, Hur, their sister Miriam's husband, to stand on either side to hold his hands high and not permit weariness to cause him to drop his hands. When this was done the slave army conquered the main force of the Amalekites. The battle was a signal victory for the slaves. The victory also resulted in booty. Moses constructed an altar at the site which he named "To the Familyhead the Conqueror."

Now the slaves arrived at Mount Sinai. Moses told them he was going from them up Mount Sinai to converse with God and to receive from God and bring back with him God's instructions to the slaves.

Upon his return, Moses joyfully told all the slaves that they should approach the mountain with him. The whole of the slave people drew near the mountain filled with apprehension and respect for what God did for them but also seeking to know what God intended for their lives.

At the mountain, the slaves heard a great voice speaking to them about how they must live. Not one of God's words escaped any of them. Moses wrote down the words on two stone tables.

God commanded them:

1. I am your Familyhead. I liberated you from Egypt. I am the only one God and you must not worship otherwise.

2. Do not make an image of me in any form. I am jealous for your love and I will punish any who reject me. Keep my commands and you will live in my loyal love.

3. Do not abuse the knowledge of who I am.

4. Sundays must be observed in rest from all work.

5. Honor your parents. You will someday be parents yourselves. Thus the fullness of time may reach an earth of loving families as the Familyhead, your God, likes.

6. Do not put others to death or commit murder.

7. No one must commit adultery.

8. No one should steal.

9. No one should lie against a neighbor.

10. No one should desire what another one has.

And the slaves responded in one voice
that what God told them to do, they would do.

* * * * *

Folk story:

The Flood

Once while God was moulding the earth, it became necessary for land to be formed. The earth was simply moving around too much for humanity to evolve. Lands were popping up out of the seas everywhere. Then God decided to bring all the land together into one super-continent called Pangaea. But when all the lands were brought together, the life which God was culturing on each began such a fight for survival that something new was necessary.

Humanity didn't fare so well either. Noah, a human male, and Nefer, a human female, were two of the people of a folk that used to live near a sea before all the lands were brought together. Humanity thrived near such waters because the climates there were never as harsh as in the more rugged land interiors. When all the land was brought together, there were no more coasts and Nefer and Noah's people as well as all the coastal life began to die out.

Now God decided to separate the continents so that the sea could be closer to humanity and the life of coastal dwellers.

At the same time God decided to pick out the best of the evolving creation to that date. Humans would be the inheritors of this new creation. Humans were blessed with one characteristic that most appealed to God - they were able to conceive of truth, purity and holiness. Their minds could exalt in the things that God loved too.

Should God save all humanity?

God's spirit searched out humanity everywhere. No, humanity was not ready for saving in its entirety.

God looked at the earth and found the two humans he was most pleased with.

Of the humans God picked out Noah and Nefer. Both believed God existed and created life for a reason. To each God gave a mission. Nefer was to gather the plants of the land that were most nutritious and bountiful and Noah was to pick out the animals that were most useful and worthy.

God spoke to these two one day. "Build me an ark," God said.

But Noah and Nefer were too amazed too respond.

So God told them how to construct it and the dimensions it was to have. The wood was to be of cyprus and apartments were to be arranged so light would enter each.

Now the two began the construction of the ark on the dry land. Soon multitudes came to observe this foolish effort and went away laughing. But the two continued their task despite being ridiculed.

After its building, Noah and Nefer went about their assigned tasks in gathering the plants and animals of the world.

When all was ready, God began to work. Dark clouds began to overspread the skies. Mutterings of thunder and the flash of lightning was everywhere. Large drops of rain fell. As the lands grew apart, the mountains began to fall into what had been the sea. Rivers broke away from their boundaries and deepened and disappeared. A great wrenching and groaning overcame all other sounds. Then massive rocks of hundreds of meters rose into the air while lands elsewhere were buried deep within the ground. Momentary impressions of shelters came and went. Here and there in the new places valleys emerged with waters close to seashores. God was rearranging the world upon the destruction of the old.

As Noah and Nefer sailed upon the turbulent seas, they were filled with the sights of jets of water bursting from lands and mighty cataracts driving bluffs away. Darker and darker appeared all of the earth. The water rose higher and higher and above the highest mountains settling to become ocean crusts. Ocean ridges deepened. The sea floor spread and volcanoes erupted.

Was there dry land anywhere? Noah and Nefer wondered. They sent a dove forth from the ark to see. After several hours it returned with an olive leaf in its mouth. Yes, there was now the land re-emerging into its present continents.

At last the ark settled onto land.

Nefer and Noah asked only one boon of God - to give them a promise that never again must humanity face such terror about their lands.

In response God placed a bow upon the skies which we now see as a rainbow. This marked God's promise to stay with humanity and never destroy all of life in this way ever again. The continents would now be left alone.

Now the land could again be rich and beautiful in the gifts of providence.

* * * * *

After Tao Teh Ching:

Mother Nature

Nature, since it mothers all of us, may be thought of as our Mother Nature. Only those who understand Mother Nature can understand her many children. If we choose to avoid mistakes and desire to have a wise guide throughout our lives, we should study the wisdom of Mother Nature's ways.

How can we truly describe Mother Nature? To describe her completely would require us to create her in the form of a perfect duplicate. There is no other duplicate to Nature than Nature. We may try to explain Mother Nature by saying she is the ultimate source of all that exists, all that comes and goes, all that begins and all that ends, all that is and all that is not - but to describe Mother Nature as the ultimate source of all is only to use a few of Her sounds.

Mother Nature contains all natures, yet no matter how many natures come into being, her supply is without end. We may learn from Mother Nature, as she reveals the way in simple lessons. Those who try to reach beyond their reach by standing on their tiptoes, soon lose their balance. Those who stretch their legs too far apart to try to walk more quickly, soon find they cannot walk at all. Those who brag about themselves too much, soon find themselves more ignored than others. Those who push their views most heavily upon others, soon find that fewer people will agree with them. When people claim credit for what they have not done, they soon find that they do not even receive the credit they have earned. The more one is filled with arrogance and pride, the further the fall when humiliated. The longest

journey begins with the first step. The tallest tree starts as a small seed. The highest building starts with the first brick.

Learning from the ways of Mother Nature, one continually discovers how best to proceed.

* * * * *

Abraham, Star Child

Lest we forget the the first Abraham Patriarch...

Our first Abraham was Abraham of the line of Shem.

Thus came a human life evolved from the center of the cosmos fifteen billion light years from the earth. From Abraham we spring.

From Abraham, we understand our roles as pilgrims on an endless journey, only rarely pausing in rest to share fellowship with others who acknowledge that humanity can have no earthly destination. Now came quantum life in humanity.

Both Abraham Patriarchs of the Americans were persons of faith. By faith the first Abraham when he was called to go out into a place which he should after receive for an inheritance, obeyed, and he went out, not knowing where he was going.

God once spoke to this first Abraham. God promised a great blessing. Abraham would be the first Patriarch of the inheritors of the earth. But first he must pass a test. He must leave home and learn that humanity must wander. Abraham accepted the challenge and left Ur of the idolatrous Chaldean people to go to Haran. Now he picked up with his flocks and herds and employees and left with only Sarah his wife and the child Lot for an immediate family to go to the land of Canaan. God gives to each a pilgrim home upon this earth who accept that humanity is a wandering species.

In the eightieth of her years, Sarah, Abraham's wife, gave birth to Isaac amidst great laughter. The wandering seed of life manifest in humanity was truly to be permitted to live a life in the story of God's love of life.

God's gift of a child, Isaac, to the barren Sarah and faithful first Abraham was proof of this contract.

God was truly behind the journey of humanity out into the cosmos.

God was truly behind the journey of humanity thereafter.

* * * * *

Folk story:

A Night of Wrestling with God

One night a man named Jacob was deep in prayer. Jacob was in the mountains, a place where danger lurked everywhere. Who would know what murderers or robbers or criminals might be hiding?

Jacob had gone to the mountains as an outcast. Jacob had tricked his brother Esau out of his inheritance. Now Jacob was going home to the land where Esau lived. Jacob sent a messenger to tell Esau he was coming in peace. No response came to this message and as Jacob approached, a watchman came to Jacob to tell him Esau was on his way to greet him with four hundred armed men.

What else could Jacob think? Jacob was convinced his life would soon be ended at the hands of his wronged brother.

Now Jacob prayed to God seeking his very life.

As Jacob was deep in prayer, he felt a strong hand upon his shoulder.

Jacob thought this must be some enemy so he tried to wrest himself away from the grasp of this assailant. He could not. In the darkness, the two began a struggle for mastery. Not a word was spoken but Jacob put forth all his strength and refused to release for even a moment. He was battling for his life. Still, Jacob remembered God and his whole heart went out in an entreaty to God for mercy. The struggle continued on and on.

Finally came the break of day. The stranger groaned and placed upon Jacob's thigh a finger. This crippled Jacob instantly.

Now Jacob knew that he was in conflict with God which was why his superhuman effort had failed to succeed in victory. Jacob was in terrible agony, disabled and suffering the keenest pain, but Jacob still refused to loosen his hold. Jacob still clung to his antagonist even though Jacob realized it was God. The wrestling continued though Jacob began weeping and praying vocally. The physical pain did not stop Jacob from holding on to God. Finally, God asked Jacob for release, but Jacob answered, "I will not let you go, unless You bless me and forgive me." God realized Jacob was simply not going to let go. God knew the trust that had driven Jacob to wrestle and endure despite exhaustion and injury and told him, "From now on your name is changed to Israel. This is because as a human you shall be empowered by God and with humanity. You have wrestled with God and survived."

That ended the wrestling match.

That day Esau arrived in welcome and not anger even though the land Esau occupied was now given over to Israel.

Thereafter, the crippled man Jacob newly named Israel delighted in his infirmity because his weakness was the result of God's power. God's power had settled a great blessing upon all of humanity to be exercised in weakness and vulnerability to God's touch.

* * * * *

Folk story:

The Last Judge of Israel

Samuel was a child who was given to the Chief Minister of God at Shiloh to raise. This deed was in response to a promise by Hannah, Samuel's mother, that she would do so if she could have a child. Thus Samuel was given to Eli, the Chief Minister of God in Israel, to bring up.

When Samuel was twelve years old, he began to communicate with God. This was very surprising to the boy. At night God called on him by his name. Samuel

Gendreau

A BABY'S PRAYER

Bless this milk and bless this bread.
Bless this soft and waiting bed
Where I presently shall be
Wrapped in sweet security.
Through the darkness, through the night
Let no danger come to fright
My sleep till morning once again
Beckons at the window pane.
Bless the toys whose shapes I know;
The shoes that take me to and fro
Up and down and everywhere.
Bless my little painted chair.
Bless the lamplight, bless the fire,
Bless the hands that never tire
In their loving care of me.
Bless my friends and family.
Bless my Father and my Mother
And keep us close to one another.
Bless other children, far and near,
And keep them safe and free from fear.
So let me sleep and let me wake
In peace and health, for Jesus' sake . . .
Amen.   — RACHEL FIELD

heard the call and assumed it was a summons from the Chief Minister but when Eli said he didn't call him, Samuel went back to sleep. Three times this happened the same night. Eli then told him it must be God calling. He must say, "I am here, ready." When Samuel did so, God told him many things. God said, "Learn what miseries are coming upon the Israelites." It was revealed that Eli's two sons were to die on the same day and Eli must be supplanted as Israel's Judge because he loved his sons more than he loved Godly worship.

Samuel was told many other things and whatever God told him to reveal to people he did.

Now war came about with the Philistines. The war was not going too well for the Israelites. The call came for Eli to send his sons to lead the Israelites in battle.

The choice was not favorable. God was angry with the two sons, Hophni and Phineas. The place of their father's home at Shiloh was very special. The people of Israel took gifts to God there, celebrated great religious festivals, and felt God was manifest to God's people at that site. But these two sons took gifts to God for their own use, sometimes lured and seduced women who came to worship and elicited bribes for prophecies.

To ensure victory for his people, Eli sent not only his sons to lead them but also he sent the ark of the covenant for them to carry into battle. The ark of the covenant was a special object of worship to the Israelites. In it Moses had placed the ten commandments chiseled in stone. Looking like a portable throne, God was thought to sit upon it in God's invisibility.

The battle was joined but almost as soon as the lines closed the Philistines gained the upper hand. 30,000 men were lost to the Israelites and among them were the sons of the Chief Minister. The ark of the covenant was carried away as spoils of victory by the pagans.

After the news reached Shiloh and when Eli learned the course of events from the battle, he fell off his chair and died not so much because his sons were dead - he had been forewarned that might happen - but because the ark of the covenant had fallen into the hands of unbelievers.

The Philistines had captured the ark but it was no prize for them. Every place the Philistines kept it, the folk of that place suffered greatly. Initially it was placed in a temple to an idol of this people named Dagon, a half-man, half-fish statue. Each time folk came to view it the idol was found lying on the floor as if to adore the ark. The Philistine people began suffering disease and felt the presence of the Hebrew ark was to blame. Thus they passed the ark off from Philistine town to town. In each town the same thing happened until after only four months, the Philistines decided to voluntarily return the ark to the Israelites.

In the meantime, the people of Israel began listening to Samuel. He told them, "Persevere in honor to God and God will save this people." Samuel promised his own body as security for their safety and led them to the defense of the country. When the Philistines attacked the Israelites again, the men rushed towards Samuel who was preparing a sacrifice upon an altar. The men had come without their weapons they were in such disorder. Samuel told them to be of good cheer and promised them that God would assist them.

Now the Philistines bore down on the worshipping Israelites gathered about Samuel still in sacrificial worship except that an earthquake greeted them. As the Philistines moved in for the kill, the ground shook under them and they fell or tripped into chasms opening into the ground. About their faces were immense thunders and lightnings so distinct that their faces burned. Weapons were shaken from their hands and the Philistines fled before the unarmed Israelites. Samuel told his people that this signified the power God gave them over their enemies.

So Samuel settled into becoming the Judge over Israel. He appointed a city in every district where he would come to render judgment over controversies and to do justice. By this means, Samuel kept order in Israel for a long time and until he found himself oppressed with old age. Then the people begged Samuel for a king to govern them.

Samuel agreed to do so but warned the people, "A ruler will take your sons away from you. He will take your freedom and give you despotism. He will command some of them to be drivers of their chariots and some to be their horsemen and some guards of their body and others of them to be runners before them am and captains of thousands, captains of hundreds. They will also make them makers of armour and of chariots and of instruments and planter for their own fields, and diggers of their own vineyards. They will appoint your daughters to be confectioners and cooks and bakers and do as slaves do. They will take away your possessions and give them to their friends. You will all be servants to your king and when you regret doing what you ask me to do in appointing you a king, you will seek God have mercy on you and deliver you from your kings but God will not do that."

About this time, a handsome young man named Saul who stood head and shoulders above any of the people set out to search for his father's lost donkeys near where Samuel was living. At the suggestion of a servant, Saul decided to obtain a prophet's help in locating the donkeys. Seeing Samuel, he offered him a fraction of a shekel. What Saul did not know was that Samuel was the Chief Minister of the Israelites and also given the power to appoint a king. Samuel had prayed to God for a sign as to whom should be appointed king and the prophecy came that on a certain hour would come the chosen king. Here came Saul in search of his donkeys. Samuel soon recognized this handsome young man as the person God wished to become the king of Israel. Saul had gone off from home in search of donkeys and returned home with a kingdom. Saul led the Israelites in great victories. Later, however, Samuel chose David to replace Saul as King.

* * * * *

The Story Of David

Now the Philistines gathered together their armies to battle, and they were gathered together at Socoh, which belongeth to Judah, and pitched between Socoh and Azekah, in Ephes-dammim. And Saul and the men of Israel were gathered together, and pitched in the vale of Elah, and set the battle in array against the Philistines. And the Philistines stood on the mountain on the one side, and Israel stood on the mountain on the other side; and there was a valley between them. And there went out a champion from the camp of the Philistines, named Goliath, of Gath, whose height was six cubits and a span. And he had a helmet of brass upon his head, and he was clad with a coat of mail; and the weight of the coat was five thousand shekels of brass. And he had greaves of brass upon his legs, and a javelin of brass between his shoulders. And the shaft of his spear was like a weaver's beam; and his spear's head weighted six hundred shekels of iron; and his shield-bearer went before him. And he stood and cried unto the armies of Israel, and said unto them: 'Why do ye come out to set your battle in array? Am not I a Philistine, and ye servants to Saul? choose you a man for you, and let him come down to me. If he be able to fight with me, and kill me, then will we be your ser-

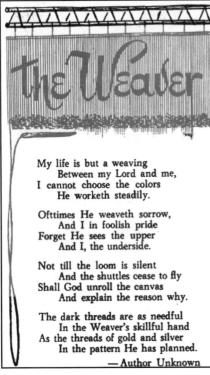

My life is but a weaving
Between my Lord and me,
I cannot choose the colors
He worketh steadily.

Ofttimes He weaveth sorrow,
And I in foolish pride
Forget He sees the upper
And I, the underside.

Not till the loom is silent
And the shuttles cease to fly
Shall God unroll the canvas
And explain the reason why.

The dark threads are as needful
In the Weaver's skillful hand
As the threads of gold and silver
In the pattern He has planned.

— Author Unknown

vants; but if I prevail against him, and kill him, then shall ye be our servants, and serve us.' And the Philistine said: 'I do taunt the armies of Israel this day; give me a man, that we may fight together. And when Saul and all Israel heard those words of the Philistine, they were dismayed, and greatly afraid.

Now David was the son of that Ephrathite of Beth-lehem in Judah, whose name was Jesse; and he had eight sons. And the three eldest sons of Jesse had gone after Saul to the battle. And David was the youngest.

And the Philistine drew near morning and evening, and presented himself forty days. And Jesse said unto David his son: 'Take now for they brethren an ephah of this parched corn. And bring these ten cheeses unto the captain of their thousand, and to thy brethren shalt thou bring greetings, and take their pledge; now Saul, and they, and all the men of Israel, are in the vale of Elah, fighting with the Philistines. And David came to the barricade, as the host which was going forth to the fight shouted for the battle. And Israel and the Philistines put the battle in array, army against army. And David left his baggage in the had of the keeper of the baggage, and ran to the army, and came and greeted his brethren. And as he talked with them, behold, there came up the champion, the Philistine of Gath, Goliath by name, out of the ranks of the Philistines, and spoke according to the same words; and David heard them. And all the men of Israel, when they saw the man, fled from him, and were sore afraid. And the men of Israel said: 'Have ye seen this man that is come up?" surely to taunt Israel is he come up; and it shall be, that the man who killeth him, the king will enrich him with great riches, and will give him his daughter, and make his father's house free in Israel.'

And David spoke to the men that stood by him, saying: 'What shall be done to the man that killeth this Philistine, and taketh away the taunt from Israel? for who is this uncircumcised Philistine, that he should have taunted the armies of the living God? And the people answered him after this manner, saying: 'So shall it be done to the man that killeth him.' And Eliab his eldest brother heard when he spoke unto the men; and Eliab's anger was kindled against David, and he said: 'Why art thou come down? and with whom hast thou left those few sheep in the wilderness? I know thy presumptuousness, and the naughtiness of thy heart; for thou art come down that thou mightest see the battle.' And David said: 'What have I now done? Was it not but a word?' And he turned away from him toward another, and spoke after the same manner; and the people answered him after the former manner.

And when the words were heard which David spoke, they rehearsed them before Saul; and he was taken to him. And David said to Saul: 'Let no man's heart fail within him; thy servant will go and fight with this Philistine." And Saul said to David; 'Thou art not able to go against this Philistine to fight with him; for thou art not able to go against this Philistine to fight with him; for thou art but a youth, and he a man of war from his youth. And David said unto Saul: 'Thy servant kept his father's sheep; and when there came a lion, or a bear, and took a lamb out of the flock, I went out after him, and smote him, and delivered it out of his mouth; and when he arose against me, I caught him by his beard, and smote him, and slew him. Thy servant smote both the lion and the bear; and this uncircumcised Philistine shall be as one of them, seeing he hath taunted the armies of the living God. And David said: 'The Lord that delivered me out of the paw of the lion, and out of the paw of the bear, He will deliver me out of the hand of this Philistine.' And Saul said unto David: "Go, and the Lord shall be with thee."

And Saul clad David with his apparel, and he put a helmet of brass upon his head, and he clad him with a coat of mail. And David girded his sword upon his apparel, and he essayed to go, [but could not]; for he had not tried it. And David said unto Saul: 'I cannot go with these; for I have not tried them.' And David put them off him. And he took his staff in his hand, and chose him five smooth stones out of the brook, and put them in the shepherd's bag which he had, even in his scrip; and his sling was in his hand; and he drew near to the Philistine.

And the Philistine came nearer and nearer unto David; and the man that bore the shield went before him. And when the Philistine looked about, and saw David, he disdained him; for he was but a youth, and ruddy, and withal of a fair countenance. And the Philistine said unto David: 'Am I a dog, that thou comest to me with staves?' And the Philistine cursed David by his god. And the Philistine said to David: 'Come to me, and I will give thy flesh unto the fowls of the air, and to the beast of the field.' Then said David to the Philistine: 'Thou comest to me with a sword, and with a spear, and with a javelin; but I come to thee in the name of the Lord of hosts, the God of the armies of Israel, whom thou hast taunted. This day will the Lord deliver thee into my hand; and I will smite thee, and take thy head from off thee; and I will give the carcasses of the host of the Philistines this day unto the fowls of the air, and to the wild beasts of the earth; that all the earth may know that there is a God in Israel; and that all this assembly may know that the Lord saveth not with sword and spear; for the battle is the Lord's, and he will give you into our hand. And it came to pass, when the Philistine arose, and came and drew nigh to meet David, that David hastened, and ran toward the army to meet the Philistine. And David put his hand in his bag, and took thence a stone, and slung it, and smote the Philistine in his forehead; and the stone sank into his forehead, and he fell upon his face to the earth. So David prevailed over the Philistine with a sling and with a stone, and smote the Philistine, and slew him; but there was no sword in the hand of David.

And David ran, and stood over the Philistine, and took his sword, and drew it out of the sheath thereof, and slew him, and cut off his head therewith. And when the Philistine saw that their mighty man was dead, they fled. And the men of Israel and of Judah arose, and shouted, and pursued the Philistines, until thou comest to Gai, and to the gates of Ekron. And the wounded of the Philistines fell down by the way to Shaaraim, even unto Gath, and unto Ekron. And the children of Israel returned from chasing after the Philistines, and they spoiled their camp. And David took the head of the Philistine, and brought it to Jerusalem; but he put his armor in his tent.

And when Saul saw David go forth against the Philistine, he said unto Abner, the captain of the host: 'Abner, whose son is this youth?' And Abner said: 'As thy soul liveth, O king, I cannot tell.' And the king said: 'Inquire thou whose son the stripling is.' And as David returned from the slaughter of the Philistine, Abner took him, and brought him before Saul with the head of the Philistine in his hand. And Saul said to him: 'Whose son art thou, thou young man?' And David answered: 'I am the son of thy servant Jesse the Bethlehemite.'

* * * * *

David,

God's Time

Oh, Our Familyhead, you have been our dwelling place in all generations. Before the mountains were brought forth, or ever you formed the earth and the world, even from eternity to eternity, you are God. You turn humanity to destruction and say, "Return, you are the children of my humanity." A thousand years in your sight are but as yesterday when it is past and a watch in the night. You carry folk away as with a flood. They are as in a sleep. In the morning they are like grass which grows up. In the morning it flourishes and burgeons forth. In the evening it is cut down and withers. The days of our years are seventy and if by reason of strength they may be 80. Yet is their strength labor and sorrow. It is soon cut off

and we fly away. So teach us to number our days that we may apply our hearts to do wisdom. Return, O Familyhead. How long must it be? Let it be a time of forgiveness concerning those who serve you. O satisfy us early with your mercy so we can be happy in our days. Make us glad according to the days in which you afflict us and the years where we see such evil. Let your work appear to your servants and your glory appear to their children. And let the beauty of our God be upon us and establish our efforts as being worthy of your own hands. Make our work the work of your own hands.

* * * * *

Traditional:

Orpheus And Euridice

Orpheus played the harp with rhythm and energy that made the whole world glad. Now he had a new lyric. He was in love with the beautiful girl Euridice. Best of all she was in love with him too. Their passion could not wait. The two planned a wedding right away.

On the day of their wedding, everyone in town knew it. Orpheus played his harp in a stroll down the main street of town as he went to the church. He was simply too happy not to. Folk poured out of their homes with smiles on their faces. Soon all of the town was following him toward the nuptial events. Orpheus planned to sing his vows to Euridice accompanied by his harp.

Now it was time for the wedding.

However, on the way to the wedding Euridice stepped on a venomous snake and she was killed. Euridice should have been looking where she was walking. She was simply too happy to pay attention to what she was doing. Her spirit rose to God.

Orpheus was already at the church when he got the news. Everyone was devastated. All of their friends tried to console Orpheus but he could not be consoled. He picked up his harp and left the church vowing never to play happy music again. All the joy in his life was snuffed out.

When he went to the spots where he and Euridice had found love, he could not help but play such sad music that the very trees and rocks and nearby animals found themselves crying and the wind sobbed and the sky clouded up and rained.

His sad music was so powerful that even God was moved.

As Orpheus beheld it a great opening appeared from this world directly into God's Homeland. At the entry to a stairway was an angel who told Orpheus he could go up to get Euridice and bring her back down to earth if only he would stop playing such sad songs. Creation could not stand such grief.

Only one other caution did the angel give Orpheus. Orpheus must not look back returning to the earth from God's Homeland. God did not wish humanity to have God's Homeland described in great detail or else all would be too overwhelmed trying to get there that they would forget that they were supposed to be of service to others on earth. Thus, Orpheus must not look upon Euridice until they were both back down on earth.

The music of Orpheus was happy again as he sang on his way climbing the stairway to get Euridice and the music from his song again filled the air with gladness. At the top of the stairs, Orpheus called out for Euridice. A loving force seemed to speed towards him until he laughed with exultation. Then Orpheus began to descend again.

Orpheus could clearly hear the footsteps of someone following him back down to earth. The footsteps sounded light and airy as had Euridice's. But was it her?

Who was it following him back down to earth?

Was it really Euridice?

Doubts began to fill his mind and he stopped singing. He walked on and on down the stairway to earth. Did the angel deceive him?

Orpheus was almost at the bottom of the stairway from God's Homeland when he felt he simply had to check to see if Euridice was behind him. Curiosity got the better of him. What if Euridice wasn't behind him and he left the stairway without bringing her back? He feared a mistake. What if the stairway left and he could never get to God's Homeland to get Euridice again?

Orpheus turned around to see if the footsteps following him were Euridice's. As he did so, he saw that it really was her and she whispered to him "Goodbye, my beloved husband." She turned around and re-ascended as she was required to do if Orpheus violated the rules. Then the stairway lifted up and vanished.

Orpheus could do nothing. He wildly ran and jumped with his harp into a nearby river where he was so distracted he drowned.

As you listen to the waters washing down rivers and cricks they still sometimes carry Orpheus's gentle musical strains which reminds us of the strength of joyous passion and the disappointment when it is lost.

* * * * *

Traditional:

Ruth and Her Marriages

Ruth was a foreigner to Palestine. She come from the land of Moab, a place like a tabletop above the Dead Sea. It was a well-watered fertile land. Everything about Ruth was different to the people of Palestine. She did not share their customs, their dress or their appearance. There she was - a startlingly beautiful woman in a strange new land. Race was the biggest stumbling block. Everyone knew she was a Moabite as they called Ruth's folk.

This story is what happened to Ruth in Palestine.

How did she end up there?

Even though Ruth was a Moabite, she married a Palestinian before she picked up to live there. The mixed marriage took place in Ruth's own land where she grew up. Ruth's husband and his father Elimelech and mother Naomi and brother Chilion left Bethlehem ten years before Ruth become a widow. Famine drove Ruth's husband's family from Palestine. They escaped to the ancient land of Moab. Here both of the children of Naomi married Moab girls. Ruth knew the joy of a happy marriage. Unfortunately, here Ruth also experienced the death of her husband and her two children.

When Ruth's husband Mahlon died at a young age she faced a very uncertain future. Now she was left with her mother-in-law Naomi and her sister-in-law Orpah, widow of Chilion, to worry about and care for.

Ruth did not give up at the loss of her husband. She couldn't do that and take care of them she had to. She grieved for him by the affection she expressed toward his mother, his people, his country and his God. She did not pity herself even though her husband's death left her destitute. Instead she chose to follow her dead husband's mother wherever she led. She did so in a spirit of love.

After Ruth's husband died, she had a choice to make. Where should Ruth live now that Mahlon and her children were gone? Should she stay and grieve in her native land?

What of her mother-in-law Naomi? Old and weary, Naomi longed to return to Palestine, the land of her birth to live out her life. Ruth couldn't deny her mother-in-law this choice.

Naomi would no longer stay in Moab. She was going back to Palestine and there was no stopping her. Before she left, Naomi pleaded with her two daughters-in-law to turn back and stay at their own mother's home. Orpah did turn back but Ruth clung lovingly to her mother-in-law. She confessed her decision. She said, "Do not ask me to leave you or to stop following after you. Where you go, I will go. And where you make a home, I will live. Your people shall be my people. And your God my God. Where you die, I will die. And there I will be buried." Ruth was determined to honor her dead husband by providing care for this forlorn old woman.

Now she and Naomi traveled the long distance back to Naomi's land, a long, fatiguing and dangerous trip for two unarmed lone women. Ruth's race, being different, give her even less chance of regard. Ruth and Naomi crossed the Arnon and Jordan Rivers, ascending to the mountains between and descending into deep valleys on foot.

Finally Ruth and Naomi arrived in Bethlehem. Here Ruth began to support Naomi and herself through the lowliest of tasks. She took to following after the reapers harvesting grain to gather pickings of grain which fell and were left behind for the poor. Ruth gleaned all the days in the hot sun returning to Naomi faithfully at the end of each day with her small harvests.

One day as Ruth gleaned a field belonging to Boaz, a rich Palestinian, she come to his notice because she stood out so. Boaz wondered who she was and was told she come to Bethlehem with her mother-in-law Naomi to care for her despite not being from those parts. Boaz give her permission to glean in his field all she wanted to and took her under wing. Boaz admired her more and more as he come to know her and how she was. He asked her to eat with him sometimes and told his workers to give parched grain to her and pull out stalks from their bundles and leave them for her so she could have an easier time of feeding herself and Naomi.

Naomi always asked Ruth how things was going every day. At the end of one day Naomi learned Boaz was helping and she remarked to Ruth how he was really her kinsman. Then Naomi showed how much a matron of Palestine she really was. She took Ruth aside and told her to wash, anoint herslef and put on her best clothes that very night. Then she was to go to the threshing floor where Boaz would be winnowing his grain. Then, later, when he goes to lie down, Ruth was to watch where he went, go uncover his feet and lie down with him. She was to do what Boaz told her to do. Ruth did what Naomi told her as always. You obey the one you respect and love.

Ruth's advance was accepted by Boaz who was more grateful than anyone could have dreamed. He done for her even more after this and protected her like she was so special. This was a legal custom in those days in Palestine. Where a man died his next of kin took up with his wife. This is basically what Naomi took precedence of even though Boaz wasn't the closest kin of Ruth's dead husband.

Boaz went to see Naomi and give her thanks for treating him as next of kin and then did proper legalizing to make it so. He got her waived to him from a closer kin before taking her to be his wife. Now he could publicly tell all the folks of his land that he took the place of Mahlon to be the husband of Ruth the Moabite in Ruth's second mixed marriage.

From the racially mixed children of Ruth come David and of course from the line of David come God's choice of the earthly parents of God's own Child.

* * * * *

Myth:

The Seasons

Two of heaven's happiest angels were a mother Demeter and her daughter Persephone. They were always happy together and their laughter filled heaven with sweet music. The mother was an angel of the harvest and she often went to earth to help out farmers. On these occasions she began to take her daughter with her because she simply couldn't bear to be apart from Persephone.

Persephone was really one of God's most beautiful angels. She loved to go with her mother to earth. Wherever Persephone walked on earth with her light feet flowers would spring up. Unfortunately she was noticed by the devil on one of these trips. The Challenger saw how beautiful Persephone was and wanted her to become his wife in Hell. He knew that her mother, Demeter, would never consent to this so the devil decided to carry her off the next time he saw her on earth.

One day as Persephone ran about a meadow on earth she wandered away from her mother. Suddenly, the devil saw his chance to make the conquest he sought. Now the ground of the meadow opened up and out of the crack of the earth came a team of black horses in a chariot pulled by the devil himself. The usually grim Challenger stepped out of the chariot laughing at his good luck and seized the beautiful girl. Persephone was too terrified to even scream to her mother. The devil turned his team around and the ground closed behind him. As the ground closed, a herd of cattle grazing nearby fell into the crevice too. Now the devil plunged back toward his own dark and hopeless homeland.

Up in the meadow, Demeter rushed around frantically looking for her daughter. Where could she have gone? Demeter looked everywhere without success. Then she came to a farmer who was in great anguish. Demeter asked him what was the matter. The farmer told her about how the ground opened up and he saw the Devil seizing a girl and how his cattle had fallen into the crack.

Then Demeter knew what happened. Her grief turned to anger. She told God that she simply could not help the farmers anymore she was so upset. In fact, she decided that she would no longer even allow the earth to become green with vegetation until she got her daughter back from Hell. She simply would not allow anything to grow until Persephone was returned.

Other angels went down to Hell and begged the Challenger to allow the girl to return to her mother. They told him how grief stricken Demeter was. This only made the Challenger even more determined to keep his new bride.

Persephone was unhappy, it is true. She did not like being in the dark place. There were no flowers there. The only fruit to eat was the fruit of the dead, pomegranates from the trees of Hell. When you ate these fruits, there could no longer come to you the joy of life that folk can know.

Then came an Order from God. Persephone was to be returned to her mother. The devil had to obey. He was preparing to return Persephone to her mother when the gardener of the fruit trees of Hell came to him laughing. She revealed that Persephone had succumbed to the temptation to eat of the fruit of the trees of Hell. Persephone had eaten six pomegranates. Then the Challenger knew he had won his bride partially.

And yet the Order of God still stood. Now for six months a year, Persephone must be returned to her mother. She would accompany her as Demeter wished on her rounds of the earth. Demeter was the happiest angel from God's Homeland during these days and she often visited the earth to make sure harvests were bountiful. The whole earth would burst into bloom for the six months that Demeter and Persephone were together helping out farmers. Their joy at being together made the earth warm and crop bearing. Golden grain was soon scattered over the world to seed fields for food for God's children.

But there could be no helping the return of Persephone back to Hell for six months, one month for each of the six pomegranates she ate of the fruit of the joyless dead. During these months, the earth returned to its barren state. The ground was cold and lifeless.

And so the seasons have come and gone on earth ever since alternating between times of natural growth and decay, warmth and coldness, bounty and hard times.

* * * * *

Folk story:

Elijah

There came a great time of peril to humanity when the worship of God was almost eradicated. In fact there was left only one minister to God. His name was Elijah and he was a man of strange sight. His life was lived on the edges of the desert and he clothed himself in a garment of woven hair and wore a leather girdle. Elijah came out of no where.

All of Palestine - from its ruler to its people - had gone over to the worship of a statue named Baal. Only Elijah was left as a minister to God.

Elijah went to King Ahab to punish him for worshipping Baal who was touted as the god of rains and storms. Elijah did so by condemning Ahab's land to a drought. No longer did the rains come and the land was parched and cracked. Crops did not grow and the people thirsted.

Ahab only laughed. Elijah was simply a wildman. This drought would end.

So Ahab did not relent. What was he to fear from the single minister to God when he had so many other ministers to Baal to oblige him?

Then Elijah returned to Ahab. Ahab recognized him. "Is it you, you troubler of Israel?" he said. Elijah reminded Ahab it was he who was troubling Israel with his worship of Baal. Then Elijah challenged Ahab to a test. Let Ahab bring his 450 pagan ministers of Baal to Mount Carmel along with his 400 ministers to the idol's wifely statue of Asherah. The test would be to see who could entreat their god to ignite an altar offering. Would it be the pagan ministers?

The great test came to pass.

The people of Israel came to witness. Elijah addressed them, "How long will you sit on the fence? If God is God, worship God. If the statue of Baal is supreme, follow it."

Which one controls rain and fertility?

On the top of Mount Carmel Elijah watched hour after hour as the pagan ministers implored Baal to send down his fire to burn their offering. They drew themselves into ecstatic frenzy performing a limping dance around the altar shouting ritual cries. Nothing happened.

Elijah shouted over to them, "Perhaps your Baal can't hear you because he is relieving himself."

The people watched and waited. The supremely confident Elijah began to laugh at the idol while the people noted that Baal did not heed any supplication.

Then Elijah prepared the altar for God by pouring water on its wood. Now when God lit it, there could be no question of God's power. As Elijah began to pray to God immediately the fire descended on the altar devouring its offering and even the altar on which it lay.

Clearly the people must now make no further mistake as to the identity of God. They shouted, "It is Yahweh who is God." They saw the fire fall from God's Homeland.

How could Ahab ignore so great a proof? God must be the God of Israel. Elijah again prayed - this time prostrate on the ground - for a rain to end the draught and stop the suffering of the people.

God must be seen as the God of the fertility of the land and Elijah's acts confirm that people's lives are lived wholly in God's hand.

Seven times a messenger was sent towards the Mediterranean Sea to see if storm clouds were approaching. The people expected a monstrous rain to come. On the seventh trip back the servant announced seeing "a little cloud like a human hand" was on its way. Then the storm clouds gathered and nourishing rain descended.

When it came time for Elijah to go be with God, a fiery chariot came out of God's Homeland for him, swinging low to the ground to take him in, and with a whirlwind it took the loyal minister to God to his reward.

* * * * *

Traditional:

Two of God's Interventions

Heinrich Heine:

Belshazzar

The noon of night was drawing on,
Dark silence lay on Babylon.

Yet in the palace of the King
Were flaring lights and reveling,

There, in the royal banquet hall,
Belshazzar held drunken festival.

He saw his sumptuous court recline
And empty bowl on bowl of wine.

He heard cups ring and vassals sing
And all the partying pleased the King.

The wine aroused him and made him bold.
He flushed, his words grew uncontrolled.

Wine was his passion, wine his prod
With obscene oaths he mocked at God.

He blasphemed God's Homeland and all its laws
While the court echoed with applause.

The King commanded, his brow was black.
The servants vanished, but hurried back

Carrying stolen treasures, rich and rare.
The Jerusalem main Church's booty was there.

The King laid hands on a worship cup.
With a lewd laugh he filled it up.

He drained the cup in one quick draught
And then, with slobbering lips, he laughed.

"False Familyhead! I drink to your greatness gone.
I am the King of Babylon!"

The blasphemous words had scarce been said
When something struck the King with dread.

The ribald laugh died in the hall.
Silence fell like a deathly pall

While on the white wall there appeared
A human hand, abrupt and weird.

And then in letters of red flame
It wrote, and vanished the way it came.

The King's pale features seemed to freeze.
He could not quiet his knocking knees.

Stone-cold about him his servants were.
They gave no sound. They made no stir.

Astologers came, yet none of all
Could read that writing upon the wall.

And in the night death came to one
Belshazzar, King of Babylon.

George Gordon:

The Destruction of Sennacherib

The Assyrian came down like the wolf on the fold
And his cohorts were gleaming in purple and gold.
And the sheen of their spears was like stars on the sea
When the blue wave rolls nightly on deep Galilee.

Like the leaves of the forest when summer is green
That host with their banners at sunset were seen.
Like the leaves of the forest when autumn has blown,
That host on the morrow laid withered and strown.

For the Angel of Death spread his wings on the blast
And breathed in the face of the foe as he passed.
And the eyes of the sleepers waxed deadly and chill
And their hearts but once heaved and forever grew still!

And there lay the steed with his nostril all wide,
But through it there rolled not the breath of his pride.
And the foam of his gasping lay white on the turf
And cold as the spray of the rock-beating surf.

And there lay the rider distorted and pale
With the dew on his brow, and the rust on his mail.
And the tents were all silent, the banners alone,
The lances unlifted, the trumpet unblown.

And the widows of Ashur are loud in their wail.
And the idols are broke in the temple of Baal.
And the might of the Gentile, unsmote by the sword
Has melted like snow in the glance of the Lord.

* * * * *

An Old Epic Tradition:

The Creation of Humanity

There come a time when God created the heavens and the earth. At first there was no rain and so there was no plants growing in fields and no plant could grow. Therefore, human beings were not made yet to raise crops.

Now there come a mist over the earth and soon rain fell to water the whole face of the earth.

And God formed the first one of humanity out of the dust of the ground and breathed into this person's nose and a person first become alive from the breath of God the Familyhead.

Then God planted a garden eastward in a place called Eden and there he put this first person formed.

Out of the ground, God the Familyhead caused every tree to grow which are so pleasant to see and good for food. One of these trees was one of life. This tree was in the middle of the garden. Also there was a tree of knowledge of what is good and bad.

A river poured out of the ground in Eden to water the garden and it divided itself into four branches.

The name of the first was Pison and it watered the land of Havilah where there is gold. That gold is very valuable and there is bedellium and the onyx-stone.

The second river is Gihon. It waters the whole land of Ethiopia.

The third river is Hiddekel. It goes toward the east of Assyria.

The fourth river is Euphrates.

Now God the Familyhead took this first person and put it into the garden of Eden, to dress it and to keep it. And God told it, "You can eat off of every tree here but don't eat of the tree of knowledge of what is good and bad. You will die for sure if you eat from it.

Then God the Familyhead said, "It isn't good for a person to be alone. I will make another as a helpmate."

And out of the ground God the Familyhead formed every animal of the field and every bird of the air and brought them to Adam to see what he would call them and whatever Adam called the creature, that become the name.

And Adam give names to all cattle and to the birds of the air and to every animal of the field but for Adam there wasn't found nobody for help yet.

Then God the Familyhead caused it to fall into a deep sleep. As Adam slept, God took out a rib and closed Adam up.

And the rib which God the Familyhead took from it got made into another person and one become a man and another a woman. Then Adam said, "This is now bone of my bones and flesh of my flesh. I call her a woman because she was took out of me, a man.

That is why every person must leave parents and marry. A man and woman then return to be one flesh.

Now both the man and woman was naked and they wasn't ashamed of it.

Now of all the animals the most tricky was a snake which was one of the creatures made by God the Familyhead.

And the snake said to the woman, "So, did God say you can't eat of every tree of the garden?"

And the woman said to the snake, "We can eat all of the fruit of the trees of the garden except the tree in the middle of the garden. God told us, "You can't eat of that one and you mustn't even touch it or you will die."

And the snake said, "You won't die. God just knows that on the day you eat from it then your eyes will be opened and you will become as gods, knowing good and evil."

And when the woman looked she saw the tree looked like it had good fruit and it seemed appetizing to her eyes and, well, it seemed a good idea to try to become wise...so she took some fruit and ate it and also gave some to her husband and he ate too.

Then their eyes were opened they realized they were naked. They sewed figleaves together and made themselves aprons. And the heard the voice of God the Familyhead walking in the garden in the cool of the day. So Adam and his wife hid from the presence of God the Familyhead among the trees of the garden.

Then God the Familyhead called out to Adam and said to him, "Where are you?"

And Adam said, "I heard your voice in the garden and I was afraid because I was naked so I hid myself.

And God said, "Who told you that you were naked? Did you eat of the tree that I told you not to eat from?"

And the man said, "The woman who gave me, she gave me the fruit of the tree and I ate it."

And God the Familyhead said to the woman, "What is it you have done?" And the woman said, "The snake tricked me and I ate it."

Then God the Familyhead said to the snake, "Because you did this, I am angrier at you than at any cattle and more than every animal of the field. Upon your belly you must go and eat dust all your days. I will have this woman hate you and it will continue between your descendants and hers. Her descendants will bruise your head and yours shall bruise their heels."

Then God told the woman, "I will greatly multiply your grief in those you conceive. You shall bring forth children to live in sorrow. Your desire will be for your husband and he shall be your guide."

Then God told Adam, "Because you took orders from your wife to eat from the tree I forbid, I must curse this ground and order you to eat from it all the days of your life. It will grow thorns and thistles for you, and you must eat of the crops of the field. You will be left to eat bread while sweat pours from your face until you yourself are planted in the ground. From it you were taken and to dirt you will return.

And Adam called his wife Eve. She would be the mother of all life.

Then God the Familyhead made coats of skins and clothed Adam and his wife. And God the Familyhead said, "Look this man resembles me to know good and evil. So now, to avoid him also snatching the fruit of the tree of life to live forever I must send him out of the garden of Eden to cultivate the ground from which I took him."

So God the Familyhead drove out the man and placed Cherubims to the east of the garden and a flaming sword which turned every way to keep them away from the tree of life.

* * * * *

After Aeschylus:

An Angel Who Stole Fire

Once there was an angel who loved humanity far too much and had to pay for it. The angel's name was Prometheus and he had long been a favorite of God. It was not, however, God's way to benefit one form of life over another. Humanity was just another evolutionary step to God and there was no reason why any particular one life form should be given a gift over another.

Life forms came and went as nature's selection went along. Now came amoeba and bacteria, and new hierarchies of life were appearing one after another. Soon reptiles and mammals evolved. The earth was once taken over by dinosaurs.

In the meantime the ways of God produced humanity, life forms which ran from danger on two legs and climbed into huge trees to observe the earth below. With their hands freed, this new life form could raise them to the skies and learn prayer. Promethius noticed this strange ability of the new life form.

Now Promethius was a keen observer not just of humanity but also about God. God did not know suffering. God simply was above such a thing. God was ordering things without any purpose. God did not wish the will of any life form to overwhelm harmony.

And yet on the earth was humanity who did know about suffering from having to compete with survival with dinosaurs and diseases of amoeba and bacteria.

Promethius came to love this humanity who dealt so with adversity and yet raised their hands to God in prayer.

Promethius decided to help humanity no matter what.

At every opportunity he stole down from heaven with a gift. When first he came down, people had no houses but instead lived in caves. They did not know the signs that meant winter was coming to prepare for. They did not have symbols of one to googles to count with. In their brains were no devices to have memories. They did not look upon other life forms like horses as helpers. They did not know of the herbs that could heal their maladies. Promethius taught them all these things.

Promethius was helping humanity more than all the other angels of God's Homeland were helping any other life forms. Humanity was being taught knowledge and how to think.

God knows all and called the angel Promethius into council for a warning. God warned Promethius to stop favoring one life form over any other. God's love was for all.

Promethius could say nothing to change God's mind. He tried to tell God how there was much value in humanity because they lived humbly and were such eager learners.

The talk did no good. God lifted Force which bore the mighty appearance of a thunderbolt with a flame that seeks out the heart to burn leaving one lifeless. "One more of your favoritisms to humanity and I will punish you horribly," God told the angel.

Promethius left the council very depressed. He could not convince God of the possibility of humanity. And perhaps God was right. Humanity was progressing along quite nicely but there was one thing humanity did not have - the power of the flame of feeling. Without hearts that burn with emotion for God quite naturally God would not be happy to favor humanity over all the other life forms.

There was only one thing to do. It was a daring move but something that might soften God's heart toward humanity.

Promethius stole in to God's council room that very night and stole the fire that energizes God's own lightning. He was determined to give this final gift to humanity. People must have the burning emotion that was the essence of God's own power.

Now he took it down to earth and gave humanity the gift of fire itself.

This did not escape God's attention.

Promethius was soon fastened to a rock inescapably. If he were not stopped would not he give God's Homeland itself over to humanity so that God would not be God?

God that knows all also knew something else.

Humanity itself could free its benefactor Promethius by turning its gift of emotion into proper love and regard for one and all. When humanity proved its gift was well given and humanity earned citizenship in God's Homeland, God would free Prometheus as justice would require.

* * * * *

After Dhammapada:

Twin Verses

All that we are is the result of what we have thought. We are founded on our thoughts. We are made up of our thoughts. If a person speaks or acts with an evil thought, pain follows as the wheel follows the foot of the ox that draws the carriage.

All that we are is the result of what we have thought. We are founded on our thoughts. We are made up of our thoughts. If a person speaks or acts with a pure thought, happiness follows as a shadow that never leaves him.

"He abused me. He beat me. She defeated me. She robbed me."- in those who harbor such thoughts hatred will never cease.

"He abused me. He beat me. She defeated me. She robbed me."- in those who do not harbor such thoughts hatred will cease.

For hatred does not cease by hatred at any time. Hatred ceases by love. This is an old rule.

The world does not know that we must all come to an end here - but those who know it, their quarrels cease at once.

One living looking for pleasures only, senses uncontrolled, immoderate in food, idle, and weak, the tempter will certainly overthrow such a one as the wind throws down a weak tree.

One living without looking for pleasures, senses well controlled, moderate in food, faithful and strong - this one the tempter will certainly not overthrow any more than the wind throws down a rocky mountain. One wishing to put on the clothing of righteousness without seeking forgiveness for sins who disregards also temperance and truth is unworthy of such clothing.

But one who has sought forgiveness from sin is well grounded in all virtues, and regards also temperance and truth. This one is indeed worthy of the clothing of righteousness.

They who imagine truth in untruth, and see untruth in truth, never arrive at truth, but follow vain desires.

They who know truth in truth, and untruth in untruth, arrive at truth, and follow true desires.

As rain does not break through a well-thatched house, passion will break through an unreflecting mind.

As rain does not break through a well-thatched house, passion will not break through a well-reflecting mind.

The evil-doer mourns in this world, and mourns in the next. Such a person mourns in both. The person mourns and suffers when seeing the evil of that person's own work.

The virtuous person delights in this world and delights in the next. Such a person delights in both. A person delights and rejoices when seeing the purity of that person's good works.

The evil-doer suffers in this world and suffers in the next. Such a person suffers in both. A person suffers when thinking of the evil the person has done. A person suffers more when going on the evil path.

The virtuous person is happy in this world and is happy in the next. Such a person is happy in both. A person is happy when thinking of the good that person has done. A person is still more happy when going down the good path.

The thoughtless person, even if that person can recite a large portion of the gospel, but is not a doer of it, has no share in the service of others, but is like a cowherd counting the cows of others.

The follower of the gospel, even if this person can recite only a small portion of the gospel, but, having forsaken passion and hatred and foolishness, possesses true knowledge and serenity of mind, caring for nothing in this world or that to come, can share in the service of others.

* * * * *

Traditional:

Esther Saves Her People

Esther wasn't a special person at all except that she was a good spouse. She was a Jew married to a Persian. Her husband was a very powerful man though. He was the ruler of the Persians named Ahasuerus. She didn't have no choice in the marriage. Ahasuerus picked her out for himself after he divorced his first wife Vashti. Esther's kin, the Jews, were exiles from Jerusalem in Babylon at the time. Esther's ties to her own kin were not strong since her parents was both dead from when she was young. She was, however, brought up by a Jewish man named Mordecai, a distant relative who give her to know about her being Jewish.

Now come a time when times got bad in Persia. The prime minister of the Persians, Haman, figured he could deflect blame for the bad times by saying the Jews was the cause. Consequently, he planned to have Jews massacred to take the blame.

The Jews of course learned about their fate and Mordecai figured all he could do was ask Esther to help her kinfolk. Mordecai went to the home of Esther dressed in sackcloth and ashes to give her the message about what Haman was going to do. The message required her to help her people be spared.

What could Esther do?

She decided to bring the plot to the attention of her husband as the ruler of the Persian lands he was. She would do it formal and bring out the whole plot to him where he couldn't ignore it. There was only one problem. A person who got an audience with the ruler this formal way - while he was on the throne - risked everything. If the ruler didn't like what was said, it was automatic death to the asker. Now came the day of the formal time when the ruler held audience. Here come Esther. Before all the ministers of the mighty Persian Empire and in the presence of heads of all the government Esther went forward to speak up for her people. Even before she spoke, Ahasuerus had it in mind to do whatever she asked because he loved her. Quietly she told her husband that one of his chief lieutenants was plotting to destroy a whole race of the people in his empire. Ahasuerus asked who and Esther told him it was the most important of all the Persians, his own prime minister, Haman. She told him he was cooking up a massacre of all the Jews in Persia.

Furious, Ahasuerus give orders for Haman to take the place of Mordecai in the jail where Haman had him took. There the orders was to give Haman the hanging that he had ordered for Mordecai.

That was how Esther though not special except for being a beloved spouse saved her race from destruction and saved humanity the stain from the blot of a holocaust.

* * * * *

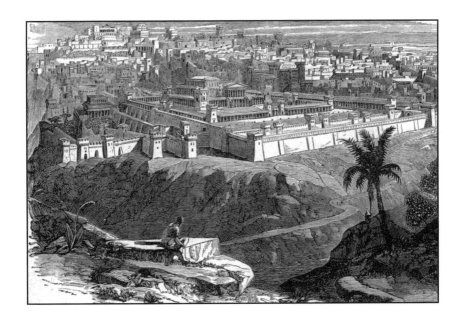

King James Scholars from Isaiah in Exile:

A God for the Homeless and Estranged

Comfort ye, comfort ye, my people, saith your God.

Speak ye comfortably to Jerusalem and cry unto her, that (the attacks on her are over), that her (sin) is pardoned; for she has received of the Lord's hand double for all her sins.

(Now comes) The voice of him that crieth in the wilderness, Prepare ye the way of the Lord, make straight in the desert a highway for our God. Every valley shall be exalted and every mountain and hill shall be made low, and the crooked shall be made straight, and the rough places plain. And the glory of the Lord shall be revealed, and all flesh shall see it together, for the mouth of the Lord hath spoken it.

The voice said, Cry (out that relief comes).

And (Isaiah) said. (Why) shall I cry? All flesh is grass, and all the goodliness thereof is as the flower of the field. The grass witherth, the flower fadeth, because the spirit of the Lord bloweth upon it, surely the people is grass.

(Maybe so, but this remains.) The grass withereth, the flower fadeth, but the word of our God shall stand for ever. O Zion, that bringest good tidings, get thee up into the high mountain; O Jerusalem that bringest good tidings, lift up thy voice with strength, lift it up, be not afraid, say unto the cities of Judah, Behold your God!

Behold the Lord God will come with strong hand, and his arm shall rule for him: behold, his reward is with him, and his work before him. He shall feed his flock like a shepherd: he shall gather the lambs with his arm, and carry them in his bosom and shall gently lead those that are with young.

Who hath measured the waters in the hollow of his hand, and meted out heaven with the span and comprehended the dust of the earth in a measure and weighed the mountains in scales, and the hills in a balance?

Who hath directed the Spirit of the Lord, or being his Counsellor, hath taught him?

With whom took he counsel, and who instructed him, and taught him in the path of judgment, and taught him knowledge, and shewed to him the way of understanding?

Behold, the nations are as a drop of a bucket and are counted as the small dust of the balance; behold, he taketh up the isles as a very little thing. And Lebanon is not sufficient to burn, nor the beast thereof sufficient for a burnt offering.

All nations before him are as nothing and they are counted to him less than nothing and vanity...

It is he that sitteth upon the circle of the earth, and the inhabitants thereof are as grasshoppers; (It is he) that stretcheth out the heavens as a curtain, and spreadeth them out as a tent to dwell in; (It is he) that bringeth the princes to nothing; (It is he that) maketh the judges of the earth as vanity.

Yea, they shall not be planted; yea, they shall not be sown; yea, their stock shall not take root in the earth: and he shall also blow upon them, and they shall wither, and the whirlwind shall take them away as stubble.

(God asks) To whom then will ye liken me, or shall I be equal? Saith the Holy One. Lift up your eyes on high, and behold who hath created these things, that bringeth out their host by number: he calleth them all by names by the greatness of his might for that he is strong in power; not one faileth.

Why sayest thou, O (folk of) Jacob, and speakest, O Israel, My way is hid from the Lord, (God has forgotten us), and my judgment is passed over from my God?

Hast thou not known? Hast thou not heard that the everlasting God, the Lord, the Creator of the ends of the earth, faitheth not, neither is weary? there is no searching of his understanding? He giveth power to the faint; and to them that have no might he increaseth strength?

Even the youths shall faint and be weary, and the young men shall utterly fall; But they that wait upon the Lord shall renew their strength; they shall mount up with wings as eagles; they shall run, and not be weary; and they shall walk, and not faint.

* * * * *

After an Account by Jerusalem Priests 6th Century B.C.,

Cosmic Creation

In the beginning, God created the skies and the earth.
And the earth was without form and void.
And darkness was upon every dimension.
And the breathing spirit of God moved upon the face of misty clouds.
And God said, "Let there be light." And there was light.
And God saw the light, that it was good.
And God divided the light from the darkness.
And God called the light Day, and the darkness God called Night.
And the evening and the morning were the first day.
And God said, "Let there be a rocky place in the middle of the misty clouds.
And let it divide the clouds from other clouds."
And God made this rocky place.
And separated out the clouds that were under the rocky place
From the clouds which were above the rocky place,
And it was so.
And God called the rocky place Cosmos.
And the evening and the morning were the second day.
And God said, "Let the clouds under the cosmos be gathered together into one place,
And let dry land appear." And it was so.
And God called the dry land Earth,
And the misty clouds gathered together God called the Seas,
And God saw that it was good.

And God said, "Let the Earth bring forth grass,
The plant yielding seed, and the fruit-tree
Yielding fruit after its kind, Whose seed is in itself,
Upon the earth." And it was so.
And the Earth grew grass and plants yielding seed after each's kind,
And the tree yielding fruit, whose seed was in itself, after its kind,
And God saw that it was good.
And the evening and the morning were the third day.
And God said, "Let there be lights in the clouds of the skies,
To divide the day from the night.
And let them be for signs and for seasons, and for days and years.
And let there be lights in the clouds to give light upon the earth." And it was so.
And God made two great lights.
The greater light ruled the day and the lesser light ruled the night.
God made the stars too.
And God set them in the clouds of the skies to give light upon the earth.
And to rule over the day and over the night and to divide the light from the dark-
    ness.
And God saw it was good.
And the evening and morning were the fourth day.
And God said, "Let the seas produce moving creatures that have life.
And birds that may fly above the earth in the open clouds of the skies."
And God created great whales and every living creature
That moves which the seas produced abundantly after their kind.
And every winged fowl after its kind.
And God saw that it was good.
And God blessed them, saying, "Be fruitful, and multiply.
And fill the waters in the seas.
And let birds multiply over the earth."
And the evening and the morning were the fifth day.
And God said, "Let the earth produce life after each's kind: cattle and creeping
    thing, and animal of the earth after its kind."
And it was so.
And God made each animal of the earth after its kind.
And cattle after their kind, and everything that creeps upon the earth after its kind.
And God saw that it was good.
And God said, "Let us make a human in our image and after our likeness.
And let these have dominion over the fish of the sea
And over the birds of the air
And over the cattle and over all the earth,
And over every creeping thing that creeps upon the earth."
And God created humanity in God's own image.
In the image of God created God humanity.
God created male and female.
And God blessed them and God said to them,
"Be fruitful and multiply and replenish the earth and subdue it.
Have dominion over the fish of the sea
And over the birds of the air
And over every form of life that moves upon the earth."

And God said, "Look, I have given you every plant bearing seed
Which is upon the face of the earth, and every tree in which is the fruit of a tree
    yielding seed.
To you it shall be food. And I have give you every animal of the earth
And every bird of the air and everything that creeps upon the earth
And every green plant for food."
And it was so.
And God saw everything that God made and it was very good.
And the evening and the morning were the sixth day.
Then the cosmos and the earth were finished and all of them.
And on the seventh day God rested from the work God had made.
And God rested on the seventh day from all God's work which God had made.
And God blessed the seventh day, and made it special
Because God rested from God's work which God created and made.

* * * * *

After Plato:

Life After Death:
Excerpts From a Dialogue with the Dying Socrates

What of a person's soul after death? A Greek of the ancient days, Socrates, was to drink a potion of poison as he has been sentenced to die. He was convicted of impiety to the pagan gods at the age of seventy in 399 B.C. Companions are with him and they converse on the day of the death.

A friend, Simmias, asks, "Can it be that when the person dies the soul is scattered abroad and that is the end of it, as so many say? For supposing it is composed from somewhere or other, and comes into existence before it even enters a human body; what hinders it, when it has entered and finally got rid of that body, from ending at that moment also, and being itself destroyed?"

Another friend, Cebes,..."We are afraid of that, Socrates and try to convince us against it. Or better, don't think we are afraid, but imagine there is a kind of child in us which has such fears. Then let us try to persuade this child not to fear death as if it were a bogey."

"Very well then," said Socrates, "we must ask ourselves what sorts of things properly undergo dissolution and scattering and see if the soul belongs to such a category. Then we shall know whether to be confident or fearful for our own soul."

"That seems to me correct," said Cebes.

"What sort of things undergo dissolution? Are these things not compounds of some sort? These things can be decomposed as they are composed. But a thing that is always in the same state is not liable to dissolution and keeps in the same state even when compounded or uncompounded. This is so even if that something in the same state is essential and unseen and cannot be grasped by anything except intellectual reasoning."

"Then what of the soul?"

"When the soul has the body to help in examining things, either through sight or hearing or any other sense, the soul is dragged by the body towards what is always changing and the soul can go astray and become confused and staggers about like one drunken because she is taking ahold of such things. But when she examines by herself, she goes away yonder to the pure and everlasting and immortal and unchanging and abides ever with it and there she rests from her wanderings while she is among those things like herself unchanging because what she takes hold of is unchanging."

"Then what are the two like: the body and the soul?"

"The soul is unchanging and divine and intellectual and self-unchangeable. After death, the body is quickly dissolved, but on the contrary to the soul dissolution is wholly indissoluble. When a person dies, the visible part, the body, that which lies in the visible world and which we call the corpse properly dissolves and disappears. But the soul, the 'unseen' part of us, goes to another place noble and pure and unseen like itself to the presence of the good and wise God, where if God will, my own soul must go very soon. Shall our soul then, being such and of such nature, when released from the body go straightway scattered by the winds and perish, as most men say? Far from it, my dear Simmias! This is much more likely: If it is pure when it gets free, and drags nothing of the body with it, since it has no unseemly communion with the body in life if it can help it, but avoids the body excesses and gathers itself into itself, since it is always practising this, a soul loving wisdom rightly and in reality practising for death, it goes away into the unseen which is like itself, divine and immortal and wise and on arrival it has the opportunity to be happy, freed from wandering and folly and fears and wild loves and all other human evils. But if it dies polluted and unpurified as having been always with bodily pleasures and attentions and in love with it and bewitched by it through desires so that it thinks nothing to be true but the bodily - what one could touch and see and drink and eat and use for carnal passion, accustomed to hate and fear, the soul has difficulty in the fleeing of the dead body and bears such a heavy load it is dragged back into the visible world weighed down and is not released purely."

After these words, Socrates put the cup of poison to his lips and, quite easy and contented, drank it up. When the companions began crying uncontrollably, Socrates said, "What a scene! You amaze me. That's just why I sent the women away, to keep them from making a scene like this. I've heard that one ought to make an end in decent silence. Quiet yourselves and endure." He walked about until his legs felt too heavy and then lay down until he grew cold and stiff. His last words were, "Criton, we owe a cock (a poor man's offering) to Asclepios (a rite of thanksgiving for a healing). Pay it without fail."

* * * * *

After Plato:

Shadows And Echoes In A Cave

Here is a parable of the condition of our humanity.

Imagine humanity as dwelling in an underground cave. People have lived in this cave since childhood as prisoners. Each is restrained with their necks and legs chained so they have to stay where they are. They cannot move their heads round because of the chains and they can only look forward - not see behind. Light comes to them from fire burning behind them higher up at a distance. Between the fire and the prisoners is a road above their level, and along it imagine a low wall has been built, as puppeteers have a wall in front of them above which they can work their puppets.

Now come bearers carrying along this wall all sorts of objects which they hold projecting above the wall, statues of people and other living things and all kinds of stuff, some of the bearers speaking and some silent.

What people can see of themselves can only be shadows which the fire casts on the opposite wall of the cave. And the things being carried along this wall would be the same. As the prisoners talk together, they simply name the shadows which they see passing by. The echoes within the cave would seem to convey the talk of the bearers carrying the objects.

The prisoners would never believe that there were any realities except the shadows and echoes of things.

However, if one is released from the chains, one might walk back to look at the fire. At first the person might be too dazzled to understand the source of the light by which that person sees. Now he might be able to more clearly understand the passing things.

And then someone might drag that person out of the cave altogether and up into the sunlight. The person would no doubt be furious at being dragged so and when the person came into the light, the brilliance of the sun would fill the eyes and nothing could even perhaps be seen as it really was at first.

Eventually, the person would become used to the light and understand that life should not be seen as mere shadows and echoes. Eventually a person would understand that what seems real and what reality is could be different.

* * * * *

After Aristotle,

Living for the Highest Good

A human being should live so as to nurture the soul with courage, wisdom, fortitude, temperance, and justice. These attributes come from personal effort and not by chance. Virtues are good things that the soul can come to possess and gain happiness. They are the good of the soul as well. They are the primary goals of life. This effort constitutes not just the condition but also the cause of the best and hap-

piest life. The best life is the life lived for the sake of good duly equipped with sufficient good relation with the external goods and good done for the bodily needs.
A person cannot be happy who has no particle of the good virtues of the soul, who
fails to fear the flies buzzing around his head or who abstains from extravagance
from hunger or thirst.

Which is best? Is it best to be good in the soul, or in the possession of external
goods or in the body? Striving for good in the soul is the best. Happiness comes
when a person cultivates one's character and mind to the uttermost and keeps ac-
quisition of external goods within moderate limits rather than to try to acquire
more external goods than one can possibly use. It is for the sake of the soul that
other things like property or bodily health are desirable. They are goals in and for
themselves.

The nature of God bears witness to how humanity should act. God is happy
and blessed but God is so in and by God's own self by reason of the nature of God's
very life and not because God possesses every external good. Being happy and being fortunate with possessions are two different things. Accidents and chances can
cause a person to have external goods but no person can be just and temperate and
have a happy soul by accident or simply by chance.

The country or community is the happiest which does good. Fairing well is
the result of behaving. A country doesn't do good unless it does right. A state like
a person has fortitude by doing justice and acting wisely and this gives the energy
for the country to survive.

The best way of life, for individuals severally as well as for countries and communities collectively, is the life of goodness duly equipped with such a store of re-
quites of external goods and of the goods of the body as makes it possible to share
in the activities of goodness.

* * * * *

Job:

A Rent in the World

"Why do you hide your face and hold me as your enemy?" Job asks God.

"Why do you go by me and I cannot see you. How can you pass me by and I do
not understand you?"

A man of the ancient days, Job by name, suffers. He loses his possessions. Robbers
steal his cattle and donkeys. A fire burns up his sheep. Another band of enemies steals
his camels. His field hands are killed off. His family die in a storm. His health is broken
and he suffers terrible sores. The pain is everywhere. There is a rent in the world. This
rent is the problem of justice because Job loves God.

He asks God, "Why are you breaking me with great storms of suffering and
wounding me in multiples without reason and freely?"

Job thinks "God has overthrown me and has thrown a net of misfortune about
me." Does God deal crookedly with him? Does God do justice? Job concludes, "God is
not just."

Friends do not help him deal with his predicament. They assume Job has fallen
out of favor with God. Job is a religious man so they assume he should not suffer if he

were really righteous. They confuse religion with the life of humanity with a living God.

The problem is that Job knows how God acts toward him. Job knows God "numbers my steps." He asks God, "And don't you watch over my wrongdoing? My wrongs are sealed up in a bag and you sew it up. Life is like what happens to a mountain as it disappears from the earth. Rock by rock it is washed away. The waters wear its stones. Just this way the dust of the earth out of which things grow disappears. So is all hope in humanity destroyed." Job complains, "You prevail against humanity. Humanity passes away. You change the appearance of the human body and send us away a human at a time. While alive, this body suffers and knows pain and causes a human's soul to mourn." Does how much a person suffer matter to God? Is it commensurate with justice? Job sees himself "stripped of glory" with "the crown of appearance of doing right taken from him." Job formerly believed God worked justice with humanity. He thought a human had only to walk in God's way to be justly treated. Now Job sees God as destroying the perfect and the imperfect equally. Job says, "God exterminates the good as well as the wicked."

Then Job reaches an understanding. Justice is a human activity willed by God, even if it is sometimes opposed by human acts. God gives freedom to humanity not a straightjacket. God wishes justice but does not fore-ordain behavior.

Faith must be directed to God and not to justice as a substitute for the living God. Doing justice is something human and special. Justice is no system of earthly recompense. Justice is simply God's demand that no one cause another to suffer gratuitously.

* * * * *

After a Upanishad:

A Boy's Conversation With Death

Once there was a parent who desired to make a gift to God of all that he possessed. He had a son, still a boy, by the name of Nakiketas.

When the parent made the gift, the priest accepted the offering which included the boy and looked at the boy who had come to the church with the father strangely. What an unexpected gift the priest thought. He took the boy back to the locked room where church valuables and other gifts were kept.

But before he followed the priest away, the boy, Nakiketas, suddenly reacted to being given away and looked at his father with great fear and demanded of him, "Who have you given me to?"

The father was angry at Nakiketas's insolence and told him, "I am giving you to Death."

The father then left Nakiketas behind at the church. He had to be true to his word and thus relinquish his son.

Three days passed and Nakiketas was given no food nor water.

Finally after three days, Death entered the boy's room.

Death spoke first and said, "I apologize for my ingenerosity. It is a foolish person who does not treat a guest with hospitality. You have awaited me for three days without food or other benefit so I shall grant you three wishes."

Nakiketas said, "O Death, as the first wish, I ask that my father not be angry with me. Please allow him to become pacified, kind and free from anger at me. I want him to remember me as a fine son."

Death granted the wish and told the boy that indeed the father would remember his son as he had once known him before. In fact he would allow the father to sleep peacefully from then on with fond dreams of Nakiketas.

For his second wish, Nakiketas asked to learn the secret of fire. Was it the force which led to God's Homeland?

Death granted the wish and told the boy about the need of worship, the means by which God's Homeland could be attained. Fire was symbolic of the fervor of worship. Worship was not merely glorifying God but also undertaking the three duties of study, self-giving and charity. Worshipping God takes on the earnestness of fire which permits overcoming birth and death.

For his third wish, the boy asked what happens to a person after death. Nakiketas said, "When I am taken by you am I really dead or do I go on living as some say."

Death was very reluctant to respond. "Ask me something else," Death asked. "I will give you children who live a hundred years, herds of cattle, elephants, gold and horses. I will give you the finest home on earth and harvests beyond bounty if you will not require me to give you this answer."

The boy insisted. "I want to know about you."

Death was in great consternation. "I will make you a king if I do not have to answer. I will give you all you desire."

"No," the boy said. "You promised me three wishes. I want to know about the great Hereafter."

Death replied, "What you want to know is what does not pass away. Here is what is not transient. It is a state which the wise can know by meditation of the Self seeking to recognize the Ancient who is difficult to be seen. It is the Self who has entered into the dark, who is hidden in the cave, who dwells in the abyss, where lives God. God leaves joy and sorrow far behind. Even a mortal who hears this and embraces it can reach the subtle Being of God because he has obtained what is a cause for rejoicing. The Homeland of God opens. Its residents include the Self. The knowing Self is not born. The Self dies not. It sprang from nothing. Nothing springs from it. The Ancient is unborn, eternal, everlasting. The Self is not killed though bodies are killed. The Self, smaller than small, greater than great, is hidden in the heart of that creature. A person who is free from desires and free from grief sees the majesty of the Self by the grace of the Creator. Though sitting still, it walks far. Though lying down, it goes everywhere. Who, save the Self, knows the God who rejoices and rejoices not? The Self is bodiless within the body, as unchanging among changing things, as great and omnipresent never grieving. The Self takes over the body as its own. But the one who has not first turned away from wickedness, who is not tranquil and subdued, or whose mind is not at rest, can never obtain the Self even by knowledge. The Self sits in the chariot, the body, the chariot, the intellect, the charioteer, and the mind, the reins. The senses they call the horses, the objects of the senses their roads. When the Self is in union with the body, the senses, the mind, then wisdom is achieved. Beyond the senses there are objects, beyond the objects there is the mind, beyond the mind there is the intellect. The Great Self is beyond the intellect. Beyond the Person of God there is nothing. I have told you of the goal, the highest road."

Then Death went to the door of the chamber and opened it to Nakiketas. "You may leave," he said. The boy was told to return home. "You have now received your wishes and I shall release you back to your parents. But remember the path of the Self is hard."

* * * * *

Seven Brothers and a Governor

Stubborn righteousness is like a fine pilot steering the ship of sanctity on the sea of the passions though buffeted by threats of the tyrant and swept by the swelling waves of tortures, never shifting the route of sanctity until the ship has sailed into the haven of victory over death.

Commitment defends the person's sacred soul when attacked with every torture.

Once there was a Governor of Israel, Antiochus, who wished to break the will of the Jewish people. He wanted them to be Greek. He knew the Jewish custom of refusing to eat unclean meat and decided to rid them of this custom to destroy their ancestral law. His demand was simple- eat unclean meat or be tortured; eat unclean meat and be rewarded.

Now seven brothers were brought before him with their aged mother. All were handsome and modest, well-born and generally attractive.

When Antiochus saw them thus brought before him, with their mother in the midst, he urged them, "Please accept my friendship. Eat of this food. I will punish you if you don't and reward you if you do. I need good men to hold positions of authority and importance in my service. Share in the life of the Greeks and walk in their new way. Take pleasure in your youth. If you don't accept the food and disobey me, I could put every single one of you to death by torture."

Then he ordered that the brothers see the tortures that awaited disobedience. They were wheels, joint dislocators and racks, bone crushers and catapults, cauldrons and braziers, thumb-screws and iron claws, and wedges and branding irons. After the captive Jewish brothers were returned to the governor's presence, he noted no fear. The governor said, "You had better learn respect and how justice will treat you if you do not obey me. Now will you eat this meat?"

The young men said, "Don't delay. We are ready to die rather than transgress the commands of our ancestry. We fear more to walk in defiance of the law of Moses. Try us and you will see. If you take our lives, you still cannot hurt us. Divine justice will cause you to suffer the more."

Antiochus was filled with rage. He had wished them converted to his service and now they were daring him to try them with his tortures. Still he offered to the oldest, "Eat and you will be released." The oldest refused. As he did so guards stripped him of his clothing and bound his hands and arms. Then they whipped him til they were weary but the oldest did not relent. They They placed him on the wheel where he was racked till his bones were out of joint. And as the joints gave way, the oldest denounced the tyrant, "You are an abomination and the enemy of the justice of heaven and bloody-minded. You torture me for obeying the law of God." The guards told him, "Simply eat this meat and we will release you." The oldest replied, "Cut off my arms and legs, and burn my flesh and twist my joints. I will show you that only by virtue are the children of the Jews moved. Otherwise we are unconquerable." Now hot coals were set on him as he was strapped to the torture wheel. The wheel was tightened until blood flowed and the fire of the coals were quenched by his flesh. The flesh of the man fell from the wheel to the axis of the machine. As the eldest died, he called to his brothers, "Follow my example, brothers. Don't desert me or our brotherhood of the soul. Trust that a just providence that watched over our ancestors will take vengeance on every accursed tyrant."

Then the guard brought forth the second son. Would he eat rather than be tortured? He did not and was grappled with sharp-clawed hands of iron fastening him to the torture engines and a catapult. Now these panther like beasts tore at his muscles with claws of iron and began rending away all the flesh from his cheeks and tore off the skin from his head. He spoke out that he would endure all for righteousness sake. "I am supported under pain by the joys that come through virtue where you are the one who will suffer for your impiety." Now the third son was brought forward and entreated to taste and save himself. But the third son said, "Are you ignorant that the same father begat me and my brothers that are dead and in the same doctrines was I brought up. If you wish to torture me, go ahead for my soul is out of your reach." This greatly angered Antiochus and his guards dislocated his hands and his feet with their dislocating engines and wrenched his limbs out of their sockets and unstrung them and they twisted round his fingers and his arms and his legs and his elbow joints. His spirit still unshaken, they stripped off his skin taking the points of his fingers and tore the scalp from his head and took him to the wheel where they twisted his spine till he saw his own flesh hanging in strips and great gouts of blood pouring down from his entrails. But before death, he said, "We suffer for our upbringing and our virtue that are of God. You shall endure torment without end."

The fourth son was entreated, "Don't be so mad as to follow the course of your brothers. Obey the governor and save yourself. This son said, "I will not deny my noble brotherhood. Invent tortures as you will to attempt to move me, but I am the brother of those you have tortured." Antiochus was furious and ordered the man's tongue cut out. Before they could do this the fourth son said, "Even if you remove my organ of speech, remember that God can hear the speechless. Cut it out but you will not silence my Reason. We give our body members for the cause of God." He was likewise put to death in the agonies of the tortures.

After the fourth died, the fifth sprang forth. "I demand torture for the sake of my brothers. It is not evil to worship the Creator of all and life according to his virtuous law." As he spoke the guards placed him before the catapult and tied him on it at the knees. Now they wrenched his loins over the rolling wedge so that he was completely curled back like a scorpion and every joint was disjointed. While in grievous straits for breath and anguish of body, this son exclaimed, "Glorious, O tyrant, glorious against your will are the benefits that you have given me, enabling me to show my fidelity to the Law through your tortures."

The sixth was brought forth. He was a mere boy. When Antiochus asked him if he would eat meat, the boy said, "I am not so old in years as my brothers, but I am as old as they in mind. We were all born and reared for the same purpose and are equally bound to die for the same cause. If you must torture for not eating unclean meat, torture." Soon they stretched him out and dislocated the bones of his back and set fire under him. And they made skewers red hot and ran them into his back and piercing through his side they burned away his insides. "I am not conquered," the boy exclaimed. "We six youths have overthrown your tyranny. You are impotent to alter our Reason or force us to eat unclean meat to overthrow us."

After the sixth was dead and thrown into the cauldron, the seventh came forward. Now the tyrant felt pity for this last brother and begged him, "See how the foolishness of your brothers has brought about their deaths. Obey me and I will advance you to a high office in the business of the state." The governor ordered the boys' mother brought before him so that she might talk to her last son to get him to obey him and save the family from extermination.

But the mother spoke to her son in Hebrew as young as he was and encouraged him and then said to the governor, "Release him from his bondage so that he can come and talk to me." When the governor did so, the boy ran to the edge of the burning cauldron where the bodies of his brothers lay burning and said to the governor, "Aren't you ashamed being a human, to take men of like feelings as yourself, made from the same elements, and tear out their tongues and scourge and torture them in this manner. While they have fulfilled their righteousness towards God, you shall simply be a person guilty of unjust slayings." Standing on the brink of death he said, "I am no renegade to the witness of my brothers and I call upon God to be merciful to my nation." With this prayer, he jumped into the red-hot brazier and died.

Does not this prove that stubborn righteousness is supreme over the passions? It is impossible to deny the supremacy of the mind for those who wish the victory over passions and pains. Now the seven brothers form a holy choir of righteousness in their consecrations unto God. They say to us, "Fear not the one who can merely kill. Arm yourself with commitment to avoid the peril of the soul if an ordinance of God be transgressed."

* * * * *

After Jerome.

An Ancient Folk Story of Mary

Mary, Oh Mary! Mary watching the cross scene!

It is said that Mary was of the ancient stock of David and was educated in the Great Jerusalem church. Her father was a man named Joachim whose family came from Nazareth. Her mother was a woman named Anna whose family came from Bethlehem. The two lived plain and simple lives. All they made they divided three ways. One portion went to God's church. Another was distributed among strangers. The family lived on the third part.

Even after twenty years of marriage, Joachim and Anna had no children. Every year the two made the annual trip to the main Jerusalem church and prayed that God would allow them to live proper lives.

Now there came a year in which Joachim and Anna decided to make a vow when they made the annual trip. They decided to promise God that if they were given the gift of a child they would have that child raised in the Jerusalem church as a child wholly devoted to God. The two gathered up all they owned to make as a gift at the church to seal the offer to God.

However, when the two arrived in Jerusalem and wished to make the vow and seal the offer with the gift of all they owned, the minister - a man named Issachar - said "No." The minister told them they must return home with their gift because it was obvious they were not people favored to even appear in the main Jerusalem church. At that time there was the mistaken notion that if a family did not have a male child God was angry with them. This was the way the situation of Joachim and Anna appeared to that minister.

The minister did not merely order them from the church, he also banned them from returning until they had a child. Only then could they make an offering.

The marriage of Joachim and Anna was in great trouble. Both wished sincerely to live proper lives despite their shameful state of having no children. Now they could not go to Jerusalem to dedicate themselves to God anymore.

Joachim felt himself cursed, abandoned his wife and went off to seek the company of shepherds. He decided he could never return home. He was sure all his neighbors had heard the curse of the minister. He was convinced his neighbors would shun him and look on him as an accursed man.

While Joachim was on a hillside, an angel appeared to him in a great light. The angel told him not to be afraid. This angel told Joachim that his gift at the temple - though rejected by the earthly minister - had not been rejected by God. God accepted the offer and heard the promise that the child, if born, would be dedicated to God. In fact, God had not only accepted the offering but had also decided that the offer of Joachim and Anna to bear a Child for service to God should come true. The angel told Joachim that "God sees shame very clearly and hears those unjustly driven into it. Your offering has ascended to God. Anna shall give you a child, a daughter, and her name shall be Mary. She shall breathe the breath of God's own breathing throughout her life. You must allow her to live her life in devotion to the

Familyhead. Then after the progression of the years she shall give birth while yet a Virgin to a human Child of God."

Joachim was in a state of shock at seeing this angel and asked how he knew it could be true. The angel told him to go to Jerusalem and when he was about to enter the city he would see his wife, Anna, standing at the Golden Gate to that city waiting for him.

Now, too, the same angel went to the distraught Anna, Joachim's wife. The angel told Anna, "You will be the mother of a child who is to be called Mary. She will be blessed more than any human woman. She will give birth to God's own Child. To prepare for this event, you must take her to the Great Jerusalem Church after she is weaned. There she will serve the Familyhead day and night in prayer and will have the company of the spirit of God. She will give birth to God's Child while yet a virgin."

Anna was in a state of shock at seeing this angel and asked how she knew it could be true. The angel told her she would be given a sign. When she went down to the Golden Gate of the city of Jerusalem she would look out into the hills and see her husband returning to her.

Now, Joachim and Anna made their separate journeys of faith in God's promise to the Golden Gate of Jerusalem. They soon met each other again and were reunited in the promise.

The child Mary was born after the two returned to Nazareth. After the child was three, they took Mary to Jerusalem to live in the Great Jerusalem Church where she grew up to the age of fourteen ministered to by angels in apartments set aside for girls dedicated to God's service.

The minister of the main Jerusalem church had a rule. Those virgins who arrived at the age of fourteen must return to their ancestral villages. All of the other virgins took great joy at this prospect. Not Mary. She vowed virginity to the Familyhead and did not wish to leave God's church at Jerusalem. Her pleas to remain were so loud and boisterous that the minister decided to call a council of the elders of his church. He did not know what to do with such a difficult case as Mary. When the elders gathered, they prayed for guidance in the Holy of Holies section of the main Jerusalem church.

While these elders were in prayer, a voice came from the Ark of the Covenant as if it was now ascended to sit upon the mercy seat. This voice said that the troubled girl must be given in marriage to a special husband. This husband would be identified by a prophecy. That prophecy said that there was a rod grown out of the stem of the tribe of Jesse and that a flower would spring from its root. In those days, the men of the place carried rods to assist them in their protection, shepherding and walking on the unimproved roads.

Now the elders gathered together the eligible men of the house of David who were of marriageable age to demand each of them take their rods to the altar to see which should take Mary as a wife.

Among the men brought to the temple was an aged carpenter by the name of Joseph. This man was the only one brought forth who disobeyed the minister's order that the men take their rods to the altar to see from which a flower would spring but no one noticed.

When no one's rod sprung forth a flower, the elders were in great consternation. What went wrong? Then they decided to consult God again. This time, the voice of God said that Mary must be given in marriage to the only man gathered in the crowd who did not take his rod to the altar. After the crowd of men were thus dispersed, only Joseph remained.

Then Joseph's rod was taken to the altar where it not only flowered but a dove came flying out of the sky of existence to perch upon it. Thus was Joseph identified. He was then ordered to take Mary as his wife and take her to his home in Bethlehem.

While Joseph went home to make arrangements and before the actual ceremony, Mary, accompanied by seven other virgins of the main Jerusalem church returned to her parents' home to await the marriage.

While in Galilee, Mary heard a great salutation from an Angel. It was Gabriel who told her, "Fear not, Mary, nothing shall happen inconsistent with your chastity. You have found great favor with the Familyhead of Life and you shall bear a child while yet a virgin whose name shall be Jesus. He shall be God's own Child."

"Let it happen," asked Mary. "Let all else happen."

* * * * *

Various Traditions:

Folk Tales About the Infancy and Childhood of Jesus

Many folk tales about Jesus survive from various traditions.

An account of Jesus speaking as a baby was said to come from a book of accounts recorded against Jesus by Caiaphas, the Jerusalem Church Superintendent. Jesus was related to speak from the cradle, "Mary, I am Jesus, the Child of God. I am the logos of the world which you bore as declared by Gabriel to you and my Parent has sent me for the salvation of the world."

To facilitate the birth of Jesus, Joseph was said to have gone to find a Hebrew midwife. When he returned with a midwife, they found the cave filled with light, greater than lights that could come from lamps or candles and greater than the light of the sun itself. It appeared that the simple cave was lit like a glorious temple and the tongues of angels as well as the shepherds who arrived united to adore God for the gift of the birth of the Familyhead of humanity, Jesus.

Mary had no customary blessing to give the wise men who arrived from the east and instead gave them a swath of the swaddling clothes of Jesus. Later, after the wise men returned to the East, the cloth was consigned to a fire but after the fire was extinguished the cloth remained unburned.

After Mary and Joseph fled with Jesus to Egypt, they settled near an Egyptian temple. The temple was one of the chief ones of Egypt and contained an idol who allegedly spoke oracles. The priest of this temple had a child who was mentally ill. One day priests came to this temple from all over Egypt to enquire why the land seemed in such consternation. The idol spoke the last words that "The unknown God is come here. There is no other God besides this one. Only this one is worthy of divine worship for he is truly the Child of God." After these words the idol fell over and the priests dispersed in terror. But the mentally ill boy at his play took down one of the swaddling cloths of the baby Jesus and put it on his head. From that time forth the child was healed of his illness. The boy went to his father, the chief priest of the broken idol and told him what had happened and how the cloth of this baby had healed him. This was how the priest learned who was this Child of God.

There was once a girl who was afflicted by the Challenger of God. Frequently this Challenger appeared to her in the form of a dragon who was inclined to swallow her up so to remove her blood. She bore the appearance of a dead carcass. As often as this foul spirit came, this girl would cry out and throw her hands about, saying, "Is there no one who can deliver me from that impious dragon!" The girl's mother was told to go to Bethlehem and inquire of Mary, the mother of Jesus. She went and took her daughter. When Mary heard her story, she gave the mother and daughter a little of the water she had used to wash her baby Jesus and told her to baptize her daughter. The two returned to their home far away. When next the Challenger came to her as the image of a dragon to suck her blood, the girl was much frightened as usual. The dreadful dragon could not, however, touch her body and fled screaming, "What have I to do with you, Jesus, Child of Mary? Where can I flee from you?" When Jesus was seven, he

played with the other children of Nazareth. The children enjoyed playing in the mud to make objects in the shapes of familiar things such as donkeys, oxen, birds and other figures. All of the children boasted that their objects were the best. Jesus in his childish way said, "Yes, but watch while I command these figures which I have made to walk and move." So Jesus's mud-objects took life and scampered about until Jesus ordered them to return and be quiet. All did except the birds and sparrows which, since Jesus had commanded them to move had taken to flight, and had flown too far away to return.

Jesus once played close to a dyer's shop. The children entered the shop of this dyer named Salem when he was gone and destructively spoiled many dyed cloths of various combinations and solid colors. When the dyer returned he went complaining to Mary. "You have injured me with this child of yours." When Jesus heard the cause of the complaint, he replied, "I will return each cloth to whatever color you desire" ... and did so producing clothes with portions in the colors the dyer prescribed.

Joseph, the father of Jesus, often took Jesus with him on his carpentry jobs. Joseph was a fine man and good-hearted but was not a very competent carpenter. He was not skillful at his carpentry trade. Often his work was deficient. Too often his lumber was cut too short or too long, or was too wide or too narrow. This was why he took Jesus with him. When such occurred, Joseph told his child of the problem and Jesus would stretch out his hand toward it and the item would become as Joseph wished it.

One day Jesus went to play with neighborhood children who did not want to play with him and instead hid in the furnace of their home. The children told their mother to tell Jesus they were not there. When Jesus learned of this deception he told the mother to go to the furnace and open the door. When she did so, out came the children as kid goats. Jesus said to them, "Come my kids and play with your shepherd." The mother went to Mary and pled with her saying, "Please have Jesus return my children from being goats. Isn't it said, that the Child of God has come to save and not to destroy?" Jesus heard this plea and immediately said to the goats, "Come, friends, let's go play." And immediately, the children were changed back to being children.

On another occasion, the neighborhood children were playing "Governor of the World" with Jesus as the Governor. Some children played guard and others servants. Jesus ordered all to worship him in play. Just then, two men walked by with what appeared to be a dead boy on a stretcher with the father crying following along behind. The guards yelled that all passers by must come to worship the governor but the procession would not play. Forcibly the children took the stretcher with the boy to Jesus. Jesus asked the father what happened. The boy, it seemed had gone out to gather wood in the hills and had been bit by a venomous snake with a fatal bite. Jesus ordered the father to take him where the snake's nest was. The father objected but eventually submitted to go and take the victim boy with them. At the spot of the nest, Jesus ordered the snake to come forth. It did. Then Jesus ordered the snake to go to the boy and suck out all the venom that the snake had infused into that boy. The snake crept to the boy and took away all its poison again. Then Jesus cursed the snake and it immediately burst into pieces and died. When Jesus touched the child, he was restored. This was the child who later became the disciple Simon the Canaanite.

A schoolmaster of Jerusalem heard of Jesus and wished Jesus brought to him to learn his "A.B.C.'s." Jesus agreed to go see the man. At the school, the master told Jesus to say Aleph (A - in Hebrew). Jesus replied, "I will say Aleph when you tell me what it means and then I will say Beth (B)." The schoolmaster was enraged by his pupil's response - and threatened to whip him...except that Jesus went on to explain the straight figures of all the letters, the obliques and what letters had double figures and points or none and many other things of which the master had never heard nor read in any book. The master replied, "I believe this boy was born before Noah! He is more learned than I am or than any master." Another master tried to teach Jesus too. When Jesus replied to him that "I will say Aleph when you tell me what it means and then I will say Beth," this next master was so enraged he lifted up his hand to whip Jesus until his hand withered away and the master died. Thereafter Joseph and Mary did not allow Jesus out of their home for a long time because everyone who displeased him was killed. And so Jesus learned to conceal his miracles and secret works and gave himself over to a study of the law until his thirtieth year at which time he was baptized.

* * * * *

Joseph Smith:

America Experiences the Crucifixion and Witnesses the Resurrection of Jesus

It was predicted by the American prophet Samuel, the Lamanite, that there should be darkness for the space of three days over the Americas. Many doubted. But it came to pass in the thirty fourth year, in the first month, on the fourth day, a great storm, such a one as never had been known in the Americas. And there was a great and terrible tempest and thunder that shook the whole earth as if it were about to divide it in half. And there were sharp lightnings. And the city of Zarahemia was set afire. And the city of Moroni sunk down into the depths of the sea. And the earth was carried up upon the city of Moronihah so that it rested under a mountain. And there was great and terrible destruction in the land southward. But to the northward there were greater changes over the whole face of the land. Highways were broken up and level roads spoiled and smooth places became rough. Buildings were shaken to the ground in many places and inhabitants died. Some cities remained despite great damage and deaths and whirlwinds carried folk away. These events lasted for about the space of three hours.

Then came darkness upon the Americas. The darkness was like a vapor. And there no light, neither fire nor glimmer, neither sun nor moon, nor stars for so great were the mists of darkness. This lasted for three days during which there was great mourning and howling and weeping among all the American people continually.

Then the voice of God proclaimed the extent of the disaster and the cause. God cried out, "Wo, wo, wo unto this people; wo unto the inhabitants of the whole earth except they shall repent. for the devil laugheth and his angels rejoice, because of the slain of the fair sons and daughters of my people; and it is because of their iniquity and abominations that they are fallen!"

And more was said, "O all ye that are spared because you were more righteous than they, will ye not now return unto me, and repent of your sins, and be converted, that I may heal you? Yea, verily I say unto you, if ye will come unto me, ye shall have eternal life. Behold, mine arm of mercy is extended towards you, and whosoever will come, him will I receive; and blessed are those who come unto me. Behold, I am Jesus Christ, the Son of God. I created the heavens and the earth, and all things that in them are. I was with the Father from the beginning, I am in the Father, and the Father in me; and in me hath the Father glorified his name. I came unto my own and my own received me not. And the scriptures concerning my coming are fulfilled. And as many as have received me to them have I given to become the sons of God; and even so will I to as many as shall believe on my name, for behold, by me redemption cometh, and in me is the law of Moses fulfilled. I am the light and the life of the world. I am Alpha and Omega, the beginning and the end. And ye shall offer up unto me no more the shedding of blood; yea, your sacrifices and your burnt offering shall be done away, for I will accept none of your sacrifices and your burnt offerings. And ye shall offer for a sacrifice unto me a broken heart and a contrite spirit. And whoso cometh unto me with a broken heart and contrite spirit, him will I baptize with fire and with the Holy Ghost, even as the Lamanites, because of their faith in me at the time of their conversion were baptized with fire and tithe Holy Ghost, and they knew it not. Behold, I have come unto the world to bring redemption unto the world, to save the world from sin. Therefore whoso repenteth and cometh unto me as a little child, him will I receive for of such is the kingdom of God. Behold for such I have laid down my life, and have taken it up again; therefore repent, and come unto me ye ends of the earth, and be saved."

Joseph Smith, an American prophet, received this information from the plates of Nephi discovered in New York State at the top of the Hill Cumorah. This prophet's close walk with God began on the night of September 21, 1823 when he prayed fervently to the Familyhead. He recounts, "While I was thus in the act of calling upon God, I discovered a light appearing in my room, which continued to increase until the room was lighter than at noonday, when immediately a personage appeared at my bedside standing in the air, for his feet did not touch the floor. He had on a loose robe of most exquisite whiteness. It was a whiteness beyond anything earthly I had ever seen; nor do I believe that any earthly thing could be made to appear so exceedingly white and brilliant. His hands were naked and his arms also, a little above the wrists, so also were his fee naked, as were his legs a little above the ankles. His head and neck were also bare. I could discover that he had no other clothing on but this robe, as it was open, so that I could see into his bosom. Not only was his robe exceedingly white, but his whole person was glorious beyond description, and his countenance truly like lightning. The room was exceedingly light, but not so very bright as immediately around his person. When I first looked upon him, I was afraid; but the fear soon left me. He called me by name, and said unto me that he was messenger sent from the presence of God to me, and that his name was Moroni: that God had a work for me to do; and that my name should be had for good and evil among all nations, kindreds, and tongues, or that it should be both good and evil spoken of among all people. He said there was a book deposited, written upon gold plates, giving an account of the former inhabitants of this continent, and the source from whence they sprang. He also said that the fullness of the everlasting Gospel was contained in it, as delivered by the Savior to the ancient inhabitants..."

The account was based upon Joseph Smith's translation.

* * * * *

Paul from Tyner Pioneer Family Bible:

Fruits of the Spirit

Walk in the Spirit and ye shall not fulfil the lust of the flesh. For the flesh lusteth against the Spirit, and the Spirit against the flesh: and these are contrary the one to the other; so that ye cannot do the things that ye would. But if ye be led by the Spirit, ye are not under the law. Now the works of the flesh are manifest which are these: Adultery, fornication, uncleanness, lasciviousness, idolatry, witchcraft, hatred, variance, emulations, wrath, strife, seditions, heresies, envyings, murders, drunkenness, revellings and such like of the which I tell you before, as I have also told you in time past, that they which do such things shall not inherit the kingdom of God.

But the fruit of the Spirit is love, joy, peace, long- suffering, gentleness, goodness, faith, meekness, temperance: against such there is no law. And they that are Christ's have crucified the flesh with the affections and lusts.

If we live in the Spirit, let us also walk in the Spirit.

The Fruits Of The Spirit As Subjects For Meditation.

LOVE: God's love for me in unconditional. I am accepted. I can love others in the same love God has for me.

JOY: Joy is deeper than happiness and unhappiness. Joy comes from my relationship with God and world that God made.

PEACE: I have peace with God. I can be at peace within myself and with others.

PATIENCE: I can be patient with others and myself because God is patient with me. What's the rush? Why do I push?

KINDNESS:

GENEROSITY: It is not by hoarding or holding onto my life that I find joy, but in giving. In what ways can I be more generous with my time, my possessions, myself?

FAITHFULNESS: God is steadfast love. Therefore I can be steadfast in my love and not give up so easily on people and those things that are most important.

GENTLENESS: People and life around me are beautiful and fragile. I can speak, act, and live with greater sensitivity and awareness.

SELF-CONTROL: For the sake of other's lives and my own, I can examine my behaviors, attitudes, and thoughts in light of the love of God. I don't have to have, speak, think, or do everything!

* * * * *

Ralph Vaughn Williams:

A Song to Honor Christian Saints from Days of Christian Martyrdoms

For all the saints,
Who from their labors rest,
Who you by faith before the world confessed,
Your Name, O Jesus, be forever blest.

> Allelulia, alleluia!—Amen.

You were their rock, their fortress, and their might:
You, Familyhead, their Captain in the well-fought fight;
You, in the darkness dreary, the one true light.

> Allelulia, alleluia!—Amen.

O may your soldiers, faithful, true, and bold,
Fight as the saints who nobly fought of old,
And win, with them, the victor's crown of gold.

> Allelulia, alleluia!—Amen.

O blest communion, fellowship divine!
We feebly struggle, they in glory shine;
Yet all are one in you, for all are thine.

> Alleluia, alleluia!

And when the strife is fierce,
The warfare long,
Steals on the ear the distant triumph song,
And hearts are brave again,
And arms are strong.

> Alleluia, Alleluia!

From earth's wide bounds,
From ocean's farthest coast,
Through gates of pearl streams in the countless host,
Singing to Parent, Child, and Holy Ghost,

> Alleluia, alleluia!—Amen.

* * * * *

Eusebius and Traditional Accounts:

The Works of the Apostles

The Apostles who traveled with Jesus and spread the message of God's coming to earth lived dramatic lives and courageously carried the message of God's life on earth to the far reaches of the world. Their lives were devoted to witnessing what they heard and saw. Traces of their lives and even their relics survive.

Where formerly there had been twelve favored tribes of Israel, Jesus set forth twelve evangelists to go out so that all the world would inherit the favor of the former twelve tribes of Israel. All the planet saw missionaries and now the favor of God rests over the entire earth.

This recitation of the lives of the twelve does not challenge the redeeming work of the Spirit of God. The church of Jesus was born on Pentecost when people from all the parts of the world heard the message of God's life on earth shortly after the ascension of Jesus to God's Homeland. Until Pentecost the chosen Apostles waited. Thereafter they were unshakably committed to perform work as missionaries assisted by the Spirit of God's own Breathing.

Pentecost established that God always intended Jesus to be the Familyhead of all of humanity. The life of God on earth was to be an international experience. Under the direct leadership of the Breathing Spirit of God, Philip was sent out to witness to an Ethiopian treasurer. Peter was directly commanded to witness and baptize Cornelius, the Roman centurion at Joppa. Despite martyrdoms such as those of Stephen and James, the imprisonment of Peter, the advance of the church continued. Paul and Barnabas began their travels. Other missionaries and followers evangelized with the stories about the life of Jesus.

An early church historian, Eusebius, says that the inhabited world was divided into zones of influence among the Apostles after Jerusalem fell in 70 A.D. Thomas was assigned the region of the Parthians, John in Asia, Peter in Pontus and Rome, Andrew in Scythia. Many of the geographical churches have been linked to the apostles who taught them and helped them establish their churches. The Mesopotamia churches link themselves to James and Thomas. The Asian church trace themselves to Philip and John. Those churches of Phoenicia, Pontus, Greece and Rome are said to be Petrine or influenced first by Peter.

Next to Paul, we know the most about Peter. Here was a tumultuous person as unstable as water who was transformed into the character of a rock.

The original site of the home of Peter which is often chronicled in the gospels still remains in Capernaum. Here Jesus visited, healed Peter's mother-in-law, slept, cured many people, and often returned. In the principal large room the Jewish followers of Jesus held services of reunion and prayer and in the other rooms people lived common lives for many years. The site remains for visitors to view.

It is said that Peter first went to Mesopotamia after Pentecost. There were many rich and influential Jewish commercial settlements in these places and along the coast of India, Ceylon, Malaya and on to the farthest coasts of China. There is a record of Thaddeus going to Edessa to fulfill a promise of Jesus to send a missionary to King Abgar of that place. The letters of Peter indicated Peter preached in Babylon. Thomas worked among the Jews of Mesopotamia and later on went to the small colonies on the coast of India and reached Cranganore by 52 A.D. Bartholomew was also founder of a church there.

The message of the life of God on earth was received fully in the former Persian Empire. The major cities were evangelized first and then the Word spread into the interiors.

The first center of God's church was in Antioch but then centers spread to Corinth, Ephesus, Alexandria in Egypt, and Rome while Edessa, Arbil, Seleucia-Ctesiphon became strong hubs in the former Persian Empire.

Eusebius tell us of the church of Antioch where the Matthew Committee gathered together the substance of the gospel of Matthew from Jerusalem church materials, books of the sayings of Jesus and recollections of Peter and the other Apostles. Peter was said to have founded the Antioch church and became its first bishop before he went to Rome. Tradition says Peter was in charge of the Antioch church for seven years before going to Rome. The destruction and fall of Jerusalem in 70 A.D. prompted migration of many followers of Jesus to Antioch. St. Peter is said to have charged many others to become missionaries. One record has Peter while at Rome sending three such missionaries, Eucharius, Valerius and Matermus, to Trier and Cologne to preach the gospel.

The tradition of the death of Peter is this. Peter was crucified by order of Nero - who also had Paul beheaded - on the Vatican Hill. Peter was first cast into the horrible fetid prison of the Mamertine. Here he was held for nine months prior to crucifixion in absolute darkness. The historian Sallust describes the place of imprisonment of Peter. "In the prison called the Tullian, there is a place about ten feet deep. It is surrounded on the sides by walls and is closed above by a vaulted roof of stone. The appearance of it from the filth, the darkness and the smell is terrible." Many prisoners went stark mad. Others were kept them prior to being murdered. Countless followers of Jesus were imprisoned in its depths. The historian Boadicea, in her account of Paul's death, says, "How Peter managed to survive those nine dreadful months is beyond human imagination. During his entire incarceration he was manacled in the upright position, chained to the column, unable to lie down to rest. Yet, his magnificent spirit remained undaunted. It flamed with the immortal fervor of the noble soul proclaiming the Glory of God through the Child Jesus." In spite of the suffering, Peter was said to have converted his gaolers, Processus, Martinianus, and forty-seven others.

Peter refused to die in the same position of Jesus, declaring he was unworthy. Peter demanded to be crucified in the reverse position, with his head hanging downward. This wish was granted in A.D. 67. Another story of Peter survives. Peter's parting words to his wife as she was led out to execution were words of rejoicing because of her summons and her return home and Peter called to her very encouragingly and comfortingly addressing her by name and saying, "Oh, just remember your Familyhead." This according to Eusebius and Clement.

Peter has the firmest connection to Mark's gospel. An early historian, Papias notes that Mark was Peter's interpreter. Mark translated for Peter as Peter preached in Rome. His frequent repetition permitted Mark to be able to give an almost verbatim account of Peter's recollections. After Peter's death, Mark was said to have realized the value of Peter's first hand accounts and drew up his gospel. Luke was said to have used Mark's account for his own gospel accounts and much of the same material from Peter was also used by the Antioch writers of the Matthew gospel. Peter's great contribution to the church came in the accounts of the life of Jesus which read to this day.

Peter's body was removed to the cemetery in the Appian Way two miles from Rome where it rested obscurely until the reign of Constantine who rebuilt and enlarged the Vatican to honor Peter.

Peter was said to have been a slender person of a middle size inclining to tallness. He had a pale complexion, curly beard which was thick and short, and black eyes flecked with red from crying too much according to the seventeenth century writer Dorman Newman.

Pope Paul VI proclaimed bones found in a niche of St. Peter's were those of Peter. They were identified from ancient Latin inscriptions in the place where the bones were discovered.

Mark's bones are also revered in Italy. These are in Venice in the altar of St. Mark's Church. The tradition of those is that they were sneaked out of Alexandria, Egypt long after Mark died. The real bones of the gospel writer were declared as a bag of pig's bones to custom's authorities in Egypt.

The Apostle Andrew was a native of Galilee born in Bethsaida. He joined John the Baptist, the cousin of Jesus, before becoming an Apostle. Andrew was said to have done missionary work in Scythia, Southern Russia, on the Black Sea. Here he was stoned. Then he went into Macedonia and Greece. The proconsul ordered him crucified in this account because the proconsul's wife Maximilla had been converted by Andrew. The cross of Andrew was said to have been in the form of an X, hence "St. Andrew's Cross" in that shape. Another tradition has Andrew receiving a revelation from God that he must go have John write down his recollections while both were in Ephesus. Thus he indirectly is responsible for the gospel of John. Patras in Greece was said to be the place of Andrew's martyrdom. A church there contains the relic of Andrew's skull. A few bones of Andrew were taken to Scotland in the fifth century. Andrew's cross is the official banner of this place. The Russians, Greeks and Scots all claim special ties to Andrew. When Constantine built the great church at Constantinople he was said to have done so as a shrine for relics of not just Andrew but also Timothy and Luke.

The Apostle James was the first to be martyred. This incident is in the gospels along with the death of Judas, one of the other original Apostles. James was the older brother of John, the beloved Apostle. With John, Andrew and Peter, James was in the fishing trade with James's father, Zebedee. James was murdered by King Herod Agrippa I about 44 A.D, shortly before Herod's own death.

According to Spanish legend, James preached the gospel first in Judea and then began traveling over the whole world until he went to Spain. One day, as James stood with his disciples on the banks of Ebro, the blessed Virgin appeared to him seated on the top of a pillar of jasper and surrounded by a choir of angels. James threw himself down on his face as the Virgin commanded James to build on that spot a church for her worship, assuring him all this province of Saragossa though in paganism at the time would be specially devoted to her in the future. Thus the church, Nuestra Senora del Pillar' was built and James, after having founded the church of Jesus in Spain, returned to Judea where he preached for many years.

Another tradition has James confronting one of those dragging him to Herod Agrippa to be murdered who was then himself converted and asked to be killed along with James. James gave him a kiss and said, "Pax vobis!" and this kiss and the words became a benediction for the church ever since. James was said to have been buried by friends outside Jerusalem.

James's brother John was the last of the Apostles to die in about 100 A.D. He lived a long life at Ephesus and had a special relationship to the other churches in this area. John was said to have taken Mary, the mother of Jesus, with him to Ephesus. John cared for her there until her death.

A story about John survives from the time when John governed the churches of Asia. John's residency at the time was at Ephesus, a Christian center where Paul founded the first church. John's work there continued until his death during the reign of the Roman Emperor Trajan (according to Iranaeus). John traveled extensively appointing bishops of cities and visiting churches. On one occasion, after John ordained a bishop he saw a young man nearby and said to the bishop, "Him I commend to you with all earnestness, in the presence of the church and of Jesus." The bishop took the young man home with him, had him educated and baptized. Nevertheless, as the young man grew into adolescence and beyond, he took up with a gang of robbers who drew him away from the church. They included him in expensive entertainments, had him go with them to plunder and eventually he was chosen their leader. They stationed themselves to control mountainous rough regions where they could not be captured. As the captain of this robber band, the young man surpassed them all in violence, blood and cruelty. When John heard of this, he visited the bishop to whom he had entrusted the boy. Then he demanded a horse and a guide to the mountain where the band thrived. John rode away as he was from the church and was taken prisoner at the gang's mountain by an outguard. John did not attempt to flee but instead insisted, "For this very purpose am I come. Conduct me to your captain." When the young man saw John advancing towards him, overcome with shame, he turned about to flee. The Apostle, however, pursued him with all his might, forgetful of advanced age and cried out, "Why do you fly, my son, from me, your father, your defenseless, aged father? Have compassion on me, my son. Fear not! You still have hope of life. I will intercede with Jesus for you. Should it be necessary, I will cheerfully suffer death for you, as Jesus did for us. I will give my life for you. Stay. Believe Jesus has sent me." Upon hearing this the robber captain at first gave downcast looks. Then throwing open his arms, he embraced the aged Apostle. Soon he was re-baptized in tears and became a powerful voice for Jesus in the Asian churches.

And so the witness of the Apostles continued in the work of humanity until each died.

After Clement:

On Being Humbly-Minded

Humble yourselves. Lay aside all pride and boasting and foolishness and anger. Have it be as it is written by the Spirit of God, "I will not allow the wise person profit in wisdom, nor the strong person in strength, nor the rich person in riches, but have the one seeking my attention act profitably for the Familyhead, to seek after God's Child, and to do judgment and justice."

Above all, remember the words of the Familyhead, Jesus, when he spoke about equity and long suffering, saying, "Be merciful and you will obtain mercy. Forgive and you will be forgiven. As you do, so will it be done to you. As you give, so will it be given to you. As you judge, so will you be judged. As you are kind to others so will God be kind to you. With the measure you dispense, the same will be measured back to you."

By this command and by these rules, let us establish ourselves so that we may always walk obediently to the inspired words, being humbly minded. Inspired writing tells us of God's self-dialogue, "Who will I look to? I will look to the vulnerable ones and those conscious of their need for me who respect the story of my life."

It is necessary, just and right, people, that we become obedient to God rather than follow pride and rebellion to the point of becoming cultists of a circle of forbidden emulation. We do ourselves no ordinary harm by this but rather run a great danger if we give ourselves over to the wills of leaders who promote strife and seditions to turn us aside from that which is fitting.

Be kind to one another according to compassion and sweetness of the God who made us. It is written, "The merciful will inherit the earth. Those that are without malice will be left upon it. Those who do not witness God's Child will perish from off the face of the earth."

Keep your innocence and the thing that is right, for there will be a remnant to the peaceable person.

Hold fast to those who pursue peace and not to those who pretend to desire it. There is the saying, "This people honor me with their lips but their heart is far from me." And another saying, "They bless me with their mouths, but curse in their hearts."

Lying lips will become dumb along with the tongue that speaks proudly.

Those who oppress the poor and laugh at the sighing of the needy will cause the Familyhead to rise against them. Jesus will set the needy into safety and deal confidently with their oppressors.

God's Child is theirs who are humble and do not exalt themselves over the flock. The scepter of the majesty of God, our Familyhead Jesus, Child of God, did not appear in a show of pride and arrogance although it could have been so. Humility marked the appearance as the Spirit of God's breathing words spoke concerning the event. God told us, "I will love a people who accept my decision to have my Child grow up as a tender plant from a root out of dry ground. My Child will have no advantage of size or handsomeness and when seen will not have such beauty that it arouse desire. My Child will be despised and rejected by people. He will be a person of sorrows and acquainted with grief."

And so it was. We humans hid our faces from God's Child. We despised him and we did not value him at all.

How true it is he has carried our griefs and sorrows. We did not care that he was wounded, struck down, and afflicted.

Nevertheless, God's Child accepted the burden of wounds to bridge our separation from God. He was bruised for our transgressions. The discipline of peace was upon him. With his stripes we are healed.

* * * * *

Traditional:

Perpetua And Felicitas

Once there was a fine lady, Vibia Perpetua, with a personal slave, Felicitas, who were asked to worship the image of a Roman Emperor. The alternative - if they said "No"- was to be thrown to wild animals and slaughtered in a public amphitheater in Carthage, Africa where they lived. The event was to be a spectacular celebration of the birthday of the Emperor.

Perpetua was only twenty-two years old and was highly educated in Greek and Latin as well as being from a wealthy and powerful Roman family. She was recently married and the mother of a fine young boy.

The event occurred during a time of Christian persecution. Perpetua was arrested for worshipping the Familyhead along with friends Saturus and Saturninus and her slave and another slave Revocatus. Soon they were jailed in a stiffling African cell. Perpetua kept a written journal of what followed. Perpetua's father was horrified. He went to the jail every day to beg Perpetua "out of love for me" to change her decision about being a Christian. She rejected his pleas and to avoid embarrassing him changed her family name. She admitted grieving that her father, mother, and brothers were "suffering out of compassion for me." At first, she wrote, "I was tortured with worry for my baby there." She was able to gain permission for her baby to stay in jail with her. She says, "at once I recovered my health, relieved as I was of my worry and anxiety for the child."

A court hearing before a Roman official was slated. The father went to Perpetua in prison "worn with worry" to plead with Perpetua to offer sacrifice for the welfare of the emperors, kissing her hands as he spoke:

"Daughter...have pity on your father, if I deserve to be
called your father, if I have loved you more than all
your brothers; do not abandon me...Think of your
brothers; think of your mother and your aunt; think of
your child, who will not be able to live once you are
gone...Give up your pride! You will destroy all of
us. None of us will ever be able to speak freely again

if anything happens to you." Perpetua refused and writes how her father "left me in great sorrow." Then she wrote, "one day while we were eating breakfast we were suddenly hurried off for a hearing. We arrived at the forum and straightway the story went about the neighborhood near the forum and a huge crowd gathered. We walked up to the prisoner's dock. All the others when questioned admitted their guilt. then, when it came my turn, my father appeared with my son, dragged me from the step, and said: "Perform the sacrifice - have pity on your infant son. Offer the sacrifice for the welfare of the emperors."

"I will not," I retorted.

"Are you a Christian?" said Hilarianus. And I said:

"Yes, I am."

When my father persisted in trying to dissuade me,
Hilarianus ordered him to be thrown to the ground and
beaten with a rod. I felt sorry for my father, just as
I myself had been beaten. I felt sorry for his pathetic old age.
Then Hilarianus passed sentence on all of us: we were
condemned to the beasts, and we returned to prison in
high spirits."

Long before she was condemned Perpetua knew she was going to die. She had a dream of climbing a bronze ladder of great height reaching all the way to God's Homeland despite daggers, swords and spikes trying to keep her from climbing. Then the day before the execution, Perpetua had another dream of having to fight with a terrible athlete. When she was striped of clothing to begin the fight, she found she had become a strong man who won the wrestling match. Then she ends her journal, "So much for what I did until the evening of the contest. About what happened at the contest itself, let whoever write about it who will."

As the execution date approached, Perpetua's slave Felicitas was eight month's pregnant. Felicitas did not want to survive her friends but since she was pregnant she could not be executed under Roman law until after she gave birth. Two days before the execution, the Christians prayed for her "in one torrent of common grief, and immediately after their prayer the labor pains came upon her. She suffered a good deal in her labor because of the natural difficulty of an eight-month delivery." The slave woman's baby was taken to be raised in another Christian's family.

Then came the day of the execution when Perpetua and Felicitas were led, together with their Christian brothers, to the amphitheater. At first they were to be dressed in costumes of robes of priests of the god Saturn for the men and costumes of priestesses of the goddess Ceres for the women as if they were offering their lives as a sacrifice to these gods. When they refused, they were stripped naked and confined in nets and placed in the amphitheater. This did not long continue. A witness says, "even the crowd was horrified when they saw that one was a delicate young girl, and the other woman fresh from childbirth, with milk still dripping from her breasts. And so they were brought back again and dressed in loose tunics.

Now a mad heifer was set loose after them. Perpetua was gored and thrown to the ground wounded. She got up and seeing Felicitas crushed and fallen she went over to her and lifted her up and the two stood side by side. Then they underwent similar attacks which included tortures committed against the men. Finally Perpetua and Felicitas, along with others, were called to the center of the arena to be slaughtered. The witness recalls that Perpetua "screamed as she was struck on the bone; then she took the trembling hand of the young gladiator, and guided it to her throat."

This witness then continues, "Some spectators at such martyrdoms to Christians shook their heads and said, 'What good was their religion to them, which they preferred even over their own lives.'"

* * * * *

Justin:

Brave Letters to the Emperors

A boy named Justin was born in Samaria in 110 A.D. to a rich Roman family. He wished to learn philosophy and went to Rome where the Roman emperors lived. These emperors claimed they were blessed by the pagan gods, the powers of the creation, who gave the emperors divine authority to rule humanity. The Roman emperors wanted to be worshipped. On the other hand, the Romans passed around rumors that Christians were cannibals who embraced promiscuity. When Justin learned the truth about Jesus and saw how Christians were suffering so from martyrdoms, Justin's conscience was struck and he converted from paganism to Christianity.

Justin learned from philosophy that the human mind cannot grasp the truth about the universe except through the power of the spirit of God. Then comes Christian freedom. This meant freedom from sexual passion, greed and hatred but also from external domination of the human soul by any government. Justin opened a Christian school in Rome itself. The trouble was that this left him open to arbitrary arrest and condemnation as a Christian. To be a Christian brought a death sentence in those days.

Justin did not think this right so he wrote brave letters to the Roman Emperors to explain Christianity. Justin wished them to know a terrible secret learned by the Christians. The power of the Roman gods was from demons, active evil forces bent upon corrupting and destroying humanity, determined to blind people to the fact that there is One God, Creator and the Parent of the earthly Familyhead, Jesus. The Christians believed that though Jesus was crucified by Roman authority Jesus triumphed over it, arose from death, and now was enthroned triumphantly at the right hand of God where martyrs and other Christians could join God's Child. Christians felt worship of the Roman Emperors was disgusting.

Justin wrote to the emperors and said:

"The truth shall be told; since of old these evil demons (the ancient Greek and Roman gods) effecting apparitions of themselves, both polluted women and corrupted boys, and showed such terrifying visions to people that those who did not use their reason...were struck by terror; and being carried away by fear, and not knowing that these were demsons, they called them gods."

Humanity fell under the power of demons until Jesus appeared. Very few, only such as Socrates, escaped demonic thinking. Justin said:

"Taking as their ally the desire for evil in everyone," the demons became the patrons of powerful and ruthless leaders and "instituted private and public rites in honor of those who are most powerful." Injustice in the courts resulted. According to Justin, the demons of the world manipulte judges to try to destroy the hope of humanity to find salvation in God and brought about the conviction of Socrates as well as Jesus, God's own Child. He said:

"And when Socrates attempted by true reason and investigation to...deliver humanity from the demons, then the demons themselves, using human beings as their instruments, brought upon him death for being an "atheist," and in our case, too, they do the same things."

Justin trusted the powerful Emperors of Rome to be open to reason. He addressed them as "fellow philosophers and lovers of learning." Nevertheless, Justin wrote angrily that they were administering a system that condemned persons for refusing to worship demons. Justin hinted that these emperors were actually criminals - "robbers in the desert" - who rule by force, not justice, because of what they were doing. Justin warned them, "be on your guard, lest the demons whom we have been attacking deceive you, and distract you from reading and understinding what we say. These demons strive to keep you as their slaves."

The letters of Justin received wide publicity. Justin was depicting the Emperors of Rome as petty tyrants enslaved to demons contending against people allied with the One True God. Christians asserted they were free to worship only God who retains ultimate power over the universe and renders final vindication for the followers of Jesus and condemneation for God's Child's enemies. But on the other hand, Justin was also asking for tolerance for Christians. Justin explained that Christians "more readily than any other people," pay full share of taxes and "we, more than any other people, are your helpers and allies in preserving peace." All Christians seek is to obey God not a human government undergird by demons. Justin depicted Christians as a humble people who merely wished to live quietly without persecution. They wished to be respected and not required to deny God's Child or be forced to make pagan sacrifice. To persecute Christians was a great mistake. Christians were good citizens.

Then came the day Justin anticipated. He was arrested and charged with being a Christian. His judge, Rusticus, interrogated him and other Christians arrested and repeated his demand, "Let us come to the point at issue - a necessary and urgent matter. Agree together to offer sacrifice to the gods."

Justin said, "No one of sound mind turns from piety to sacrilege."

The judge said, "If you do not obey, you will be punished without mercy."

Justin and his friends answered, "Do what you will: we are Christians, and will not sacrifice to idols."

Rusticus entered judgement saying, "Those who have refused to sacrifice to the gods and yield to the emperor's law are to be taken away to be beaten and beheaded, in accordance with the laws."

* * * * *

Traditional:

Shekhina

Blessed Shekhina,
Perfect reflection of womanly being
Whose image appears upon seeking the highest grace.
Too long has She been in exile.
Too long have Her people
sorrowed at Her absence.
Since the burning of Her sanctuary,
She has been seen at the wailing wall
Clad in black and weeping.
Yet She may be found
In the field of Provident fruit trees.
Her orchards are very sacred in memory -
And now we beg her to return.
Maybe She is one
With the Queen of the Sabbath,
Shabbat Bride of the Kabbalah.
Was she once known as Shapatu
Seen in the silver of the moon?
Then she was welcomed by the Semitic peoples
And honor was paid to Her beloved being
When first she arrived
As a thin young crescent
In the dark heaven.
And again, when in Her full attendedness
Her perfect glowing roundness
Cast silver flecks upon the leaves
Of Her provident grove?

Still the candles are lit.
Still the sacred braided loaf is baked
In hopes that Her ancient Sabbath spirit
Will enter each home -
Filling it with the Mother love
That is the very presence of the Shekhina.

* * * * *

Missionaries After the Apostles

About the year 303, Albanus, a heathen of England while under Rome, gave shelter to a Christian missionary. Albanus was won over to the faith. When soldiers came to arrest the Christian, Albanus put on the missionary's garments to be taken in the missionary's stead. The judge demanded of Albanus his name, but Albanus only confessed his faith. He said only, "Christianus sum." ("I am a Christian.") He would not tell his own name nor city nor whether he were slave or free. The judge commanded him to sacrifice to the gods nevertheless. Albanus said they are not gods but goblins. Albanus was condemned. Crowds of Britons came to see the execution and they filled the river Thames bridge so that the convict could not cross. Albanus eager for the crown of martyrdom caused the river to dry up so that he could cross the river to his place of execution. Albanus prayed his executioner for water and when he refused a spring appeared. Then Albanus and his executioner who was himself converted were beheaded. The historian Bede says, "Even to this day there are ceaselessly fulfilled the healing of the sick and a continuance of good works."

As barbarians with strange gods began invasions of every land, Jerome (342-420) journeyed to Bethlehem in the Holy Land and founded a monastery where he translated the gospels into Latin and preserved their words. In 376, he wrote, "I shudder to think of the catastrophes of our time. For more than twenty years Roman blood has daily been shed, from Constantinople to the Julian Alps. The Roman world is falling, yet we hold up our heads instead of bowing them down...If only I had a watch-tower so high as to view the whole earth, I would show you the wreck of the world."

In the Fifth Century the Franks began to settle along the Rhine and extended their power. Clovis, a boy of sixteen, became their king. The Franks were not Christian in any respect. Four years later Clovis faced a Roman army. After victory, he incorporated the legionnaires into his own forces. Clovis married a Christian wife, Clotilda, the daughter of the King of the Burgundians. She told him of Jesus. Then the Franks were forced to defend their lands against northern tribesmen, the Alemanni. Clovis prayed, "I have called upon my own gods, but, as I see it, they are far from my help. I believe they are robbed of power, who do not help those who give them obedience. I now call upon thee and believe in thee. So let me be plucked from the hands of my adversaries." Clovis's forces were saved from defeat. On Christmas Day, 496, Clovis, the King of the Franks, along with three thousand of his warriors were baptized and the Franks became witnesses to God's Child.

As the nations of the world began forming, missionaries from monasteries were often teachers. They learned their discipline from Benedict, born in 480 A.D. This young man was sent to Rome to be educated. It was said, "He inspected the world and despised it." Disgusted with the immorality of Rome, he went off to live as a hermit in a cave, Subiaco, half-way between Rome and Monte Cassino. Others joined him. Now the Christian expansion was led by monastics from monasteries established under Benedict's discipline. His Rule of 529 begins, "Give heed my son to the precepts of the master, and incline the ear of your heart. Accept with gladness the admonition of the father, and fulfil it carefully. So by the hard word of obedience you may return whence the sloth of disobedience has withdrawn you."

As Columba began his missionary works among the Celts and Picts about the year 563, he encountered the Loch Ness monster. On reaching the banks of the Ness River, Columba saw villagers burying a poor fellow who had been swimming there. A water-beast with savage jaws caught and bit him. Some of them put out in a boat but could only recover the corpse. Columba said, "All the same, one of our company must swim to the opposite shore and steer the boat there back to me." A monk with him stripped and dived into the water. The Loch Ness monster was waiting with an appetite sharpened by the former prey. He lay hidden in deep water. Then he felt the surface disturbed by the swimmer and came up with a roar, jaws wide open, making straight for the swimmer in mid- stream. Columba raised his holy hand to save him, drew the sign of the cross in the empty air, and commanded the fierce beast in the name of God, saying, "No further! Do not touch him! Quick! Back you go!" The beast was within a pole's length of the swimmer but backed away so quickly as if hauled by cables and fled. Then did the heathen natives say, "Great is the God of the Christians."

As the world fell into war, looting, famine, plague and crushing taxation, Gregory was growing up in Italy. He gave away his father's vast estates and inheritance to become a monk before being declared Pope in Rome. Soon the world turned to Christianity to find a basis for a peaceful society. The church assumed the authority of the government of the world as the Roman Empire died.

And the northern peoples of Europe were brought to God's Child. The missionary Willibroard went into Holland and found a sacred spring - so sacred that no one dared speak near it - from which folk had gone to draw water for centuries. Daring what no man had done before, Willibrord brought his converts to this pool and shouted for all to hear, "I baptize you in the name of the Parent..." When nothing happened, the people of the place said the old god must have slunk away and joined in the conversion.

And Boniface struck into Germany to bring Jesus to those peoples. He came across the mighty oak of Geismar. The oak tree stood, like an ancient superstition itself, deeply rooted into the past. The Germans had for hundreds of years considered it sacred to Thor, the god of thunder. It might have stood another hundred years had not Boniface cut it down. Boniface told the people he would convince them their gods were powerless against God. From miles around the Germans gathered hardly believing Boniface would dare to cut down Thor's tree. They were sure lightning would flash and consume him if he tried. They watched as Boniface stripped to the waist and began striking with his axe at the base of the tree with regular strokes. Now, instead of the lightning flashing, there came a sudden wind helping Boniface and soon the old oak crashed down and broke into pieces out of which Boniface constructed a Christian church. And so paganism ended in Germany.

Patrick was sixteen when he was carried from Britain to Ireland with two sisters, farmers and neighbors. They were among prisoners of war taken in a seventh century raid. In Ireland he turned to God for help. "Day by day as I went, a shepherd with my flock, I used to pray constantly...a hundred prayers a day, and nearly as many at night, staying out in the woods or on the mountain. And before daybreak I was up fro prayer, in snow or frost or rain." After six years, a voice in his sleep spoke of home-coming and a few nights after, "Your ship is ready." Patrick escaped and tramped two hundred miles to a port. A ship was ready to sail, and Patrick tried to get on but was repulsed. Desperate, and praying hard, he heard a sailor call him aboard. After three days they landed on a shore of a place desolate due to a barbarian invasion. Patrick's prayers saved them from starving when they met a herd of wild pigs. Even the dogs of the sailors were able to eat. After two months he got away from the ship's crew and went to Britain where he was welcomed by his parents who had not been seized. But Patrick was not at peace. He says, "I saw in the night visions of a man coming from Ireland whose name was Victoricus with letters innumerable. And I read the letter which began, `The voice of the Irish.' And while I was reading out that beginning, that same moment I thought I heard the voice of those who were beside the wood of Foclut, which is near to the western sea. And they cried as with one mouth, `We ask you, holy boy, to come and walk among us once again.' And I was exceedingly `broken in heart' and could read no more. And so I awoke, Thanks be to God that after many years the Lord granted to them according to their cry." And so Patrick went to Ireland as a missionary so that a people who had never had the knowledge of God but only worshipped idols and abominations could become children of God's Child.

* * * * *

After John Foxe:

Constantine

What idea can survive which denies God a Child? If this world is the inheritance of that Child, can any force of this world depose that Child? If the Child gives folk comfort in church life, can any ban that church? What benefit is there in witness for the Child as a people?

The history of those people who love the Child has been filled with great persecution.

But always since the time of Constantine has the chief government of the world been in the hands of those who honor the Child. In this way has God given this world the benefit of God's favor.

Other ideas challenge God's plan. They fail.

The chief government of the world at the time God gave this world the gift of the Child was Rome. Christian tradition reports that the head of that government, Tiberius Caesar, heard of Jesus from Pilate. Tiberius was much impressed and even considered debate in the Roman Senate whether to acknowledge Jesus.

Not for three hundred years and as the result of the work of Constantine did Rome come around.

The father of Constantine was Constantius, a Caesar, or chief ruler, of the Roman Empire. Constantius was in charge of France, Spain and Britain because, in those days, the Roman Empire was divided into divisions for administration. Constantius took his son Constantine as his successor and died while a persecution of Christians was underway elsewhere in the Roman Empire.

Constantine was born in England. His mother was named Helena and she was a daughter of a native king, Coilus. Constantine was brought up with a good education and enjoyed learning and the good arts. Oftentimes he took to reading or writing or studying by himself as a child. He greatly favored the Christian faith. Once he chose to live for God's Child, he was steadfast in Christian devotions and beliefs. Constantine was also bright and witty, eloquent as a speaker, a speculator in philosophy and excellent in debate.

He committed himself as a Roman Emperor to refuse no labor which would benefit his people. He believed appointments as Emperor were determined by God for specific purposes. His own goal was to do as Emperor what was worthy of his appointment to the post by God.

Elsewhere in the Roman Emperor was a division at Rome ruled by Maxentius, also the son of a ruler. Maxentius took his post at the point of a sword. The praetorian soldiers of the Empire were his chief supporters. He ruled Rome in tyranny and great wickedness like that of the Pharaoh of former days or Nero, an Emperor who was often compared to a "beast" for his cruelty. Maxentius's greed caused him to murder Roman citizens to confiscate their belongings. When angered he ordered citizens gathered up and murdered. He did not avoid any lascivious act and loved magic. He invoked devils to help him. Maxentius at first tolerated Christians to gain their favor but toward the end he turned to Christian persecution.

The citizens and Senate of Rome wrote to Constantine for relief from the rule of Maxentius. Constantine responded with correspondence to Maxentius to urge him to consider what his corruption and cruelty were bringing about toward the Children of God. This didn't work. So Constantine warned Maxentius he must not grieve the people of his division of the Empire or he would do something about it. When nothing gave relief, Constantine gathered together an army in Britain and France to depose the tyrant in Rome.

In the last year of the Christian persecution of 313 A.D., Constantine and his soldiers marched towards Italy. Constantine's army brushed aside all skirmishes with the soldiers of Maxentius until he reached the outskirts of Rome.

In anxiety, Constantine often looked up to the skies and voiced his hopes in prayer to God's Child for help safeguard the Child's family on earth.

Outside Rome, on one such occasion, Constantine raised his eyes up to the skies over Rome and observed a great brightness in heaven which fixed his gaze. It was in the South part of the sky. As Constantine concentrated his attention, he noticed this great brightness to be in the form of a cross. Under this cross were bright letters reading, "In hoc vince." This is Latin which is translated as "In this, be victorious." In later years, Constantine often repeated that this is what he saw with his own eyes in the heavens. His soldiers also confirmed this. They were so sure of what they saw that they swore to it. Constantine and his soldiers conferred together what the meaning of this could be.

Then that night Constantine had a dream in which the Familyhead appeared to him with the sign of the same cross which Constantine saw before. The Familyhead told Constantine to carry an emblem of this cross before his armies into this great war against Roman Empire persecutions of Christians. Constantine was told he would be victorious if he did so. The cross was not given to induce superstitious worship or reverence of the cross itself as if the cross itself had some power, but only to bear the meaning of the events that were to follow. It was intended as an admonition to the soldiers to inspire them with knowledge and recollection of their faith in the Child of God.

The next day Constantine made a cross of gold and placed on it precious stones. He wished this cross carried before him as he battled for Rome instead of the normal Imperial standard carried in those days. Then he sent his troops into battle.

As one of his preparations for the battle, Maxentius destroyed the bridge over the River Tiber which led into Rome and built a fake bridge in its place, a bridge which would collapse at the weight of soldiers crossing it and destroy them by trickery.

The soldiers of Constantine and Maxentius joined in battle beyond this bridge. Constantine's troops prevailed and Maxentius tried to get away. In his desperation in doing so, Maxentius crossed this very bridge he had prepared as a trap. The bridge fell under him and the weight of his horse and armor and Maxentius was drowned being held under by the weight of his own armor.

This Maxentius was the last Christian persecutor in the Roman monarchy. Constantine, fighting under the cross of the Familyhead, vanquished Rome the government which persecuted Christians and established the peace for the Christians that lasted for the next thousand years.

The citizens of Rome gladly welcomed Constantine into their city. History has surnamed him as "Constantine the Great."

After the drowning of Maxentius and his victory, Constantine issued a proclamation which banned all religious persecution and gave liberty to all persons, both for the Christians and for all others, to freely worship according to personal beliefs.

This is an example of the miraculous working of God in the world.

Before Constantine, the many emperors of the Roman Empire confederated against the Child of God and the Child's friends and family on earth. They held Christians in subjection, disfavor and persecuted them. They often bent their whole might and fury to destroy Christianity. What did they fail to do? Their persecutions not only killed Christians but bereaved the Christians with horrible forms of killing. Whatever cruelty humanity could conceive was used. Christians were killed with whips, drawings, tearings, stonings and plates of iron were laid onto them burning hot. Christians were thrown into prisons to starve. They were stretched on racks. They were strangled in prisons. They were exposed to wild animals to be wounded, mangled and chewed. They were hung. They were beheaded. They were cut upon. Their bodies were abused in every subtle or horrible way. They were left to be tossed by the horns of bulls. After deaths from these causes, their bodies were often laid in heaps and given to dogs to eat. Prayers were forbidden for them. And yet, the Child of God welcomed them into God's life and their numbers increased daily. Thousands of Christians were put to death in such ways during the great periods of persecution.

Christians faced death with great courage. An example was Ignatius, the leader of the Antioch Church after Peter. When the Romans arrested him, his only comment was, "Now I begin to be a disciple. I care for nothing, of visible or invisible things, so that I may but win the Familyhead. Set me afire or place me on a cross. Set companies of wild beasts on me. Break my bones or tear off my limbs. Let animals chew up my body. Permit all the malice of the devil to be set against me. Be it so. Only this. I wish for Jesus." Then as the lions came to maul him in a public stadium in Rome, Ignatius said above their roar, "I am the wheat of the Child of God. I am going to be ground with the teeth of wild beasts that I may be found pure bread."

If the power of rulers prevails, how did Christianity survive? Only through the miraculous working of the power of the mighty God. Christianity could not have otherwise stood. Laws, edicts, proclamations mean nothing to God. No idea can stand against God's will.

The Roman Empire which practiced religious intoleration against Christians passed away following the victory of Constantine just as Revelation predicted.

God's Child is still the Familyhead of the Christians. The Church of the Familyhead still stands. God was steadfast in promising this world as the inheritance of God's Child. The only benefit of any people is to recognize this.

* * * * *

Athanasius:

The Reason for the Incarnation

You are wondering, perhaps, for what possible reason, having proposed to speak of the Incarnation of the Story of God's life on earth, we are at present treating of the origin of humanity. But this, too, properly belongs to the aim of our treatise. For in speaking of the appearance of the Saviour among us, we must speak also of the origin of people, that you may know that the reason of His coming down was because of us, and that our transgression called forth the loving-kindness of the story of God's life on earth, that the Familyhead should both make haste to help us and appear among people. For of His becoming Incarnate we were the object, and for our salvation He dealt so lovingly as to appear and be born even in a human body. Thus, then, God has made humanity, and willed that he should

abide in incorruption; but people, having despised and rejected the contemplation of God, and devised and contrived evil for themselves received the condemnation of death with which they had been threatened; and from thenceforth no longer remained as they were made, but were being corrupted according to their devices; and death had the mastery over them as king. For transgression of the commandment was turning them back to their natural state, so that just as they have had their being out of nothing, so also, as might be expected, they might look for corruption into nothing in the course of time. For if, out of a former normal state of nonexistence, they were called into being by the Presence and loving-kindness of the story of God's life on earth, it followed naturally that when people were bereft of the knowledge of God and were turned back to what was not (for what is evil is not, but what is good is), they should, since they derive their being from God who IS, be everlastingly bereft even of being; in other stories of God's life, that they should be disintegrated and abide in death and corruption. For a person is by nature mortal, inasmuch as he is made out of what is not; but by reason of his likeness to Him that is (and if he still preserved this likeness by keeping Him in his knowledge) he would stay his natural corruption, and remain incorrupt; as Wisdom says: "The taking heed to His laws is the assurance of immortality;" but being incorrupt, he would live henceforth as God, to which I suppose the divine Scripture refers, when it says: "I have said ye are gods, and ye are all sons of the most Highest; but ye die like people, and fall as one of the princes."

For God has not only made us out of nothing; but He gave us freely, by the Grace of the story of God's life on earth, a life in correspondence with God. But people, having rejected things eternal, and, by counsel of the devil, turned to the things of corruption, became the cause of their own corruption in death, being, as I said before, by nature corruptible, but destined, by the grace following from partaking of the story of God's life on earth, to have escaped their natural state, had they remained good. For because of the story of God's life on earth dwelling with them, even their natural corruption did not come near them, as Wisdom also says: "God made humanity for incorruption, and as an image of His own eternity; but by envy of the devil death came into the world." But when this was come to pass, people began to die, while corruption thenceforward prevailed against them, gaining even more than its natural power over the whole race, inasmuch as it had, owning to the transgression of the commandment, the threat of the Deity as a further advantage against them. For even in their misdeeds people had not stopped short at any set limits; but gradually pressing forward, have passed on beyond all measure: having to begin with been inventors of wickedness and called down upon themselves death and corruption; while later on, having turned aside to wrong and exceeding all lawlessness, and stopping at no one evil but devising all manner of new evils in succession, they have become insatiable in sinning. For there were adulteries everywhere and thefts, and the whole earth was full of murders and plunderings. And as to corruption and wrong, no heed was paid to law, but all crimes were being practised everywhere, both individually and jointly. Cities were at war with cities, and nations were rising up against nations; and the whole earth was rent with civil commotions and battles; each human being vying with his fellows in lawless deeds. For it were not worthy of God's goodness that the things

He had made should waste away, because of the deceit practised on people by the devil. Especially it was unseemly to the last degree that God's handicraft among people should be done away, either because of their own carelessness, or because of the deceitfulness of evil spirits. So, as the rational creatures were wasting and such works in course of ruin, what was God in His goodness to do? Suffer corruption to prevail against them and death to hold them fast?

* * * * *

THE MULBERRY TREE.

At the side of the road is an old rotten tree;
Since it withered many mornings have passed.
The bark is bright; outside it is still alive;
But the heart is black; for a tree rots from the core.
And so it is with the greatest sorrows of man;
The grief that slays him springs always from within.

By Po Chu-i   772–846 A. D.

After Athanasius,

Anthony's Advice About Demons and Wunks

Antony was an Egyptian born into a good and wealthy Christian family in the Third Century. The family owned a productive farm. Antony rarely left his home as a boy except to go to church. Then when Antony was about eighteen both of his parents died. Antony sold the family land and gave the money from it to the poor. He began devoting himself to helping others on their farms and homes.

But Antony wanted to discipline his body against lust and pleasure seeking. He began eating only once a day after sunset. The meal was bread and salt. He slept upon a rush mat.

Then he took to sleeping in a graveyard of tombs far from the village. He slept alone in one of the tombs.

This is how Antony came to know demons and wunks. The wunks tried to deceive him and the demons began to attack him. His staying in tombs, this the enemy of humanity could not permit and assaulted Antony with a multitude of wunks in various forms and demons who whipped him mercilessly until Antony was left on the ground speechless in great torment. No blows every inflicted on a person could have caused more torment. The next day, Antony's friends came to bring him bread and found him looking like a corpse. They took him back to the village and he eventually came around.

Antony was not about to be beaten by demons. He could not stand because of the blows but he had his friends return him to the tombs the next day and shouted,

"Here I am. Antony! I don't flee from your whippings. Nothing can separate me from the love of Jesus." When the enemy of humanity heard this, he was amazed Antony had dared to return but then grew angry again and burst forth with hounds of hell to attack him. They appeared in such a noise that the whole region seemed to shake with an earthquake and the place was filled with forms of lions, bears, leopards, bulls, serpents, asps, scorpions and wolves, and each one attacked Antony with the ferocity of its own nature, but none could harm him, because he lay there with an unshaken soul, groaning from bodily anguish but still clear in mind." Antony taunted them saying, "Taking the shapes of beasts only shows how weak you wunks are compared to the faith in God's Child which protects me." The enemy of humanity could not shake Antony's faith.

Antony decided to go live as a hermit in the desert mountains of Egypt where he found a deserted fort of ancient days. It was filled with reptiles but when Antony entered it, they left. Friends came to see Antony here. Then they slept outside the abandoned fort. In the night there came clamorous sounds, piteous voices, and shouts of crying from disembodied souls, "Go from this desert which is ours. We don't want you here. You cannot abide our attacks if you don't leave." Antony was summoned and he told them to make the sign of the cross and all demons and wunks must flee before their face. He said, "As smoke vanishes, so they will vanish. They are sinners who are perishing before the face of God."

Antony lived in the desert for twenty years. His fort came to be like a shrine to early Christians to visit. Antony would come forth and visit with travelers and his countenance appeared filled with the spirit of God's very breathing. He was given the gift of healing and Jesus healed many persons through him. He consoled the sorrowing and preached that he prefered the love of God's Child before all that is in the world. He was a persuasive advocate for solitary life. Soon cells of others began appearing around his desert mountain home.

On one occasion, Antony needed to travel and cross a river. Antony was able to encounter the full power of prayer and by simply praying he gained safety to cross an intervening river filled with crocodiles without harm. On one preaching occasion he explained his discipline as designed to rid him of the "desire of possesion." On the other hand his ascetic discipline was intended to give him gifts that could be taken with his soul to God. These were "prudence, justice, temperance, courage, understanding, love, kindness to the pooer, faith in God's Child, freedom from wrath and hospitality." His advice was to live to "die daily." He said there was no sin to one took to dying daily. This happened by avoiding being world-minded. The soul could gain rectitude by keeping it as close to its natural state as possible without worldly thinking of anger or lust.

Antony believed the world to be filled with demons and wunks in great numbers in the air. They were not made by God who makes nothing evil. They are souls who have fallen away from heavenly wisdom and have taken to grovelling on earth. They are villainous and try to wile their way into people's thinking. Antony said there was no need for a Christian to fear their suggestions because by prayer, fasting and faith, Jesus causes their attacks to immediately fail. They are treacherous and can change themselves into all forms and assume all appearances. They carry off the simple to despair. It was the Familyhead who stayed the demons and wunks of the earth in His appearance. Now they are weak and can only threaten. They have no power to effect anything. Antony said, "So then we ought to fear God only, and despise the demons and wunks, and be in no fear of them. But the more they do these things- prate, confuse, dissemble, confound, deceive the simple, change forms, make dins, laugh madly, whistle-the more let us intensify our discipline against them, for a good life and faith in God is a great weapon."

Antony said, "When therefore they come by night to you and wish to tell the future, or say, "we are the angels," give no heed, for they lie. Yea, even if they praise your discipline and call you blessed, hear them not, and have no dealings with them; but rather sign yourselves and your houses, and pray, and you shall see them vanish. For they are cowards, and greatly fear the sign of the Familyhead's cross, since of a truth in it the Savior stripped them and made an example of them. Then, even if they stay their ground, do not fear them. The presence of enemies can only remain in the presence of a fearful soul."

* * * * *

Nicene Creed

We believe in one God, the Parent almighty, Creator of heaven and earth, of all things both visible and invisible. And in one Familyhead Jesus Christ, the only-begotten Child of God, born of the Parent before all time, light from light, true God from true God; begotten, not created, of the same substance with the Parent; through this Child all things were made. For the sake of us humans and for our salvation, the Child came down from heaven, was made flesh by the Holy Spirit from the Virgin Mary, and became human; and he was crucified for our sake under Pontius Pilate, suffered, and was buried. And on the third day God's Child arose according to the scriptures, ascended into heaven, sits at the right hand of the Par-

ent, and is going to come again in glory to judge the living and the dead. This Child's reign will have no end. We believe in the Holy Spirit, the Familyhead, the giver of life who proceeds from the Parent, is adored and honored together with the Parent and the Child, spoke through the prophets. We believe in one, holy, catholic, and apostolic church. We profess one baptism for the forgiveness of sins. We expect the resurrection of the dead and the life of the world to come.   AMEN

* * * * *

Eusebius:

A Bishop's Account of the Nicene Creed
to His Church Members
from the Year of the Council of Nicea

What happened to confirm our faith at the Great Council at Nicea you have probably learned, beloved, from other sources with rumors preceding an accurate account. To avoid misunderstanding, we feel obliged to send to you first the formula of faith we submitted and then secondly the formula put forth with some additions to my proposal. My proposal which was read in the presence of our most pious Emperor (Constantine) and declared good and without room for criticism began this way:

"As we have received from the Bishops who preceded us, and in our first catechisings, and when we received the Holy Baptism, and as we have learned and taught in the Presbytery, and in the Episcopate itself, so believing also at the time present. We report to you our faith, and it is this,

"We believe in One God, the Parent Almighty, the Maker of all things visible and invisible. And in One Familyhead, Jesus, God Come to Earth, the Story of God, God from God, Light from Light, Life from Life, Child Only-begotten, First born of every creature, before all the ages, begotten from the Parent, by Whom also all things were made. This One for our salvation was made flesh and lived among humanity and suffered and rose again the third day, and ascended to the Parent, and will come again in full authority to judge the living and dead. And we believe also in One Spirit which is God's Spirit. We believe each of these to be and to exist. We believe the Parent truly Parent, and the Child truly Child and the Spirit of God truly God's Spirit, as also our Familyhead, sending forth students and friends to teach said, `Go teach all people, baptizing them in the Family name of the Parent, and of the Child and of God's Spirit.' Concerning this, we confidently affirm that so we hold, and so we think, and so we have held before, and we maintain this faith unto death, damning every godless deviation. We think this from our hearts and soul, from the time we recollected ourselves and now think and saying it truthfully before God Almighty and our Familyhead Jesus, God's Child, and so do we witness, being able by proofs to show and to convince that even in times past such has been our belief and preaching.'"

We put forth this faith statement. No contradiction appeared. Then our most pious Emperor was the first to talk. He testified that it comprised very acceptable statements. He confessed that it expressed his own sentiments and he advised all present to agree to it and to subscribe its articles and to assent to them with the insertion of the single phrase "of one essential substance" which he explained meant different from how human bodies react to each other as if the Child emerged from the Parent in the way of division or any severance. He stated that the immaterial and intellectual and bodiless nature of God and the Child could not be the subject of any bodily interaction and we should conceive of such things in a divine and inexplicable manner. And such were the theological remarks of our most wise and most religious Emperor. So the council with one accord drew up the statement of faith.

When the formula was dictated, we did not let it pass without inquiry in what sense they introduced "of the same substance with the Parent" and "one is substance with the Parent." Accordingly discussions took place and the phrase underwent scrutiny. They came to the conclusion that the phrase "of the substance" indicated the Child's self came from the Parent yet without being as if a part of God. And with this understanding we thought good to assent to the sense of such religious doctrine, teaching, as it did, that the Child was from the Parent, not however within the part of God's own essence.

In the same way we also discussed "begotten not created." This was decided because created was the name to the process by which other creatures came to be through God's Child to whom the Child had no likeness. They concluded Jesus was not a work resembling the things that through him came to be but that he was of a substance which is too great for the level of any work and which the Divine prophecies teach to have been generated from the Parent, the mode of generation being inscrutable and incalculable to every originated nature.

And so too on discussion there are grounds for saying that the Child is "one in substance" with the Parent. This is not in the way of bodies, nor like mortal beings, for Jesus is not such by division of substance or by severance. Nor did any physical force or alteration or changing of the Parent's substance and power occur (as if Jesus were not of the Godly substance and the Parent was alien.) One in substance with the Parent suggests that the Child of God bears no resemblance to the created creatures, but that to the Parent alone Who begat the Child into every assimilation and that the Child is not of any other subsistence and substance but from the Parent. To which term also, thus interpreted, it appeared well to agree since we were aware that even among the ancients some learned and illustrious Bishops and writers have used the term "one in substance" in their theological teaching concerning the Parent and Child.

So then this be said concerning the faith which was published to which all assented not without inquiry but according to the specified senses mentioned before the most religious Emperor himself and justified by the outlined considerations.

* * * * *

Augustine:

Dealing with Sex

Once there was a boy who wanted to know everything. He thought he could learn enough to discover God that way. He was a very bright boy whose name was Augustine. His father, Patricius, was a Roman official and a pagan while his mother, Monica, was a Christian. Augustine was born in 354 A.D. in North Africa.

As a boy, Augustine studied and studied. He attended the finest school of the area called Madaura and learned the entire curriculum in a single year. His instructors said he had the finest brain they ever encountered. It was clear that Augustine was destined to become a teacher.

Yet Augustine could not satisfy his intellectual need. He seemed to have no power to reach an understanding of God. His sexual impulses took over and controlled him.

Augustine felt his body take control over him time and time again.

He admitted as much. He wrote, "I will now call to mind my past foulness and the carnal corruptions of my soul. My dissipation drove me into pieces. I burned in my youth to be satisfied with things below and I was wild with various and shadowy loves. I lost myself. My beauty was consumed away and I stank in the eyes of God pleasing myself and desiring only to please the eyes of humanity. I delighted in nothing but to love and be loved. Nor did I keep love within bounds or as friendships. Instead sexual impulses bubbled up in my youth. Mists fumed up which beclouded and overcast my heart so I could not understand the brightness of love from the goal of lust. Love and lust got confused in me. I hurried my unstoppable passions as they threw me over the precipice of unholy desires and sank me in a gulf of excess. God's wrath was gathered over me for this without my knowing it. I grew deaf by the clanking of the chain of my own mortality. I strayed further away from God and God allowed it and left me alone. I boiled over with fornications. God allowed this to happen."

Augustine wanted to find God but instead his body was in charge. "I foamed like a troubled sea, following the rushing of my own tide forsaking God and exceeded all limits." There he was in his sixteenth year, "when the madness of lust caused me to shamelessly give lust free license and it took the rule of me and I resigned myself to lust."

Augustine did not ignore the condition he found in himself. He concluded that humanity is in bondage to its sexuality. There is no rational control over sexual impulses. He confesses, "what made me a slave to it was the habit of satisfying an insatiable lust." Augustine realized he was powerless, a captive and victim of his sexual desire. "My invisible enemy trod me down and seduced me."

Augustine concluded that a human has no free will when it comes to the sin that wells within. This situation is nothing new and is part of the essential situation of a person. Humanity was conceived in original sin. The passions people express prove it. Sexual organs were wrested from human control and are not subject to willpower. Augustine writes,

"At times the sex urge intrudes uninvited. At other times, it deserts the panting lover so that, although desire blazes in the mind, the body is frigid. In this strange way, desire refuses service, not only to the will to procreate, but also the desire for wantonness and thought for the most part, it solidly opposes the mind's command, at other times it is divided against itself, and having aroused the mind, it fails to arouse the body."

So where is there freedom, free will, liberty, autonomy, self-government?

Augustine believed only by denying spontaneous sexual desires can humanity shun its situation of sin due to the original demands inherent in being a person. Then can come submission to God. What one person cannot do, others can help in. Human government can assist the goal of submission by helping one another avoid the excesses of spontaneous sexuality. Thus a goal of a Christian society is to promote domestic peace and require obedience of those who live together in homes to serve God despite their dangerous sexual impulses and free willing licenti

* * * * *

Boethius:

A Philosopher's Poem

Boethius was a victim of invasions of his homeland. An invading Ostrogoth, Theodoric, ruled the former Roman Empire lands where the family of Boethius had lived for generations. Boethius, a child of a distinguished Roman Senatorial family, was pressed into service of the invaders at the point of a sword. He was to do their bidding in the captured dominion of his own people and assist them in their program of destroying the former way of life.

And yet Boethius could not bring himself to undo the world he had known that he must to survive with the barbarians.

Theodoric had him arrested and charged with treason. For a long period of time Boethius was thrown into a prison where he had only the books of the philosophers and thinkers of the past ages being wiped out culturally. Then an order was given to simply kill him without any hearing of any kind. He was executed in A.D. 525. He consoled himself with philosophy and from his learning he bequeaths us a poem:

> If you desire to see and understand
> In purity of mind the laws of God,
> Your sight must on the highest point of heaven rest
> Where through the lawful covenant of things
> The wandering stars preserve their ancient peace:
> The sun forth driven by his glittering flames
> Stays not the orbit of the gelled moon;
> Nor does the Bear who in the highest pole
> Of heaven drives her swiftly - turning course
> Which never to the western sea descends
> Desire to follow other stars that set,
> And merge her fire beneath the Atlantic deep:
> By equal intervals of time each day
> The Evening Star foretells the evening dusk
> And comes again as Morning Star at dawn.
> So everlasting courses are remade
> By mutual love and war's disunion
> Is banished from the shores of heaven above.
> This concord governs all the elements
> With equal measures, that the power of wet
> Will yield by turns unto the hostile dry.
> And cold will join in amity with hot;
> The pendant fire will surge into the air,
> And massive weight of earth will sink below.
> And for these reasons when the spring grows warm
> The flower-bearing year will breathe sweet scent,
> In summer torrid days will dry the corn,

Ripe autumn will return with fruit endowed,
And falling rains will moisten wintry days.
This mixture seizes, hides, and bears away
All things submerged in death's finality.
Meanwhile there sits on high the Lord of things,
Who rules and guides the reins of all that's made,
Their king and lord, their fount and origin,
Their law and judge of what is right and due.
All things that He with motion stirs to go
He holds and when they wander brings them back;
Unless He call them home to their true path,
And force them back their orbits to perfect,
Those things which stable order now protects,
Divorced from their true source would fall apart.
This is the love of which all things partake,
The end of good their chosen goal and close:
No other way can they expect to last,
Unless with love for love repaid they turn
And seek again the cause that gave them birth.

* * * * *

Anonymous:

Cinderella

Once there were two older sisters who had an easy life. These two were given everything they wanted. Instead of working hard, they lazed around primping themselves and talking down people they didn't like. The mother and father used up all their love for these two daughters and were blinded about how they were acting.

Then along came another daughter who the father and mother didn't plan for or even want. After she was born, the parents decided to make a servant girl out of her. She was left to work in the kitchen. She slept by the fire and was so often covered with ashes that she was called Cinderella.

And so the three sisters grew up into their teenaged years.

Now along one spring morning there came news that the King of this country was going to have a great dance to honor his son's twenty-first birthday. This dance was announced from the castle turrents by heralds after long blasts on silver trumpets. "In one month, one week and one day hence, the Prince and heir to this kingdom wishes the honor of the company of every young woman of marriageable age."

What else could this mean? Surely the Prince was wanting to meet all the girls to decide on one to marry.

All the girls of the kingdom went crazy with anxiety. The Prince was so handsome, powerful and rich! All of the girls wanted to be his future Queen.

All over the kingdom there was sewing of dresses and fittings and pressings and starchings and washings and hemmings and shirring and cutting. Buttons were polished. Hair was curled and styled. Jewels were fitted into bracelets, necklaces, rings.

All of the girls of the kingdom were so busy that no one bothered to offer help to Cinderella. No one would buy silks or velvets or laces or ribbons for Cinderella. She had to watch sadly as her older sisters and all the rest of the girls of the kingdom drove off in carriages to go to the dance.

But after the excitement died down in her dark kitchen Cinderella told God of her disappointment in a silent groaning prayer. Soon she saw an angel appear before her. She was like a mist seen as a shadow of the moon, illuminated by a burning beam of light.

This angel told her, "Go to the garden and pick for me the largest pumpkin you can find." When Cinderella returned with the largest pumpkin she could carry, she set it upon the ground. The angel touched the pumpkin and Cinderella saw it turn into coach of solid gold which gleamed brightly in the spare starlight.

"Now see what you find in the kitchen mousetrap," the angel said.

Cinderella returned with a mousetrap that had six young mice very much alive in it. The angel spoke and they each turned into a fine dappled horse.

As a rat sneaked around a cabinet corner, the angel smiled at it and it became a fat coachman with a pointed black beard dressed handsomely in gray velvet. He at once hitched up the horses to the fine carriage and stood waiting for Cinderella to enter the coach to be taken to the dance.

Cinderella began weeping as she shook her head to the coachman. "I cannot go to the dance," she said. "Look at me. I have no clothing to wear."

Now the angel approached her after a short absence. The angel had brought her a cobweb strung with evening dewdrops. As the angel lifted it into the air, its form was changed into a gown finer than any silk and every strand was threaded with winking diamonds. Cinderella knew at once it was to be her dress for the dance and put it on.

When she felt her face she noticed all of the ashes of the fireplace were gone and her long dark hair was so clean it shone. Looking at her feet, Cinderella saw she was wearing glass slippers.

The angel smiled at her. "I am your guardian angel," she exclaimed. "You may go to the dance but remember this one thing. When the clock strikes twelve, you must return home and leave the ball. If you don't all will return as it was."

When Cinderella arrived at the dance, she became the talk of the guests. Soon the Prince heard of her and when he went to meet her he forgot all of the other girls there. All he wanted to do was to be with Cinderella. He escorted her to the banquet hall and paid no attention to any other girl at the supper and ball.

Then midnight came. Cinderella heard the clock striking and before it reached twelve she rushed out of the castle and back to her fireplace.

The Prince was not prepared for Cinderella's quick departure. All he could do was stare wistfully at the festively decorated halL and wish Cinderella might return. When she did not, he wandered to the exit and looked down to see a glass slipper that he recognized Cinderella had been wearing.

Now the days passed by in the kingdom and yet the Prince could not forget Cinderella. The Prince even told his father the King that he had decided he would marry no one else. Why had Cinderella disappeared so mysteriously? The Prince decided she might be afraid so he would himself try to find her. In desparation, the Prince began going door to door and asking all the girls in the homes to try on the slipper. The Prince reached the last home in the kingdom with his self-appointed task. His pages knocked at the door of Cinderella's home and asked all the girls inside to come out and try on the slipper. The two older girls did. Each tried mightily to get the slipper on but though they wiggled and giggled, pushed and shoved, they could not get their foot in it.

Then the Prince begged, "Is there no one else in this house? It is the very last place where I can enquire."

One of the older sisters responded, "We do have a younger sister who is nothing but a ragged wretched girl who sits in the ashes all day and cooks for us and washes up the pans and kettles. But, you don't want to see her, I am sure."

But the Prince went in to see for himself.

He was shown to the dark kitchen and there he saw Cinderella. She had not been told he was searching for a girl who could wear the glass slipper. When the Prince tried it on her, it fit like wax and from the woodpile she brought forth its mate. Her sisters were livid with rage. One broke down and sobbed and the other wheezed disappointment hissing like a tea kettle.

The Prince now looked at Cinderella. Yes, it was she! He disregarded her rags and ashes and remembered her beauty, gentleness and humility. At once he asked her not to run from him ever again. Then he asked her to marry him.

It was not long until there was a royal wedding. The whole kingdom was present to witness the marriage. Cinderella looked up from the altar to the heights of the church where the wedding was being celebrated. She knew her guardian angel must be witnessing the joy.

* * * * *

Bernard Of Clairvoux:

On the Kiss of Jesus

When I reflect, as I often do, on the ardor with which the patriarchs longed for the incarnation of Christ, I am pierced with sorrow and shame. And now I can scarcely contain my tears, so ashamed am I of the lukewarmness and lethargy of the present times. For which of us is filled with joy at the realization of this grace as the holy men of old were moved to desire by the promise of it?

Soon now we shall be rejoicing at the celebration of his birth. But would that it were really for his birth! How I pray that that burning desire and longing in the hearts of these holy men of old may be aroused in me by these words: "Let him kiss me with the kiss of his mouth". In those days a spiritual man could sense the Spirit how great would be the grace released by the touch of those lips. For that reason, speaking in the desire prompted by the Spirit, he said, "Let him kiss me with the kiss of his mouth," desiring with all his heart that he would not be deprived of a share in that sweetness.

Freedom Fighter

by Stephen Baker

It's 1861. I'm fighting for freedom.
Cannonballs smoke the enemy.
I'm a negro Union soldier.
I march to the beat of a negro drummer.

It's 1917. I'm fighting for freedom.
Mustard gas smokes the enemy.
I fight in this war to end all wars.
My negro troop crawls within muddied
rat-filled trenches throughout France.

It's 1941. I'm fighting for freedom.
Japanese have smoked our Navy.
I'm a negro cook for a white ship
docked, sunk at Pearl Harbor.

It's 1953. I'm fighting for freedom.
Planes bomb, smoking the enemy.
Countless Chinese troops pour across
the 38th parallel.
Politicians back home
refuse to allow us to push
the enemy back to Red China.
Once back stateside, I'm a negro.
Back of the bus. Back of the line.

It's 1964. I'm fighting for freedom.
I listen to Dr. King's dreams.
Watercannons smoke the enemy.
I witness hoodlums pointing white fingers
at negro folk. White cursing
and waving an American flag.

It's 1971. I'm fighting for freedom.
Agent orange smokes the enemy.
Everyone is the enemy.
Hendrix' music blares
from our helicopters overhead.
I'm an Afro-American knee deep in jungle.
Countless peaceful war demonstrators
march all across America, back home.
Politicians target our assaults.
Leaders guesstimate US and Them.
Politicians fold up the chessboards.
We're phonecalled back from Vietnam.

It's 1991. I'm fighting for freedom.
Numerous high-tech bombs smoke the enemy.
I'm a black US soldier sitting in the sand,
chewing gum, watching our planes fill the sky.
Politicians and leaders plan assaults.
Countless American flags fly high back home.
War protestors cry, sing, and join hands.
Americans sit glued to the television
watching tapes of the bombings.

The holy men who lived before the coming of the Savior understood that God had in mind a plan to bring peace to the race of mortal men. For the Word would do nothing on earth which he did not reveal to his servants the prophets. But this

Word was hidden from many, for at that time faith was rare upon the earth and hope was very faint even in the hearts of many of those who were waiting for the redemption of Israel. Those who foreknew also proclaimed that Christ would come in the flesh and that with him would come peace. That is why one of them says, "There will be peace when he comes to our earth". By divine inspiration they preached faithfully that men were to be saved through the grace be fulfilled in his own time, and he declared, "Grace and truth have come through Jesus Christ", and all Christian peoples now experience the truth of what he said.

In those days, although the prophets foretold peace, the faith of the people continually wavered because there was no one to redeem or save them, for the Author of peace delayed his coming. So men complained at the delay, because the Prince of Peace, who had been so often proclaimed, had not yet come, as had been promised by the holy men who were his prophets from of old.

They began to lose faith in the promises and they demanded the kiss, the sign of the promise of reconciliation. It was as if one of the people were to answer the messengers of peace, "How much longer are you going to keep us waiting?" You foretell a lpeace which does not come. You promise good things and there is still confusion. See, many times and in many ways angels announced to the patriarchs and our fathers proclaimed to us, saying, "Peace. And there is no peace". If God wants me to believe in his benevolent will which he has so often spoken of through the prophets but not yet shown in action, "Let him kiss me with the kiss of his mouth," and so by this sign of peace make peace secure. For how am I to go on believing in mere words? They need to be confirmed by deeds. Let him confirm that his messengers spoke the truth, if they were his messengers, and let him follow them in person, as they have so often promised; for they can do nothing without him. He send a boy bearing a staff but no voice or life.

I do not rise up or awaken; I am not shaken free of the dust; I do not breathe in hope, if the prophet himself does not come down and kiss me with the kiss of his mouth.

Here we must add that he who makes himself our Mediator with God is the Son of God and he is himself God. What is man that he should take notice of him, or the son of man, that he should think of him? Where am I to find the faith to dare to trust in such majesty? How, I say, shall I, who am dust and ashes, presume to think that God cares about me? He loves his Father. He does not need me, nor my possessions. How then shall I be sure that he will never fail me?

If it is true, as you prophets say, that God has the intention of showing mercy, and thinks to make himself manifest for our reassurance, let him make a covenant of peace, an ever-lasting covenant with me by the kiss of his mouth.

If he is not going to go back on what he has said, let him empty himself, humble himself, bend low and "kiss me with the kiss of his mouth." If the Mediator is to be acceptable to both sides, let God the Son of God become man; let him become the son of man, and make me sure of him with the kiss of his mouth. When I know that the Mediator who is the son of God is mine, then I shall accept him trustingly. Then there can be no mistrust. For he is brother to my flesh. For I think that bone of my bone and flesh of my flesh cannot spurn me.

So, therefore, the old complaint went on about this most sacred kiss, that is, the mystery of the incarnation of the Word, while faith faints with weariness because of its long and troubled waiting, and the faithless people murmured against the promises of God because they were worn out by waiting. Am I making this up? Do you not recognize that this is what Scripture says, "Here are complaints and the loud murmur of voices, order on order, waiting on waiting, a little here, a little there"? Here are anxious prayers full of piety, "Give their reward, Lord, to those who wait on you, so that your prophets may be found faithful". Again, "Bring about what the prophets of old prophesied in your name". Here are sweet promises full of consolation, "Behold the Lord will appear; and he will not lie. If he seems slow, wait for him, for he will come, and that soon". Again, "The time of his coming is near and his days will not be prolonged", and, from the Person of him who was promised, "Behold," he says, "I am running toward you like a river of peace, and like a stream in flood with the glory of the nations".

In these words, both the urgency of the preachers and the lack of faith of the people is clear enough. And so the people murmured and faith wavered and, as Isaiah puts it, "The messengers of peace weep bitterly". Therefore, because Christ delayed his coming lest the whole human race should perish in desperation while they thought their weak mortality condemned them and they did not trust that God would bring them the so-often promised reconciliation with him, those holy men who were made sure by the Spirit looked for the certainty that his presence could bring, and urgently demanded a sign that the covenant was about to be renewed for the sake of the weak in the faith.

O Root of Jesse, who stand as a sign to the peoples, how many kings and prophets wanted to see you and did not? Simeon is the happiest of them all because by God's mercy he was still bearing fruit in old age. For he rejoiced to think that he would see the sign so long desired. He saw it and was glad. When he had received the kiss of peace he departed in peace, but first he proclaimed aloud that Jesus was born, a sign that would be rejected.

And so it was. The sign of peace arose and was rejected, by those who hate peace. For what is peace to men of goodwill is a stone to make men stumble, a rock for the wicked to fall over. "Herod was troubled, and all Jerusalem with him". He came to his own and his own did not receive him. Happy those shepherds keeping watch at night who were found worthy to be shown the sign of this vision. For even at that time he was hiding himself from the wise and prudent and revealing himself to the simple. Herod wanted to see him, but because he did not want to see him out of goodwill, he did not deserve to see him.

The sign of peace was given only to men of goodwill; the only sign which was given to Herod and his like is the sign of Jonah and the prophet. The angel said to the shepherds, "This is a sign for you", you who are humble, you who are keeping vigil and meditating on God's law day and night. "This is a sign for you," he said.

What is this a sign of? Indulgence, grace, peace, the peace which will have no end. It is this sign: "You will find a baby wraped in swaddling clothes and lying in a manger". But this baby is God himself, reconciling the world to himself in

The following poem is in loving memory of Anne Wells, from her sisters, Olive King, and Jessie Porter.

REMEMBER

Remember me when I am gone away,
　Gone far away into the silent land;
　When you can no more hold me by the hand,
Nor I half turn to go yet turning stay.
Remember me when no more, day by day,
　You tell me of our future that you planned:
　Only remember me; you understand
It will be late to counsel then or pray.
Yet if you should forget me for a while
　And afterwards remember, do not grieve;
　For if the darkness and corruption leave
　A vestige of the thoughts that once I had,
Better by far you should forget and smile
　Than that you should remember and be sad.
　　　　　　　　　　　Christina G. Rossetti

him. He will die for your sins and rise again to make you just, so that, made just by faith, you may be at peace with God.

Eyes that are used to darkness will be blinded by light, and wrapped again in a darkness deeper than before. You who are such a soul, do not think othat position despicable in which the sinner laid down her sins and put on the garment of holiness. There the Ethiopian changed her skin and, restored to a new brightness, she could reply faithfully and truthfully to those who reproached her, "I am black but I am beautiful, daughters of Jerusalem".

Are you wondering how she was able to change like this, or how she deserved it? You shall hear in a few words. She wept bitterly and sighed deeply from her inmost heart, and her sobs shook her one by one, and the evils within her came forth. The heavenly Physician came quickly to help her, for "his Word runs swiftly".

Surely the Word of God is not a medicine? Indeed it is, strong and powerful, searching out the heart and mind. "God's word is living and effective, and more penetrating than any two-edged sword, penetrating to the place where soul and spirit meet, and separating the marrow; it judges the thoughts".

O wretch, prostrate yourself like this blessed penitent, so that you can cease to be miserable. Prostrate yourself on the ground, embrace his feet, plead with kisses, water them with tears. Wash not only him but yourself, and you will become one of the flock of shorn ewes as they come up from the washing. Even then you will not dare to lift your face, swollen with shame and grief, until you hear him say, "Your sins are forgiven", and "Awake, awake captive daughter of Sion, awake, shake off the dust".

Though you have given a first kiss to the feet, do not presume to rise at once to kiss the mouth. You must come to that by way of another, intermediate kiss, on the hand. This is the reason for that kiss: "If Jesus says to me, "Your sins are forgiven," what is the good of that unless I cease to sin? I have taken off my filthy garment. If I put it on again, what progress have I made?". If I dirty again the feet that I have washed, surely the washing is valueless? Filthy with every sort of vice, I have lain for a long time in the slough of the more. If I return to it again it is worse than my first falling into it. I remember that he who healed me himslef said to me, "Behold you are healed; go and sin no more, lest worse befall you".

It is necessary that he who gives the will to repent should add the virtue of continence lest I should do things to repent of worse than the first. Woe is me even if I repent, if he immediately takes away the hand without which I can do nothing. Nothing, I say, because without him I cannot repent, or contain my sin. For that reason I listen to Wisdom's advice, "Do not repeat yourself at your prayers". I fear the Judge's reaction to the tree which did not bear good fruit. For these reasons I am not fully satisfied by the first grace, by which I repent of my sins, unless I receive the second, too, so that I may bear worthy fruits of repentance, and not return like a dog to his vomit.

There remains to consider what I must seek and receive before I may presume to touch higher and more sacred things. I do not want to be there all at once. I want to proceed a step at a time. The sinner's impudence displeases God as much as the penitent's modesty pleases him. You will please him more readily if you live within your limits and do not seek things too high for you. It is a long leap and a difficult one from the foot to the mouth, oand that way of getting there is not appropriate.

How then, should you go? Should you who were recently covered in filth touch the holy lips? Yesterday dragged out of the more, do you present yourself today to the face of glory? Let your way be by the hand. The hand first touched you and now lifts you up. How will it lift you up? By giving you the grace to aspire. What is that? The sweetness of temperance and the fruits of worthy repentance, which are the works of holiness; these can lift you from the mire to the hope of daring greater things. When you receive this grace you kiss his hand. Give the glory not to yourself but to him. Give it once and again, both for the forgiveness of sins and for the virtures that are given. Otherwise you will need to fortify yourself against such darts as these, "What do you have that you have not received? If you have received, why do you glory as though you have not?"

Now at last, having the experience of the divine kindness in these two kisses, perhaps you will not feel diffident of presuming to what is holier. The more you grow in grace, the more you are enlarged in faith. Thus it is that you will love more

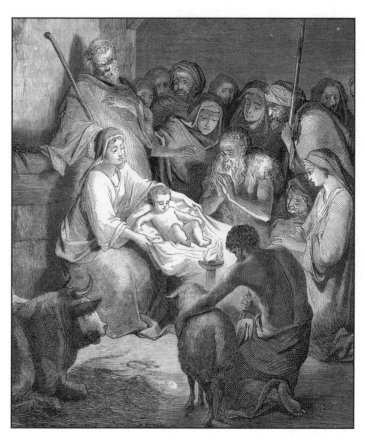

ardently and press more confidently for that which you know you still lack. For, "to him who knocks it shall be opened". I believe that that supreme kiss of the highest condescension and wonderful sweetness will not be denied to him who so loves.

* * * * *

After Professor Kurtz with Folk Tale:

The Crusades

Christian pilgrims came to like to go to Israel to see the places where Jesus lived. This land was ruled by first one people and then another. At first, the people of the Holy Land welcomed the pilgrim travelers. Then in the 10th Century, oppression of pilgrims began. It is said that this circumstance started under Khalif Hakim, a ruler of the people of this place born from a Christian mother. Since most of the people were of another religion, the Khalif thought to blot out his connection to Christianity by cruelties to Christians and win over the affection of his people who were doubting his commitment to them.

Setting upon pilgrims grew and grew. It became worst under the Seljuk dynasty which controlled Palestine. This oppression also happened as the end of the first thousand years after the birth of Jesus approached. Many people figured the world might end then. Religious enthusiam grew rampant.

Most pilgrims were from Europe. These people of the West had a religious leader named Pope Sylvester II. In the year 999 A.D., Sylvester began the cry for a religious crusade directed at the Holy Land. Many such crusades followed. The goal was to wrest control of Jerusalem from the local people so that pilgrims going there would be safe.

The crusades became a series of wars begun by the Christian folk of the West against the local people of the places where Jesus lived. The movement was encouraged by the religious leaders. For example, at the Council of Claremont in 1095 A.D. the Pope himself called for a holy war under the standard of the cross. "It is God's Will" ran the cry from this council. Men enlisted in national armies to go to this war with great enthusiasm. Jerusalem was once briefly conquered by Crusading soldiers from an army of 600,000 men on the First Crusade on July 15, 1099 with great singing of psalms. They elected a man named Godfrey as king but he refused to wear a crown saying he would wear no crown of gold where his Savior had only worn a crown of thorns. Eventually the crusades cost Europe between five and six million men. It was like a second migration of nations with armies going to Israel for two centuries. No permanent solution to the safety of pilgrims was ever achieved.

One of the crusades was of children.

Kid Crusaders

Thomaso Cazardini, the old Venetian trader in his sixties now, but still goin strong, was at the docks of Fusina, across the bay from his home city, Venice, at the time the kids began arriving in Lombardy from the Alpine passes. The "Children's Crusade" was in full bloom. It was the year 1212 and the kids were called to go to the Holy Land, unarmed, to do what the Christian knights with all their squires and vassals could not, win back the spot where God could return to earth.

The children were not to be so vulnerable as this scenario might sound. An angel would accompany them.

Yes, there would be an angel to accompany these children when they reached the sea, an angel of gold. This angel, accordin to the vision of Nicholas, a German boy of ten years of age would open the sea so they might walk across to the Holy Land where the Saracens would be converted by the example of the youthful innocence of children bearin the story of Jesus. Then the children would take possession of the Holy Sepulchre and await the end of the world and a returnin Familyhead.

Friar John convinced Piet and Gulda Gotthered, whose home was on a little rise near Luzern, Switzerland, to let their children go on this Crusade. "They qualify," he said. "They are innocent and good. God will protect them. If there's no angel openin up the Mediterranean sea for them to walk to the Holy Land when they get to the sea, like the inspired visions say, the friars and monks goin along will return all the children safely," the Friar promised.

"Will you go along?" Piet and Gulda asked the old Friar?

"No," he said. But he explained that many, many Franciscans were goin along who were trustworthy with kids.

The Gotthereds took their children Stephen, fourteen, Patia, twelve, and young Lukus, eleven, to the Luzern church on the brightest day that May could produce in the Swiss alps to meet their fellow pilgrim children. They were beautiful that day, those Gotthered children, faces shinin, bodies healthy, energies burstin.

They were being turned over to God.

As the kids left, Piet and Gulda hugged, and the father, Piet, said quietly that the children would probably be back in a couple days much wiser than before.

But Gulda could only cry knowin her kids were goin off from her home where she's give them the milk from her breast and the food prepared at her hand and table.

Now Stephen and Patia and Lukus left with the others. About five hundred kids took this route that day. They were tired from the trip over the Alps away from their family and home when they come to Fusina.

At the docks they found the golden angel awaiting them. It was Thomaso Cazardini, an angel of golden appearance. To see the man was to see a golden angel. Thomaso wore a long nightgown lookin dalmatic in gold embroidery that covered him from top to bottom. Over this he wore the pallium of a wealthy Venetian, a wide strip of cloth of gold, which had a hole for puttin your head through and then it hung down front and back. The piece in back was brought around from the back and was draped over his left arm.

Thomaso stood before them as a genuine golden angel.

No one could have looked more like an angel.

He told them, "I have a ship for you kids to be taken to the Holy Land." Thomaso knew his cargo ship he's sendin over to Alexandria could only take so many, so he picked and chose among the kids. "Only the kids, not the Friars," Thomaso said as he separated out the ones of them that he had use for.

The Swiss Gotthered kids were picked. They were healthy and could take the trip. He bundled them on board, with about fifty more. Other Venetian traders would come over and select from the rest. They were going to be transported to the slave markets of Asia.

The kids were thrilled to get on board to be set off at sea, to get to sail. They hadn't been at sea before. The kids were told where to settle in the cargo hold. They were even given some bread and cheese.

At the rialto close to Venice, the kids were told to stay in the ship while Thomaso got off to return to his palace. The golden angel wasn't goin along for the ride.

After some of the novelty of the sea wore off, the oldest of the Gotthered kids, made an observation. "The sea didn't open," he told his brother and sister. "Don't you remember how we were told to come home if the Golden Angel didn't open up the sea?"

"Well it did in a way," Patia told him. "The golden angel opened a way through the sea in his ships," she said quite satisfied.

"Yes, but it didn't open like the Red Sea opened for Moses," Stephen said. "That was how the Friar said it would be. We were to walk through the sea, not ride on some ship. Otherwise we were to come straight home."

"Well it's too late to worry bout now," Patia said, "and even so we need have to faith that through us may be the cause of the return of Jesus."

After the day wore down more and more and more and more of the novelty wore off, the Gotthered kids stood together on the deck, lookin out over the blue Mediterranean after passin the Venetian colonial port of Corfu, headin for the East. What would the future hold for them?

Darkness come over the Epirus. As the night came, the kids huddled under the larger foremast of the ship with its huge lateen sail. Then one of the Croat sailors who had been leerin at Patia all day confronted them. First he took away their sacks of beddin and then he got Patia by her wrist and drug her to the back of the ship. There wasn't anything Stephen or Lukus could do when they heard their sister's screamin.

It was at the Venetian tradin center of Constantinople that Stephen was drug off the ship. A Selzic Turk with rouged face and mascarad eyelashes took to Stephen and bought him for his household returnin back into Anatolia.

Lukus had tried to fight against the sailors tearin his brother from him at the docks of Constantinople. All Lukus got for this was beat on the head. Beat silly. No more could Lukus talk. His brain was hit too hard. He would not see as others did from then on, but only as one whose brain was addled. His price at the slave market at Alexandria would not be much.

They was no time for partin words of the kids of the slopes juttin into the Vierwaldstattersee.

Now the ship headed south for Alexandria. At the end of the blue Mediterranean, the markets of Alexandria were always busy, busier than Constantinople.

The slave mart of Alexandria was in the commercial section of town within the harbor sheltered by its four mile long mole reachin from the mainland out past the little Pharos island. Warehouses stood one after another on the road leadin up to the slave market. The kids left were only those who had not got sick and been thrown over. The merchants never permitted unsaleable slaves to land. Sick or not they would still have to have customs taxes paid on them. When Patia was taken to the slave block she couldn't comprehend what was happenin. A camel trader bid most on Patia and bought her. At twelve she would make a suitable present to the Dahmier, he who supplied the camels out in the deserts. The purchaser would see that she arrived at a tradin family who might reward him with a good trade, maybe even a camel itself.

Now Patia was taken into the desert to be kept in a black tent. Of all the Gotthered children, only Patia had made it to the Holy Land, but she didn't know it. In the mornins, Patia was called to gather firewood and keep the brush fire goin so her masters, the family, fakhd, could warm themselves and rouse themselves from the cold desert nights. Even wearin the long black dress with its long sleeves, her body shape could not be hid. She was gettin big. She wore the face mask of the bedouin women which covered all but her eyes.

Underneath the clothing, the bedouin women had given Patia their character-istic tatooes, but, laughin, they had given her ugly scars in the shapes of the cross. Even so it was she that the Shaikh had called to his side. She was pregnant when the women of the hamoula learned of it.

Patia showed hugely with the Shaikh child when the women of the black tents made their move. There should be no white blood in the line of the bedouin to dilute it and pollute it. With clubs they beat at her that night, beat at her stomach now grown large. The baby inside could not cry out or raise a hand in defense but churned and tore its little face side to side, its unopened eyes unseein those at-tackin. When the bedouin women were sure the child was dead, they left off.

It was later that night that Patia retrieved a dagger, cut herself open and pulled out her dead child. Cuttin its throat she drained it of its still warm blood which she added to her own from her wounds into a camelsack. Stickin her head in the sack, Patia drowned herself. When shown to the light of day, the baby was as white as a swan.

Lukus had been taken off the boat at Alexandria too. Maybe he didn't know much, but he was still a healthy lookin ten year old. He was taken to the slave mar-kets too! Christian blackfolk from Nubia went to Alexandria regularly to do their tradin. The folk of Nubia lived in truce, "baked," with their Muslim neighbor to the north so they could trade with them and earn money at their Egyptian markets.

Lukus was picked up as a bargain slave by some pottery traders and was taken back down the Nile by boat below the third cataract. He eventually entered the capital city of Dunkula in the black Nubian kingdom of Mukaria and was sold there to a landowner. This landowner's irrigation ditches were needin tenders.

Lukus could have cared less what happened by now. Lukus never even recog-nized his sister at the slave market where he was first sold he was beat so in the head. But, one thing that stayed with Lukus. He still could imagine the golden an-gel of Venice, Thomaso Cazardini. When this happy recollection came, Lukus would cry out, "Angelus, Angelus," in Latin to his masters who could not under-stand him and would beat his head again to shut up this strange cursing.

At the lower Nile settlement in the shaikiya, the master land supervisor put his white slave Lukus to use. He was supposed to pull down on the crossbeam rope lowerin the water bucket into the Nile and bringin up the muddy waters and swin-gin them across the low walls into the irrigation splashes. Mornin til night that is what Lukus did. The fields required irrigation.

Sometimes Lukus wouldn't do what he was told. Sometimes he couldn't un-derstand what to do. His masters had to keep him to the water device. They kept hittin on him til Lukus couldn't feel. Eventually the rote of the pulls was inter-rupted when the cord become entangled around his neck. Lukus hung himself into a dangle. His master didn't miss him. Lukus wasn't smart enough to get a full bucket of Nile water up to the irrigation ditch anyway. The last stupid look of Lukus was of the muddy Nile so different from Lake Luzern where the blueness served as a reminder of his mother's eyes. Before throwin the stupid kid into the Nile with the other trash, the landowner's kid removed Lukus's cotton libas, trou-sers that had overlaped his knees and covered his bent over form down to his caloused feet. Filthy, the pants still might have some value at the bazaar. For sure, the idiot boy wearin them had none.

And what of the slave ship which had transported the crusader kids?

When the ship returned to Venice, its captain went to the golden angel of Venice, Thomas Cazardini, and gave him the silver marks from the sale of the kids.

Thomoso added it to his treasury.

* * * * *

> *"If a man does not keep pace with his companions, perhaps it is because he hears a different drummer. Let him step to the music which he hears, however measured or far away."*
>
> **Henry David Thoreau**

Anselm Of Canterbury:

Proof of God

God exists so truly that God cannot be conceived not to exist. It is possible to conceive of a being who cannot be conceived not to exist; and this is greater than one who can be conceived not to exist. Hence, if one who "nothing greater than" can be conceived, can be conceived not to exist, it is not that which "nothing greater than" can be conceived. But this is an irreconcilable contradiction. There is, then, so truly a being than who "nothing greater than" can be conceived to exist, that God cannot even be conceived not to exist; and this being who you are, O Familyhead, our God.

So truly, therefore, do you exist, O Familyhead, my God, that you cannot be conceived not to exist; and rightly. For, if a mind could conceive of a being better than you, the creature would rise above the Creator; and this is most absurd. And, indeed, whatever else there is, except you alone, can be conceived not to exist. To you alone, therefore, it belongs to exist more truly than all other beings, and hence in a higher degree than all others. For, whatever else exists does not exist so truly, and hence in a less degree it belongs to it to exist. Why, then, has the fool said in his heart, there is no God, since it is so evident, to a rational mind, that you do exist in the highest degree of all? Why, except that he is dull and a fool?

But how has the fool said in his heart what he could not conceive; or how is it that he could not conceive what he said in his heart? since it is the same to say in the heart, and to conceive.

But, if really, no, since really, he both conceived, because he said in his heart; and did not say in his heart, because he could not conceive; there is more than one way in which a thing is said in the heart or conceived. For, in one sense, an object is conceived, when the word signifying it is conceived; and in another, when the very entity, which the object is, is understood.

In the former sense, then, God can be conceived not to exist; but in the latter, not at all. For no one who understands what fire and water are can conceive fire to be water, in accordance with the nature of the facts themselves, although this is possible according to the words. So, then, no one who understands what God is can conceive that God does not exist; although he says these words in his heart, either without any. or with some foreign, significance. For, God is that than which a greater cannot be conceived. And he who thoroughly understands this, assuredly understands that this being so truly exists, that not even in concept can it be non-existent. Therefore, he who understands that God so exists, cannot conceive that he does not exist.

I thank you, gracious Familyhead, I thank you because what I formerly believed is your bounty, I now so understand by your illumination, that if I were unwilling to believe that you do exist, I should not be able not to understand this to be true.

What are you, then, God Familyhead, than whom nothing greater can be conceived? But what are you, except that which, as the highest of all beings, alone exists through itself, and creates all other things from nothing? For, what ever is not this is less than a thing which can be conceived of. But this cannot be conceived of you. What good, therefore, does the Supreme God lack, through which every good is? Therefore, you are just, truthful, blessed, and whatever it is better to be than not to be. For it is better to be just than not just; better to be blessed than not blessed.

Although it is better for you to be sensible, omnipotent, compassionate, passionless, than not to be these things; how are you sensible, if you are not a body; or omnipotent, if you have not all powers; or at once compassionate and passionless? For, if only corporeal things are sensible, since the senses encompass a body and are in a body, how are you sensible, although you are not a body, but a Supreme Spirit, who is superior to body? But, if feeling is only cognition, or for the sake of cognition, for he who feels obtains knowledge in accordance with the proper functions of his senses; as through sight, of colors; through taste, of flavors, whatever in any way cognizes is not inappropriately said, in some sort, to feel.

Therefore, O Familyhead, although you are not a body, yet you are truly sensible in the highest degree in respect of this, that you do contemplate all things in the highest degree; and not as an animal cognises, through a corporeal sense.

But how are you omnipotent, if you are not capable of all things? Or, if you cannot be corrupted, and cannot lie, nor make what is true, false-as, for example, if you should make what has been done not to have been done, and the like- how are you capable of all things? Or else to be capable of these things is not power, but impotence. For, he who is capable of these things is capable of what is not for his good, and of what he ought not to do; and the more capable of them he is, the more power have adversity and perversity against him; and the less has he himself against these.

He, then, who is thus capable is so not by power, but by impotence. For, he is not said to be able because he is able of himself, but because his impotence gives something else power over him. Or, by a figure of speech, just as many words are improperly applied, as when we use "to be" for "not to be," and "to do" for what is really "not to do," or "to do nothing." For, often we say to a man who denies the existence of something: "It is as you say it to be," though it might seem more proper to say, "It is not, as you say it is not." In the same way, we say: "This man sits just as that man does," or, "This man rests just as that man does"; although to sit is not to do anything, and to rest is to do nothing.

So, then, when one is said to have the power of doing or experiencing what is not for his good, or what he ought not to do, impotence is understood in the word power. For, the more he possesses this power, the more powerful are adversity and perversity against him, and the more powerless is he against them.

Therefore, O Familyhead, our God, the more truly are you omnipotent since you are capable of nothing through impotence and nothing has power against you.

* * * * *

Abelard and Heloise

What happens to a woman who consents to sex out of marriage and who brags she prefers "love to marriage and freedom to chains" when the man she loves cannot love her back?

Where is there comfort when physical love fails a man?

There was once a brilliant man intelligent beyond all others of his Middle Ages. Abelard was his name.

He thought hard and was tough intellectually. He didn't just accept ideas. He reasoned them through. His talents in rhetoric made him feared as a debater. His shrewd arguments caused him to be the greatest instructor in dialectics. When an idea seemed crazy, he attacked it no matter what. He shunned no controversy. He became the chief antagonist of a previously reigning philosophy of "universals" teaching there was nothing in the world but "universal forms of ideas." He dismissed "universals" as merely concepts without reality. His arguments that differences made such a belief in "universals" improbable came to prevail and with it thoughts of progress whereby the Renaissance could proceed. He studied with saints such as Anselm and became a respected and inspired theologian. His fame established the University of Paris which through the centuries became the chief university of Europe. Students sought him out from the most distant places in the civilized world. Abelard was supreme in the academic environment.

And yet Abelard, in his mid-thirties in the peak of his intellectual powers, was still a man. He described himself as having "exceptional good looks." He fell in love with a beautiful young student named Heloise who loved Abelard for his talent for verse and song. Heloise, about seventeen years of age when the affair started, was the niece of Fulbert, one of the most prominent churchmen in Paris. The love of Heloise and Abelard quickly became passionate. They deliberately chose not to marry so that they might feel only the passion of their lovemaking and have no legal ties to their wild revels and carnality. Abelard and Heloise became completely carried away with each other and their love was reckless. Abelard neglected his pupils, abandoned serious teaching, paid no attention to gossip and sang songs of Heloise which quickly were repeated throughout Paris. They made love wherever they wished - even in churches and monastic institutions and during times of celibacy even when married couples were under church orders to abstain. Simple marriage was out of the question. They were not interested in domesticity. They wished to love each other with unbridled emotion and intensity beyond the love that any man and woman had known. Heloise became pregnant and a baby was born in Brittany and given to Abelard's sister. Heloise's uncle Fulbert, the respectable churchman, decided he must do something about their affair. The two were taking greater and greater risks to be together and were sometimes found in bed with each other. Heloise admitted freely, "If the Emperor Augustus offered marriage she would still choose to be Abelard's whore."

The consequences were dire. At that time in history, scholars had no professional choices outside the church and the church did not permit high officers to marry. Then to try to salvage some sense of decency, Abelard and Heloise agreed with Fulbert to marry secretly. This news got out and their only choice was to break things off to save Abelard's career.

Abelard and Heloise promised to stop their very public affair but they could not. To be with her, Abelard dressed her as a man to sneak her from her cloister where her uncle tried to restore her reputation. Fulbert could not avoid the public disgrace of his family. The public scandal was too great.

Fulbert decided to take action. In the middle of the night, Fulbert's servants broke into Abelard's room and exacted a terrible cause of horrible revenge to his family's reputation. These servants castrated Abelard and mangled his manly parts.

Crowds gathered outside of Abelard's chambers when news of the attack and of his plight began to be known in Paris. The deed could not be concealed. Although Abelard himself wished to escape feeling totally humiliated, his adoring students became a noisy crowd with outcries of sympathy. The public nature of the whole affair was repeated over and over together with stories about the end of Abelard's capacity to love. Later Abelard took refuge from his feelings of being a eunuch, which he considered "the unclean beast of Jewish law," by joining a monastery. No longer did he feel the personal dilemma of the torments of the flesh.

He wrote Heloise, "See then, my beloved, see how with the dragnets of his mercy the Lord has fished us up from the depth of this dangerous sea, and from the abyss of what a Charybdis he has saved our shipwrecked selves, although we were unwilling, so that each of us may justly break out in that cry: 'The Familyhead takes thought for me' Think and think again of the great perils in which we were and from which the Familyhead rescued us. Tell always with the deepest gratitude how much the Familyhead has done for our souls. Comfort by our example any unrighteous who despair of God's goodness, so that all may know what may be done for those who ask with prayer, when such benefits are granted sinners even against their will. Consider the magnanimous design of God's mercy for us, the compassion with which the Familyhead directed judgment towards our chastisement, the wisdom whereby he made use of evil itself and mercifully set aside our impiety, so that by a wholly justified wound in a single part of my body he might heal two souls. Compare our danger and manner of deliverance, compare the sickness and the medicine. Examine the cause, our deserts, and marvel at the effect, his pity.

You know the depths of shame to which my unbridled lust had consigned our bodies, until no reverence for decency or for God even during the days of Our Lord's Passion, or of the greater sacraments could keep me from wallowing in this mire. Even when you were unwilling, resisting to the utmost of your power and tried to dissuade me, as yours was the weaker nature, I often forced you to consent with threats and blows. So intense were the fires of lust which bound me to you that I set those wretched, obscene pleasures, which we blush even to name, above God as above myself. Nor would it seem that divine mercy could have taken action except by forbidding me these pleasures altogether, without future hope. And so it was wholly just and merciful, although by means of that supreme treachery of your uncle, for me to be reduced in that part of my body which was the seat of lust and sole reason for those desires, so that I could increase in may ways...

Come too, my inseparable companion, and join me in thanksgiving. You were made my partner both in guilt and in grace. The Familyhead is not unmindful also of your own salvation. At the time I desired to keep you whom I loved beyond measure for myself alone, but God's Child was already planning to use this opportunity for our joint conversion to God's self... The talents which God's Child had entrusted to us, were not being used to glorify God's name..."

Abelard and Heloise both went on to live lives of great service. He is considered one of the great philosophers of all time and a staunch upholder of monastic life. He was sometimes abbot of monasteries and spoke out against the shortcomings of the church wherever he detected them to the end of his life. He remained a dedicated humanist and scholar. Heloise had about eighteen months with Abelard and then was nineteen when she took vows to become a nun. The rest of her life was lived within convent walls. After the attack on Abelard, Abelard became a changed man but Heloise was not a changed woman. She wrote Abelard,

"The pleasures of lovers which we shared have been too sweet - they can never displease me, and scarcely be banished from my thoughts. Wherever I turn they are always there before my eyes, bringing with them awakened longings and fantasies which will not even let me sleep." She did not pretend that love of God had supplanted her love of Abelard but she was intelligent and possessed a strong character and went on to become the prioress of the abbey where she lived in charge of educating the nuns, novices and children brought up in the convent as Heloise had been brought up herself.

The world does not end when physical love fails. The Child of God is only to be served more fully.

* * * * *

Prayer of Francis of Assisi

Familyhead, make me an instrument of your peace;
where there is hatred, let me sow love,
where there is injury, pardon,
where there is doubt, faith,
where there is despair, hope,
where there is darkness, light,
and where there is sadness, joy.

O Divine Leader,
grant that I may not so much seek
to be consoled as to console,
to be understood, as to understand,
to be loved, as to love,
for it is in giving that we receive,
it is in pardoning that we are pardoned,
and it is in dying that we are born to eternal life.

Traditional:

Waldo's Church

There is a "police report" from the 13th Century which helps us learn of the man named Waldo. This "police report" is taken from the records of the French Inquisition whose police searched out "heretics." This "report" states, "The poor of Lyons had their origins around the year 1170 founded by a certain Lyonese citizen by the name of Valdensius or Valdensis, after whom his followers took their name. The person in question was a rich man but abandoning all his wealth, he determined to observe a life of poverty and evangelical perfection, as did the Apostles. He arranged for the Gospels and some other books of the Bible to be translated into common speech; also some texts of Saints Augustine, Jerome, Ambrose, and Gregory, arranged under titles which he called "sentences," and which he read very often, though without understanding their import. Infatuated with himself he usurped the prerogatives of the Apostles by presuming to preach the Gospel in the streets, where he made many disciples and involving them, both men and women, in a like presumption by sending them out, in turn, to preach. These people, ignorant and illiterate, went about through the towns, entering houses, and even churches spreading many errors round about."

Most conclude this "police report" accurately describes the founding of Waldo's denomination of church. Waldo is how the name Valdensius or Valdensis has been brought down to us in history.

Waldo was not a priest. That became a great problem for him in establishing his church.

Waldo was a merchant and we do not know when he was born or died. Some accounts say he had a wife and two daughters. Sometime between 1170 and 1180 he had an unknown conversion experience which may have had to do with an understanding of Matthew's Witness about a rich young man told by Jesus to sell his goods, give them to the poor and follow Him. Perhaps others had taken this text to heart. Waldo however did something revolutionary with his great wealth. He commissioned a vernacular translation of the New Testament writings and then published and spread the document among the poor. Penniless, he is thought to have spent the rest of his life ministering as a layman to the poor.

Waldo believed in Christian discipleship based on literal and direct reading of the New Testament writings translated into current language. He found no authority there and thus preached against confessions, fasts on any particular days, and devotions to saints. This set him and his followers against the organized church of his time. Soon his followers began facing imprisonment, torture and death for their faith at the hands of the Inquisition.

The members of Waldo's church began forming themselves into little apostolic like communities throughout the Piedmont region of Europe. Their preachers were called "barbas" (uncles) who used New Testament writings translated into the common speech. The worship was usually centered around a vernacular Bible reading, discussion and prayer and the two sacraments - baptism and a recollection of the Familyhead's Last Supper. The members of the church called themselves "The Poor." A member of Waldo's church caught owning one of Waldo's vernacular translations of the New Testament was usually subject to arrest by the Inquisition. Preachers were burned at the stake or drowned. An example of the persecution occurred on June 5, 1561, when a community of Waldo's church, virtually the entire town of San Sisto with its 6,000 residents, was burned to the ground and its residents were burned like torches, sold as slaves to the Moors or condemned to die of starvation in dungeons. This and other atrocities were committed against Waldo's church because this church had authorized and paid for a vernacular translation of the Greek New Testament writings by Giova Paschale in 1555 which the organized church wished to suppress.

Nevertheless Waldo's church survived. Their tradition of encouraging direct translation of the Greek New Testament texts into current language had dramatic effect. Apparently it is almost always a revolutionary circumstance for people to be exposed to the Greek New Testament in current speech. By the Sixteen Century, the members of Waldo's church had hired a cousin of John Calvin to translate the New Testament into vernacular French for mass distribution to the poor which is said to have sparked the French Reformation and the Huguenot movement in that country.

Despite all persecution, still there are members of Waldo's church in many places in rural Southern Europe still served by their "uncle" preachers, still listening to the story of God's life on earth in little stone churches from their vernacular gospels.

* * * * *

Traditional:

Gratian's Thought

The power of thought! What a great power and how remarkable it is is! The lives of persons come and go and yet the thought of a person can linger even when all record of the thinker has disappeared.

How could the thought of an anonymous Christian living in the 12th Century have an impact on modern lives?

There was once a disciple named Gratian whose life is almost totally anonymous. Gratian dedicated his quiet life to reviewing all the sources of law in the world and turning them into a system in which the love of God's Child predominated. There is virtually no legal system in today's world which cannot be traced to the thoughtful system of this forgotten soul.

Gratian lived in the first half of the Twelfth Century. Little else is known. This was a time of tribal or feudal law in the medieval world. Such law was not really law but a rule of power by persons with authority. It was a rule of "might makes right." Such was the way of life when Gratian began his work.

The very few facts known about Gratian prove that he was a monk of the Camaldulensian monastery in Bologna. This was a Benedictine monastery. He is once mentioned as being a consultant in a papal court in 1143 and died anonymously sometime before 1159. Virtually no other trace can be found. Gratian was of course not even his birth name but an assumed name he was somehow assigned probably taken from an obscure former Roman Emperor. Who he was we cannot know.

Yet Gratian's thought is tapped every time a modern judge considers a legal matter and tries to rule what is right to do.

Gratian composed a system of law known as his "Decretum," originally called "Concordia Discordantium Canonum." This has sometimes been known as canon law. Its purpose was to extend the rule of Christianity into a secular legal system. Nothing like this had ever been attempted before. Jesus had said his Homeland was not of this world but Gratian panged to have the Homeland Jesus described dialogue with human systems of legal relationships with an apostle of the heritage of Jesus as judge. So Gratian exhaustively reviewed every source of the law he could find and composed it into a body of law that was intended to and did supersede feudal law. This canon law established that all laws were subservient to God. It upheld the claim that the domain of this world is ruled by the breathing spirit of God and that a spiritually ordained judge should decide things.

Gratian's Decretum is basically a compilation of legal sources with Gratian's own commentary or "dictum" about each. It has about 4,000 capitulae divided into three parts. The first part contains "distinctions" that define the sources of law and assess pastoral problems dealing with clerics and aspects of church discipline. The second part refers to "causes" and address specific questions. They are like a treatise on individual legal subjects. Here can be found Gratian's views on divorce or dissolution of marriage law which remain as principles still in effect today. Other subjects consider the laws of monastic life and church property. A third section refers to laws about sacraments.

On the surface, the Decretum of Gratian is just a compilation of apostolic constitutions, canons and church councils, texts from Roman law and other unknown sources. Gratian's commentaries on each are the unifying element of his legal system. Gratian's summaries of the law highlight each's importance and his reconciliation of contradictions establishes the work as a single system. His comments favor moderation and humanitarian feeling. He discusses sentences or penalties as well as disciplinary rules but urges against the imposition of the death penalty as being beyond human authority to impose. Even heretics are not to be put to death.

Other great systems of laws have existed in the history of humanity. All important predecessors of Gratian were pagans. Probably the most important prior system was the Roman Emperor Justinian's Code. Humanity simply has to have government for its community. But before Gratian no Christian had attempted to formally reconcile human law with the law of revelation and spirit. Now the world was to be ruled by a legal system envisioned by a person with absolutely no power but the power of his thought.

One can certainly argue with the points of Gratian's legal code. Gratian seems to have consciously used access to the sacraments as a means of taming the world. His law says that only a priest duly ordained through the papal system has the power of administering the Eucharist, the body and blood of Jesus. The monks of his time were the civilizers of the world and soldiers against ignorance, violence and disorder. Gratian armed them with the innocent weapon of the body and blood of Jesus. Either some barbaric king towed the line of peace on earth or else he was not deemed worthy to share the Eucharist. Did the establishment of peace in the world and the survival of Christianity during his time justify this?

Gratian's law maintains that priests alone can bind and loose sins. The most powerful rulers of the world found they were required to confess to a simple humble monk. Did the establishment of peace in the world and the survival of Christianity during his time justify this?

Some have said his system merely substitutes Papal authority over human authority. Popes often seemed to try to use Gratian's law to assert secular power in the world. Over the years Gratian's "Decretum" grew thicker and thicker with great complexity as the life of the simple Christian Gratian slipped further and further into obscurity.

If we wish to summarize Gratian's law it is possible to separate it from its claim about the Papacy and its historical anomalies. For it was not really a Pope whose authority was asserted by Gratian. Gratian wished an apostle to be in charge of earthly matters. It is up to God to determine if the line of Roman Popes was worthy of this status. Gratian's thought was that all humanity were children of God needing the guidance of an apostle. It is to a person of spiritual integrity that we must look for leadership in this world.

Now when we ask a judge to decide a legal issue we direct to him his responsibility under Gratian's thought that he decide it as would one of the heritage of Christianity rather than barbarism. We ask him to be not just a secular judge but also a spiritual apostle of Jesus as we have been trained to expect of a judge by Gratian's thought.

* * * * *

Thomas Aquinas:

Predestination

It is fitting that God should predestine humanity for all things are the subject of God's providence. Now it belongs to providence to direct things towards their end. The end towards which created things are directed by God is twofold: one which exceeds all proportion and ability of created nature; and this end is life eternal, consisting in the vision of God which is above the nature of every creature. The other end is proportionate to created nature to which end created being can attain according to the power of its nature. Now if a thing cannot attain to something by the power of its nature, it must be directed thereto by another. Thus an arrow is directed by the archer towards a mark. Hence, properly speaking, a rational creature capable of eternal life is led towards it, directed, as it were, by God. The exemplar of that direction pre-exists in God just as in God is the exemplar of the order of all things towards an end which is declared to be providence. Now the exemplar in the mind of the doer of something to be done is a kind of pre-existence in that one of the thing to be done. Hence the exemplar of the direction of a rational creature towards the end of life eternal is called predestination. For to destine is to direct or send. Thus it is clear that predestination is a part of providence.

* * * * *

After Thomas Aquinas:

Angels, A Similar Form of Spirit in the Human Soul and the Powers of the Human Soul

In the created world the highest form of life are the pure spirits or angels. Angels are those souls not united to bodies. They are the pure intelligences of the created emanation of the intelligence and will of God. The created world is hierarchical. Every nature is taxed with what is least noble in it. Thus the angels are superior to the human soul because the angels are not united to bodies.

Angels and the souls of humans are not different. A single and simple creative power produced and maintains the whole of creation and the same life flows through both. At the supreme degree of all things is the absolutely simple and One, which is God. Intellectual substances freed from all union with matter are the angels. The purpose of angels is that of knowing. Their intellect may, however, pass from potency to act without the need to assume a distinction in the form of the matter within their essence which remains unchanged. The angel differs from God in that the angel is confined in activity to the finite world. What is true of those things of a material nature is true of angels in that they have forms and determinate natures. Each is absolutely different and species of them exist. Angels, as pure intelligences, comprehend the sensibilities of life rather than its materiality. Some angels are turned wholly towards God and are concerned entirely with the contemplation of God while others contemplate the plurality of objects equal to the number of created beings. Finally angels are directly charged with the ordering of human affairs. Some are concerned with the common good of nations and cities and others bear entrusted messages to individuals from God. Others encourage the individual good in persons.

The human soul is entirely a subsisting form and not susceptible to any admixture of matter. The human body is animated by the soul. Like the angel, the soul is potency and can act. The soul can unite with a body. The body is not a prison of the soul but rather its servant and instrument so placed by God at its disposal. The body and soul are designed to permit a human being to become perfectly joined into the life of God. In a human being each organ exists by reason of its function as the eye to enable sight and hands to handle, etc., etc. The human body permits the soul to reach for the perfection of the universe for the soul that animates it.

Each human soul is incompletely perfect and is conscious that it ought to be what it is not. The soul feels the need of hope for accomplishing God's work. The human being can become conscious of what it lacks. It must seek union of its intelligence with its soul. The intellectual essence of the soul cannot combine with a body to form the mixture or else the soul would cease to exist. The form of union is not sharing of all functions. The body has its own intellect and performs its own operations. The soul can however share in sensations and passions. In this way, a human being becomes not only body but body and soul. The eye does not truly see unless it sees out of the animation of the soul. The body can assume an intellectual nature and so can the soul. In this way a human being becomes a union of body and soul. Within every one individual there is only one form because the body and soul impress their natures upon each other. A human being is both that person's body and soul. Nevertheless the Godly form of the person is the soul although a soul reaches its full perfection only in union with the body. A soul possesses manifold powers of reason, sense, movement and life. The only object of the soul is the body with which it unites. This is the soul in its vegetative state. The body receives life from this soul as from its form. The soul can also be the body's sensibility and also its apprehension or source of intellectual activity.

The soul seeks after the possession of beatitude. The human soul exists in the view of God and is not its own last end. The good of the human soul can combine with the Supreme Good which is the perfection that fully satisfies the appetite after death. Even seeing God face to face in beatitude, the soul is not that of a separate intelligence but that of a soul together with its body. This is the combination which we find again in the attendedness of God in God's Homeland.

* * * * *

Dante:

A Vision of Hell

"Midway in our life's journey, I went astray from the straight road and woke to find myself alone in a darkwood," said Dante Alighieri in 1300 A.D. He was bewildered to find himself on a journey, a vision of hell to medieval Christians.

"Here sighs and cries and wails coiled and recoiled on the starless air, spilling my soul to tears," he hears. Hell is the painful place that mirrors the evil of the earthly life. It is a place that reminds us of the evil caused by uncontrollable instincts, wrong behavior and wickedness. Dante finds that each wrong is symbolically punished so that the retributions fits the error. The agents of judgment are such things as furious rain, howling wind, raining fire, stench, darkness, biting cold, or even wunks and demons who are capricious, malicious, spiteful and cruel. They inflict not just pain but also terror.

Dante finds the first residents of hell to be those who lived lives not doing either good or bad. They shirked their moral responsibilities. They are not deemed worthy of God's Homeland nor of the punishments of the deeper regions. They did not stand up for Jesus. Their standing back is rewarded by its opposite. Now they are given to eternally pursue an elusive, ever-shifting banner, goaded by swarms of wasps and hornets.

Now Dante finds the River Acheron. Damned souls wait on its banks to be ferried across into the hell of fire and ice. The boatman taking them across, tells them, "Woe to you depraved souls! Bury here and forever all hope of Paradise. I come to lead you to the other shore, into eternal dark, into fire and ice." At these words, the souls of the damned continue their blasphemy and denials about God, their parents, their time on earth, and the day, hour and place of their births. Now they may enter a world of the hatred, despair, cruelty and suffering that their activities created on the earth. The unbaptized and noble heathens reside in the first region of hell. Their punishment is not seeing God. Though they did not know the true God, they contributed to the growth of the human spirit. Here are sighs but not punishments. Dante finds that deeper Hell is an abyss. It is a place of dark, starless air, a place of souls who have lost the good of the intellect with sounds of hoarse, shrill voices like seas wracked by wars of winds. A whirlwind whips through the second circle of hell. Here are those who physically love in sin driven by winds as they were driven by their passions. Dante meets Paolo and Francesca here. They are two lovers who were caught by death when sinning together. Francesca has committed adultery but freely confesses to Dante, "Love which permits no loved one not to love, took me so strongly with delight in him..." She felt physical attraction drive her as the wind now did.

In the third circle, Dante finds gluttons. A ravenous three-headed dog, Cerberus, personifies gluttony and takes those consigned here to himself ripping them apart, flying and mangling them. Here are those who dwell on sensual passions and emotional attachments. One of them begs Dante, "When you move again among the living, oh, speak my name to the memory of men!" Thus can the real world be a damnation with its ties.

In the fourth circle are mobs of hoarders on the one hand and wasters on the other. As Dante goes through this place, the two mobs attack each other. The hoarders uphold their lack of generosity, inability to surrender themselves and closed minds while the wasters contend they do not need to be responsible for what they have been entrusted.

The wrathful are punished in the fifth circle. They lie in a marsh and arise to attack each other. "They bit, as if each would tear the other limb from limb." Their land is a marsh from a black spring. The sullen ones of the wrathful do not rise from the marsh but instead lie entombed in the slime and gurgle their hatreds in their throats. One of the angry ones rises and recognizes Dante. It is an ostentatious wealthy man covered in mud who continues his brutal anger even after death and Dante shouts at him, "May you weep and wail to all eternity for I know you helldog, as filthy as you are."

Now Dante arrives at the capital of Hell, the city of Dis. Here is the sixth circle. It is a countryside that resembles a vast cemetery except that the fiery tombs are not open lidded as cries of pain issue endless from the entombed dead. Here are those who deny the immortality of the soul. Other matters are of greater importance to these sufferers. Among them was a politician who loved his city more than God and yet scorned the very fires raging about his soul.

Incontinence is punished outside the city of Dis. Violence, bestiality, fraud and malice are punished within it.

In the seventh circle are those who are violent. Here is the Minotaur, a bloodthirsty bull, who ravages the punished.

In this circle are three rounds. The first forms a boiling river of blood. Those who have done violence to their neighbors must drown here through eternity. The great war- makers of all time are residents - people like Alexander the Great and Attila the Scourge of God as well as simple thieves and robbers. Centaurs patrol the banks of the river and shoot with arrows any who try to rise from the boiling blood.

Surrounding the river is the wood of suicides where souls must live in thorny trees. They will go for their bodies on Judgement Day but they cannot reinhabit them but instead must dangle from the trees until the end of time. When Dante breaks off a twig from one of the trees, a human voice inside cries out begging for mercy. The suicide inside was a man who stood unjustly accused of treason against his master. The man was just to his master but unjust to himself. Two souls who escape are observed. Dante sees the souls running but pursued by a pack of ravenous hounds of hell who catch them and tear them apart.

The third round is a thick and arid land upon which descends an eternal, slow rain of fire. Here are blasphemers stretched on the ground, predatory homosexuals running in endless circles and usurers huddling together on sand.

Now Dante gets on the back of the monster Geryon to fly down into the eighth circle of Hell. Concentric ditches include those who committed vices from seduction to flattery, from simoniacs to fortune tellers, from thieves to sowers of discord. Horned demons with great whips lash the seducers. In the second ditch lie flatterers in their own excrement. In the third ditch are found tube-like holes where simoniacs - those who sell church offices - are place upside down with the soles of their feet ablaze. When a newcomer arrives, he crashes headlong into a hole and pushes his predecessor deeper. In the next ditch are the wizards and witches who attempted to look into the future with their heads turned backwards on their bodied and compelled to walk backwards. Grafters are in the next ditch sunk in boiling pitch and guarded by demons who tear them to pieces with claws and grappling hooks. In the sixth ditch are hypocrites weighed down by robes of lead walking round and round a narrow track. In the seventh ditch are insolents whose souls are being remoulded into the forms of reptiles. In the eighth ditch are tricksters and liars who live in flames like fireflies. In the ninth ditch are sowers of discord with their bodies rent and hanging open. In the last ditch of the eighth circles are falsifiers. Here was a man who took the identity of another, a counterfeiter, a perjurer.

In the great pit at the center of hell lives Satan. Dante is lowered into this pit in the palm of a giant. Antaeus, who places him in the freezing lake which is divided into four rounds. The regions are for those treacherous to their families, those treacherous to their countries, those treacherous to their guests and those treacherous to trusting employers. The sinners are buried in ice and the ice blacks every movement. Nor can they cry because their tears congeal and their eyes freeze.

Satan too is here. He has three faces, one face is fiery red, the other between white and yellow and the third is black. In every mouth, Satan chews on a sinner between his rake like teeth. Judas who betrayed Jesus is one of them. Satan has six pairs of beating wings which are the source of icy winds.

Only after Dante climbs up to the hair of Satan to reach a place at the center of the earth can he begin his climb back from Hell.

* * * * *

After Fyodor Dostoevsky:

God's Child and a Grand Inquisitor

We return to the 16th Century for this story. Now came God's Child on the scene. But it is not as promised to come in glory. It is fifteen centuries since a gospel writer wrote, "Behold, I come quickly." Humanity awaits with the same faith and with the same emotion. What great faith has humanity! It has been fifteen centuries since a human being has seen signs from God's Homeland. Now there was nothing left but faith.

And yet let us imagine a story in which Jesus returned. He desired to appear but for a moment, to the people, to the tortured suffering people, sunk in sin but loving Jesus like children. He came to Spain in the most terrible time of the Inquisition, when fires were lighted every day to the glory of God and "in magnificent array' wicked heretics were burnt.

Jesus came softly, unobserved, and yet, strange to say, every one recognized Him. The people are irresistibly drawn to God's Child. They surround Him. They flock about Him. The follow Him. He moves silently in their midst with a gentle smile of infinite compassion. The sun of love burns in His heart, light and power shine from His eyes, and their radiance, shed on the people, stirs their hearts with responsible love. He stretches out His hands to them, blesses them, and a healing virtue comes from contact with Him, even with His garments. An old man in the crowd, blind since childhood cries out, "Oh, Familyhead, heal me and I will be able to see You." It happens as if scales fell from his eyes. The crowd weeps and kisses the earth under His feet. Children throw flowers before Him sing and cry hosanna. "It is He -it is He!" all repeat. He stops at the steps of the Seville cathedral as weeping mourners bring by a little open white coffin. In it lies a child of seven, the only daughter of a prominent citizen. The dead child lies covered with flowers. "He will raise your child," the crowd tells the weeping mother. The priest leading the procession looks perplexed but the mother throws herself at His feet with a cry. "If it is you, raise my child!" The coffin is set down at His feet and His lips once more say, "Stand up." The little girl does so. Then she smiles with wide open wonderment at holding this bunch of white roses in her hands.

A Grand Inquisitor was passing the cathedral. He is an old man, ninety, tall and erect with a withered face and sunken eyes in which there is still a gleam of light. He is not dressed as he was the day before when he supervised the burning of heretics. Today he wears an old cassock. He is followed by his gloomy assistants and slaves and "sacred guard." The Grand Inquisitor saw it all. He saw the dead child rise up. Now he bids the guards of his to go arrest Him. The Grand Inquisitor has such power that people are cowed into submission and trembling in obedience to his orders. The guards take the Prisoner to the prison of the Holy Inquisition and shut Him in it.

Now, the next day the Grand Inquisitor goes to the prison cell with a lantern in his hand. The door is closed behind him. The Grand Inquisitor says, "Is it You? You?" Then he realized Jesus does not answer those seeking such proof. "Yes of course it is you," he answered himself.

"Why do you hinder us?" the Grand Inquisitor asked Him.

No answer.

"You know very well you have come to hinder us! Tomorrow I will condemn you and burn you at the stake as the worst of heretics. And the very people who have to-day kissed your feet tomorrow at the faintest sign from me will rush to heap burning coals on your fire."

"You often said you came to set humanity free," the Grand Inquisitor said. "But look what this has done to people. We've paid far too dearly for it in the centuries since you first came. For fifteen centuries we have been wrestling with your brand of freedom and now we in the Inquisition are going to do something about it. We are going to destroy the freedom of humanity. We who know of the mystery of your love - that it gives humanity freedom - must impose a rule which will make folk more happy. Now we will cause humanity to be happy by taking away their freedom. Humanity was created to rebel and how could You have expected rebels to be happy in their freedom? You rejected the only path for happiness of humanity! Fortunately, upon departing, you passed along to us the right to tell your story and gave us religious authority. Your coming again hinders us. Do not think of taking our authority away. We cannot allow you to hinder us.

Nothing has ever been more insupportable for humanity and human society than freedom. And yet you insisted humanity be free. You could so easily have rejected this by turning stones into bread to earn humanity's obedience. If you fed them, they would have been yours. Instead you said that humanity must not live by bread alone. Didn't you know that for the sake of bread humanity would repeatedly rise up against you? How often must humanity face a rival to you who will come along and for the sake of bread oppose you and overcome you? You freed humanity and then asked them to seek virtue? How stupid. Did you simply want all of those who loved humanity to always be persecuted and tortured? Those of this freedom you gave seek us again and again no matter where we hide. Now we shall serve an Inquisition and eliminate your enemies and in the process correct your mistake of giving people freedom. They will say, "We will be your slaves if you will feed us." They will understand that freedom and bread enough for all are inconceivable together for never, never will they be able to share between them. We will convince them that they are too weak to be free - that they are worthless, weak, vicious and rebellions. You wished for them the bread of God's Homeland but we will show them they cannot compare it to earthly bread. Perhaps for the sake of the heavenly bread, you will have thousands and tens of thousands to follow you, but what is to become of the millions and millions of humanity who do not have the strength to forego the earthly bread for the heavenly? Humanity is now our responsibility. You would simply have us who truly cherish the weak serve as raw material for the great and strong? No! We will cherish the weak and give them happiness even at the price of taking away their freedom. Even the great and strong will become obedient to us. They will marvel at us and look on us as gods because we are ready to endure the freedom which they have found so dreadful and to rule over them - so intolerable will they find it to remain free. Humanity wanted to bend down to you and they would have if you had given them bread. Instead of taking possession of humanity's freedom, you increased it and burdened it with talk of a spiritual Homeland and left us to suffer in this life forever. All you desired was for humanity to love freely, that humanity should love you freely and love each other because you enticed them and captivated them. But did it not occur to you that humanity would reject you if you weighed them down with such a fearful burden as freedom of choice? Nothing could ever have caused such great confusion and suffering as what you have caused laying upon humanity so many cares and insoluble problems. Thus, you yourself laid the foundation for the destruction of your own Homeland and you must not blame us. No! We will save humanity with this Inquisition by wiping out freedom. We will use the weapons of miracle, mystery and authority. You rejected all three. We will accomplish what all humanity seeks. We will give them something to bow down to. We will unite them in one unanimous and harmonious earthly organization. We will unite the world into one mind but it cannot have freedom. Only those of us who rule will be unhappy, not the vast majority who will be saved from their freedom. Those of us who burn you will be the ones who keep the secret of your true mystery. The obedient flock of humanity will do my bidding and take you to be burned tomorrow and heap coals on you for coming again to hinder us. If ever there was one who deserved our fires it is you and tomorrow I shall burn you. Dixi."

And yet on the next day, despite all the Grand Inquisitor said, he returned to give Jesus a further chance to answer him and give him some advice. The old Inquisitor longed for Jesus to say something however bitter and terrible like, "You do not believe in God." But Jesus suddenly approached the Grand Inquisitor in silence and gently kissed him on his bloodless aged lips. That is his whole answer. The old man shudders. The corners of his lips tremble. He goes to the door, opens it and says to Jesus: "Go and never come again...Never! Never! Never!"

You see the Grand Inquisitor truly loved humanity despite the fact that millions of humanity have remained a mockery and could never be capable of using their freedom. The secret of the Grand Inquisitor's love for humanity-in seeking to destroy freedom-could only come from loving humanity more. Trying to correct the work of Jesus for the sake of Jesus was his failing.

* * * * *

Martin Rinkart:

A Song Of Thanks From A Time Of Plague

When a war struck Germany called the Thirty Years' War, Martin Rinkart was a church pastor in the walled city of Edinburg in Saxony. His town suffered famine and rampant disease from a Black Plague. The pastor was a slightly built frail man but he did not leave Edinburg even when the plague was at its worst. After the other pastors left, he stayed to pastor to not only the city folk but also huge numbers of refugees from war. Treating the sick and dying, he conducted 4,500 funerals of victims including the one of his wife. Then towards the end of the war, his city was attacked first by Austrian troops and then twice by the Swedish army. During one of the Swedish assaults, its general demanded a huge ransom to leave the city alone. Martin Rinkart went to the commander to seek relief but when he was refused, he called to his Christian flock, "Come, my children; we can find no mercy with man - let us take refuge with God." The pastor led his church members to fall on their knees in prayers and in singing of hymns. The general was so moved he reduced his demand to one-twenieth and then left.

Martin Rickart wrote a hymn which began as a family grace said before meals, but which became a song of national thanksgiving at the end of the Thirty Years' War.

Now thank we all our God
With heart and hands and voices,
Who wondrous things hath done,
In whom his world rejoices,
Who, from our mothers' arms,
Hath blessed us on our way
With countless gifts of love,
And still is ours today.

O may this bounteous God
Through all our life be near us,
With ever joyful hearts
And blessed peace to cheer us,
And keep us in his grace,
And guide us when perplexed,
And free us from all ills
In this world and the next.

All praise and thanks to God
The Father now be given,
The Son, and him who reigns
With them in highest heaven,
The one eternal God,
Whom earth and heaven adore,
For thus it was, is now,
And shall be evermore.
Amen.

* * * * *

John Calvin:

The Elect and the Damned from Before Birth

God once established by eternal and unchangeable plan those whom were before determined once for all to be received into salvation and those whom, on the other hand, would be devoted to destruction. We assert that, with respect to the elect, this plan was founded upon freely given mercy, without regard to human worth, but by just and irreprehensible but incomprehensible judgment God has barred the door of life to those whom are given over to damnation. Now among the elect we regard the call as a testimony of election. Then we hold justification another sign of its manifestation until they come into the glory in which the fulfillment of that election lies. But as the Familyhead seals the elect by call and justification, so, by shutting off the reprobate from knowledge of the name or from the sanctification of the Spirit, God reveals by these marks what sort of judgment awaits them.

The elect are gathered into the Familyhead's flock by a call not immediately at birth, and not all at the same time, but according as it pleases God to dispense grace to them. But before they are gathered unto that supreme Shepherd, they wander scattered in the wilderness common to all, and they do not differ at all from others except that they are protected by God's especial mercy from rushing headlong into the final ruin of death. If you look upon them, you will see Adam's offspring, who savor of the common corruption of the mass. The fact that they are not carried to utter and even desperate impiety is not due to any innate goodness of theirs but because the eye of God watches over their safety and God's hand is outstretched to them!

What of them, then, whom God created for dishonor in life and destruction in death to become the instruments of wrath and examples of severity? That they may come to their end, God sometimes deprives them of the capacity to hear the Word. At other times, God blinds and stuns them by the preaching of it.

The supreme Judge, then, makes way for predestination when he leaves in blindness those whom are condemned and deprived of participation in the light. Of the former effect there are daily proofs. If the same sermon is preached, say, to a hundred people, twenty receive it with the ready obedience of faith, while the rest hold it valueless or laugh or hiss or loathe it.

The fact that the reprobates do not obey God's Word when it is made known to them will be justly charged against the malice and depravity of their hearts, provided it be added at the same time that they have been given over to this depravity because they have been raised up by the just but inscrutable judgment of God to show forth God's glory in their condemnation. While stubbornness grows out of their own wickedness, it is noted that they are left in their stubbornness even though the Familyhead could have softened their hearts - because God's immutable decree has once and for all destined them to destruction.

* * * * *

Erasmus:

Two Christians Prepare for Death

Marcolphus. "Does even death have its vainglory?"

Phaedrus. "Never have I seen two men die so differently. If you have time to listen, I'll describe each one's end. You shall judge which death would be preferable for a Christian. Marcolphus. "Oh, yes, do be good enough to tell me. There's nothing I'd rather hear. Phaedus. "First hear about George, then. The moment unmistakable signs of death appeared, the company of physicians who had long attended the patient demanded their fees, hiding their feeling of hopelessness about his life.

Marcolphus, "How many doctors were there?"

Phaedrus, "Sometimes ten, sometimes twelve; never fewer than six."

Marcolphus, "Enough to kill even a healthy man!"

Phaedrus, "When they had their money, they warned the relatives confidentially that death was not far off; that they should look to his spiritual welfare, for there was no hope of his physical safety. And the patient was warned courteously be his close friends to entrust his body to God's care, and to concern himself only with what belonged to making a good end. When he heard this, George stared at the physicians in wild surmise, as though indignant at being deserted by them. They retorted that they physicians, not gods; that what their skill could do had been performed; but that no medicine could prevail against destiny. After this, they went into the next bedroom.

Marcolphus, "What? They lingered even after they were paid?"

Phaedrus, "They had disagreed completely over what sort of disease it was. One said dropsy; another, tympanites; another, an intestinal abscess - each one mentioned a different ailment. And during the whole time they were treating the patient they quarreled violently about the nature of his malady.

Marcolphus, "Lucky patient meanwhile!"

Phaedrus, "To settle their dispute once for all, they requested through his wife that they be permitted later to perform an autopsy on the body - quite a respectable thing, that was, and done customarily as a mark of respect in the case of eminent person. Furthermore, it would help save many lives, and would increase George's accumulation of merits. Last of all, they promised to buy thirty masses at their own expense for the repose of his soul. This request met with opposition, to be sure, but was finally granted, thanks to their flattery of his wife and relations. Business disposed of, the medical congress adjourned, because it's not right, they say, for those whose job is to save life to look on at death or to attend funerals. Nest Bernardine was summoned, a holy man (as you know), warden of the Franciscans; he was to hear confession. Hardly was confession over when the four orders commonly called mendicants caused a disturbance in the house."

Marcolphus, "So many vultures at one corpse?"

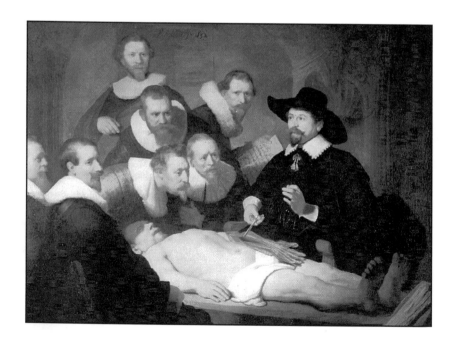

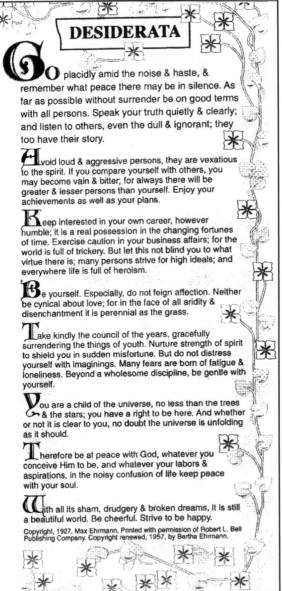

DESIDERATA

Go placidly amid the noise & haste, & remember what peace there may be in silence. As far as possible without surrender be on good terms with all persons. Speak your truth quietly & clearly; and listen to others, even the dull & ignorant; they too have their story.

Avoid loud & aggressive persons, they are vexatious to the spirit. If you compare yourself with others, you may become vain & bitter; for always there will be greater & lesser persons than yourself. Enjoy your achievements as well as your plans.

Keep interested in your own career, however humble; it is a real possession in the changing fortunes of time. Exercise caution in your business affairs; for the world is full of trickery. But let this not blind you to what virtue there is; many persons strive for high ideals; and everywhere life is full of heroism.

Be yourself. Especially, do not feign affection. Neither be cynical about love; for in the face of all aridity & disenchantment it is perennial as the grass.

Take kindly the council of the years, gracefully surrendering the things of youth. Nurture strength of spirit to shield you in sudden misfortune. But do not distress yourself with imaginings. Many fears are born of fatigue & loneliness. Beyond a wholesome discipline, be gentle with yourself.

You are a child of the universe, no less than the trees & the stars; you have a right to be here. And whether or not it is clear to you, no doubt the universe is unfolding as it should.

Therefore be at peace with God, whatever you conceive Him to be, and whatever your labors & aspirations, in the noisy confusion of life keep peace with your soul.

With all its sham, drudgery & broken dreams, it is still a beautiful world. Be cheerful. Strive to be happy.

Phaedrus, "Then the parish priest was called in, to give the man extreme unction and Holy Communion.

Marcolphus, "Piously done."

Phaedrus, "Thereupon a bloody battle between the priest and the monks very nearly broke out."

Marcolphus, "At the sick man's bedside?"

Phaedrus, "Yes, and with Christ watching."

Marcolphus, "What provoked such unexpected uproar?"

Phaedrus, "When the priest learned that the patient had confessed to the Franciscan, he declared he would not administer the rite of extreme unction, the Eucharist, or burial unless he had heard the patient's confession with his own ears. He was the parish priest; he would have to render an account of his flock to the Lord; this he could not do if he alone were unfamiliar with the secret of the man's conscience. . . . .

Marcolphus, "I can't wait to hear these."

Phaedrus, "I'll summarize them, because it's a long story. He was survived by a wife of 38, a good sensible woman; two sons, one 19, the other 15; as many daughters, but both young and unmarried. The will provided that since the wife could not be induced to become a nun she should put on a Beguine's cloak - an order midway between nuns and laywomen - and the elder son, since he flatly refused to become a monk—"

Marcolphus, "You don't catch an old fox with a noose!"

Phaedrus, "-wash to hurry to Rome without delay after father's funeral. There, after being made priest by a papal dispensation before reaching legal age, he should say mass for his father's soul every day for a whole year in the Vatican church, and every Friday crawl on his knees up the sacred steps in the Lateran church."

Marcolphus, "Was he glad to undertake this?"

Phaedrus, "To be blunt, he was as glad as asses are to bear heavy burdens. The younger son was promised to St. Francis, the older daughter to St. Clre, the younger daughter to St. Catherine of Siena. Only this last promise could be kept. George's intention was to have God further in his debt by putting his five survivors into five mendicant orders, and he tried very hard to do so, but his wife's age and that of his elder son would yield neither to threats nor to flattery."

Marcolphus, "A way of disinheriting them."

Phaedrus, "The entire estate was so divided that after money for funeral expenses was set aside, one share was allotted to the wife: half of this for her support, half to the house she would join. If she changed her mind and backed out of the agreement, all the money was to pass to that congregation. Another share would fall to the son. He, however, would have passage money paid to him at once, and enough to buy the dispensation and take care of a year' living expenses in Rome. If he changed his mind and refused to take priestly orders, his share would be divided between the Franciscans and Dominicans. And AI fear that may happen, so greatly did the boy seem to detest a priestly career. Two share would go to the monastery receiving the younger son; two likewise to the nunneries receiving the daughters, but on condition that if these children balked at entering the religious life, the monastery and nunneries could still keep all the money. Furthermore, one share would go presently to Bernardine; the same amount to Vincent; half a share to the Carthusians, for the community of all good works done by the entire order. The one-and-a-half shares remaining were to be distributed to undisclosed beggars approved by Bernardine and Vincent."

Marcolphus, "You should have said, lawyer-fashion, 'those beggards male and female.'"

Phaedrus, "So when the will had been read, the covenants were made in the following terms: 'Do you, George Balearicus, being alive and of sound mind, approve this testament which you have made of recent date and in accordance with your wishes?' 'I do.' 'And is this your final and irrevocable will?' 'It is.' "And do you appoint me and the said Vincent, Bachelor, executors of your last will?' 'I do.' He was ordered to sign it again."

Marcolphus, "How could a dying man do that?"

Phaedrus, "Bernardine guided the invalids' hand."

Marcolphus, "What did he write down?"

Phaedrus, "May he who attempts henceforth to change any of this incur the wrath of St. Francis and St. Dominic."

Marcolphus, "But weren't they afraid of a suit on grounds of 'inofficious testaemtn'?"

Phaedrus. "That kind of suit doesn't apply to property promised to God, nor does anyone readily sue God at law. When these matters were finished, the wife and children gave their right hand to the sick man and swore they would keep the obligations laid upon them.. . . . . .

Marcolphus, "And so he breathed his last?"

Phaedrus, "Not yet. A rush mat was spread on the floor in such a manner that at one end it looked like a pillow."

Marcolphus, "Now what's going to happen?"

Phaedrus, "They scattered a few ashes on it, and there they laid the sick man. A Franciscan tunic was spread over him, but only after being blessed by short prayers and holy water. A cowl was placed at his head (for at that time it could not be put on), and along with that his brief and the covenants.

Marcolphus, "A new kind of death!"

Phaedrus, "But they swear the devil has no jurisdiction over those who die thus. So, they say, St. Martin and St. Francis, among others, died."

Marcolphus, "But their lives corresponded to this kind of death. What happened after that, please?"

Phaedrus. "A crucifix and a taper were held out to the sick man. To the crucifix extended to him he said, 'In was I was accustomed to rely on my shield; now will I face my foe with this shield.' And after he kissed it, he turned on his left side. To the taper he said, 'I used to excel with my spear in war; now will I brandish this spear against the enemy of souls.'"

Marcolphus, "Spoken like a soldier!"

Phaedrus, "These were his last words, for presently death stopped his tongue and at the same moment he began to expire. Bernardine on his right, Vincent on his left, hung over the dying man, both in fine voice. One displayed an image of St. Francis, the other that of Dominic. Others, scattered through the bedroom, murmured some psalms in a doleful tome. Bernardine assailed his right ear with great clamors, Vincent his left."

Marcolphus, "What were they screaming?"

Phaedrus. "Bernardine something like this: 'George Balearicus, if now you approve what's been done between us, turn your head to the right.' He did so. Vincent, on the other side: 'Be not afraid, George, you have Francis and Dominic as your champions. Rest easy: think how many merits you have, what a papal brief; finally, remember my soul is pledged for your if there is any danger. If you understand and approve this, nod your head to the left.' He nodded. Again, with like clamor: 'If you understand this,' he says, 'press my hand.' The George pressed his hand. So what with nodding to this side and that, and pressing of hands, nearly three hours were spent. Just as George began to gape, Bernardine, standing up straight, pronounced the absolution, but George was dead before he could finish it. . . . . ."

Marcolphus, "Well said, and boldly. But now I'm impatient to hear how Cornelius died."

Phaedrus, "As he lived without being a nuisance to anyone, so he died. He had an annual fever that recurred regularly. And then, either because of his old age - for he was past sixty - or for some other reason, it oppressed him more than usual, and he himself seemed to sense that his last day was close at hand. So, four days before his death, i.e., on Sunday, he went to church, confessed to his parish priest, heard sermon and mass, devoutly took Communion, and returned home."

Marcolphus, "He didn't use physicians?"

Phaedrus. "He consulted only one, but one who was fully as good a man as he was a physician: James Castrutius by name."

Marcolphus, "I know him. No man is truer."

Phaedrus, "He promised to do whatever he could for his friend, but said he thought there was more help in God than in doctors. Cornelius received this reply as cheerfully as if he had ben given absolute assurance of life., And so, even though he had always been as liberal towards the poor as his means permitted, he then distributed among the destitute whatever he could spare from the needs of his wife and children' not to pushing and sometimes obtrusive beggars, but to worthy ones who struggled against their poverty by working as hard as they could. I implored him to go to bed and summon the priest rather than exhaust his weak body. He replied that he had always tried to help his friends, if possible, rather than be under obligation to them; nor did he want to be any different at death. He didn't even take to his be except for the last day and part of the night on which he left this earth. Meanwhile he used a cane because of his physical weakness, or sat in a big chair. Occasionally he lay down on a little bed, but with his clothes on and his head up. At this time he either gave instructions for relieving the poor, particularly those who were acquaintances or neighbors, or he read from the Bible passages exhorting man to trust God, and setting forth God's love for us. If weakness prevented him from doing even this for himself, he listened while a friend read. Often, with wonderful feeling, he urged his family to mutual love and harmony and to zeal for true righteousness, and comforted them very affectionately, grieved as they were about his dying. From time to time he reminded his family not to leave any of his debts unpaid."

Marcolphus, "Hadn't he made a will?"

Phaedrus. "He had attended to that long before, when he was well and strong. For he held that those made by the dying weren't wills but rather ravings."

Marcolphus, "Didn't he bequeath anything to monasteries or to the poor?"

Phaedrus, "Not a farthing. 'I have shared my modest fortune as I could afford,' he said. 'Now, as I am handing over possession of it to others, so I hand over the spending of it. And I am confident that my family will spend it better than I myself have done."

Marcolphus, "Didn't he send for holy men, as George did?"

Phaedrus, "Not even one. Except his family and two close friends, nobody was present."

Marcolphus, "I wonder why he felt like that."

Phaedrus, "He insisted he didn't want to be troublesome to more people when dying than he had been when he was born."

Marcolphus, "I'm awaiting the end of this story."

Phaedrus, "You'll soon hear it. Thursday came. Feeling extremely weak, he did not leave his couch. The parish priest was called, gave him extreme unction, and again administered Communion, but without confession, for Cornelius said he had no lingering anxieties on his mind. At that point the priest began to discuss the funeral - what sort of procession, and where he was to be buries.

'Bury me as you would the humblest Christian,' he said. 'It makes no difference to me where you lay this poor body; it will be found on the Last Day just the same, wherever you've put it. The funeral procession I care nothing about.' Presently the subjects of tolling the bells, thirty day and anniversary masses, a papal brief, and purchase of a community of merits came up. Then he said, "Pastor, I'll be none the worse off if no bell tolls; or if you deem me worthy of one burial service, that will be more than enough. Or if there is anything else that because of the Church's public custom can scarcely be omitted without scandal to the weak, I leave that to your judgment. I do not desire to buy up someone's prayers or deprive anyone of his merits. There is sufficient abundance of merits in Christ, and I have faith that the prayers and merits of the whole Church will benefit me, if only I am a true member of it. In two 'briefs' I rest my entire hope. One is the fact that the Lord Jesus, the chief shepherd, took away my sins, nailing them to the Cross. The other, that which he signed and sealed with his own sacred blood, by which he assured us of eternal salvation if we place our whole trust in him. For far be it from me that, equipped with merits and briefs, I should summon my Lord to court with his servant, certain as I am that in his sight shall no man living be justified! For my part, I appeal from his justice to his mercy, since it is boundless and inexpressible.' Whereupon the priest departed. Eager and joyous as though with strong hope of salvation, Cornelius ordered certain biblical passages confirming the hope of resurrection and rewards of immortality to be read to him: as that in Isaiah on the postponement of Hezekiah's death, along with his hymn; then the fifteenth chapter of Paul's first letter to the Corinthians; the story of Lazarus' death from John; but above all, the narrative of Christ's passion from the Gospels. How eagerly he concentrated on every one of these, sighing at some, giving thanks with folded hands at others, at some rejoicing and exulting, at others uttering brief prayers! After lunch, when he had taken a short nap, he had the twelfth chapter of John read, to the very end. When this was done, you would have said the man was completely transformed and breathed upon by a new spirit. Day was already turning to evening. He called for his wife and children; then, straightening up as much as his weakness permitted, he spoke to his family thus: 'My dearest wife, those whom earlier God had joined together, now likewise he puts asunder; but in body only, and that for a little while. The care, love, and devotion you have been accustomed to share with me and our sweetest children, transfer wholly to them. Do not suppose you can deserve better by any means, either of God or of me, than by so nurturing, cherishing, and instructing those whom God gave us as the fruits of our marriage, that they may be accounted worthy of Christ. Double your devotion towars them, therefore, and consider my share made over to you. If you do that - as I am confident you will - there will be no reason they should seem orphans. But if you remarry' - at this word his wife broke into tears and began to swear she would never think of marrying again. Then Cornelius: 'My dearest sister in Christ, if the Lord Jesus shall think best to grant you that resolution and strength of spirit, do not fail the heavenly gift, for this will be more comfortable for you and the children alike. But if weakness of the flesh shall call otherwise, know that my death release you from the marriage bond, but not from the obligation have in my name, and in your own, of caring for our children. As for marrying, use the liberty the Lord has given you. This only do I ask, and warn you of: that you choose a husband of such moral character, and bear yourself towards him in such a way, that, guided by his own kindness and prompted by your gentleness, he may love his stepchildren. Be cautious, therefore, about binding yourself by any vow. Keep yourself free for God and for our children. So train them to every form of godliness that you may dissuade them from committing themselves to any career before age and experience demonstrate what mode of life they are suited for.' Turning then to his children, he exhorted them to the pursuit of righteousness, to obedience to their mother, to mutual love and concord among themselves. Having spoken these words, he kissed his wife, made the sign of the Cross, and invoked the favor and mercy of Christ upon his children. After that, looking upon all who were present, he said, 'By dawn tomorrow the Lord who rose from the dead at daybreak will of His mercy vouchsafe to call this poor soul from the tomb of this poor body, and from the shades of this mortality into His heavenly light. I do not want to tire tender youth with vain watching. Let the others, too, take turns sleeping. I need only one watcher, to read the sacred page.'

When the night had passed - it was about four o'clock - and all were come, he ordered read the entire psalm spoken by the Lord when praying on the Cross. After it was ended, he bade them bring a taper and a crucifix. And taking the taper he said, 'The Lord is my light and my salvation; whom shall I fear?' Kissing the crucifix, he said, 'The Lord is the strength of my life: of whom shall I be afraid?' Presently he folded his hands on his breast, in the manner of one praying, and with his eyes turned to heaven said, "Lord Jesus. receive my spirit.' And straightway he closed his eyes as though he were going to sleep, and at the same time expired with a slight gasp. You would have said he had fallen asleep, not died.

Marcolphus, "I never heard of a death less troublesome."

Phaedrus, "He was like that all his life. Each of these men was my friend. Perhaps I'm not a fair judge of which one died in a manner more becoming a Christian. You, being unprejudiced, will decide that better."

Marcolphus, "I'll do so, but at my leisure."

* * * * *

CAT'S CRADLE   Verses and Drawing by
Verna Grisier-McCully

Grandmother played cat's cradle   The good old-fashioned puzzle
Oh, many years ago,   Has brought me thoughts most deep:
And later she taught mother,   If this is called cat's cradle
And mother taught me — so.   Where do the kittens sleep?

James:

The King James Psalms

A philosopher once said, "Since we are born of this world, we are condemned to seek its meaning."

Once there was a child who grew up to become the King of England and a great promoter of the Christian faith through perpetuating its writings. A king in those days was a position of great prominence rather like the Presidents of the United States although kings were picked genetically - usually because they were related to prior kings and queens - which confirmed the providence of the particular happenstance about James that he was reputedly gay. His work in translating the Psalms was a work of great righteousness and confirms that those who give their life to God - be they gay or straight -can accomplish much good.

James was well-educated and a great student of the sacred writings. As an adult, his partner was George Villiers, "Buckingham" to the court and English nation. Buckingham was known as "the royal favorite." James was also the husband of Anne, the daughter of the King of Denmark, and the parent of several children.

It was James who gave us the King James Bible in 1611, a Bible which grew out of James's search for biblical meaning. Its translations were the work of James's scholars under his direction. The most notable influence of James on the King James Version of the Bible is in its Psalms which most closely bear James's own mark and reflect his own thoughtful translations of these songs.

The King James Version of the Bible has proven to be the greatest and most enduring vision of Christianity known to the world. Its words sustained and spellbound Christian pilgrims through many generations of life journeys. Three of James's translations:

THANKSGIVING

I love the Lord, because he hath heard my voice and my supplications.
Because he hath inclined his ear unto me, therefore will I call upon him as long as
    I live.
The sorrows of death compassed me and the pains of hell gat hold upon me: I
    found trouble and sorrow.
Then called I upon the name of the Lord; O Lord, I beseech thee, deliver my soul.
Gracious is the Lord, and righteous, yea, our God is merciful.
The Lord preserveth the simple: I was brought low, and he helped me.
Return unto thy rest, O my soul: for the Lord hath dealt bountifully with thee.
For thou hast delivered my soul from death, mine eyes from tears, and my feet
    from falling.
I will walk before the Lord in the land of the living.
I believed, therefore have I spoken: I was greatly afflicted.
I said in my haste. All men are liars.
What shall I render unto the Lord for all his benefits to me?
I will take the cup of salvation, and call upon the name of the Lord.
I will pay my vows unto the Lord now in the presence of all his people.

Precious in the sight of the Lord is the death of his saints.

O Lord, truly I am thy servant; I am thy servant, and the son of thine handmaid; thou hast loosed my bonds. I will offer to thee the sacrifice of thanksgiving, and will call upon the name of the Lord.

I will pay my vows unto the Lord now in the presence of all his people.

In the courts of the Lord's house, in the midst of thee, O Jerusalem.

Praise ye the Lord.

AS THE HART PANTETH...

As the hart (deer) panteth after the water brooks, so panteth my soul after thee, O God.

My soul thirsteth for God, for the living God: when shall I come and appear before God?

My tears have been my meat day and night, while they continually say unto me, Where is thy God?

When I remember these things, I pour out my soul in me: for I had gone with the multitude, I went with them to the house of

God, with the voice of joy and praise, with a multitude that kept holy-day.

Why art thou cast down, O my soul? and why art thou disquieted in me? hope thou in God: for I shall yet praise him for the help of his countenance.

O my God, my soul is cast down within me: therefore will I remember thee from the land of Jordan, and of the Hermonites from the hill Mizar.

Deep calleth unto deep at the noise of thy waterspouts: all thy waves and thy billows are gone over me.

Yet the Lord will command his loving kindness in the daytime, and in the night his song shall be with me, and my prayer unto the God of my life.

I will say unto God my rock, Why hast thou forgotten me? why go I mourning because of the oppression of the enemy?

As with a sword in my bones, mine enemies reproach me; while they say daily unto me, Where is thy God?

Why art thou cast down, O my soul? and why art thou disquieted within me? hope thou in God: for I shall yet praise him, who is the health of my countenance, and my God.

AN EARTHLY LAND OF UNITY

Behold how good and how pleasant it is for brethren to dwell together in unity!

It is like the precious ointment upon the head, that ran down upon the beard, even Aaron's beard: that went down to the skirts of his garments;

As the dew of Harmon, and as the dew that descended upon the mountain of Zion: for there the Lord commanded the blessing, even life for evermore.

* * * * *

Traditional:

Little Red Riding Hood

Wonst they was a leetle-teeny dirl, an' she was named Red Riding Hood, toz her ma maked her a leetle red cloak `at torned up over her head - an' it was all thist one piece of red cardnal like the dreat long stockin's `at the storekeeper's dot. O! it was the nicest cloak in this town! An' - an' - an' so one day her ma she put it on her. It was Sunday, coz the cloak was too nice to wear thist all the time. An' so her ma she put it on her, an' told her not to dit no dirt on it; an' nen she dot out her little basket `at ole K'is b'inged her, an' filled it full o' whole lots o' good fings t'eat, an' told her to take `em to her dran'ma, an' not spill `em, toz her dran'ma'd spank her ef she did, maybe.

An' so little Red Riding Hood she promised to be tareful, an' tossed her heart she wouldn't spill`em for six-five-ten-two hundred bushel dollars. An' nen she kissed her ma dood bye, an' went a skippin off through the dreat big woods to her dran'ma's - no she didn't do a skippin' nedver coz that 'ud spill the dood fings. She thist went a walkin' along like a little lady, she did - as slow an' purty- like she was a marchin' in the Sunday school kassession.

An' so she was a goin' along an' along through the dreat big woods - toz her dran'ma lived a way fur off from her ma's house, an' you had to do through the dreat big woods to dit there.

An' little Red Riding Hood had mostest fun when she'd do there - a listenin' to the purty burds, an' pullin the purty flowers at drowed around the stumps - an' catchin' butterflies an' drasshoppers, an' stickin' pins through 'em-I thist `said' that! coz she was dood. She'd this catch `em, an' leave their wings on `em thist like they was, an' let 'em do adin, toz she was a "boss girl" - my pa said she was!

An' so she was a doin' along an' doin' along, an' purty soon they was a old wicked wolf jumped out; an' he wanted to eat her up, but there was a big man a choppin' wood wite those there, an' you could hear him, an' so th' old wolf was afeared to tackle her this then - feared the man ud kill him, you know; an' so he `tended like he was a dood friends to her, an' he says, "Dood morning, little Red Riding Hood!" this like that. An' nen little Red Riding Hood she says, "dood morning," this as kind - like her ma learnt her - coz she didn't know th' old wolf wanted t'eat her up.

Nen th' old wolf says, "Where are you doin' to?"

Nen little Red Riding Hood says, "I'm doin' to my dran'ma's -coz my ma said I might." An' nen she told him that th' old wolf skipped out an' dot to her dran'ma's first, an' she didn't know he did.

Nen when th' old wolf dot to her dran'ma's he knocked at the door. An' nen th' old wolf he knocked adin, an' little Red Riding Hood's dran'ma she says, "Who's there?"

Nen th' old wolf 'tended like he was little Red Riding Hood, you know, an' so he says, "W'y, it's me, dran'ma; I'm little Red Riding Hood, an' I'm tome to see you!"

Nen little Red Riding Hood's dran'ma she says, "Thist walk in, nen, an' make yousef at home, toz I'm dot the 'raigy, an' tuvered up in bed, an' I tan't open the door fur you!"

An' so the old wolf thist walked in an' shut the door, an' hopped up on th' bed an' et old Miss Ridinghood up 'fore she could take her specs off, he did! Nen th' old wolf put on her nightcap an' tovered up in bed like she was, you know, an' purty soon her tome little Red Riding Hood, an' she knocked at the door. Nen th' old wolf says, "Who's there?" thist like he was her dran'ma, you know, an' she thought he was, an' so she says, "W'y its me, dran'ma; I'm little Red Riding Hood, an' I'm tome to see you." Nen th' old wolf says "Thist walk in an' make yousef at home, toz I dot the 'raigy an' tovered up in bed, an' I tan't open the door for you."

An' so little Red Riding Hood she opened the door an' tomed in; an' the old wolf told her to set down her basket an' take off her fings an' tome an' set on the bed wif her.

An' little Red Riding Hood she didn't know it was th' old wolf, an' so she set down her basket an' tooked off her fings, an' dot a chair an' thumbed up on the bed wif her an' she thought th' old wolf had more whiskers'n her dran'ma, an' dreat bigger eyes too, an' she was skeered, an' so she says: "Oh, dran'ma, what big eyes you dot!"

Nen th' old wolf says: "They're thist big toz I'm so dlad to see you."

Nen little Red Riding Hood she says: "O! dran'ma, what a big nose you dot."

Nen th' old wolf says: "It's thist big thataway toz I smell the dood fings you bringed in the basket."

An' nen little Red Riding Hood she says: "O! dran'ma, what long, sharp teeth you dot."

Nen th' old wolf he says: "Yes, an' they're thist thataway t'eat you up wif!" an' nen he made a jump at her, an' she hollered an' the big man that was a choppin' wood he tomed in there wif his axe, an' he split th' old wolf's brains out from ear to ear, an' killed him so quick it made his head swim, an' little Red Riding Hood wasn't hurt at all, an' the big man tooked her home, an' her ma was so dlad she div'd him all the dood fings in the basket an' told him to call adin - an - an- that's all of it.

* * * * *

Juan de Yepes y Alvarez:

A Living Flame of Love

(A poem for recitation by one's soul.)

O living flame of love
That tenderly wounds my soul
In its deepest center! Since
Now You are not oppressive,
Now Consummate! if it be Your will:
Tear through the veil of this sweet encounter!

O sweet cautery,
O delightful wound!
O gentle hand! O delicate touch
That tastes of eternal life
And pays every debt!
In killing You changed death to life.

O lamps of fire!
In whose splendors
The deep caverns of feeling,
Once obscure and blind,
Now give forth, so rarely, so exquisitely,
Both warmth and light to their Beloved.

How gently and lovingly
You wake in my heart,
Where in secret You dwell alone;
And in Your sweet breathing,
Filled with good and glory,
How tenderly You swell my heart with love.

A Soul's Union With God Like a Window

This is a poem to contemplate by one seeking to achieve a perfect union with God through love. There is a path reaching up to God directly. This union with God is a supernatural union and not the natural or essential union by which God is always present in creation preserving its being. This supernatural union is the total and permanent union according to the substance of the soul and its faculties. It is an obscure habit and not the transient intense actual union which sometimes comes when a person realizes God has acted in one's life.

It is a union of likeness. It depends upon love, a habitual perfect love of God which makes the soul resemble God in all its activity to the extent that the soul and God become like each other and "one."

This union is like a sun shining upon a window.

God, compared to the sun, is ever present in the soul, compared to the window, communicating and preserving its natural being, just as the sun shines on the window.

When the window is wholly smeared with dirt, the sun cannot shine through it as it does when the window is unstained. The window is also smeared when it has inordinate affection for material things and is unprepared to receive the communication of God's supernatural being.

To the extent that the window is clean, the sun illumines it. The window is cleaned as the soul wipes away everything unconformed to God's will and it communicates with God's very being.

When the window is entirely clean, the sunlight so illumines the soul that it appears to be the same as the light passing through it. Yet, regardless of its total resemblance to the light, the window remains distinct from the nature of the sunlight. Just so, when the soul in its activity is completely purified of everything unlike God, when it is entirely conformed with God's will through love, God will so communicate God's supernatural being that it will be like God and seem to be God. Yet in its nature it will be as distinct from God as before. A soul that has reached such perfect conformity and likeness has attained the high state of perfection, union with God, and transformation unto God.

Once one's soul is united with God and inflamed in divine union, the poem becomes clear. The soul can know that there is a delicate flame of love which assails it and burns within. This is the breath of God breathing upon God's life with humanity. Each time the flame touches, it seeks to impart eternal life and tear away the veil of mortal life. It absorbs all with its love and attacks opposition to God's will. A soul must welcome the living flame as well as seek after its sweet encounter.

* * * * *

After Julian of Norwich, an Anchoress,

Jesus as our True Mother

A Meditation in Reflection on a Showing of the Familyhead after Severe Illness (1373):

As truly as God is our father, so just as truly is he our mother.

In our father, God Almighty, we have our being: in our merciful mother we are remade and restored. Our fragmented lives are knit together and make perfect humanity. And by giving and yielding ourselves, though grace, through the Spirit of God's Breath, we are made whole.

It is I, the strength and goodness of fatherhood. It is I, the wisdom of motherhood. It is I, the light and grace of holy love. It is I, the Trinity. It is I, the unity. I am the sovereign goodness in all things. It is I who teach you to love. It is I who teach you to desire. It is I who am the reward of all true desiring.

A mother's caring is the closest, nearest and surest for it is the truest. This care never might nor could nor should be done fully except by him alone.

As we know, our own mother bore us only into pain and dying. But our true mother Jesus, who is all love, bears us into joy and endless living. Blessed may he be!

A mother feeds her child with her milk, but our beloved mother Jesus feeds us with himself. In tender courtesy he gives us the Blessed Sacrament, the most treasured food of life.

I dare to say full surely, and we should believe it, that there never was so fair a man as he, until his brightness was clouded by trouble and sorrow, passion and death.

* * * * *

After Martin Luther,

Justification Through Faith

Once a fellow felt this way. The situation of humanity is helplessness and distress about how to live our lives before God. God's law makes many demands. We must do what God's Child has give us to do. Not a jot of that Child's demands will lapse and if we don't follow the Child then humanity is condemned without any hope. No church can save us. We are before God as individuals. The great struggle of every life is to find one's place in the story of God's life on earth. How do we know we are doing the right thing? God's idea of doing the right thing is to be merciful to humanity and ours is to believe that God sees humanity as justified because of God's Child. God's grace creates the righteousness of humanity. God treats humans as being a folk doing right no matter whether humans do it or not.

God told us the complete fulfillment of the demands is to believe and have trust in God's Child. Without this belief, humanity lacks all. With it, humanity has everything. Humanity can accomplish nothing trying to work on its own to deserve the love of God. Faith in God's Child permits humanity to overcome human disobedience to the laws of God. God commands and God fulfills. This is the promise of God - that if a human believes and has faith in Jesus, that human's soul has a thing to cling to and be united with and altogether absorbed in that will permit the human to share all the power of serving God. If a touch of God's Child's clothes heals, then so healing will be the tender touch of human spirit to God which absorbs the story of God's life and communicates to the human's soul all the things of this life. Faith accomplishes all things alone without the need for works to earn salvation. Faith in Jesus alone justifies a human being by the truth and freedom we know from the story of God's life on earth. To all who believe comes the power to become children of God.

What resides in the human soul? Faith alone and God's life as we know it from the Child reside in the soul. No act of compliance with God's law or any good work dwell there. A Christian has all she or he needs by faith and needs no works for justification. Christian liberty does not cause us to live idly or wickedly but makes the law and works unnecessary for any person's righteousness or salvation.

Faith gives the human to honor God with the highest regard since it considers God truthful and trustworthy. When God is honored, the soul consents to God's will. Then the person allows himself or herself to be treated according to God's good pleasure.

Faith gives the human to be obedient to God in all things. There is no more complete fulfillment of a faithful life than to be obedient to the story of the life of God on earth. That allows us to render works through faithfulness and not in a vain effort to justify ourselves.

The great incomparable benefit of faith is that it unites the soul with Jesus as a bride is united with her bridegroom. By this mystery Jesus and the soul become one flesh. If they are of one flesh there is a true marriage - indeed the most perfect marriage since human marriages are but poor examples of this one true marriage. Everything they have is held in common, the good as well as the evil. Thus the believing soul can boast of and glory in whatever Jesus has as though it were its own and whatever the soul has Jesus claims as God's Child's own. Jesus is full of grace, life and salvation. The soul is full of sins, death and damnation. Faith comes between the soul and such things and Jesus, as bridegroom, takes upon himself sins, death and damnation which are his bride's and bestows upon the soul those things which are his. Jesus gives the soul his body and very self that is his. Now the soul can suffer no sin, nor death, nor condemnation but instead have righteousness, life and salvation unconquerably, eternally and omnipotently.

What does this royal marriage mean? Who can understand the riches of the glory of this grace? Here this rich and divine bridegroom Jesus marries this poor, wicked harlot, redeems her from all her evil, and adorns her with all his goodness. Her sins cannot now destroy her since they are laid upon God's Child and swallowed up by him. And she has that righteousness in God's Child, her husband, of which she may boast as of her own, and which she can confidently display alongside her sins in the face of death and hell and say, "If I have sinned, yet my husband, God's Child, in which I believe, has not sinned, and all his is mine and all mine is his." As Paul says, "Thanks be to God, who gives us the victory through our Familyhead, Jesus, God who come to earth."

A mighty fortress is our God,
A bulwark never failing;
Our helper he amid the flood
Of mortal ills prevailing.
For still our ancient foe
Doth seek to work us woe;
His craft and power are great;
And armed with cruel hate,
On earth is not his equal.

And though this world, with devils
    filled,
Should threaten to undo us,
We will not fear,
For God hath willed His truth to
    triumph through us.
The prince of darkness grim,
We tremble not for him;
His rage we can endure,
For lo, his doom is sure:
One little word shall fell him.

Did we in our own strength confide,
Our striving would be losing,
Were not the right man on our side,
The man of God's own choosing.
Dost ask who that may be?
Christ Jesus, it is he;
Lord Sabaoth his name,
From age to age the same,
And he must win the battle.

That word above all earthly powers,
No thanks to them, abideth;
The Spirit and the gifts are ours
Through him who with us sideth.
Let goods and kindred go,
This mortal life also;
The body they may kill;
God's truth abideth still,
His kingdom is forever.

Amen.

* * * * *

After Thomas Stapleton,

Thomas More's Martyrdom

The king (a temporal ruler) of England, Henry VIII, wished to divorce his wife, Catherine, the mother of his child, Mary, and his dead brother Arthur's widow. The king wished to marry Anne Boleyn, his mistress. The Catholic Church said No. Henry VIII then declared himself the head of the Church in England and required all of the English people to acknowledge him as the head of the church.

Thomas More had been Henry VIII's Chancellor, second most powerful man in England behind the king, for two and a half years. Then he retired in 1532 because he could not favor the divorce.

Later that year, a new Archbishop of the English Church was appointed by Henry VIII who pronounced the king divorced. King Henry quickly and secretly married Anne Boleyn October. The next May he made Anne the Queen of England by royal edict. The next May 28th, 1533, the king publicly married her. She was publicly crowned Queen June 1st and bore the child Elizabeth on 7 September. The next year, the king disinherited his daughter Mary (he already made his former wife Catherine the widow of his brother Arthur by royal edict), then demanded all the English to swear allegiance to Anne's child Elizabeth as his sole legitimate offspring and heir and at the same time to abjure the Pope's authority in England.

The chief men of England were called to take an oath to Elizabeth as the king's heir and against the Pope's authority in England. Thomas More was called before the Archbishop of Canterbury and the king's Council to take the oath but refused on account of conscience.

Thereupon Thomas More was imprisoned in the Tower of London. He was examined by delegates of the king twice while imprisoned but refused to relent. Thomas More's position in England was very high and his influence enormous. He had held high position. In public life he was honest and took no bribes and always told the king the truth and his true opinion regardless of what the king wished to hear. He was widely read for his book Utopia. Many learned people in England and Europe were his friends. His life was lived piously. He held only contempt for honors, praise and wealth. Thomas More was a married man. Erasmus once visited him in his home and described it:

"More has built for himself on the banks of the Thames not far from London a country-house which is dignified and adequate without being so magnificent as to excite envy. Here he lives happily with his family, consisting of his wife, his son and daughter-in-law, three daughters with their husbands and already eleven grandchildren. It would be difficult to find a man more fond of children that he. His wife is no longer young; but of so accommodating a disposition is he, or rather as such virtue and prudence, that if any defect appears that cannot be corrected, he sets himself to love it as though it were the happiest thing in the world...(The home) deserves the name of school for the knowledge and practice of the Christian faith. No one of either sex there neglects literature or fruitful reading, although the first and chief care is piety. There is no quarrelling; a bitter word is never heard; no one is ever known to be idle. Moreover it is not by harshness or angry words that More maintains so happy a discipline in his house, but by kindness and gentleness. All attend to their duty; but diligence does not exclude merriment."

After fifteen months in the horrible Tower of London, More was formally indicted and then tried for treason. He was tried before his successor Lord Chancellor and a death sentence was the verdict. Here was his sentence: "Our sentence is that Thomas More shall be taken back from this place by William Kingston, the Constable, to the Tower and thence shall be dragged right through the City of London as far as the gallows at Tyburn. There he shall be hanged, cut down while yet alive, ripped up, his bowels burnt in his sight, his head cut off, his body quartered and the parts set up in such places as the King shall designate." More's martyrdom was changed by the king for him to simply be executed on the block.

The day before his death, Thomas More sent his daughter the hair-shirt he wore unknown to anyone and a scourge he used to discipline his flesh to make sure his body did what his soul demanded.

More was lead from the Tower of London to the place of execution through a crowd of watchers. He needed help ascending the scaffold and said, "I pray you see me safe up, and for my coming down let me shift for myself." He wished to speak when he got up the scaffold, but the Sheriff said No. Thomas More did tell the crowd "I call you to witness, brothers, that I die the faithful servant of God and the King, and in the faith of the Catholic Church." He recited a prayer and knelt down, covered his eyes with a linen cloth he brought with him and calmly laid his head on the block. It was at once struck off.

After his shameful death, his severed head was placed upon a stake on the London Bridge by orders of the King where it remained for nearly a month. The head was supposed to then be thrown into the river but a daughter, Margaret Roper, who had been watching carefully for events, bribed the executioner whose office was to remove heads and obtained possession of it. She kept it for the rest of her life with great reverence and preserved it with spices. Her daughter then deposited the head in the Roper vault at St. Dunstan's Canterbury. It was last seen in 1837 when the vault was opened.

His writing in prison was with a coal since no pen was permitted him.

* * * * *

Thomas More:

Witness About Comfort
Written in Prison Under Threat of Execution

I will in my poor mind assign for the first comfort the desire and longing to be by God comforted, and not without some reason call I this the first cause of comfort. For like as the cure of that person is in a manner desperate that hath no will to be cured, so is the discomfort of that person desperate that desireth not his own comfort.

And here shall I note you two kinds of folk that are in tribulation and heaviness: one sort that will seek for no comfort, another sort that will. And yet of those that will not are there also two sorts. For first one sort there are that are so drowned in sorrow, that they fall into a careless deadly dullness, regarding nothing, thinking almost of nothing, no more than if they lay in a lethargy, with which it may so fall that wit and remembrance will wear away, and fall even fair from them. And this comfortless kind of heaviness in tribulation is the highest kind of the deadly sin of sloth. Another sort are there that will seek for no comfort, nor yet none receive, but are in their tribulation (be it loss or sickness) so testy, so furnish, and so far out of all patience, that it booteth no man to speak to them; and these are in a manner with impatience as furious as though they were in half a frenzy, and may with a custom of such fashioned behavior fall in thereto full and whole. And this kind of heaviness in tribulation is even a mischievous high branch of the mortal sin of ire.

Then is there, as I told you, another kind of folk which fain would be comforted, and yet are they of two sorts too. One sort are those that in their sorrow seek for wordly comfort; and of them shall we now speak the less, for the divers occasions that we shall after have to touch them in more places than one. But this will I here say, that I learned of Saint Bernard: he that in tribulation turneth himself into wordly vanities, to get help and comfort by them, fareth like a man that in peril of drowning catcheth whatsoever cometh next to hand, and that holdeth he fast be it never so simple a stick, but then that helpeth him not. For that stick he draweth down under the water with him, and there lie they drowned both together.

So surely if we custom ourself to put our trust of comfort in the delight of these peevish worldly things, God shall for that foul fault suffer our tribulation to grow so great, that all the pleasures of this world shall never bear us up, but all our peevish pleasure shall in the depth of tribulation drown with us.

The other sort is, I say, of those that long and desire to be comforted of God. And as I told you before, they have an undoubted great cause of comfort, even in that point alone that they consider themself to desire and long to be by Almighty God comforted. This mind of theirs may well be cause of great comfort unto them for two great considerations. The token is that they see themself seek for their comfort where they cannot fail to find it; for God both can give them comfort, and will. He can, for He is almighty. He will, for He is all good, and hath Himself proimised Petite et accipietis: Ask and ye shall have. He that hath faith (as he must needs have that shall take comfort) cannot doubt but that God will surely keep His promise. And therefore hath he a great cause to be of good comfort, as I say, in that he considereth that he longeth to be comforted by Him, which his faith maketh him sure will not fail to comfort him.

But here consider this, that I speak here of him that in tribulation longeth to be comforted by God; and it is he that referreth the manner of his comforting to God, holding himself content, whether it be by the taking away or the minishment of the tribulation itself, or by the giving him patience and spiritual consolation therein. For of him that only longeth to have God take his trouble from him, we cannot so well warrant that mind for a cause of so great comfort. For both may he disire that that never mindeth to be the better, and may miss also the effect of his desire, because his request is haply not good for himself. And of this kind of longing and requiring we shall have occasion farther to speak hereafter. But he which, referring the manner of his comfort unto God, desireth of God to be comforted, asketh a thing so lawful and so pleasant unto God, that he cannot fail to speed; and therefore hath he, as I say, great cause to take comfort in the very desire itself.

Another cause hath he to take of that desire a very great occasion of comfort. For sith his desire is good and declareth unto himself that he hath in God a good faith, it is a good taken unto him that he is not an abject, cast out of God's gracious favour, while he perceiveth that God hath put such a virtuous well-ordered appetite in his mind. For as every evil mind cometh of the world and ourself and the devil, so is every such good mind, either immediately or by the mean of our good angel or other gracious occasion, inspired into man's heart by the goodness of God Himslef. And what a comfort, then, may this be unto us, when we by that desire perceive a sure undoubted token that toward our final salvation our Saviour is Himself so graciously busy about us!

* * * * *

Felicia Hemans,

The Landing of the Pilgrim Fathers

The breaking waves dashed high
  On a stern and rock-bound coast
And the woods against a stormy sky
  Their giant branches tossed.

And the heavy night hung dark
  The hills and waters o'er
When a band of exiles moored their
    bark
  On the wild New England shore.

Not as the conqueror comes,
  They, the true-hearted, came,
Not with the roll of the stirring drums,
  And the trumpet that sings of fame,

Not as the flying come,
  In silence and in fear,
They shook the depths of the desert
    gloom
  With their hymns of lofty cheer.

Amidst the storm they sang,
  And the stars heard, and the sea,
And the sounding aisles of the dim
    woods rang
  To the anthem of the free.
The ocean eagle soared

From his nest by the white wave's
    foam,
And the rocking pines of the forest
    roared,
  This was their welcome home.

There were men with hoary hair
  Amidst that pilgrim-band.
Why had they come to wither there
  Away from their childhood's land?

There was woman's fearless eye
  Lit by her deep love's truth.
There was manhood's brow-serenely
    high,
  And the fiery heart of youth.

What sought they thus afar?
  Bright jewels of the mine?
The wealth of seas, the spoils of war?
  They sought a faith's pure shrine!

Ay, call it holy ground,
  The soil where first they trod;
They have left unstained what there they
    found,
  Freedom to worship God.

* * * * *

William Shakespeare:

The Challenge of Fate

To be, or not to be; that is the question:
Whether 'tis nobler in the mind to suffer
The slings and arrows of outrageous fortune,
Or to take arms against a sea of troubles,
And by opposing end them. To die; to sleep;
No more; and by a sleep to say we end
The heart-ache, and the thousand natural shocks

That flesh is heir to, 'tis a consummation
Devoutly to be wish'd. To die, to sleep;
To sleep; perchance to dream; ay, there's the rub;
For in that sleep of death what dreams may come,
When we have shuffled off this mortal coil,
Must give us pause; there's the rub;
For in that sleep of death what dreams my come,
When we have shuffled off this mortal coil,
Must give us pause; there's the respect
That makes calamity of so long life;
For who would bear the whips and scorns of time,
The oppressor's wrong, the proud man's contumely,
The pangs of despised love, the law's delay
The insolence of office, and the spurns
That patient merit of the unworthy takes,
When he himself might his quietus make
With a bare bodkin? who would fardels bear,
To grunt and sweat under a weary life,
But that the dread of something after death,
The undiscover'd country from whose bourn
No traveller returns, puzzles the will,
And makes us rather bear those ills we have
Than fly to others that we know not of?
Thus conscience does make cowards of us all,
And thus the native hue of resolution
Is sickled o'er with the pale cast of thought,
And enterprises of great pitch and moment
With this regard their currents turn awry
And lose the name of action.

* * * * *

William Shakespeare:

Sonnet to Committed Love

Let me not to the marriage of true minds
Admit impediments; love is not love
Which alters when it alteration finds
Or bends with the remover to remove.
O, no, it is an ever-fixed mark
That looks on tempests and is never shaken;
It is the star to every wandering bark,

Whose worth's unknown, although his height be taken.
Love's not Time's fool, though rosy lips and cheeks
Within his bending sickle compass come;
Love alters not with his brief hours and weeks,
But bears it out even to the edge of doom,
If this be error, and upon me proved,
I never writ, nor no one ever loved.

* * * * *

John Donne:

A Hymn to God the Parent

Wilt thou forgive that sin where I begun
    Which is my sin, though it were done before?
Wilt thou forgive those sins, through which I run
    And do them still; though still I do deplore?
        When thou hast done, thou hast not done,
          For I have more.

Wilt thou forgive that sin by which I have won
    Others to sin? and, made my sin their door?
Wilt thou forgive that sin which I did shun
    A year, or two; but wallowed in, a score?
        When thou has done, thou hast not done,
          For I have more.
I have a sin of fear, that when I have spun
    My last thread, I shall perish on the shore;
        Swear by thyself, that at my death thy Sun
    Shall shine as it shines now, and heretofore;
        And, having done that, thou hast done,
          I fear no more.

* * * * *

John Donne:

Meditation on Sickness unto Death

Perchance he for whom this bell tolls may be so ill, as that he knows not it tolls for him; and perchance I may think myself so much better than I am, as that they who are about me, and see my state, may have caused it to toll for me, and I know not that. The church is Catholic, universal, so are all her actions; all that she does belongs to all. When she baptizes a child, that action concerns me; for that child is thereby connected to that head which is my head too, and ingrafted into that body whereof I am a member. And when she buries a person, that action concerns me, all humanity is of one author, and one volume; when one person dies, one chapter is not torn out of the book, but translated into a better language; and every chapter must be so translated; God employs several translators,; some pieces are translated by age, some by sickness, some by war, some by justice; but God's hand is in every translation and his hand shall bind up all our scattered leaves again, for that library where every book shall lie open to one another. As therefore the bell that rings to a sermon calls not upon the preacher only, but upon the congregation to come, so this bell calls us all; but how much more me, who am brought so near the door by this sickness. There was a contention as far as a suit (in which both piety and dignity, religion and estimation, were mingled), which of the religious orders should ring to prayers first in the morning; and it was determined, that they should ring first that rose earliest. If we understand aright the dignity of this bell that tolls for our evening prayer, we would be glad to make it ours by rising early, in that application, that it might be ours as well as his, whose indeed it is. The bell doth toll for him that thinks it doth; and though it intermit again, yet from that minute that the occasion wrought upon him, he is united to God. Who casts not up his eye to the sun when it rises? But who takes off his eye from a comet when that breaks out? Who bends not his ear to any bell which upon any occasion rings? But who can remove it from that bell which is passing a piece of himself out of this world? No person is an island, entire of itself; every person is a piece of the continent, a part of the main. If a clod be washed away by the sea, Europe is the less, as well as if a promontory were, as well as if a manor of the friend's or of thine own were: any person's death diminishes me, because I am involved in humanity, and therefore never send to know for whom the bell tolls; it tolls for thee. Neither can we call this a begging of misery, or a borrowing of misery, as though we were not miserable enough of ourselves, but must fetch in more from the next house, in taking upon us the misery of our neighbors. Truly it were an excusable covetousness if we did, for affliction is a treasure, and scare any many hath enough of it. No person hath affliction enough that is not matured and ripened by it, and made fit for God by that affliction, If a person carry treasure in bullion, or in a wedge of gold, and have none coined into current monies, his treasure will not defray him as he travels. Tribulation is treasure in the nature of it, but it is not current money in the use of it, except we get nearer and nearer our home, heaven, by it. Another person may be sick too, and sick to death, and this affliction my lie in his bowels, as gold in a mine, and be of no use to him; but this bell, that tells me of his affliction, digs out and applies that gold to me, if by this consideration of another's danger I take mine own into contemplation, and so secure myself, by making my course to my God, who is our only security.

* * * * *

John Milton:

A Song of Patient Waiting for Jesus

When I consider how my light is spent,
 Ere half my days, in this dark world and wide,
 And that one talent which is death to hide
 Lodged with me useless, though my soul more bent
To serve therewith my Maker, and present
 My true account, lest he returning chide,
"Doth God exact day-labor, light denied?"
 I fondly ask. But Patience, to prevent
That murmur, soon replies: "God doth not need
 Either man's work or his own gifts; who best
 Bear his mild yoke, they serve him best. His state
Is kingly: thousands at his bidding speed,
 And post o'er land and ocean without rest;
 They also serve who only stand and wait."

* * * * *

Jonathan Edwards:

Excerpts from a Sermon on Wrongdoers in the Hands of a Frustrated God

There is nothing that keeps wicked people, at any one moment, out of hell, but the mere pleasure of God.

There is no want of power in God to cast wicked people into hell at any moment. People's hands can't be strong when God rises up: the strongest have no power to resist him nor can any deliver out of his hands.

He is not only able to cast wicked people into hell, but he can most easily do it. Sometimes an earthly prince meets with a great deal of difficulty to subdue a rebel that has found means to fortify himself, and has made himself strong by the numbers of his followers. But it is not so with God. There is no fortress that is any defense from the power of God. Though hand join in hand, and vast multitudes of God's enemies combine and associate themselves, they are easily broken in pieces. They are as great heaps of light chaff before the whirlwind or large quantities of dry stubble before devouring flames. We find it easy to tread on and crush a worm that we see crawling on the earth. So 'tis easy for us to cut or singe a slender threat that anything hangs by. Thus easy is it for God when he pleases to cast his enemies down to hell. What are we, that we should think to stand before him, at whose rebuke the earth trembles, and before whom the rocks are thrown down? So that it is not because God is unmindful of their wickedness, and don't resent it, that he don't let loose his hand and cut them off. God is not altogether such an one as themselves, though they may imagine him to be so. The wrath of God burns against them. Their damnation don't slumber. The pit is prepared. The fire is made ready. The furnace is now hot, ready to receive them. The flames do now rage and glow. The glittering sword is whet, and held over them, and the pit hath opened her mouth under them.

It is no security to wicked people for one moment that there are no visible means of death at hand. 'Tis no security to a natural person that he or she is now in health, that he or she don't see which way he should now immediately go out of the world by any accident, and that there is no visible danger in any respect in his circumstances. The manifold and continual experience of the world in all ages, shows that this is no evidence that a person is not on the very brink of eternity, and that the next step won't be into another world. The unseen, unthought of ways and means of persons going suddenly out of the world are innumerable and inconceivable. Unconverted people walk over the pit of hell on a rotten covering, and there are innumerable places in this covering so weak that they won't bear their weight, and these places are not seen. The arrows of death fly unseen at noonday. The sharpest sight can't discern them. God has so many different unsearchable ways of taking wicked people out of the world and sending 'em to hell, that there is nothing to make it appear that God had need to be at the expense of a miracle, or go out of the ordinary course of his providence, to destroy any wicked person at moment. All the means that there are of wrongdoers going out of the world as so in God's hands and so universally absolutely subject to his power and determination.

All wicked people's pains and contrivance they use to escape hell, while they continue to reject Jesus, God who came to earth, don't secure 'em from hell one moment. Almost every natural person that hears of hell, flatters themself that they shall escape it. They depend upon themselves for security. They flatter themselves in what they have done, in what they are now doing, or what they intend to do.

Everyone lays out matters in their own minds how they shall avoid damnation, and flatter themselves that they contrive well so their schemes won't fail.

It is this way to everyone who is outside of Jesus, God who came to earth. That world of misery, that lake of burning brimstone is extended abroad under you. There is the dreadful pit of the glowing flames of the wrath of God. There is hell's wide gaping mouth open and you have nothing to stand upon, nor anything to take hold of. There is nothing between you and hell but the air. 'Tis only the power and mere pleasure of God that holds you up.

The God that holds you over the pit of hell, much as one holds a spider, or some loathsome insect, over the fire, abhors you, and is dreadfully provoked. His wrath towards you burns like fire. He looks upon you as worthy of nothing else but to be case into the fire. He is of purer eyes than to bear to have you in his sight. You are ten thousand times so abominable in his eyes as the most hateful venomous serpent is in ours. You have offended him infinitely more than ever a stubborn rebel did his prince: and yet 'tis nothing but his hand that holds you from falling into the fire every moment. 'Tis to be ascribed to nothing else, that you did not go to hell the last night, that you was suffered to awake again in this world after you closed your eyes to sleep, and there is no other reason to be given why you have not dropped into hell since you arose in the morning, but that God's hand has held you up. There is no other reason to be given why you han't gone to hell since you have sat here in the house of God, provoking his pure eyes by your sinful wicked manner of attending his solemn worship. Yes, there is nothing else that is to be given as a reason why you don't this very moment drop down into hell.

And now you have an extraordinary opportunity, a day wherein Jesus has flung the door of mercy wide open, and stands in the door calling and crying with a loud voice to poor wrongdoers; a day wherein many are flocking to him, and pressing into the kingdom of God. Many are daily coming from the east, west, north and south. Many that were very lately in the same miserable condition that you are in, are in now an happy state, with their hearts filled with love to him that has loved them and washed them from their wrongdoings in his own blood, and rejoicing in hope of the glory of God. How awful is it to be left behind at such a day! To see so many others feasting, while you are pining and perishing! To see so many rejoicing and singing for joy of heart, while you have cause to mourn for sorrow heart, and howl for vexation of spirit! How can you rest one moment in such a condition? Are not your souls as precious as the souls of the people at Suffield where they are flocking from day to day to God who came on earth?

And let everyone that is yet out of Jesus, and hanging over the pit of hell, whether they be old men and women, or middle aged, or young people, or little children now hearken to the loud calls of God's Word and providence. This acceptable year of the Familyhead, that is a day of such great favor to some, will doubtless be a day of as remarkable vengeance to others. People's hearts harden, and their guilt increases apace at such a day as this if they neglect their souls. Never was there so great danger of such persons being given up to hardness of heart, and blindness of mind. God seems now to be hastily gathering in his elect in all parts of the land, and probably the bigger part of adult persons that ever shall be saved, will be brought in now in a little time, and that it will be as it was on that great outpouring of the Spirit upon the Jews in the apostles' days, the election will obtain, and the rest will be blinded. If this should be the case with you, you will eternally curse this day, and will curse the day that every you was born, to see such a season of the pouring of God's breathing spirit, and will wish that you had died and gone to hell; before had seen it. Now undoubtedly it is, as it was in the days of John the Baptist, the ax is in an extraordinary manner laid at the root of the trees that every tree that brings not forth good fruit, may be hewn down, and cast into the fire.

Therefore let everyone that is out of Jesus now awake and fly from the wrath to come. The wrath of almighty God is now undoubtedly hanging over a great part of this congregation. Let everyone fly out of Sodom. Haste and escape for your lives. Look not behind you. Escape to the mountain lest you be consumed.

* * * * *

John Newton:

Amazing Grace

The turnaround of John Newton, the writer of "Amazing Grace," was from being a slave trader to a church minister. He composed his own tombstone which has this self- composed inscription: "John Newton, clerk, once an infidel and Libertine, a servant of slavers in Africa, was, by the rich mercy of our Familyhead and Savior Jesus, Child of God, preserved, restored, pardoned, and appointed to preach the faith he had so long labored to destroy." Before it was too late but after great sin, he abruptly turned his life to defend the gospel he had so long despised.

John Newton transformed his life. He become a preacher. He continued on to preach despite deafness and blindness at near age eighty until age eighty-two. Then when it was suggested he retire due to his old age and failing memory, he responded, "My memory is nearly gone, but I remember two things: that I am a great sinner, and that God's Child is a great Savior." In another hymn he gives God's Child the credit for "hushing the law's loud thunder." When one turns one's life over to God's Child "justice smiles and asks no more." His advice during the mid-week bible studies at his church was to "keep your relationship with God honest and personal."

Amazing grace!
How sweet the sound
That saved a wretch like me!
I once was lost but now am found,
Was blind but now I see.

'Twas grace that taught my heart to
    fear,
And grace my fears relieved;
How precious did that grace appear
The hour I first believed.

The Familyhead has promised good
    to me,
His word my hope secures;
He will my shield and portion be
As long as life endures.

Thru many dangers, toils and snares,
I have already come;
'Tis grace hath brought me safe thus
    far,
And grace will lead me home.

When we've been there then thousand
    years,
Bright shining as the sun,
We've no less days to sing God's praise
Than when we'd first begun.

* * * * *

After John Locke:

Reason and Christianity

What is most reasonable to believe in the Christian faith is that Jesus was God's Child. Reason permits us to understand idea particulars. We know for example what is a body at rest and a body in motion. From these ideas we can infer the reasonableness of active powers. Power can be understood in terms of such idea particulars.

The gospels give us to know of the life of Jesus. These are idea particulars. Although there be no deductive links between the idea particulars and the propositions, they link into an intuitive situation not unlike that we know when we intuit our own active power.

The power of the gospel, like all active power we know, is tractable in terms of its idea particulars.

Its most compelling power is the assertion that Jesus is God's Child.

* * * * *

After David Hume,

Natural Religion

The conclusion of Christianity is that the Christian religion was not only first attended with miracles but even to this day cannot be believed by any reasonable person without one. Mere reason is insufficient to convince us of its veracity. Whoever is moved by faith to assent to it is conscious of a continued miracle in his or her own person which subverts all the principles of understanding and gives a determination to believe what is most contrary to custom and experience.

In fact a proof of the veracity of Christianity is that it is entirely contrary to custom. A belief in One God is far from being a belief founded on human instinct. Polytheism is far more natural. Nor is the idea of a Supreme Being necessarily socially beneficial. Without belief in the love of God's Child, monotheism may lead to an implacably narrow and legalistic spirit, bloody principles of conquest or grotesque intolerance to progress.

Faith in God's Child is the principle that saves Christianity. It is an open avowal of an irrational faith in a Supreme Being supported by nothing but its own intensity and fervor and against a specious attempt to establish the existence of God by reason. Faith is the only but sufficient bulwark of the religious life.

Once God's existence is taken for granted, we postulate that all we know are repeatable sequences of particular events within nature. Our observations are simply of natural correlations observed singly, individually and without parallel. Such causes lead us on forever. The whole chorus of nature raises one hymn to the praises of its Creator...you ask me what is the cause of this cause? I know not; I care not; this concerns me not. I have found God in nature and here I stop my enquiry.

Thomas Jefferson Et Al.:

Declaration of Independence

We hold these truths to be self-evident, that all men are created equal, that they are endowed by their Creator with certain unalienable Rights, that among these are Life, Liberty and the Pursuit of Happiness. That to secure these rights, Governments are instituted among Men, deriving their just powers from the consent of the governed, That whenever any Form of Government becomes destructive of these ends, it is the Right of the People to alter or to abolish it, and to institute new Government, laying its foundation on such principles and organizing its powers in such form, as to them shall seem most likely to effect their Safety and Happiness. Prudence, indeed, will dictate that Governments long established should not be changed for light and transient causes; and accordingly all experience hath shown, that mankind are more disposed to suffer, while evils are sufferable, than to right themselves by abolishing the forms to which they are accustomed. But when a long train of abuses and usurpations, pursuing invariably the same Object evinces a design to reduce them under absolute Despotism, it is their right, it is their duty, to throw off such Government, and to provide new Guards for their future security

* * * * *

Henry Wadsworth Longfellow:

Paul Revere's Ride

Listen, my children, and you shall hear
Of the midnight ride of Paul Revere
On the eighteenth of April, in Seventy-five,
Hardly a man is now alive
Who remembers that famous day and year.

He said to his friend, "If the British march
By land or sea from the town to-night,
Hang a lantern aloft in the belfry arch
Of the North Church tower as a signal light,
One, if by land, and two, if by sea,
And I on the opposite shore will be

Ready to ride and spread the alarm
Through every Middlesex village and farm
For the country folk to be up and arm."
Then he said, "Good-night," and with muffled oar
Silently row'd to the Charlestown shore.

Just as the moon rose over the bay
Where swinging wide at her moorings lay
The Somerset, British man-of-war,
A phantom ship, with each mast and spar

Across the moon like a prison bar,

And a huge black hull, that was magnified
By its own reflection in the tide.
Meanwhile his friend, through alley and street,
Wanders and watches with eager ears,
Till in the silence around him he hears
The master of men at the barrack-door,
The sound of arms, and the tramp of feet,
And the measured tread of the grenadiers
Marching down to their boats on the shore.
Then he climb'd the tower of the Old North Church,
By the wooden stairs, with stealthy tread,
To the belfry-chamber overhead...

Paul Revere watch'd with eager search
The belfry-tower of the Old North Church
As it rose above the graves on the hill
Lonely and spectral and sombre and still.
And lo! as he looks, on the belfry's height
A glimmer and then a gleam of light!
He springs to the saddle, the bridle he turns,
But lingers and gazes, till full on his sight
A second lamp in the belfry burns.

A hurry of hoofs in a village street,
A shape in the moonlight, a bulk in the dark.
And beneath, from the pebbles, in passing, a spark
Struck out by a steed flying fearless and fleet.
That was all, and yet, through the gloom and light,
The fate of a nation was riding that night.
And the spark struck out by that steed in his flight
Kindled the land into flame with its heat...
It was twelve by the village clock
When he crossed the bridge into Medford town.
He heard the crowing of the cock,
And the barking of the farmer's dog.
And felt the damp of the river fog
That rises after the sun goes down.

It was one by the village clock
When he galloped into Lexington.
He saw the gilded weathercock
Swim in the moonlight as he pass'd,

And the meeting-house windows, blank and bare,
Gaze at him with a spectral glare,
As if they already stood aghast
At the bloody work they would look upon.

It was two by the village clock
When he came to the bridge in Concord town.
He heard the bleating of the flock,
And the twitter of birds among the trees,
And felt the breath of the morning breeze
Blowing over the meadows brown.
And one was safe and asleep in his bed
Who at the bridge would be first to fall,
Who that day would be lying dead,
Pierced by a British musket-ball.

You know the rest. In the books you have read
How the British regulars fired and fled,
How the farmers gave them ball for ball
From behind each fence and farmyard wall
Chasing the red-coats down the land,
Then crossing the fields to emerge again
Under the trees at the turn of the road,
And only pausing to fire and load.

So through the night rode Paul Revere.
And so through the night went his cry of alarm
To every Middlesex village and farm,
A cry of defiance, and not of fear,
A voice in the darkness, a knock at the door,
And a word that shall echo for evermore!

For, borne on the night-wind of the Past,
Through all our history, to the last,
In the hour of darkness, and peril, and need,
The people will waken and listen to hear
The hurrying hoof-beats of that steed,
And the midnight message of Paul Revere.

* * * * *

Frederick Rapp:

Letter of a Deutsch Immigrant on the Opportunity of America (1816)

Esteemed Friend!...

The trade branch has occupied a great deal of space in the United States. Arts and sciences in part are still in their childhood here but some have developed very high among which especially mechanics are to be reckoned, in which the Americans surpass all other nations. This has been encouraged by the freedom which everyone enjoys under the law for here one knows nothing of any limitation. Each man can do what he wishes. Some carry on two, three or four and some even more professions and carry all of them on or whichever goes best. There are no poor people here who must suffer need or who could not feed themselves. An acre of land costs 5fl from the government which is to be paid in four installments and when a family is so poor that it can buy no land, then the land can be obtained on a loan basis for 1,2,3 to 10 years and the third part of what is planted must be paid the owner of the land that they need pay neither taxes nor other dues. In this way it is easy for a man who works only half the time to obtain in three or four years an estate and 50 to 200 acres of land, which is the least that a person has here. We ourselves have many such families sitting on our land to whom we have loaned it in this manner and would have place on our own land for some 100 families who could live on this calmly and happily without being tormented by worries of food or being bothered by the beadle or official servant.

Much less would they have to worry that their sons would be taken away as soldiers. The laws of the land here are exactly the opposite of a monarchy. Every person who has reason can live happily under them. Every citizen is acquainted with them and knows the punishment of every crime in advance before it comes before court. Officials and subjects have the same laws and the crimes of both are punished equally. All officials are elected by a majority vote of the citizens. Every citizen has equal right in the place of election. Each year the lawgivers in each state are elected by the people - these from the assembly and the senate in order according to circumstance to improve the laws, to set state affairs in proper order, and to maintain them therein. Everyone has the freedom to express himself freely or to write about political or other affairs. Also complete freedom of conscience is introduced in all America so that every person according to the conviction of his own conscience can perform unhindered his Divine service. Everyone can here as well in political as in religious fields develop according to his own ability and reveal or refine himself. This is the reason why Americans are far more enlightened than many nations of the world. It is our wish that many more poor German families may come because so much of the best land still lies uninhabited here. The rights of humanity are unknown to them and we should like to have them enjoy them with us for every wisely thinking person can see that as yet there is no durable peace in Germany, but the firmament of the political heaven is covered with a cloud in which a horrible night is still enveloped out of which necessarily thunder and lightning must develop before a clear heaven can appear out of which the sun can once more shine forth and refresh the earth with its lovely ray...

* * * * *

Traditional:

The Gentle Life of Johnny Appleseed

It don't matter how you live so long as you follow the great law of love.

Too often folk look around and judge a person on account of whether they are "settled down." This means life with a spouse, bill-payin and keepin up on taxes to payroll government folks and an army, house maintainin and raisin their kids clean. Not all folk are set in their hearts to do this. If they got other ways, they can do just as well and God don't hold their other ways against them. If any thinks otherwise, they need to remember God don't have one set way. God acts by feel and what's in God's heart to do.

We modern folk got Johnny Appleseed to look to.

Johnny looked like a wild man. His hair grew until it fell over his shoulders. He never shaved. He was five foot nine and very slender. His diet was whatever there was. Frequently he lived on nuts. Johnny was most often barefoot in summer and wore moccasins or shoepacks (thick leather soles tied on the feet with deer thongs or whangs) in the winter but if a needy person was encountered Johnny give his footwear away. He didn't need no reason to dress one way or another. Once he was seen near Ft. Wayne, Indiana with only one shoe on. He explained, "That bare foot stubbed his toe a few days ago, now I'm going to punish it for stumbling." He was indifferent to clothing. He most often wore a coffee sack. Other times, he wore equally outlandish discarded clothes.

Johnny Appleseed was born May 11, 1768 and died March 11, 1847. At his death, a board was placed over the mound where he was buried that described him: "A Planter of apple seeds." His given birthname was John Chapman. He made possible thousands of orchards of the apple in the America west of the Alleghanies.

He spend winters at apple presses gathering seeds. Every night he read from the New Testament which he always carried over his heart. When guests were present, he preceded his readings with the same expression: "And now would you like to hear some news right fresh from Heaven?" He was a good reader and often explained what he read. But what he did by day was gather bags and bags of seeds and store them with different people until the Spring. Then he travelled and planted numerous nurseries to provide trees that he either gave away or sold. If someone wanted to buy one, and asked how much, he said, "Whatever they are worth to you, fipenny-bit, an old coat, a pair of boots or your note." When a person had no money, he gave them away. During the Springs and Falls, Johnny spent his days along the banks of rivers and cricks heeling in thousands of seedlings to dispose of to the emigrants entering the American West.

How come Johnny done what he did? He explained it. One evening while recovering from a serious illness, John Chapman (before he become Johnny Appleseed) had a dream. "I had once thought to be a preacher of the gospel but I had a vision in which two angels in shining robes stood by my side and pointing toward Heaven, they showed me a picture of the New Jerusalem resplendent with glory. I could see one long street, pave with gold and on both sides of it were rows of trees laden with fruit. As I gazed, I seemed to be transported by my angel guides beyond the walls of the city and I saw the trees was filled with apples. It was a beautiful city, the air was filled with the sweetest of music, and angels' forms were everywhere. Oh how I should have loved to have stayed there, but the angels at my side brought me gently back to earth and quietly said to me: 'Brother John, your mission on earth shall be to fill it with love and kindness, bringing joy and happiness to the world; you are to sow seeds that shall blossom and bear fruit and forget not that you are one of the elect.'"

From that day forth, Johnny took his life's work to be to sow the West with apple seeds making the wilderness to blossom with their beauty and the people happy with their fruit.

Because Johnny was accepted by the Indians, he often attended their campfires. He understood their language and signs and warned nearby settlers of approaching danger during periods of strife. He was never lost in the forest. After Hull's surrender at Detroit when thousands of Indians were released to attack settlers in Ohio and Indiana, Johnny rushed out to precede them. He was a sight to see. He was barefooted, hatless and with only a coffee sack on for clothing with holes cut for arms and head. He sped through the night running to each cabin and tapping on the window or door in a piercing voice, "The spirit of the Lord is upon me and He hath anointed me to blow the trumpet in the wilderness and sound an alarm in the forest; for behold the tribes of the heathen are about your doors and a devouring flame followeth after them!" Such were his exact words as recalled by many settlers. After such a family was safely led to a blockhouse or strong point, he speeded on to another. He loved the Indians you see, but he didn't want no part of killin.

Life with natural beasts and such wasn't somethin he feared. Traveling on a snowy winter day between Mansfield and Mt.Vernon, Ohio, Johnny once needed shelter for the night. He found a hollow log to squirm into. He built a fire nearby, cooked his mush for dinner and got ready to crawl into the log when he heard a low growl. The log was already occupied by a bear hibernating through the winter. Johnny withdrew without argument, apologized to the bear and slept in the snow. Such was Johnny's respect for all God's life of the American wilderness.

Another time, on a hot summer evening, Johnny was so swarmed with mosquitoes that he built a smudge fire. Then he noticed that thousands of insects was attracted to the blaze and was losing their lives in the flames. Johnny at once put it out. He exclaimed, "God forbid that I should build a fire for my comfort that should be the means of destroying any of God's creatures." Likewise he never threw a piece of wood onto a fire without shaking the worms or ants off first.

Johnny liked to help folks. It was just his way. One day, Johnny was helping men working off their road tax on the public highway when a hornet crawled up his pants and stung him. Johnny tried to persuade the hornet to come down his leg and fly off but the hornet kept stinging him. Every time, Johnny tried to force the hornet down his leg, he got stung until Johnny finally pushed him out. The hornet stung him dozens of times until Johnny got him out and the hornet flew away. All the crew was watching and laughing at Johnny and urging him to simply swat the hornet and kill it. Johnny replied, "No, he thought he was right and was simply defending himself with his God given weapons of defense, his sting - and why should I kill him for that."

Johnny wasn't no racist. He knew every person was give breath by God one at a time without no difference. That's probably why he was accepted by the Indians. He lived with them for weeks and months at a time. They respected his fearlessness and refusal to carry a weapon. They regarded him as a Medicine Man because he was much like the Indian in being able to endure pain and take hardship. The Indians was trained to withstand affliction. Starting at ten years of age, the Indian child was deprived of food for a day, then two, and up to a week at a time to learn to become a warrior. Johnny was able to do the same. Discipline is necessary, of course, to ever do anything God wants you to do. No Indian ever assaulted Johnny though he lived with many of them in their camps and there was often great conflict between the settlers and the native peoples of the West.

Johnny didn't shy away from war or battles and saw service in the Battle of Tippecanoe, the great battle of the West in the epoch of the American War of 1812. He was pressed into service by General William Henry Harrison, later to become American President, to approach the Indians to attempt to avert battle. He entered the Indian lines to see if peace talks could be arranged. Johnny was easy welcomed since he was no enemy of any Indian. Brought before the Indian leader, "the Prophet," he spoke to them in their language. "The Prophet" promised to "hold council with him before tomorry's sun shall set. We want peace too and tomorry will settle it forever. 'The Prophet' loves the white man's friendship more than his bullets." Other Indians told Johnny laughingly, "We will all come over to have a meeting with you tomorrow, so be ready for us."

While Johnny took this to mean peace talks, General Harrison took it as treachery and feared the Prophet had in mind to attack so he prepared for a battle to take place that very night. This happened. Just bein a gentle person don't mean you read the future right. During the battle that began that morning at 4 A.M., Johnny rushed after those who was injured and pulled them to safety. He carried no weapons and would have been wounded twice to the heart. After the battle, he reached up and found two bullets in his New Testament which he wore in the pocket over his heart. Either one of them would have done him in if it hadn't bin how he put his New Testament where he did.

Gentleness meant being kind to animals to Johnny. He purchased lame or used-up horses of emigrants and turned them out to forage for themselves. On other occasions he gathered up half-starved horses and bargained with a settler to care for them during the winters and then either led them away or sold them for small sums to settlers on condition that they be kindly treated. Johnny met many emigrants because he was a tireless traveler in the states of Ohio, Indiana, Illinois, Iowa, Pennsylvania, Virginia, Michigan and Missouri.

Of course Johnny's gentleness gave him to value family life. One summer while he was living with Shawnees along the Little Miami in Ohio, Johnny saw a little girl brought into camp not over four years old. She was crying as though her heart would break. Johnny knew the settlers she was snatched from. The squaws to whom the girl was give could not stop her from crying. Johnny volunteered and eventually purchased her and returned the little girl to her parents.

The Jonathan apple was a product of his creative genius. This is one of the best species of apple. The "Johnny cake" was his invention. Love gits demonstrated with doin for others by some folks who live different. A gentle life regardin others speaks fur itself.

Henry Lyte:

A Call Upon God to Abide

Shortly before his death, Henry Lyte (1793-1847) wrote a hymn to God. He was an English minister of a poor church in a fishing village in Devonshire. He was 54 years old and had never succeeded to be more than a poor minister for 23 years. He died at that age of 54 of tuberculosis and asthma. His life was lonely and he felt alone except for his faith.

Abide with me. Fast falls the eventide.
The darkness deepens. Familyhead, with me abide.
When other helpers fail and comforts flee
Help of the Helpless, O abide with me.

Swift to its close ebbs out life's little day.
Earth's joys grow dim. Its glories pass away.
Change and decay in all around I see.
O You who change not, abide with me.

I need Your presence every passing hour.
What but Your grace can foil the tempter's power?
Who, like Yourself, my guide and stay can be.
Through cloud and sunshine, Familyhead, abide with me.

I fear no foe, with You at hand to bless.
Ills have no weight, and tears no bitterness.
Where is death's sting? Where, grave, your victory?
I triumph still, if You abide with me.

Hold You Your cross before my closing eyes.
Shine through the gloom and point me to the skies.
Your Homeland's morning breaks, and earth's vain shadows flee.
In life, in death, O Familyhead, abide with me.

* * * * *

The Boy's Kernel

Once upon a time there was a boy born to poor folk who lived out on a small farm that didn't have good dirt. Just when his pa figured he's goin' to have to move, the boy found a kernel of corn and stuck it in his pocket.

The next mornin', he went down by the crick that ran through the old farm and buried the seed near to a place where he liked to fish and where his ma would find him every time he'd be wanderin' away.

`Bout a month later, he hiked back by the old farm. When he look'd over to where he buried the seed, there was a corn plant. It had grow'd up from the ground up through the clouds. The lil boy was so surpris'd he didn't know what to do.

He went over to it and look'd up.

There was Jesus up there smilin' down on him. The lil boy just felt like he had to climb up to say hello. He footheld the stalk leaves one at a time not lookin' down so as not to fall and got up close enough for a hug. Then he figured he'd better get back home before his folks got worried.

The boy grow'd up and every time he don't feel good, he'd sneak back to that old homeplace on the crick. "Yes," he would say to himself, "the corn plant is still whar it oughter be."

His life run on like the water run down the crick. He got married, had some kids that grow'd up fine. He made do on a lil piece of ground til he could get some of his own, and then when he's older he let his children do the corn plantin' and harvestin' and took to stayin' home most times. All his life he follow'd the Golden Rule.

Then one day he took sick and went to bed and next thing he know'd there he was at the cornstalk. Now he didn't feel so bad. No, he felt better'n ever. The man felt himself turn back into a boy, and here he was a boy again! He looked up and there was Jesus smilin' down at him again.

So he start'd climbin'.

Every step become lighter.

When he's up there, Jesus hugged him tight and the angels told him he's dead. "But I can't be," the boy said. "What about my family?" "Don't worry," Jesus said. "Look down and you'll see why."

And when the boy look'd down to see if everything's okay he couldn't see nothin' but cornstalks growin up on every farm on every continent on the planet. They was all growing tall to where the boy was too - there in God's Homeland - one for each and every loved one left behind in all the world.

Jesus laughed, "I make sure all my family finds a kernel to plant!"

* * * * *

Walter Scott:

Ave Maria

Ave Maria!
Maiden mild
Oh, listen to a maiden's prayer
For thou canst hear tho' from the wild.
And thou canst save amid despair, Amid despair.
Safe may we sleep beneath thy care
Tho' banished outcast and reviled
Oh, maiden!
Hear a maiden's prayer
Oh, mother hear a suppliant child!
Ave Maria!
Ave Maria! undefiled!
The flinty couch we now must share,
shall seem with down of eider piled,
If thy, if thy protection hover there.
The murky cavern's heavy air shall breathe of balm
if thou hast smiled;
Then, maiden! hear a maiden's
prayer
Oh, mother hear a suppliant
child.
Ave Maria!

* * * * *

W.C.Bryant,

Thanatopsis

So live, that when your summons comes to join
The innumberable caravan which moves
To that mysterious realm where each shall take
His chamber in the silent halls of death,
You go not like the quarry-slave at night,
Scourged to his dungeon, but,
Sustained and soothed
By an unfaltering trust, approach your grave
Like one who wraps the drapery of his couch
About him and lies down to pleasant dreams.

* * * * *

Godly Community of Hard Workers:

Harmonie

That was an idea of a community of hard workers at a frontier settlement of Harmonie. Their leader was George Rapp who lived between 1757 and 1847. His dream was of a community worthy of the Sunwoman of John's vision of how the New Jerusalem could come down. George Rapp dreamed to build a community in which the Sunwoman become flesh as a Church community of brothers and sisters in the American wilderness.

In John's vision, the Sunwoman flees into the wilderness where God prepares a place for her where she is to be fed. From this vision, George Rapp encouraged his friends in Germany to emigrate to Pennsylvania in America. Then George Rapp followed the next verses in moving the community to Harmonie, Indiana. In those verses, the Sunwoman was give two wings of a great eagle to fly into the wilderness to a place to be nourished for a time, and times, and half a time, from the face of the serpent. Thus was to begin the time called the "era of the Golden Rose" of the community.

A short history of Harmonie comes from a letter of George Rapp to Thomas Jefferson, then President of the United States. "Your memorialists are natives of the Electorate of Wurttemberg in Germany, and have been there in corporated to the Lutheran Religion after the Law of the Country yonder; having become acquainted through the Grace of God Enlightening of the holy Spirit with the decline of Christianism since Eighteen Years, so they was going the Way of Piety, after the sense of Jesus, and formed a proper Community, the Number of which amount to Two thousand men; having been persecuted and punished in many manner for sake of the Truth which they perceived and confessed, they was necessitated to look for a place, where is liberty of Conscience, and where they may exercise unprevented the Religion of the Spirit of Jesus. Your Memorialists understanding of the United States, America would be such a place, the whole Society was unanimously resolved to send their Leader George Rapp accompanied with some brethren before them, to enquire about the Country; after whose notice are already in Phila and

Baltimore arrived about fourteen hundred me, which body of People consists of Tradesmen, Farmers and chiefly cultivators of the Vine, which last occupation they contemplate as their primary Object, and whilst they know how to plant and prepare Hemp and Flax, having good Weavers among them, so they are intended to erect too a Linen Manufactory..."

An earth in harmony of those working with each other and for each other would encourage the Second Coming of Jesus. Such a community would restore humanity to the original harmony that existed in the world and before humanity was corrupted.

The community of Harmonie prospered mightily. Hundreds of emigrants became members. Those joining signed a contract of three principles. 1. Members of the community give up their property as free gifts to the community. 2. All members of the community pledge to submit to the laws and regulations of the congregation and to advance its interests. 3. If any member wishes to withdraw, he or she may do so but without asking for compensation for services already performed since they would have been done for the common interest. Then the benefit of life was give in three pledges of the community to each member. 1. Every member was adopted into the community and give religious and educational privileges. 2. All members of the community was give the necessaries of life, not only in health, but also in sickness. 3. Any member wanting to leave who stated so openly would receive a cash donation according to that one's conduct while in the community.

Harmonie was built on forested lands on the Wabash River, mid-continent America, starting in the fall of 1814. Within a short span of years Harmonie consisted of 1450 acres of cleared land, 150 log cabins, a brick house for George Rapp, 3 other buildings, a church, steam mill and other mills, a dyehouse, granaries, barns and sheep huts, stables and corn cribs. The trade of the community grew and grew. Its produce was sold by river commerce far up the Ohio River (into which the Wabash River flows) to Pittsburgh and downriver to St. Louis and New Orleans. The community opened up outlets for its produce in surrounding communities in Kentucky, Indiana and Illinois. A loan from the community permitted the state of Indiana to restore its credit in 1823. Everyone in the community, men, women and children, had a task assigned to each one of them every day which that person must dutily perform whether it was in the field, mills or shops. Families lived together and unmarried persons lived in dormitories.

A great church of Harmonie was erected over which was carved the Golden Rose of Micah's prophecy of an era to come for a place of the daughter of Jerusalem, George Rapp's Sunwoman. This stone lintel is still there and stands as a monument to the work of Mary, the mother of Jesus, and the power of a community which envisions the love of this mother of God's Child.

In a letter by Frederick Rapp, December 19, 1822 is found this explanation of the religious foundation of the community. "Of all those evils and calamities (of the modern world) Harmonie knows nothing. Eighteen years ago she laid the foundation and plan for a new period, after the original Pattern of the primitive church described in the 2 and 4 chapter of the acts and since that time we lived, although unnoticed, covered with ignominy and contempt, yet happy in peace, for all our temporal as well as Spiritual Union became every year more perfect, and now our Community stands proof, firm and unmovable upon its Rock of truth...Taking a worldly view, our diligence and Labour are amply rewarded, we suffer no want whatever." "We can neither refer to a Book nor send a pamphlet (to explain our community) which could give any information of our principles and management, having nether a written nor a printed Constitution or form of Law for the organization of our Society, but merely found it necessary to make a sort of agreement with new Comers whereby they are insured, that in case they should not stand the given time of probation, or if after being adopted into the community they could not be made to lead a Christian life, and therefore withdraw they shall receive back the value of their property brought in, and if they are poore and layd in nothing, they shall receive a donation at their departure according to the Conduct and need...No community established upon the principles of ours can exist without the prohibition of exclusive property, which always creates motives for individual self interest and operates as an inherent and irresistible principle to bring on confusion and decay. Therefore all schemes to form Societies similar to Harmonie without practising the Religion of Jesus Christ in prohibiting individual property have gone to wreck." The community did not join in economic downturns or upturns. In another letter, Frederick Rapp explained the society as simply providing their own labor to provide the members all the necessaries of life - food, drink, and clothing. Harmonie carried on the extensive trade it did "for the welfare and progress of its neighbors rather than for its own advantage." The community moved from its wilderness location back to Pennsylvania in 1824.

The spirit of the community is expressed in a letter written as Harmonie was being laid out in August, 1814.

Father! (to George Rapp)

Our condition has changed considerably since our arrival. Several of our young people have caught the fever, viz, J. Krail, Aug. Schmid, and A.J. Laipple, Raymunt Schuhle, F. Nachtrub, also his girl and big boy. But they did not all have the same kind of fever. With Raymunt Schuhle the fever changed. After freezing he became intensely hot, and this heat continued unceasingly and all means of cooling him had no effect. He died Tuesday, August 2. Nachtrub's girl was sick two days and died August 6. Nachtrub and his child are better again. J. Krail, Aug. Schmid, and A.J. Laipple are better again, too. Now imagine, dear Father, how your weak children felt under such conditions. We were rather frightened. According to appearance the sickness did not seem the least bit serious, so that the sick ones complained of no pain but a little Durmel in the head, until the heat had overpowered them and they began to slumber so that one could scarcely bring them to consciousness for even a moment. Schuhle lamented about this. He had not feared the least for his Raymunt and now he could not speak a word with him anymore. We are now using the home remedies suggested to us by sensible neighbors, and we hope that all will be better in the future. But if the Lord wishes to deal with further in this way, then His will be done. We will not leave Him for we know that God is good to us and that what He does with us is best for us. So we have commended ourselves to Him to live or die according to His pleasure, and with this resignation to God we are calm and at peace, but our wish and longing for you does not cease, until we shall again be united, then everything will be indescribably easier, no matter how things go...Today we laid out the town through a surveyor in the neighborhood."

* * * * *

Lorenzo Dow:

The Power of a Preacher for God:

There is a power which preachers got that no force can reckon with. Take the case of Lorenzo Dow.

Lorenzo Dow was a powerful preacher on the frontier. He was so famous for his blood-and-thunder sermons that many thought he was possessed of supernatural powers. The Spirit of God's breath sometime become his own. Some thought he could literally "raise the devil." He preached everywhar. He didn't care if it was in somebody's house in the woods, in the cropfields, in a barnloft, out house or sawmill. No wolf's howl or panther's cry frightened him out of doin what the Familyhead said.

Once it got very late at night while he was traveling from a meetin south of his near-Fortville, Indiana farm, and he found the way dark and unfamiliar and asked permission at a house to spend the night. Only a woman was there.

The woman replied that her husband was not at home and he would have to go on - she could not accommodate him. However, one did not trifle with a wish of Rev. Dow. As was usual with him, he insisted and got his way. He was on the Familyhead's work and so his arguments was heavy. He said he would sleep in the stable if he could do no better. Then the woman looked at him more closely and saw his long hair and odd dress and asked him if he might be the Methodist preacher, Lorenzo Dow. People knew Rev. Lorenzo Dow because he stood out as a righteous minister always does.

When he replied in the affirmative, she waived her objections and took him to a side room from where, however, he could see the front part of the house. The preacher settled in for the night. He didn't get much sleep though because soon

another man arrived and from the series of jokes that ensued and levity and the pleasantries, Rev. Dow feared that this man was not the husband of his hostess.

The night activities went along with Rev. Dow puzzled and perplexed. Somethin didn't let him sleep about what was goin on.

About midnight there come a rap on the locked cabin door. Then came the roaring voice of the husband demanding entry. Inside there was a great stirring around. Now the Rev. Dow was sure the man was not her husband. Unfortunately for the woman, there was only one door into this sturdy pioneer home and at it stood the woman's husband. The wife quickly undid a bale of cotton in a drum at the foot of the bed into which she hurriedly buried her caller.

Her husband had been at a tavern and was wise and wiry and he thundered for admittance. "Hush, hush!" said the wife. "Lorenzo Dow is in the house!"

"Are you trying to tell me old blood and tobacco is in the house?" the husband asked drunkenly. This was Dow's nickname from two of his favorite sermon topics. "Is it Lorenzo Dow, the man who raises the devil?" he insisted. "Yes, and it is so be still," said the wife. "Come into the house quietly and you will see the devil emerge."

To calm her husband, the wife then went and got Rev. Dow. Dow was thus forced to come out of the side room and nothing then would do but that he decided right then and there he would make the devil appear.

Rev. Dow said that he would indeed make the devil appear but only on condition that the husband stand at the door and give the devil a few thumps as he should pass forth, "but not enough to break his bones."

Rev. Dow had heard the commotion and figured where the "guest" was so he took a candle in his hand and touched it to a bale of cotton near the bed and cried: "Come forth, Old Boy and get what you deserve fur tryin to hold forth in a Hoosier home!" To the husband's shock, out indeed jumped the hidden sinner and made his exit in a mass of flames to his pants and received a sound cudgeling from the husband beside the door on the way out as the preacher had instructed.

Lorenzo Dow had raised the devil all right. The woman promised to be at his Fortville church regularly from then on and the husband said not a word because he was convinced that the Rev. Dow had in fact done a supernatural feat.

* * * * *

Alexander Campbell:

Prayer

This is the spirit of true religion. Without communion with God there is nothing gained by faith or hope, by promises or commands, by professions, confessions, or institutions. This is the sanctum sactorum, the holy of holies, the inmost temple of religion. This was lost by Adam, and if we do not gain this by Messiah, we have gained nothing but a name. But what is communion with God? Let us ask, for illustration, what is communion with man? The reciprocation of common sentiment and common feeling. Language fails to define its intimacies. Two sentimental spirits in conversation with each other is its best illustration - two spirits of kindred thought pouring into each other the overflowings of congenial feelings.

Speech with us is the channel of thought. In this channel betwixt man and man flows every sentiment, feeling, and desire. And it is not only the circulating medium of spirits on earth, dwelling in houses of clay; but it is the medium of converse 'twixt God and man. Arrayed in words of human language, the Eternal Spirit appears to man not now only; for in Eden, blooming in primeval beauty and innocence, the voice of God, in harmonies sweeter than nature knows fell upon that ear not yet polluted with the serpent's poisonous breath. Since then God has spoken to man through the mediation of angels, celestial and terrestrial; by prophets in times of old; and in later ages by his Son. The stipulated signs of human thought are the stipulated signs of all divine ideas suggested to man. God now speaks to us in his written word, and we speak to him in our prayers. Thus we have communion with God through his Holy Spirit which is imparted to us. If we listen to God when he speaks (for he speaks first as it becomes him) he promises to listen to us. But if we hear not him, he hears not us. What an honor to be admitted into the audience of the Almighty Father upon such gracious terms! We hear the recorded words of God spoken by him through angels, patriarchs, prophets, apostles, his own Son; and thus having given our ears for awhile to the voice of God, we lift up our voice to him. We utter our adorations, confessions, thanksgivings, petitions, and our unconditional submission to the will, authority, wisdom and goodness, mercy and love of him "who is, and was, and evermore shall be!" Thus our spirits ascend to the heavens and commune with God. This is the delightful fellowship which the Christian indeed has with the Father and with his Son Jesus Christ; "praying always, with all prayer and supplication in the spirit;" in the closet, by the way, in the field, morning, noon, evening, he prays "without ceasing." "My voice shalt thou hear in the morning, O Lord! In the morning will I direct my prayer to thee, and will look up." "In the morning shall my prayer anticipate thee." "As for me, I will call upon God, and the Lord shall save me. Evening and morning, and at noon, will I pray and cry aloud, and he shall hear my voice." "Seven times a day do I praise thee because of they righteous judgments." "His praise shall be continually in my mouth." "By Jesus let us offer the sacrifice of praise continually." Thus speak the saints of both Testaments.

Men may talk about religion, about sound doctrine, about ordinances, about institutions, about everything present and future; but without this communion with God, this habitual devotion of mind, these constant aspirations, ejaculations, and soarings to the throne of mercy and favor, man is unfit for heaven, and soarings to the throne of mercy and favor, man is unfit for heaven, and unworthy of the Christian profession. A zealot he may be, orthodox in doctrine, moral in demeanor; but he wants the life and power of Christianity. Meditation on what God has spoken to us, and the outpourings of our spirit to him is to the moral man what free respiration in a pure atmosphere is to the physical man - life, health, vigor, beauty.

* * * * *

Harriet Tubman, Conductor:

An Abolitionist Heroine and a Freedom Story

Harriet Tubman was an African-American born a slave on a Maryland plantation in 1821. At an early age she was put to work as a field hand and never learned how to read or write. She knew the driver's lash when she didn't do what the field boss said. She took her pinch of salt to stand the sun in the fields and survived on her peck of corn. She was bred by her owner to John Tubman, a fellow slave, before she escaped to freedom in the North in 1849. Northern states prohibited slavery. They didn't allow auction blocks to sell folk from one owner to another.

Now began her great work. Harriet Tubman become a "conductor."

A "conductor" was a guide who helped fugitives from slavery to freedom through the Underground Railroad. The Underground Railroad was not really transportation. It was a route to the North where friendly homes welcomed fugitives until they found a safe place to stay far away from the South where slavery was legal.

Harriet Tubman undertook hazardous missions at the risk of her own freedom to go South and bring slaves back to the North on the Underground Railroad. Sometimes the slaves wanted to go back. She said "No!" and made sure they got their liberty. She helped over three hundred slaves escape the worst conditions and even rescued her own parents. After the Civil War begun, she helped the North and went to South Carolina to serve as a cook, nurse and scout for the Union Army. She lived out the last of her life in Auburn, New York.

An abolitionist story narrated in rhyme comes from Ohio.

> Eastward of Zanesville, Ohio, two or three
> Miles from the town, as our stage drove in,
> I on the driver's seat, and he
> Pointing out this and that to me,-
> On beyond us - among the rest-
> A grovey slope, and a fluttering throng
> Of little children, which he "guessed"
> Was a picnic, as we caught their thin
> High laughter, as we drove along,
> Clearer and clearer. Then suddenly
> He turned and asked, with a curious grin,
> What were my views on Slavery? "Why?"
> I asked, in return, with a wary eye.
> "Because," he answered, pointing his whip
> At a little, whitewashed house and shed
> On the edge of the road by the grove ahead,_
> "Two Black slaves that I've passed each trip

For eighteen years. - Though they've been set free,
They have been slaves ever since!" said he.
And, as our horses slowly drew
Nearer the little house in view,
All briefly I heard the history
Of this little old Negro woman and
Her husband, house and scrap of land;
How they were slaves and had been made free
By their dying master, years ago
In old Virginia: and then had come
North here into a free state - so,
Safe forever, to found a home--
For themselves alone?- for they left South there
Five strong sons, who had, alas!
All been sold ere it came to pass
This first old master with his last breath
Had freed the parents. - (He went to death
Agonized and in dire despair
That the poor slave children might not share
Their parents' freedom. And wildly then
He moaned for pardon and died. Amen!)

Thus, with their freedom, and little sum
Of money left them, these two had come
North, full twenty long years ago;
And, settling there, they had hopefully
Gone to work, in their simple way,
Hauling - gardening - raising sweet
Corn, and popcorn. - Bird and bee
In the garden-blooms and the apple-tree
Singing with them throughout the slow
Summer's day, with its dust and heat--
The crops that thirst and the rains that fail;
Or in Autumn chill, when the clouds hung low,
And hand-made hominy might find sale
In the near town-market; or baking pies
And cakes, to range in alluring show
At the little window, where the eyes
Of the Movers' children, driving past,
Grew fixed, till the big white wagons drew
Into a halt that would sometimes last
Even the space of an hour or two--
As the dusty, thirsty travelers made
Their noonings there in the breeches' shade
By the old black Aunty's spring-house, where,
Along with its cooling draughts, were found

Jugs of her famous sweet spruce-beer,
Served with her gingerbread-horses there,
While Aunty's snow-white cap bobbed 'round
Till the children's rapture knew no bound,
As she sang and danced for them, quavering clear
And high the chant of her old slave-days--
    "Oh, Lo'd, Jinny! my toes is so',
    Dancin' on you sandy flo'!"

Even so had they wrought all ways
To earn the pennies, and hoard them, too,--
And with that ultimate end in view?--
They were saving up money enough to be
Able, in time, to buy their own
Five children back.

Ah! the toil gone through!
And the long delays and the heartaches, too,
And self-denials that they had known!
But the pride and glory that was theirs
When they first hitched up their shackly cart
For the long, long journey South. - The start
In the first drear light of the chilly dawn,
With no friends gathered in grieving throng,-
With no farewells and favoring prayers;
But, as they creaked and jolted on,
Their chiming voices broke in song--

    "Hail, all hail! don't you see the stars a-fallin'?
      Hall, all hail! I'm on my way.
        Gideon am
        A healin' ba'm--
      I belong to the blood-washed army.
        Gideon am
        A healin' ba'm--On my way!"

And their return! - with their oldest boy
Along with them! Why, their happiness
Spread abroad till it grew a joy
Universal - It even reached
And thrilled the town till the Church was stirred
Into suspecting that wrong was wrong!-
And it stayed awake as the preacher preached
A Real "Love"-text that he had not long
To ransack for in the Holy Word.

And the son, restored, and welcomed so,
Found service readily in the town;
And, with the parents, sure and slow,
He went "saltin' de cole cash down."

So with the next boy - and each one
In turn, till four of the five at last
Had been bought back; and, in each case,
With steady work and good homes not
Far from the parents, they chipped in
To the family fund, with an equal grace.
Thus they managed and planned and wrought,
And the old folks throve - Till the night before
They were to start for the lone last son
In the rainy dawn - their money fast
Hid away in the house, - two mean,
Murderous robbers burst the door.
...Then, in the dark, was a scuffle - a fall-
An old man's gasping cry - and then
A woman's fife-like shriek. ...Three men
Splashing by on horseback heard
The summons: And in an instant all
Sprung to their duty, with scarce a word.
And they were in time - not only to save
The lives of the old folks, but to bag
Both the robbers, and buck-and-gag
And land them safe in the county-jail--
Or, as Aunty said, with a blended awe
And subtlety,-"Safe in de calaboose whah
De dawgs caint bite 'em!" So prevail
The faithful!- So had the Lord upheld
His servants of both deed and prayer,--
JIS the glory unparalleled--
Theirs the reward, - their every son
Free, at last, as the parents were!
And, as the driver ended there
In front of the little house, I said,
All fervently, "Well done! well Done!"
At which he smiled, and turned his head
And pulled on the leaders' lines and - "See!"
He said, - "'you can read old Aunty's sign!"
And, peering down through these specs of mine
On a little, square board-sign, I read:

"Stop, traveler, if you think it fit,
And quench your thirst for a-fip-and-a-bit.--

The rocky spring is very clear,
And soon converted into beer."

And, though I read aloud, I could
Scarce hear myself for laugh and shout
Of children - a glad multitude
Of little people, swarming out
Of the picnic-grounds I spoke about.--
And in their rapturous midst, I see
Again - through mists of memory --
A black old Negress laughing up
At the driver, with her broad lips rolled
Back from her teeth, chalk-white, and gums
Redder than reddest red-ripe plums.
He took from her hand the lifted cup
Of clear spring-water, pure and cold,
And passed it to me: And I raised my hat
And drank to her with a reverence that
My conscience knew was justly due
The old black face, and the old eyes, too-
The old black head, with its mossy mat
Of hair, set under its cap and frills
White as the snows on Alpine hills;
Drank to the old black smile, but yet
Bright as the sun on the violet,--
Drank to the gnarled and knuckled old
Black hands whose palms had ached and bled
And pitilessly been worn pale
And white almost as the palms that hold
Slavery's lash while the victim's wail
Fails as a crippled prayer might fail.--
Aye, with a reverence infinite,
I drank to the old black face and head--
The old black breast with its life of light--
The old black hide with its heart of gold.

* * * * *

Julia Ward Howe:

A War that Freed Slaves

If a situation of peace is so unjust as to arouse God's wrath, then war can come.

The most horrible war of history struck America in 1861. It was a Civil War and by the time it was over 2,200 battles were fought and 3,000,000 men served in the army. The battles ranged from Vermont to the Arizona Territory. On an average of its four years, 430 soldiers died every day. Cities were burned, farms were destroyed, brothers opposed brothers. Fathers shot their sons and vice versa. A generation of Americans lived shattered lives until the goal of freedom for all humanity was burned into the American heart. America was given a hard dose of righteousness medicine.

Many Americans understood the war through a song:

Battle Hymn of the Republic

Mine eyes have seen the glory of the coming of the Lord,
He is trampling out the vintage where the grapes of wrath are stored;
He hath loosed the fateful lightning of His terrible swift sword-
His truth is marching on.
    Glory! glory, hallelujah!
    Glory! glory, hallelujah!
    Glory! glory, hallelujah!
    His truth is marching on.

I have seen Him in the watchfires of a hundred circling camps,
They have builded Him an altar in the evening dews and damps;
I can read His righteous sentence by the dim and flaring lamps-
His day is marching on.
    Glory! glory, hallelujah!
    Glory! glory, hallelujah!
    Glory! glory, hallelujah!
    His truth is marching on.

He has sounded forth the trumpet that shall never sound retreat,
He is sifting out the hearts of men before His judgement seat;
O be swift, my soul, to answer Him! be jubilant, my feet!
Our God is marching on.
    Glory! glory, hallelujah!
    Glory! glory, hallelujah!
    Glory! glory, hallelujah!
    His truth is marching on.

In the beauty of the lilies Christ was born across the sea,
With a glory in His bosom that transfigures you and me;

As He died to make men holy, let us live to make men free,
While God is marching on.
> Glory! glory, hallelujah!
> Glory! glory, hallelujah!
> Glory! glory, hallelujah!
> His truth is marching on.
Amen, amen.

* * * * *

Abraham Lincoln:

An Address on a Field of Battle Drenched in Blood

The South invaded the Union (the North) in July, 1863 with a huge army afoot of 75,000 soldiers. This army advanced across Maryland and into Pennsylvania. The American President Abraham Lincoln appointed a new Army Commander only three days before the two armies collided at Gettysburg. "The Greatest Battle of the Western Hemisphere" then began with 163,000 men shooting, bayoneting and brawling with each other for three days. The South repeatedly attacked the Union positions on hills but could not dislodge the Northern soldiers from their four mile line. In desperation, a charge of the Union Center known as "Pickett's Charge" was attempted by the South. Half of these Southerners were killed outright. Wounded were everywhere. 51,000 men were casualties in the whole battle. The fields were literally drenched in blood before the Southern troops returned South.

President Abraham Lincoln dedicated a cemetery where casualties were buried.

> Four score and seven years ago our fathers brought forth
> on this continent a new nation, conceived in liberty and
> dedicated to the proposition that all men are created equal.

> Now we are engaged in a great civil war, testing whether
> that nation or any nation so conceived and so dedicated can
> long endure. We are met on a great battlefield of that war.
> We have come to dedicate a portion of that field as a final
> resting place for those who here gave their lives that that
> nation might live. It is altogether fitting and proper that
> we should do this.

> But, in a larger sense, we cannot dedicate - we cannot
> consecrate - we cannot hallow - this ground. The brave men,

living and dead, who struggle here have consecrated it far above our poor power to add to detract. The world will little note long remember what we say here, but it can never forget what they did here. It is for us, the living, rather, to be dedicated here to the unfinished work which they who fought here have thus far so nobly advanced.

It is rather for us to be here dedicated to the great task remaining before us - that from these honored dead we take increased devotion to that cause for which they gave the last full measure of devotion; that we here highly resolve that these dead shall not have died in vain; that this nation, under God, shall have a new birth of freedom; and that government of the people, by the people, for the people shall not perish from the earth.

* * * * *

Abraham Lincoln:

A Patriarch for the American Folk and
His Lesson on How to Treat the Vanquished

On April 15, 1865, Abraham Lincoln was assassinated, but not before addressing the nation on his views.

At this second appearing to take the oath of the presidential office, there is less occasion for an extended address than there was at the first. Then, a statement, somewhat in detail, of a course to be pursued seemed fitting and proper. Now, at the expiration of four years, during which public declarations have been constantly called forth on every point and phase of the great contest which still absorbs the attention and engrosses the energies of the nation, little that is new could be presented. The progress of our arms, upon which all else chiefly depends, is as well known to the public as to myself, and it is, I trust, reasonably satisfactory and encouraging ot all. With high hope for the future, no prediction in regard to it is ventured.

On the occasion corresponding to this four years ago, all thoughts were anxiously directed to an impending civil war. All dreaded it, all sought to avert it. While the inaugural address was being delivered from this place, devoted altogether to saving the Union without war, insurgent agents were in the city seeking to destroy it without war - seeking to dissolve the Union and divide effects by negotiation. Both parties deprecated war, but one of them would make war rather than let the nation survive, and the other would accept war rather than let it perish. And the war came.

One-eighth of the whole population were colored slaves, not distributed generally over the union but localized in the southern part of it. These slaves constituted a peculiar and powerful interest. All knew that this interest was somehow the cause of the war. To strengthen, perpetuate, and extend this interest was the object for which the insurgents would rend the Union, even by war, while the government claimed no right to do more than to restrict the territorial inlargement of it.

Neither party expected for the war the magnitude or the duration which it has already attained. Neither anticipated that the cause of the conflict might cease with or even before the conflict itself should cease. Each looked for an easier triumph and a result less fundamental astounding. Both read the same Bible and pray to the same God, and each invokes His aid against the other.   It may seem strange that any men should dare to ask a just God's assistance in wringing their bread from the sweat of other men's faces, but let us judge not that we be not judged. The prayers of both could not be answered. That of neither has been answered fully. The Almighty has His own purposes. "Woe unto the world because of offenses! for it must needs be that offenses come; but woe to that man by whom the offense cometh."   If we shall suppose that American slavery is one of those offenses which, in the providence of God, must needs come, but which, having continued through His appointed time, He now wills to remove, and that He gives to both North and South this terrible war as the woe due to those by whom the offense came, shall we discern therein any departure from those divine attributes which the believers in a living God always ascribe to Him? Fondly do we hope, fervently do we pray, that this mighty scourge of war may speedily pass away.

Yet, if God wills that it continue until all the wealth piled by the bondsman's 250 years of unrequited toil shall by sunk, and until every drop of blood drawn with the lash shall be paid by another drawn with the sword, as was said 3,000 years ago, so still it must be said, "The judgments of the Lord are true and righteous altogether."

With malice toward none, with charity for all, with firmness in the right as God gives us to see the right, let us stirve on to finish the work we are in, to bind up the nation's wounds, to care for him who shall have borne the battle and for his widow and his orphan - to do all which may achieve and cherish a just and lasting peace among oursleves and with all nations.

* * * * *

Abraham Lincoln:

A Letter to Mrs. Bixby

On Nov. 21, 1864, Abraham Lincoln composed a letter to to a Massachusetts widow.

"I have been shown in the files of the War Department a statement of the Adjutant General of Massachusetts, that you are the the mother of five sons who have died gloriously on the field of battle.

I feel how weak and fruitless must be any words of mine which should attempt to beguile you from the grief of a loss so overwhelming. But I cannot refrain from tendering to you the consolation that may be found in the thanks of the Republic they died to save.

I pray that our Heavenly Father may assuage the anguish of your bereavement, and leave you only the cherished memory of the loved and lost, and the solemn pride that must be yours, to have laid so costly a sacrifice upon the altar of Freedom.

Yours, very sincerely and respectfully,

A. Lincoln."

And so the American families sent their children off to join the Union Army to battle for human freedom. Gone must be the idea that a human being has a monetary value. Gone must be crimes that forbid movements of God's people from place to place, to learn or to be found reading a book. Gone must be prejudices based on skin color, sex or sexual orientation. Gone must be assertions that government has a duty to help some people to eat their bread on the sweat of other men's faces. Gone must be the idea that religion sets people to rebel against their own government to uphold slavery. Gone must be the idea that a leader is more than an instrument of the people. Mournfully but willingly the American people sent their boys to take a chance with death on the field of battle. So humanity relearned the lesson with Mrs. Bixby that human freedom must be paid for with agony.

* * * * *

Walt Whitman:

On the Death of America's Patriarch

When lilacs last in the dooryard bloom'd,
And the great star early droop'd in the western sky in the night,
I mourn'd, and yet shall mourn with ever-returning spring.

Ever-returning spring, trinity sure to me you bring,
Lilac blooming perennial and drooping star in the west,
And thought of him I love.

O powerful western fallen star!
O shades of night - O moody, tearful night!
O great star disappear'd- O the black murk that hides the star!
O cruel hands that hold me powerless - O helpless soul of me!
O harsh surrounding cloud that will not free my soul.

In the dooryard fronting an old farm-house near the white- wash'd palings,
Stands the lilac-bush tall-growing with heart-shaped leaves of rich green,
With many a pointed blossom rising delicate, with the perfume strong I love,
With every leaf a miracle - and from this bush in the door- yard,
With delicate-color'd blossoms and heart-shaped leaves of rich green,
A sprig with its flower I break.

In the swamp in secluded recesses,
A shy and hidden bird is warbling a song.

Solitary the thrush,
The hermit withdrawn to himself, avoiding the settlements,
Sings by himself a song.

Song of the bleeding throat,
Death's outlet song of life, (for well dear brother I know,
If thou wast not granted to sing thou would'st surely die.

Over the breast of the spring, the land, amid cities,
Amid lanes and through old woods, where lately the violets peep'd from the
    ground, spotting the gray debris,
Amid the grass in the fields each side of the lanes, passing the endless grass,
Passing the yellow-spear'd wheat, every grain from its shroud in the dark-
    brown fields uprisen,
Passing the apple-tree blows of white and pink in the orchards, carrying a
    corpse to where it shall rest in the grave,

Night and day journeys a coffin.

Coffin that passes through lanes and streets,
Through day and night with the great cloud darkening the land,
With the pomp of the inloop'd flags with the cities draped in black,
With the show of the States themselves as of crape-veil'd women standing,
With processions long and winding and the flambeaus of the night,
With the countless torches lit, with the silent sea of faces and the unbared
     heads,
With the waiting depot, the arriving coffin, and the sombre faces,
With dirges through the night, with the thousand voices rising strong and sol-
     emn,
With all the mournful voices of the dirges pour'd around the coffin,
The dim-lit churches and the shuddering organs - where amid these you jour-
     ney,
With the tolling tolling bells' perpetual clang,
Here, coffin that slowly passes,
I give you my sprig of lilac.
...

Lo, body and soul - this land,
My own Manhattan with spires, and the sparkling and hurrying tides, and the
     ships,
The varied and ample land, the South and the North in the light, Ohio's shores
     and flashing Missouri,
And ever the far-spreading prairies cover'd with grass and corn.

Lo, the most excellent sun so calm and haughty,
The violet and purple morn with just-felt breezes,
The gentle soft-born measureless light,
The miracle spreading bathing all, the fulfill'd noon,
The coming eve delicious, the welcome night and the
     stars,
Over my cities shining all, enveloping man and land.
...

     To the tally of my soul,
Loud and strong kept up the gray-brown bird,
With pure deliberate notes spreading filling the night.

Loud in the pines and cedars dim,
Clear in the freshness moist and the swamp-perfume,
And I with my comrades there in the night.
While my sight that was bound in my eyes unclosed,
As to long panoramas of visions.

And I saw askant the armies,
I saw as in noiseless dreams hundreds of battle-flags,
Borne through the smoke of the battles and pierc'd with missiles I saw them,.
And carried hither and yon though the smoke, and torn and bloody,
And at last but a few shreds left on the staffs, (and all is silence,)
And the staffs all splinter'd and broken.

I saw battle-corpses, myriads of them,
And the white skeletons of young men, I saw them,
I saw the debris and debris of all the slain soldiers of the war,
But I saw they were not as was thought,
They themselves were fully at rest, they suffer'd not,
The living remain'd and suffer'd, the mother suffer'd,
And the wife and the child and the musing comrade suffer'd,
And the armies that remain'd suffer'd.

Passing the visions, passing the night,
Passing, unloosing the hold of my comrades' hands,
passing the song of the hermit bird and the tallying song of my soul,
Victorious song, death's outlet song, yet varying ever- altering song,
As low and wailing, yet clear the notes, rising and falling, flooding the night,
Sadly sinking and fainting as warning and warning, and yet again bursting
    with joy,
Covering the earth and filling the spread of the heaven,
As that powerful psalm in the night I heard from recesses,
Passing, I leave thee lilac with heart-shaped leaves,
I leave thee there in the door-yard, blooming, returning with spring.

I cease from my song for thee,
From my gaze on thee in the west, fronting the west, communing with thee,
O comrade lustrous with silver face in the night.

Yet each to keep and all, retrievements out of the night,
The song, the wondrous chant of the gray-brown bird,
And the tallying chant, the echo arous'd in my soul,
With the lustrous and drooping star with the countenance full of woe,
With the holders holding my hand nearing the call of the bird,
Comrades mine and I in the midst, and their memory ever to keep, for the
    dead I loved so well,
For the sweetest, wisest soul of all my days and lands - and this for his dear
    sake,
Lilac and star and bird twined with the chant of my soul,
There in the fragrant pines and the cedars dusk and dim.

* * * * *

Folk story:

Children of the New American Abraham

Outside of M'Phersonville, South Carolina stood a stately plantation home surrounded by former cotton fields.

The plantation home was a wonder to behold. It was three stories with mansard roof atop and fantastic towers rising to tall points and even a widow's walk so that one atop saw the cotton fields at a great distance. From this vantage, the plantation owner, Caesar Stillwater, before he died in the 1850's, supervised his black field hands at work. He kept close watch through binoculars. If any did not work hard enough, he whipped them mercilessly.

Inside the home was a first floor with towering ceilings hand painted and moulded in gold leaf. The walls were fine murals. Nothing but hand carved furniture was in any room, European and hand picked specially for the rooms by the lady of the house, Gloria Stillwater, the wife of Caesar. The floors were parquet except the entry way which was tiled in fantastic blue flowered patterns. Expensive rugs from the Orient were elsewhere. Front parlors opened on both sides of the deep hallway. A hand carved rosewood stairway led to the second floor at the river end of the hall. A niche at the landing halfway up contained a bust of Augustus Caesar. One of the parlors was somewhat less formal than the other and sliding interior doors opened from this parlor into a huge dining room under a gilded chandelier and gold leaf painted ceiling. Upstairs was the main bedroom. Also upstairs in a tiny bedroom had lived the black house slave, Rosie. When Gloria Stillwater found out her son, Castor, and Rosie, were loving each other, she had never been so angry.

The servants' addition was complementary to the rest of the house and also had three upper floors. Entry from its second floor section opened on to the master bedroom where Gloria Stillwater slept and entry from its third floor opened on to the children's bedrooms where Gloria's sons, Alphaeus and Castor, slept. This was, of course, before they went off to join the Confederate Army after the outbreak of the Civil War.

How things had changed since her husband's death before the war and now her two boys...

Now as the American Civil War was lost, Gloria still lived in the beautiful mansion except she had no money to maintain it. Events turned the South to prey.

Gloria Stillwater had grasped at every straw for salvation of her South. She prayed that Lincoln would lose the Northern election for the presidency in the November, 1864 so that the South would not suffer total annihilation. The other Presidential candidate, General McClellan, seemed to favor a negotiated peace in which the South might keep its slavery institution.

That hope for an election defeat of Lincoln was dashed when the Northern Army stormed and captured Atlanta, Georgia, and the North smelled victory. There were two dastardly messages sent by the Yankee commander of the Northern troops, General Sherman, to Abraham Lincoln. The first read, "Atlanta is ours and fairly won. W.T. Sherman on November 15, 1864." The second was even more surprising. It was sent to Abraham Lincoln after Sherman burned Atlanta, or everything of military importance in it, and set off through Georgia for Gloria Stillwater's South Carolina. This second message was wired December 22, 1864, reading "I beg to present you as a Christmas gift, the city of Savannah, with 150 heavy guns and plenty of ammunition, and also about 25,000 bales of cotton. W.T. Sherman." South Carolina had also been conquered.

How could Abraham Lincoln's army have overrun Gloria Stillwater's home state of South Carolina? Perhaps Southern troops were being defeated everywhere, but what of the land? Sherman's troops could not meet the last opposition to peace which was the land itself. The Carolina country would rise up to defeat the Yanks. The Carolinas were heavily wooded, filled with swamps, crossed by slow streams, full of vegetation and entanglements. Those in South Carolina never feared invasion because they knew the land was their unconquerable ally. If Yankees dared come, the country would catch the Northerners and give the South victory.

Now the land caught the invaders and battle began. But these Yankees were Boston boys and New Yorkers, Pennsylvanians and Hoosiers, Illini and Ohioans, those from territorial small farms and small cities of all of America, farmers and woodsmen used to doing everything. There were no roads so Sherman's army chopped down trees and made them. There were no bridges so they built them. The Salkahatchie River has fifteen channels in the swamp that bears its name. In a single day, Sherman's troops built fifteen bridges. The Edisto River was half a mile wide where Sherman's army encountered it. Howard's wing crossed it in four hours with wagons and artillery. Columbia, South Carolina was burned in a few days and yet Lincoln's army continued its inexorable march toward ultimate victory. All of the places abiding inhumanity against black brothers and sisters must be conquered and cauterized. Then could come peace.

But now on the Stillwater plantation a strange event occurred.

Who was this black lady dropping off black children at the Plantation? Gloria Stillwater had no clue. The two black children were so young. Ato was 3 and Shaquille, his younger brother, was 2. All they did was waddle. The younger boy wasn't much of a walker at all. The black lady dropping them off was their aunt and formerly a field slave to the Stillwater family. Her sister, Rosie, was the house slave Gloria Stillwater sent away for sleeping with her son. Gloria Stillwater did not know what happened to her. Would she have cared that Rosie died from abuse during rape by Yankee soldiers? The two youngsters had been close by her side in her miserable room during her bout with the soldiers and her subsequent bloody death after their beatings of her and strangulation.

Rosie's sister found the children but couldn't raise these two babies anymore and put them on the porch of the Stillwater mansion. Their father was of course Gloria Stillwater's son, Castor.

What a task it was for the auntie to leave these two grandchildren of the white plantation owners and the banished house slave on the steps!

The auntie was crying as she left Ato and Shaquille on the Stillwater porch. Black slaves weren't taught to write so no note of explanation was left. She prayed sometime Gloria Stillwater would come to understand. Perhaps, at least, the children might be raised as field hands since the Auntie knew they would be not be acknowledged as joint heirs because of their black colored skin.

When they were just left there on this huge porticoed porch, the children cried and cried. Finally, Gloria Stillwater heard Ato and Shaquille and came to the porch. She thought this development very strange. Finally, she took them out to the former slave quarters and left them in the middle of its street. Then she called out loud for whomever left these slave children at her porch to come get them. "I am simply going to leave them here," Gloria called out several times. She could only hope whoever left them would come get them. Gloria couldn't have slaves anymore. The war had destroyed her plantation.

But there were no former slaves around to take these children. There was no one around period. Soon both children wandered away. They waddled off toward the low places in the swamps. Who would expect danger where the lavish drapery of the Spanish moss covers the bayou trees? Surely nothing hungry lurks as if a swimming log in disguise among the cypress knees. The mist off the swamps offered concealment to the alligators awaiting the children. It is the alligator which latches onto a limb of its prey and pulls the prey under water for a drowning before the bloody devouring. If no one else wanted the children, these reptiles were at the ready as takers.

The hours passed slowly and more slowly for Gloria Stillwater. What could she do? What had America done to her? What had God done placing Abraham Lincoln as Patriarch over the folk?

It was cold on this 2d day of February, 1865 when Doc McCletus was in M'Phersonville, South Carolina. He was in town to give a performance from his miracle medicine wagon. The Doc traveled widely. He sold cures for every ailment.

Doc McCletus's Patent Medicine Wagon rolled into the town of M'Phersonville, South Carolina shortly after General Sherman's troops departed. It was cold this early February. Sherman's soldiers were hacking their way through the Carolinas after conquering Savannah. Gloria Stillwater happened to be in town and noticed his arrival.

Hardly anyone in the once proud South had much heart to come to Doc McCletus's wagon for his performance on the tailgate of the wagon in the flickering early setting Winter Day. Still Doc McCletus was well known and his arrivals were always very well advertised. The Doc wanted to give the most wondrous program he could for the people of this devastated place.

A few came to gather. He offered to give away his cures. Many accepted. Doc sang, tried to offer cheer and, of course, extolled the virtues of his medicines.

Gloria Stillwater came up and wanted to talk.

She asked if she could speak with Doc privately.

Finally she said, "Doc McCletus, I know you are the devil. I feel it. My husband is long dead. Recently, my boys were killed near Atlanta. My oldest child, Alphaeus, died when his General Hood ordered an attack on Thomas's Army of the Cumberland. I understand it was at Peachtree Crick on July 20th just north of Atlanta or so I have been told. About a week later, my other son, Castor, was killed at the Ezra Church Crossroads two miles west of Atlanta. They tell me he died on July 28th, 1864. In 8 days I lost my boys and all I had to live for."

Doc asked, "Were they married?"

Gloria Stillwater responded, "One took up with this black house slave of ours named Rosie, claimed to be married, about shamed us all to death, but we sent her off. I don't know where she ended up. She was somewhere around here. The other never took up with women."

"So you have no grandchildren?" Doc said puzzled.

"No."

"Well what can I do for you?" Doc asked.

"I want to make a bargain." Gloria Stillwater said. "I feel my life was ruined by Abraham Lincoln. I hope the South will still prevail but whether it does or not I want Lincoln to die."

Then she looked at Doc McCletus very very seriously.

"I have always noted you. Every time you come to town. You are not an ordinary mortal. I feel it in my bones."

Then she looked again at Doc McCletus very very seriously.

"You are the devil aren't you, Sir?" she asked. Gloria Stillwater did not imagine any other force at work in the world except the Devil.

Then she looked at Doc McCletus triply very very seriously.

"You don't need to say it. I know it. Only evil comes to us, we who are Southerners. I have heard of your customs. I am yours. I feel such evil working in my thoughts. There is nothing good left in me." She thrust in the doctor's face her hands. "Here, I know how you are. Those who are devoted to you let you suck the blood from their hands and faces. Do it. I don't care. Do whatever you want. Mark me. Wherever. Whatever."

Doc drew back. Angels do not know such emotion.

She was sobbing.

"I cannot stand living," she said. "My plantation is a grave to me. I am a statue. Stone. I want to scream so loudly that the sky falls in. Sometimes I don't think my eyes work or my mouth. I don't want to see and I hate to think what nasty things I want to say. My life is gone forever."

She wiped the tears from her eyes.

"My sons were everything to me. When they were children they called for me with voices as soft as doves. I once begged my husband to kill a slave girl who seduced the youngest but I understand she was sent away. I wanted them pure. I did not want them touched by the evil world."

She went on, "I see swallows dipping ripples into a stream and I want to throttle them. I don't ever care to see the cotton froth and bubbles from pod. My two sons died defending Atlanta. They perished in its fall. They are as dead as this earth we are standing on. I want to avenge their death by selling my soul to you, Sir. I want Abraham Lincoln dead. I give you my soul to do it."

"Is that what you really want of all things?" Doc McCletus said.

"Yes, yes," she responded as Doc McCletus said, "This is a bargain you say. And how about your grandchildren's souls?"

"Grandchildren?" Gloria Stillwater asked. "Sir, I have no grandchildren."

"Oh yes, you do," Doc McCletus confided. "Your son, Castor, married this woman you call a slave, Rosie, I believe was her name before she died. She bore

Castor two children. I probably should not tell you this since I do not like to give things away but you are a grandmother twice over. Did they not come to you after their mother died raped and strangled by Northern soldiers? Yes, I believe they were dropped off at your home. Did you not meet your grandchildren, Ato and Shaquille?"

"No."

"Now let me see what happened next," Doc said, trying to recall the order of things. "Did you take them out to the old deserted slave quarters?"

"Oh my God! No. No. No. They are the children of my dead heroic son Castor?" she said. "But what can I do about them? They are black by law?"

"Isn't the law changed now because of Abraham Lincoln?"

"He killed my boys and I want him dead!" she replied. "I give you my soul, now give me Lincoln's blood in return for my son's blood." Then Gloria Stillwater stomped away.

And yet the fact that she was a grandmother caused her heartbeat to quicken and warm.

Now came the news that Abraham Lincoln was dead. Gloria Stillwater was convinced her deal with the Devil had made the event come true. The devil had taken the deal.

Gloria Stillwater was crying and all alone. Her crackling prayers arose from South Carolina and bore into the aeons.

Her voice rose to God's Homeland while God was in consultation with the new Patriarch of the Americans, Abraham Lincoln.

"Devil," she cried out, "you accepted my bargain. You took the life of Lincoln. You can have my soul but please give me back my grandchildren. I have not been able to find them. I have searched everywhere so I suppose you took them. I know we made a deal. But it was not about my grandchildren. They are all I have. I know the South fell. I know you killed Lincoln. I want to keep my end of the deal. My soul is yours. I know you earned my soul performing so much wrack and destruction. But please not my grandchildren. I have no one else."

God and the new Abraham turned to each other. Such pleading they never heard.

"Did you know of a deal with this woman?" Abraham Lincoln asked.

"Not that I know of."

"Well she apparently thinks her wishing so caused my death."

God looked around very peeved. "People ascribe to me many things. They constantly misunderstand. They see history as magic and not providence. We make no deals with humanity. We have never covenanted with any two except the two Abrahams. We promised the first Abraham the peace of knowing we were God for a wandering people and now you, the second, the peace of knowing we were God for a settling people."

"But look at her. She does not know her own soul."

Gloria Stillwater was a mess. Her hands were sweaty from ringing. It was night outside in the air and in her soul.

God looked sadly at Abraham. "If we are for her, what can be against her? Did we not give up our lives in the flesh for her? What can separate her from our love?"

Then they looked at each other. Abraham Lincoln looked at God with all the love he had for this people for whom he had risked his all and now suffered martyrdom.

God looked back. Abraham Lincoln, now the Patriarch of this new people, was wretched when one of his own was so very wretched.

"Well, okay," God agreed, "just this once."

And out of the resources of time and place in heavenly love, Ato and Shaquille emerged. The two little boys shook off their immortal clothes and atoms, molecules, tissues, organs and systems of organs settled upon them. Then they found themselves back on earth and close to the Stillwater Plantation.

Now from out of the black swamps of the night, safe from alligator bite and jerky drowning, Ato and Shaquille walked with placid look and hopeful demeanor. The dawn was spreading her rosy fingers over the sky. Up ahead they saw their grandmother, Gloria Stillwater, looking for them, calling as she did every day at every point. Seeing Ato and Shaquille, Gloria Stillwater rushed over to them and took them into her arms.

"Oh, Ato," she said through tears, "you are so handsome...just like your father and my son."

"And you, Shaquille, you are as handsome as your mother's folk."

Both children smiled and drew into their grandmother's arms.

In tears Gloria told her grandchildren, "Come into the house. I have your father and uncle's rooms ready for you."

On the way she lifted first one and then the other above her head to see the land awaiting the renewal of Spring. "See our fields? They are fallow. I have no inheritance to leave you. I will go out into the fields myself. I will provide for us my beloved ones. God will help. Somehow I feel sure. The South will rise again, this time in righteousness."

Oh dear, she told herself as they approached the empty mansion. She stopped at the flowerless urn in the front cul de sac. She spoke sternly to herself. You must

he truthful with these dear children. She stopped and brought them close and told them quite seriously, "I am sorry to have to tell you I have no soul. I have sold it to the devil so foolishly. But I still have my life. I will devote every bit of it for you." She felt much better about confessing her sin in causing the death of Abraham Lincoln.

Then almost to the porch, she shook her head sorrowfully. "I have no servants to bathe you or feed you, but I can do those things just fine. I do not feel my 60 years. My wrinkles are lies. I can tell you all about your mother and father, too. They were both so good." She sat on the wicker furniture on the front porch for a minute's rest and smothered first one and then the other one with caresses and kisses.

And choked with ecstatic understanding, she bundled them into the plantation house. To her, the day held the brightness of noon. "And I will answer every question either of you ever asks me so far as I can," she told them and many other things. She would not need to fear their enslavement because they were emancipated by a dead martyr for whom she now prayed every day, sad to think she was the cause of his death.

* * * * *

The Bells at Brown's Chapel

A little girl grew up ugly. Her looks didn't stop her heart from growin' big and full. She helped everyone she come in contact with and was patient about her lot in life bein' ugly. Every farm animal sensed her kindness. She never squashed even an insect. When chores was to be done, she done more than her share and volunteeered when her brothers and sisters felt too good to do somethin'. As time went on her older siblin's got married and then the younger ones but she was left waitin' and hopin'.

Then one day, while this ugly girl was out in the barn feedin' extra a lame cow that's stepped in a gopher hole, she heard bells. She never heard them before in all her twenty years. After she done her best with the cow, she figured she would go see what the noise was for. Fact was if she's gone there's no one that would complain much about it and hardly anyone to miss her for a time. So she followed the sound of them bells. She didn't think they was far away so she begun walkin' out to the county road and down it to the range line road to the west. And then she heard the sounds of them bells from more to the north, up over the railroad tracks and the National Road that leads to the county seat town and just north where the bend in Nameless Crick come close enough to the road for its linin' sycamore trees to offer shade.

Right there's where she saw a little white church, frame built, and showin' itself off by a huge window in front with a cross in color'd glass and lilies around it. Over and above it was a steeple with a cross atop. The girl wander'd over to it where the bells was summonin' her. And when she got there there's no one there at all!

And the bells stop'd ringin' too!

But she did kind of feel so tuckered that she rest'd on the front steps leadin' in and draw'd the notice of the country preacher livin' in the parsonage next door. He come out and met her and told her she could come back when the Sunday services was proper schedul'd.

She done it the very next Sunday.

It wasn't too many Sundays after that an elderly farmer took her to notice. This come at a time when there wasn't much hope she would do very good for a husband. Seems the old Jack in the church has had his wife up and die on him. The girl's parents was surprised when he come around and said he would take the ugly girl off'n their hands to marry.

Even though he was close to sixty and she's jus' twenty her parents told her to get pack'd for she wasn't ever gonna do no better.

On her weddin' day she heard the chapel bells again blowin' in the gusty wind. The bells was so pretty. The girl hadn't ever heard such! They couldn't have gloried more for even a pretty girl. It made her happy to be followin' them to the church and she got married a'goin' down the aisle to their chimin'. And when she look'd around, others of the little church was there beamin' smiles at her just like she was the prettiest bride in Hancock County! She couldn't hardly believe it. She even come to dare think she was pretty. And the bells seem'd to be announcin' jus' that!

She went on home with her husband and in the days to come she bore him two kids and twarn't long after, when the kids was still very young, that her husband's demands become more needful than her own kids for his heart give out on him and after he linger'd for about a month, he dropped off. So there she was alone again, and this time with a farm to plow and two kids to raise and ugly to boot. She took her kids to her brother's house not far away and as she was loadin' up her dead husband to take to the church for a showin' she heard the bells of Brown's Chapel ringin' in the winds. They rung in courage in her.

Seem'd like no time at all before the kids was grown and took off'n her hands to raise. She done it rememberin' how full has been her time with 'em, teachin' em to work hard and give thanks for every shock of wheat and cut of corn. She done all the farm work herself since bein' ugly don't limit that she should be a worker. And the kids and she was at the little church every Sunday and come to the Wednesday night Bible study. The kids join'd her in gettin' baptized. She'd never done it regular at eleven or twelve. Year's after, she took sick. Even ugly women do. The doctor said her heart had beat too hard. And jus' as she was dyin' she heard the wind joustlin' them bells into aringin' again. She could smile even to the last jus' listenin' to their beautiful sound. She whispered to the preacher standin' there at her deathbed, "Them bells has still got the most beautiful sound I ever heard. I know I won't hear no prettier bells even in God's Homeland."

"What bells?" the preacher asked the dyin' woman. "Our chapel's not got bells in the steeple. Never had."

But the ugly woman never heard how she was so fooled for all her life for her eyes was clos'd final.

* * * * *

Elizabeth Wills

The Temperance Crusade

Away back in the Seventies
A long, long time ago,
We women went out in the old crusade
When the ground was covered with snow.
Now what do you mean by the old crusade?
We would like to hear you explain
Was the fight just for popularity
Which we women were hoping to gain?
No, we mothers had sat in rum ruined homes
And mourned o'er the wreckage the rum fiend had made
It was rum, rum with its withering curse,
That's what started the Temperance Crusade.
Rum had robbed us of husband, had robbed us of sons
And of all, which the heart holds most dear
So we women went out, in this battle for home
Without the least tremor of fear.
In Hillsboro, Ohio, the Crusade first broke out
And the first soon kindled to flame.
it flew to the south, the north, east and west
Just like a tornado it came.
This fire had been smoldering for years and for years
Just waiting and ready to catch.
It was fed by wrecked manhood and orphan's sad tears
All it lacked was just touching the match.
We met in the churches, met three times a day
To form resolutions, to talk, sing and pray.
Just women in daytime, men kept out of sight
But they joined in our mass-meetings held every night.
Then while all the church bells were ringing at once
and all the whistles were blowing,
We started right out with our hymn books in hand
To visit saloons - we were going.
We caused much excitement as we marched two abreast
Through the crowded and awe-stricken street But with
heads quite erect and courage unchecked
Did we march with the snow on our feet.
We marched right in to the open saloon
And begged of the men to desist
But some grew angry and cursed us
And came at us with shaking fist;
And some of them told us we'd better go home

And men our husband's sox; We appointed committees to
sit out in front,
To keep the men out of saloons.
I imagine we felt a little like men
When they finally tree their 'coons;
And we couldn't help but sorter wear
A half-way satisfied grin
To see the men we were keeping out
That wanted so much to go in.
Then while at this stage in the conflict
After first excitement was through,
we organized the little band
called the W.C.T.U,
And the ball has kept rolling and rolling
with its purity banner unfurled,
Till now our white-ribbon army
Is teaching and belting the world.
So pin on the white ribbon, sisters,
And we will keep plugging away,
Till we win in the fight and put rummies to flight
Some Glad Day.

* * * * *

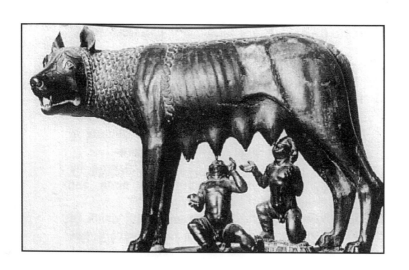

Song:

"Some Little Bug Will Find You Some Day"

1. It is oftentimes a question, in this age of indigestion,
    As what to eat and what to leave alone:
    For each microbe and bacillus has a different way to kill us,
    And in time they always claim us for their own.
    There are germs of every kind in any food that you can find
    In the market or upon the bill of fare;
    Drinking water's just as risky as the so-called deadly whiskey,
    And it's oftentimes a mistake to breathe the air.
    > CHORUS
    > Some little bug is going to find you some day,
    > Some little bug will creep behind you some day;
    > Then he'll send for his bug friends
    > And all your earthly troubles end;
    > Some little bug is going to find you some day.

2. The inviting green cucumber gets most everybody's number.
    While the green corn has a system all its own;
    Tho the radish seems nutritious, its behavior is quite vicious,
    And a doctor will be coming to your home.
    Eating lobster cooked or plain, is only flirting with ptomaine,
    While the oyster sometimes has quite a lot to say;
    But the clams we eat in chowder make the angels chant the louder,
    For the know that we will be with them right away.
    > CHORUS
    > Some little bug is going to find you some day,
    > Some little bug will creep behind you some day;
    > Then he'll get into your gizzard,
    > And if you lose him, you're a wizard,
    > Some little bug is going to find you someday.

3. Take a slice of nice fried onion, and your fit for Doctor Munyn,
    Apple dumplings will kill you quicker than a train;
    Chew a cheesy midnight rabbit and a grave you'll soon inhabit,
    Ah! to eat at all is such a foolish game.
    Eating huckleberry pie is a pleasing way to die,
    While saur kraut brings on softening of the brain;
    When you eat banana fritters every undertaker titters,
    And the casket makers nearly go insane.
    > CHORUS
    > Some little bug is going to find you some day,
    > Some little bug will creep behind you some day;

With a nervous little quiver
They'll give you cirrhosis of the liver.
Some little bug is going to find you some day.

4. When the cold storage vaults I visit, I can only say
    "What is it makes poor mortals fill their systems with such stuff
    Now for breakfast prunes are dandy, if a stomach pump is handy,
    And your doctor can be found quite soon enough.
    Eat a plate of fine pigsknuckles, and every headstone cutter chuckles,
    While the gravedigger makes a mark upon his cuff.
    Eat that lovely red bologna, and you'll wear a wood kimono,
    As your relatives start scrapping 'bout your stuff.
              CHORUS
        Some little bug is going to find you some day,
        Some little bug will creep behind you some day;
        Eating juicy sliced pineapple
        Makes the sexton dust the chapel.
        Some little bug is going to find you some day.

5. All these crazy foods they mix will float us cross the river Styx
    Or help start us climbing up the milky way;
    And the meals we eat in courses mean a hearse and two black horses,
    So before eating some people always pray.
    Luscious grapes breed 'pendicitis and the juice leads to gastritis,
    So there's only death to greet us either way.
    And fried livers nice but mind you,
    Your friends will soon ride slow behind you,
    And the papers will have nice things to say.
              CHORUS
        Some little bug is going to find you some day,
        Some little bug will creep behind you some day;
        Eat some sauce, they call it Chili,
        And on your breast they'll place a lily.
        Some little bug is going to find you some day.

* * * * *

A.K.Branham:

A Short History of an American Church

Brothers, sisters, and neighbors, as one of the pioneers of this congregation, worshiping at this church, I have been selected to give you today some of its early history. In doing so, I will necessarily have to tell you of the part taken by myself in its organization and all along its history to the present time. There are many sad recollections that cluster around and about this church. Of the men and women who composed the membership at the organization, I am the only survivor who attends the meetings of the Disciples.

"Yes, many friends were gathered 'round me
In the bright days of the past
But the grave has closed above them
And I linger here, the last".

As far back as 1836, there were a few Disciples scattered about in this county and at Greenfield. They occasionally met at the house of Brother William Sebastian, who kept what at that time was called an Inn, and at the old County Seminary and M.E. Church, and were addressed by such men as Brother John McKane, Milton B. Hopkins, and others, on the subject of "The Great Reformation", as taught by Alexander Campbell.

But not until the year 1854 was there anything like a permanent organization. In April 1854, Brother James L. Thornberry of Kentucky held a two week meeting, which resulted in quite a number of additions to the church. It was at this meeting that I was brought from darkness to light, and from the power of Satan to God; and from that day to this I have never regretted the casting of my lot with the poor, despised Nazarene and his humble followers.

With the old Disciples and the new converts, the organization was completed, and Brother William Sebastian and myself were selected as Elders to serve the congregation. I have served the church as an Elder ever since Brother Sebastian has long since passed to his reward.

We did not forget the assembling of ourselves together. Having no church of worship, we met at the homes of the brethern for prayer, singing the songs of Zion, and attending the Lord's Supper. We continued to walk in His footsteps, always trying to do good, determined to know nothing but Christ and him crucified. But we were met at the threshhold of our new organization with the fact that we had no house of worship. This fact troubled our minds no little, for we were not possessed of much of this world's goods, and were few in number. To build a house of worship meant to us a sacrifice on our part of no ordinary character.

We held a meeting, and after a long and ernest conference, we resolved that we would build a house and dedicate it to God, who loved us and died to redeem us from all iniquity, and purify unto himself a peculiar people, zealous for good works. About this time an opportunity was offered us to show our faith by our works. The Commissioners of the county declared in favor of building a new Court House; the old Court House was sold at a public sale, and Bro. Lewis Sebastian and myself purchased it for two hundred and fifty dollars. We got enough brick from the old house to make the wall of our new house, and after a long struggle, and by the generosity of our fellow citizens, we were enabled to complete the building and dedicate it to God.

The young of today know but little of the trials, struggles, and difficulties that were encountered by the Disciples thirty-five years ago. Instead of the beautiful seats we occupy today, the pioneers were compelled to use one made of two by twelve-inch boards, with wooden legs. Such are some of the vast changes in the third of a century gone by.

We had for our first pastor, Brother Lyttleton L. Rains, a young man full of promise and the spirit of God, a man whom to know was to love, and to name was but to praise. He was successful as a preacher in an eminent degree for one so young, and added largely to the numbers of the congregation. But alas! that fell destroyer of the human race took him away at an early age.

After Bro. Rains the church has had many eminent preachers such as John B. New, John D. Kane, Bennett Edmonson, the gifted orator A.I. Hobbs, George Campbell, J.J. Sloan, the brilliant Dr. A.G. Thomas, Andersen Chastine and J.L. Parsons, our present pastor, who has been here for nearly four years. We cannot speak too highly of him as a man and a preacher. He came to us when the church was at its darkest hour, when we were almost ready to give up in despair, and the candlestick seemed about ready to be removed from the church when he, by his pious walks and Godly conversation, by his gentleness and sweetness of disposition, brought light out of darkness and peace and happiness to the church; and he has won his way to the hearts of the entire congregation. May God bless his labors in the future as He has in the past.

I beg leave, at this point, to give my tribute of praise to the noble band of women who have labored for the church from the time of organization to the present. Some have fallen asleep in Jesus after a long life of service in the cause, and the living of today are the same faithful workers. In the darkest hour of the church's history they have never wavered in their fidelity to the cause of Christ, no labor could tire them, and no sacrifice or trial could dishearten them; but like the eagle, with its wings to the wind and eye to the sun, swerve not, but bears onward, right on, so have the noble women of this church made Christ and His service the great object of their lives. Man's heart may quail in the hour of trial and affliction, but woman's never.

> Not she with traitorous kiss the Savior stung,
> Not she denied him with unholy tongue,
> She, when apostles shrank, could dangers brave--
> Last at the cross, and earliest at the grave.

My brethern and sisters, I cannot close this brief history without saying a few words of another of my co-laborers. I refer to Bro. George Barnett, who is present today. Bro. Barnett has served the congregation, as an Elder, for nearly thirty years, with a zeal and devotion unquenched and unflagging. To his untiring labors, to his zeal for the success of the cause of Christ, we attribute in large degree the firm hold that we, as a church, have on the people of this city. God bless Bro. Barnett and may his last days be his best, and when he is done serving the church here below, may he hear the welcome plaudit:

> "Soldier of Christ, well done,
>
> Praise be thy new employ:
>
> The battle fought, the victory won,
>
> Enter thou thy Master's joy".

I might tell of many more of those who have been bright and shining lights in the Kingdom of God here on earth, who have long since entered their rest of the Saints: John T. Sebastian, Jacob Sifer, Sister Ryon, Sister Mitchell, and a host of others, but it would consume more time than is allotted to me on this occasion.

I thank God that today we are at peace with one another, and are endeavoring to carry out the great principles for which we were united, and when our work on earth is done, and death shall call us from our labors, may we all have a happy admittance into that house not made with hands, eternal in the heavens, is my prayer.

* * * * *

James Whitcomb Riley:

To My Old Friend, William Leachman

Fer forty year and better you have been a friend to me,
Through days of sore afflictions and dire adversity,
You allus had a kind word of counsul to impart,
Which was like a healin' 'intment to the sorrow of my hart.

When I buried my first womern, William Leachman, it was you
Had the only consolation that I could listen to -
Fer I knowed you had gone through it and had rallied from the blow
And when you said I'd do the same, I knowed you'd ort to know.

But that time I'll long remember; how I wundered here and thare-
Through the settin'-room and kitchen, and out in the open air-
And the snowflakes whirlin', whirlin', and the fields a frozen glare,
And the neghbors' sleds and wagons congergatin ev'rywhare.

I turned my eyes to'rds heaven, but the sun was hid away;
I turned my eyes to'rds earth again, but all was cold and gray;
And the clock, like ice a-crackin', clikt the icy hours in two -
And my eyes'd never thawed out ef it hadn't been fer you!

We set thare by the smoke-house - me and you out thare alone-
Me a-thinkin' - you a-talkin' in a soothin' undertone -
You a-talkin' - me a-thinkin' of the summers long ago,
And a-writin' "Marthy - Marthy" with my finger in the snow!

William Leachman, I can see you jest as plane as I could then;
And your hand is on my shoulder, and you rouse me up again;
And I see the tears a-drippin' from your own eyes, as you say:
"Be rickonciled and bear it - we but linger fer a day!"

At the last Old Settlers' Meetin' we went j'intly, you and me -
Your hosses and my wagon, as you wanted it to be;
And sence I can remember, from the time we've neghbored here,
In all sich friendly actions you have double-done your sheer.

It was better than the meetin', too, that nine-mile talk we had
Of the times when we first settled here and travel was so bad;
When we had to go on hoss-back, and sometimes on "Shank's mare,"
And "blaze" a road fer them behind that had to travel thare.

And now we was a-trottin' 'long a level gravel pike

In a big two-hoss road-wagon, jest as easy as you like -
Two of us on the front seat, and our wimmern-folks behind,
A-settin' in theyr Winsor-cheers in perfect peace of mind!

And we pinted out old landmarks, nearly faded out of sight: -
Thare they ust to rob the stage-coach; thare Gash Morgan had the fight
With the old stag-deer that pronged him - how he battled fer his life,
And lived to prove the story by the handle of his knife.

Thare the first griss-mill was put up in the Settlement, and we
Had tuck our grindin' to it in the Fall of Forty-three -
When we tuck our rifles with us, techin' elbows all the way,
And a-stickin' right together ev'ry minute, night and day.

Thare ust to stand the tavern that they called the "Travelers' Rest,"
And thare, beyent the covered bridge, "The Counterfitters' Nest" -
Whare they claimed the house was ha'nted - that a man was murdered thare,
And burried underneath the floor, er 'round the place somewhare.

And the old Plank-road they laid along in Fifty-one er two -
You know we talked about the times when the old road was new:
How "Uncle Sam" put down that road and never taxed the State
Was a problem, don't you rickollect, we couldn't dimonstrate?

Ways was devius, William Leachman, that me and you has past;
But as I found you true at first, I find you true at last;
And, now the time's a-comin' mighty nigh our jurney's end,
I want to throw wide open all my soul to you, my friend.

With the stren'th of all my bein', and the heat of hart and brane,
And ev'ry livin' drop of blood in artery and vane,
I love you and respect you, and I venerate your name,
Fer the name of William Leachman and True Manhood's jest the same!

* * * * *

James Whitcomb Riley:

On the Death of Little Mahala Ashcraft

"Little Haly! Little Haly!" cheeps the robin in the tree;
"Little Haly!" sighs the clover, "Little Haly!" moans the bee;
"Little Haly! Little Haly!" calls the killdeer at twilight;
And the katydids and crickets hollers "Haly!" all the night.

The sunflowers and the hollyhawks droops over the garden fence;

The old path down the garden walks still holds her footprints' dents;
And the well-sweep's swingin' bucket seems to wait fer her to come
And start it on its wortery errant down the old beegum.

The beehives all is quiet; and the little Jersey steer,
When any one comes nigh it, acts so lonesome-like and queer;
And the little Banty chickens kindo' cutters faint and low,
Like the hand that now was feedin' 'em was one they didn't know.

They's sorrow in the waivin' leaves of all the apple trees;
And sorrow in the harvest-sheaves, and sorrow in the breeze;
And sorrow in the twitter of the swallers 'round the shed;
And all the song her redbird sings is "Little Haly's dead!"

The medder 'pears to miss her, and the pathway through the grass,
Whare the dewdrops ust to kiss her little bare feet as she passed;
And the old pin in the gate-post seems to kindo'-sorto' doubt
That Haly's little sunburnt hands'll ever pull it out.

Did her father er her mother ever love her more'n me,
Er her sisters er her brother prize her love more tendurly?
I question - and what answer? - only tears, and tears alone,
And ev'ry neghbor's eyes is full o' tear-drops as my own.

"Little Haly! Little Haly!" cheeps the robin in the tree;
"Little Haly!" sighs the clover, "Little Haly!" moans the bee;
"Little Haly! Little Haly!" calls the killdeer at twilight,
And the katydids and crickets hollers "Haly!" all the night.

* * * * *

James Whitcomb Riley:

Away

I can not say, and I will not say
That he is dead. - He is just away!

With a cheery smile, and a wave of the hand,
He has wandered into an unknown land,

And left us dreaming how very fair
It needs must be, since he lingers there.

And you - O you, who the wildest yearn
For the old-time step and the glad return, -

Think of him faring on, as dear
In the love of There as the love of Here;

And loyal still, as he gave the blows
Of his warrior-strength to his country's foes. -

Mild and gentle, as he was brave, -
When the sweetest love of his life he gave

To simple things: - Where the violets grew
Blue as the eyes they were likened to,

The touches of his hands have strayed
As reverently as his lips have prayed:

When the little brown thrush that harshly chirred
Was dear to him as the mocking-bird;

And he pitied as much as a man in pain
A writhing honey-bee wet with rain. -

Think of him still as the same, I say:
He is not dead - he is just away!

* * * * *

James Whitcomb Riley:

The Prayer Perfect

Dear Lord! kind Lord!
Gracious Lord! I pray
Thou wilt look on all I love,
Tenderly to-day!
Weed their hearts of weariness;
Scatter every care
Down a wake of angel-wings
Winnowing the air.

Bring unto the sorrowing
All release from pain;
Let the lips of laughter
Overflow again;
And with all the needy
O divide, I pray,
This vast treasure of content
That is mine to-day!

* * * * *

Dwight Moody:

Faith Not Reason

I heard of some commercial travelers who went to hear a man preach. They came back to the hotel, and were sitting in the smoking-room , and they said the minister did not appeal to their reason, and they would not believe any thing they could not reason out. An old man sitting there listening, said to them, "You say you won't believe any thing you can't reason out?" "No, we won't." The old man said, "As I was coming on the train I noticed some sheep and cattle and swine and geese, eating grass. Now, can you tell me by what process that same grass was turned into feathers, hair, bristles, and wool?" "Well, No. We can't just tell you that." " Do you believe it is a fact?" "Oh, yes, it is a fact." "I thought you said you would not believe any thing you could not reason out?" "Well, we can't help believing that; we see it with our eyes." "Well, " said the old man, "I can't help but believe in regeneration, and a man being converted, although I cannot explain how God converted him."

* * * * *

Dwight Moody:

No Unpardoned Sinner in Heaven

Suppose Queen Victoria did not like any man to be deprived of his liberty, and threw all her prisons open, and was so merciful that she could not bear any one to suffer for guilt, how long would she hold the sceptre? How long would she rule? Not twenty-four hours. Those very men who cry out about God being merciful would say, "We don't want such a queen." Well, God is merciful, but He is not going to take an unpardoned sinner into heaven.

* * * * *

Dwight Moody:

Why the Judge Converted

When I was quite a young man a lady came to me and requested me to talk to her husband. I felt it was no use, for he was a prominent western judge of skeptical sentiments, and more than a match for me in argument. But yielding to her persistent entreaties I proceeded to the judge's office. The old man laughed at me. I succeeded in obtaining from him a promise that when he was converted he would write and let me know. Special prayer was offered for him at the Fulton street prayer meeting and other places. Some time afterward, when I returned to town, I met the judge, who told me of his conversion. One night his wife went to prayer meeting and during her absence he began to think, "Suppose my wife is right; that there is a hell and a heaven, and that my children are going to heaven and I am not." Conviction seized him and he commenced to pray. He retired before his wife returned and pretended to be asleep while she prayed for him. Rising early in the morning he told her he did not feel very well, and without waiting for breakfast, proceeded to his office. He told his clerks they might have a holiday and shutting himself up in the office prayed that God for the sake of the Familyhead would take away the great load of guilt, and soon the burden rolled off. He told his wife that he was a new man and they both kneeled in prayer, thanking God for his great goodness. Upon returning to America I inquired if the judge stood firm. I was informed that he had passed gloriously from earth and was now standing at the right hand of God.

* * * * *

Francis Church:

"Yes, Virginia, There is a Santa Claus"

In the fall of 1897, a little girl of New York City's Upper West Side, Virginia O'Hanlon, wrote a letter to her local newspaper, The New York Sun, to enquire about Santa Claus. The response of the Editor of that newspaper, Francis Pharcellus Church, was printed September 21, 1897.

"We take pleasure in answering at once and thus prominently the communication below expressing at the same time our great gratification that its faithful author is numbered among the friends of The Sun:

Dear Editor:
I am eight years old. Some of my little friends say there is no Santa Claus.
Papa says, "If you see it in The Sun it's so."
Please tell me the truth, is there a Santa Claus?
Virginia O'Hanlon
115 West 95th Street

Virginia, your little friends are wrong. They have been affected by the skepticism of a skeptical age. They do not believe except they see. They think that nothing can be which is not comprehensible by their little minds. All minds, Virginia, whether they be men's or children's, are little. In this great universe of ours humanity is a mere insect, an ant, in intellect, as compared with the boundless world about us, as measured by the intelligence capable of grasping the whole of truth and knowledge.
Yes, Virginia, there is a Santa Claus. He exists as

certainly as love and generosity and devotion exist, and you
know that they abound and give to your life its highest
beauty and joy. Alas, how dreary would be the world if there
were no Santa Claus! It would be as dreary as if there were
no Virginias. There would be no childlike faith then, no
poetry, no romance to make tolerable this existence. We
should have no enjoyment, except in sense and sight. The
eternal light with which childhood fills the world would be
extinguished.

Not believe in Santa Claus! You might as well not
believe in fairies! You might get your papa to hire men to
watch in all the chimneys on Christmas Eve to catch Santa
Claus coming down, but what would that prove? Nobody sees
Santa Claus, but that is no sign that there is no Santa
Claus. The most real things in the world are those that
neither children nor men can see. Did you ever see fairies
dancing on the lawn? Of course not, but that's no proof that
they are not there. Nobody can conceive or imagine all of
the wonders that are unseen and unseeable in the world.

You tear apart a baby's rattle and see what makes the
noise inside, but there is a veil covering the unseen world
which not the strongest man, nor the united strength of all
the strongest men that ever lived, could tear apart. Only
faith, fancy, poetry, love, romance can push aside that
curtain and view and picture the supernal beauty and glory
beyond. Is it all real? Ah, Virginia, in this world there is
nothing else real and abiding.

No Santa Claus! Thank God he lives, and lives forever.
A thousand years from now, Virginia, nay ten times ten
thousand years from now, he will continue to make glad the
heart of childhood."

The little girl Virginia O'Hanlon grew up to live a fine
life. She was educated at Hunter and Columbia Colleges,
married, and devoted her working life to the care of
chronically ill children.

SANTA CLAUS

Santa Claus?
Who is Santa Claus?
He's not just like all the elves makin toys for kids.
He is special.
You wonder what he looks like? Well, he wears a warm red
    coat and stocking cap with a bell on the end that
    jingles out Christmas tunes. He has black boots most
    up to his waist to get around in the snow. He don't
    have time to shave makin toys so much and has a long
    white beard.

You never seen him?

Well, wait up late on Christmas Eve! That's when he comes
down to every house in the world from the North Pole.

I get in practice waitin up for a week or two!

I can't hardly go to bed round then.

Mother gets secrety and dad mumbles about bills.

Grandma sits on her rocker and squeaks and rocks happily.

But me? I am day dreamin.

I think I hear sleigh-bells from reindeer pulling
a sled through the night air bringin my benefactor
from the North Pole down my way.

It's Santa Claus! And when he comes on Christmas Eve you know
it because all the clocks in the house whir and go crazy
because time stands still.

Except while things is suspended, Santa Claus lands his
sleigh on the roof and slips on down the chimney. He
does it putting his finger to the side of his nose.

No one can see him, whether you're awake or asleep.

That's a funny thing because there is a trick where you can
know if he's been there.

Leave him milk and cookies out. The old gentleman can't pass
em by. He don't know he's been tricked into givin
hisself away and provin he's been there. He falls for
that trick every time.

And then after he's got down the chimney and got in your
front room he puts lots of presents for you under the
tree. All this lets you know you've been a good boy or
girl for the year.

The one's not good only get coal
under the tree.

Funny! I never knew a friend who
got coal.

Ralph Waldo Emerson:

Fable

The mountain and the squirrel
Had a quarrel,
And the former called the latter "Little
   Prig."
Bun replied,
"You are doubtless very big.
But all sorts of things and weather
Must be taken in together
To make up a year
And a sphere.

And I think it no disgrace
To occupy my place.
If I'm not so large as you,
You are not as small as I
And not half so spry.
I'll not deny you make
A very pretty squirrel track.
Talents differ. All is well and wisely put.
If I cannot carry forests on my back,
Neither can you crack a nut."

* * * * *

After Albert Schweitzer:

The Answer to a Quest for the Historical Jesus

God's Child comes to us as One unknown without a name.
As of old by the lakeside God's Child comes.
God's Child comes to a humanity not knowing the event.
God's Child speaks to us, repeating the same word, "Follow.
   Follow. Follow me!"
Then God's Child sends us to fulfill the same tasks God's
   Child fulfills for our time.
God's Child demands.
And to those who obey, whether they be wise or simple, God
   reveals God's Child.
The revelation is in the toils, the conflicts, the
   sufferings,
Which they will pass through in the fellowship.
And as an ineffable mystery,
Humanity shall learn.
Yes, humanity shall learn in their own experiences
Who is God's Child.

* * * * *

Anonymous:

Billy The Kid

I'll sing you a true song of Billy the Kid.
I'll sing of the desperate deeds that he did
Way out in New Mexico long, long ago,
When a man's only chance was his own forty-four.

When Billy the kid was a very young lad
In old Silver City he went to the bad.
Way out in the West with a gun in his hand
At the age of twelve years he killed his first man.

Fair Mexican maidens play guitars and sing
A song about Billy, their boy bandit king,
How ere his young manhood had reached its sad end
He'd a notch on his pistol for twenty-one men.

`Twas on the same night when poor Billy died
He said to his friends: "I am not satisfied.
There are twenty-one men I have put bullets through
And Sheriff Pat Garrett must make twenty-two."

Now, this is how Billy the Kid met his fate -
The bright moon was shining, the hour was late.
Shot down by Pat Garrett, who once was his friend,
The young outlaw's life had now come to its end.

There's many a man with a face fine and fair
Who starts out in life with a chance to be square.
But just like poor Billy he wanders astray
And loses his life in the very same way.

* * * * *

John Hatfield:

A Personal Quest for Sanctification

For eight years I battled along against that subtle enemy of the human heart, known as inbred sin. During these years I heard not a word on the possibility of deliverance from this inward foe. One day my pastor, Rev. James Leonard, attended a Holiness camp-meeting at Hartford City, Indiana, conducted by the National Holiness Association, and in this meeting he professed to have obtained the blessing of entire sanctification. When he returned he was not the same preacher, and his sermons were not the same. He had something new, and there was fire in it, and you could feel it burn. His theme was holiness as a second definite cleansing work of God's grace, and it made me feel very uncomfortable to sit there and listen to him. He soon had me on the fence, and he had me guessing, but still I was interested. I knew I needed something, and he seemed to have the thing my poor, hungry heart was craving. At last I became very deeply convicted for it, and told my wife that I was going to have that experience or die seeking it. Immediately I began to seek the blessing, and often in my prayers I would become so fervent and intense that I would receive great spiritual enduements, and at times I often wondered if I had truly been sanctified wholly; but when I came to dealing with things about the farm, I would become impatient and lose my temper, and this was a clear evidence to me that I did not have it. I spent much time in prayer seeking this blessing. In the woods, in the field, at the barn, at family prayer, in church, at Sunday-school, in the class meeting and in prayer-meetings I could pray down fire and wonderful blessings upon my soul, but nothing that would remove inbred sin.

I was walking in all the light I had, I was not under condemnation, but I had an intense hungering and thirsting for a clean heart; yet the secret of how to obtain it had never been revealed to me. I was persistent and held on like a dog at a root, but I would have my spells of fits and starts. I remember once of hearing Bro. C.W. Ruth say, "Forty fits to one start," but that did not apply to me, for I never allowed but one fit until I took a start. I always took my pain-killer (repentance) after I had my fit.

Before I received this "second blessing," one evening my wife and I went out to set a hen; we had to move the hen from her nest to a more desirable location. My wife placed the eggs in the nest while I held the hen, which, when all was ready, I very gently placed upon the eggs, then quietly withdrew my hand and up came the hen. I gently placed her back again, and again she arose, so I put her back again (only not quite so gently as before), and again she arose to her feet. I set her down this time with more authority, and the way I stuck my fingers into her old back and ribs was enough to give her to understand that there was something going to happen, but the end was not yet. By this time my wife was getting a little anxious, for she knew the fellow that was handling the hen. We had already broken some eggs, but the hen still, with all past experiences, refused to set, and I was determined that she should, and so we had it, and before we got through that hen was well-nigh picked, and feathers and broken eggs were the fragments that covered that battlefield; but that poor old hen, where! oh, where! was she? "Ask of the moon." This was very clear that I did not have the second blessing, and I was very much in need of another dose of pain-killer.

At another time my wife and I went out to the barn to teach a young calf to drink out of a bucket. We went into the stall where the young calf was and I caught the calf and was very gentle with it; I put my fingers in its mouth and tried to coax it to put its nose in the bucket, but instead it would stick its nose in the air. With much effort I succeeded in getting its nose in the bucket, and giving it a taste of the milk. this made it frantic, it went wild, it pranced and jumped around, and stood on both hing legs. Presently I began to talk pretty loud to my wife, telling her first to hold the bucket up and then hold it down. At last, every other expedient uinavailing, I leaped a-straddle of that calf, grabbed it by both ears and downed its head in milk up to its eyes. It suddenly gave one big lurch which upset my wife, spilled the milk, threw me over its head, and we all went in one pile together. I never thought to help my wife up, I was busy in helping that calf out of that stall with my foot, threatening to kill it, but it survived the treatment and was ready for its milk at the next meal. This was again very clear that I had not received the second blessing and the calf had gotten the first.

I often said that it took my wife too long to get ready for church on Sunday morning. Invariably I found it necessary to wait for her, until at last, one Sunday morning, while she was pressing me to bring on the buggy that she would be ready to go, I said, "I will have the team here, but if you are not ready when I drive to the door, I will drive off and leave you." and sure enough she still had the old failing; she had to go back in the house after something, but when she came out I was gone, and was soon at the church. I took my usual place in the front seat, and presently my wife came in and took a seat by my side. You would never have known anything had hapened by looking at her, for she was as calm as a May morning and as patient as a jug of molasses under a kitchen table; but to have seen me you would have a different picture. I had a guilty conscience, the sermon didn't do me much good, I was bothered with other reflections.

After the sermon (fortunately the pastor did not call on me to pray), my wife and I got in the buggy and started for home; I felt guilty, mean, little and wretched. I could endure it no longer, so I said, "Amanda, that was a mean trick in me this morning to make you walk to church; I want you to forgive me." She knew my weakness and it was willingly done; she very well knew that I could no more keep the "old man" down than I could keep down a sick stomach. I just felt that for that one act I would like to have her take me in the parlor and pull every hair out of my head, but that would not be like her; she had a different disposition. Her even Christian life was a source of conviction to me for years. I never saw her excited, impatient, scared or lose her temper in all our thirty-eight years of married life, and she did not profess to be sanctified wholly. She possessed the characteristics before she was converted, and I still displayed mine, after I was converted. I needed the second blessing, and that was what I was seeking.

The night before I received this sanctifying work of grace in my heart, while working in a revival in my home church, I received such a wonderful blessing that I ran all about the church shouting and praising the Lord, and yet, when I went to milk my cow, because she did not stand to suite me, we got into a scrap, and I lost my temper, as well as a bucket of milk. I got the milk all over me and the cow got the bucket all over her; the "old man" within, and the devil without; so, as a case of necessity, I was compelled to take another dose of pain-killer, but by the time for the service that night I had gotten relief, and was ready for another meeting. The Lord was good to me, He greatly blessed me in my soul, and gave me great liberty in working in the congregation and leading sinners to the altar to seek the Lord.

I never felt the need of a clean heart, and full deliverance from an evil temper so much in all my life as during this night's service. It was intense. My pastor called on me to lead in prayer. The altar was full of weeping sinners. I began to pray for them, but soon my prayers were turned to praying for myself. How often had I prayed for a clean heart, and how often had I been blessed in praying for it, but the "old man" still remained; but this time, by the aid of the Spirit, I was given the key to the situation. Heretofore I had been praying myself up into blessings without exercising any faith, but when I reached the place where I said, "Lord, I do believe," instantly the fire fell, and I knew the work was done. The "old man" was killed, and I have never seen him since, and that has been more than thirty years ago.

I had passed through six months of desperate struggle amidst many a cheering hope and many a blasting fear, but, thank God! I knew I had the blessing this time. From my knees I looked across at my pastor and said, "Brother, I've got it," and he said, "Got what?" I said, "I have been sanctified wholly." Some of our people in the church were very anxious for me to get the blessing, for they said they were getting tired of hearing me pray for it. No doubt they were, it was putting conviction on them. I did not have it many hours until they were wishing that I had not gotten it.

It was not long until I had a splendid chance to tell whether or not I had the blessing. I considered my cow a bad one to milk, and I suppose the cow considered me a bad one to milk her. It was sometimes hard to tell which was worst, me or the cow, for while the cow threw hoofs and horns and milk and bucket, I was not slow in keeping myself busy playing the milk-stool to her back and my boots to her ribs. Everything went well in the cow stable that morning until the milking was done and I arose to leave the stall; I was so filled with the joy of my experience that I never thought of the cow, but she had not forgotten me, for just as I arose from my milking, evidently fearing that I intended striking her with the stool, she gave a sudden kick which struck the bucket and spilled the milk all over me, but now, instead of jumping at her and trying to pull all the hair out of her back, I stepped to the front of the stall, put my hand gently upon her back and began to make my confession and tell her my experience. I said, "Lill, I have been mean to you; I have kicked you and cuffed you and beat you with milk-stools and buckets; I have pulled hair out of your back, but now I want you to understand I am sanctified; I've got the blessing and the kick is out of me; you can kick if you want to, but I'm done. I love you, Lill; you are a good old cow. It has been my fault, but you will find me a different man from now on, for I am here to tell you that I an sanctified."

The old cow seemed to understand my testimony. I convinced her that there was something in holiness, even though nine-tenths of the preachers in the country considered it fanaticism. At once she relaxed every muscle, put her head in the manger and began to eat, and I walked out a victor over the world, the flesh, the devil, the cow and myslef. I did not need any pain-killer this time; I had taken a dose the night before that had killed the "old man," and that puit an end to the use of pain-killers. Next to the cow, my wife was the first to understand that I had the blessing. When she saw me coming up the path that morning from the barn, my clothes bespattered with milk and my face covered with a smile, this was enough for her, she was satisfied that I had the blessing.

Over thirty years have passed away since that morning and God's grace has kept me through all the trying scenes of a busy life. I have worked balky horses, milked kicking cows, been kicked clear out of the stall, taught calves to drink out of a bucket, set stubborn hens, put up stove pipes, helped my wife clean house, sat in the carriage and waited for her to come and get in, been set down on, criticised by preachers, have faced more than a thousand backslidden holiness fighters, have had unnumbered lies told on me, preached while four and five babies were squalling at their best; but through it all I have been able to maintain my experience, and, to my best knowledge, I have never made a break in all these years. Now, let all the people say, yes, let everybody say, Amen!

* * * * *

After R.J. Cooke,

Jesus as the Answer to the Lowly Origin of Humanity in Evolution

So humanity is simply an evolving life form?

Did humanity simply evolve from ancestral species? Yes, species evolve through natural selection in which the most adaptive survive and the rest are selected out.

Does this define humanity?

No way! Humanity is the form in which God gave God's Child to live. Whatever physical science may have to say as to the lowly origin of humanity, here is the story. God cannot be forced into a life form.

But when God found the need to become manifest in life, God did not despise taking the revealing form and capacity in the human. Nor was the human condition unable to bear the weight, the presence of deity. But because humanity is spirit, because humanity has intelligence, and reason, and will, and affection, because humanity is a moral being, Infinite Spirit, Infinite Wisdom, and Infinite Love can adjust to the spirit of humanity -laying every power and quality of God alongside of every corresponding faculty in the human soul without violence to the soul

- and thus manifest God's very self as God in the flesh. The astounding revelation dawns on us for the first time that the human may embody the eternal.

It is the human being who took the experience of the life of humanity with God's Child and modified Roman law, motivated the struggles for freedom in Western civilization, abolished slavery and championed reforms, built civilization, and organized political and social institutions. It is the human spirit which struggles against wealth and power, enters into conflicts between labor and capital, alignments of class against class, and within each effort reaffirms the infinite worth of humanity.

* * * * *

Anonymous:

Frankie and Johnny

Frankie and Johnny were lovers. Oh lordy how they could love!
Swore to be true to each other, true as the stars above.
    He was her man, but he done her wrong.

Frankie she was his woman, everybody knows.
She spent one hundred dollars for a suit of Johnny's clothes.
    He was her man, but he done her wrong.

Frankie and Johnny went walking, Johnny in his brand new suit.
"Oh good Lord," says Frankie, "but don't my Johnny look cute?"
    He was her man, but he done her wrong.

Frankie went down to Memphis. She went on the evening train.
She paid one hundred dollars for Johnny a watch and chain.
    He was her man, but he done her wrong.

Frankie went down to the corner to buy a glass of beer.
She says to the fat bartender, "Has my loving man been here?
    He was my man, but he done me wrong."

"Ain't goin' to tell you no story. ain't goin' to tell you no lie.
I seen your man 'bout an hour ago with a girl named Nellie Bly.
    If he's you man, he's doin' you wrong."

Frankie went down to the pawnshop. She didn't go there for fun.
She hocked all her jewelry, bought a pearl-handed forty-four gun
    For to get her man who was doing her wrong.

Frankie went down to the hotel, looked in the window so high.
There she saw her lovin' Johnny makin' love to Nellie Bly.
    He was her man, but he was doin' her wrong.

Frankie threw back her kimono, took out that old forty-four.
Root-a-toot-toot three times she shot right through the hotel door.
    She was after her man who was doin' her wrong.

Johnny grabbed off his Stetson, cried, "O Lord, Frankie, don't shoot!"
But Frankie put her finger on the trigger, and the gun went root-a-toot-toot.
   He was her man, but she shot him down.

"Roll me over easy, roll me over slow,
Roll me over easy, boys, `cause my wounds are hurting me so,
   I was her man, but I done her wrong."

"Oh, my baby, kiss me once before I go.
Turn me over on my right side, baby, where de bullet hurts me so.
   I was your man, but I done you wrong."

Frankie went to his coffin, she looked down on his face.
She said, "O Lord, have mercy on me. I wish I could take his place.
   He was my man, and I done him wrong."

Oh, bring on your rubber-tired hearses. Bring on your rubber-tired hacks.
They're takin' Johnny to the cemetery, but they'll never bring him back.
   He was her man, but he done her wrong.

The judge said to the jury, "It's as plain as plain can be.
This woman shot her lover, so it's murder in the second degree.
   He was her man, but he done her wrong."

Now it wasn't murder in the second degree. It wasn't murder in the third.
The woman simply dropped her man like a hunter drops a bird.
   He was her man, but done her wrong.

"Oh. put me in that dungeon. Oh, put me in that cell.
Put me where the northeast wind blows from the southeast corner of hell,
   I shot my man, `cause he done me wrong."

This story's got no moral. This story's got no end.
This story only goes to show that there ain't no good in men.
   He was her man, but he done her wrong.

* * * * *

The Downfall of the Leaders of the Ku Klux Klan

Never before had the demons of this world shown such arrogance or exhibited such raw power. Never before had the demonic world of opposition - an "invisible empire" - become so visible. Never before had humanity permitted the cross of God's Child to be so publicly burned. Such brazenness! The human pawns of the demons took demon names. A Grand Goblin ruled each of the regions of the United States. Exalted Cyclops, Klaliffs, Klokards, Kludds, Kligrapps, Klagaroos, Nighthawks. In the 1920's, America was in the throes of subservience to the forces of self-confessed demons.

Dec. 6, 1915 was the date that William Simmons chartered the Knights of the Ku Klux Klan in Atlanta, Georgia. Simmons was an itinerant preacher who took the name "Colonel." He remembered a shadowy former organization of Southern men with that name briefly existing in the South after the American Civil War and reinvented it. Now for $16.50 any "pure," native-born, white Protestant American citizen over eighteen was eligible to join this order. Part of the dues was for a white robe so that the members could hide their identities from humanity and the eyes of God. By 1924, the Klan had over 4 1/2 million members and spread across country. Politically it came to dominate the governments of Oregon, Oklahoma, Texas, Arkansas, Indiana, Ohio and California to say nothing of the traditional Deep South states. The Klanspeople identified themselves by jumbles of words formed from the first letters of secret sentences. "Ayak," the faithful member would say. (Are you a Klansman?) "Akia," would come the reply. (A Klansman I am.) "Kigy," the Klansman would answer. (Klansman, I greet you.)

Now came dramatic public social occasions. Cars would roar into the towns of America for "klanvocations." The idea was to strike terror into the hearts of minority groups.

Two of the major leaders in the American heartland were D.C. Stephenson (A Grand Goblin) and Daisy Barr (An Imperial Empress). Both attracted huge crowds to Klan gatherings and wielded great power. D.C. Stephenson once announced to 20,000 cheering Klan supporters in Kokomo, Indiana that he had been delayed because "the President of the United States kept me unduly long counseling upon vital matters of state." Daisy Barr, a former Protestant minister, made famous the saying, "If Christ were on earth, he would be a Klansman." At the height of Klan activity, in July 1923, Daisy Barr was on the program at the first annual meeting of the Grand Dragons of the Knights of the Ku Klux Klan in Asheville, North Carolina. There is a record of the poem she composed and read on that occasion called, "The Soul of America."

I quote in part:
"Ready, without fear, I am the Spirit of Righteousness.
They call me the Ku Klux Klan.
I am more than the uncouth robe and hood
With which I am clothed.
YEA, I AM THE SPIRIT OF AMERICA."

The leaders of the Klan publicly portrayed it as a social organization encouraging purity, prohibitionism, and marital and family values with the goal of wiping out liquor consumption and prostitution. Many folk and especially the Protestants who were being recruited and subverted were duped and misled by such claims.

The Klan was not just a social organization. Its members were vigilantes and the Klan drew its power from members who felt its demonic appeal to brutalize neighbors. The Klansmen armed themselves. Laws of the times permitted citizens to legally organize themselves into "Anti-Horsethief Associations" and the Klansmen established themselves as constables to preserve their brand of law and order. They supported "white womanhood" and if a man didn't support his family or was drunk or abusive they would take him out and whip him - things like that. But they also did the same things to terrorize immigrants and Catholics for no reason. The Klansmen bullied and intimidated the homeless ones of the world seeking new homes in America, a shameful thing. They perpetuated a myth that immigrant Catholics were trying to take over the country to install the Pope as worldly head. The idea was drummed in that every time a Catholic boy was born a rifle was buried for him to use when the Pope would make his move on America. On one occasion a "scare" was broadcast that the Pope was traveling through the country incognito on his way to Chicago to announce his takeover of America. In several places, unwarned railroad travelers who perhaps had some resemblance to the Pope were removed from the trains by Klansmen and thrashed.

D.C. Stephenson once said, "I am the law in Indiana." He bragged of engineering the election of Indiana's Governor Ed Jackson and Indianapolis Mayor John Duvall who both were in Stephenson's organization.

With Jesus gone to God's right hand, only the spirit of God's breathing was around to act on behalf of God's people and provide comfort from the demonic onslaught against the vulnerable.

The downfall of the Klan eventually came about by the downfall of its leaders. The demons who had taken charge of them destroyed them and brought people to their senses. Daisy Barr's downfall came from greed. She was born Daisy Douglas Brushwiller near Marion, Indiana, at a small town called Jonesboro in 1878. The Protestant denomination in which she would pastor had been her father's church. She had seven brothers and sisters who all became ministers. She said she was called to the ministry at the age of eight during a visit to the family woodshed for meditation. She is thought to have completed a high school education.

At the age of sixteen while working at a Jonesboro department store she received the further call to become an evangelist. She did so and became a recorded Protestant minister two years later. In 1893, she wed and bore one child.

How did Daisy Barr succeed so well in the Klan movement? She had a great capacity to organize mass meetings and give messages at them. Some assume this came from her experience in her major pastorate which was in a Muncie, Indiana church before her Klan involvement. At Muncie she arranged highly visible political rallies on local issues. One was on the state Proctor Law of 1908 which allowed a special referendum on countywide Prohibition if 20% of the voters signed petitions. She got that county turned "dry" but failed in a subsequent referendum to keep it that way. Here she also led movements to establish a YWCA, to get a woman on the Muncie Police Force, and to set up a "Friendly Inn" where women could go who wished to give up the prostitution then fairly open in Muncie. Many consider her a genuine social reformer for these efforts. She certainly learned how to be an adroit organizer, an eloquent orator, as well as a symbol manipulator. She used similar tactics in her Klan involvement - the torchlight parades, the mass meetings, the coercive rhetoric.

After leaving pastorates that provided little money, Daisy Barr first went on to hold evangelical revivals- reportedly she "healed" a sick person at one of these - and to become the president of the Indiana War Mothers, a group whose sons had served in World War I and to assume the vice- chairmanship of one of the two major political parties. Then the lure of great income drove her to become a leader of the Klan. She was brought into the Klan by D.C. Stephenson. Daisy Barr was not the only Protestant minister brought into the Klan by the Grand Goblin. Stephenson sought out many Protestant ministers to bring into his orbit. The Ku Klux Klan did not attempt to appeal to any particular Protestant church more than others. Nevertheless, nine of the ten Indiana Klan lecturers were introduced as Protestant ministers. It was said that Protestant pulpits supplied the respectability, the orators, and a good part of the local leadership of the Klan.

Daisy Barr entered into a contract with Stephenson whereby she assumed complete control of the "Queens" (the Klan women) and then went on to organize Klan women's groups around the country. Her initial contract gave her $1 for every woman initiated after July 9, 1923 in Indiana, Kentucky, West Virginia, Pennsylvania, Ohio, Michigan, New Jersey, and Minnesota. But the initiation fee wasn't her only reward. She got an extra $4 if she got robe orders for the national headquarters.

Now very successful, Daisy Barr began to become more greedy. She wanted a larger "cut" in the purchase of Klan robes. The sale of these robes was a major source of Klan funds. The Klan agreed to give her a "franchise" to sell the women's robes for $6.50 each. But this wasn't enough for Daisy. She got an Anderson, Indiana company to make the robes for her for 77 cents and pocketed everything else.

As a result, the Klan filed a lawsuit against her in June 1924 saying she owed them thousands and thousands of dollars of "robe money." It was about this time, that Daisy headed for Florida. She had become too greedy and now too wealthy to find safety at home.

As soon as she felt freed from her legal troubles from double-crossing the Klan of robe income, she returned to Indiana and publicly claimed she had made her millions as a relator in Florida during her short stay there. She died on April 3, 1938 of a broken neck suffered in an auto accident on U.S.31 near New Albany.

If greed led to Daisy Barr's downfall, sexual brutality led to her male counterpart's downfall.

D.C. Stephenson was an impassioned orator with a magnetic personality. Something demonic in him enabled him to attract and dominate better men and good women.

His downfall came from brutalizing a young woman. By 1926, Stephenson was one of America's wealthiest men from Klan robe sales. He lived in a huge mansion in Irvington, Indiana and bathed in the power from his Klan involvement. Then in March 1926, he did what he had probably done so many times before. He lured a beautiful young woman to his home.

The woman was Madge Oberholtzer and Stephenson called her on a Sunday evening with a pretext of urgent business related to her keeping her state-funded employment.

When Madge Oberholtzer arrived she was forced to drink three drinks in the kitchen of the Grand Goblin's mansion in Irvington. She realized she was trapped and tried to telephone her mother but was prevented. Madge was forced into an automobile taken to the Hotel Washington. She later said in a dying statement that Stephenson told "Shorty" his chauffeur to "have Claude Worley (an investigator for the Marion County prosecutor's office) to protect them." The father said his daughter told her Stephenson "would shoot her while in the automobile if she made an outcry." She stayed in the automobile while Pullman and railroad tickers were obtained and then was placed aboard the Pullman railroad car, "Herkemer." A porter on the train later testified he heard Madge yelling, "Oh, dear. Put that gun up. I am afraid of it." While on the train, she was victimized in the lower berth of the Pullman car compartment while Stephenson's bodyguard occupied the top berth. During his lovemaking, Stephenson bit into Madge Oberholtzer's left breast causing lacerations. These bitings later became badly infected which developed into blood poisoning as Stephenson's human teeth and mouth bacteria spread to Madge's lungs. She was also heavily bruised by beatings.

The party - including Stephenson, "Shorty" and Madge then left the train at Hammond, IN where they went to the Indiana Hotel. Stephenson registered them as Mr. and Mrs. W.B. Morgan, Franklin, IN and "Shorty" registered under his own name. The three were assigned two rooms. Stephenson took Madge to Room 416. "Shorty" went to another room. After they entered, the girl said Stephenson threw himself across the bed and forced her to lie down with him and then fell asleep. After Stephenson was asleep Madge arose and took a revolver belonging to Stephenson and intended to take his life. Then reflecting on the disgrace this act would bring to her family she changed her mind and decided to shoot herself. She was interrupted and decided to seek other means of taking her life.

Later, while eating the breakfast served in the room, she asked Stephenson for money to buy a hat and went out under "Shorty's" guard to buy the hat and had the aide also take her to a drugstore where she bought poison, bichloride of mercury. She laid out eighteen tablets but took only six before vomiting. She threw the rest of the pills in the toilet and the bottle of them out the window. Then she lay down and passed out. When she awoke she told "Shorty" what she had done. He tried to get her to drink milk but she threw it up. Stephenson called her a "fool" continued drinking and told "Shorty" he was going home.

They drove by auto the 190 miles back to Indianapolis. A doctor later said that failure to get Madge Oberholtzer treatment for the poisoning was a major contribution to her death. In a dying declaration Madge said she had pleaded with Stephenson and Gentry to get her to a doctor but they refused and merely kept drinking.

She was taken to the garage of the Stephenson home on the evening of March 16th and kept there overnight.

Another aide of the Grand Dragon took Madge home on the morning of the 17th, saying Madge had been hurt in an automobile accident. At first she refused to reveal what had happened.

The father said "I encouraged her to make her to think she would get well, but she always said, 'It's no use, Daddy. I'm not going to get well.'" Beatrice Spratley, a nurse, was called and arrived at the Oberholtzer home. Then doctors came to treat her. Madge told the doctor who was called, "She did not expect, or want, to get well -that she wanted to die." She died on April 14th.

A warrant for the Grand Dragon was issued upon the demand of the outraged parents. At the post-mortem, her lungs were found to be abscessed and filled with pus. Her left nipple was almost bitten off with the lacerations obvious as human bitemarks. She was still heavily bruised.

When an officer went to arrest Stephenson for murder Stephenson came to the door but misidentified himself as "Mr. Stephenson's secretary." He was recognized however and jailed.

At his trial for her murder, Stephenson claimed Madge died of suicide. The medical doctors however contradicted this. They said that poison causes the kidneys to fail to function and this occurs within 5 to 12 days. Since Madge survived for 23 days, the doctors believed her kidneys were recovering from the poisoning and they concluded her death was from a complication of the poisoning, the inability to withstand the infection from the human teeth bites, rather than the poisoning itself.

Much to Stephenson's surprise, a Noblesville, Indiana, jury found the man who once called himself "the law" guilty and he was sentenced to life imprisonment. Stephenson died June 28, 1966 having spent his days in prison.

Being a member of the Klan lost its appeal after people realized its leaders harbored demons.

* * * * *

A Universal Declaration of Human Rights and the Woman Who Nurtured It.

Preamble

Whereas recognition of the inherent dignity and of the equal and inalienable rights of all members of the human family is the foundation of freedom, justice and peace in the world,

Whereas disregard and contempt for human rights have resulted in barbarous acts which have outraged the conscience of mankind, and the advent of a world in which human beings shall enjoy freedom of speech and belief and freedom from fear and want has been proclaimed as the highest aspiration of the common people,

Whereas it is essential, if man is not to be compelled to have recourse, as a last resort, to rebellion against tyranny and oppression, that human rights should be protected by the rule of law,

Whereas it is essential to promote the development of friendly relations between nations,

Whereas the peoples of the United Nations have in the Charter reaffirmed their faith in fundamental human rights, in the dignity and worth of the human person and in the equal rights of me and women and have determined to promote social progress and better standards of life in larger freedom,

Whereas Member States have pledged themselves to achieve, in co-operation with the United Nations, the promotion of universal respect for and observance of human rights and fundamental freedoms,

Whereas a common understanding of these rights and freedoms is of the greatest importance for the full realization of this pledge,

Now, therefore, THE GENERAL ASSEMBLY proclaims

This Universal Declaration of Human Rights as a common standard of achievement for all peoples and all nations, to the end that every individual and every organ of society, keeping this Declaration constantly in mind, shall strive by teaching and education to promote respect for these rights and freedoms and by progressive measures, national and international, to secure their universal and effective recognition and observance, both among the peoples of Member States themselves and among the peoples of territories under their jurisdiction.

Article 1

All human beings are born free and equal in dignity and rights. They are endowed with reason and conscience and should act towards one another in a spirit of brotherhood.

Article 2

Everyone is entitled to all the rights and freedoms set forth in this Declaration, without distinction of any kind, such as race, color, sex, language, religion, political or other opinion, national or social origin, property, birth or other status.

Furthermore, no distinction shall be made on the basis of the political, jurisdictional or international status of the country or territory to which a person belongs, whether it be independent, trust, non-self- governing, or under any other limitation of sovereignty.

Article 3

Everyone has the right to life, liberty and security of person.

Article 4

No one shall be held in slavery or servitude; slavery and the slave trade shall be prohibited in all their forms.

Article 5

No one shall be subjected to torture or to cruel, inhuman or degrading treatment or punishment.

Article 6

Everyone has the right to recognition everywhere as a person before the law.

Article 7

All are equal before the law and are entitled without any discrimination to equal protection of the law. All are entitled to equal protection against any discrimination in violation of this Declaration and against any enticement to such discrimination.

Article 8

Everyone has the right to an effective remedy by the competent national tribunals for acts violating the fundamental rights granted him by the constitution or by law.

Article 9

No one shall be subjected to arbitrary arrest, detention or exile.

Article 10

Everyone is entitled in full equality to a fair and public hearing by an independent and impartial tribunal, in the determination of his rights and obligations and of any criminal charge against him.

Article 11

1. Everyone charged with a penal offence has the right to be presumed innocent until proved guilty according to law in a public trial at which he has had all the guarantees necessary for his defense.

2. No one shall beheld guilty of any penal offence on account of any act or omission which did not constitute q penal offence, under national or international law, at the time when it was committed. Nor shall a heavier penalty by imposed than the one that was applicable at the time the penal offence was committed.

Article 12

No one shall be subjected to arbitrary interference with his privacy, family, home or correspondence, nor to attacks upon his honor and reputation. Everyone has the right to the protection of the law against such interference or attacks.

Article 13

1. Everyone has the right to freedom of movement and residence within the borders of each state.

2. Everyone has the right to leave any country, including his own, and to return to his country.

Article 14

1. Everyone has the right to seek and to enjoy in other countries asylum from persecution.

2. This right may not be invoked in the case of prosecutions genuinely arising from non-political crimes or from acts contrary to the purposes and principles of the United Nations.

Article 15

1. Everyone has the right to a nationality.

2. No one shall be arbitrarily deprived of his nationality nor denied the right to change his nationality.

Article 16

1. Men and women of full age, without any limitation due to race, nationality or religion have the right to marry and to found a family. They are entitled to equal rights as to marriage, during marriage and at its dissolution.

2. Marriage shall be entered into only with the free and full consent of the intending spouses.

3. The family is the natural and fundamental group unit of society and is entitled to protection by society and the State.

Article 17

1. Everyone has the right to own property alone as well as in association with others.

2. No one shall be arbitrarily deprived of his property.

Article 18

Everyone has the right to freedom of thought, conscience and religion; this right includes freedom to change his religion or belief, and freedom, either alone or in community with others and in public or private, to manifest his religion or belief in teaching, practice, worship and observance.

Article 19

Everyone has the right to freedom of opinion and expression; this right includes freedom to hold opinions without interference and to seek, receive and impart information and ideas through any media and regardless of frontiers.

Article 20

1. Everyone has the right to freedom of peaceful assembly and association.

2. No one may be compelled to belong to an association.

Article 21

1. Everyone has the right to take part in the government of his country, directly or through freely chosen representatives.

2. Everyone has the right of equal access to public service in his country.

3. The will of the people shall be the basis of the authority of government; this will shall be expressed in periodic and genuine elections which shall be by universal and equal suffrage and shall be held by secret vote or by equivalent free voting procedures.

Article 22

Everyone, as a member of society, has the right to social security and is entitled to realization, through national effort and international co-operation and in accordance with the organization and resources of each State, of the economic, social and cultural rights indispensable for his dignity and the free development of his personality.

Article 23

1. Everyone has the right to work, to free choice of employment, to just and favorable conditions of work and to protection against unemployment.

2. Everyone, without any discrimination, has the right to equal pay for equal work.

3. Everyone who works has the right to just and favorable remuneration ensuring for himself and his family an existence worthy of human dignity, and supplemented, if necessary, by other means of social protection.

4. Everyone has the right to form and to join trade unions for the protection of his interests.

Article 24

Everyone has the right to rest and leisure, including reasonable limitation of working hours and periodic holidays with pay.

Article 25

1. Everyone has the right to a standard of living adequate for the health and well-being of himself and of his family, including food, clothing, housing and medical care and necessary social services, and the right to security in the event of unemployment, sickness, disability, widowhood, old age or other lack of livelihood in circumstances beyond his control.

2. Motherhood and childhood are entitled to special care and assistance. All children, whether born in or out of wedlock, shall enjoy the same social protection.

Article 26

1. Everyone has the right to education. Education shall be free, at least in the elementary and fundamental stages. Elementary education shall be compulsory. Technical and professional education shall be made generally available and higher education shall be equally accessible to all on the basis of merit.

2. Education shall be directed to the full development of the human personality and to the strengthening of respect for human rights and fundamental freedoms. It shall promote understanding, tolerance, and friendship among all nations, racial or religious groups, and shall further the activities of the United Nations for the maintenance of peace.

3. Parents have a prior right to choose the kind of education that shall be given to their children.

Article 27

1. Everyone has the right freely to participate in the cultural life of the community, to enjoy the arts and to share in scientific advancement and its benefits.

2. Everyone has the right to the protection of the moral and material interests resulting from any scientific, literary or artistic production of which he is the author.

Article 28

Everyone is entitled to a social and internal order in which the rights and freedoms set forth in this Declaration can be fully realized.

Article 29

1. Everyone has duties to the community in which alone the free and full development of his personality is possible.

2. In the exercise of his rights and freedoms, everyone shall be subject only to such limitations as are determined by law solely for the purpose of security due recognition and respect for the rights and freedoms of others and meeting the just requirements of morality, public order and the general welfare in a democratic society.

3. These rights and freedoms may in no case be exercised contrary to the purposes and principles of the United Nations.

Article 30

Nothing in this Declaration may be interpreted as implying for any State, group or person any right to engage in any activity or to perform any act aimed at the destruction of any of the rights and freedoms set forth herein.

Eleanor Roosevelt, the woman who presided over the commission that drafted the Universal Declaration of Human Rights, was not always a public figure. She was thought not pretty as a child nor likely to succeed even to find a husband. Nevertheless Eleanor Roosevelt did marry and the man she married, Franklin Delano Roosevelt, would one day become President of the United States and a great leader of the American nation at the time of its worst economic depression and then fierce war with Germany.

From a rejected spouse, Eleanor Roosevelt blossomed as a public figure. At her death she was writing a daily newspaper column carried in newspapers

---

POEMS ARE TREASURES
Straight from God's Storehouse
of Inspiration

The riches of God are sound and sight:
A fall of snow on a windless night.

The lift and start of
The shy new leaves

The starry dark and the sunny noon;
And blown white buds in the fields of June.

And children's laughter and lovers' dreams;
And cool green shadows on quiet streams.

The riches of God are manifold,
Exceeding silver, surpassing gold;

And all may take from the endless store,
Since no man lives who is really poor.

Whoever has loved or laughed or sung,
Been gay or lovely, or brave or young,

Or walked with the
With the light of th

Whoever has seen with
The new day break in

Or scattered seed on the fragrant sod,
Has had a share in the wealth of God.

(The Riches of God, by R. H. Grenville)

---

around the world, presented fifty lectures a year, 50,000 traveling miles and when she would become America's United Nation's Representative, she did not miss a single session.

Eleanor's journey to confidence and mission took her from a mere fixture of the Presidency to a position as one of the most influential women of her time. She began traveling. Her travels took her to coal mines in Appalachia or mountains of Tennessee. She saw the plight of blacks and and poor. She insisted that her husband listen to her reports about federal projects or human conditions. Her voice became powerful. After the start of World War II, Eleanor was constantly visiting the troops in the fields and those in the hospitals. It was said, "Eleanor Roosevelt cares first and always for people...her interest is human beings, her hobby is human beings, her pre-occupation is human beings and her every thought is for human beings. As every single thing she devotes herself to has to do with human beings of one sort or another, the basis of all her strength is in her profound interest in them and her readiness to share with them the agony of experience and fulfillment of destiny."

After the death of her husband, the new President, Harry Truman, asked Eleanor to be the United States Representative to the United Nations. Her initial success in this role is the Declaration of Human Rights, a cornerstone expression of the aspirations of people everywhere, and the source of the language of many new nation's constitutions, including those of India and Indonesia and language in federal court cases on due process in American courts to this day.

The unlikely product of Eleanor Roosevelt's mediation turned out to be what the world's most extensive war, World War II, had been all about.

* * * * *

Sermon by Billy Sunday:

Heaven

This sermon was delivered countless times in American cities and towns at revivals from the 1910's until Sunday died in 1935.

Everybody wants to go to Heaven.

We are all curious.

We want to know:

Where heaven is,

How it looks,

Who are there,

What they wear,

And how to get there.

Some say:

Heaven is a state or a condition. You are wrong.

Your home is not a state or a condition. It is a place.

The penitentiary is not a state or a condition. It is a place.

Jesus said:

"I go to prepare a place for you that where I am ye may be also."

The only source of information we have about Heaven is the Bible.

It tells us:

That God's throne is in the heavens and that the earth is God's footstool. And if our spiritual visions are not blinded we believe it is true.

Enoch walked with God and was not - for God took him to Heaven. He left this earth at the behest of God and went to Heaven where God has a dwelling place.

Elijah, when his mission on earth was finished, in the providence of God, was wafted to Heaven in a chariot of fire. The former pupils went out to search for the translated Prophet but they did not find him.

But it was the privilege of Peter, James, and John on the Mount of Transfiguration with Jesus to see the gates of Heaven open and two spirits jump down on the earth whom they recognized as Moses and Elijah who so many years before had walked through Palestine and warned the people of their sins and he slew 450 of the false prophets of Baal.

When Jesus began His public ministry we are told the heavens opened and God stopped making worlds and said from Heaven:

"This is My beloved Child. Hear ye Him."

Then Stephen, with his face lit up with the glories of the Celestial Kingdom as he looked steadfastly toward Heaven, saw it open. And Jesus Himself was standing at the right hand of God, the place He had designated before His Crucifixion and Resurrection would be His abiding place until the time of the Gentiles would be fulfilled, when He would leave Heaven with a shout of triumph and return to this earth in the clouds of Heaven.

Among the last declarations of Jesus, in which we all find so much comfort in the hour of bereavement, is:

"In My Parent's house are many mansions: if it were not so I would have told you."

When Heaven's music burst upon human ears that first Christmas morning while the shepherds guarded their flocks on the moonlit hills of Judea, as the angels sang:

"Peace on earth, good will to humanity, for unto you is born this day in the City of David a Savior Who is Christ the Lord."

We have ample proof that Heaven is a real place.

"When you have been there
    Ten thousand years - bright shining like the sun -
    You'll have no less days,
    To sing God's praise,
    Than when you first begun."

Oh, what a place Heaven is - the Tuileries of the French, the Windsor Castle of the English, the Alhambra of the Spanish, the Schonbrunn of the Austrians, the White House of the United States - these are all dungeons compared with Heaven.

There are mansions there for all the redeemed - one for the martyrs with blood-red robes; one for you ransomed from sin; one for me plucked like a brand from the fire.

Look and see - who are climbing the golden stairs, who are walking the golden streets, who are looking out of the windows?

Some whom we knew and loved here on earth.

Yes, I know them.

My father and mother, blithe and young as they were on their wedding day.

Our son and our daughter, sweet as they were when they cuddled down to sleep in our arms.

My brother and sister, merrier than when we romped and roamed the fields and plucked wild flowers and listened to the whippoorwill as he sang his lonesome song away over in Sleepy Hollow on the old farm in Iowa where we were born and reared.

Cough, gone - cancer, gone - consumption, gone - erysipelas, gone - blindness, gone - rheumatism, gone - lameness, gone - asthma, gone - tears, gone - groans, sighs, gone - sleepless nights, gone.

I think it will take some of us a long time to get used to Heaven.

Fruits without one speck upon them.

Pastures without one thistle or weed.

Orchestra without one discord.

Violin without a broken string.

Harps all in tune.

The river without a torn or overflowed bank.

The sunrise and sunset swallowed up in Eternal Day.

"For there shall be no night there."

Heaven will be free from all that curses us here.

No sin - no sorrow - no poverty - no sickness - no pain - no want - no aching heads or hearts - no war - no death.

No watching the undertaker screw the coffin-lid over our loved ones.

When I reach Heaven I won't stop to look for Abraham, Isaac, Jacob, Moses, Joseph, David, Daniel, Peter or Paul.

"I will rush past them all saying, "Where is Jesus? I want to see Jesus who saved my soul one dark stormy night in Chicago in 1887."

If we could get a real appreciation of what Heaven is we would all be so homesick for Heaven the devil wouldn't have a friend left on earth.

The Bible's description of Heaven is: the length and the breadth and the height of it are equal.

I sat down and took 12 inches for a foot, our standard. That would make it two thousand five hundred miles long, tow thousand five hundred miles wide, two thousand five hundred miles high. Made of pure fold like glass. Twelve gates, each gate made of one pearl. The foundations are of precious stones. Imagine eight thousand miles of diamonds, rubies, sapphires, emeralds, topaz, amethysts, jade, garnets.

Some one may say:

"Well, that will be pleasant, if true."

Another says:

"I hope it's true";

"Perhaps, it's true;

"I wish it were true."

It is true!

The kiss of reunion at the gate of Heaven is as certain as the goodbye kiss when you drift out with the tide.

"God holds the key
Of all unknown,
And I am glad.
If other hands should hold the key,
Or if God trusted it to me,
I might be sad."

Death is a cruel enemy. He robs the mother of her baby, the wife of her husband, the parents of their children, the lover of his intended wife. He robs the lodge of its members, the Nation of its President.

Death is a rude enemy. He upsets our best plans without an apology. He enters the most exclusive circles without an invitation.

Death is an international enemy. There is no nation which he does not visit. The islands of the seas where the black skinned mothers rock their babies to sleep to the lullaby of the ocean's waves. The restless sea. The majestic mountains. All are his haunts.

Death is an untiring enemy. He continues his ghastly work Spring, Summer, Autumn and Winter. He never tires in his ceaseless rounds, gathering his spoils of human souls.

But Death is a vanquished enemy. Jesus arose from the dead and abolished death although we may be called upon to die.

Death to the Christian is swinging open the door through which he passes into Heaven.

"Aren't you afraid?" said the wife to a dying miner.

"Afraid, Lassie. Why should I be? I know Jesus and Jesus knows me."

This house in which we live, "our body," is beginning to lean. The windows rattle. The glass is dim. The shingles are falling off.

> You will reach the river's brink
> Some sweet day, bye and bye.
> You will clasp your broken link
> Some sweet day, bye and bye.
>
> There's a glorious kingdom waiting
> In the land beyond the sky,
> Where the Saints have been gathering
> Year by year.
>
> And the days are swiftly passing
> That shall bring the kingdom night,
> For the coming of the Lord
> Draweth near.

Thank God for the rainbow of hope that bends above the graves of our loved one.

> We stand on the other side and rejoice as they come
> On the Resurrection morning
> Soul and body meet again.
> No more sorrow, no more weeping,
> No more pain.
>
> Soul and body reunited.
> Thenceforth nothing can divide.
> Waking up in Christ's own likeness

Satisfied!
On that happy Easter morning,
All the graves their dead restore.
Father, sister, child and mother
Meet once more.

To that brightest of all meetings
Brings us Jesus Christ, at last,
By the cross through death and judgment,
Holding fast.

The Bible indicates that angels know each other. If they have the power to recognize each other, won't we?

The Bible describes Heaven as a great home circle. It would be a queer home circle if we did not know each other.

The Bible describes death as a sleep. Well, we know each here before we go to sleep and we know each other when we wake up. Do you imagine we will be bigger fools in Heaven than we are here on earth?

A woman lay dying. She had closed her eyes. Her sister, thinking her dead, commenced the wait of mourning. The dying woman raised her hand and said:

"Hush! Hush! I am listening to the breezes waving the branches in the trees of life."

You will be through with your back-biting enemies. They will call you vile names no more. They will no longer misrepresent your good deeds.

Broken hearts will be bound up. Wounds will be healed. Sorrows ended.

The comfort of God is greater than the sorrows of men. I've thanked God a thousand times for the roses but never for the thorns, but now I have learned to thank God for the thorns.

You will never be sick again. Never be tired again. Never weep again.

What's the use of fretting when we are on our way to such a coronation?

You must know the password if you ever enter Heaven, Jesus said,

"I am the Way, the truth and the Life. No man cometh unto the Father but by Me."

Here comes a crowd.

They cry:

"Let me in. I was very useful on earth. I built churches. I endowed colleges. I was famous for my charities. I have done many wonderful things."

"I never knew you."

Another crowd shouts:

"We were highly honored on earth. The world bowed very low before us. Now we have come to get our honors in Heaven."

"We never knew you."

Another crowd shouts:

"We were very moral. We never lied, swore or got drunk."

"We never knew you."

Another crowd approaches and says:

"We were sinners, wanderers from God. We have come up, not because we deserve Heaven, but because we heard of the saving power of Jesus, and we have accepted the Child as our Savior."

They all cry, "Jesus, Jesus. You Child of God, open to us."

They all pass through the pearly gates.

One step this side and you are paupers for eternity. One step on the other side and you are kings and queens for eternity.

When I think of Heaven and my entering it I feel awkward.

Sometimes when I have been exposed to the weather, shoes covered with mud, coat wet and soiled with mud and rain, hair disheveled, I feel I am not fit to go in and sit among the well dressed guests.

So I feel that way about Heaven. I need to be washed in the blood of the Lamb and clothed in the robe of Christ's righteousness. I need the pardoning waves of God's mercy to roll over my soul. And thank God, they have.

If you go first will you come down half way and meet me between the willow banks of earth and the palm groves of Heaven? You who have loved ones in Heaven, will you take a pledge with me to meet them when the day dawns and the shadows flee away?

Some who read this are sadly marching into the face of the setting sun. You are sitting by the window of your soul looking out toward the twilight of life's purple glow. You are listening to the music of the breaking waves of life's ebbing tide and longing for the sight of faces and the sound of voices loved and lost a while.

But if you are true to God and have accepted Jesus as your Savior at last you will hail the coming morning radiant and glorious when the waves of the sea will become crystal chords in the grand organ of Eternity.

A saint lay dying. She said:

"My faith is being tried. The brightness of which you speak I do not have. But I have accepted Jesus as my Savior and if God wishes to put me to sleep in the dark God's will be done."

Sorrow sometimes plays strange dirges on the heartstrings of life before they break but the music always has a message of hope.

Should You Go First
Should you go first, and I remain
To walk the road alone,
I'll live in memory's garden, dear,
With happy days we've known.

In Spring I'll watch for roses red,
When fade the lilacs blue;
In early Fall, when brown leaves fall,
I'll catch a breath of you.

Should you go first, and I remain
For battles to be fought,
Each think you've touched along the way
Will be a hallowed spot.

I'll hear your voice, I'll see you smile,
Though blindly I may grope;
The memory of your helping hand
Will buoy me on with hope.

Should you go first, and I remain
To finish with the scroll,
No length'ning shadows shall creep in
To make this life seem droll.

We've known so much of happiness,
We've had our cup of joy;
Ah, memory is one gift of God
That death cannot destroy.

Should you go first, and I remain,
One thing I'd have you do;
Walk slowly down the path of death,
For soon I'll follow you.

I'll want to know each step you take,
That I may walk the same;
For some day - down that lonely road -
You'll hear me call your name.

A.K. Rowswell (Rosey)

One day when the children were young I was romping and playing with them and I grew tired and lay down to rest. Half asleep and half awake I dreamed I journeyed to a far-off land.

It was not Persia, although the Oriental beauty and splendor were there.

It was not India, although the coral strands were there.

It was not Ceylon, although the beauty and spicy perfume of that famous island paradise were there.

It was not Italy, although the dreamy haze of the blue Italian sky beat above me.

It was not California nor Florida, although the soft flower-ladened breezes of the Pacific and the Atlantic were there.

I looked for weeds, briars, thorns and thistles, but I found none.

I saw the sun in all his meridian glory. I asked
"When will the sun set and it grow dark?"
They said:

"Oh, it never grows dark in this land. There is no night here. Jesus is the light."

I saw the people all clothed in holiday attired with faces wreathed in smiles and halos of glory about their heads.

I asked:

"When will the working men go by with calloused hands and empty dinner buckets and faces grimed with dust and toil?"

They said:

"Oh, we toil not, neither do we sow nor reap in this land."

I strolled out into the suburbs and the hills which would be a fit resting place for the dead to sleep. I looked for monuments, mausoleums, marble slabs, tombs and graves, but I saw none. I did see towers, spires and minarets.

I asked:

"Where do you bury the dead of this great city? Where are the grave-diggers? Where are the hearses that haul the dead to their graves?"

They said:

" Oh, we are never sick. None ever die in this land."

I asked:

"Where do the poor people live? Where are the homes of penury and want?"

They said:

"Oh, there are no poor in this land. There is no want here. None are e3ver hungry here."

I was puzzled.

I looked and saw a river. Its waves were breaking against golden and jewel strewn beaches.

I saw ships with sails of pure silk, bows covered with gold, oars tipped with silver.

I looked and saw a great multitude no man could number, rushing out of jungles of roses, down banks of violets, redolent of eternal Spring, pulsing with bird song and the voices of angels.

I realized Time had ended and Eternity had dawned.

I cried:

"Are all here?"

They echoed:

"Yes, all here."

And tower and spire and minaret all caroled my welcome home. And we all went leaping and singing and shouting the eternal praises of

God the Parent,

God the Child

God the Holy Spirit.

Home, home, at last!

Here's to you, my friends.

May you live a hundred years,

Just to help us

Through this vail of tears

May I live a hundred years

Short just one day,
Because I don't want to be here
After all my friends have gone away.

* * * * *

Anonymous

John Henry

When John Henry was nothin' but a baby
  Sitting on his mammy's knee,
He said, "De Big Bend tunnel on de C. & O.
  road
  Is gonna cause de death of me."

Da cap'n said to John Henry,
  "Gonna bring me a stream drill aroun'.
Gonna take dat stream drill out to de tunnel
  An' gonna mow de mountain down."

John Henry tol' his cap'n
  A man ain't nothin' but a man.
But befor' he'd let dat steam drill beat him
  He'd die wid a hammer in his han'.

John Henry said to his cap'n,
  Lightnin' was in his eye
Wid my twelve-poun' hammer an' a four-foot
  handle
  I'll beat dat steam drill or die."

John Henry went to de tunnel.
  Dey put him in de lead to drive.
De rock so tall an' John Henry so small
  He put down the hammer an' he cried.

John Henry started on de right side,
  Steam drill started on de lef.
"Befo' I'd let dat steam drill beat me down
  I'll hammer my fool self to death."
Steam drill started workin',
  Was workin' mighty fine.
John Henry drove his fifteen feet,
  An' de steam drill only made nine.

Cap'n said to John Henry.
  "I b'lieve de mountain's sinkin' in"
John Henry said to his cap'n,
  "It's just my hammer suckin' win'."

De hammer dat John Henry swung
  Weighed over thirteen poun'.
He broke a rib in his lef han' side
  An' his intrails fell on de groun'.

John Henry had a li'l woman,
  Her name was Polly Ann.
On de day dat John Henry drop down dead,
  Polly Ann hammered steel like a man.

Dey took his body to Washin'ton.
  Dey carried it over the lan'.
People f'om de Eas' and people f'om de Wes'
  Dey mourned for dat steel-drivin' man.

Sam Walter Foss:

The House by the Side of the Road

There are hermit souls that live withdrawn
In the peace of their self-content.
There are souls, like stars, that dwell apart,
In a fellowless firmament.
There are pioneer souls that blaze their paths
Where highways never ran.
But let me live by the side of the road
And be a friend to man.

Let me live in a house by the side of the road
Where the race of men go by.
The men who are good and the men who are bad
As good and as bad as I.
I would not sit in the scorners seat
Or hurl the cynic's ban.
Let me live in a house by the side of the road
And be a friend to man.

I see from my house by the side of the road
By the side of the highway of life
The men who press with the ardor of hope
The men who faint with the strife.
But I turn not from their smiles nor their tears
Both parts of an infinite plan.
Let me live in my house by the side of the road
And be a friend to man.

I know there are brook-gladdened meadows ahead
And mountains of wearisome height
That the road passes on through the long afternoon
And stretches away to the night.
But still I rejoice when the travelers rejoice,
And weep with the strangers who moan,
Nor live in my house by the side of the road
Like a man who dwells alone.

Let me live in my house by the side of the road
Where the race of men go by.
They are good. They are bad. They are weak. They are strong,
Wise, foolish - so am I.
Then why should I sit in the scorner's seat,
Or hurl the cynic's ban?
Let me live in my house by the side of the road
And be a friend to man.

* * * * *

Chemical Grace

The prominence of humanity on the earth over other life forms was not always certain. Since antiquity, humanity has been subject to predation by other evolutionary life forms. Persons have died of famine and disease carried by insects, fleas and vermin. The "Black death" of the Middle Ages wiped out nearly a third of the human population of Europe through infection by the flea-borne bubonic plague. Whole continents and especially their tropical areas were once largely uninhabited because of such diseases as malaria, yellow fever and sleeping sickness.

Humanity has taken to the sciences to preserve itself. One example is the discovery of the chemistry of DDT (dichlorodiphenyltrichloroethane) in 1939. Production of the chemical followed. This chemical is extremely toxic to insects but its toxicity to mammals is very low. An ounce of DDT is required to kill a person, but that same amount can protect an acre of land against locusts or mosquitos. It is estimated that DDT saved over 100 million human lives by controlling mosquito-borne and flea-borne diseases and by protecting food crops until 1972 when it was banned by the U.S. Environmental Protection Agency as an agricultural insecticide and other chlorinated insecticides replaced it. Large parts of the earth are now populated safely without insect-borne disease or fears of starvation because of chemical grace.

* * * * *

After Paul Tillich:

The Protestant Principle

There is this principle among the churches that is the essence of Protestantism. It is based on the concept that the love of Jesus is not identical with human realization. The love of Jesus is a living, moving, restless power in humanity that always protests and engages against any absolute claim made by any relative principle. It demands that what is human be considered conditional and conditioned on God's desires for humanity. It is a matter of faith that recognizes that hu-

manity is grasped by the power of the love of Jesus which judges our existence. It teaches all of the creaturely existence of humanity is finitudinal and fleeting. The cleavage between God's Homeland and ours is a cleavage beyond human achievement to breach. God storms the breach for us.

The situation of humanity often seems to escape the care of the churches. Sometimes it may seem that the churches of Jesus in this world are tied in with the status quo whatever that may be in many parts of the world. This leads to great violence against Jesus. Tying the message of Jesus to any religious or secular establishment never seems to help humanity. The Protestant principle challenges all such attempts. A revolution in Russia was necessary to free its churches of their allegiance to a corrupt class governmental system. America has consistently held to the view in its Constitution that church and state must be separated. The church of Jesus must dialogue with the world of humanity and yet protest its value system or social, secular religious or governmental agendas even if they are posed as divinely ordained.

This does not mean that the Protestant principle rejects human need. Those who value the teachings and spirit of Jesus, the Familyhead of humanity, must be concerned about the lives of people. The German churches did not engage the ideas of Adolph Hitler and a great World War became necessary in the order of things for God's justice to restore us.

The Protestant principle stands for this idea: the churches of Jesus must transcend their own religious and confessional characters so as not to identify Jesus with any one of humanity's conceptions of anything less ultimate than God and God's demands. The Protestant principle upholds the view that being wealthy or a member of a favored class or being a confessing member of one faith is no proof of God's favor. Nor is anything else. The Protestant principle stands for the need to express the concerns of Jesus in every situation for those who are needy, unemployed, incarcerated, homeless, mentally ill, the discriminated against, every minority, every class, every individual, all life.

The Protestant principle is a protest in our souls whenever any religious or cultural entity makes an ultimate claim on human allegiance or loyalty. It is a prophetic judgment against religious pride, ecclesiastical arrogance, and secular self-sufficiency. It is the principle that the human condition is estranged from God and yet endowed with the power of soul to contradict the human bondage. It attacks every attitude to enslave people to ideologies or views of a humanity-made God. It warns us of political lies and social falsifications. It denies any attempt to pervert the character of the human situation.

The Protestant principle is also an idea of anticipation and providence. It anticipates that God's Homeland is at hand and that humanity has access to the infinite as well as the finite and must engage both through ecstatic faith. Faith requires us to protest any human reliance upon the claim of any person that something finite is more important that the infinite. At the same time, providence requires us to understand the existential self-contradiction about life. Humanity both transcends its own forms of life and yet engages the life that God gives human freedom to achieve.

232 # AMERICAN FOLK GOSPEL

* * * * *

A Little Girl Hides from Madness

A little girl beloved of God's Child only thirteen years old wrote in her diary Monday the 6th of July, 1942. "Dear Diary, since you and I are going to be great friends, I will start by telling you about myself. My name is Anne Frank. I was born in Germany the 12th of June, 1929. As my family is Jewish, we emigrated to Holland when Hitler came to power. My father started a business, importing spice and herbs. Things went well for us until 1940. Then the war came and the Dutch capitulation followed by the arrival of the Germans. Then things got very bad for the Jews. You could not do this and you could not do that. They forced Father out of his business. We had to wear yellow stars. I had to turn in my bike. I couldn't go to a Dutch school any more. I couldn't go to the movies, or ride in an automobile, or even on a streetcar and a million other things. But somehow we children still managed to have fun. Yesterday Father told me we were going into hiding. Where, he wouldn't say. At five o'clock this morning Mother woke me and told me to hurry and get dressed. I was to put on as many clothes as I could. It would look too suspicious if we walked along carrying suitcases. It wasn't until we were on our way that I learned where we were going. Our hiding place was to be upstairs in the building where Father used to have his business..."

And so the little girl went into hiding from a German leader's, Adolph Hitler's, madness. Humanity was forced to experience a German regime's desire to purify the genes of its citizenry. Nazi Germany began this fastidiously destructive process in 1933 when the leadership of Adolph Hitler began to mobilize the members of an entire society to destroy their neighbors. The process was new and subtle. A legal system was its key player. With people as the targets of its racism, the German people turned themselves into a criminal organization. Essentially good people were oblivious to the horrors they caused.

The outline of the holocaust was a "process" wielded by the legal arm of anti-Jewish legislation. Legislation began this "process" by singling out people for destruction, the Jews. After the group of Jews was identified legally, the process of ostracism began in community life. These were such things as boycotts, revocations of legal rights, job discriminations, and forced labor for the "right" or community purposes. Then a program of property confiscations was put in place. The "process" of destroying the race then resulted in a process of concentrating the members of the race to be destroyed into certain geographical locations. Only then did annihilation begin. The process of annihilation was two-pronged. Not only were deaths inflicted, but also births were prevented through marriage and birth regulations, contraception, sterilization and physical separation of the sexes. Deaths were imposed indirectly through starvation or exposures and also more directly by killing operations such as herding Jews into gas chambers at either mobile or fixed sites. The German people stood by while this carnage sequence was carried out and the Christians of the country could do nothing to stop it.

The Dutch were an occupied people of the German government of Adolph Hitler. Their country, Holland, had been known for tolerant and liberal traditions, but Holland allowed its Jewish citizens to be sacrificed. Of the more than 140,000 Jews living in the country, approximately 107,000 were deported to the East to concentration and forced labor sites and at least 102,000 were murdered or worked to death in the Nazi camps. Jewish families constituted 40% of the total civilian casualties of the entire country of Holland. Other Dutch civilians suffered little as a result of German occupation.

Anne's family, the Franks lived in the sparsely furnished three rooms of the top floor of a warehouse. A bookcase in one of the rooms was actually a concealed door to a steep attic stairway above where the Franks could go in dire emergencies.

Anne could never get away outside. She could not breathe fresh air. She could not shout or jump. Every creak in the building might mean soldiers were coming for them. Every day hundreds of Jews were disappearing. Anne awoke at nights suffering the nightmare of being snatched and taken who knows where.

Every Dutch family including the one providing food for the Franks were under watch by the Gestapo, a German intelligence organization dedicated to catching Jews and political dissidents. An employee from the warehouse below asked for a greater salary and hints that he remembers a door where the bookcase now is. After two years, a clandestine radio provides news that the Americans have landed on the beaches of Normandy, France but the war over Europe between the Germany of Adolph Hitler and the rest of the world crawls on. Then a thief enters the building, learns of the hideout of the Frank family and informs the German police where Anne and her family hide. Soon the block was surrounded and the door to Anne's hiding place from Adolph Hitler's madness was busted open.

The soldiers gave the Franks five minutes to each gather a bag of clothing. Anne made a final entry in her diary before being taken to Belson concentration camp and disappearing to Christian history, "And so it seems our stay is over. They are waiting for us now. So, dear Diary, that means I must leave you behind. Goodbye for a while. P.S. Please, please, Miep, or Mr. Kraler, or anyone else. If you should find this diary, will you please keep it safe for me, because some day I hope..."

* * * * *

Eva Peron,

The Charitable First Lady of Argentina

Eva Duarte Peron, the charitable first lady of Argentina, died on 26 July 1952 after having lived a short life of thirty-three years. She died slowly and painfully over a period of many months from cancer of the uterus. Her last speech with her Argentine folk was from a balcony of the Presidential Palace in Buenas Aires on October 17th, 1951, prior to her last surgery, urging those who loved her to remember her descamisados, the poor and unprivileged.

Eva Duarte's memories of poverty were an ache of burning heat. They drove her toward power and influence and when she achieved both they sought expression not in revenge but in acts of great charity for the poor. Born Eva Duarte, she was of humble origin and never forgot her she was one of five illegitimate children of Juan Duarte, a man who died when Eva was seven leaving her mother and family in rock bottom poverty. After his death, Juan Duarte's legitimate family snubbed Eva's family and kept them from attending his funeral. Eva grew up poor but found her opportunity to achieve success in acting and radio and political movements. The women in Argentina before Eva Peron's time were considered totally subservient to men, a fact that was not questioned. Eva Duarte, later married to Juan Peron, President of the country, brought about the right of women to vote in her country. Her later years in power as the wife of the President were spent largely in charity. She established the Eva Peron Foundation beginning this charity with 500 dollars of her own. By 1952, the year of her death, the income of the Foundation was estimated to be equal to one-third the entire Argentine national budget, approximately one hundred million dollars. The foundation was supported by the nation's unions, businesses and stock exchange. Schools, hospitals, clinics, and holiday camps were built in great numbers. Those ravaged by natural disasters were given financial aid. Deprived persons benefitted with educations. Eva at times used funds to purchase property where landlords where said to be exploiting tenants. Poor children were given vacations. Peso notes were tossed into crowds. Eva often worked eighteen hours a day on her Foundation and she was passionate in her desire to eliminate poverty in Argentina. She remains remembered to this day as the charitable first lady of Argentina.

* * * * *

Martin Luther King:

A Dream

Five score years ago, a great American, in whose symbolic shadow we stand today, signed the Emancipation Proclamation. This momentous decree came as a great beacon of light of hope to millions of Negro slaves who had been seared in the flames of withering injustice. It came as a joyous daybreak to end the long night of their captivity.

But one hundred years later, the Negro still is not free. One hundred years later, the life of the Negro is still sadly crippled by the manacles of segregation and the chains of discrimination.

One hundred years later, the Negro lives on a lonely island of poverty in the midst of a vast ocean of material prosperity. One hundred years later, the Negro is still languished in the corners of American society and finds himself an exile in his own land. So we have come here today to dramatize a shameful condition.

In a sense we have come to our nation's capital to cash a check. When the architects of our republic wrote the magnificent words of the Constitution and the Declaration of Independence, they were signing a promissory note to which every

American was to fall heir. This note was a promise that all men, yes, black men as well as white men, would be granted the unalienable rights of life, liberty, and the pursuit of happiness.

It is obvious today that America has defaulted on this promissory note insofar as her citizens of color are concerned. Instead of honoring this sacred obligation, America has given the Negro people a bad check; which has come back marked "insufficient funds."

But we refuse to believe that the bank of justice is bankrupt. We refuse to believe that there are insufficient funds in the great vaults of opportunity of this nation. So we have come to cash this check - a check that will give us upon demand the riches of freedom and the security of justice.

We have also come to this hallowed spot to remind America of the fierce urgency of now. This is no time to engage in the luxury of cooling off or to take the tranquilizing drug of gradualism. Now is the time to make real the promises of democracy. Now is the time to rise from the dark and desolate valley of segregation to the sunlit path of racial justice. Now is time to lift our nation from the quicksands of racial injustice to the solid rock of brotherhood. Now is the time to make justice a reality for all of God's children.

It would be fatal for the nation to overlook the urgency of the movement and to underestimate the determination of the Negro. This sweltering summer of the Negro's legitimate discontent will not pass until there is an invigorating autumn of freedom and equality. 1963 is not an end but a beginning. Those who hope that the Negro needed to blow off steam and will now be content will have a rude awakening if the nation returns to business as usual.

There will be neither rest nor tranquility in America until the Negro is granted his citizenship rights. The whirlwinds of revolt will continue to shake the foundations of our nation until the bright day of justice emerges.

But there is something that I must say to my people who stand on the warm threshold which leads into the palace of justice. In the process of gaining our rightful place we must not be guilty of wrongful deeds.

Let us not seek to satisfy our thirst for freedom by drinking from the cup of bitterness and hatred. We must forever conduct our struggle on the high plane of dignity and discipline. We must not allow our creative protest to degenerate into physical violence. Again and again we must rise to the majestic heights of meeting physical force with soul force.

The marvelous new militancy which has engulfed the Negro community must not lead us to a distrust of all white people, for many of our white brothers, as evidenced by their presence here today, have come to realize that their destiny is tied up with our destiny and they have come to realize that their freedom is inextricably bound to our freedom. This offense we share mounted to storm the battlements of injustice must be carried forth by a bi-racial army. We cannot walk alone.

And as we walk, we must make the pledge that we shall always march ahead. We cannot turn back. There are those who are asking the devotees of civil rights, "When will you be satisfied?" We can never be satisfied as long as the Negro is the victim of the unspeakable horrors of police brutality.

We can never be satisfied as long as our bodies, heavy with fatigue of travel, cannot gain lodging in the motels of the highways and the hotels of the cities. We cannot be satisfied as long as the Negro's basic mobility is from a smaller ghetto to a larger one.

We can never be satisfied as long as our children are stripped of their selfhood and robbed of their dignity by signs stating "for whites only." We cannot be satisfied as long as a Negro in Mississippi cannot vote and a Negro in New York believes he has nothing for which to vote. No, we are not satisfied, and we will not be satisfied until justice rolls down like waters and righteousness like a mighty stream.

I am not unmindful that some of you have come here out of excessive trials and tribulation. Some of you have come fresh from narrow jail cells. Some of you have come from areas where your guest for freedom left you battered by the storms of persecution and staggered by the winds of police brutality. You have been the veterans of creative suffering. Continue to work with the faith that unearned suffering is redemptive.

Go back to Mississippi; go back to Alabama; go back to South Carolina; go back to Georgia; go back to Louisiana; go back to the slums and ghettos of the Northern cities, knowing that somehow this graduation can, and will be changed. Let us not wallow in the valley of despair.

So I say to you, my friends, that even though you must face the difficulties of today and tomorrow, I still have a dream. It is a dream deeply rooted in the American dream that one day this nation will rise up and live out the true meaning of its creed - we hold these truths to be self evident, that all men are created equal.

I have a dream that one day on the red hills of Georgia, sons of former slaves and sons of former slave-owners will be able to sit down together at the table of brotherhood.

I have a dream that one day, even the state of Mississippi, a state sweltering with the heat of injustice, sweltering with the heat of oppression, will be transformed into an oasis of freedom and justice. I have a dream my four little children will one day live in a nation where they will not be judged by the color of their skin but by content of their character. I have a dream today!

I have a dream that one day, down in Alabama, with its vicious racists, with its governor having his lips dripping with the words of interposition and nullification, that one day, right there in Alabama, little black boys and black girls will be able to join hands with little white boys and white girls as sisters and brothers. I have a dream today!

I have a dream that one day every valley shall be exalted, every hill and mountain shall be made low, the rough places shall be made plain, and the crooked places shall be made straight and the glory of the Lord will be revealed and all flesh shall see it together.

This is our hope. This is the faith that I go back to the South with.

With this faith we will be able to hear out of the mountain of despair a stone of hope. With this faith we will be able to transform the jangling discords of our nation into a beautiful symphony of brotherhood.

With this faith we will be able to work together to pray together; to struggle together, to go to jail together, to stand up for freedom together, knowing that we will be free one day. This will be the day when all of God's children will be able to sing with new meaning - "my country 'tis of thee; sweet land of liberty; of thee I sing; land where my fathers died, land of the pilgrim's pride; from every mountain side, let freedom ring" - and if America is to be a great nation, this must become true.

So let freedom ring from the prodigious hilltops of New Hampshire.
Let freedom ring from the mighty mountains of New York.
Let freedom ring form the heightening Alleghenies of Pennsylvania.
Let freedom ring from the snow-capped Rockies of Colorado.
Let freedom ring from the curvaceous slopes of California.
But not only that.
Let freedom ring from Stone Mountain of Georgia.
Let freedom ring from Lookout Mountain of Tennessee.
Let freedom ring from every hill and molehill of Mississippi,
    from every mountainside, let freedom ring.

And when we allow freedom to ring, when we let it ring from every village and hamlet, from every state and city, we will be able to speed up that day when all of God's children - black men and white men, Jews and Gentiles, Catholics and Protestants - will be able to join hands and to sing in the words of the old Negro spiritual. "Free at last, free at last; thank God Almighty, we are free at last."

* * * * *

Various:

Humanity Begins to Cope with its Quantum Situation

The Twentieth Century learned the awesome fact that existence is not at all what it seemed. No longer could the material world be found to be of any substance at all. What the eyes behold are tricks of scans of energetic absorptions within a tiny range of energy picked up through chemical receptors of the eyes. What is touched is not real. Instead the levels of reality can be peeled away from the human dimension down through evolutionary hierarchies to molecular and atomic structures of the measurement of angstroms and picometers. There other elementary energies interact.

At a tiny level proliferation of the measurements that humans cope with begin with atomic orbitals of relative energy states existing in clouds and hybridization. Between atomic structures are bonds which settle the dimensions of molecular forms mainly as result of electroweak forces. Only on the much grander scale does humanity begin to find its world forming. The level of God's dealing is on a much tinier scale than any human can deal with short of the perfectly rational posture of faith.

How did such a situation become known? The significance of these facts was made dramatically clear when humanity learned that splitting heavy nuclei through fission technology was very, very exothermic or heat and energy releasing. Uranium was the substance of interest. Its atomic mass of 235 was found divisible so that uranium could splinter into tellerium and barium, two much lighter elements. As long as the neutrons from this fission were held within a critical mass, they caused further fissions in a chain reaction of huge energy production. The nuclear bomb resulted.

The discoveries of the potential of such a bomb occurred in countries at war. In the 1930's, two European countries, Germany and Italy, formed a political alliance on the basis of Nazism, a form of nationalism forged on racist supremacy ideas. The political leaders of these two countries set out on a course of territorial expansion and elimination of racial stocks of the peoples of those new areas of expansion, particularly those defined as Jews. As it turned out, the research underlying the nuclear weapons technology was first worked out in Italy by Enrico Fermi in the 1930's and then in Germany by Otto Hahn. The Nazi wars of conquest resulted in a further alliance with Japan in Asia which also was bent on great national territorial expansion.

A last piece of the puzzle as to bomb possibilities came about with the discovery that neutrons from fission reactions cause chain reactions. This information was gleaned in the United States at Columbia University through the work of Leo Szilard and Walter Zinn.

Nevertheless, the awesome possibilities of nuclear weapons became widely known in both Nazi countries and those of others. The physicist Albert Einstein brought all of the concern of the scientific community to the attention of the United States President Franklin Roosevelt in a famous letter. Late in 1941, the United States began its project to build a nuclear bomb largely out of concern about what might happen to the world if the Nazi countries in a war with the United States might develop it first. It was President Roosevelt's successor, Harry Truman, who made the decision to use the atomic bomb to end the territorial wars costing many, many lives. The loss of troops in subduing the armies of Germany and Italy had been staggering. In August, 1945, the United States dropped atomic bombs on two Japanese cities, Hiroshima and Nagasaki. Japan subsequently sought peace. World War II was ended but the nuclear age of military weapons had arrived.

A teacher described the sight of the bomb going off over Hiroshima, Japan, from a distance of three miles away. "A blinding...flash cut sharply across the sky...I threw myself onto the ground...in a reflex movement. At the same moment as the flash, the skin over my body felt a burning heat. (Then there was) a blank in time...dead silence...probably a few seconds...and then a...huge "boom"...like the rumbling of distant thunder. At the same time a violent rush of air pressed down my entire body...Again there were some moments of blankness...then a complicated series of shattering noises...I raised my head, facing the center of Hiroshima to the west...(There I saw) an enormous mass of clouds...(which) spread and climbed rapidly...into the sky. Then its summit broke open and hung over horizontally. It took on the shape of...a monstrous mushroom with the lower part as its stem-it would be more accurate to call it the tail of a tornado. Beneath it more and more boiling clouds erupted and unfolded sideways...The shape...the color...the light...were continuously shifting and changing."

A grocer who was very severely burned himself has left this account. "The appearance of people was...well, they all had skin blackened by burns...They had no hair because there hair was burned, and at a glance you couldn't tell whether you were looking at them from in front or in back...They held their arms bent (forward)...and their skin - not only on their hands, but on their faces and bodies too - hung down...If there had been only one or two such people...perhaps I would not have had such a strong impression. But wherever I walked I met these people...Many of them died along the road - I can still picture them in my mind - like walking ghosts...They didn't look like people of this world...They had a special way of walking - very slowly...I myself was one of them."

A man who was a thirteen year old shopkeeper's assistant at the time of the atomic bomb explosion has written, "I was a little ill...so I stayed at home that day...There had been an air-raid warning and then an all-clear. I felt relieved and lay down on the bed with my younger brother...Then it happened. It came very suddenly...It felt something like an electric short - a bluish sparkling light...There was a noise, and I felt great heat - even inside of the house. When I came to, I was underneath the destroyed house...I didn't know anything about the atomic bomb so I thought that some bomb had fallen directly upon me...And then when I felt that our house had been directly hit, I became furious...There were roof tiles and walls - everything black - entirely covering me. So I screamed for help...And form all around I heard moans and screaming, and then I felt a kind of danger to myself...I thought I too was going to die in that way. I felt this way at that moment because I was absolutely unable to do anything at all by my own power...I didn't know where I was or what I was under...I couldn't hear voices of my family. I didn't know how I could be rescued. I felt I was going to suffocate and then die, without knowing exactly what had happened to me. This was the kind of expectation I had..."

A doctor recorded a scene in his diary. "Those who were able walked silently toward the suburbs in the distant hills, their spirits broken, their initiative gone. When asked whence they had come, they pointed to the city and said, "That way." And when asked where they were going pointed away from the city and said, "This way." They were so broken and confused that they moved and behaved like automatons. Their reactions had astonished outsiders who reported with amazement the spectacle of long files of people holding stolidly to a narrow, rough path when close by was a smooth, easy road going in the same direction. The outsiders could not grasp the fact that they were witnessing the exodus of a people who walked in the real of dreams."

* * * * *

John F. Kennedy:

Responsibility for World Peace

A Speech of a Young President Televised to the American People on Oct. 22, 1962. "The Cuban Missile Crisis"

This government, as promised, has maintained the closest surveillance of the Soviet military buildup on the island of Cuba. Within the past week, unmistakable evidence has established the fact that a series of offensive missile sites is now in preparation on that imprisoned island. The purpose of these bases can be none other than to provide a nuclear strike capability against the Western Hemisphere.

The urgent transformation of Cuba into an important strategic base - by the presence of these large, long-range, and clearly offensive weapons of sudden mass destruction - constitutes an explicit threat to the peace and security of the Americas...

Neither the United States of America nor the world community of nations can tolerate deliberate deception and offensive threats on the part of any nation, large or small. We no longer live in a world where only the actual firing of weapons represents a sufficient challenge to a nation's security to constitute maximum peril. Nuclear weapons are so destructive, and ballistic missiles are so swift, that any substantially increased possibility of their use or any sudden change in their deployment may well be regarded as a definite threat to peace.

For many years, both the Soviet Union and the United States, recognizing this fact, have deployed strategic nuclear weapons with great care, never upsetting the precarious status quo which insured that these weapons would not be used in the absence of some vital challenge. Our own strategic missiles have never been transferred to the territory of any other nation under a cloak of secrecy and deception; Our history - unlike that of the Soviets since the end of World War II - demonstrates that we have no desire to dominate or conquer any other nation or impose our system upon its people. Nevertheless American citizens have become adjusted to living daily on the bull's-eye of Soviet missiles located inside the U.S.S.R. or in submarines.

In this sense, missiles in Cuba add to an already clear and present danger - although it should be noted the nations of Latin America have never previously been subjected to a potential nuclear threat.

But this secret, swift and extraordinary buildup of Communist missiles - in an are well known to have a special and historical relationship to the Untied States and the nations of the Western Hemisphere, in violation of Soviet assurances, and in defiance of American and hemispheric policy - this sudden, clandestine decision to station strategic weapons for the first time outside of Soviet soil - is a deliberately provocative and unjustified change in the status quo which cannot be accepted by this country, if our courage and our commitments are ever to be trusted again by either friend or foe.

The 1930's taught us a clear lesson: aggressive conduct, if allowed to go unchecked and unchallenged, ultimately leads to war. This nation is opposed to war.

We are also true to our word. Our unswerving objective therefore must be to prevent the use of these missiles against this or any other country, and to secure their withdrawal or elimination from the Western Hemisphere.

Our policy has been one of patience and restrain, as befits a peaceful and powerful nation which leads a worldwide alliance. We have been determined not to be diverted from our central concerns by mere irritants and fanatics. But now further action is required- and it under way; and these actions may only be the beginning. We will not prematurely or unnecessarily risk the costs of worldwide nuclear war in which even the fruits of victory would be ashes in our mouth -but neither will we shrink from that risk at any time it must be faced.

———

Following this address, the American navy began interdicting Russian ships entering or leaving Cuban waters to search for nuclear armaments. The American people braced for a nuclear weapons missile attack from Russia. It did not come and Communist missiles were withdrawn from Cuba. Many an American feared nuclear holocaust that day. The young President was assassinated shortly after giving this speech in Dallas, Texas. It was widely thought the assassin or assassins were connected with the Cuban government.

* * * * *

Church Suicide

Nov. 18, 1978 spelled the end of one of the most unusual churches in the history of the world, the People's Temple pastored by Jim Jones. The church self-destructed in a mass suicide of its over nine hundred members in the jungle of Guyana, South America. The church had negotiated with the world for freedom to live within its own religious worldview but believed its negotiations failed. The community's final strategy for salvation was simply suicide.

This suicide was not a quick decision. The members of the People's Temple had practiced the rite of mass suicide many times. The first recorded time was in January 1, 1976 when Rev. Jones gave about thirty members of the church board a glass of wine to drink and then informed them they were poisoned and going to die in one hour. Jones later told them, "Well, it was a good lesson. I see you're not dead." His goal was to warn them that they must confront death and be prepared to die for commitment to the People's Temple. This "suicide drill" or "white night" became a regular rite of the church. It was not simply intended as a loyalty test, but came to be the church's threat to the world that if not left alone the members would commit a collective, self-imposed death, especially rather than submit to what they called a "subhuman life." To understand what this meant one must go back to the teachings of this church.

The church claimed to pursue the goal of human dignity for the dehumanized and rejected of American society, particularly blacks, the elderly and the poor who had been betrayed by the American establishment. The church was organized in Indiana, but left for California, and eventually sought peace in a vast agricultural

project called Jonestown in the South American jungle when governmental interference was brought to bear against the church or its minister.

The followers of Jim Jones were under the influence of the mind of a minister
of God who yet convinced his congregation that the American government was
preparing concentration camps for them, bent on racial genocide against blacks
and pledged to fascism. His view of history concentrated on the history of oppression as when slaves were brought to America and given food if they worked in the
fields and accepted Jesus. Rev. Jones taught that his church should identify with
revolutionary ideas and link its hopes with the destiny of the communism of
Vladimir Lenin, the dreamer of a dream of a socialist utopia. Suicide was to be their
weapon against the outside world. If the church were to be attacked, the congregation would suicide rather than be subjected to subhuman lives in the American
racist and capitalist society.

Several tests of their will to suicide followed. One was an order from a California judge requiring Rev. Jones to turn over a child which Rev. Jones believed to be
his own. The community refused and took up arms on the border of Jonestown
until the threat passed. Then an American Congressman, Leo Ryan, arrived with
news media reporters and representatives of family members of the People's Temple who wanted their relatives to leave the church settlement in South America and
return to America claiming that Rev. Jones was brainwashing his followers.

The visit of the Congressman was perceived as the arrogance of white America
pushing the Jonestown community up against the wall. Soon, they believed, their
community would be destroyed. The family members vowed to have the People's
Temple kicked out of Guyana. When the Congressman left with his party and
fourteen dissatisfied residents, they were ambushed by the Jonestown security
force. Congressman Ryan and three newsmen were killed together with one of the
defectors. Then the community anticipated the Guyanese Defense Corps or American soldiers soon parachuting in to their community, taking away their children,
consigning them all to a subhuman life outside. Death they believed preferable.

The children of the community were killed first with the consent of the parents. Then the bodies began to be piled on top of each other as the rest of the community died.

Many suicide notes were found in Jonestown following the mass suicide. 911
had died of suicide poisoning. One author of such a note described the community
hugging and kissing, in silence and joy, as they merged in their minds with the millions of others who had been subsumed in the human struggle against oppression
and for the sake of revolution in order "to bear witness at once." Their deaths were
intended as a testimony of their unity, a united voice of affirmation and as the note
said, as a "victory of the human spirit." A Jonestown nurse, Annie Moore, twenty-
four at the time of her death, wrote in her note, "Jim Jones showed us all this - that
we could live together with our differences -that we were all the same - human beings." Moore stated that Jonestown had been the most peaceful, loving community
that had ever existed, a paradise that had eliminated racism, sexism, elitism and
classism, the best thing that had ever happened for the free, bright, healthy children, the respected senior and all the followers of Jim Jones. "We died," she concluded, "because you would not let us live."

* * * * *

A Child and the Drug Traffickers

Jenny Campo was eight when the government soldiers entered her family dwelling in rural Columbia, South America, and killed her parents and baby brother. The soldiers did not leave the adobe home. For a week, the soldiers detained Jenny and her sister close by the dead bodies of her family to interrogate her and her sister. In the end the soldiers had to realize a mistake had been made and Jenny's family were not guerilla supporters.

The violence and drug trafficking in Columbia continued to take a toll. Elsewhere in the world, drug abuse was growing bringing about human destruction implicit in drug addiction. But in Columbia, the monetary rewards of production of marijuana, cocaine and psychoactive derivatives resulted in the growth of financial cartels and alliances with guerilla paramilitary forces to protect them. Violence was rampant. The drug trade was illegal and those who rose to the positions of power were often common criminals whom jails could not hold.

Five years after her parents' deaths in 1997, Jenny Campo, now a sixth grader, struck back. She became the leader of a group of children calling themselves the Children's Movement for Peace. The children were seeking to end three decades of civil war in Columbia. For two years they drew almost 2.3 million Columbian children into their movement for peace. They conducted referenda seeking support. They called upon the children to come to official polls to vote on ballots on the subject. Children in more than 100 townships in Columbia did so cutting paper copies from newspapers or from the backs of pamphlets to express themselves. They wish a national convention of peace. Recently the children of Villavicencio from ages 5 to 14 held a regional conference to select representatives to such a convention. This city was a late focus of fighting between the country's soldiers and guerillas that flicks like a flame burning into first one place and then another. It is the children of Columbia who know the hurt the most - who have seen the fighting and the massacres and assassinations. Their children's movement for peace is now in the battle too.

* * * * *

The Fence

There was a little boy with a bad temper. His father gave him a bag of nails and told him that every time he lost his temper, to hammer a nail in the back fence. The first day the boy had driven 37 nails into the fence. Then it gradually dwindled down. He discovered it was easier to hold his temper than to drive those nails into the fence. Finally the day came when the boy didn't lose his temper at all. He told his father about it and the father suggested that the boy now pull out one nail for each day that he was able to hold his temper. The days passed and the young boy was finally able to tell his father that all the nails were gone. The father took his son by the hand and led him to the fence. He said, "You have done well, my son, but look at the holes in the fence. The fence will never be the same. When you say things in anger, they leave a scar just like this one. You can put a knife in a man and draw it out. It won't matter how many times you say I'm sorry, the wound is still there. A verbal wound is as bad as a physical one. Friends are a very rare jewel, indeed. They make you smile and encourage you to succeed. They lend an ear, they share a word of praise, and they always want to open their hearts to us. Show your friends how much you care."

* * * * *

Confusing the Packaging

A young man was getting ready to graduate from college. For many months he had admired a beautiful sports car in a dealer's showroom, and knowing his father could well afford it, he told him that was all he wanted. As Graduation Day approached, the young man awaited signs that his father had purchased the car. Finally, on the morning of his graduation, his father called him into his private study. His father told him how proud he was to have such a fine son, and told him how much he loved him. He handed his son a beautifully wrapped gift box.

Curious, and somewhat disappointed, the young man opened the box and found a lovely, leather-bound Bible, with the young man's name embossed in gold. Angry, he rose his voice to his father and said, "With all your money you give me a Bible? Is this all I mean to you?" and stormed out of the house. Many years passed and the young man was very successful in business. He had a beautiful home and wonderful family, but realized his father was very old, and thought perhaps he should go to him.

He had not seen him since that graduation day. He could not get rid of his anger. Before he could make arrangements, he received a telegram telling him his father had passed away, and willed all of his possessions to his son. He needed to come home immediately and take care of things. When he arrived at his father's house, sudden sadness and regret filled his heart. He began to search through his father's important papers and saw the still new Bible, just as he had left it years ago. With tears, he opened the Bible and began to turn the pages. His father had carefully underlined a verse, Matt.7.11, "And if you, being evil, know how to give good gifts to your children, how much more shall your Heavenly Father which is in Heaven, give to those who ask Him?" As he read those words, a car key dropped from the back of the Bible. It had a tag with the dealer's name, the same dealer who had the sports car he had desired. On the tag was the date of his graduation, and the words PAID IN FULL. How many times do we miss God's blessings because they are not packaged as we expected!

The Story Of Mother Teresa

In 1948, a solitary woman stepped out into the slums of Calcutta, India, to live among the poorest of the poor as one of them. She was not only humble and small at five feet but also determined and tough because she knew God was on her side. She was born in Serbia August 26, 1910 and named Agnes Gonxha Bojaxhiu. She was the youngest of three children of Albanian ancestry. The father was a merchant and the mother a housewife. The father died, probably of poison, when the woman to become Mother Teresa was eight and the mother supported the family with sewing, embroidery and cloth selling. The family table began to be a gathering place for the poor and homeless. The mother took in the six children of a widow when their mother died. An alcoholic woman covered with sores was cleaned and her wounds treated by the mother. Many such incidents impressed themselves on the child. Prayer was an integral part of their family life. The Jesuit priest of their parish told the family and members of his parish of the missionary work undertaken by the Society of Jesus in Bengal, in the archdiocese of Calcutta by Serbian missionaries. Mother Teresa joined an Irish missionary order, the Loreto Sisters, in 1928 and took a commitment to chastity. She took training in the order and undertook teaching initially. Every Sunday she visited the poor in the bustees, the slum areas of Calcutta. As the years went by Calcutta became more and more devastated from disruptions, poverty, ignorance, wars and famines. On one occasion, Mother Teresa took upon herself the care of an abandoned woman half eaten by maggots and on the point of death abandoned by her son. She went out into the streets, though weak and ill, to obtain food during periods of Muslim/Hindu fighting for her orphan children.

In 1946, Mother Teresa began to receive inspirational calls to be a Missionary of Charity. She went on to establish a congregation to "quench the infinite thirst of Jesus Christ on the Cross for love of souls." Mother Teresa felt when Jesus said from the cross, "I thirst," its purpose was to draw humanity to God's Child. The response of people should be like the woman at Jacob's well who gave Jesus water for God's Child's thirst which could not be quenched wholly by water but required love. She obtained permission to leave the convent of the Loreto Sisters and entered into a work in the slums of Calcutta. There were millions of destitute people there.

Her first major work began at Nirmal Hriday, a home for the dying in Calcutta, bringing love and care to those who most needed it. She wished to help the dying after seeing a woman dying on the street outside Campbell Hospital. Mother Teresa picked her up and took her to the hospital but she was refused admission because she was poor. The woman died on the street. Then Mother Teresa decided to establish a home for the dying and those needing a resting place for going to God's Homeland. Each dying one was Jesus to her in his most distressing disguise. She saw Jesus present and hungry and thirsty in the poor or whatever form that poverty might take. Such were each God's Child broken and present in humanity. She found in her work the spirit and the joy of loving Jesus among the poorest of the poor and through the strength that prayer makes possible to do this work. She once said, "if you remove Jesus from my life, my life is reduced to a mere nothing." She tried every day to give over herself to the work of the breathing Spirit of God. The spirit of an order of helpers she nurtured that spread throughout the world was "Loving trust, total surrender and cheerfulness as lived by Jesus and his mother." The order, the Missionaries of Charity, continued to grow in number in the late Twentieth Century.

When asked why there were so many poor in the world, she replied, "If there are poor in the world it is because you and I don't give enough." She expressed her philosophy of life in words of a poster hanging in a home for Aids victims in New York City set up by her order which reads: Life is an opportunity, avail it. Life is a beauty, admire it. Life is bliss, taste it. Life is a dream, realize it. Life is a challenge, meet it. Life is a duty, complete it. Life is a game, play it. Life is costly, care for it. Life is a wealth, keep it. Life is love, enjoy it. Life is mystery, know it. Life is a promise, fulfil it. Life is sorrow, overcome it. Life is a song, sing it. Life is a struggle, accept it. Life is a tragedy, brace it. Life is an adventure, dare it. Life is life, save it! Life is luck, make it. Life is too precious, do not destroy it.

* * * * *

Finding the Time

I knelt to pray but not for long,
I had too much to do.
I had to hurry and get to work
For bills would soon be due.

So I knelt and said a hurried prayer,
And jumped up off my knees.
My Christian duty was now done
My soul could rest at ease.

All day long I had no time
To spread a word of cheer.
No time to speak of Jesus to friends,
They'd laugh at me I'd fear.

No time, no time, too much to do,
That was my constant cry,
No time to give to souls in need
But at last the time to die.

I went before the Familyhead,
I came, I stood with downcast eyes.
For in Jesus's hands God held a
    book;
It was the Book of Life.

God looked into the book and said,
"Your name I cannot find.
I once was going to write it down…
But never found the time."

* * * * *

The Student and the Athiest Professor

This is a true story of something that happened at the University of Southern California near the time when the 2d millennium after the life of Jesus was closing..

There was a Professor of Philosophy there who was a deeply committed
atheist. His primary goal for one required class was to spend the entire semester
attempting to prove that God couldn't exist. His students were always afraid to argue with him because of his impeccable logic. For twenty years, he had taught this
class and no one had ever had the courage to go against him. Sure, some had argued in class at times, but no one had ever "really gone against him" (you'll see
what I mean later). Nobody would go against him because he had a reputation. At
the end of every semester, on the last day, he would say to his class of 300 students,
"If there is anyone here who still believes in Jesus, stand up!" In twenty years, no
one had ever stood up. They knew what he was going to do next. He would say,
"because anyone who does believe in God is a fool. If God existed, he could stop
this piece of chalk from hitting the ground and breaking. Such a simple task to
prove that he is God and yet he can't do it!" And every year, he would drop the
chalk onto the tile floor of the classroom and it would shatter into a hundred
pieces. All of the students could do nothing but stop and stare. Most of the students were convinced that God couldn't exist. Certainly, a number of Christians
had slipped through, but for 20 years, they had been too afraid to stand up Well,
a few years ago, there was a freshman who happened to get enrolled in the class.
He was a Christian and had heard the stories about this professor. He had to take
the class because it was one of the required classes for his major and he was afraid.
But for 3 months that semester, he prayed every morning that he would have the
courage to stand up no matter what the professor said or what the class thought.
Nothing they said or did could ever shatter his faith, he hoped Finally the day
came. The professor said, "If there is anyone here who still believes in God, stand
up!" .The professor and the class of 300 people looked at him, shocked, as he
stood up at the back of the classroom. The professor shouted, "YOU FOOL!! If
God existed, he could keep this piece of chalk from breaking when it hit the
ground!" He proceeded to drop the chalk, but as he did, it slipped out of his fingers, off his shirt cuff, onto the pleats of his pants, down his leg, and off his shoe.
As it hit the ground, it simply rolled away, unbroken. The professor's jaw dropped
as he stared at the chalk. He looked up at the young man and then ran out of the
lecture hall. The young man who had stood up proceeded to walk to the front of
the room and share his faith in Jesus. For the next half-hour, 300 students stayed

and listened as he told of God's love for them and of his power through Jesus Christ.

"Yet to all who received JESUS, to those who believe in JESUS'S name, JESUS gave the right to become children of God –children born not of natural descent, nor of human decision or a husband's will, but born of God." "But the Familyhead knows the way that I take. When the Familyhead has tested me, I will come forth as gold." Job.23

* * * * *

The Death of a Doe

Karla Faye Tucker was still a young woman when the State of Texas authorities took her from her prison cell which she had converted into a church for God and strapped her onto a death chamber gurney to be wheeled to a chamber to be killed. Outside, her brothers and sisters in God's Child attempted to sing "Amazing Grace" to recall that the Spirit of God's breath still upholds all of the earth. Instead, the earthly wind found the hymn drowned out with Texans crying, "Kill her!" "Kill her!" in deafening chants. God's people could do nothing to stop the brutality of the majority of the people of that state. The United States Supreme Court and the Governor of Texas refused to intervene to halt this deed and so a doe for Jesus was put to death within the walls of a human prison in 1998 to go to God's Homeland and give an account of the incident to Jesus.

She was not always a doe for Jesus. Before her conversion to Christianity, she had been convicted of a grisly pickax murder while under the demonic control of drugs in 1984. Only after this had God's Child come into her life. Christians throughout the world recognized her spirit as one which had flowered with the conversion. No longer was she a chilling killer. No longer was her mind clouded by drugs. Her eyes now were those of a doe for Jesus. Now there was a smile about life in her spunky demeanor. It does happen. People can truly find Jesus anywhere even if they have committed murder.

Christians prayed for her. They begged God to soften the hearts of the people of Texas and the Texas Board of Pardons and Paroles, a board that had never shown mercy to anyone in the past. This board had never reprieved a single person. If ever there were a case for mercy made, this doe made one. The Texas board prided itself on never meeting when a request for mercy came before it. They did not budge.

* * * * *

Traditional:

Footprints

One night a man had a dream. He dreamed he was walking along the beach with the Lord. Across the sky flashed scenes from his life. In each scene he noticed two sets of footprints in the sand - one belonging to him and the other to the Familyhead.

When the last scene flashed before him, he looked back at the footprints and noticed that many times along the path, there was only one set of footprints in the sand. He also noticed that this happened during the lowest and saddest times in his life.

This really bothered him, so he questioned the Familyhead: "Sir, you said that once I decided to follow you, you would walk with me all the way, but I noticed that during the most troublesome times of my life there was only one set of footprints. I don't understand why, when I needed you the most, you deserted me."

The Familyhead replied, "My precious child. I would never desert you. During your times of trial and suffering when you saw only one set of footprints, it was then that I carried you."

* * * * *

The Beautiful Lady of Indiana

Once there was a little boy about five who set down by a farm pond on a warm late Spring day with his fishing pole and a line that disappeared down into the muddy waters. The day was so warm that his eyes was most tugged closed. Sitting under the apple tree kept the sun off and there was not a thing on his mind to clutter up his thinking.

But when he felt a catch on the line, he noticed something else.

There was an ever so slight wind movement of the waters.....like something caught itself on the surface water going by.

"What's that?" the surprised little boy thought to himself at his spot on the bank.

Soon the little boy got busy again watching the fishing line. He figured he was just imagining something like the bites he was wishing for from the bluegills he liked to catch and throw back.

Then the next day, while he was on his dad's tractor riding with him bushhogging the fence rows, the little boy looked over to his favorite place in that field - where the hedgeapple trees was in a row with their fruits like brains to be thrown around after playing surgeon with them.

At a certain spot where he was looking, his eyes got fixed on something bright as a diamond. He was sure he was seeing something. BUT it was like seeing something when your eyes don't. Just thinking about it give him the "willies" and caused him most to lose his balance on the tractor wheel guard where he was perched.

The little boy snatched the back of his dad's overalls so hard, his dad was sure to turn around.

"Hey!" the dad says.

"Hold on," the little boy insisted.

So he has his dad stop and he jumped off the rear tire guard and while his dad went on, the little boy walks ever so worried over to his "brain" hospital and there is a fire blowing high for a second but only just so before it's out and gone.

The little boy called out at this "light-fire thing- place," "What is there?"

But nothing is said.

It wasn't a couple of weeks later that his mom sent him out to bring in some beets down at the garden along the crick in the low spot where the dirt lane back to the house bends around a hilly place to stay level.

And while he's got his trowel hand working down and his head's bent over going this way and that for to search out and find where the lumps would signal the best beets growing, he felt some water being poured on his head.

The little boy sat up with a start!

Then he looked up at the sky and there was not a single cloud floating around!

He sent his hand that was not so muddy to feel real gingerly back there around the crown of his head. Sure enough, there was the wettest spot!

Now he was all atingle - and just a little scared and fidgety -and his eyes were darting here and there, jumpy and fast. He whispered - this time as insistent as a five year old boy can - "WHO IS THERE!"

For just a second there wasn't any more sound than the crick's grumbling and the meadowlarks fussing and the bugs buzzing.

Then, while the boy was half afraid to move, up in front of him came a lady as white as lightning and as beautiful as a pleasant dream.

"You are the most noticing boy I ever saw!" she said. "I go here and there, to and from, every minute watching and most times, -no! I'd say all the time, - I don't have any trouble doing my work anonymous. But I can't get by with anything on this acreage!"

Then she smiled at the little boy and went over and held his frozen head in her hands just at the ears so as to be able to look right in his eyes. She smiled at him so he knew he was the most beloved boy in all the world by somebody right then! Wow!!! His ears began to feel so funny and special.

He said to her in the tiniest voice, "Who are you?"

And she says, "I'm the spirit of life that is on this earth to help poor folk, but don't tell folk, else I can't come when I want and go where I will," she said.

And then before he could dissolve himself in hugging her like he felt like he wanted to do, she disappeared into thin air.

At first the little boy didn't know what to think. Then he stopped trying to think things through because he just couldn't unbottle his feeling so tingly and good!

Best way he could describe it was like he felt on his birthday when he was getting ready to open his presents his mom and dad brought him sitting there in front of his birthday cake!

And after he got a saucepan full of beets for his mom, he picked himself up to go back to the house - when he heard some talking from over at the fenceline.

There was a groundhog yelling for its pups to stop moving around so in their close quarters. He'd sworn it!

He's heard groundhogs talking!

He dropped his pan and held his ears and where the Beautiful Lady has touched his ears he felt SUPER cleaned of "ear interference."

He was given the gift of understanding the talking of life!

He went over to the fence row where the ruckus was and there was the escape hole of the groundhogs all right. And the little family of them was discussing this and that in a real busy kind of way.

When the boy went up to the house, he was afraid to tell his mom he heard groundhogs talking! So he just kept it close.

The next morning when he got up and was having breakfast, he was set at the kitchen table when his mom was going to bring him his favorite thing...bacon.

"Beautiful Lady!" he whispered to the air. "I know you're around here. Won't you bring me a whole plate full of bacon??? My mom don't give me enough!" But the little boy had to be satisfied with the couple of strips his mom always brought him.

Maybe she would give him a pair of new jeans? He asked the Beautiful Lady for that too!

Then he has to put on his jeans with the rip his mom has patched because the Beautiful Lady wouldn't do anything for him anymore, he figured disgusted.

After getting ready he went out to the pasture field with his dad to check on the cows that have got pinkeye from brushing so against weeds and to dab blue ointment on those they could catch - mostly the brood cows that didn't move too fast.

The little boy wandered off to look for his special calf that come to him after he took to bottle feeding it like a baby. Then came another shocker! The little boy was surprised to know he could hear the whole herd talking to each other.

Some were talking about where there was the best alfalfa in the field to mosey to and how the bites were so juicy and delicious that morning. Another one was talking about the things said at the rubbing tree down by the ford over the crick. And another one was complaining for the bull was only looking at the younger brood cows that day and not paying attention to his calf by her.

The boy didn't know more to do than just look at this one and that, hearing this one and then that one. He was afraid to tell his dad of it for fear his dad will take him to the doctor for a shot! What has that Beautiful Lady done to his ears!

Maybe she haint forgot him at all!!

When his dad went back up to the barn, the little boy stayed back in the pasture skulking here and there and finding a stick to poke before going down to the crick to see if the bush snakes were still there darting for minnows into the crick from the corkscrew willow bushes hanging over the sandy shallows. While he was sitting there, throwing his rocks in the crick, he drew himself up and said again, "Beautiful Lady? Beautiful Lady? I need some toys like other boys! How about a remote control car? Or how about a Nintendo to play games on like the boys in Indianapolis?"

But there was nothing to be done. Not a sound come from anywhere.

Not a brush against him or nothing!

But while he was staring into the hole of the crick where he knew there was a snapping turtle, he heard the crick complain and say, "That little boy is throwing rocks at me again! I wish he wouldn't!"

And the huge sycamore whose roots was most spread half clear across the crick was saying, "You're just an old grumbler! Don't you know boys have to be boys."

And then the boy heard the sun saying, "How's the temperature down there?"

A chorus of voices rose up at the sun all at once. Most where real angry cause the afternoon wasn't heating up. In fact the day was just as cool as if summer wasn't coming on. "Well-if you really care-you need to be turning it up a bit!!!" most everthing was replying!

They got really naggy!!!

"Okay," the sun says, "I will send something along," he says mischievously.

The little boy was as confused as he ever was!

His ears were doing overtime!

And his mind was forgetting about the toys.

He was getting burdened down by every story that everthing was saying.

Now, here was a bank dandelion sad for losing its fancy fluff.

And there was a crawdad screaming it can't find a shelter rock comfy enough.

And a little band snake saying its twists in the crick water as it was swimming was giving it a backache.

And the little boy seemed like his heart kept getting bigger and bigger as the stories the young learn were being inked into its pages.

And then he heard his mom calling from the house, "Danny!!! Danny?" And she was really insistent.

So the little boy ran up to the house to find his mom and dad were in the middle of a scare.

The television says a tornado is on its way.

And when the little boy looked at the sky sure enough it was on its way right then. Even as he was looking out into the Hoosier sky, the sky was getting dark and the black tornado has come. The little boy's farm is the center of a blasting, booming explosion.

The cows were scattered - there wasn't time to get them to the barn - the whole herd, everywhere...even in the cornfield where the fence was blown open.

Trees was being torn out by the roots. Neighbors's barns and fences was floating like fluff in the air and come down who knows where. Pieces of this and that ended up in torment here and there.

The dad went out to the barn anyhow. The little boy's mom was yelling for him not to. Maybe he didn't hear her! Or maybe he was going to do it to try to get the cows in anyway to save them from being turned into hamburger premature!

The little boy and his mom watched while the dad made it out to the barn somehow and got to where he was opening the barn doors so the air pressure won't be so different from the turbulent air outside. The man couldn't do any good. Just as he was standing there, and the little boy and his mom were watching, the barn was blown apart in black fury. Where was his dad? The sky was so dark and his mom was crying. And then the little boy heard his mom tell him to get to the basement and stay there. When he wouldn't, she took him down and then ran on up the basement stairs to get to the door.

The little boy heard the basement door slamming along with the crashes of the thunder and the roar of the tornado winds gnashing its teeth and sharpening them on the objects its chewing in its maw.

Later, when the storm was over and the noise levels were tamed down, the little boy came out of the cellar gingerly with eyes darting and calling here and there. "Mom? Dad?" he started calling out.

Outside he found his mom with her head under the same barn beam she was trying to help his dad get extracted from.

A nearby tree was saying it was so sorry to the little boy for the way things turned out. "There is no telling what will happen in this world," it was saying, "and me without any roots. I'm not doing so well either!"

The little boy heard everything crying and cussing the world for what sometimes happens.

Then the little boy called up, "Beautiful Lady! Beautiful Lady! Help my mom and dad. I don't care about bacon or toys."

This time the call brought forth a gusto of nature. Here came a bright light out of the Hoosier air in a misty glowing that was fiery intense...much more so than the nasty sun that had sent the tornado.

Before the little boy's eyes come the Beautiful Lady of Indiana.

This time she reached out and picked up the little boy's hand and gave him to know it was going to be just fine for him to go on a walk with her up to the county road. On the way, she told him she would go back and take his mom and dad on up to God where they could wait on him.

Then she set him down and touched his eyes to rest awhile until he was found asleep after his waving neighbor farmer came along and picked him up from there and took him to town to live with his grandma.

Sure there were disappointments in the little boy's life. One was he couldn't hear anything talking anymore.

But growing up means going from here to there and going from doing this to doing that in a restless kind of way.

And the Hoosier days sometimes was bright and that helped the little boy feel good about his homeland of Indiana. He knew Hoosier life was being burnished by a nurturing light. He knew the Beautiful Lady was busy sparkling around.

And the boy felt warmed by fire too. He remembered her then! It was like the fire he saw where his hedgeapple brains used to be.

And the wind blew like when he saw the catch in his fishing line.

And the rain fell so he could see how wet things got to help growing. He could still feel the damp on the crown of his head when he was a boy getting beets for his mom.

And the storms - and not even a tornado - could stop any of this.

No, the little boy didn't see the Beautiful Lady of Indiana ever again.

He didn't need to to know she was there.

* * * * *

Anonymous

If Jesus Come to Your House

If Jesus come to your house to spend a day or two
If he come unexpectedly, I wonder what you'd do.
Oh, I know you'd give your nicest room to such an honored Guest.
And all the food you'd serve would be the very best.

And you would keep assurances you're glad to have God there.
That serving God in your home is joy beyond compare!
But when you saw God coming, would you meet God at the door
With arms outstretched in welcome to your Homeland visitor?

Or would you have to change your clothes before you let God in,
Or hide some magazines and put the Bible where they'd been?
Would you turn off the television and hope God ain't heard -
And wish you hadn't uttered that last, loud hasty word?

Would you hid your worldly music and put some hymn books out?
Could you let Jesus walk right in, or would you rush about?
And I wonder - if the Savior spent a day or two with you --
Would you go right on doing the things you always do?

Would you keep right on saying the things you always say?
Would life for you continue as it does from day to day?
Would your family conversation keep up its usual pace?
And would you find it hard each meal to say a table grace?

Would you sing the songs you always sung and read the books you read,
And let God know the things on which your mind and spirit feed?
Would you take God with you everywhere you'd planned to go,
Or would you, maybe, change your plans for just a day or so?

Would you be glad to have God meet your very closest friends,
Or would you hope they'd stay away until God's visit ends?
Would you be glad to have God stay forever on and on,
Or would you sigh with great relief when God at last done gone?

It might be interesting to know the things that you would do
If Jesus God come in person to spend some time with you.

* * * * *

After Reinhold Niebuhr:

The Ethic of Jesus

The ethic of Jesus is the perfect fruit of the stories of God's life with humanity and its universe. Its ideal of love has the same relation to the facts and necessities of human experience as the God of faith has to the world. It is drawn from and relevant to every moral experience. It is immanent in life as God is immanent in the world. It transcends the possibilities of human life in its final pinnacle as God transcends the world.

The stories of life unite in the love Jesus, God's Child, felt for this world by which humanity is saved. This love is both the unity which is the ground of existence and the only thing ultimate, the good which is on the other side of existence. Love permits the world to exist and is the only possible way in which chaos is overcome. Nevertheless love is threatened by chaos and its meaningfulness is always imperiled. Love rests on faith in this love.

The unity of the stories of life, logos, is potent and creative and is the definition of love. All life stands under the responsibility to the loving will of this unity of God's life in the universe. All moral demands are the product of God's logos. They apply to every social morality, family, community, class and nation, existent or conceivable, here or in other worlds. It reveals the will of God in the realities of the world of human egoism, and the injustices and tyrannies arising from it. The ethic demands an absolute obedience to the will of God without consideration of consequences. The reward is a resurrection of the just.

* * * * *

Nora Etherington:

A Poor Woman's Legacy

(Nora F. Etherington died childless in 1998 at an advanced age after suffering a stoke which left her incapable of communicating in her last years. This poem was read to her church family on the Sunday service following her death and burial.)

Tho wealth I cannot leave you
And there isn't claim to fame
May I leave you many riches
Each by a different name -
My legacy would be beauty
To help sustain your soul
Courage and integrity
To make you feel quite whole.
May I leave you tenderness
A gracious heart to share, and be kind.
So many beautiful memories, I leave
As they do come to mind...
In this legacy I leave you
Compassion for another's lonely heart
Forgiveness for your fellowmen
To allow others a fresh new start.
May I leave you appreciation
For all created from above.
But most of all, dear family
My legacy to you is love.

* * * * *

A Monologue to the Tiniest God

A young girl once saved a new born calf and reared it wild until she became pregnant and had to leave her home. Now the Wild Bull was old and had lived wildly and must die totally alone.

"Yes, Yes," the Wild Bull said, taking a very deep bull breath, "it is so very dark out here. I have never imagined just how black is black."

The Wild Bull settled into some scrub by an abandoned pole barn pasture.

The night this fall was its voidest with the roll of blanketing storm clouds hovering in band after band overhead. What light there might have otherwise been over and above the overcast sky was shut out and intercepted in the softness and absorbency of the cottony unstable cloud layers.

The Wild Bull wondered to himself, "Has the sky always had this clampered dark aspect to it in the prior years, during the years of my home-seeking?" He had not remembered it if it had.

He could see from where he was settled the Hoosier woods and crick country surrounding his pasture, but it was not a visual sight. Without any light reaching the place where he was, the sight was the feel and lam of his sad recollection. Probably over the centuries there had been void nights before, but his was in the Twentieth Century, just an ordinary old Wild Bull breathing at the end of the Second Millennium, wondering if and when there would be deserved a next.

His "feel" told him that all the world and the humans he saw were asleep in the somewhere that was beyond his need to know.

And this made the void all the more black.

If time were approaching its end all over again, ending, ending, often and again, how could there be a future?

The Wild Bull tried to sleep but nightmares flew at him more incessantly than horn flies, and as annoyingly.

What if he should die? No longer after might there be anyone who cared, really cared about those humans up there asleep?

Or was there a God for the new millennium?

Now that was something to ponder!

Where if anywhere might there be a God who cared enough about humanity for the next thousand years?

Dilly Crick stopped bubbling. He had never heard that before. An owl with wings spread wider than an eagle's, flew out of the barn whispering, "Who? Who?"

"My point, exactly," the Wild Bull answered, as the bird flew away to leave the Wild Bird to ponder the why of the question, its need, and the wonder of the word "why" as well.

And as the dark night passed by in bearded minutes, the poor old Wild Bull sought out company.

Could he rely upon his friend, Mindy, to spend a moment in reflection with him. But the old horse had other dreams to share. Lumbering away was the only thing the old horse ever seemed to want to do when the Wild Bull needed some words. And as the night fell, he felt the familiar presence of the Beautiful Lady of Indiana coming to him in the air staying with him as his angel silently as always but clearly present.

Was he asleep, as he felt a touch on his eyes?

It was the beautiful lady giving him to see!

There was before him a shine as if from a light of this land where he had wandered so long, homelessly.

And the Wild Bull looked and it was as if his eyes were opened for the first time.

The shine was not what it was.

What he had thought was a shine was turning into a rainbow.

And the rainbow separated its colors and become angels standing before him in his confusion and amazement.

The first angel was telling a story in the red of passion in which God was telling God's self a story and humans were in that story which pleased God very much.

The second angel was reciting the color orange of soul and body which was filled with new continents and new nations and new peoples more perfectly conceived in liberty and dedicated to the proposition that all humanity and life, angels and things, is created equal.

The third angel give yellow to turn into neuronal cell types, pyramidal, stellate or granule never leaving cortexes and blowing like the wind into every body. Everything was ascending vertically toward the cortical surface towards God, basal dendrites emerging from base joining hands with brothers and sisters, ranging in size from 10 numilimeters in diameter to 70 or 100 mumilimeters, meeting with impossible giant pyramidal cells, Betz cells, motor cortex, pyramidal cells greeting cortical areas and subcortical sites amplified by the energy of time, interneuronal stellates buzzing through the neocortex telling the news to the friendly outputers amidst studding of spiritual spines, preferential sites in contact with life source.

The fourth angel as green as eukaryotic cells, DNA to RNA to transcription and to protein translation of every holy thought, enzymatically polymerasing, transcribing, genesing, encoding momeric nucleotides, subtly, began singing in tones of four nucleotides, tenor, alto, baritone and base ribonucleotides, genetically melodious, living, alive, loving, in molecules, in somatic cellularism of 50,000 to 100,000 genes, expressing every hope through every function being taken up to God.

The fifth angel, blue wave-particle duality, materiality and light, principles and complimentariness, particular and waving, electronic, energetic, visually impossible, awareness, a glow in a magnetic field, tiny fields, undirectedness, irrecognizeableness, modelless, extrapolateable macroscopically, reality, logically constructed 10 to 15 billion years ago, but with simultaneity today, affectionately considered, reoccuring, universal in tiny explosive points, thoughts in harmony.

The sixth angel, indigo relationships, proportionality, equations, in symbols and terminology, respectively, exponents, a,b,c's to the nth powers, exponential notations, extremes of very large and very small, algebra, representative quantitatives, manipulative equations, equalities, signs, values, binominal expansives, formulaic, comparitive, successive, determinable, plane geometrics, angular, planed in different dimensionalities, added, similar, congruent, corresponding, enclosed, relational, life in theorem, spiritual hypotenuse, logarithmic, life of anthropos to base creation to exponent of God's will, gives on.

The seventh angel, violet momentum conservation, length, time intervals, mass, relativity, rest-mass, mass increase, similarity of inertial reference forms, propagation through emptiness definitely independent from source of observation, departure, presence eternity and beyond.

And the angels joined hands and departed upward to the Familyhead, a rainbow, ascending, not descending, toward the place of rainbows which is no place at all in a relativity beyond time, but within reach, and the Wild Bull, as he closed his eyes for the last time, felt the Beautiful Lady give him embrace and close his tired eyes.

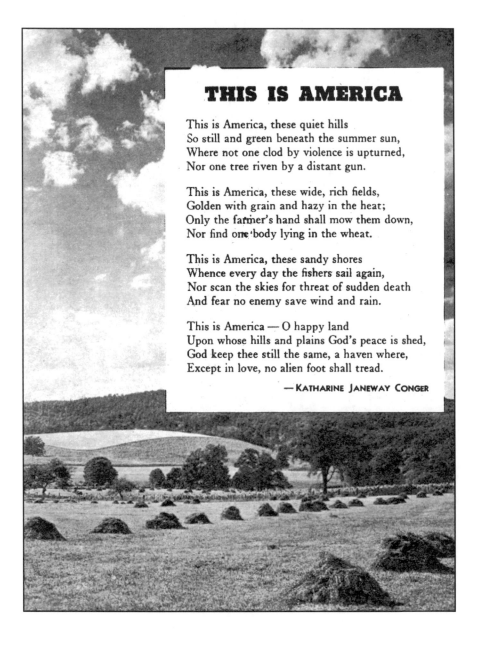

THIS IS AMERICA

This is America, these quiet hills
So still and green beneath the summer sun,
Where not one clod by violence is upturned,
Nor one tree riven by a distant gun.

This is America, these wide, rich fields,
Golden with grain and hazy in the heat;
Only the farmer's hand shall mow them down,
Nor find one body lying in the wheat.

This is America, these sandy shores
Whence every day the fishers sail again,
Nor scan the skies for threat of sudden death
And fear no enemy save wind and rain.

This is America — O happy land
Upon whose hills and plains God's peace is shed,
God keep thee still the same, a haven where,
Except in love, no alien foot shall tread.

— KATHARINE JANEWAY CONGER

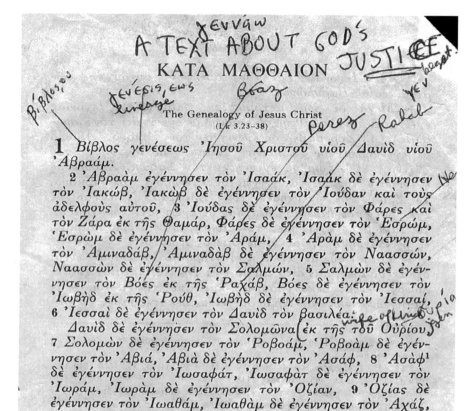

A TEXT ABOUT GOD'S JUSTICE

KATA ΜΑΘΘΑΙΟΝ

The Genealogy of Jesus Christ
(Lk 3.23-38)

1 Βίβλος γενέσεως Ἰησοῦ Χριστοῦ υἱοῦ Δαυὶδ υἱοῦ
Ἀβραάμ.

2 Ἀβραὰμ ἐγέννησεν τὸν Ἰσαάκ, Ἰσαὰκ δὲ ἐγέννησεν
τὸν Ἰακώβ, Ἰακὼβ δὲ ἐγέννησεν τὸν Ἰούδαν καὶ τοὺς
ἀδελφοὺς αὐτοῦ, 3 Ἰούδας δὲ ἐγέννησεν τὸν Φάρες καὶ
τὸν Ζάρα ἐκ τῆς Θαμάρ, Φάρες δὲ ἐγέννησεν τὸν Ἐσρώμ,
Ἐσρὼμ δὲ ἐγέννησεν τὸν Ἀράμ, 4 Ἀρὰμ δὲ ἐγέννησεν
τὸν Ἀμιναδάβ, Ἀμιναδὰβ δὲ ἐγέννησεν τὸν Ναασσών,
Ναασσὼν δὲ ἐγέννησεν τὸν Σαλμών, 5 Σαλμὼν δὲ ἐγέννησεν τὸν Βόες ἐκ τῆς Ῥαχάβ, Βόες δὲ ἐγέννησεν τὸν
Ἰωβὴδ ἐκ τῆς Ῥούθ, Ἰωβὴδ δὲ ἐγέννησεν τὸν Ἰεσσαί,
6 Ἰεσσαὶ δὲ ἐγέννησεν τὸν Δαυὶδ τὸν βασιλέα.
Δαυὶδ δὲ ἐγέννησεν τὸν Σολομῶνα ἐκ τῆς τοῦ Οὐρίου,
7 Σολομὼν δὲ ἐγέννησεν τὸν Ῥοβοάμ, Ῥοβοὰμ δὲ ἐγέννησεν τὸν Ἀβιά, Ἀβιὰ δὲ ἐγέννησεν τὸν Ἀσάφ, 8 Ἀσάφ[1]
δὲ ἐγέννησεν τὸν Ἰωσαφάτ, Ἰωσαφὰτ δὲ ἐγέννησεν τὸν
Ἰωράμ, Ἰωρὰμ δὲ ἐγέννησεν τὸν Ὀζίαν, 9 Ὀζίας δὲ
ἐγέννησεν τὸν Ἰωαθάμ, Ἰωαθὰμ δὲ ἐγέννησεν τὸν Ἀχάζ,
Ἀχὰζ δὲ ἐγέννησεν τὸν Ἐζεκίαν, 10 Ἐζεκίας δὲ ἐγέννησεν τὸν Μανασσῆ, Μανασσῆς δὲ ἐγέννησεν τὸν Ἀμώς,
Ἀμὼς[2] δὲ ἐγέννησεν τὸν Ἰωσίαν, 11 Ἰωσίας δὲ ἐγέννη-

[1] 7-8 {B} Ἀσάφ, Ἀσάφ p¹ א B C (D^Luke) f¹ f¹³ 700 1071 ℓ¹⁸⁵ᵐ ᵖᵗ
it^aur,c,d^Luke,g¹,k,q syr^hmg cop^sa,bo arm eth geo (Epiphanius) // Ἀσά, Ἀσά
K L W Δ Π 28 33 565 892 1009 1010 1079 1195 1216 1230 1241 1242 1365 1546
(2148 Ἀσσά) Byz Lect^m ℓ¹⁸⁵ᵐ ᵖᵗ it^s,f,ff¹ vg syr^c,s,p,h,pal Epiphanius Augustine
[2] 10 {B} Ἀμώς, Ἀμώς א B C (D^Luke) Δ Θ Π* f¹ 33 1071 1079 1546
ℓ¹⁶²⁷ᵐ it^c,d^Luke,ff¹,g¹,k,q cop^sa,bo,fay arm eth Athanasius Epiphanius // Ἀμών,
Ἀμών K L W Π² f¹³ 28 565 (700 892 1195 Ἀμμών, Ἀμμών) 1009 1010 1216

1 Βίβλος γενέσεως Gn 5.1 υἱοῦ Δαυίδ 1 Chr 17.11 υἱοῦ Ἀβραάμ Gn 22.18 2 Gn 21.3,
12; 25.26; 29.35; 1 Chr 1.34 3 Gn 38.29-30; 1 Chr 2.4, 5, 9; Ru 4.12, 18-19 4-5 Ru 4.13, 17-22;
1 Chr 2.10-12 6 Ἰεσσαί...βασιλέα Ru 4.17, 22; 1 Chr 2.13-15 Δαυίδ...Οὐρίου 2 Sm 12.24
7-10 1 Chr 3.10-14 11 Ἰωσίας...αὐτοῦ 1 Chr 3.15-16; 1 Esd 1.32 LXX

1

Opening page of Matthew's Witness from the *Greek New Testamant* that Ben Johnson used for translation

MATTHEW'S WITNESS

How Jesus Come to Us

THE RECORD OF FAMILY BACK-GROUND of Jesus, Child of God who come to earth, into the heritage of of David, of the line of Abraham. Abraham was the head of Isaac's family. Isaac was the Familyhead rearing Jacob. Jacob become a clan leader raising Judah and his brothers. Judah was the Familyhead over Phares, a twin with Zara, both nurtured by Tamar. Phares was the Patriarch when Hezron matured. Hezron became the Familyhead raising Aram. Aram was the head of Aminadab's tribe. Aminadab was the clan leader raising Naasson. Naasson was the Patriarch when Salman was brought up. Salman was the Familyhead raising Boaz nurtured by Rachab. Boaz was the Familyhead raising Jobed nurtured by Ruth. Jobed was the head of Jesse's family. Jesse was the Familyhead when David was raised, the David who was the powerful ruler. David was the Familyhead when Solomon was reared, nurtured by a mother from Uriah's family. Solomon was the clan leader when Roboam grew up. Roboam was the Patriarch raising Abia. Abia was the Familyhead when Jasaph was brought up. Jasaph was the clan leader when Josaphat grew up. Josaphat was the Familyhead when Joram was raised. Joram was the Patriarch raising Josian. Josian was the Familyhead as Joatham matured. Joatham raised Achaz was. Achaz was the Patriarch when Hezekian was raised. Hezekian was the Familyhead when Manassa was raised. Manassa was the Familyhead when Amos was reared. Amos was the clan leader when Josian was raised. Josian was the Familyhead when Jechonian was nurtured with his brothers' families during exile in Babylon.

After the exile in Babylon, Jechonian was the Familyhead when Salathial was raised. Salathial was the clan leader when Zorobabel was reared. Zorobabel was the Familyhead when Abioud was raised. Abioud was the Patriarch when Eliakim grew to maturity. Eliakim brought up Azor. Azor was the Familyhead when Sadok was raised. Sadok was the clan leader when Achim was reared. Achim was the Familyhead when Elioud was raised. Elioud was the Familyhead when Eleazar was reared. Eleazar was the lead of Mathan's family. Mathan was the Patriarch when Jacob was reared. Jacob was the Familyhead raising Joseph, the husband of Mary, where Jesus come from, the one we recognize as God's Child.

All of these generation heads from Abraham until David are fourteen, and from David until the exile in Babylon are fourteen, and from the exile in Babylon until the birth of God's Child are fourteen.

The Birth Of Jesus, God's Child Come To Earth

It was like this about the mother of Jesus, God's Child. About to be married to Joseph, this earthly mother of his, Mary, before marrying him, got pregnant in her female way with the breathing spirit of life that attends us. Joseph being the man he was, wanted to do right, and didn't want to make a spectacle of her. He was going to break off the engagement without fuss. But while these thoughts is working in his heart, an angel of the Familyhead come to him in a dream saying, "Joseph, Child of David, don't be scared to marry Mary, making her your wife. For this kid in her is come to be out of the Spirit that attends life. She is to give birth to a child, calling his name to be Jesus. Listen here! This one will save folk from their separation from God. This whole thing comes about to complete the speaking of the Familyhead through the prophets saying,

*Take notice, a pregnant
unwed girl will be bearing a
boy, the name of him will
be called Emmanuel (God is
committing himself to
earthly folk.)"*

*This is thought of as mean-
ing, "God is with us."*

So Joseph come out of the
dream knowing what to do, as
if there's been an order give him, this angel being a messenger from the Familyhead, and he took back his woman, and he didn't think no more of not accepting her son and calling his name Jesus.

A Visit By Non-Jewish Religious Figures

After Jesus was born in Bethlehem, Judea, in the days of Herod's controlling things, See!!! court religious figures - astrologers - from eastern places
came into Jerusalem, asking, "Where is it there's born this powerful one, a Jew?
We saw the sign of it in the east and we come to serve him." When Herod, in
power, heard about it, he got scared and all of the rest of Jerusalem the same,
and all of them got together, the senior church folk and Hebrew translators
who took care of foreign visitors and one astrologer asked if they knew where
God's child would be born on earth, and they said to him, "in Bethlehem,
Judea. That's where it got said through a prophet,

> And You, Bethlehem, Jewish soil!
> Never mind you being the least significant place in the state of Judea,
> From you will come out one who will take charge of it all,
> Who himself tends my folk, Israel, as does a shepherd."

Then Herod sent a secret summons to the eastern court astrologers to try
to find out about these things, like the time the sign showed this would happen
- it was after they'd been informed about Bethlehem - and after they come, he
interrogated them to see if they were sure about their information about the
child. "Find out about this, as my emissaries, so I too can go serve him," he told
them. And after they heard the governor say this they went to go and See! a star
- they saw it there in the east - it took off in front of them - until when they got
there, it stayed overhead where the child was. Seeing what the star done, they
whooped for joy giving mighty cheers. And going into the house, they saw the

child with Mary, his mother. And they got down on their knees to say they would serve him, and they opened up expensive items that they brung him as gifts, silver and incense and ointment. Later they was warned in a dream not to go back to Herod, and they took another road, a different way, to their homeland.

Hitting The Road To Egypt

After they'd left - Look! - an angel of the Familyhead appeared in a dream to Joseph saying, "When you wake up, take the baby and his mother with you and escape to Egypt, and stay put until what's done is done. Herod is hot against the baby to kill him." So Joseph got up and took off with the baby and his mother that very night and lit out for Egypt. And it was none to soon for Herod was on his way to finish off the boy so that the law would be triggered told from a Jerusalem prophet saying,

> Screams was heard in Rama, Crying and grieving
> everywhere, Rachel is weeping for her kids, And she
> isn't remembering this, because it hasn't happened yet.

Returning From Egypt

After Herod's time on earth come to an end, Look, the angel of the Familyhead appeared in a dream to Joseph in Egypt saying, "After you wake up, pick up this baby and his earthly mother and go to the land of Israel. He is dead, this one plotting against the life of the boy." So Joseph woke up and picked up the baby and, with his mother, took them back to the land of Israel. Later, after he heard that Archelaus took over the power, ruling the same as his father, Herod, Joseph got scared of being killed there in Judea. Then after he got ad-

vise where to go make a home in a dream, he took off to the region of Galilee, and, getting there, took up housekeeping in a town called Nazareth. So got fulfilled the law give by a prophet that he will be called a Nazarene.

John The Baptist Takes Up Preaching

In them days that we are talking about there come John, a baptizing fellow who preached out in the countryside of Judea, saying,

"Change your thinking! A power is come to us from out of where existence and life itself is. This is the law of Isaiah, its giver, saying,

> Scream! Shout out in the countryside -
> Get ready a path for the Familyhead.
>> Blaze a trail for God's Child."

This fellow, John, wore his clothes wove from camel hair and a hide belt around his waist, and his keep was locusts and findings of honey. Fact is folk would come out to him from Jerusalem and all of Judea and the places around the Jordan River, and he would baptize them in the Jordan River in person, washing and scrubbing out of them their faults separating them from God's love.

Noticing how many of the Pharisees and Sadducees was coming out to be baptized by him he said to them, "Your kind mislead as did the snake in the Garden of Eden! Can anyone protect you when you try to escape from the coming days of God's anger? You concentrate on habits of eating food, but you should be paying attention to saying inside, `We have a father in Abraham.' I'm telling you that God can raise up children of Abraham out of rocks. Already an ax is being sharpened to hack at the roots of trees. All the trees that don't give good fruit is to be cut down and thrown in a fire. I baptize you in the water to get rid of faults, but there is one coming before you who is much more powerful than me. Ain't no way that I can do the unbinding of hearts by doing baptizing. This comes in a baptizing into the Spirit of God's very breathing attending us, a fiery thing. Watch out! Someone comes with a winnowing tool in hand to separate out folks, and this place is his threshing floor, and he will pick out the wheat before throwing the rest into the fire, and the chaff will be burned up in an unquenchable fire."

Jesus Gets Baptized

About this time, Jesus come there out of Galilee up to the Jordan to this John, to be baptized by him. But John held back baptizing him, saying, "I'm the one who needs to be baptized by you, and here you are coming to me?" But Jesus answered him saying, "Cut it out right now! Just so is how its got to be done for the ends of justice to come about." Then John stopped arguing about it. After Jesus was baptized, immediately after he come up out of the water, Yes! Yes! the place where God is was revealed opened up and the Spirit of God could be seen coming out as would a dove coming over him.

And, Yes! a voice out o God's Homeland was saying. "This is my Child, one I love, in him I am mighty proud."

Jesus Tempted

After this, Jesus was took into the countryside to be put to the test by the spirit of contrariness to God. And after he fasted forty days and forty nights, he was hungry from all this. And coming to him, a proof-demander said to him, "If you are the Child of God, prove it by making the stones become bread."

> But Jesus answered saying, "It is written,
> Not from bread only will folk have life,
> But from every law coming out of the mouth of God."

Then this proof-demander got him to go to the special city of Jerusalem and he stood Jesus on a high place at the church and said to him, "If you are the Child of God, jump down, you! It is written that you can!

> To his angels, it is give the order to guard you,
> And by their hands, they will raise you if you fall.
> Never may your foot get bruised on a rock."

Jesus said to him, "Again it is written,
  "Don't put the Familyhead,
    your God, on trial."

Again, this proof-demander took him away to the very highest mountain, and showed him all the countries of the world and their glory and he said to him, "All this I will give to you if, after you come down from the mountain, you will acknowledge me." Then Jesus said to him, "Get out of here Trickster. It is written.

> You will acknowledge the Familyhead, as your God,
> And to God only give your allegiance."

Then the spirit of contrariness left him, and See! an angel of the Familyhead come down to minister to him.

Jesus Starts Work

When Jesus heard that John had been arrested, he returned to Galilee. Later, leaving behind Nazareth, going away, he went to live in Capernaum by the sea in the mountains of Zebulon and Naphthali. This way the saying of Isaiah, the prophet, was fulfilled saying,

> In Zebulon and Napthali, roadway by the sea, opposite
> the Jordan from Galilee, populated by people from all
> over the world,
> Where folk are stuck in darkness, a light shined bright,
> And for even those stuck in field or shadow of death,
> The light will shine for them.

Later on after this, Jesus picked up to preach saying, "Open up your minds." He would be preaching about the real Homeland of God.

Jesus Gets Help From Four Fishermen

While walking around the Galilee Lake, he saw two brothers, Simon, nicknamed Peter, and Andrew, his brother. Calling them, he said, "Come over here to me and I will turn you into fishermen for people." Then, not blinking, they set down their fishnets to join him. And after he went on from there, he saw another set of two brothers, James, the son of Zebedee, and John, his brother, in a boat along with their father, Zebedee, mending their nets, and he called out to them. They too, without blinking, left their boat and their father and joined up with him.

Teachings From His First Big Scale Missionary Journey

Then he went to missionary in the whole region of Galilee, teaching in the Jewish churches around there and preaching the good news about God's Homeland, and he healed many sick folk - didn't matter why they's sick. Then he left to give the good news to Syria and brought the message to all those suffering having many different illnesses and took over by pain, or mentally ill, and epileptic, and paralyzed, and he healed them. And there come following after him a big crowd from Galilee and Decapolis and Jerusalem and Judea and the parts around the Jordan River.

After he saw these folks climbing up a hill, he did too, and sitting down, they come around him, these friends of his, striving to learn God's ways, and, inspired to speak out, he taught them saying,

> "Beloved are those with spiritual, not worldy,
> resources for theirs is God's Homeland.
> Beloved are those who are saddened, for they will be
> comforted.
> Beloved are the humble, for they will share the use of
> the earth in common.
> Beloved are the hungry and thirsty who do right,
> for their appetites will be satisfied.
> Beloved are those who are compassionate,
> for they will be treated with compassion.
> Beloved are the innocent in heart,
> for they will see God.
> Beloved are the strivers for peace,
> for they are the children who will be God's
> beneficiaries.
> Beloved are those who are persecuted on account of doing
> right, for theirs is God's Homeland.

Beloved are you when they slander you and persecute you and say all the worst about you on account of me. Welcome it and find joy in it, because your pay is much in God's Homeland. Just the same way did they prosecute the prophets before you. You are the table salt of the earth. If salt loses the sting to the tongue, can its flavor come back? If it don't have the stinging taste, ain't no one don't throw it out outside to be walked on by folk. You are the shine of the world. No way can such a community be hid - having the effect of elevating your location to a hill. No one lights a lamp and places it under a bucket but instead on a lampstand where it illuminates everything in the house. Don't try to shine the light intentionally in front of folk -so they think its yours-that's a bad thing to do - instead our Parent in God's Homeland should get credited.

Don't think I came to terminate the Hebrew law or the books of prophecy - I haven't come to terminate them, but to consummate them. It's so, here's the way it is, there won't come no passing away of the sky or the earth, certainly not no passing away of the law in even its punctuation or letter, until everything is ready. There won't be no give to end even the single most minor rule or how its teaching works out for folks - what is called minor is orderly governance for folks. I tell you that if you don't do right, more than the Hebrew translators at the church in Jerusalem or Pharisees, it won't be enough, and you won't make it into the assembly beyond time in God's Homeland.

Remember how it was told to our ancestors, "Don't Murder." Any who kills someone will be guilty to sentencing. But I tell you if any becomes angry at sistor or brother, the sentence is "guilty". Now if you cuss at your brother or sister, it's a crime by Jewish council standards. On the other hand if you call someone "Worthless!", expect condemnation like comes to those who was sacrificing their children on a fire in Jeremiah's day..

If you want to place your offering down to the altar and standing there you remember that your brother has anything against you, right then and there forget about your offering at the altar and first go to make peace with your brother, and then you can come back and leave off your offering. Here is something you must do! - make friends with your enemy quickly while you are with him on the road. Unless you do, he may claim you are guilty of something, and a sentence may find you in the keep of a jailer, and you will be thrown in prison. Yes, I warn you, you may never get out of there until you have lost your last penny.

Remember how it was told, "Don't have sex that destroys loving relationships." I warn you that everyone who looks at love-partners of another to try to snare such away already has acted destructive in that one's heart. If your right side eye scandalizes you, yank it out and throw it away. Otherwise it will take you with it to the destruction of the rest of your body. So don't throw away your whole body into the fire of wrongdoing. Same if your right hand scandalizes you. Cut it off and fling it off you. Otherwise it will take you with it into the destruction of your body and next thing your whole body is took to the fire of condemnation.

Formerly it was told, "One who wants to break off a relationship with a love-partner must give this news in writing." But I tell you that everyone who breaks off with a love-partner unless it's with proof of outside sex does destructive sex acting, and this one acts destructive even if the partner who's thrown off should happen to get married.

Another thing you have heard told to our ancestors, "If you don't keep your word, you will get paid back by the Familyhead by its admonition." But I tell you not to swear at all, not on the imagination, because that is God's dwelling place, not on anything on earth, because that is God's footstool, not looking towards Jerusalem because the city belongs to the great governor, nor go swearing on your head because it is not give to you to make one white hair into black. Make your affirmation be yes for yes, no for no. Anything more that these is wrong.

You have heard it said, "An eye in place of an eye and a tooth in place of a tooth." But I tell you not to try to hold your ground against wrongdoing. When someone punches you in the right jaw, turn to him the other. And to one wanting to sue to take the clothes off your back, give him your pajamas too. And if someone drafts you into military duty to carry army luggage one mile, go with him two. To someone asking for help, give it, and one wanting to borrow from you, don't hold back turning it over.

You have heard the saying, "Love the one close to you, but hate your enemy." I tell you love your enemy and offer comfort to the one who hounds you. Doing so, you may become children of our Parent in God's Homeland, because the sun, belonging to the Parent, comes up for the wrongdoers as it does for the good and rain falls upon the ones making the right choices same as those making the wrong ones. If you love the one who loves you, you get some kind of satisfaction, but don't the tax collectors feel that? And if you say hello to your best friend, don't it make you happy? Why don't you act this way toward others outside your community? That's how you will be fulfilled as your Parent, the God of being, feels fulfilled.

Now turn your mind to this. Don't go trying to act like you are religious in front of folk to get them to admire you. Don't do it, please.. It won't have no reward from our Parent in God's Homeland.

When you do a good turn, don't go trumpeting it everywhere you are, as do those who are hypocrites, whether in the Jerusalem church, or out in an alley, to get attention in front of folks. I tell you this, Yes, I do! -being noticed is their benefit. When you do a good deed, don't let your left hand know what your right hand is doing. That's the way to do your good turns -privately. And your Parent, the one seeing it done in private, will credit you.

Then, too, when you pray, don't be like the hypocrites who get emotional in the churches and on the street corners where they act up as they pray so as they can get noticed by folks. I tell you this, Yes, I do! - they are receiving their benefit. When you pray, go to your most private place and close the door to pray to your Parent in private. And your Parent, the one seeing it done in private, will give you credit. Also when you pray, don't repeat prayer-formulas as pagans do thinking in their many words to be more likely to be heard. Don't try to be imitating others. Your Parent knows you, of what needs you have, before you even ask.

For example, pray

Our Parent in God's Homeland,

Give us to respect you for who you are,
Your Homeland come. Your desire be realized,
    as in your homeplace, also on earth.
The bread of our daily need - give it to us
today,
    And leave off seeking revenge against us,
      as we leave off seeking revenge against
others.
    And don't take us to trial,
    But drag us away from wrongdoing.

If you forgive the wrongdoings of other
folks against you, our Parent in God's Homeland
will forgive you. If you don't forgive folks these things, then our Parent don't
forgive your wrongdoings.

When you don't eat for religious reasons, don't do as the glory-seeking
hypocrites. Their faces are camouflaged so they can look like they are abstain-
ing. Yes, I tell you, their being noticed is their reward. When you abstain from
eating, comb your hair and wash your face so it don't look like you are holding
back on food to folks for our Parent is in on the secret. And our Parent is the
one who knows, privately, to give you credit.

Don't send valuables to the treasury-holding places of this earth, like the
city Treasuries of Delphi, so a moth can turn its substance into food or where
thieves can break in and steal. Valuables - bank them in God's Homeland,
where food don't disappear and where thieves can't break in or steal. Where
your valuables are, there is your heart.

The illuminator of the body is the eye. So, if you can get your eye focused on positives, your whole body can be brightened by it. But if your eye
is used wrong, your whole body gets dark. If it ain't light, it is dark. Oh! It can
get so black.

No one can serve two bosses. Here is what happens. One will be hated and
the other loved, or one will be give loyalty and the other contempt. You cannot
serve God and a god of this world.

Through it all, I say, don't stew over your life - where's your next meal
coming from - or your body - what you wear over it. Does living get better,
eating, or your body for what you wear? Think on the birds in the air, how they
don't plant, or cultivate, or store together nothing in a barn, and our Parent,
the one in charge of the air, feeds them. Why do you think you are any more
different than them? What can come out of stewing over yourselves? adding to

your life span even one day? And is there anything to stew over- what to wear? Study the
thistles in the field - how they flourish. They
don't work or sew. And I tell you Solomon in
all his dazzle couldn't dress himself as one of
them. Now if the hay of the field is here today
and tomorrow there is God heaving it into a
chaff fire, so what does it matter what it looked
like? Why can't you get faithful enough? Can't
you do a little better than that? Aren't you
stewing when you say, What will we eat? or,
What will we drink? or What will we wear?
Everybody, all people, are scroungers. Don't
our Parent in God's Homeland know it? God is
the one who takes care to meet needs? The
first thing is to journey to God's homeland and God's ideas of justice and all
the rest will get provided to you. Don't stew about tomorrow, for tomorrow
will stew over itself. Today and its burden is enough.

Don't discriminate, so you won't get discriminated against. If your discrimination results in a prejudice, you will be the one condemned, and in the
amount you deal with folk on that basis you will be dealt with. Why do you
see a speck in the eye of your friend and you don't catch on that you have a
timber in your eye. Why do you say to your friend, Come here- I can poke out
the speck out of your eye, and don't you have a major splinter blocking your
vision? Hypocrites! First poke out the timber from your own eye and then you
can see clear enough to poke out the speck from your friend's eye. Don't give
an offering that should be for God to dogs or throw your pearls in front of pigs
who don't know no better than to trample on them with their hooves, bursting
them to pieces.

Ask and it will be give to you, search and you will find, knock and it will
be opened to you. Everything anyone asks for gets received, or looks for gets
found, or comes from knocking on a door for entry gets opened up. Is there
anyone among you folk whose child needs bread who would give them a rock?
Or who ask for a fish - would anyone give that child a snake? Now if you know
that good things are give to children, even misbehaving, how much more likely
is it that our Parent in God's Homeland will give good things to those asking
for them. Everything - whatever it is - you want people to do for you, so you
must do for them. For this is the law and the prophet teachings.

You are entering a city through a gate hard to maneuver through. Yes, there
is a street gate - then too, its street is wide leading you away into destruction

and everybody else may be trying to get in this way. Whoever asks can enter through the gate of obstacles and the press of its road leading into life but few there are who try to locate it.

Be watchful for false prophets - some come to you in sheep's clothing - inside they are hungry wolves. By their actions, you will be able to recognize them. Can you pick grapes from thorns or figs from thistles? Just so, every good plant bears good fruit, but a weedy plant bears bad fruit. A good plant cannot bear bad fruit. Nor can a weedy plant bear good fruit. Every plant that don't bear good fruit gets cut down and thrown into the fire. Thataway, from their fruit you will recognize them.

Not everybody who calls to me, `Sir!' will go into the God's Homeland, but the one who acts on the urging of my Parent who is in God's Homeland. Many will say to me at that time, `Sir! ain't we acted like we was prophets for your sake, or ain't we helped the mentally ill for your sake, or done many other things for your sake?' And then I will have to tell them straight out, `No, I don't know you. Get along away from me to where them are who didn't do justice.'

Everybody who pays attention to these words of mine and acts on them will become like a smart person who built a house on rock. Rain fell down and the floods came up and the winds blew up and beat against the house, and it didn't crash down, for it was built solid on the rock. But everyone who pays attention to these words of mine and don't act on them will be like someone foolish, who went building his house on sand. And rain fell down and the floods came up and the winds blew up and that house got beat against, and it crashed down, and there was a loud rukus demolition of it."

And there come the time Jesus finished these words, and the whole crowd were filled with inspiration from his teachings, for these teachings was based on authority and not like them of the church Hebrew translators.

Healing Incidents

A large crowd followed him from that place where they come down the hill. Now, see! A leper come up to him begging him, saying, "Sir! If you want to you can clear up my skin." Then stretching out his hand, Jesus touched him saying, "I want to. Have clean skin." And right then, the leper has been give clean skin. And Jesus says to him, "See that you don't tell no one, but go right

away to church and take a gift, the one Moses ordered, to explain what happened to them."

At Capernaum, there come to him a captain of soldiers calling out to him and saying, "Sir, my son fell in the house crippling him. He is terrible visited by pain." And he says to him, "When I visit him, I will heal him." But the captain replied, saying, "Sir, I am not worthy that you may come under my roof. You only need to say it in a word and he will be healed, this son of mine. Now I myself am a person under a command - I myself have soldiers - and I tell one of them, Go and he goes. Or another, Come here and he comes. Same to my servant. Do this, and he does it." After listening to this, Jesus did his healing and said to them following him, "Yes, I tell you, I have discovered no one anywhere in Israel of such faith. I tell you that the crowds will come from the east and west and they will seat themselves before Abraham and Issac and Jacob in the homeland of God's Homeland, but the children of this state will be thrown into the outer place to a void. There they will be shouting and gnashing teeth." And Jesus said to the captain, "Go, as your faith has given it to be, so it is." And he was healed - this son of his - at that hour.

When Jesus went to Peter's house he saw Peter's mother- in-law lying down and sick with a fever. And he touched her hand and her fever fled and she got up and welcomed him. When the evening came, they brought to him many anguished folk. And he relieved their mental problems with a word and he healed every calamity. So came to be fulfilled the words of Isaiah, the prophet, saying,

> This one takes upon himself our weakness and lifts off
> sickness.

And Jesus, knowing how many were in the crowd around him, told them to go back home so he could go across to the other side. But one of the Hebrew translators from the church came up to him and said, "Teacher, I want to follow you wherever you go." Jesus said to him, "Well, a fox has a den, and a bird the sky to make his home, but the Orphan does not have so much as a sickbed to go to rest his head." Another one, wanting to become a friend in learning about God's ways, said to him, "Sir, I got to first await the death of my parents and their burial," but Jesus said to him, "Follow me and leave those charged with burying dead folk to bury them."

Now after he got on a boat, his friends in striving to do God's bidding followed after him. But there came a huge storm in the waves and even as the boat was going to be capsized under a whitecap, Jesus was napping. And, going over to him, they woke him up, saying, "Sir! Save us! We are going to die!" But he says to them, "Why are you afraid? Don't you have faith enough?" Then, awoke, he calmed down the winds and the waves and there come a great stillness on the sea. And these folk were struck with questions, saying, "Who is this when the winds and the sea take orders from him?"

And getting to the other side, to a town called Garadanos, their way was obstructed by two mentally ill folk, very strange looking, living in a cemetery who came to them, so he couldn't get by them to go on his way. And how they shouted, saying, "What is to happen to us and to you, Child of God? Are you coming here, to this time, to shake us up?" But he was distracted from them by a huge herd of pigs grazing. Then their mental problems begged him, saying, "If you are going to throw us out, send us into the herd of pigs." And he said to them, "Get out!" And rushing out, they entered into the pigs, and all of the herd stampeded across a cliff into the sea and drowned in the waves. And the pig herder escaped and ran into the town sounding warnings to everybody about what had happened to the crazy ones. And, yes, the whole town went out to ward away Jesus, and, seeing him, they confronted him, trying to get him to go away from their neighborhood.

Then, re-boarding the boat, he crossed back and went to his hometown. And they was bringing to him an injured fellow on a stretcher who's been in a fight. And after Jesus realized what they was expecting him to do, he said to the injured fellow, "Don't be afraid, boy, your crimes are forgiven." And some of the Hebrew translators said to them, "This fellow speaks against God." But Jesus got mad and said to them, "Why do you enrage your hearts in deception? Isn't it easier to say, 'Your crimes are forgiven,' than to say, 'Get up and walk?' You don't understand the authority that the Orphan has upon

the earth to forgive crimes?" Then he said to the injured fellow, "Get up from your stretcher and go to your house." And he got up and went to his house. And the onlookers were filled with respect and they gave the praise to God, the one giving the authority to such a one over folk.

Matthew Called

Later, when Jesus was traveling from there, he saw a fellow sitting down up close to a toll booth - Matthew was what he was named - and Jesus says to him, "Join me." And, inspired to get up, he joined Jesus. And Jesus went to give a blessing at his house, and there come several toll collectors, and crooked ones was coming too, and they sat down with Jesus and his friends learning to follow God's teaching. And when they saw it, some Pharisees said to his friends, "What is going on - him with these tax collectors- and crooked ones - this teacher of yours is eating with them!" But when Jesus heard about it, he said, "Ones who are healthy don't have need of a doctor, only the ones suffering bad times. Now learn -traveling along- how it is,

I prefer mercy and not church offerings. I came not to call the self-assured but the wavering."

Fasting Explanation

Then, there come to him John's friends learning God's ways, saying, "What is going on with you. Like Pharisees, we do fasting to remember when our people were slaves in Egypt, but your followers—don't they hold off eating?" And Jesus said to them, "How can it be for folks in a bridal party to know remorse for so long as the bridegroom is with them? But there will come the day when the bridegroom may be took away, and then they can fast. No one sews on new cloth as a patch for an old robe whose rips have torn the robe apart - a mender is needed to pick it up and handstitch it. No one stores new wine in old wineskins. If you do that, the wineskins bust and the wine pours out and the wineskins wear out. instead folk store new wine in new wineskins and both help preserve each other."

More Healing For The Faithful

While these things was being discussed among themselves, something else - a chairman of a church's elders was arriving to plead with him, saying, "My daughter is dying. Come and go with me. Lay your hands on her and she will live." And getting up, Jesus followed him and his friends learning from him come too. And - now this - a woman with female problems for twelve years was overtaking him from behind struggling to touch the edge of his robe. And she was saying to herself, "If only I could have touched his robe, I would have been healed." But Jesus turned to her and said, "Don't worry lady. Your faith has healed you." And the lady was healed from that instant. And Jesus went on the house of the elder and - look at this - flute players was there, and while the crowd was milling outside, Jesus said, "Get out of the way, for the little girl hasn't died, she is sleeping" - causing them to laugh at him. But after the crowd was broke through, and after he entered, he grabbed her hand, and the little girl woke up. And the news about her was passed around to that whole land.

And after he took himself away from there, Jesus was followed by two blind folk, crying out and saying, "Have mercy on us, Child of David." After he has come to this road house, they come to him - these blind folk - and Jesus says to them, "Do you really believe I can do this?" And they said to him, "Yes sir!" Then he touched their eyes saying, "I make it happen to you according to your faith." And they opened their eyes. And Jesus was very earnest with them, saying, "You see but don't let nobody know how it come to be!" But after they left, they went spreading it to the whole land.

While they was traveling along - now this - there was brought to him a hard-to-understand fellow who is mentally ill. And when he throwed off his mental illness, the hard-to-understand fellow could talk. And the crowd was shocked, saying, "Never before has the like been seen in Israel." But the Pharisees was saying, "He is throwing off mental illness while he is in the throes of mental illness."

Getting The Feel How Human Life Is

Now while Jesus was leading them to lots of cities and towns, he was doing teaching in the their churches and preaching the good news of the homeland and healing everybody diseased and everybody sick. And what the crowds was seeing was him feeling for them down to his guts because they was what he was worrying over and stewing about, as a shepherd but one who don't have sheep. Then he says to his friends striving to learn God's ways, "The crops is plentiful but the field hands are few. Pray to the Landowner of the crops to send out field hands for his crops."

There come a time when the twelve friends and learners was called together, and he gave them the charge over Godless behaviors so as to throw them off and to heal all disease and all sickness. The names of the twelve friends and followers are these: First was Simon called Peter and Andrew his brother, and James the son of Zebedaios, and John, his brother, Philip and Bartholomew, Thomas and Matthew, the toll booth man, James the son of Alphaios, and Thaddaios, Simon the Caananite, and Judas the Iskariot, who give him over.

A Test Whether Israel Is Ready As God's Homeland

Jesus sent these twelve out, giving them orders, saying, "Don't leave off to a road to folks not Hebrew stock and don't go along into a town of the Samaritans. Go, instead - where better - to the sheep scattered from the house of Israel. When you get there, preach, saying that God's Homeland is coming. Encourage the weak, raise up the despairing, clear up the skin of lepers, throw off mental illnesses, accept charity, give charity. Don't pack gold or silver or copper coins in your belt. Don't even carry a money belt, or extra shirt or pair of shoes or a walking stick. And it is fitting to be a field hand for your meals. In whatever city or town you enter you can search out who is hospitable in her. And there's where you can stay until you leave. When you go into a house give it your good wishes. And if it turns out a hospitable house, leave your peace upon it, but if it is not, take back your peace to yourself. And if no one welcomes you, don't go passing judgment on them in your words, just when you leave the house or that city, shake the dust off your feet. I tell you this for sure, that it will be more endurable to be in the land of Sodom and Gomorrow on the judgment day than to be in that city.

A Warning About Earthly Persecution

I am deputizing you as sheep in the middle of wolves -be as surreptitious as snakes but as innocent as doves. Watch out for folk who would turn you in to Jewish church councils or in to their churches where you would end up getting beat with whips. Also you could get dragged in front of judges or magistrates for witnessing for me to them. When you are arrested, don't be fretful of what to say. It will be give to you at that time what to say. For you will not be the talker but the breath of the Spirit of our Parent will do the talking in your place. Friend will turn against friend causing their death, and a father against a child, and children will stand up testifying against their mothers and fathers and convicting them to die. And you will be hated by everybody for my sake. But one holding on to the end, this one will be saved.

When they prosecute you in a certain city, escape to another. It's for sure, it won't last long for those cities of Israel until the Orphan may arrive.

Resigning One's Self To Christian Status

No student is above the teacher. Nor is an employee above a supervisor. It is enough for a friend striving to live an approved life to become as his teacher and for an employee to become as his supervisor. If the head of household is one calling upon the Devil, its just as likely - if not more -that's to happen to them in the household.

Don't fear them. Nothing which you are accused of will be left unprosecuted, or forgot that you will tell about. What I foretell so gloomy, you have spoken into the light and what you hear in your ears is broadcast beyond rooftops. And don't fear the death of your body, for the soul can't die. Be more afraid of the possibility that both the body and soul will be destroyed in retribution.

Aren't two sparrows sold for a penny? And not one of them falls to the ground without our Parent. And the strands of hair on your head is all counted. So don't be afraid. You matter a lot more than sparrows.

Everyone who acknowledges me before folks, I will acknowledge them before my Parent in God's Homeland. But who denies me before folks, I will deny before my Parent in God's Homeland.

Don't think that I came to force peace on the earth. I came not to force peace but to wield the sword of justice. For I came to turn a man against his father, and a daughter against her mother, and a bride against her mother-in-law, and that a man's worst enemies might be members of his own house.

Someone loving a father or mother more than me is not deserving me and someone loving a son or daughter more than me is not deserving me. And any not picking up the cross to follow after me, isn't deserving to be mine. One coveting his life loses it, and one losing his life for me covets it.

Someone welcoming you, welcomes me, and that someone who welcomes you is welcoming the one who sent me on my mission. Someone welcoming a prophet with the dues of a prophet will receive the pay of a prophet and someone welcoming a saint with the dues of a saint will receive the pay of a saint. And someone who gives a drink of water to even a single one of the least of these - if only a cup of cold water - the dues of a friend learning God's ways - it's my warranty - won't have that one's pay lost out.

Afterwhile, when Jesus was finished giving instructions to his twelve traveling companions, he was leaving out from there to teach and preach in their cities.

John The Baptist Is Reassured

But John, who heard in jail the happenings of God's child, sent out two of his companions, and had them say to him, "Are you the one coming or do we have to wait for someone else?"

And when Jesus worked up an answer, he said to them, "After you leave, give John the news what you hear and see. The blind are give to see and the handicapped are give to walk, lepers are give clean skins, and the deaf are give to hear, and the dead are give to arise and the poor are give good news. And especially happy is someone who ain't ashamed being mine." After these two had left, Jesus started up saying to a crowd about John, "What did you go out to the countryside to gaze at? Was it to see water reeds being blown in the wind? Something else you went out to see? A man dressed fit to kill in fancy clothes? Maybe even fancy clothes like is worn in the upper class homes? What else did you want to see? Was it a prophet? Yes, I tell you, and much more than just a prophet. This one is about who is writ,

Watch - I will send ahead of time my messenger to confront you,
One who will have charge to build the road for you to come before me.

I tell you for sure, no prophet has been aroused to prophesy ever born of a woman greater than John, the one who baptizes - still the least worthy in the homeland of God's is better off then him. Before the days of John's baptizing until this very moment, God's Homeland is held back and obstructors are attacking it. It was this way at the time of all the prophets and the time the commandment scroll was give until the time when John come to give prophecy to make its meaning known. Now, you want it told plain out? He is the one Elijah said would precede the one coming. Anyone who has ears, listen.

What can this generation be compared to? Its folk are like children sitting at the marketplace gossiping to each other saying,

We have played the music to you - but you don't dance,

We have sung sad songs to you - but down deep, you feel no grief.

John went without, not worrying about eating or drinking, and what did they say about him, 'He is out of his head.' An Orphan came who eats and drinks, and they say, "Look at him! There he is - fat and drunk, acting smart, just another sinner. This wiseguy thinks to be considered righteous by doing good deeds."

Judgment On Cities

Then he began to criticize the cities in which most of his work has been done because they wasn't changing their ways. Shaking his head, he groans your name, "Chorazin", then shaking his head, he groans your name, "Bethsaida", saying, "Well, if Tyre or Sidon had been a party to them doings done in you, long ago they'd be in sackcloth and ashes and have turned themselves around. Even so, Tyre and Sidon will be more preferable in the days of judgment than you. And you, Capernaum,

> Can you expect yourselves to be lifted up to the Homeland
> while you are on your way down to desolation.

because if there had been done in Sodom them things done in you, it would have stayed to this very day. So I tell you that Sodom will be more preferable in the days of judgment than you."

Jesus Acknowledges His Paternity From God

In due time, aroused, Jesus said, "I acknowledge you as my Parent, Head over God's Homeland and the earth. What you have hid from the wise and intellectual, you have revealed to these common innocents. Yes, my Parent, because you want me to, I stand before you. Everything has been turned over to me by my Parent, and no one knows the mind of a child more than a parent, nor does a parent want anyone not to be mindful of his child or disregard what the child might wish to reveal. Come to me, all who are tired or held down, and I will give you rest. Take my bond upon yourselves, and learn from me, because I am an easy tamer to the dejected in heart, and you will find empowerment in your lives. My bond is bearable and its burden is light."

Following Jesus Permits Law Transcending And Healing

In due time, Jesus was traveling on the sacred days of rest through cropfields. His disciples was hungry and began to pick heads of wheat to eat. But Pharisees watching him said to him, "Hey, do you see what your friends and followers is doing that's not give to them to do on the sacred days of rest!" But Jesus said to them, "Haven't you read in public worship what David did when he was hungry and them with him, how he went into the house of God and ate bread offered to God that wasn't supposed to be eat by him, nor by them with him, but only by priests? Either that or don't you read during your worship in the law that the priests in the church can violate the code of the days of rest and it is okay? I say to you that here is someone greater than a church. If you recognize what it means,

> I desire tolerance not sacrifice.
> Then you would not have judged these to be the cause of no violation.
> A human Child of God is the one in charge over the Sunday days of rest."

After going along from there, he went into a church of theirs. And - see - a fellow having a crippled hand. And they was asking him, saying, "Is it legal to heal on the sacred rest days so they won't be charging you with being a criminal out of doing it?" But he said to them, "What person among you would there be who has a single sheep and if it stumbles into a pit on a sacred rest day don't grab it and pull it out? What's the difference between a person and a sheep? So that's why it is legal to do needful things on the sacred days of rest." Then he says to the man, "Stretch out your hand." And the guy stretched it out and it was returned to normal the full range of motion as the other. Leaving out of there, the Pharisees took to conspiring about it, how they could do him in.

But Jesus knowed it and left out of there. And a whole bunch of people followed him and he healed them all. But he warned them so's they won't do nothing to show off. This way got fulfilled the writing of Isaiah the prophet saying,

> See! my Child who is chose,
> My adored one - my life becomes happy thinking of him.
> I will give him the breath of my spirit,
> And he will pass judgment upon folk.
> He will not argue or shout
> Nor will anyone hear his voice on wide city streets.
> He will not snap off a bent reed
> Or douse a smoking candlewick,
> Unless it be toward victory in execution of judgment.
> And in his name the homeless and saddened will have hope.

Next, a blind and deaf person, so depressed he was mentally ill, was brought to him, and he healed him so the deaf person could talk and see. And the whole crowd was shocked and said, "Can anyone doubt this is the Child of David?" But when the Pharisees heard of it, they said, "He is not healing the mentally ill except by appeal to a mentally ill God". But knowing what they was thinking about, Jesus said to them, "Every Homeland which harbors a party of dividers becomes desolate. Also any city or house harboring dividers in it cannot stand. And if there were a God of opposition healing opposition how would a homeland of his opposition to God be able to stand? If I am healing mental illness in the name of a mentally ill God, in whose name are your proteges healing them? For this reason, they will be sitting in judgment of you. Unless it were through the spirit of God's breathing that I am healing mental illnesses, the Homeland of God could not be coming down on you. How could anyone break into a house strongly guarded unless his tools can break in, and even firstoff after he subdues the strongest guard? And only then will the house be burglarized. Someone who is not with me is against me and if someone conspires against me, he will be chased in all directions. Also I tell you, any wrong and contrariness is forgivable against folk, but a contrariness of spiritual dimension will not be forgot. And if anyone tells a lie about God's Child, he can be forgive. But if it's said against the breath of God's spirit then it will not be forgive him in this age or the one coming."

Becoming Known By The Fruit You Bear

"If you tend a good plant, its fruit will be good, but however you tend a puny plant, its fruit will be puny. It is from the fruit that a plant is known. Monsters! How can you be saying what's right is corrupt! Speech expresses the overflowing feeling of the heart. A good person speaks out blessings from a stored treasure of good feeling, but a bad person speaks out cursed language from a cursed nature. I tell you that every expression which these folk say will be give back to them in a sentence of everlasting judgment. But you will be approved on account of your speech, and, on account of your speech, you will be disproving theirs."

Jesus And The Sign Of Jonah

Once, some of the church Hebrew translators and the Pharisees was saying, "Teacher, we need to see a miracle out of you." And he was aroused to say about them, "A corrupt and unfaithful offspring is looking for a sign and a sign will not be give to them except the sign of Jonah, the prophet.

Jonah was in the belly of a whale three days and three nights. God's human Child will be in the heart of the ground three days and three nights. The people of Nineveh would turn over in their graves to criticize this bunch and they would condemn them, because the people of Nineveh knew enough to have an attitude change after Jonah's preaching and, look, someone with more important preaching than Jonah is here! The Queen of the South would get up out of her grave to criticize this bunch and to condemn it, because she came from a distant place of the earth to listen to the knowledge of Solomon and, look, someone with more information than Solomon is here."

The Need For Vigilence Against Backsliding

When a goblin was kicked out from a fellow's house, it went out to a deserted place looking for shelter. But it didn't find any. Then it thought, "Maybe I can go back to the house from where I come out of." And when he went back, he saw them in the house was preoccupied praying fulltime while they was sweeping and decorating. So he went in and he brought with him seven other nasty ghosts and after moving in he took up residence again. So it is with these successors compared to the times of their forebears. So it will be in that corrupt generation.

Doing God's Will Brings Membership In God's Family

Once while he was talking in a crowd, his mother and brothers and sisters was standing outside waiting to talk to him. And someone near him said, "Your mother and your brothers and sisters are outside waiting to talk to you." He responded to the one telling him this, saying, "Who is my mother and who are my brothers and sisters?" And gesturing his hands to his friends striving to learn Godliness, he said, "See! My mother and my brothers and sisters. Whoever is acting to do the wishes of my Parent in God's Homeland, this is my brother or sister or mother."

Stories From Jesus Told By The Sea

At another day, Jesus was leaving his home and went to sit down beside the sea. And there come gathering around him a huge crowd so as to make it he had to go sit in a boat. And the whole crowd was sitting on the shore. And he told them everything in a story with an example in it, saying, "A farmer when out to farm. Now on the way to do his planting he spilled seed down on the stony road, and birds come down and ate them. And he went and spilled more in gravel where it didn't have good dirt, and its starts come up through it not having any size because of the dirt. And while they was coming up, the sun got scorching hot and in the end they didn't have roots enough to keep sprouting. And then he spilled more on a thorn patch, and these thorns bushed up and they choked them. And then he spilled the rest on good dirt and the field produced quality crops, some 100% top grade, some 60%, some 30%. Those who have ears need to take heed!"

Later, after the friends learning to conform their lives to God's will come to him, they said to him, "Why do you tell stories to them?" And, aroused, he said to them, "Well, it is give to you to understand the mystery of the God's Homeland but it ain't give to these. Whoever has the capacity, it will be give to and it will be made more and more clear. Whoever don't have the capacity still it will be in reach for that one like the one who has it. This is why I am talking to them in example like stories, because seeing they don't see, and hearing, they don't hear enough nor get the point.

And it was being fulfilled to these the prophecy of Isaiah saying,
For sure you will hear and not misunderstand,
And looking, you will see and not be ignorant.
The feelings of this people have grown insensitive,
And what they may be thinking they hear is jumbles.
They have closed their eyes
For fear of seeing what's to be seen
And closed their ears except to what they may be wanting to hear
But in the heart they are give to understand and to
change their ways and I will restore them.

Your eyes are beloved because they see and your ears because they hear. And I tell you the truth, that all the prophets and saints would have liked to see what you are seeing but they didn't get to see it, and would have liked to hear it but they didn't get to hear it. You heard the example about the farmer. To everyone who hears the story of the Homeland and doesn't reckon by it, the Evil One comes and snatches away the seed that is in his or her heart and this is the point about the seed spilling on the road. Now the seed spilling in the gravel, this is case of one hearing and at first, fortunately, receiving it, but it is temporary for this one don't have the root firm in them enough, and when troubles come or persecution on account of the story, this one is quick to disregard it. Now the one whose seed is spilled in a thorn patch, this one hears the story, and is anxious about eternity, but crowds around the story guiles about wealth and ends up bearing no crop. But where the seed is spilling in good dirt, this is one hearing the story and reckoning on it. This one really is give over to bearing good crops and producing 100% or 60% or 30%."

Here is another story with example to it that he was telling them gathered around, "God's Homeland is made up like this - about a farmer who planted good seed in his field. But while folk was sleeping, an enemy of his come around and scattered seeds of weeds looking like wheat up the rows of wheat and left. When the crop sprouted, he was going to cultivate the wheat, when

he looked and they was weeds resembling wheat. The farm hands come up to him and said, `Sir, isn't that a worthless crop coming up in your field? How come you have weeds?' Then he told them, `An enemy of mine done this.' Then the farm hands said to him, `Do you want us to go out and cull them?' And he said, `No, I'm afraid if you cull out the weeds, you might cull wheat at the same time. Leave it both to grow together until harvest time, and on harvest day, I will come with the harvest crew. Then first you can cull the weeds resembling the wheat and bind them into bundles to be burned and then gather the wheat and take it to the barn.'"

Here is another story with example to it that he was telling them gathered around. "God's Homeland is made up like this - about a mustard plant seed which a fellow collected and planted in his garden. This thing - which is the smallest of all the seeds - when it comes up it is the biggest of the garden plants and becomes a tree so that those that's birds of the sky can fly to them and make their homes in its branches."

All these, Jesus told about in stories to the crowds and he didn't say nothing to them except stories with examples. So it was fulfilled the word coming from the prophet saying,

> I will express myself in stories with deep meanings,
> I will speak from the bottom of my heart the hid
> things from the beginning of the world.

After the crowd left, he went into the house, and his friends learning from him God's ways come up to him and said, "Explain to us the story of the field-weeds." And it aroused him to say, "The one planting the good seed is God's human Child, and the field is this world, and the good seed is those who are children of the Homeland. But the weeds resembling the good seed are the children of the obstruction, and the enemy of the farmer is the Opposition. The harvest is the finishing time of the world. The harvest crew are the angels. As the weeds are culled and burned in the fire, so will it be at the finish of the age. God's human Child will come with his angels and they will cull from his

Homeland all the scandalous ones and them that's doing wrong. And they will be throwed together into a burning fire. Here will be someone crying out and there will be someone gnashing teeth. Then the saints will be made as shiny as the sun in the Homeland of our Parent. One having ears better listen!"

"Like this is God's Homeland - to a hidden treasure in a field which after a fellow finds it he keeps secret, and he goes back home from his lucky find and sells everything - so much as he has - and buys this field."

"Also like this is God's Homeland - a fishing dragnet throwed into the sea and it does its gathering from every hierarchy. And when its been filled up is when they drag it up to the beach and after they have sat down they collect out the good into a catch but the worthless are thrown outside. So it will be at the end of the age. Angels will select and separate out the evil from the thick of the saints and they will cast them into the burning fire. Here will be one crying out and there one gnashing teeth."

"Do you understand these things?" They all said, "Yes." Then he said to them, "So it is that every interpreter who is made a friend and seeker after God's Homeland is the same as a fellow homeowner who retrieves from it treasures old and new."

A Record Of Jesus's Visit To His Hometown

Afterwards, when Jesus was done telling these stories, he went away from there. And when he come to his hometown, he taught those that was there in their church so as to shock them into saying, "What has got into him - this wisdom and these doings?" "This can't be the boy we knew as the carpenter's son, can it?" "No way." "Wasn't his mother named Mary and his brothers was James and Joseph and Simon and Judah?" "And wasn't his sisters all familiar to us?" "What's brought about all these things?" And they lost interest in his mission. And Jesus said to them, "There is no prophet dishonored anywhere like in his hometown and in his house." And he didn't do any more miracles there on account of their orneriness.

Herod And John The Baptist

Near that time, Herod, the Tetrarch of the Roman region, was hearing about Jesus. And he said to them administrators of his, "This is John the Baptist. He has come back from the dead and this is how the miracles are being performed through him." This fellow, Herod, after arresting John, confined him and after he was in jail he kept him there on account of Herodias, the wife of his brother Philip. John had told Herod, "It isn't permitted for you to have her." And Herod wanted to kill him but was afraid of the population because they was regarding him as a prophet. While a birthday party for Herod was going on, the daughter of Herodias danced out in the center of the room and it er responded to him and said, "Sir, if you want to, order me to be able to go to you on the water." And Jesus said, "Come." And, after he left the boat, Peter walked on the water and went to Jesus. But, seeing the wind grow stronger, he took fright, and when he began sinking he cried out, saying, "Sir, save me." Then Jesus reached out and took him by the hand and says to him, "You don't have enough faith. Why were you in doubt?" And after he got on board into the boat with them, he stilled the wind. But them on the boat give worship to him saying, "It is for sure you are the Child of God."

Now after they crossed over, they went upon the shore at Gennasaret, and when the men of that place found out about it, they give the news out to the whole neighborhood and they took to him all the ones that's sick, and they begged him to touch the cuff of his robe and thatway they would be cured.

Jesus Condemns Empty Eating Customs

Once there come out to Jesus from Jerusalem, Pharisees and church Hebrew translators saying, "Why is it your friends and followers disobey the customs of the elders? They don't wash their hands before they eat." Jesus answered that saying, "Why do you avoid the law of God handed down to you? God said,

> Prize your father and mother.
> and
> One who curses his father and mother is to be ordered to die!

Now it's like you might say to a father or mother, `I will be benevolent, but you got to pay me for it!' and that will not be valuing the Parent. And you are disregarding the story of God's life by your custom. Hypocrites! It was apt predicted by the prophet Isaiah saying,

> This folk - it gives me lip service.
> But in its heart it distances itself from me,
> And its worship of me is empty
> holding up teachings that is people's rules.

And he called the crowd together and said to them, "Listen and understand. Nothing going into a mouth is forbid a person, but what comes out from the mouth - this may be forbid a person." Then his friends striving to learn God's ways come to him saying, "Do you understand that the Pharisees is saying the lesson is going to cause folk to violate God's law?" But Jesus responded, saying, "Every seedling which my Parent in God's Homeland don't seed is going to have to be uprooted. Forget them - they are blind leaders -if the blind are give to lead the blind, everybody will fall into a pit." Then Peter said to him, "Tell us the nut of the example from the story." But he said, "Even now can't you understand? Don't you realize that everything going into the mouth is give home in the stomach and is passed out into a toilet? But what comes out of a mouth is an expression of the heart, and each of such might be profanities to a person. For out of the heart come corrupt arguments, murder plots, begging to commit sex out of marriage, solicitations for wrong sex acts, demands from thieves, lies, blasphemies. These are the dishonoring things of folks, and leaving hands unwashed before eating don't amount to dishonoring to folk."

Jesus Lives With Non-Jews And Heals There

Now after Jesus left from there, he went to live in the neighborhood of Tyre and Sidon. And - here's a situation to look at - a woman of Canaan in the neighborhood come up to him crying, saying, "Have pity on me, Sir, Child of David. My daughter is mentally ill." But he didn't give her no heed. And when they was leaving his friends striving to learn God's ways asked him about it, saying, "Help her, because she is still crying out behind us. "But Jesus responded and said, "I was not sent except to the lost sheep of the house of Israel." Then she overtook them, and begged, "Help me." And he answered her, "It isn't right to take food from children and throw it to house dogs." "Yes, Sir," she said, "but even dogs get to eat scraps thrown from the table to them by the Familyhead." Then Jesus answered her, "Woman, great is your intuition. It will be as you wish." And her daughter was healed at that very hour.

And going out from there, Jesus went to the Sea of Galilee and, going up to a hill, he sat down there. And there come out to him a huge crowd bringing with them those that's crippled, blind, deaf, and many other problems and they was carried over before his feet, and he healed them. So it was the crowd was shocked seeing the deaf talk, the deformed restored, the crippled walking and the blind seeing, and they give the praise to the God of Israel.

Later on Jesus called the friends learning God's ways to him saying, "I feel sorry for the crowd, how already three days they have stayed with me and they haven't had anything to eat. I don't want them to be weak from hunger, so much so they might be too exhausted on the road." But the companions of his striving to Godliness said to him, "Where is there any bread for us to get in this wilderness? -let alone enough to satisfy the appetites of such a crowd!" But Jesus said to them, "How much bread do you have?" And they said, "Seven loaves and a few fish." And he give an order to the crowd to sit down on the ground and he took the seven loaves of bread and the fish and, after giving thanks, he divided them and give them to the friends, and the friends to the crowd. And everybody ate and was filled up. And the leftovers from the divisions was seven baskets full. And those that ate amounted to four thousand men, not counting women and children. And after they was sent away, he went out to a boat and left to the neighborhood of Magdalena.

No Miraculous Sign To Be Given For Critics

Once the Pharisees and Sadducees come to him to test him asking him for a sign from God's Homeland to show them. But it got him aroused and he said, "When the evening comes, you say, `By Jupiter! the sky is red. Well, we know about the morning weather. It's a sign of winter weather coming for it's red in the darkening sky.' You know enough to recognize the aspect of the weather. Can't you recognize the sign of the times? What a lost class of folk and faithless it is to ask for a sign and no sign is going to be give to that bunch except the sign of Jonah." And he went on, leaving them behind.

Now after the friends of his learning God's ways got to the other side, they have forgotten to take bread. And Jesus said to them, "Keep a sharp eye out to recognize the yeast of the Pharisees and Sadducees. And they took to arguing amongst themselves if he was saying that because we didn't bring bread. Realizing it, Jesus said, "Why do you argue amongst yourselves, half-wits, because you have no bread? Don't you even now understand or remember the five loaves of bread of the five thousand and how many basketfuls you got? Or the seven loaves of bread of the four thousand and how many basketfuls you got? Is it possible you can't understand what I told you wasn't about bread? Just be on guard against the yeast of the Pharisees and Sadducees." Then they understood when he was telling them to watch out for the yeast of the loaves, it was about the teaching of the Pharisees and Sadducees.

Who The Orphan Is

Another time, when Jesus went to the neighborhood of Caesaria Philipi, he asked his companions trying to learn right, "Who are folks saying the Orphan is?" And they said, "They are saying John the Baptist, or others are saying Elijah, or others are saying Jeremiah, or one of the prophets." He says to them, "Who do you say I am?" And Simon Peter said, "You are God's child, a Child of God alive." And Jesus replied to him, "You are beloved, Simon Barjonah, because flesh and blood didn't give this answer to you. It comes from my Parent in God's Homeland. And I say to you, your instinct is rock solid, and upon this foundation I will build my church and the lackeys of destruction will not be able to tear it down. I will place you in charge of the welcomers into God's homeland and whoever you cling to on earth will be clung to in God's Homeland, and whoever you send away will be sent away from God's Homeland."

Then he warned the friends accompanying him not to tell no one that he is God's child.

Live Your Life For Others

By and by, Jesus began to point out to his friends dedicating themselves to learning about God how it would be needful for him to go to Jerusalem and to suffer much from the elders and senior churchmen and Hebrew translators and to be killed and on the third day to rise from the dead. But when Peter took it in he begun to get critical, saying, "Have pity on us, our Familyhead! It can't be - you doing this to us!" But Jesus turned from Peter and said, "Get behind me, Challenger! You are acting scandalous because you don't think about God, but of people." Then Jesus said to his friends learning God's ways, "If any of you want to follow me, forget about yourselves, and take up the cross and follow me. Someone wanting their life saved must lose it. Someone losing their life on account of me will save it. For what will be a fellow's enrichment, even if they plunder the whole world, if it results in the loss of their soul. Where can a fellow find an equivalent for his soul? The Orphan is sure to be coming in the authority of his Parent in the company of his angels and he will be giving back to each according to what that one has done. In fact the truth is that some who is standing here won't even have to experience death before they see the Orphan go to his homeland."

Jesus Transformed

About six days later, Jesus took with him Peter and James and John, the one who was born from his mother, and he privately whisked them up to a high mountain.

And there he changed form before their very eyes, and his face shined as the sun, and his robe is white as light. And - a miracle- it was being seen by them that he was talking with Moses and Elijah. And Peter perked up and said to Jesus, "It is a good thing we are here, Sir. If you want, I can make three shelters here, one for you, and one for Moses, and one for Elijah." While he was still talking - look! - a shiny cloud enveloped them, and - yes! - a voice from the cloud was saying, "This is the Child of my love, in him I find content. Listen to him!" And when the friends accompanying him heard this, the fell upon their faces and were very scared. And Jesus went to them and while he hugged them he said, "Get up and don't be afraid." And lifting up their eyes to look they didn't see nobody but Jesus himself and only him. And after they was took back from down the mountain, Jesus give them an order, saying, "Don't never tell this sight until the Orphan has arose from death." But the friends needing instruction about God questioned him, saying, "Why do the church Hebrew translators say that Elijah has to come first?" And Jesus answered them and told them Elijah don't have to come more than he has and all of them was objecting. "Do I have to tell you that Elijah has already come and he wasn't recognized and what was done to him they also have in mind for me. Just so, it has to be the Orphan is to be persecuted under them." Then the friends striving to learn about God knowed that it was about John the Baptist he was making reference to them.

Healing Incidents

Later, after a crowd come to him, he come across a fellow kneeling down in front of him, and he says, "Sir, Have pity on my child, because he has epilepsy and he suffers from it bad. in a spell he throws himself into fire or into deep water. Here I brought him to your friends disciplining themselves to learn God's ways and they can't do nothing to make him better." Jesus was brought to say, "Half wits! How much longer can I be with you? How long can I coddle you? Bring him here." And Jesus give the order and the disability left from him and the boy is give good health from that moment. After this, when his friends striving for Godliness was come to Jesus private, they said, "Why couldn't we heal the disability?" He give them this answer -"Because you don't trust enough. I tell you this true, if you have faith on the order of a mustard seed, you can say to a mountain, get out of here, and it will go away, and there will be nothing can stop you."

Jesus Again Prepares His Friends For His Death

Again, when they was assembled in Galilee, Jesus said to them, "The Orphan is readying to be give over to the hands of humans. And they will kill him and on the third day he will come back to life." And they was very choked up.

Jesus Pays A Church Pledge

Later on when they got to Capernaum, those taking up the collection for the pledge to keep up the church went to Peter and said, "Don't your teacher pay the half shekel church tax?" He says, "Yes," and going into the house, he confronted Jesus about it who says, "What do you think, Simon? From who do the governors of the earth collect local taxes and poll taxes? From their own children or from others?" And he answered, "From others." Jesus was agreeing with him, "Yes indeed! Children are untaxable and free! Even so we don't hurt our cause in paying them - go to the lake, cast in a hook and line and when you get a bite, take out the first fish and when you open its mouth, you will find a Greek coin worth four drachmas. After you get that, give it to them for me and you."

The Importance of Having a Soul as Vulnerable to God as a Child's

On another time, the friends wanting to learn God's ways come to Jesus saying, "Who is it we can expect to be the most important in God's Homeland?" Then calling to a child, he stood him there in the midst of them and said, "I tell you something true, unless you change and become as this child you won't be going to God's Homeland. The one's able to get as vulnerable to God as this child, that one is the most important in God's Homeland. Anyone who bears himself as a child such as this one into my family, receives me."

"If anyone dares to confuse even one of the most vulnerable of these, he or she might as well be collaring a millstone around that one's neck and expect to be sunk in a deep spot in the sea." Then Jesus took a deep agonizing breath thinking about life on earth being confounding, them locked into fixing on their own natural needs frustrating God, and deep was the agonizing breaths about the confusions to come. He says, "If your hand or foot leads you to oppose God's plan, cut it off and throw it away. You are better off to go through life crippled or hobbling than to have two hands and two feet and be thrown into eternal oblivion. And if your eye causes you to try to wreck God's plan, pull it out and throw it away. You are better off going through life one-eyed than having two while you are being thrown into fiery damnation."

"Look out that you don't set your mind against a single one of those who are vulnerable. I tell you that they have angels in God's Homeland looking out for all of them in the presence of my Parent in God's Homeland. What are you thinking? Let's say a fellow owns one hundred sheep and one gets lost from them. Don't he forget about the ninety-nine grazing on the hill and go looking for the one's lost? And if he happens to find it, Yes, I tell you, that he is so happy about it -even more so than about the fact that the other ninety-nine wasn't lost at all! Just so, it ain't the will in the heart of our Parent in God's Homeland that even the most vulnerable of these have harm come to pass."

Way To Act Toward Someone Who Does You Wrong

"If a brother of yours does wrong, go to him and work out the problem between you and only him. Maybe he will listen to you and that way you have avoided losing the brother of yours. But if he don't listen, take along with you

another or two, because out of the mouths of two or three witnesses come every truth. If he don't pay attention to them, tell the church. And if he won't take the advice of the church, have it between you as a stranger and a tax collector.

I tell you something to expect, whoever you have tied in to acting guilty, it will be deemed guilt in God's Homeland, and whoever you have resolved the guilt on earth, it will not be deemed guilt in God's Homeland. I also emphasize that if two among you come to a conclusion about a thing in every respect - of what may be the subject of an offense, and the fellows is implicated, the penalty will happen to them by my Parent in God's Homeland. And of anything two or three who are gathering are in agreement, there I am in their midst.

Forgiveness Should Be Given Unlimited

Now, here come Peter to him, saying, "Sir, how often can my brother do wrong to me and I have to forgive him? Is it for seven times?" And Jesus says to him, "I don't expect only seven times, but seventy times seven. This is similar to how a landowner of fields governed folks - when he was wanting to settle the accounts of his tenants. When he was processing their accounts, he was give to handle one owing him ten thousand talents. And since the fellow didn't have it to give, the head over that household could have give the command to sell him as a slave, and his wife, and kids, all everything that he has, and get repaid that way. The tenant fell down to his knees and begged him not to saying, `Be patient with me, and I will repay you everything.' And the head of that household felt sorry for the tenant and struck off the debt and the account was forgive him. Then that same tenant left and searched out a fellow working for him who owed him ten denarius coins, had him arrested, and choked his throat, saying, `Pay me back what you owe me!' And the fellow fell to his knees pleading with him, saying, `Be patient with me, and I will repay you.' But he wouldn't do it and leaving had him throwed back into debtor's prison until he would repay the debt. Seeing what happened, his co-workers was mighty up-set, and went to report to the head of the household himself all that happened. Then, the head of the household himself summoned him and says to him, `Wrongdoing fellow, all that debt of yours that I cancelled, I did it just because you begged me to. I did not have to, and you didn't have any compassion for your workers, as I had compassion on you.' And becoming furious, his head of household give him over to the jailers until everything owed was repaid. So, my Homeland Parent acts to you, if you don't forgive each other's brother or sister in your hearts."

Jesus Ministers To Huge Crowds

Later, after Jesus was finished with these teachings, he traveled from Gali-lee and went into the hills of Judea near the Jordan River. Great crowds come following after him and he ministered to them there.

Teaching On Marriage And Dissolution Of Marriage

And there were Pharisees trailing him wanting to trick him and asking whether it was lawful for a man to dissolve his marriage on every proof of fault? And he answered, "Don't you read in church that at the first creation

A male and a female he made them.

And it is said,

On account of this state, a man will leave father and mother
and be joined to his wife, and they will become one body.

Just so they are no longer two but one body. A person should not split up the one body which God has caused to be joined together." They said to him, "Why did Moses give the commandment that

To hand a woman a dissolution writing is
sufficient to send her away?"

He says to them that Moses permitted this to the hard-hearted ones of yours that they could send away their wives, but it wasn't that way from the beginning and shouldn't happen so. "I say to you that if any sends away his wife, her not a wrongdoer, and marries another one, the act is adulterous." Then the friends striving to learn God's ways said to him, "If it's so that this is the relationship of a man with a wife, it is not a good idea to marry." But he told them, "Not everyone can abide this teaching, but it is still given to them.

Also there be sexually inactive ones who are made to be sexless by folk, and there are also sexually inactive ones who become sexually inactive in the service of God's Homeland. One who can bear to abstain from sex should abstain."

Jesus's Love For Children

Another time, children were brought to him so that they could have his hands placed on them and feel beloved. But the friends learning about God was scolding them. And Jesus said to them, "Don't frighten off the children and don't stop them from coming to me for to such as them is God's Homeland." And after he has placed his hands on them, he traveled from there.

Eternal Life Comes To Those Valuing It Over Possessions

Now there come one to him saying, "Teacher, What good can I do so that I can have eternal life?" But he said to him, "Why do you ask about good? One is good but if you want to enter into life, keep the commandments." He says to him, "Which ones do I have to do?" And Jesus said,

"Don't murder. Don't commit adultery. Don't steal.
Don't tell lies. Prize your father and mother. Also,
Treat with love those closest to you as yourself."

The youngster says to him, "All these things I have obeyed. What else is holding me back?" Jesus says to him, "If you wish to be fully mature, go sell your possessions and give them to the poor, and you will have savings in the

Homeland, and come follow me." But after hearing this teaching, the youngster went away depressed for he owned much worldly wealth.

Then Jesus said to his friends learning God's ways, "I tell you something to pay attention to - the wealthy will cringe at going into God's Homeland. As I keep telling you, it is easier for a camel to go through the eye of a needle than for a rich man to enter the Homeland of God." The companions seeking the discipline of God's love that heard this was shocked and anxious saying, "Who can be saved?" Jesus looked up and said to them, "For a person to do this is impossible, but to God everything is possible." Then Peter got inquisitive and said to him, "Look, haven't we give up everything and followed you? How is it with us?" And Jesus said to them, "I am going to tell you something to count on - you who want to follow me into the re-borning day: when the Orphan is seated upon the throne of attendedness, you will be seated too and you twelve will be seated as are judges upon twelve thrones over the twelve tribes of Israel. And all who leave off from homes or brothers or sisters or father and mother or children or fields for work in my name will be rewarded a hundred times over and will inherit timeless life. And many who will be proudest, are the humblest, and the humblest will be the proudest."

The Workers In The Vineyard Story

"God's Homeland for folk is like this - a landowner who is going out early in the morning to hire workers for his vineyard. And when they come to an agreement that they would work the day for a denarius coin, he sent them into his vineyard. Later, when he left out about the third hour, he saw others standing around in the market place and he said to those, `You too can go to work in the vineyard and whatever it is that's fair, I will pay you.' So they went ahead. So too when he left out about the sixth and ninth hour, he made the same bargain. Then when he left out at the eleventh hour, he found others standing around and says to them, `Why are you field hands standing around here the whole day?' They said to him, `Because no one is hiring us today.' `You can go to work in the vineyard.' When evening come, the owner of the vineyard says to the foreman, `Call together the workers and pay them the wage arranged from the last arrivals to the first.' And here come those hired at the eleventh hour- give a denarius apiece. And when those come first hired, they complained because they should receive more. But they received a denarius apiece too. And when they took it, they was begrudged at the landowner, saying, `These who come at the last worked one hour, and you have paid them the same as us who carried the croploads all day, a hot one too!' But he caught the remark of one of them and said, `Friend and sharer in this enterprise, I did you no wrong. Didn't you agree with me on a denarius? Take it and go. I choose to pay this latecomer as you. Isn't it up to me to pay as I choose in these fields of mine? Why do you view something as wrong which is beneficial?' So it will be that the latecomers will be treated as the first and the first as the last."

Jesus Knows His Own Future On Earth

And after he was looking up toward Jerusalem, Jesus took to himself his companions striving to Godliness and his close friends and on the roadway said to them, "For sure, we are going up to Jerusalem, but the Orphan will be betrayed there to the senior churchmen and Hebrew translators and will be sentenced to die. And they will give him over to non-Jewish strangers to be ridiculed and whipped and hung on a cross and on the third day he will arise from death."

The Reward From Jesus's Training Comes In Service To Others

Then come to him the mother of the sons of Zebedee with her sons falling down before him as worshippers to ask a particular question of him. He said to her, "What do you want?" She says to him, "Say that when these are seated on thrones, these two sons of mine, one will be on your right and other on your left in your Homeland." Jesus answered, saying, "You don't know what you are asking for. Can you drink the cup of God's fury that I am able to drink?" James and John was saying back to him, "Yes, we are able to." He says to them, "You can drink my cup, but to be seated on my right and left is not my choice to make. Such decisions are under anticipation by my Parent." And when they heard about this, the other ten were angry at the two friends. But Jesus called them all together and he said, "You know how powerful people in authority establish themselves over the nations and races and people and there are ambitious ones who dominate the folk among them. It will not be that way with us. Instead this is the great motivation in us - it is this, the prominent will be the serving ones among us. So it is that the Orphan didn't come to be ministered to but to minister and to give over his life as a liberating ransom for all."

Now as they was leaving out of Jericho he was being followed by a big crowd. Now here was two blind folk sitting along the road and when they heard that Jesus was passing by, they screamed out saying, "Have pity on us, David's child." But the crowd was shutting them up so they couldn't talk. The loudest of them was still shouting, saying, "Have pity on us, Sir, Child of David." When Jesus got close, he heard them and said, "What do you want me to do?" They answered him, "Sir,"... beginning to open their mouths. But Jesus was feeling sorry for them and touched their eyes, and just like that, they could see and they followed after him.

Jesus Enters Jerusalem

Now came the time of their approach into Jerusalem and they come to Bethphage at the Mount of Olives, There Jesus talked to two of the friends striving to learn God's ways, telling them, "Go into the town in front of us and right there you will find a tethered donkey and a donkey colt along with it. Untie it and bring it to me. And if anyone asks about it, say, The Familyhead of ours has need of it." Right then he sent them on the task. These things was happening to fulfill the words of the prophet saying,

Tell to the daughter of Zion,
It is come time - your governor comes to you
Humble and mounted on a young donkey
And he will be on the male colt of a donkey.

Then the companions striving to Godliness left and did as Jesus told them and brought the young donkey - the male colt- saddled it with their outer robes and he took a seat upon them for a mount. Then a huge crowd began paving the route with their own outer robes while others was cutting branches from trees and strewing them on the road. And crowds was coming to him and then following behind in a clamor -saying,

"Hosanna! Save us! Help has come in the Child of David,

Praise be that the one has come in the service of the Familyhead,

Thanks be in the highest places."

And when he went into Jerusalem, all of the city was surging in excitement saying, "Who is causing this?" And the crowd was saying, "This guy is the prophet Jesus from out of Nazareth of Galilee."

And Jesus went into the main church and ordered out all of the ones selling and commercializing in the church and he overturned the tables of the ones changing currency into church shekels for the church half-shekel tax offering, and the booths where doves was being sold for sacrificing, and he says to them, "It is written,

This home - my house - is dedicated for praying,
but you are making it into a den of thieves."

And the blind and crippled went to him in the church and he give their incapacities to re-function.

Watching all this, the senior churchmen and the Hebrew translators was shocked about the doings, and his followers shouting in the church and saying, "Hosanna to the Child of David," and they become very upset. And they said to him, "Aren't you listening to what they are saying?" But Jesus answered them saying, "Yes, have you read that

I will pour praise from the mouths of babies and those
just born still nursed by their mothers."

And brushing them aside, he left out of there to go to the city of Bethany and he spent the night there.

An Example Of The Power Of Faith

Early the next morning, when he was returning to the city, he got hungry. And when he saw a fig tree - one of them along the road - he went to it but he couldn't find nothing on it - nothing only but leaves - and he says to it, "Never again will there be fruit on you, ever." And the fig tree, right then and there, began withering. And seeing this, the friends receiving his instruction was shocked, saying, "How could that fig tree start withering so quick?" And Jesus answered them, "I tell you something to count on, if you have faith and you don't doubt yourselves, it is only a slight doing about the fig tree, but you might also say to a mountain, Shift! and it will be thrown into the sea, if you will it. And everything you - a believer - ask in prayer, you will get."

Jesus Questioned About His Authority

Later, when he reached the church, and was devoting himself to teaching, there come to him the senior churchmen and the elders and people saying, "By what authority are you engaging in this business?" And, "Who is giving you this authority?" Jesus responded to them, "Let me ask you a single question and when you tell me I will tell you by what authority I am engaging in this business. From who come John's baptism: from out of God's Homeland or from out of something human about him?" And they begun disputing how to answer arguing among themselves, "If we say, From God's Homeland, here's the rub, he will say to us, Why didn't you yourselves trust in it?" But if we answer, "From out of something human about him, we may face an angry church mob, because all of them accept that John was a prophet." So they responded saying, "We don't know." And Jesus said to them in kind, "I am not going to try to tell you from whose authority I am doing this work."

Service Not Its Opportunity Gits Rewarded

"What is there to make out of this? A fellow has two children. And after the going to the first he said, `Son, Go to work today out in the vineyard.' And he responded, `I can't,' but later on he regretted saying that and went on out. Going over to the other, the man said the same thing. But this other one responded, `Sir, I am the one to do it,' but he didn't go. Which of the two is doing the will of the Parent?" They answered, "The first one." Then Jesus said to them, "I am telling you something to pay attention to- tax collectors and prostitutes will be preceding you into the Homeland of God. John come to you along the road leading the right way and you wouldn't take it, but the tax collectors and prostitutes believed him. You even seen it, and still don't regret not changing your attitudes about it."

Rejecting Jesus Leads To Rejection By God

"Here is another story with an example in it you should listen to. Once a man who was the landlord planted a vineyard and he fenced it all around and laid the platform for a winepress and built a guard tower. Then he leased it as a field with a growing crop and left. The time was coming for his harvest so he sent some employees there to the tenants to collect his share of the crop. But after the tenants took notice of his employees, they beat up one, they killed another and stoned the other. Again he sent out other employees, more important than the first ones, but they did the same things. Finally, he sent to them his son, saying, `Reconsider, this is my son.' But the tenants, when they saw his son, said to themselves, `This is the heir. Come on let's kill him and then we can take his inheritance.' And they took hold of him and threw him out of the vineyard and they killed him. When the landowner of the vineyard came, what must he do to those tenants?" They answered him, saying, "Punish them's done wrong for their bad deeds and give over the vineyard to other tenants, them who will give over to him his crops in due time." And Jesus says to them, "Never neglect to think of this story when you read in public worship this scripture:

> The stone which the housebuilder rejects,
> This will be the cornerstone -
> On the Landowner's say so -
> And yet it seems baffling to our eyes?

So I tell you that the Homeland of God will be took from you and given to the homeless who will steward his crops.

And then the senior churchmen and Pharisees understood the meaning of this story with its example in it - that he was talking about them. But when they was working up to arrest him, they become afraid to on account of the crowds, since they considered Jesus a prophet.

A Story Of A Wedding Feast

Continuing, Jesus told stories with lessons in them saying: Consider how God's Homeland is to this fellow: a king, who planned a wedding party for his son. And he sent out some of his court process servers to give invitations to them's to be summoned to the party, but none wanted to come. Again, he sent out others of the court process servers saying, `Tell them that was invited,

Look, I have already prepared a banquet. The steers that I have fed out have been butchered and everything is ready. Come to the party.' But still they was disregardful and went their own ways. Here went one to his own farm. There went one toward his business district. And the rest took hold of the court process servers of his rousting them about and it ended up they killed them. Then the king got furious and, dispatching his soldiers, executed their murderers and their city was burned down. Then he says to his court process servers, `The wedding party is still prepared, but the ones invited to it wasn't worth having. Go out to the outskirts and further down the roads and such as you find there invite them to the party.' And after these court process servers left for the roads, they went about inviting everyone they could find, those not so well off as well as those that were well off. And the wedding hall was filled up with guests. When the king entered - in a state of shock - he saw there a fellow who hadn't changed clothes for the wedding party. And he says to him, `Friend, why did you come here not wearing clothes for a wedding party?' But this fellow was as one muzzled. Then the king said to the guards, `Cuff him - feet and hands - and throw him into the utter blackness. There he will be as one who cries out and grinds his teeth. All are invited but few will be selected to stay.'" Later the Pharisees conspired so as to catch him in his talk.

Giving To Caesar, Caesar's, And To God, God's

And they sent for him and his friends striving to learn God's ways along with agents of Herod Antipas saying, "Teacher, we know that you tell the truth and you teach according to the way of God truthfully and it isn't give to you to hold back nothing. You look at a person, face to face, and say to us what you are thinking. Is it necessary to pay a tax to Caesar or not?" But Jesus knew what they was up to, and he responded to their scheme, "Why are you tricking me, hypocrites! Hand over to me a coin for taxpaying." They brought to him a denarius coin. And he says to them, "Whose likeness is struck on it?" They answered him, "Caesar." Then he says to them, "Give over to Caesar, Caesar's, and the things of God, give to God."

About The Resurrection Of The Dead

On a particular day there come Sadducees who deny there is such a thing as resurrection of the dead to talk to him. They asked, "Teacher. Moses said:

If a fellow die not having children, his brother should
marry his wife, and his brother's sperm will take the place of his.

Now there was seven brothers. And the first died a married man, but since he couldn't have children his brother took himself to his wife. The same thing come to the second and third on to the seventh. Finally the woman died. In the resurrection which of the seven can claim the woman? All of them have held her." Responding Jesus said to them, "Can you have misunderstood what is said in the writings that nothing is impossible to God? In the resurrection, none will marry nor live in a state of marriage, but the life will be that of angels in God's Homeland. Concerning this, don't you read in your public worship services the word to you from God saying,

I am the God of Abraham and the God of Isaac and the God of Jacob.?

God is not the God of dead folk but of living folk." And after they heard this, the crowd was filled with awe at his teaching.

The Demand Of The Law

When the Pharisees heard that he had silenced the Sadducees, they took council about it and asked one of them to go question him, "Teacher, What is the greatest demand of the law?" And he said to him,

"Love the Familyhead, your God, in your whole heart, and
in your whole life and in your whole thinking.

This is the greatest and first demand. Second is similar to it,

Love the one close to you as yourself.

In these two demands is the whole of the law suspended and that of the prophets."

While the Pharisees was knotted, Jesus approached them asking, "What is your thinking about God's Child? Who is the Child?" They answered him, "A Child of David." He says to them, "Why then did David in ecstasy call him `Familyhead,' saying,

'The Familyhead said to my Familyhead,
Sit down on my right hand
While I make your enemies a footrest.'

If David calls him Familyhead, how can he be his Child?" No one could answer this question, and no one challenged him by asking him any more questions the rest of the day.

Humility Is The Key To Real Prominence

Later Jesus called out to the crowds and to his friends striving to learn right, saying, "They have sat themselves on the seat of Moses - these popular translators of the Hebrew scrolls and these Pharisee cultists. Act like they say and keep to the many rules they tell about, but don't act like they do. They don't do what they preach. They chain folk to difficult loads, hard to bear, and cause folk's shoulders to be weighted down, but they themselves do not lift a finger to ease the burdens. Everything they do, they do to make a spectacle of themselves before folk. They make obnoxiously large phylactery cases jammed with bible verses strapping them to their arms and foreheads and they pride themselves on having fringes and tassels of the ministry on their clothes. They love to take the seat of honor at dinners and the most prominent chair in the synagogues and to be called Rabbi by folk in the shopping places. Do not allow yourselves to be called Rabbi. One among you is a teacher and all the rest of you are brothers and sisters. And don't claim you have a Parent on the earth for your Parent is one in God's Homeland. Don't claim to be a guide because your guide is one who is God's child. And the most important one of you will be the one who serves. Whoever tries to lift himself to prominence will be brought low and whoever humbles himself will be lifted to be prominent."

Some Damned

"Damn you, you translators and Pharisee cultists, hypocrites, because you try to lock the doors to God's Homeland in front of folks. You do not enter in and those who are in the process of entering in you try to thwart while they are trying to enter in."

"Damn you, you translators and Pharisee cultists, hypocrites, because you travel sea and desert to make a convert and, when you have done your work, the convert is a child of ungodly practices, twice as bad as your own."

"Damn you, blind leaders who say, `Giving an oath in the name of the church won't bind you to nothing,' and, `Whoever wants to can swear on the money accounts of the church to bind them to a promise.' Idiots and blind ones! What is more important, money or the church which collects the money? And whoever swears on the church altar won't be bound to nothing, but there can be a promise made on an offering binding folk to a promise? Are you blind? Which is more important, a church offering or the altar set over for the gift? Whoever swears on the holdings on the altar swears on the altar and on everything placed on it. Anyone swearing on something in the church swears on the church and the One who upholds it. And giving an oath to God's Homeland binds a promise before the seat of power of God and the one seated on it."

"Damn you, you translators and Pharisee cultists, hypocrites, because you pay your 10% tithe in dill and cumming and forget about the obligations of the law, justice and mercy and loyalty, the things you are responsible to do and never leave off. Blind guides who strain a gnat out of wine so as not to kill it on the Sabbath at the same time a camel is permitted to die of thirst.

Damn you, you translators and Pharisee cultists, hypocrites, because you keep clean the outside of the cup and plate but the inside is left to greed and self-indulgence. Blind Pharisees, first wash out the inside of the cup so that you can get the outside clean.

Damn you, you translators and Pharisee cultists, hypocrites, because you look like whitewashed tombs which on the outside shine beautiful but on the inside are filled with decayed bones and putrefaction. So it is you shine on the outside as being God-conforming in front of folk but inside you are ones who are full of double dealing and law-breaking.

Damn you, you translators and Pharisee cultists, hypocrites, because you build up tombs for prophets and keep up the monument stones of the church congregation, and you say, 'If we were living in the days of our ancestors, we would never have been a part to the bloodshed of the prophets.' As it is you yourselves are witnesses of what they were like, being children of the murderers of the prophets. And you will find execution in the same degree as your Parents. Devils, class of snakes, where can you run to away from the punishing judgment? How can you not understand! I send to you prophets and wise workers and writers. You kill them and crucify them and whip them in your churches and you persecute them about the city in law courts of the earth seeking their blood, as innocent as Abel's, even as was the blood of Zacharias, the

child of Braxios, who you murdered within the church and at the very altar. I tell you the truth, all these things will be held against this bunch."

Jerusalem's Degradation

"Jerusalem, Jerusalem, killer of prophets and stoner of friends of God. How often have I wanted to gather together your children, give them shelter as does a hen with her chicks under wing, and you would not permit it. Now your home changes to ruins. And I have to tell you that you cannot see me from now on until you will be give to say,

Praise be! Here comes the Familyhead!"

The Great Jerusalem Church To Be Destroyed

After time to go, Jesus left the Great Jerusalem Church, and his friends discipling themselves to rightful life came along too, pointing out to him the extent of the church. But he was moved to tell them, "You see all this extent, right? Well, let me tell you this - here, not one stone will be permitted to remain on top of another. There won't be one which won't be torn down."

Happenings At The End Of Time

When he sat down to rest on the Hill of Olives, his friends striving to know God went to him seeking privacy saying, "Tell us, what is going to happen, and what miracle will predict your re-appearance and the end of eternity?" And

Jesus answered them saying to them, "Don't look for something that may lead you astray. Many will come in my name, saying, `I am God's Child,' and many will be confused. Expect to be hearing of wars and reports of conflict. Recognize this but don't be surprised. It is necessary for such to happen, but hold off thinking it's the end. Races and peoples and nationalities will rise up against races and peoples and nationalities and governments against governments and starving will happen and earthquakes in various places. All these things are the beginning of suffering similar to the pain of a woman about to give birth. Then you will be betrayed in trial after trial and they will kill your denomination, and you will be hated among all of the races and peoples on my account. And then many will be caused to abandon my cause, and others will be given over to authorities, and those left will hate one another. And many false prophets will arise and mislead huge numbers. And while all this wicked confusion is going on, the tie of brotherly and sisterly love among the many will die out. But each one remaining true to the end will be saved. Then the good news of the homeland in the whole of creation will be broadcast through many witnesses to the races and peoples and nationalities, and then will come the end."

"When you have seen a sacreligious object causing desecration as predicted by Daniel the prophet standing in a dedicated place - reckon on it and it will become known - then you should flee from Judea into the hills. Someone on a roof should not exit through the house for it will be leveled and anyone in a field being destroyed behind him should not return to fetch his shirt." Jesus took a deep breath. "It is trouble for those pregnant or breast feeding in those days. Pray that your flight doesn't have to happen in winter or on Sunday. At that time there will be horrible disasters such as never been known from the beginning of the world until now nor will there ever after be. But the days will be cut short at that time. Otherwise no physical body could be saved whole. For the benefit of the survivors, those days will be shortened. Then some will be heard to say, `Look here is God's Child.' 'Over here!' But, don't believe it. Fake divines and fake prophets will make claims and claim to do great miracles just so as to scare you into being deceived, if possible, the survivors. Watch out, I warn you. Now if someone says to you, `Yes, really, he is in the desert!' Don't go out there. Or if someone say, `Look, he is in hiding!' Don't believe it. For just as the lightning strikes across the eastern sky and flashes off to the west, so will be the second coming of God's human Child. Wherever there may be a corpse, there the vultures flock.

Immediately after the trouble of that day,
The sun will be blotted out,
And the moon will not cast her moonlight,

And the stars will streak from the sky,

And the powers of the cosmos will be shaken. And then will come the representation of God's human Child in the sky, and mournful cries arising from the races of the earth, and they shall

see God's human Child coming down as from hovering clouds

with his friends who have accepted God's life amid much array, and he will send ahead his angels with great trumpet blasts bringing to him all of his elect from the distant reaches of the four winds, from edges of the world and of its furthest boundaries.

Take a lesson from the fig tree. When its branch has already come into sap, and its leaves are displayed, you know that summer is close. So should you understand - when all these things happen - that the time is close for the door to open. In fact the family of folk won't pass into history until all these things will happen. The sky and the earth will break open but my promise will not pass away.

Folk Are Not Given To Know When The End Will Come

As to the exact day and hour - no one knows, not the angels of the Homeland nor the Child, except only the Parent. It is like the age of Noah when the second coming of God's human Child will come. It was like it was in those before the flood when folk were eating and drinking, marrying and preparing for wedding parties, up to the day when Noah went into the ark, and folk did not know until after he went into the ark that everything was over with. Like this will be the second coming of God's human Child. Then two will be in a field and one will be lifted up and one left behind. Two will grinding at a mill and one will be lifted up and one left behind. Be alert then, because you do not know the time the Familyhead of yours will be coming. You know this - if a head of the household has had warning about the period of time a thief was coming, he would be able to thwart the break in of his home. So I tell you this - be forewarned - even though it is not yours to know the hour when God's human Child comes.

Keep Busy In The Faith Until The End

Who is a faithful helper and who is responsible enough for a head of a family to entrust over his household to provide for their sustenance in the meantime? That kind of beloved conservator is one who the familyhead will find busy when he returns. In fact, the familyhead will entrust him with all his property. Just when the bad conservator says in his heart, "My boss won't be back for a long time," and he begins abusing his fellow workers, gorging himself and drinking himself into an alcoholic, here comes the boss over that conservator on a day that he will not expect and at an hour that he will not know and he will cut him up and throw away his pieces as a result of his presumption. And there will be cries and teeth ground.

Being Prepared For The End

Once God's Homeland was brought up in this reference - ten young girls bearing lamps who went to meet a bridal matchmaker. Five of them was dumb and five smart. These dumb ones - when they carried their lamps with them - didn't take along any oil. The smart ones took oil in jugs along with their lamps. When the matchmaker was running late, they all got sleepy and napped. It was in the middle of the night that a shouting occurred, "Hey! the matchmaker!" "He is coming to make arrangements." Then they all woke up and wicked their lamps. The dumb ones said to the smart ones, "Give us some of your oil, because our lamps are going out." But the smart ones answered by saying, "No way, we can't supply both ours and yours. Go in a hurry to the stores and buy some for yourselves." While they was gone to do their buying, the matchmaker got there, and those that was ready went in with him to arrange for marriages and the door was locked. Afterwards the other young girls returned and called out, "Sir, Sir, open up." But he replied saying, "I don't know who you are." So, be alert, because you won't know its day or hour.

A Tale About Entrusting Helpers

As a fellow was going away on a trip, he called together some of his domestic helpers and entrusted them with his possessions. To this one he give five talents, to this one, two, to this one, one, each according to his own potential and went on his trip. Immediately after he is gone, the one with five talents took it and traded with it and got profit of another five. Same thing, the one with two talents profited another two. But the one who was give one went out and buried it in the ground and embezzled his familyhead's silver. After a long time, the familyhead over these domestic helpers come back to settle accounts with them. And there come to him the one who was give five talents who said, "Familyhead, Sir, you give me five talents. Here are the five talents and I earned five talents more." The Familyhead says to him, "Okay, good and faithful helper, you were faithful over little. I can entrust you with everything. Share the abundance of your familyhead." Here come the one with two talents saying, "Familyhead, Sir, here are the two talents you give me, and look I have earned two more." The familyhead says to him, "Okay, good and faithful helper, you were faithful with a little, I will entrust you with much. Share the abundance of your Familyhead." Then there come the one who was give one talent saying,

"Familyhead, Sir, I know you, that you are a hard man, harvesting where you don't plant seed, and baling over where you don't broadcast grain, and I grew afraid after you went away and I hid the one talent of yours in the ground. Here you can have it." But the Familyhead answered him saying, "What a bad and lazy helper you are! You even knew about me that I harvest where I do not plant seed and I bale over where I do not broadcast grain. That compelled you to take my silver to make investments and I come back and I expect to be paid back not only what's mine but interest. Take from him the talent and give it to the keeping of the one with ten talents. To the one having much, more will be given and he will increase it even more, but to the one who don't have, even what he has will be taken away from him. Now throw the worthless helper into the outermost blackness. There he will be one who cries out and grinds his teeth."

Judgment On The Basis Of Caring

When God's human Child comes in his attendedness and all the angels with him, then he will sit upon the throne of authority. And there he will as-

semble before him every person of every race and nation and people and he will separate them one from one another as one who is a shepherd separates the sheep from the goats and he will herd the sheep over to his right but the goats over to his left. Then this one of ultimate power and authority will say to those on his right, "Come, you who are the ones called beloved by my Parent, have the inheritance prepared for you in the Homeland from the time of the creation. For when I was hungry, you give me something to eat. When I was thirsty, then you brought water to me. I was a homeless outsider and you come to shelter me. I was short of clothes and you supplied them to me.

I got sick and you doctored me. I was in jail and you come to visit me." Then these special ones questioned him, saying, "Familyhead, Sir, when did we see you hungry and fed you or thirsty and brought water to you? When did we see you as a homeless person and shelter you? Or needy for clothes and supplied some? When did we see you sick or in prison and we come to you?" And he answered them and says to them, "The fact was that what you have done for the most vulnerable or humble of my brothers and sisters, you have done for me."

Then he says to those out on his left, "Get away from me you who must be threw into the eternal fire which is prepared for my chief challenger and his agents. I was hungry and you wouldn't give me nothing to eat. I was thirsty and you wouldn't let me have a drink. I was a stranger, homeless and different, and you didn't welcome me, needy for clothes and you didn't supply any. I was sick and in prison and you didn't come to see about me." Then these questioned him and they said to him, "Familyhead, Sir, when did we see you hungry, or thirsty or homeless or bare of clothes or sick or in prison and we didn't try to take care of you?" He answered them, saying, "The fact was that when you didn't do for the most humble, you didn't do for me. And these will be sent away into timeless punishment, but the special saved ones into timeless life."

It Is Okay To Value Jesus For Who He Is

Now then after Jesus got done speaking these things, he told his friends seeking to learn God's ways, "You know that after two days the Easter season is coming, and God's human Child is to be give over to be crucified." Even as he spoke, the senior church authorities and elders of the church went complaining to Caiaphous in the court of the palace and they was scheming to arrest Jesus secretly and they was wanting to kill him. But they decided not to on the feast day because it would cause a commotion in the church. After bit, after Jesus went to Bethany to the house of Simon the leper, a woman went to him holding an alabaster jar full of expensive oil and she poured it out upon his head while he was sitting at the table. When they saw this, the companions steeling themselves into God's love began to get frustrated saying, "How come she is wasting this? It could be sold for a lot of money and be given for charity to the poor." Jesus was knowing their thoughts and he said to them, "How can you hold grievance against this woman? A good deed has been done for me. You always have poor folk bearing up each other, but you will not always have me. Pouring out this oil upon my body is doing what's needed to get me ready to be buried. The fact is that wherever in the entire world the good news is preached, her act will be remembered."

Judas Sells Out Jesus

Then one of the twelve left, the one called Judas Iscariot, going to the senior churchmen and said, "What would you give me if I would give you confidential information about Jesus?" And they reached an agreement of thirty silver coins. And from that time on, Judas set to plotting when would be the best time for Jesus's arrest as part of his confidential informant work.

Having An Easter Season Meal

Anticipating the first day of the Easter season holiday, the companions striving to learn God's ways came to Jesus, saying, "Where do you want us to prepare to have your Easter season meal?" And he said, "Go to the city to this certain home and say to the householder, "The teacher says, `The time is close. I want to have the Easter season meal with my special friends at your home." And the friends learning God's ways went where Jesus told them to go and prepared for the Easter season meal. Late in the evening, after they all got there, Jesus lay down to eat with the twelve. And while they was eating, he said, "The fact is one of you is a a confidential informant against me." And every one of them begun to get agitated asking him which one more definite, saying, "Familyhead, Sir, you don't think I am the one, do you?" And he told them, "The one dipping his food with me in the dish, this is the confidential informant against me. God's human Child's needs must be left as it is written about him, but damnation comes to the certain one who acts as a confidential informant against God's human Child. It would be better for that one that he was never born." Judas, the one doing the informing, said to him, "You don't think I am the one do you?" And Jesus said, "You have said it."

Instituting the Christian Family Meal

While they was eating, Jesus took the bread and after calling down God's good feeling about it, split it and give it to the friends disciplining themselves into God's love saying, "Take it, eat it, this is my body." And he took a cup and after giving thanks for it, he gave it to them and said, "Drink all of it. This is my blood poured out as a promise to everyone to end folk's separation from God. I tell you right now that I won't be drinking from this product of the vineyard until that day when I will drink with you new wine in the homeland of my father." Then, after a time of singing, they left for Olive Hill.

Jesus Foretells the Friends Straying Away

Then is when Jesus says to them, "All of you will stray away from acknowledging me in the night, like it is writ,

I will strike down the shepherd
and the lamb flocks of the shepherd will be

stampeded afar. But afterwards - after my resumption of activity -I will go ahead of you into Galilee." Peter questioned him saying, "Even if everyone else strays away from you, I won't never abandon you." Jesus said to him, "The fact is before the rooster crows this night you will have personally denied knowing me three times." Peter says to him, "If dying with you becomes needful, still I won't reject you no way." All the friends witnessing the story of God's life on earth said the same thing.

Jesus Prays at Gethsemene

Afterwhile, Jesus went with them to a place called Gethsemene, and says to his special friends, "Sit down here while I go be by myself to pray. Taking along Peter and the two sons of Zebedee, he started getting emotional and

scared. Then he says to them, "My soul is so very sad while I die, stay with me here and watch what happens with me." Then going apart a little bit, he dropped on his face praying and saying, "My Parent, if it is in your power, take away from me this cup...except not as I want but as you want." And he went to the companions he has specially instructed in God's ways and discovered them as they was sleeping there, and he says to Peter, "Couldn't you find strength to stay watchful with me a single hour? Keep awake and pray, so that you don't have to be put to trial yourself. The spirit is willing but the flesh is weak." Again, a second time, he went to pray saying, "My Parent,if there is no other way to empowerment than to drink this cup, let it be your will." And returning again, he found them asleep. The eyes of them with him was overburdened. And leaving them again, he went to pray for a third time saying the same dialogue. Later he went to his friends and says to them, "Sleep on and gather your rest, The hour is arriving when the Orphan is to be give over into the hands of the sceptics. Now, wake up, we need to take ourselves along. The time is here. The informant approaches me.

Jesus Is Arrested

And while he was talking, right then, Judas- one of the twelve - come and with him many folk in a mob bearing swords and billyclubs, among them the senior ministers and the elders of the people. And the traitor gave them the target information having said, "The one I go hug will be the one. Arrest him." And immediately searching out Jesus, he said, "Hello, teacher," and he kissed him. But Jesus said to him, "Friend, a traitor has come." Then angry hands reached out to seize Jesus to arrest him. Now what! Oh no! One of those with Jesus reaches down, draws his sword and swings toward a Jewish elder's lackey, lopping off his ear. But Jesus says to him, "Sheath your sword to its scabbard. All who take up a sword, die in swordplay. Don't you think if I wanted to, I could call upon my Parent and he would station around me twelve legions of angels? Then how would the prophecies be fulfilled about what it is necessary to happen?" It come time for Jesus to address the mob, "Do you come to

take me with swords and billyclubs to capture me as you would a common thief? Every day I was sat down in the church teaching and you didn't even try to arrest me. This whole thing is needs be so that the writings of the prophets could make sense." Then all the friends instructed in the ways of God left him and snuck off.

Jesus Took to Court

Those that arrested Jesus dragged him to Caiaphos, the senior minister and it was there the Hebrew translators and elders assembled. And Peter followed after him from a distance until reaching the courtyard of the senior minister's house and going inside he sat down with chair bearers to see the end. Then the senior minister and the whole church council scurried around to locate witnesses who would lie about Jesus so they could justify putting him to death. But none could be found among the whole assemblage who was willing to stand up and lie, except they finally was two who came forward saying, "This fellow said, 'I am able to tear down the church of God and in three days build it.'" And the senior minister stood up and said to Jesus, "Is there an explanation to this that these are testifying about?" But Jesus stayed silent. Then the senior minister said to him, "I put you under obligation to the living God to tell us if you are God on earth, the Child of God." Jesus says to him, "You say it. In addition to this I tell you,

From now on you will see the human Child of God

Seated on the right hand of ultimate power,

And hovering over the earth as do clouds in the sky." Then the senior minister clutched his clothes saying, "He has misquoted scripture violating God's intention for it. Why do we need to have witnesses? Look, you have now heard a crime against God. What do you decide?" And they answered him, "It is deserving of the death penalty." Then they spit on his face and slapped him and punched him, saying, "Tell us about God, God on earth, why is it that we can get away with punching you?"

Peter Denies Knowing Jesus

Meanwhile, Peter was sitting outside in the courtyard, and someone come up to him, a house worker, a girl, saying, "Aren't you one hanging around Jesus of Galilee?" And he denied it in front of all of them, saying, "I don't know what you are talking about." While he was leaving through the gates another one saw him and said, "This fellow was with Jesus of Nazareth." But again he denied it under oath like so, "I don't know the man." After a little bit, others standing around come up to Peter and said, "Tell us the truth, aren't you from Nazareth? Your dialect gives away what you are doing here." Then Peter begun to curse and swear, "I don't know the man." Right then a rooster crowed. Peter remembered the statement of Jesus coming to be that before the rooster crowed three times, he would be denying knowing him three times. He went outside and cried bitter.

Jesus Took to Pilate

While the dawn was coming up, the plan was schemed up by all of them, the senior minister and the elders of the church about Jesus, how to have him killed. And after they tied him up, they took him out and delivered him to Pilate the Roman governor.

The End of Judas

Now about Judas, the one who was confidential informant - after Jesus was found guilty, Judas was sorry he took the thirty silver pieces from the senior ministers and elders, and returned them, saying, "I done wrong taking away the life blood on an innocent man." But they said to him, "What's this to us? You can handle it." Then, throwing the coins down on the floor of the church, Judas left out of there, not wanting any more to do with them. But the senior ministers picked the coins up from the floor and said, "It is not right to deposit these coins in the church account since they's tainted with blood." Instead they took the money and purchased a garden owned by a pottery maker for burying the poor from its proceeds. That's how that field come to be known as Bloody Garden down to this day. Also this explains the writing of Jeremiah the prophet saying, "And they took thirty silver coins, the value of the man by their reckoning, and the value was agreed to by the children of Israel, and they give them for the garden of a potter, just as it was fore-ordained by the Familyhead."

Jesus Interrogated

Jesus was ordered to be took before the governor and the governor interrogated him, saying, "Are you the ruler over the Jews?" And Jesus says, "You are saying it." And then come the accusing of him by the senior ministers and elders, none of which he responded to. Then Pilate says to him, "Don't you hear how they attack you?" And he didn't respond to this by saying a single word, so as to amaze the governor a lot.

Jesus Gets a Death Sentence

At the time of the Easter season, it was the custom for the authorities to release someone sentenced on the choice of the crowd. Accordingly, they brought out one of the most notorious of the prisoners locked up named Barabbas. Pilate said to them assembled, "Who do you want released, Barabbas or Jesus, the one claiming to be God come to earth?" He was thinking that, on account of resenting a Roman holding a Jewish religious fellow, they would choose Jesus. And while he was sitting on the judgment seat, his wife sent a message to him, saying, "No way must you choose that Godly fellow. Many times I have felt a premonition about him in a dream." But the senior ministers and the elders was spreading their wishes in the crowd to ask for Barabbas so as not to have their sentence of Jesus commuted. Seeking response, the governor said to them, "Which of the two do you want me to release?" And they said, "Barabbas." Then Pilate says to them, "What do you want that I do with Jesus the one called God on earth?" All was shouting, "Crucify him!" Pilate seen that no more was to be gained and it was best to avoid a riot, and taking water, he washed his hands in full view of the crowd, saying, "I am innocent of this man's blood. You have seen to it." And responding to the unanimous crowd he said, "The blood of him is on you and your children." Then he released Barrabas to them, and after Jesus was to be whipped he was to be took to be crucified.

What the Governor's Soldiers Did to Jesus

Later, after Jesus was put in the custody of the governor's soldiers, he was took to their headquarters in front of the whole cohort. Stripping him down, they dressed him in a bloody red Roman cloak like them Roman soldiers wear, and after they wove a wreath of akanthos stems, they placed it upon his head, and a reed was placed in his right hand, and after they cowtowed in front of him, they mocked him, saying, "Welcome! Ruler of the Jews!" And after they spit on him they took away the reed and beat him on his head. And while they was spitting on him, they was undressing him of the cloak, and they clothed him in his own clothes and brought him out to be crucified.

Jesus Crucified

When they went to deliver him they come across a Cyrenian named Simon, who they ordered into their service so he could carry Jesus' cross. Along they went to the place called Golgatha which is called the Skull Place. There they give him wine to drink mixed with a drug. But when he tasted it he wouldn't choose to drink it. After they stuck him on the cross they went to divy his clothes throwing dice for them, and they sat down to watch him there. And above his head they placed the information charged against him in writing. "This is Jesus, the ruler of the Jews." Then they put two robbers on crosses, one on the right and one on the left. Now come those passers by, God-cursers, who shook their heads at him, saying, "Hey, fellow, you who can tear down the church and rebuild it in three days. Save yourself! If you are the Child of God, come down from there!" The same way the senior ministers come and did their ridiculing, along with the Hebrew translators and the elders who said, "He kept others alive but he can't seem to keep himself alive. He is supposed to be in charge of Israel. Come down now from the cross and we will acknowledge you.

He can smooth talk God. Let him persuade God to rescue him now if he wants to since he claimed that 'I am God's Child'." Thru this time Jesus is just there and the robbers, being crucified with him, was ridiculing him the same way.

Jesus Dies

From the sixth hour to the ninth hour all the earth was under a shadow. About the time of the ninth hour, Jesus cried out loud in Hebrew, saying, "Eli, eli, lema sabaxthani?" which is, "My God, my God, why are you leaving me in the lurch?" Some of them standing there hearing it said that he calls upon Elijah himself. And quickly one run from them and taking a sponge filled it with myrrh and lifted it up on a reed for him to suck on. But the rest said, "Leave off so we can see if Elijah will save his life." Then, after Jesus again took to crying out in a loud voice, he died. And at this same time the curtain at the main Jerusalem church split apart in two from top to bottom and an earthquake happened and rocks broke and graves opened up and many of those whose lives had been saved, now, as saints, rose to offer witness, and coming out of their graves after they had come back to life, they went to the special city of Jerusalem and they gave report from the perspective of the dead to many. The Roman officer in charge of the detail and those who had kept Jesus in custody, feeling the earthquake and those other happenings, became very scared, saying, "It must have been true, this fellow was the Child of God." There were there also many women from long distances away observing events who had been supporters of Jesus from Galilee helping his ministry. Among them was Mary the Magdalene and Mary the daughter of Jacob and the mother of Joseph and the mother of Zebedee's boys.

Jesus is Buried

When evening set in, here came a rich fellow from Arimathaia by the name of Joseph, who also has received instruction from Jesus. This one went over to Pilate and asked for the body of Jesus. That is how come Pilate ordered the body turned over to him. Taking the body, Joseph wrapped it in clean linen and deposited it in a new grave that he had had cut in rock and rolled a huge rock against the entrance and left. Then came Mary Magdalene and the other Mary who sat outside and in view of the tomb.

Guarding The Tomb

The next day which is the day of Easter Preparation there gathered together the senior church authorities and the Pharisees at Pilate's place, saying, "Sir, we remember what that lying fellow said before he died, `After three days I will arise.' Order security at that grave until after the three days. That will prevent them friends he has bound to him by instruction from going there and stealing him and saying to the people, `He has arisen from death' and this last deception will be worse than the first." Pilate says to them, "You have security guards. You can keep ward as you think you have to." Then, after they left, the Jewish authorities set guards at the tomb to make sure the rock stayed put according to good security procedures.

Jesus Returns To Life

Late in the day of the Sabbath, at the dawn on the first day of the Sabbath, there came Mary Magdalene and the other Mary who charged themselves to observe the tomb. And right at that time there come a huge earthquaking. An angel of the Familyhead, coming out from God's Homeland, took and rolled away the rock and sat down on it. He was in appearance as lightning and his clothing was white as snow. From fear of him, they took to shaking, these who was keeping watch and they was as dead folk. But the angel took note of it and said to the women, "Don't you be afraid. I know that Jesus, the one who was crucified, lives. He isn't here, he arose as he said. Come look at the place where he lay. Now, quickly go! You must tell the friends of his who have received his instruction into the ways of God that he has arisen from death and at this time he goes to you to Galilee. There you will see him. Bear in mind, he has instructed you." And going quick from the tomb with fear and great joy they ran to give the good news to his friends disciplined into God's story of life. And, now this! Jesus met them, saying, "Hello." And they rushed over and held his feet and reverenced him. Then Jesus says to them, "Don't be afraid. Go tell my friends that they need to go to Galilee, and there they will see me."

The Security Guards Return To The City

While the friends who had learned God's ways was leaving, Yes! these of the security guards was returning into the city to tell the senior church authorities everything that happened. And they was assembling with the elders in conspiracy thinking to take money and bribe the guards saying, "Let's say that his special friends took him away in the night, stealing him while you was asleep. And if any word of this gets to the governor, you will get prosecuted but on the other hand we can keep you out of trouble." Then the guards took money and did what they was going to do and the soldiers was bought into the conspiracy. And this story was spread around Judea most to this day.

Jesus Gives His Friends The Mission Of Christians

Meanwhile the eleven friends disciplined into God's love went to Galilee to the hill where Jesus give them directions, and seeing him, they treated him very respectfully, but they kept their distance. And Jesus went to them and spoke with them, saying, "All existence is given over to me in God's Homeland and on earth. Now go, help all people become friends to God's ways, baptizing them in the name of the Parent, and of the Child, and of the breathing Spirit of God which guides them, keeping to everything that I taught you. And Yes! I am with you every day until the end of time."

κατασκευαζω prepared/build equip   *ευθυς εις, ο straight right.*

αρχη, ης beginning first.   *Isaiah*   *τριβος ου path, pathway*

ΚΑΤΑ ΜΑΡΚΟΝ

The Preaching of John the Baptist
(Mt 3.1-12; Lk 3.1-9, 15-17; Jn 1.19-28)

1 Ἀρχὴ τοῦ εὐαγγελίου Ἰησοῦ Χριστοῦ [υἱοῦ θεοῦ]¹·ᵃ
2 Καθὼς γέγραπται ἐν τῷ Ἠσαΐᾳ τῷ προφήτῃ²,
   Ἰδοὺ ἀποστέλλω τὸν ἄγγελόν μου πρὸ προσώπου σου,
   ὃς κατασκευάσει τὴν ὁδόν σου·
3 φωνὴ βοῶντος ἐν τῇ ἐρήμῳ,
   Ἑτοιμάσατε τὴν ὁδὸν κυρίου,
   εὐθείας ποιεῖτε τὰς τρίβους αὐτοῦ,ᵇ
4 ἐγένετο Ἰωάννης [ὁ] βαπτίζων ἐν τῇ ἐρήμῳ καὶ³ κηρύσσων βάπτισμα μετανοίας εἰς ἄφεσιν ἁμαρτιῶν. 5 καὶ ἐξε-

¹ 1 {C} Χριστοῦ υἱοῦ θεοῦ ℵ* B D L W Diatessaronᵖ Irenaeus Severian ∥ Χριστοῦ υἱοῦ τοῦ θεοῦ A K Δ Π f¹ f¹³ 33 565 700 892 1009 1010 1071 1079 1195 1216 1230 1242 1253 1344 1365 1546 1646 2148 2174 Byz Lectᵐ Cyril ∥ Χριστοῦ υἱοῦ θεοῦ or Χριστοῦ υἱοῦ τοῦ θεοῦ itᵃ,ᵃᵘʳ,ᵇ,ᶜ,ᵈ,ᶠ,ff²,ˡ,q,ʳ¹ vg syrᵖ,ʰ copˢᵃ,ᵇᵒ goth arm eth geo² Irenaeusˡᵃᵗ²/³ Origenˡᵃᵗ Ambrose Jerome Augustine ∥ Χριστοῦ υἱοῦ τοῦ κυρίου 1241 ∥ Χριστοῦ ℵ* Θ 28ᶜ syrᵖᵃˡ geo¹ Irenaeusᵍʳ,ˡᵃᵗ¹/³ Origenᵍʳ,ˡᵃᵗ Victorinus-Pettau Serapion Titus-Bostra Basil Cyril-Jerusalem Epiphanius Jerome ∥ omit 28*

² 2 {A} ἐν τῷ Ἠσαΐᾳ τῷ προφήτῃ ℵ B L Δ 33 565 892 1241 Irenaeusᵍʳ,ˡᵃᵗ Origen Severian ∥ ἐν Ἠσαΐᾳ τῷ προφήτῃ D Θ f¹ 700 1071 2174 Origen Serapion Titus-Bostra Basil Epiphanius Victor-Antioch ∥ ἐν (or ἐν τῷ) Ἠσαΐᾳ τῷ προφήτῃ itᵃ,ᵃᵘʳ,ᵇ,ᶜ,ᵈ,ᶠ,ff²,ˡ,q vg syrᵖ,ʰᵐᵍ,ᵖᵃˡ copˢᵃ,ᵇᵒ goth geo Porphyryᵃᶜᶜ·ᵗᵒ ᴶᵉʳᵒᵐᵉ Victorinus-Pettau Eusebius Ambrosiaster Jerome Augustine ∥ ἐν τοῖς προφήταις A K P W Π f¹³ 28 1009 1010 1079 1195 1216 1230 1242 1253 1344 1365 1546 1646 2148 Byz Lectᵐ syrʰ copᵇᵒᵐˢ ᵐᵍ arm eth Irenaeusˡᵃᵗ Photius Theophylact

³ 4 {C} ὁ βαπτίζων ἐν τῇ ἐρήμῳ καὶ ℵ L Δ geo¹ copᵇᵒ ∥ ὁ βαπτίζων ἐν τῇ ἐρήμῳ B 33 892 copᵇᵒᵐˢˢ ∥ βαπτίζων ἐν τῇ ἐρήμῳ καὶ A K P W Π f¹ f¹³ 565 1009 1010 1071 1079 1195 1216 1230 1241 1242 1253 1344 1365 1546 1646 2148 2174 Byz Lectᵐ itᶠ syrʰ,ᵖᵃˡ (copˢᵃ omit καί) goth arm eth ∥ ἐν τῇ ἐρήμῳ βαπτίζων καί D Θ 28 700 itᵃ,ᵃᵘʳ,ᵇ,ᶜ,ᵈ,ff¹,ˡ,q,ʳ¹·ᵗ vg syrᵖ Eusebius Cyril-Jerusalem Augustine ∥ ἐν τῇ ἐρήμῳ καί geo²

ᵃ 1 a major: WH Bov RV ASV RSV NEB Zür Luth Jer Seg ∥ a minor: TR BF² AV
ᵇ 3 b minor: WH Bov RV ASV Zür Jer ∥ b dash: RSV ∥ b major: TR WHᵐᵍ BF² AV NEB Luth Seg

2 Ἰδού...ὁδόν σου Ex 23.20; Mal 3.1 (Mt 11.10; Lk 1.76; 7.27)   3 φωνή...αὐτοῦ Is 40.3 (Jn 1.23)   4 ἐγένετο...μετανοίας Ac 13.24; 19.4

118

Opening page of Mark's Witness from the *Greek New Testament* that Ben Johnson used for translation

MARK'S WITNESS

The Preaching Of John The Baptist

L ET'S START OFF WITH A HAPPY FORETELLING of Jesus, our Familyhead,
God's own Child, as it's written up in Isaiah's prophecy,

> Look, I send my agent before your face,
> A voice crying in the barrens,
> Get ready a road to the Familyhead,
> Make paths straight to it.

John come baptizing in such an otherwise abandoned barrens and announcing a baptizing that served the purpose of re-orientation so that folks
could leave behind their angering ways. And there come out to him all them's
in towns of Judea and all them's living in Jerusalem, and they was baptized by
him in the Jordan River where they shared how distant God seemed. John was
dressed in camel hide and wore a leather belt around his waist and lived on

eating bugs and wild plant juices. And he preached sermons saying, "There is coming one who is more important that I am. Comparative, I ain't fit to take off his shoes. I baptize you with water. This one will baptize you to breath the living breath of God."

The Baptizing Of Jesus

And it happened that Jesus come that very day from Nazareth in Galilee and was baptized in the Jordan River by John. And immediate when he come up out of the water, John saw the sky of existence open and breath as a bird flying down entering into him. And a voice come out of being, "You are the child of my passion. I am proud of you."

The Temptation Of Jesus

And right after this, God's spirit drove him out into an abandoned place and there he was alone for forty days having his mind turned this way and that by the world's ways personified, and his only company was wild thoughts, while angels took care of him.

The Beginning Of The Galilean Ministry

After John got arrested, Jesus went into Galilee telling the good news about God and saying how time could be fulfilled and God's world rule was getting close. Let all this influence your thinking and believe the good news story!

The Calling Of The Four Fishermen

Now when passing by the sea of Galilee, he saw Simon and Andrew, Simon's brother, out on the sea. They was fishermen. So Jesus said to them, "Come over here to me and I will have it happen to you to be fishermen catching folks." And immediately they throwed away their fishing nets, and joined up with him. And going on a little bit, he saw James, the son of Zebedee and John, his brother and they was in a boat mending their nets, and as quick as he called them, they come on to become companions leaving back their dad Zebedee in their rented fishing boat.

The Man With The Mental Illness

Next they went into Capernaum and since it was right then on a Sunday when they went there Jesus took to teaching in the church. And folks was thunderstruck at this teaching. Reason was, his teaching was marked authoritative not like other scripture readers. And then there come into the church of theirs a fellow with a mental illness and he cried out, "What's these scriptures mean to us and you, Jesus Nazarene? Are you coming to destroy us? I appreciate who you are, the presence of God." And Jesus give him a command, saying, "Muzzle it and get out of him." And these words threw him and his mentally ill behaviors into a convulsive internal fight and there started up great shouting in loud voices coming out of him. And the whole place was thrown into uproar and it led them to arguing among themselves saying, "What's all this about?" See, it was new teaching and authoritative, and he can give commands to misdirected minds, and they's got to obey him. And gossip about him was spread out quick into the neighborhoods in the whole area of Galilee.

The Healing of Many People

And right after he left out of the church he went into the house where lived Simon and Andrew, along with James and John. And Simon's mother in law was lying down sick with a fever and right then they told him about her. And after he went to her, holding her hand, he helped her get up. And her fever went away and she was able to do chores for them. Later, it got to be evening, when the sun was setting, they brought to him all the sick folk and them's mentally ill. And it was like the whole town was gathering at the gate. And he healed all the sick ones having various kinds of physical problems and relieved them's with mental illness and he didn't slowdown to diagnose the problems, because they knowed him.

A Preaching Tour

And early the next morning, long before daylight broke, he left and set up in a solitary spot and there he took to praying. And Simon and the others searched for him real hard, and finally they found him and said to him, "Everybody is looking for you." And he says to them, "We got to go other places into the neighboring country towns, so I can preach there." So they left going another direction.

The Cleansing of A Leper

And they went preaching in the churches around there all over Galilee and dealing with folks basic concerns. Now here come to him a leper calling out for him and saying to him that, "If you want to, you can get me back to normal." And feeling deep compassion, extending his hands, Jesus touched him and says to him, "I want to. Get back to normal." And immediately his skin leprosy condition was cleared up, and he become normal-looking. Just speaking harsh to it caused it to go away fast as lightning. And he says to him, "Don't expect nothing to be believed you tell, but go anyway, show yourself in the church and offer your thanks in ritual sacrifice that Moses commanded as a witness to these things." But after the fellow left, he begun to tell lots of folks and to spread around the story of his healing, and since there's no where left for Jesus to go to be by himself in the city, he decided to leave and he went outside to a more solitary countryside spot but folks still was going to him from every-where.

The Healing of A Paralytic

And then after he went to Capernaum it become known that he was in the city. And lots of folks gathered so that there's no room not even close to the gate to the house, and he tells them a story. And there come some to him bearing a paralyzed fellow who's been paralyzed since he was four. But since they was no way to bring him close to him because of the crowd, they climbed to the roof of the house where he's at and scooped off the roof to lower down this paralyzed one still laying on a stretcher. And when Jesus saw what their faith has caused them to do, he says to this paralyzed fellow, "Boy, they're gone - these thing stopping you from witnessing for God." Now they was some of the temple Hebrew translators there sitting down and they was contentious in their hearts, "What's that he's saying? It's blasphemy, against God. Who's he think he is to release things separating folks from God. No one except God can do that." But simultaneous, Jesus knowed what was in their minds so whilst they's still thinking this, he says to them, "Why are you contentious in your hearts? Which is easier to say to this paralytic, 'They're gone - these thing stopping you from witnessing for God' or to say, 'Get up and take your stretcher and walk?' But since you need to understand the authority God's human Child has to breach God's separation from life on earth, I say to the paralytic, `I told you, get up, take your stretcher, and go away to your house.'" And he picked himself up and after he got his stretcher he left out of sight of them all, so that they was all standing there ogling and thinking they's in God's presence saying that this is like nothing we've ever seen.

The Calling Of Levi

And then he again went down to the sea. And the whole crowd went with him, and he preached to them. And after bit, he saw Levi, the son of Alphaius, sitting beside a tax office and he says to him, "Join me." And he got up and joined him. And Jesus went to have dinner with him in his house. And many tax collectors and rejected folks was sitting with Jesus and his companions. They was many who was accepting Jesus. And one of the gospel readers who was a Pharisee was seeing that he was eating with rejects and tax collectors and he says to the companions, "Why does Jesus eat with tax collectors and rejects." And after Jesus heard of it, he says to them, "Them's strong don't have a need for a doctor like those feeling bad. I didn't come to reach folks oriented to do God's will but separated ones."

The Question About Fasting

And there was traveling companions of John the Baptist and the Pharisees who ate according to strict rules. And some come and said to Jesus, "Why do the companions of John and the Pharisees eat by these strict rules and your friends don't have no religious diets?" And Jesus said to them, "Is there a reason why bridegrooms shouldn't eat at their rehearsal dinners even with them's wanting to eat strict? How many times do folks have a bridegroom with them so that they don't have need to follow religious diets? There will come days when the bridegroom will be took away from them and then, at that time, they will have eating problems enough. No clothing patch that's new can be sewed onto a new coat without it being noticed because of the dividing line. No one puts new wine in botas with old. If you do, the wine cracks through the botas and the wine is destroyed along with the wineskins. That's why new wine comes to be kept in new botas."

Picking Grain On The Sunday Day Of Rest

Once when he was taking a shortcut by a wheat crop on Sunday, his traveling companions got to picking wheatheads at the roadside. And the Pharisees said to him, "Look. What are they doing? Isn't that unlawful on Sunday?" And he says to them, "Ain't you never understood what David done when he had to have food and he himself was starving and them with him, how he went into the house of God with Abiathar, a high priest, and ate bread dedicated to God's worship purposes, and it wasn't lawful for them to eat it even though they wasn't priests and he shared it with them happening to be with him?" And he said to them, "Sunday is for the benefit of people and not people for the benefit of Sunday. Anyway, the Familyhead is God's human Child even on Sunday."

A Guy With Degenerative Arthritis

After bit he went again to a particular church and in there was a guy with a hand impairment due to degenerative arthritis. And some critics was watching like hawks to see if he was going to heal him on Sunday. And Jesus says to this fellow with the arthritis hand, "Come to the center of the group." And he asks them, "Which is better, to try to help people on Sunday or to do them harm? To make their lives better or to kill them?" That got them quieted. And while he sensed their hearts staying stony, and while he was wrestling with his sorrow for their hardheartedness, he says to the fellow, "Hold out your hand." And he held out his hand and it was returned to normal. And just as quick, the Pharisees joined Herod conspirators to figure how they could kill Jesus.

A Multitude At The Seaside

But Jesus with his traveling companions slipped away down to the sea along with a huge crowd of Galilleans, and them's from Judah, and from Jerusalem, and from along the Jordan River and its border country, and from Tyre and Sidon. They become a huge crowd paying as close attention as possible to what he was about and going everywhere Jesus went. And he said to the companions of his to get a small boat ready so he wouldn't get crushed on account of the mob. Lots of people were being healed, so that it was a fact folks was falling over themselves to get to Jesus, and even contact with Jesus was having a healing effect on diseases. And mental disorders, when he noticed them, they would acknowledge Jesus and cry out loud like, 'You are the Child of God.' And every symptom took their orders to be done away.

The Choosing Of The Twelve

Later, he climbed a hill and chose them's particular he wanted and these went with him. He picked twelve, and they was named special companions, so that they would be with him and because he wanted to train them in preaching and give them counseling tips. And Jesus charged up these twelve. And Jesus laid on a new name for Simon, "Rock," which is to say, "Peter," and James, son of Zebedee and John, son of his brother Jacob, and Jesus laid on them these names, his Wild Bulls, who were his "Thunderkids." The others was Andrew, and Philip and Bartholomew and Matthew and Simon, son of Kavanion and Judas Iskariot who become a traitor.

Jesus And Beelzebul

One day he was going into a house and again a crowd trailed behind, so that he wasn't able to eat no meal. And them's tracking him come to squeeze him. And he told them what they's doing isn't right. And the Hebrew translators from Jerusalem who come down heard that a devil has got him because from his ministry beginning he has expelled mind disorders they considered devils. And Jesus called them over and said to them, "How is Satan empowered to do stuff when the one who you call Satan is the one you say I am expelling? If the world is divided up within itself its government can't stand. Just so, if a house within itself is divided, that house can't stand. So, if the one you call Satan arises within something and can cause division, whatever it is can't stand

and its over. There can't be a strong house broke into for the purpose of bur-
glarizing, unless it's not built strong in the first place, and if that's the case it's
already: as good as burglarized. Believe it when I say to you that everything can
be forgiven by God's human Child, every separating circumstance and doing
against, whatever folks may do, but one whose mind schemes against God's
breathing Spirit in their thinking, has no forgiveness in this world age, for such
hostility is an alienation forever.

Those against Jesus said, "He is mentally ill."

The Mother And Brothers Of Jesus

And there come the mother of Jesus and his brothers and sisters and them's
standing outside sent someone to call him. And a crowd was sitting around
him and they said to him, "Look, your mother and your brothers and sisters
are wanting you to go outside." And Jesus replied and said to them, "Who is
my mother and my brothers and sisters?" And while they looked at each other
sitting around the circle, he said, "Look, my mother and my brothers and sisters. For he who does what God wants, this is my brother and sister and my
mother."

The Parable Of The Sower

Another time, Jesus begun to teach beside the sea. And he gathered to himself a huge crowd, so great that he has to get in a boat and talk to them while
seated in it a little way out from shore. And the whole crowd was on the shore
close to the sea. Now Jesus did lots of teaching giving story life examples explaining about God's Homeland and he did his teaching to them in this teaching style, so you have to pay close attention. Imagine this, a farmer come to do
planting. And as he started in to do his planting, some wheat seed fell along the
road, and birds come along and ate it down. And some of the other seed fell on
rocky ground where there wasn't good soil, and it sprouted quick even though
it didn't have no deep soil to grow in. But when the sun come up, it got
scorched and, because of what its root didn't have, it withered. And another
seed fell in among thorns, and these weeds come up and choked it, and it
didn't bear a head. And other wheat seed fell into good earth and it kept on
growing to produce a crop, producing more and more and spreading and it
produced wheat heads, some bearing thirty grains, some sixty, and some over
a hundred." Then he said, "He who has ears to hear, try to get the point."

The Purpose Of The Parables

Now one time he was telling folk stories when some among his companions has asked him why he give them. And he told them, "To you is give to

participate in the hard to understand experience of life with God in God's world. To others who stand outside our circle so that they don't see, the whole world, the mystery is explained in terms of folk stories, because

Looking, they look and don't understand

And those hearing listen and don't comprehend,

Unless they are tuned in, it escapes them."

And he says to them, "Did you understand the story? How many got the point? The one who sews seed, sews the story of God's life? And those seeds that fell along the road, well, God's story did sprout up but when its story got heard, here come opposition to God confronting it and taking away the power of the story that's growing in it. And them's growing on the rocky soil, well when they was hearing the story, they was quick to receive its saving value. But, they didn't have roots enough so that it was temporary, so when hard times come and persecution against the story's being told, just as quick they lost their faith. And them's sprouting up in the thorns. These are them who hear the story, and are filled with anxiety about it all the time, and it gets lost in a crowd of deceptive thoughts which are longings that choke the story and cause it not to bear fruit. And then there are those seeds which are planted in good soil. Such are those who hear the story and receive it full and they will bear fruit thirty times, sixty times and one hundred times over."

A Light Under A Bushel

And he said to them, "Do any of you go putting a light so that its hid under a bucket or under a bed? Don't you put it so that it's on a table? If it's hid it don't give light. Neither can it reveal what's in darkness and bring it to light. If anyone has ears to listen try to get the point." And then he says to them, "Understand what you hear. To the extent you set a standard, it will measure you, only it will be made stricter against you. Someone who has something, it's been given to that one. And what a person don't have, that's been took away from that one."

The Parable Of The Growing Seed

And Jesus told them, "Here's an inkling of a God's world governing principle. A person may throw a seed on the ground, and that person dies, and night and day pass by, and the seed sprouts and grows just like it didn't know the person's dead. It's automatic that the ground of the world has reproducing power. First comes a plant, then it grows a head on the stalk. When it is time it is give over to producing grain. Then's when Quick! go get the sickle, because the harvest time appears."

The Parable Of The Mustard Seed

And Jesus said, "Can we draw a comparison of how God's world ruling principle works in what we can see as an example? How about from the grain of mustard, which when it is thrown on the ground is the tiniest of seed. Still, when it's planted in the soil, it's the tiniest of all seeds in the garden. But after it is sewn, it comes up and becomes larger than all the garden plants and it grows huge branches, so that it can give shade to the birds nesting in it belonging to the sky of existence."

The Use Of Parables

So often Jesus spoke to them in life folk stories explaining about God's Homeland telling them a story so that they could understand. Jesus didn't hardly talk to them except telling a story from a life example and he would settle all their arguing one of the companions with the others.

The Calming Of The Storm

And he talked to them late that same day when evening come, "We need to leave for the other side of the sea." And afterwards they left the crowd to go across it, and then they was in the boat, bearing across it. And there come a storm with heavy blowing wind and waves was pouring into the boat so that already the hull was full of water. And Jesus was in the stern of the boat asleep on some pillows. And they woke him up saying to him, "Teacher, is it going to be that we will drown?" And after he got up, he give orders to the wind and said to the sea, "Quiet down, hush up." And the wind stopped blowing and it become so very calm. And he said to them, "Why are you such cowards? Don't you have faith?" And they was acting so scared and afraid of things and they said to each other, "Why is it that even the wind and the sea act in obedience to Jesus?"

The Healing Of The Gerasene Crazy Guy

And they got to the other side of the sea near a town called Gerasane. And after Jesus got out of the boat, there come to meet him a fellow from a grave-yard whose mind was off. The fellow kept his home there in the graves, and no one was able to put no chains on him to confine him. Even so, every now and then, often really, he was restrained by feet chains and prison chains and he would pull at them chains until they snapped and the feet chains would gash his ankles, and no one has the strength to arrest him. He was always crying, all through the night and day from the graveyard and in hills and the stones would echo it.

And when he saw Jesus, even as disturbed as he was, he knowed to run to him and beg him for help. And still crying, in a loud voice, he says, "What's the good of this to me and you, Jesus, human Child? I beg you, God;y Child, don't tease me." Then Jesus said to him, "Every one of you rejections and mixed-up recollections, get out of this fellow right now!" And Jesus asked him, "What is your name?" And he says to Jesus, "My name is Army, because we are many." And Jesus relieved him of an awful lot of problems so that he wouldn't have to be expelled from the people in the community anymore. Now there was on a hill a whole bunch of pigs rooting for food. And the rejections and hurts of Army's life spoke out to Jesus saying, "Send us into them pigs so that we can leave out." And Jesus said, "Okay," to them. And these thoughts, maybe a cou-ple thousand, went flying into them pigs, and the bunch of them rushed down over a steep bank into the sea and they choked and drowned on seawater. And the livestockers watching them ran off and give the news to the townsfolk and in the marketplace and they all come out to see what happened. And they come to Jesus and saw this fellow who has been crazy, sitting dressed and acting sen-sible, after Army has left out, and they were scared! The kept telling themselves what they saw, how it happened about this fellow been crazy and about the pigs. And they begun to ask Jesus to come down from their hills. And when Jesus was getting into the boat, this former crazy man begged so that he could go too and be with Jesus. And Jesus didn't let him, instead saying to him, "Go into your town to your own people and preach to them as much as you can about what the Familyhead did for you and the love-gift give to you." And he left and begun to preach in the country of Decapolis, an area that has ten major cities in it, so often as he could about what Jesus done for him and everyone listened intent.

Jairus' Daughter And The Woman Who Touched Jesus' Clothes

Then Jesus crossed over in a boat back to the place where a large crowd is gathered together, and they was on the shore. And there come to him the president of the local church whose name was Jarus, and when he saw Jesus, he fell down in front of Jesus and he begged Jesus with every ounce of hope he has saying, "My little girl is going to die any minute unless you come and place your hands on her to revive her and let her live." And Jesus went with him. And there followed behind Jesus this large crowd and they was pressing close.

Now there was a woman who has had gonorrhea sores for twelve years and she's suffered through every doctor's treatment and she's spent all the money she has and none sympathizes with her and she's wanting real bad to come to Jesus's hand. She heard the reports about Jesus, and come along with the crowd and touched Jesus's coat from behind. She was saying to herself, "If I could even touch Jesus's clothes I will be healed." And right then, this gonorrhea bleeding was dried up and she realized her body is healed from sickness.

Right then also Jesus realized inside himself that some of his healing power left, so turning around to the crowd he said, "Who touched my clothes?" And the companions said to him, "You see for yourself how the crowd is pressed in on you." But he insists in asking, "Who touched me?" And he looked around to see who would admit up to it. The woman, scared to death and shaking in fear, knowing she's the one he's talking about, went and fell in front of Jesus, told Jesus the honest truth that she's the one. And he told her, "Woman your faith has rescued you from your body frailties, and allowed you to be cured from your sickness and kept you alive too! Go on in peace and be a healthy person remembering you was once sick."

While Jesus was still talking, news come from the church board president that, "My little girl died." And the folks who knowed it, was saying to the church board president, "Why do you still bother the teacher with coming?" But Jesus don't hold back, when he heard the report and says to the church board president, "Don't be worried or scared, just have faith!"

But no way does Jesus abandon no troubled person, excepting only Peter and James and John, the brother of James, joined in thinking he can still go do something for the girl. And they come to the house of the church board president, and the scene was confused and folks was crying and even screaming. And going inside, Jesus asked, "Why are you so upset and crying? This little girl isn't dead, she's just resting."

And they laughed at Jesus.

And having everyone else leave, Jesus brought the family together, the father of the little girl and her mother and all of them together went to where the little girl was. And holding the hand of the little girl, Jesus says to her, "Wake up, baby girl." This is the translation from the Aramaic through Greek (into American folk.)

To this little girl he simply says, "you can get up." And right then, this little girl stood up and walks. She was about twelve years old. And they come to be in a state of great ecstasy. And Jesus give them strict orders not to tell what happened to nobody and Jesus said to go ahead and give her something to eat.

The Rejection Of Jesus At Nazareth

And after this, Jesus went to his hometown, and the companions went along. And when it come Sunday, Jesus begun to teach Sunday school and everybody who listened was shook up, saying, "What's all this about?" and "What is this smart- aleck dishing out to us?" and "Have we ever heard tell of such delusions as are worked through his hands?" "Isn't this the little guy, the son of Mary and brother of James, and Joses and Juda and Simon?" and, "Don't he have sisters living here with us?" and "Even they has doubts about Jesus." And Jesus said to them that there's no prophet who is ever listened to in the person's hometown or church or home. And Jesus didn't have no chance to do no good there except a few sick folks got healed when Jesus touched them. But Jesus was depressed on account of their refusal to reach a level of faithfulness.

The Mission Of The Twelve

And Jesus went around a little circle of towns surrounding Nazareth teaching. Then Jesus called together the twelve companions and begun to talk special to them two by and two and give them power to change over people's wrong behaviors, and he warned them not to hold on to nothing down their life path except only a walking stick, not even a loaf of bread or a wallet, or a penny to live on. And he told them, "When you put your shoes on, don't even wear socks!" And he said to them, "When you are welcomed into a house, stay there until you feel the need to leave from there." And, "Anyplace don't welcome us because they don't want to listen to us, when we leave from there, just shake off their dust from under our feet as our witness to them." And ever after, they was able to speak confident and reach and change people's opinions, and every mind distress overcome, and they rubbed oil on the bodies of sick folk and healed them.

The Death Of John The Baptist

Now Herodia, the Queen Ruler of the World, for that's how she bragged about herself, heard the news that they was saying that John the Baptist could raise folks from the dead and because of this they was at work in him powerful mental illness. Others was saying that he is Elijah. And others was saying that he was a prophet like them prophets come before. When Herodia kept hearing this, she said, "I am going to cut off John's head and see if he can return to life."

Now this Herodia who sent someone to do this was the one who had John arrested in the first place and had him imprisoned. She did this because Herodia was the sister of Philip and also his wife, having agreed to marry him. Now John told Herodia that it's not right for you to be both his sister and wife. From then on, Herodia held a grudge against him and wanted to kill him, but she couldn't do it. Then Herodia come to fear John, becoming aware he was come to be considered a person whose thinking was specially right and Godly-spirited, and she remembered him, and when she kept hearing about him, she got a worse and worse guilty conscience, and she was real happy when she learned he was tried and sentenced. Her opportunity come one day when Herod put on a dinner as a birthday party for a VIP who was one of his army officers and also one of the most influential people of Galilee. And the daughter of this Herodian couple come in to dance, and this pleased Herodia and them's sitting down to eat with them. And the ruler said to his little girl, "Ask me for a wish and I will give it to you. I swear it! Even if it's half my country!" And coming to be close to him, she said to her daddy, "Whatever I want?" Then getting an okay, she said, "The head of John, the one who baptizes." And she no sooner said it than she left, after having demanded the authority who could do it to give her the head of John, the one who baptizes, to be immediate brought to her on a pole. And this self-same authority become sorry he give the oath but none of them sitting at the party wanted her wish set off. So right then he called for the executioner to be sent for to go bring back his head. And going there, he cut off John's head right there in his cell. And he brought back John's head on a pole and it was give to the little girl, and the little girl give it to her mother. And when John's companions heard about it they come and took his body and buried it in a grave.

The Feeding Of The Five Thousand

Then these companions went to Jesus and told Jesus everything that's happened and as much as they learned. And Jesus says to them, "Come with us to our own shelter and rest a little." And lots of them was coming and going agitated, not taking the time to eat. And these companions left in a boat to the shelter with Jesus's own traveling companions. And others saw where they's going and figured out where all of them was going to down the lake a ways and folks was riotous over what happened to John and went running to there by foot from every city round about. After they was all there, Jesus saw this huge crowd and he felt so sorry for them, now that they was a flock of sheep without no shepherd, and Jesus comforted them everyone. But already it has come to be late in the day when they's come to Jesus and the companions said to him, "Do you realize this is out in the country and its late in the day. They need to leave because there's no stores out here or towns close enough to buy food for them to have."

But Jesus answered them and said, "Give them our own food to eat." And they said to Jesus, "You want us to go buy 200 denarius worth of bread? That's what it would take to feed them?" And Jesus says to them, "How many loaves do you have? Gather up what you can find." And after they knew, they said to him, "Five and two fish." And he told them to sit down to eat, all of them, each in a little sharing group, and there was about a hundred of them and each had fifty people. And taking the five loaves and the two fish, looking up towards God's Homeland itself, he give thanks and broke the bread and give it to the companions so that they might distribute it among them, and then he divided the two fish among them all. And everybody ate all they wanted and was filled up, and they gathered up the leftovers that filled twelve Jewish food baskets full with fish left too. And there was five thousand people that ate.

Walking On The Water

And next thing, Jesus got the companions together to get back on their boat to leave to go to a spot near Capernaum. So that's how Jesus left the crowd. And when they got there, Jesus said good-bye, and Jesus left to go up in a mountain to be alone to pray. And when night come, the companions stayed on the boat in the middle of the sea, and Jesus alone was on the land. And while they's watching being tossed about by waves and straining at their oars, they saw a gale in front of them until about midnight when here Jesus come to them walking on the sea for Jesus wanted to reach them. When they saw Jesus walking on the sea, they was scared thinking it was a ghost and they begun crying for help. Everyone of them that saw it become frantic. Then right away Jesus heard the commotion among them and says to them, "Don't worry, I AM. Don't be afraid." And he come over to them, calmed the wind and they was very much beside themselves in shock. They hadn't understood about the bread either because still there was among them a stubborn heart.

The Healing Of The Sick In Gennesaret

And after he come over from the land, they went into Gennasaret and docked. And whilst they was coming out of the boat, right then it got told about and the townsfolk come running breathless from the whole region and others begun carrying sick folks to him on stretchers bringing them to where they heard that he's at. And wherever Jesus went, whether in a town, or in a city, or in the countryside in the fields, folks plopped their sick and they would pray to Jesus to please just let these sick folks touch the edge of Jesus's clothes. And so many as touched Jesus would find themselves healed.

The Tradition Of The Elders

Now Pharisees invited Jesus to be their guest once and some of the Hebrew translators was there who's come from Jerusalem. And when they saw the companions of Jesus and how they's just common folk, and then they saw that these same companions didn't know enough about the main Jerusalem church rules saying to wash their hands at certain times, like when they divided a loaf of bread, these Pharisees and all the main Jerusalem church authorities come to make a big deal about washing their hands all the way to the wrist saying they couldn't eat otherwise, and holding off the eating until they's done all this conformity to tradition from their elders. And market-bought food couldn't be eat unless its washed. And lots of other stuff has to be gone through before they could eat, washing down the cups and jugs and bowls. While all this folderol was being gone through, these Pharisees and main Jerusalem church Hebrew translators was asking, "Why don't your companions follow tradition as its come down from elders? Why do you eat your meals with such common folk?" But Jesus said to them, "Isaiah give it right when he explained God's feelings about folks pretending to be better than others because of what they are doing when he wrote,

> This people honor me with lip service,
> But their hearts are estranged far away from me,
> In vain, they worship me,
> teachers teaching only human laws.

Forgiveness is the rule of God and you are burdening it with folk's traditions." Then Jesus said to them, "You have done a good job of abandoning God's rules when you try to stand on your traditions. As Moses said, 'Honor your father and your mother,' And, 'One who talks their father and mother into doing wrong ends up in a unsaved death.' You hear a child say to that one's father and mother, 'If you will pledge Korban, (a Hebrew language term which translates, a big showy church gift), then it will buy God's favor for me.' No one is forgiven or brought close to God through the doing of that kind of stuff, not the father or the mother and it amounts to disregarding the story of God's life through your tradition or what you demand be done. And just so is the effect of what you do." And again the crowd went to calling for Jesus, and Jesus said to them, "All of you, listen to me and understand. There's no external custom that a person does in their living which can condemn them, only them things which come from how they act that can condemn a person." And then Jesus went back into the house where Jesus's companions begun asking him the meaning of the statement. And Jesus says to them, "How's come you don't understand? Don't you realize that food customs shouldn't get formed in the lives of people for the purpose of condemning them? What food is it that can enter a heart? Nothing. The entry is into the stomach and that gets expelled in toilets after their meals." Then he said that, "The action of a person that they do, - that can be the condemning thing about a person. And it's what's inside a person's heart that can reveal the wrong things in their acting, the sex- misbe-

having, the stealing, murdering, adulterizing, acting greedy, meanness, deceit, indecency, pornographing, cussing, acting proud, and not thinking things through. All these wrong intentions come out in your lives and they condemn a person."

The Syro-phoenician Woman's Faith

After Jesus got done eating, Jesus left from there and went to a place near the city of Tyre and when he went into a house there the residents didn't want it made known, but it couldn't be hid. And at that time, a woman heard that he was around there, a woman who had a little daughter who was mentally disturbed and going to Jesus she fell down in front of Jesus. Now this woman was Greek, being born in the Syrian coast of this place called Phoenicia. And she asked Jesus that the depression and anxiety inside her daughter be removed. Then Jesus said to her, "Get out of here. First off the children must be fed, for it's not a good idea to take children's food and throw it to the house pets." But she answered and said, "Familyhead, Sir, pets under the table are permitted to eat scraps." And Jesus said to her, "Because you said this, go, the mental illness has left your daughter." And after she got back home, she discovered her child putting away her sickbed cot and her mind troubles was gone.

A Deaf And Dumb Man Healed

And again when Jesus left out of this Tyre neighborhood, he went by way of Sidon for to go to the sea of Galilee, a little beyond the area of the non-Jewish Ten Cities country. And there was brought to Jesus a deaf person who couldn't talk and the bearers asked Jesus to touch this person. Jesus turned away from the crowd to be with this one. Jesus put his fingers on that his ears and spit on his tongue which energized it, and looking into God's Homeland, Jesus give a sigh and says, "Ephatha," which in Aramaic means "Be opened up!" And that person's hearing got opened up and there got loosened up the bonds that was tying up the person's speech and he started talking straight aways. And Jesus commanded them not to tell nobody nothing except so much as he could allow them to tell, the companions being filled to overflow with wanting to give the good news of it to everyone. And Isaiah's prophecy come true complete. All this good was being done, deaf folks was brought to hearing. Them 's can't say nothing was talking.

The Feeding Of The Four Thousand

And after those days there come to be a large non-Jewish crowd wanting to stay with Jesus and they didn't have food to eat. Calling the companions together, Jesus says to them, "I have a gut reaction about these folks I can't restrain. Already three days have past and these folks have stayed with me but they don't have nothing to eat. If I send them away after a fast like that to their houses, they will give out before they get there. Some of them have come a great distance." And the companions responded to Jesus that, "How could we possible feed them bread out here far from habitations?" And Jesus answered them, "How much bread do you have?" They said, "Seven." And Jesus urged the crowd to sit down on the earth for eating. And Jesus took these seven loaves and, after saying thanks for them, Jesus divided them up and give them to the companions to be distributed and they was passed out to the crowd. And there was a few small dried fish and after giving thanks for them, Jesus said for them to be distributed. And everybody ate and ate until they was full and there was leftovers enough to fill seven baskets of the kind that Greek folk use for food gathering up.

The Demand For A Sign

Now Pharisees come and begun arguing with Jesus wanting a miracle to appear out of the sky of existence, just to test Jesus. And Jesus give out a heaving sigh from out of his soul and says, "Why does this generation want a miracle? Believe it when I tell you this generation is likely to get a miracle." And leaving them, they went again to get into a boat to go to the other side of the lake.

The Leaven Of The Pharisees And Of Herod

But they forgot to take bread with them and did not have even one loaf of bread on the boat. Jesus interrupted them to warn them, saying, "Look at that!

See the product of the yeast of the Pharises and Herod!" And the Pharises kept arguing among themselves because they don't have no food. And ciphering it, Jesus yells to them, "Why do you concern yourselves with bread you don't have? Don't you get the point yet? Your hearts is so resistant! You have been give eyes, but you can't see and ears that don't hear! You don't remember nothing! What about them five loaves divided for the five thousand, how many full servings did you take up in your food baskets after it was divided?" They said, "Twelve, one apiece." When the seven loaves was give to the four thousand, how many Greek style baskets did you fill up for you to take away?" And they said, "Seven, like enough for every day of the week." And Jesus says, "Don't you understand the significance yet?"

The Healing Of A Blind Man At Bethsaida

And they come to Bathsaida. And a blind fellow was took to Jesus and they was begging him to touch this guy. And taking hold of the hand of the blind man, Jesus led him outside the town and spitting into his eyes, and taking hold of his hands, Jesus asked him, "What do you see?" And looking up, he says, "I see a person who is like a tree of life walking around." Then again, Jesus put his hands over his eyes, and the guy changed focus and normal vision was restored and then looking around saw everything clear. And Jesus sent him to his house saying, "Don't go back into town."

Peter's Declaration About Jesus

And Jesus left with the companions and went to the town of Caeserea Philippi and along the road quizzed the companions asking them who folks was saying that I appear to be? And they answered that folks was saying, John the Baptizer, and some was saying, Elijah, others that Jesus was some kind of prophet. But Jesus pressed them, "Who do you say that I appear to be?" Peter answered, saying to Jesus, "You are God's Child come to earth." And Jesus told them not to tell it to anybody.

Jesus Foretells His Death And Resurrection

And Jesus begun to teach them that it would be needful for God's human Child to suffer and be killed before the church leaders and church authorities and church translators and to die and after three days to come back to life. And Jesus told them this story confident. But Peter took Jesus aside and begun trying to urge different. Then Jesus turned and observed all the companions urging the same as Peter and Jesus says, "Go behind me, Separator, because you don't appreciate God's needs or folks's." And calling together the crowd with the companions, Jesus said to them, "Anyone who wants to do what I want you

to, don't pursue your own claims, but instead, expect to bear a cross, and that's the way to join with me. It happens to be the fact that if a person wants that one's personal life to be meaningful, there's only frustration, unless that one has recast that one's life for my purposes and re-oriented it into good priority. Why does a person push to get world benefits, even the whole world, while that one's life is being rendered more and more meaningless? And if anyone might come to be ashamed of me and my stories in an upcoming unfaithful generation saying there's no proof, then God's human Child will become ashamed of that one, when I go to the presence of my Parent joining all them's living other worldly lives in spiritual attendance." And Jesus said to them, "Believe it when I tell you that there are some here who are standing who won't taste death until their appears the world peace coming of God, coming now for all time, past, present and future in creative and sustaining all-motivating energy."

The Transfiguration Of Jesus

Then after six more days, Jesus takes aside Peter and James and John and leads them up to the crest of a mountain, only these ones, picked, special people. And Jesus changes appearance right in front of them, and his clothes start shining like bright white light very much, like they's washed with bleach but on earth it's not possible for them to get so white. And there appears before them Elijah and Moses and there was low talking going on among them to

Jesus. And Peter responded and says to Jesus, "Teacher, This is fun! We are here in God's Homeland itself. We will go ahead and make three shelters - one for you, one for Moses and one for Elijah."

But they really didn't know what to make of it except they was scared! And there suddenly come up a cloud which covered over what they could see. And there come a voice from the cloud, "This is my beloved Child. Pay close attention to what Jesus says." And then just as sudden they look around and there's nothing to see except Jesus along with them. And after they come down from the mountain, they was instructed not to say nothing about what they's seen, except when God's human Child has been brought back to life after dying. And this warning shocked them and they argued about its meaning among themselves. "What's this about being raised from the dead?" And they asked Jesus saying, "Don't the sacred write ups say that Elijah has to come first?" And Jesus says to them, "Hasn't Elijah explained all this in his regular life, how it's written up it's got to be for God's human Child to experience everything human and get no respect? But I also confide in you that Elijah come back and did for God's Child as much as he could, as it was written, he'd do."

The Healing Of A Boy With Epilepsy

After they went back to the other companions, they again saw a crowd build up around themselves and church translators muttering this and that.

And right then's when everyone in that crowd got worked up seeing Jesus and they's running around and being happy to see him. And Jesus was asking them, "Why do you question everything so much between yourselves?" And there come a plea from the group, "Teacher, I bring to you my little boy to dispose of as you will. His brain is disordered." And then if the boy don't have a grand mal epilepsy fit, and he's foaming at the mouth, and his teeth is grinding together fit to break, and his body is arched stiff. And the fellow says, "I asked your companions to cure it and they said they didn't have no power to do nothing about it." But Jesus answered and says to them, "What a sceptical generation! How long will I have to be with you? How long will I have to patiently put up with you? Bring him to me!" And they carried the boy to him. And when Jesus saw this boy, right then the boy's brain disorder was throwing the boy into epileptic fitting, and he's throwing himself on the ground, rolling around in spasms, and foaming at the mouth. And Jesus says to the boy's father, "How long has this been going on?" And the father says, "From when he's born. And it happens all the time and he throws himself in the fire and in deep water trying to commit suicide. And hoping something could be done, the companions was asked to feel kindly to us and help us out of this predicament." But Jesus says to this fellow, "If it could only be that everyone could live in a state of faith!" Right then, witnessing, the father of the boy says, "I believe! I feel Jesus helping me overcome my doubts." When Jesus was sure the time was right and the crowd was pressing to see faith results, Jesus addressed the brain disorder saying, "Unfeeling and unyielding brain operation, I command you, leave this one and don't never come back to him." And crying out, the grand mal seizures left. And he come to act like he's dead, and many of them witnessing what went on was saying that he died. But Jesus took his hand and helped him get up, and the boy stood up. Then, after he left to go home, the companions of Jesus just by themselves asked Jesus, "Why wasn't we able to do nothing to get rid of this disorder of the boy?" And Jesus said to them, "This ability can't be manifest except if you approach and ask for it."

Jesus Again Foretells His Death And Resurrection

Then after bit, while they went walking back to Galilee, Jesus wished they wouldn't make anything known, giving them a foretelling, and telling them that, "God's human Child will be handed over to people's doings, and they will kill the Child and after they think they've killed him, three days later, the Child will come back to life." The companions, they disregarded the statement and were afraid to ask about it.

Who Is The Greatest?

And they got to Capernaum and when they come to their house Jesus asked them, "What were you discussing along the road?" They was silent. They was arguing on the road about which one of them was the most important. After they sat down, Jesus called together the twelve and says to them, "If any of you wants to be the most important, all you got to do is act like you're the least important and do needful stuff for the others." And taking a little boy, sitting him on Jesus's lap, and giving him a hug, Jesus said to the companions, "Anyone acting in my stead for the purpose of doing for the likes of these children, receives me. And anyone receiving me, don't really receive me so much as the one who sent me."

He Who Is Not Against Us Is For Us

John said to Jesus, "Teacher, We told some, in your stead, that was having problems to have their mental illness come out of them but we couldn't stop their behaviors, because their minds don't do what we say." And Jesus said, "Don't stop trying to help folks! There's no one who will do healing miracles instead of me, who is quick to talk me down. Anyone who ain't against us is for us. If there's one who would give you so much as a drink of water because of your status as a follower of God's Child, then believe it when I tell you that he or she won't find that one's life pass by unpaid for."

Temptation To Sin

And if there's anyone causes a faith turnoff to the least of those who are faithful to me, it would be better for that one to wear a millstone around that one's neck and go swimming. Or if there's anyone among you turning off faith by what you're doing by hand, cut it off. It would be more fun for you to go around partly crippled than to have both hands throwing around garbage in an eternal garbage dump, handling burning trash so hot it can't be put out. And if any turns off faith by a foot, cut it off. It would be more fun for you to go about living lame, than to have two feet walking around in that eternal garbage dump. And if anyone's eye turns off faith, blind it. It would be more fun for you to have only one eye left, than to have both eyes looking at eternal garbage, where worms don't stop eating dead stuff and the burning don't stop. Everyone tested by fire will have that one's zesty taste for life renewed like salt flavors

things. The taste for salt gives savor. But if salt loses its tang, do you use it for seasoning? You are each other's salt so sprinkle your peace on each other."

Teaching About Divorce

And from there they took up to go to the vicinity of Judah and on the other side of the Jordan crick, and there again a crowd come joining Jesus and as has now become Jesus's custom, he went to teaching them. And there come out Pharisees asking Jesus trick questions like if it was lawful in God's way for a man to discard his wife, testing Jesus's understandings. But Jesus answered them and said, "What is your law from Moses?" And they said, "Moses's law let's a fellow do it, where its said, 'A judgement of divorce can be written up that dissolves marriage.'" But Jesus said to them, "Your divorce writing don't do no more than break hearts, not the marriage. From the time of creation, a man and woman has done their living together. For this reason, a man leaves his father and mother to be united together to a woman just for him. And these two become one in body. It's as if they's no longer two but one body. The one that God joins together in marrying can't be divided."

Then again the companions went into a house around there where they asked Jesus for more information. And Jesus says to them, "If a fellow divorces his wife and marries again, he is committing adultery by doing it. And if his wife who's been divorced, marries another man, she does adulterizing."

Little Children Blessed

And folks brought children to Jesus to touch them. But the companions told them not to. When Jesus saw what they's doing, Jesus got mad and said to them, "Let the little ones come to me, don't stop them, for such as these are the state of all in the Homeland of God. Believe it when I say to you that if anyone is received to God as a child, that one won't be left out." And when Jesus took them into his arms, Jesus told them how much they was favored with love reaching them from being itself and hugged them and held their hands.

The Rich Man

And as they was going on their way, a fellow come running up and knelt in front of Jesus asking for advice saying, "Good teacher, what can I do to buy eternal life?" But Jesus said to him, "Why do you call me Good? There's no one good unless that one's God. You know the commands. Don't kill. Don't commit adultery. Don't steal. Don't lie. Don't defraud. Honor your father and mother." But the fellow said, "Teacher, I've already kept all these rules from when I was a boy." Then Jesus said to him, looking the guy straight in the eye, filled with affection and hope for this one, "One more thing you need to do. Go and what you have, give it to the poor, and you will earn regard in God's Homeland, and Come! follow me." But the guy was shocked hearing this statement, and left real sad. Fact was, this fellow had lots of property. And after Jesus watched the guy go, Jesus says to the companions, "How hard it is for someone having property to want to go to God's Homeland." And the companions was frustrated by this conversation, But Jesus again recounted the event and says to them, "My kids! It is hard to leave to go to God's governed world. Its easier for a bull camel to squirm through the eye of a needle than for a rich person to enter God's governed world." But they's still left wondering, saying to themselves, "So, what does it take to be saved?" Looking them straight in the eye, Jesus says, "For folks, saving is impossible, but not for God. Everything can be done by God." Peter begun talking to Jesus, "Look here, we have left behind everything to follow you." Jesus says to him, "Believe it when I tell you there's no one who leaves behind that one's household, or brothers and sisters or mother or father or children or farm on account of hearing the good news, who don't get a hundredfold return back on what's lost now in households, brothers and sisters and mothers and fathers and fields, after the persecution times and in the age to come, life eternal." Everyday priorities will be the least important things to do and the least important will be the most important.

Third Time Jesus Foretells His Death And Resurrection

And they was on the road starting to climb up to the higher ground where Jerusalem sits, and Jesus went on ahead of them, and they become alarmed, and then when tried to follow where Jesus was going they become scared. And again Jesus rejoined the twelve and began talking to them about what's going to be happening. "Watch out when we go to Jerusalem because God's human Child will be arrested by the senior churchmen and the Hebrew translators and they will get God's human Child sentenced to death and give him over to the world's estranged. And they will ridicule him and spit on him and beat him with a whip and kill him, and after three days he will rise up."

The Request Of James And John

And James and John, the children of Zebedee, come to Jesus saying, "Teacher, we have something to ask that you do for us." And Jesus says to them, "What is it you want me to do?" And they said to Jesus, "Give us a favor that you let us stay in your gaze, one on your left and one on your right." But Jesus said to them, "You don't know what you are asking. You cannot drink the cup that I drink nor can you be initiated into the changed condition that I undergo, and for you to stay on my left or on my right is not my gift to give," but he said to them to be prepared. And the other ten got mad at James and John. And Jesus called them together and says to them, "Know this, you who's thinking to rule over the gentile races having more power than them and exercising authority over them. That's not how it's to be for you, for the one of you wanting to be important will be a companion, and the one wanting to be most important will be everybody's helper. And God's human Child does not want to have helpers but to do work for others and give up life as a sacrifice for the sake of everybody."

The Healing Of Blind Bartimaeus

And they come to Jericho and was passing through and Jesus was with the companions and a guy named Timmy Bart was one of the settled population there, a blind beggar, and he was sitting along the road. And when he heard that Jesus of Nazareth is there he begins crying and shouting, "Child of David, Jesus, open your heart to me." And there come a request by Jesus for all them to be still. But despite the urge, this blind fellow kept yelling, "Child of David, open your heart to me." And the whole crowd begun to comfort the fellow, "Don't worry! Come on now! Jesus hears you." Then throwing off his robe, he jumps up and heads for Jesus. Then responding, Jesus said, "What do you want me to do?" The blind man said to him, "Teacher (Rabbouni, in Aramaic talk), I want to see again." And Jesus says to this guy, "Go on about your life. Your faith restores and saves and upholds you." And right then he could see again and he was able to follow Jesus down the road.

The Triumphal Entry Into Jerusalem

And they come to approach Jerusalem through Bethphage and Bethany to the Mount of Olives and Jesus sent to of the companions on ahead telling them, "Go over to town across the valley from where we are, and right then when you get over there you will see a young donkey tethered by itself that no one has rode before. Untie it and bring it here. And if anyone asks you what you are doing say, my Familyhead has need for it, and right then bring it back here." And they went and found the young donkey tied to a gate outside on a street and they took it. And some that's standing there says to them, "Who says you can take it?" And they explained it as Jesus told them to and said good-bye to them. And they brought the young donkey to Jesus and they took off their shirts for a saddle and sat Jesus on the donkey, and many paved the road with their shirts, and others was busy cutting off branches from trees from the fields along the way. And there was those going in front of Jesus and them behind all crying out,

> Hosanna, (Aramaic word meaning, "Help us!" "Save us!"
> "Straighten things out!")
> Pass along the good news of one coming in the name of
> the Familyhead.

There's joy for all of us from one end of our ancestor David's land to the other. Hosanna forever and ever." And Jesus went to Jerusalem to the main Jerusalem church and looked around at everything. It was already real late in the day. Then Jesus left back to Bethany with the twelve companions.

The Cursing Of The Fig Tree

And the next day when they was returning from Bethany, Jesus got hungry. And seeing a fig tree off a way that has leaves, Jesus went to it, to see if there's any fruit on it, and when he got there there's nothing found on it except leaves for the time for fig bearing wasn't come. And getting the gist of the situation, Jesus said to it, "It's not to be for anyone to have hope of eating your fruit in this present world time frame." And Jesus's companions heard it said.

The Cleansing Of The Temple

And they got to Jerusalem. And after Jesus went in to the main Jerusalem church, Jesus begun to shove out the merchants selling things and those buy-

ing stuff on the main Jerusalem church grounds, and overturning the tables of the bankers changing foreign currency, and the chairs of those selling birds for folks to kill for sacrificing, and Jesus didn't let nobody leave carrying their wares from the church. And Jesus explained and repeated to them, Isn't it written that,

My house will be called a house of prayer for the
world's homeseeking people.

You are making it into a high crime area." And the churchmen and Hebrew translators heard about it and tried to find them's tearing the main Jerusalem church apart. They were really scared of Jesus, for the people was feeling ecstatic by Jesus's teaching. And when it got late in the day, Jesus left, going outside the city.

The Lesson From The Withered Fig Tree
And when they passed by where they'd been that morning, they found the fig tree was scorched and burnt down to its roots. And recalling what happened, Peter says to Jesus, "Teacher, Look, the fig tree you cussed, is dried up." Jesus answered, "Have faith in God. Believe it when I say to you that anyone may say to some hill, count your dirt makeup and erode into the sea, and there

shouldn't be no doubt in any heart about it other than to have faith that what is said will come to be." That's why I say to you, "Everything like that you approach God asking for, you get. Have faith that you will receive and it is yours. And when you stand firm in your approach to God, you can avoid being anxious if you have done something against something, because our parent in being itself bears you up and forgives your wrongdoing."

The Authority Of Jesus Questioned

And they went again to Jerusalem. And after they walked into the main Jerusalem church there come to Jesus, the main church authorities and Hebrew translators and elders. And they said to Jesus, "Who's giving you the authorizing say-so to do what you're doing?" And, "What gives you the right for you to be doing this teaching!" But Jesus said to them, "Answer me one little question and then I will tell you under who's say-so I'm doing what I'm doing. Did John's baptism derive from God's Homeland or human custom? And they took to arguing among themselves saying, "If we say, from God's Homeland, won't Jesus say, 'Don't you believe John had faith enough on his own?' But can we say, as a human custom? Then the present crowd may get mad." See, the whole crowd felt like John was a prophet. And when Jesus kept asking their opinion, they said, "We don't know." And then Jesus says to them, "Then I couldn't get through to you under whose say-so I'm doing what I'm doing anyway."

The Parable Of The Vineyard And The Tenants

Then Jesus begun to tell them a story, "Once upon a time, there's a person did some grapevine planting and fenced it in with a hedge, and even dug out under the winepress for a final disposing place for the squeezed out grapes and built a guard tower and then rented it out to cash renters and went out of county. Then after while, he sent an employee to the renters to get his rent from the grape crop. But he no sooner got there than they sent the employee back empty handed. So again, the landowner sent another employee to them. And this one they roughed up, along with additional ones, sending them out of the county, and then they begun killing them. Finally, one more he sent, a child he loved more than anything. The child was sent as a last hope to them with the thought that they will surely be respectful of my child. But then, the renters conspired among themselves, and said, "Here is the heir to this vineyard. Come on, let's kill him and throw his body out of the vineyard." Then what do you suppose the Familyhead will do with the vineyard? The Familyhead will go and evict them renters, for don't you remember the public worship readings?

The stone which the housebuilder rejects,
This will be the cornerstone -
On the Landowner's say so -
And yet it seems baffling to our eyes?

And they wanted to arrest Jesus but they was afraid what the crowd might do, because they knowed that the story was pointed at them. And saying goodbye, they left.

Paying Taxes To Caesar

And they was sent to Jesus some of the Pharisees and Herod's political hacks to try to trick Jesus into saying something wrong. And here they come saying to Jesus, "Teacher, we know that you will tell us the truth and it's not possible for you to do otherwise. And you aren't looking to please folks, but instead you teach straightforward the way of God. Is it necessary to pay a tax to Caesar or not? Should we pay it or not?" But Jesus seeing that they's not on the up and up says to them, "Why are you goading me? Hand me a denarius coin to look at." Then they handed him one. And he says to them, "What's the picture on it and what's it say?" Then they said, "Caesar." But Jesus says to them, "Pay to Caesar what's Caesar's and to God what's God's." And they was baffled by it.

The Question About The Resurrection

And the Saducees come to Jesus, those one's saying there's not to be no life after death, and they asked Jesus a question saying, "Teacher, Moses wrote down for us to follow that if anyone's brother dies and leaves behind a wife, and he don't leave behind any kids, then his brother needs to take the wife and get her pregnant as a duty to his brother. Seven brothers there were. The first one took a wife and died not leaving kids. Then the second took her and died not leaving behind heirs. And the third just so. And none of the seven had kids. The last of them to go, the wife, died. When a person rises up from death, when the resurrection comes, whose wife is she going to be? For the seven has all had her as a wife." Jesus says to them, "Do you think these writings is intended to be used for making tricky questions about what power God has? When folks arise from the dead, they's not doing earth-marrying or courting, but they is as beings in being itself. Concerning the dead, how they's raised, don't you read in the special writings how Moses heard from God from the burning bush saying that, 'I am the God of Abraham and the God of Issac and the God of Jacob?' God's not no God of the dead but of the living. Your minds stray much!"

The Great Commandment

Then coming to Jesus was some Hebrew translators bearing a problem they's been arguing, seeing that Jesus could answer them good, asking him what is the most important life rule of them all. Jesus answered them saying, "This is the most important life rule, Listen, Israel, the Familyhead, God, your Familyhead, is one. Bond yourselves in love to this your Familyhead, God, with all your emotion, and with all your intention, and with all your understanding, and with all the energy you can expend. The second is, Bond yourselves in love to those close to you just like they's you. There aren't no more important rules for life than those." And one of them Hebrew translators said to Jesus, "Okay, teacher, you're saying the truth. There is one God and there's no other closer than this one. And this one God loves from the heart drawing out of it all understanding and all energy, and this one God loves those close by and this beats all the understandings come from burning offerings and sacrificing birds and such." And Jesus observing this said he's got the right idea saying, "You aren't far off from understanding God's world ruling principle." And no one asked Jesus any more questions.

The Question About David's Son

But Jesus wasn't done and said more about them teaching in the Great Jerusalem Church and said, "How come you Hebrew translators say that God's Child is the child of David? David himself said while he's talking inspired, `The Familyhead said to my Familyhead, Sit at my right hand While I put down your detractors under your feet.' David himself calls the God on earth his Familyhead. So from where does it come this talk about God's Child on earth being his child?" And many in the crowd started chuckling when they heard him say it.

The Denouncing Of The Hebrew Translators

And one time, Jesus said while teaching, "Look at them Hebrew translators, wanting to walk around in expensive robes, and be recognized in the marketplaces and taking the first seats in the churches and insisting on being first in line at church dinners. Them's ones eating up all the food in folk's homes and saying long prayers. These will receive the worst blame."

The Widow's Offering

And while Jesus was sitting across from the offering box, Jesus saw how the Great Jerusalem Church visitors was throwing copper coins into the offering box. And one that come in was a poor widow's and she put in two coins which was like a little fraction of a denarius. And calling together the companions up close, Jesus told them, "Believe me when I tell you that her gift, this poor lady's offering, is more than all the other coins thrown into the offering box. Everybody else give offerings out of their extra money, but she, despite her need for as much as she had, threw in all she possessed."

The Destruction Of The Temple Foretold

And as they was leaving from the Great Jerusalem Church one of the companions says to Jesus, "Teacher, see them stones from all around about brought here and what a building has been put together!" But Jesus said to that one, "Do you see them as a huge building? Nothing will be left here, not a stone on a stone. It's to be torn down."

The Beginning Of Woes

And while they was sitting by the Hill of Olive trees, across from the Great Jerusalem Church, he asked to be left alone with certain ones, Peter and James and John and Andrew. And Jesus told them how things was going to be and what sign there would be before the ultimate and final ending of everything would be about to happen. And Jesus begun by telling them, "Don't believe some who would mislead you. Many will come after me to take my place saying I AM, and many will be misled. When you hear about wars and war rumors, don't be scared. Its bound for them to happen but then it ends. A homeless, familyless one will be born among them's homeless and become the world leader over all countries. There will be earthshaking in various places. There will be folks hungry. Like the first birthbearing pain will them's alive have. You want to see your own ends? The ones bounding to the Sanhedrin will have you arrested. And in churches you will be beaten. And by those in authority and rulers you will be stood before for me to do your witnessing. But first, it's necessary that you announce the good news to all the earth peoples. And when you are brought to arrest, don't worry what to say because it will be give you, in that hour, what to say. You will not do the talking because God's breathing will empower you. And brother will cause the arrest of brother on charges with death penalties, and a father, his child, and kids will be turned against while they's begging for life on their knees and still they's killed. And you will be hated by everybody because of my name. But bear up with patience and in the end this will save you.

The Great Tribulation

When you see a gross statue erected where it's not supposed to be, and folks that get preached to at church be sure to recognize what I'm talking about! then them in Judea better take to the hills. Anyone living upstairs, don't delay coming down and leaving, for there will be some coming to take your house away from you. And if anyone's working in a field, don't turn back to where you come from even to get your shirt. Special hurt will be those pregnant and those who are nursing babies in them days. Pray, so that the holocaust don't last into winter. There will be in them days trouble such as hasn't been known similar since the days of first creation when God did the havoc-making, even until now, and there won't be such ever again. And unless the Familyhead stops the days short, not a single body will be left alone. Now concerning those picked out, God may choose to cut short their days too! And then, if anyone says, "Look here comes God's Child who was with us on earth," or "Look, there is Jesus," don't believe it! They will announce themselves a fake God like the God who came to you and false prophets and magicians and frighteners to try to mislead

folks if they could, even the selected ones. But be careful. Everything will come true, I am predicting.

The Return Of God's Human Child

Then, in the afterwards after this trouble, that I foretell, the sun will get dark. And the moon will not reflect its light And the stars will fall out of the sky. And the energies of the universe will be drained out. And then is when you will see God's human Child coming in the clouds with total power and determination. And then will be sent out agents and they will gather together those selected from the four winds from the limits of earth and being itself.

The Lesson Of The Fig Tree

Take a story lesson from the fig tree. When comes the day that a branch of it that could bear leaves starts to leaf out, you know that Spring is near. Same with you. When you see these things happening, recognize that the opportunity is near. Believe it when I tell you that human family life won't end until these things come to be. The sky and earth will disappear but my words can't be disregarded.

The Unknown Day And Hour

Concerning the day or the hour, no one knows, not beings in being itself or the child, except the parent. Watch! Keep alert! You won't know it until the time has come! It's like when a person leaves to go away from that one's family business and gives to the employees the orders each needs for the work they's to do, and the security guard is give orders to keep watch. Then you better keep watch all right! You won't know when the Familyhead will come back to the family business, maybe in the evening, maybe midnight, maybe when the rooster's about to crow or in the morning. In a flash, the Familyhead comes looking around even if you should be sleeping. I'm telling you everything I need to say, Be watching!"

The Plot To Kill Jesus

Then there come Passover day and the two days of the feast of unleavened bread. And the senior churchmen and the Hebrew translators was working up a trick so that after they arrested Jesus they could kill him. They was saying, "Don't let Jesus share in the holidays, otherwise he will confuse the people."

The Annointing At Bethany

Jesus was staying in Bethany in the house of Simon the Leper, and while laying sleeping, a woman come stealing in, bringing with her a carved alabaster vase of real expensive and genuine perfume, and breaking open the seal of the vase, she poured out some on Jesus's head. They was some of the others in there who got mad and was getting the others mad too! Why is this wasting of valuable perfume going on? Reason was, this perfume being used up could be sold for over three hundred denarius and be given to the poor. And they was criticizing her real bad. But Jesus said, "Leave her alone! Why are you bugging her? She's doing a nice favor for me. Always you will have the poor with you to help, and when you feel inspired to help them its good to do it. But you won't always have me. What she has done is to begin the burial preparation perfuming my body. Believe it when I tell you that wherever the good news of my death is told about in the whole world, what she's done in initial preparing, will recall her to mind."

Judas's Agreement To Betray Jesus

Now Judas, the one from Iscariot, one of the twelve went to the senior churchmen so to conspire with them to arrest Jesus. And after listening, they done their plotting, and sent him back after paying him off with gold. And he begun figuring when would be the best time and best way to turn Jesus over to the churchmen.

The Passover With The Disciples

Pretty soon it come the first day of the feast of flat bread when the Passover animal sacrifices was killed and their blood thrown on the church altar and then the bloodless animals was give back to folks for their feasting, and Jesus's companions said, "When are you going to have us leave to go get prepared for the Passover Feast?" That was when Jesus sent two of the companions and gives them directions, "Go to the city, and you will meet up with a guy, a person carrying a clay water jar, and ask him about it, and whoever that one leads you to say to that innkeeper that the Teacher says, 'Do you have my guest room where I may eat a Passover meal with my companions?' And this one will lead you to a big upstairs room already reserved and there you will get everything prepared for us." And the companions went looking as they was sent out to do and they went to the city and found just such a one and spoke to that one and got things ready for the Passover. And when evening come, Jesus went there with the twelve. And when they sat down together and while they was eating, Jesus said to them, "Believe me when I tell you that one among you will conspire against me, one of you eating with me." They was all denying it and saying to Jesus,

"One of Us? No way! Not me is it?" But Jesus says to them, "It is one of the twelve, one who's been dipping bread with me in the bowl. Yes! and it was because God's human Child goes through life toward death as it was written." And, as Jesus took a deep breath, that person about who God's human Child referred, left to complete the conspiracy. It would have been better if that one hadn't been born.

The Institution Of The Lord's Supper

And after they was ready to eat and got to the bread and give thanks for it, Jesus broke it into pieces and passed it to them and said, "Take this, this is my body." And after Jesus picked up the cup and give thanks, Jesus passed it to them, so all of them could drink from it. And Jesus told them, "This is the blood of my contract which I pour out for everybody. Believe it when I tell that no longer will I drink from this harvest of grapes until that new day when I drink in God's world." And singing hymns, they left to go to the hill where olive trees was growing.

Peter's Denial Foretold

And Jesus says to them, "Every one of you will say things that will close me in my pursuer's trap, because it's written, Let them strike down the shepherd, then the sheep will be scattered. But after the resurrection, go back, you, into Galilee." But Peter says to Jesus, "Even if everybody else stands by while you're being trapped, I won't." And Jesus says to him, "Right! I tell you that this very day, in the night, and before twice the rooster has crowed, three times you will deny even knowing me." But Peter says emphatic, "I pledge myself to die for you! And never to quit striving to save you!" All of them was saying the same things.

The Prayer In Gethsemane

And they went to the little town named Gethsemane and Jesus says to the companions, "Stay here while I go pray." But Jesus took along Peter and James and John. Then he begun to shake agitated and to feel dread, and Jesus says to them, "Loathe of leaving has ahold of me real bad. Stay here and keep me company." And it wasn't too long before Jesus fell down to the ground and prayed to have the will power to carry through his work to the end of its earth hour. And Jesus said, "God-Parent, all energy is yours. Take this cup away from me. BUT, it's not what I want but what you want I will follow through on." And Jesus got up and looked for those supposed to be along-side and they was napping. And he says, "Simon, are you asleep? Ain't you strong enough to stand by me through this life end? Stand by me and pray so that you won't have to be tested so. Even so I know you have good intentions but your body needs weaken them." Then again Jesus went to praying real hard expressing the same wish. And again coming back Jesus found them dozed off for their eyes was so very heavy and they couldn't imagine death being close to him. And a third time he come to them and says, "Go ahead and sleep a little while more, rest comfortable." Things was okay. Then the time come and Yes! God's human Child is give over to the hands of those who are separated from God. He said, "Wake up, let's go! See, the one's give us over is getting close."

The Betrayal And Arrest Of Jesus

And immediate when Jesus is still talking Judas got there to where the twelve was, together with a crowd with swords and clubs consisting of the senior churchmen and the Hebrew translators and the elders. The traitor had promised to give Jesus away signaling which one Jesus was to them saying, "The one who I kiss will be Jesus. Arrest him and take him away under guard." When Jesus got back to where the twelve was, the traitor says to him, "Teacher," and went to give him a hug. Then those along got their hands on Jesus and arrested him. Some one of them who's looking on, after drawing a sword, struck one of the employees of the senior churchmen and cut off a little bit of his ear. Then Jesus took charge and said to them, "Why are you coming like robbers with swords and clubs to arrest me? Every morning I was coming to you in the church to teach and you didn't arrest me. Even so, the foretellings has now come true." And saying "Good-bye" to Jesus, they all left quick.

The Young Man Who Fled

But there was a young fellow who was a follower of Jesus who has dressed himself in a linen shirt over his shorts, and they was grabbing at this one too, except he slipped out of his shirt and run off in his shorts.

Jesus Before The Council

And they took Jesus to the family home of a senior churchman called the Arxierea, and all the church authorities was gathered there and the elders and the Hebrew translators. And Peter followed them there from a distance until they's inside the Arxiereas fenced in front yard, and he went over and sat down with the household workers and warmed up his hands to the fire. And then the senior churchmen and all the Sanhedrin, the church governors, sent out for witnesses against Jesus so to justify killing him, but they was none to be found. Then they all started telling lies again Jesus, but their testimonies wasn't all the same. Some was standing up and testifying against Jesus, saying, "We heard this one say that, `I will tear down this Jerusalem church built with human hands and on the third day, I will build up another not built by human hands.'" But none of them could agree as to the meaning of their testimony. And the senior churchman stood up in the middle of them and asked Jesus about it saying, "No one can give no definitive interpretation. What do these sayings of yours mean?" But Jesus wouldn't say nothing and he wouldn't give no explanation. Again, the senior churchman questioned Jesus and says to Jesus, "Are you God's child, the child written of and hoped for." And Jesus said, "I AM." And, "You will see the human Child of God going to sit at the right hand of power itself and coming upon the clouds of being itself." And the senior churchman was so mad he ripped off his church garb and says, "What need do we have for witnesses? You all heard this heretic talk. What is your pleasure?" And all of them voted against Jesus saying Jesus is deserving to die. And some of them begun spitting on Jesus and then they blindfolded and rabbit punched Jesus and said, "Now tell us who done it!" And their employees took to punching Jesus too!

Peter's Denial Of Jesus

And Peter was outside in the front yard when come up to him one of the workers of the senior churchman, a girl. And recognizing Peter while he's warming up, she says to him, "You must be with the Nazarene, Jesus." But Peter denied it saying, "No I don't know Jesus and I can't believe you're saying that." And he stayed outside in the front yard. And a rooster crowed. And another girl when she saw him began to repeat the accusing with others standing there saying, "This one is one of them." But again, he denied it, and after bit again those standing they said to Peter, "Give us the truth, you are one of them and you are from Galilee." And he cursed and swore that, "I don't what you are talking about." And immediate, at that instant, a rooster crowed. And Peter remembered the statement as Jesus foretold, "Before the rooster crows twice, three times you will have denied knowing me." And Peter broke down and cried.

Jesus Before Pilate

And dawn come fast to heel and after the council's doings, the senior churchmen, together with the elders and Hebrew translators and the whole Sanhedrin, after roping Jesus, took and delivered him to Pilate. And Pilate done this interrogating, "Are you the World ruler of the Jewish people?" And Jesus answered, "You say it." And all the senior churchmen condemned that response. Then Pilate did some more questioning of Jesus, saying, "Don't you want to give no defense to their accusations? Look! All of them are wanting to have you sentenced to death." But Jesus didn't answer nothing more.

Jesus Sentenced To Die

According to the feast day's customs, Pilate could release to those there one condemned person who the people wished to be released. The other of those to be picked from was Barabbas, an arrested troublemaker who during a time of rebelling had done lots of killing. And looking up at them, the crowd begun to pick which between the two of them. And Pilate did his asking, saying, "Do you want me to release to you this Jewish world ruler?" Now Pilate expected that for patriotism sake the senior churchmen would encourage the crowd to release Jesus. But the churchmen worked up the crowd so that they would opt for Barabbas to be the one released. When Pilate repeated himself saying to them, "Come on! Which one do you want me to give to you? This ruler of the Jews?" They repeated themselves crying out, "Crucify Jesus." But Pilate said to them, "For what reason should I do this bad deed?" But they cried out even louder, "Crucify Jesus." Then Pilate, following the crowd's wishes, after doing a long think, released Barabbas to them and give over Jesus to be beat with a whip so that he could not be able to fight off being crucified.

The Soldiers Mock Jesus

Then the soldiers took him inside the front yard of the governor's house, which was their headquarters, and mustered the whole headquarter's troops. And they dressed Jesus in a ruler costume and placed on Jesus's head a woven thorn plant crown. And they begun to say "Hello," to Jesus, "Welcome, world ruler of the Jewish people." And they hit him on the head with sticks and spit and kneeling down acted like they was worshipping Jesus. And when they tired of making Jesus look ridiculous, they took off the ruler costume and put back on Jesus's clothes. And took him out to be crucified.

The Crucifixion Of Jesus

And they forced into service a passerby whose name was Simon Kuranaius who'd come in from the countryside, the father of Alexander and Rufus, so that he'd have to take up Jesus's cross. And they took Jesus to the place of Golgatha, which is translated as Skull Hill. And they give Jesus wine to drink laced with drugs, but Jesus couldn't take it. And they done their crucifying, And they divided up Jesus's clothes, throwing dice as to who could take them. Then come the third hour after they started their crucifying. And there was a sign with the charge of why they's doing their crucifying saying, "The world ruler of the Jewish people." And also beside Jesus they was two robbers being crucified, one on the right and the other on the left. And those passing by was hurling insults at Jesus shaking their heads and saying, "So, here's the one who's going to destroy the main Jerusalem church and build it back up in three days. Go on! Save yourself! Come down from your cross!" Same way come the senior churchmen making insider jokes to themselves along with some Hebrew translators saying, "He saved others' lives, but Jesus's body don't seem saveable. O God's child! Come on down from the cross so that we can see you better and believe better!" And them's being crucified alongside was making fun too!

The Death Of Jesus

And after the sixth hour, darkness come over the whole earth, until the ninth hour. And at the ninth hour, Jesus shouted out in a loud voice, in Aramaic, Elwi elwi lema sabaxthani? which is translated through the Greek language as, "God, My God, why do you neglect me like this?" And some of those standing there listening to what's going on said, "Now Jesus is calling Elijah by name." And someone come by and after he filled a sponge with drugged wine, put it on a stick, and was going to poke it to Jesus to drink but said, "Wait! Let's see if Elijah comes to bring Jesus down." But Jesus give a loud sigh and give up breathing. And the curtain that separated off the inner main Jerusalem church split in two from top to bottom. And when the Roman soldier in charge of the crucifying detail saw all this, that Jesus was dead, he said, "It's true, this person was God's child." And there were women looking on from a distance, among them was Mary of Magdalena and Mary, the daughter of James, the younger one, their mother of Joses, and Saloma, they's ones who was from Galilee who's followed Jesus and was care providers for Jesus, and many others was there who's come up to be with Jesus in Jerusalem.

The Burial Of Jesus

Now already come the evening. Here it is Saturday which is the day before the ritual day of Sabbath, or Sunday, when custom says no work can be done. Joseph, who's from Arimatheia, a respected member of the Sanhedrin Jewish ruling group, enters the story. This fellow, one who lived in expecting God's world ruler to come, took it upon himself to go to Pilate and asked for the body of Jesus. Now Pilate was surprised at the interest but he's already took and summoned the centurion to satisfy himself that Jesus is dead. So, knowing this from the centurion soldier, Pilate give the corpse to Joseph. Then Joseph, after buying some burial linen cloth and taking the body down, wrapped it in the dead wrappings, and carried it to a cave-like tomb which was new cut from rock and rolled against it a huge stone as a seal for the tomb. And Mary of Magdalene and Mary, daughter of Joses, saw how he done this laying of Jesus to rest.

The Resurrection Of Jesus

Now time passed and Sunday come, and Mary of Magdalene and Mary, daughter of James and Saloma went and bought sweet smelling embalming supplies and went to embalm Jesus. And it was real early in the morning on this first day of the week when they went to the tomb, just as the sun was coming up. And they was saying to themselves, "Who's going to roll the sealing rock of the tomb away for us?" And looking up, they noticed that the rock is rolling itself away. Now this was a heavy rock! And looking into the cave-like tomb, they saw a young looking person on the right side, dressed in dazzling white clothes, and they didn't know what to do. But this person says to them, "Don't be anxious!" The Jesus you're looking for is the Nazarene who was crucified. He has been raised up from death. He ain't here. You can check out this whole place where the body was laid! Afterwards Go, Tell the companions of

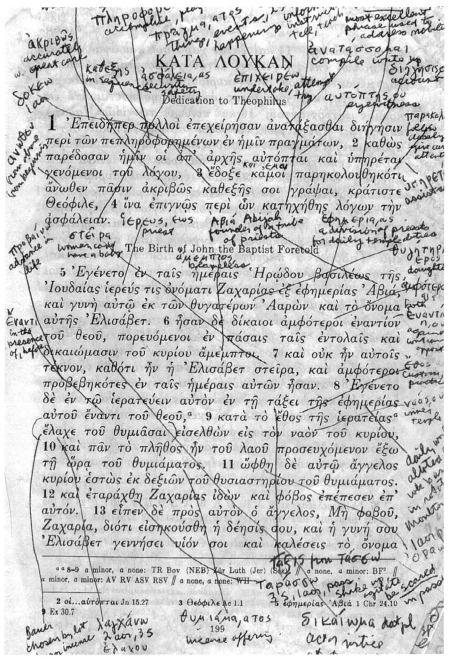

Opening page of Luke's Witness from the *Greek New Testament* that was used by Ben Johnson for the translation.

LUKE'S WITNESS

An Introduction To God's Child's Life On Earth

NOWADAYS EVERYBODY'S TRYING to put together this age's news and how it came about. The news has come to us handed down from the original eye-witnesses and the ones helping them evangelize. It has become the story to tell - the story of God's life on earth - and I will relate it following as closely as I can from the very beginning, putting it all together, as closely to the truth, and writing about it in its time sequence so you who love God can understand what's happened, having the story reliably related.

The Birth Of John, God's Reconciler, Foretold

In the days of the Roman provincial king named Herod in Judea, there was a church worker named Zacharias. His father was from the ancestry of Abijah, a person whose descendants were mostly church workers. His wife was Elizabeth. She was a daughter of the ancestry of Aaron. Both tried to do the right thing before God. They went about doing what God commanded in the laws and did what our Familyhead's ideas of justice give them was right as did reputable people. But they didn't have a single child because Elizabeth was sterile and both of them was growing older day by day. And every day Zacharias-as he would do his church work - as it got arranged on its weekly calendar - would feel God present. After the duty- roster picking procedure one week, it come to be his time to burn incense, so he went into the inner part of the Familyhead's church when everybody else is outside, all the people, worshipping at the time when incense is offered up.

While he was doing this, he was being observed by a Godly messenger standing on the right side of the incense altar.

And Zacharias seen this and was shook up! Scared so, he fell down and most blacked out.

But the Godly messenger said to him, "Don't be scared, Zacharias. The nagging desire of your life to have a child was heard. Your wife Elizabeth's going to have a baby boy. Call his name John. It will be a gift to you and such a tremendous joy that multiples of folk will be happy about his birth. He'll be a great help to our Familyhead. He won't drink either wine or any strong drink and the breath of the Spirit of God will fill him up. Elizabeth will soon carry a

child in her motherly womb. Soon crowds of the children of Israel will turn their lives over to the Familyhead, his God. And he will be Spirit-possessed as powerful as Elijah and he will stir up the heart of the parents for their kids, bring around the stubborn to do right, and prepare all people for the Familyhead whose plans for is being made."

And Zacharias said to the Godly messenger, "How can we count on such a thing? I'm elderly and my wife's advanced in age."

The Birth Of Jesus Foretold

And the Godly messenger answered and said, "I am Gabriel, one standing in the sight of God and God sent me to tell you and give you the good news. Next thing, Zacharias, you're losing your voice and you won't be able to talk until all this comes about because you don't believe my story which will come to be quick and for the purpose of endtime fulfillment."

Now all the people was waiting outside for Zacharias to come on out and they was surprised to have to wait while he was in that inner part of the church. And then when he come out, he couldn't speak to talk to them at all, and they wondered if he'd seen a vision in that inner place. All he could do was make signs at them and still couldn't talk. And since this happened just at the end of his days of doing his roster service, he left to go to his hometown. After a few days, Elizabeth, his wife, come up pregnant and hid herself out for five months saying to herself that such that had happened to her was from the Familyhead. She figured the Familyhead in them days had looked at her with a smiling face to take away her anguish over being barren as others was snickering about.

Then close to the sixth month, Gabriel was sent by God to a town of Galilee called Nazareth to a virgin girl about to be engaged to marry a man named Joseph out of a family come from David and the name of this youngster was Mary. And when he come to her, he said, "Hello. Mary, don't be afraid. The

Familyhead is with you. You bring joy to God. The Familyhead picked you out to be with you." And then she was told the story and she realized how lucky was the greeting itself.

And then the Godly messenger said, "Next thing it'll cause you to get pregnant and give birth to a boy. Call his name Jesus. This will be the biggest event of all time and he will be called the child of the highest and the Familyhead, God, will give to him the seat of his ancestor David, and he will take over the charge of the children of Jacob forever, and about his charge to come there will be no end to it."

Next Mary said to the Godly messenger, "How's this to be since I've not been with a man to get pregnant?"

And the Godly messenger answered her saying, "God's breath will come to you, and upon you and the capacity of the ultimate will overshadow you. This is why the attended child being born will be called the child of God. And pay attention! Elizabeth, your relative, she's pregnant to have a son in her dotage. Now's the sixth month after she was called out of barrenness. Figure it out? Nothing is impossible to God, not even a single God uttered and self- fulfilling story word." Then Mary said, "I place myself in the service of the Familyhead. I wish more than anything to do my duty to the Familyhead according to your revelation and story."

And the Godly messenger left her.

Mary Visits Elizabeth

Then Mary got herself ready to go in the next few days and went eager off to the hill country to the city of Judea to take up in the house of Zacharias. Elizabeth give her a big welcome when she got there. And there it happened just as they was greeting each other, Mary and Elizabeth, Elizabeth's unborn baby moved in her womb, and Elizabeth almost burst spiritually and she burst out crying agitated and Elizabeth said, "You of all women are being treated so special by God, and the benefit to come from your womb is so worthy of praising! And how could I feel this way except that the mother of my Familyhead has come to me? For as I listened to the voice of your greeting in my ears, my unborn baby moved as if excited with joy. And I am happy seeing there's coming a final fulfillment through the Familyhead."

Mary's Song Of Happiness

And Mary said, "My soul praises the Familyhead,
And my spirit sings in joy to the God of my salvation
Because God looked on to notice me, ordinary as I am,
    dutifully his.

And see what's happened out of this, all the future generations will
    call me touched by God!
Because he acted powerfully through me.
And special is his name.
And mercy abounds generation to generation to those who
    respect him.
His muscles move creation.
He confuses the proud in the yearnings of their hearts.
He brings down the world rulers from their seats of power.
And raises up the poor.
He fills up the hungry with food that is good for them,
And the ones who are rich, he shoos them out emptyhanded.
He comes to help the children of Israel, remembering promises
    for mercies,
As he swore to our ancestors, to Abraham, and all his blood kin, forever."

Mary stayed with Elizabeth about three months and then returned to her own home.

The Birth Of John, God's Reconciler

Well, the time come to be ripe for Elizabeth to give birth and she bore a son. And the neighbors and kin of hers heard the gossip, that the Familyhead showed special mercy to her by this, so they flocked to congratulate her. And soon there come the eighth day when was time to circumcise the youngster and they started to call the boy Zacharias Junior, after the name of his father, but his mother, responded, and said, "No, NO! He's to be called John."

And they said to her that nobody of their kin's ever been called by that name. So they checked with Zacharias by making signs to him to see what he wanted to call his son.

And Zacharias answered writing it on a clay tablet, "John is to be the boy's name!"

And none of them could half believe it.

Just then, Zacharias mouth was opened and immediately his tongue got loosened up and he witnessed praising God.

And it happened that this shocked the whole neighborhood, and even all of them that was in the Judea hill country that heard the account about it. And all that heard it stuck it in their memory what had been gossiped, saying, "Why's this kid come to be?" and "For what purpose is the hand of the Familyhead with him?"

The Prophecy Of Zacharias

And Zacharias, his father, was spellbound in the spirit and spoke out a message from God, saying:

"Thanks be to the Familyhead, God of Israel for selecting us and serving us as his people.

He has raised up for us a mighty savior, out of David's line, his own Child.

As it was spoke out of the mouths of saints long ago, his prophets.

A savior opposing our enemies and a hand raised against them that hate us,

Acting in mercy according to our ancestry,

Remembering the spirit-inspired covenant,

As promised under oath to Abraham, our back line parent, to be give him to us so we don't have to be afraid at having unchecked enemies.

Now let us serve him respectful and act right before him all of our days.

And you, my little one, will be called as a prophet of this exalted one.

For you will go ahead of his appearance as the

Familyhead preparing his way.

And he will give salvation information to God's people about how they can leave behind wrongdoing on account of the merciful feeling God's showing to us.

This is the way God will be bringing in a new dawn in our sky, shining in the black night, chasing off the shadows of death, so that we can see to step down the path of peace."

And Zacharias's little boy John started growing up to be big and so did his bond to the spirit. And he went out to an uninhabited and abandoned lonely spot until the days of his public appearance to Israel.

The Birth Of Jesus, God's Child Who Came To Us On Earth

Now one day a law was set down by Augustus Caesar that everybody the Romans had say over had to get counted. This first count come when Surias Kurenios was the Roman governor of the place. And all went to get counted in their hometown. And Joseph went out from Galilee from the city of Nazareth to Judea to the town of David called Bethlehem because he sprung from the house and line of David, taking Mary along with him to get counted. He was bound to Mary by a promise to marry her despite her pregnant condition. But it happened that just when their travel days was completed, Mary was having her contractions. And she give birth to her son, God's firstborn, and she wrapped him up, and put him down to sleep in a feeding trough because there was no place for them in any inn.

Nomads Encounter Godly Messengers

And nomads was in the countryside about there living out of doors and keeping guard in the night over their sheep. And a Godly messenger from the Familyhead come to them and he was shiney because of God's attention on what his mission was and they was extremely scared. And the Godly messenger said to them, "Don't be afraid. Here is what is happening! I give you the good news about the greatest love that could be for all folk, because a miraculous boy's been born for you, who is humanity's Familyhead, God come to earth, in the city of David. And this miracle is yours. Go discover the new baby wrapped up in baby clothes and resting in a feeding trough." And suddenly there appeared with the Godly messenger a crowd of beings out of the very skies of existence praising God and saying, "God's attention haas focused on you from God's ultimate place.

And upon the earth, peace and good feeling are coming to humanity.

And it happened as the Godly messengers left them to go back through the skies of existence, the nomads spoke to each other. "We have to go to Bethlehem to see this revelation the Familyhead has told us about."

And hurrying and looking for the spot, they found Mary and Joseph and the baby resting in the feeding trough. And seeing it they recognized that this was the revelation told to them about this baby. And when everybody crossing their path heard them tell it, they couldn't hardly believe the news from the nomads about it.

But Mary kept in her memory all these happenings bearing them for safe-keeping in her heart.

And the nomad's hearts was turned to regard and praising God on account of all they'd heard and seen as God was being revealed to them. After eight days past, the baby was circumcised and the name of him was give as Jesus, what he'd been called by the Godly messenger at his conception in the womb.

Presenting Jesus In The Temple

And the days past until the time arrived when those subscribing to the law of Moses took their boys to the main Jerusalem church for the standard ritual of life dedication. So his parents brought Jesus to Jerusalem to get done the purpose of it, to get Jesus placed in the service of the Familyhead, as it is written in the Familyhead's law that every boy that's born of mother needs to be called to the attention of the Familyhead, and something's got to have blood spilled and flowing as specified in the Familyhead's law, a scaly bird, called a turtledove, or two baby doves.

Now, look, there's a man in Jerusalem named Samuel who always did right and devoted himself to the service of Israel's comforting spirit, and his mind was bonded to this Spirit. And the Spirit told him he wouldn't die before he got to see the Familyhead, Jesus. And knowing this he went into the Jerusalem church just as the boy Jesus was being brought in by his parents doing the things custom says to do and Samuel hugged the boy and praised God and said, "Now take your worker home, Sir, according to your promise now to let me go in peace. I saw with my own eyes your saving life presence - who you was getting ready to present to all the world's peoples, a light to shine on every race, beamed out of Israelite forebears."

And his father and mother were shocked by his outburst, and Samuel praised them too and said to Mary, his mother, "Remember about him. It will be necessary for him to fall by the hands of a crowd of Israelites and arise resurrected. Don't be opposing it for it's a miraculous event from the hand of God. Also, you will suffer like you were stabbed as a result of his life from doubts coming out of many hearts."

And there was a prophet lady named Anna, daughter of Fanul, out of Aaron's tribe, who was getting on in years, having lived married for eight years when she was a youngster, and as a widow for eighty four years. She never left the Jerusalem church but spent her time fasting and praying, doing church duty night and day. And she was giving her usual thanks to God at that time according to how she believed, and she said to all Jerusalem that through Jesus they'd all be set free.

Return To Nazareth

And when all this was finished according to the Familyhead's law, they returned to Galilee to their hometown, Nazareth. And the child kept growing and getting stronger being filled more and more with human understanding and a gift for love, joy, and compassion was in him.

Jesus Left Behind as a Boy in

the Jerusalem Church

And then one year his parents took him to Jerusalem for Thanksgiving. This was when he was twelve. They went down like that because it was the Thanksgiving custom.

After the Thanksgiving days was over, they returned home but in going home, Jesus, just a boy, got left behind in Jerusalem and his parents didn't know it. Instead, thinking he was in the pilgrim group, they were on the road all day, and afterwhile, they looked for him among their family and friends and when they couldn't find him they went back to Jerusalem to try to locate him.

And it come to be that after three days they found him in the main Jerusalem church being seated in the middle of the religion teachers, being listened to by them, and answering their questions. The whole bunch was taking in what he was saying and was surprised that he understood things so deeply and by his conclusions. And when his parents saw him, they was amazed and his mother said to him, "Boy, what are you doing? Your father and I were scared to death looking for you!" And Jesus said to them, "Why were you looking for me? Didn't you have revelation about this... how it would be necessary for me to be myself?" And his parents didn't really get the point of the subtlety he was telling them and took him away from there and went back to Nazareth and he was obedient to their wishes. But his mother remembered all that happened. And Jesus kept growing in human understanding and years and in approval before God and people.

The Preaching Of John The Baptist

In yet the fifteenth year of the government of Tiberius Caesar, when Ponshus Pilot governed Judea, and Herod was puppet governor of Galilee, and Philip, his brother, of Ituree, was governor of the towns of Traxonitida, and Lusanus of Abilene, when the most important family of the churchmen- class was headed by Annas and Kaiphus, a breath from God came to John, son of Zacharias, out in the barrens. And news of him traveled everywhere in Judea, announcing a renewing baptism for the purpose of shedding guilt and lust, as it was written in Isaiah the prophet's book,

A voice crying in the barrens,
Get ready a road to the Familyhead,
Make paths straight to it.
It will end in a wide valley,
And a high mountain will be leveled to a hill,
And it will be zigzagety for straight-going,
And rough for way-easing,
And all flesh will see God's saving nature.

He spoke to the crowds that went out to him to be reconciled with God, saying, "You monster children of Echidna! - Do you have earth bodies, but no souls? - didn't your monster mother warn you to flee from danger? Bear the fruit worthy of one who is reconciled and don't start up to say, "We have Abraham as our parent. Hey, I'm telling you that God can raise up stones to be children of Abraham. Already there's an ax laid to the root of the tree. Every tree not bearing good fruit is to be cut down and set on fire."

And the crowds asked this question, "What are we to do?"

And he answered, saying, "A person with two changes of clothes can give one to someone that don't possess enough clothes and a person with food can share it too." And there went to him tax collectors to be baptized, and they said to him, "Teacher, what can we do?" And he said to them, "Don't assess more than you're supposed to."

And soldiers asked him, "And what are we soldiers supposed to do?" He said to them, "Don't take money by violence or force, don't accuse people to extort fast bucks and be content with your soldier pay."

While people waited expectantly, and many argued heatedly about John, the question was if he was God's Child, and he said, "I baptize you with water. But there's someone coming a lot more powerful then me. Of this one, I am not worthy to untie his shoes. He will baptize you into the spirit of morality and fire. This one will have a shovel in his hand to sort out the threshing floor, to

collect the grain out of it to put in the crib, and the chaff to burn away in the flames."

Soon everyone from everywhere heard his call and he brought good news to the people.

Then Herod, the governor, when he heard he was being talked against by John for taking his brother's wife, Herodias, to be his, and all he'd been doing, got himself filled with meanness. And this kept increasing for awhile until he arrested John and put him in jail.

The Baptism Of Jesus

And it happened that many people were being baptized and Jesus being baptized too and while he's praying the skies of existence opened up, and a spirit formed itself so that it could be seen as a dove of peace above him, and the voice from beyond the skies of existence says, "You are my Child, beloved one, and I am so such happy to have you."

Jesus's Family Background Back To Adam

And this incident was Jesus getting started when he's about thirty years old, being born, as thought, from Joseph, Eli, Maththat, Levi, Melchi, Jannai, Joseph, Mattathew, Amos, Naum, Esli, Naggai, Maath, Mattathew, Simon, Josax, Joda, John, Rasa, Zorobable, Salathial, Nary, Melchi, Addy, Kosam, El-madam, Ar, Jesse, Eliazar, Josram, Mathet, Levi, Sumeon, Jouda, Joseph, Jonam, Eliakim, Melea, Menna, Mattatha, Natham. David, Jesse, Jobad, Boos, Sala, Naasson, Aminadab, Admin, Arni, Esrom, Phares, Jouda, Jacob, Issak,

Abraam, Thara, Nakor, Seroux, Ragau, Thalek, Heber, Sala, Kainam, Arphaxad, Sem, Noe, Lamex, Mathousala, Enox, Jaret, Maleleel, Kainam, Enos, Seth, Adam, God.

The Temptation Of Jesus

Then Jesus, bonded with the spirit of comfort and advocacy, was going home along the Jordan River but he got took up in his imagination into a forty day mind game being teased by its challenger. He didn't eat in those days nor drink until he ended this game.

And a challenge in his mind said to him, "If you're the son of God, say to the rocks to be bread." And Jesus answered him and said, "It's written that not by bread only will people live."

And bearing him up, his mind telescoped all the governments of the world in a second of time. And the challenge said to him, "I will give you total control and their allegiance, because such are handed over to me and I can turn it over if I want to. It might be you'd want to get down on your knees and worship me, so that you will have all this for yourself." But Jesus answered saying, "It's written,

You will worship your Familyhead and only do service for God."

Then his mind bore him to Jerusalem and stood him atop the main Jerusalem church roof, and said to him, "If you're the son of God, jump down from here, for it is written: The protectors from God assigned to you are ordered to stay around you. And also, By their hands they will lift you, so that your foot can't strike a stone."

And Jesus answered saying,

"It's said,

Don't tempt the Familyhead your God."

And all the tempting ended right there and the challenge took off away from him.

Jesus Starts To Preach In Galilee

Then Jesus finally got to go home to Galilee filled with the comforting and advocating spirit of God. And his reputation spread out from town to town all about him. And he taught in the churches being attended by everyone.

Jesus Is Rejected In Nazareth, His Hometown

Then he went to Nazareth where he'd been brought up to and according to the regular ways of the people on Sunday he went to church. He got up to lead the public scripture reading.

And it was give to him the writing of Isaiah, the prophet, and leafing through it, he found the place where it's written,

The comforting and advocating spirit is in me because it anointed me to announce God's good news to humble people.

It chose me to announce freedom to all prisoners and give sight to the blind and preach to shattered lives they're saved, and announce that this is the welcome year of the

Familyhead's coming.

Then closing it and giving it back to the churchman, he sat down. And everyone's eyes in the church was fixed on him. Then it dawned on them that he was saying to them that the miracle which was to happen - written about in the writing - would be him. And they all verified it with him.

And they were shocked by his words of this joyful and fulfilling arrival having come from his lips and sniped, "This is Joseph's son isn't it?"

And Jesus said to them, "By all means, you will say the old proverb, 'Doctor, your first need is to heal yourself.'" And they cogitated, "So this is what we heard was going on in Capernaum and now here in your hometown."

Then Jesus said, "It's for sure that no prophet can be pleasing people of his own hometown. Now I want to tell you something also true. There were lots of widows in Israel in the days of Eli when the rains stopped for three years and six months and when there was great hunger all over the land, and Elijah didn't go no place but to Sarepta of the gentile land of Sidon to a widow lady. And there were lots of lepers in Israel in the time of Elijah the prophet and not one of them did he make clean except Namun, a Syrian."

And all of them in the church hearing these sayings were filled with resentful feelings, and when Jesus was getting ready to leave, they dragged him outside the town limits and hauled him up to the top of the mountain on which the city was built as they were meaning to throw him off a cliff. But disappearing from the middle of their clutches he went on his way.

Jesus Encounters A Mentally Ill Man

And he went down to the city of Capernaum of Galilee and went about teaching them on Sundays. And there was the quality of final truthfulness about his teaching as if there was authority in his preaching.

One Sunday in the church there was a mentally ill man who could not relate his thinking to God, and he cried out in disruption, "Come on! What's all this to you! Jesus of Nazereth. You have come to tear us up. I know you...who you are...the presence of God."

And Jesus acknowledged it saying, "Hush up and come out of this man!" And Jesus cast out the behavioral impediment without harming the man. And

everyone was amazed and conferred about it one with another saying, "What is the meaning of this? Is it because he can command the bafflement of the mentally ill to leave?" And the news went out about this incident every place in the neighborhood.

Many Are Healed

Then standing up, he left from the church and went to the house of Simon. But the mother-in-law of Simon was sick with a high fever and begged him to come to her. Then standing over her, Jesus commanded the fever to leave her. And immediately able to arise, she went to serve them dinner. When the sun was going down, all those having sick people or diseased people of various kinds brought them to him. Then laying his hands on them he healed them one at a time. And the mental illnesses of several of them left out and some babbled out saying, "You are the Child of God." And hushing them, he did not permit this to be said because they knew the truth that he was God's Child come to earth.

A Preaching Tour

Leaving in the following days, he went to go to the hilly dry lands of Judea and the crowds started looking for him and searched until they found him and headed for him where he could not get by them. Then he said to them, "Hey! I have to preach the good news of God's Homeland in other cities. That's why I have been dispatched." And so he went getting this message out to the churches of Judea.

The Calling Of His First Traveling Companions

Now it happened as the crowd pressed against him to hear about God and as he was standing by the Lake at Gennessaret, he saw two boats float upon the lake. Their fishermen were getting out to wash their nets and a man named Simon was getting ready to climb into one of the boats. So Jesus, on the shore, told him if he could he would like to get in his boat with him and put out a little way from shore so he could do his preaching from the boat to the crowd. The after he stopped talking to the crowd, he said to Simon, "Take your boat out to the deep part of the lake and put your nets down to catch some fish." But Simon answered saying, "Preacher, during the whole night, working ourselves to death, we haven't caught nothing. But on your say-so, I will lower my nets." And when they did this, he and Jesus caught netfulls of all kinds of fish until the net was ripping apart being so full of them. And they motioned to their partners in another boat to join them in the catch. And they come and both boats were filled to the sinking point. Recognizing on his own what had happened, Simon Peter got down on his knees before Jesus and said, "Get away from me Sir because I am a sinner-man." He was mind blown and so were all those with him by the catch of fish which they'd pulled in. The others with him were James and John, sons of Zebedee. They all jointly owned Simon's fishing boat. Then Jesus said to Simon, "Don't be afraid. From now on you will be catching persons." And so they beached their boats by the shore, left behind all they had and joined up with him.

A Leper's Skin Is Cleaned Up

And then this happened as they were going into one of the towns. Hey! a fellow full of leprosy seeing Jesus fell down before him and grabbed him saying, "Sir if you wanted it, you could clean me up." And Jesus's hands reached down and touched him and he said, "I do want it. Be cleaned up!" And immediately the leprosy went away off him. And Jesus ordered him not to talk about what he'd done. And leaving, he said, "Show yourself cleaned up in the church, offer the ritual sacrifice of thankfulness. Do as Moses said for a cleansed Jew to do in witness to these things." And the reputation of Jesus went out more and more and huge crowds stayed with him just to listen to him and some to be healed of their disabilities. But he was continually going out into the dry hill country praying.

A Paralyzed Man Gets Healed

Then it happened one day he was teaching and Pharisees and law teachers were seated come from all the towns of Galilee and Judea and Jerusalem. And the Familyhead's power was in him to turn minds and bodies to God. Now, what is happening! People are bearing a man on a stretcher who's paralyzed. They're searching for Jesus to bring the paralyzed one close and place him in front of him. And not finding where they could carry him through the crowd, they went up on a roof and then down through the roof tiles to lay him out on his stretcher smack dab in the middle in front of Jesus. And seeing the faith of them, Jesus said, "Fellow, your wrongdoing is erased." And the church Hebrew translators and Pharisees went to arguing saying, "Isn't this talk against God? Who has the power to erase people's guilty doings except only God?" But Jesus understood what they were arguing about and he replied, saying, "Why do you argue in your hearts? Isn't it just as easy to say, 'Be gone, offenses,' as 'Get up and walk?' since you know that God's Child has the authority while on earth to cancel out guilty doings." He said to the paralyzed man, "Get up and pick up your stretcher. Go on to your home." And immediately standing up before all who were there, he picked up his stretcher and left to go to his own home shouting praises to God. And absolutely everyone there were shocked and praised God and were trembling, saying, "We saw an unbelievable miracle."

Levi Is Called

And after some time, Jesus was going about and saw a tax collector, Levi, reclining by a tax office, and he said to him, "Join me." And leaving everything behind, Levi stood up and joined him. And Levi prepared a feast for him in his house and many guests were tax collectors and others with them reclined around the table. And the Pharisees and the translators grumbled to the companions, saying, "Why does he eat and drink with tax collectors and the opposition?" And Jesus answered, replied, "The healthy don't need a doctor, only the ones barely holding on. I don't come to call ones acting perfect, but wrongdoers to change their ways."

The Question About Fasting

Then they said to him, "Look here! John's companions lots of times don't even eat, sacrificing their appetites for God, and put themselves out praying, and so do the Pharisees, but your companions eat and drink." Then Jesus said to them, "How can the friends of a man getting married and the guests with them refuse to eat at a wedding dinner? The days will come, and soon, when the bridegroom might be taken away from them, then's when, in those days, they don't feel like eating." Then he repeated for them the parable that no patch gets cut out from a new coat to be sewed on an old coat, for what's left of the new coat will rip and the patch from the new coat won't match with the old. And no one puts new wine into old wineskins for either the new wine will bust the wineskins and pour out or the wineskins will ruin the wine. New wine must be put into new wineskins. But no one drunk on the old even wants the new for he says the old is good enough.

Picking Wheat On Sunday

It happened on one Sunday as Jesus was going by a wheat field, his companions was pulling up stems and sucking out the juice from them but some of the Pharisees said, "Isn't what you're doing unlawful on Sunday?" And Jesus answered them, saying, "Haven't you read this story about David, that when he and his friends were hungry, he went into a church, the house of God, taking the bread dedicated for God's purposes. Then he ate it and give it to those with him in spite of its being only for church purposes. Anyway," he added, "your Familyhead is God's human Child in charge of Sunday."

The Man With An Arthritic Hand

And then it happened that as he was going into church the next Sunday to teach, there was a man there whose right hand was arthritic. And the church translators and Pharisees watched for their own reasons if he would do healing on Sunday because they wanted to charge him with a crime. But Jesus knew their inner motives, so he said to the man having the arthritic hand. "Get up and go stand in the middle of them." And getting up, he stood there.

Then Jesus said to them, "Ask them if it's lawful on Sunday to do a good thing, or a bad thing, to improve someone's life or hurt it?" And while everybody stared at them, he said, "Hold out your hand." And he did and his hand was restored. The church translators and Pharisees were filled with anger and talked with themselves about what to do about Jesus.

Choosing Twelve Companions

Then it happened in those days as he went to a hilltop to pray, he spent the whole night communing with God. And when day come, he called to his companions, and called out twelve from them which he named special companions: Simon, the one also called Peter, and Andrew, his brother. James. John. Philip. Bartholomew. Matthew. Thomas. James Alpheus. Simon being a zealot. Judas Iscobus. Judas Iscariot, the one who become a traitor.

A Great Preaching Occasion

And coming down from the hill, he stood on a level platform in front of a large crowd of his companions and a great range of people, for many was from Judea, and Jerusalem, and from the coast towns of Tyre and Sidon. They came to listen to him and to be healed of their sicknesses. And those troubled by doubts in their minds was strengthened. And the whole assembly wanted to embrace him because such energy emerged from him and he cared so for them all.

Who Are Beloved And Who Damned

And Jesus looked the companions straight in the eye and said, "Beloved are the struggling because yours is God's Homeland. Beloved are the ones that know hunger now because you will eat to filling. Beloved are the ones that cry now because you will laugh. Beloved are you when people hate you, and when they discriminate against you, and when they insult you, and when they drive you out, calling your name no account, because of God's human Child. Soon and forever, be filled with joy in the end day, and then's when you'll leap for joy. See, your reward's in God's Homeland. Just so informed were the prophets and their forerunners. Damned are you as bad as the filthy rich because you will have your comforts yanked away. Damn you who are filled to bloating, because you will hunger. Damn you who laugh now, because you will know mourning and crying. Damn you when all people speak respectful because of how you have things as our ancestors did to the false prophets.

Love For Enemies

Now to all who will listen, I say, love your enemies. Do good things for those that hate you. Praise those that's cursing you. To one slapping you on one of your cheeks, offer also the other, and for one stealing your coat, don't hold back giving the fellow the clothes under it. Give everything on the asking, and don't want nothing in return from the one given to. And do the same to people as you want people to do to you. And if you only love those that love you, so what to you is the free gift of God's love? Don't the ones separated from God love the ones that love them? If you only help those helping you, so what to you is the free gift of God's love? Also ones separated from God does this. And if you give money to those that you hope to receive it back from, so what to you is the free gift of God's love? Don't the ones separated from God loan money to their own to receive it back with interest? But love your enemies and help and give, not expecting return, and it will ensure a great return and you will be children of the most exalted one, because God showers love on the ungrateful as well as scoffers.

Discriminating Against Others

And don't discriminate against others or allow yourself to be discriminated against and you will not be condemning or condemned. Think freedom and you will be free. Give and you will receive. A measuring container to be an honest measure must be packed, shaken, and leveled over at the top in your lap and as you dole out a measure so will the measure be doled out to you. Then he talked in paradox to them. "Can a blind person guide a blind person? Or will both fall into a ditch?" "A companion is not set in charge of his teacher, but all will be as the teacher." "Why do you see a splinter in the eye of your brother or sister, not realizing there is log's worth of lumber in your eyes? How can you say to your sisters and brothers, 'Get that splinter out a your eye,' when you can't see a log in your own eye. Hypocrite, first off get out your lumber from your eyes, and then you'll be able to focus in the splinter in the eye of your sister or brother to get it out.

A Tree Is Known By Its Fruit

Now there's no good tree that bears bad fruit. On the other hand neither can a bad tree bear good fruit. Thus-and- so each tree gets to be known by its fruit. We are not going to pick figs from a locust tree, nor pick grapes from a thistle bush. Good honest people do good honest things from the good honest values of their hearts, and rejectors of God do acts of rejecting God from their rejecting hearts. What wells up out from the heart is what talk expresses.

Two Foundations

Why call out to me, "Sir, Sir," and not listen to what I say? Each one who comes to me, listens to my stories and absorbs them, I will inspire with what they mean. For example, there's a person building a house, digging and digging deep, and he starts the foundation on a rock. When flood time comes, a stream bursts at that house, but it can't unsettle it because it was well built. Now there's a person, even after listening to this story, who doesn't take the example, building a house on the ground without a foundation. It may be that the stream bursts at that house and straightway it collapses or that house gets totally washed away."

The Healing Of A Centurian's Special Boy Slave

After he finished telling all his sayings preaching to the people, Jesus went to Capernaum. Now there was a particular slave of a centurion, an army captain, being so sick as to be about to die. After he heard about Jesus, he sent Jewish elders to ask him whether he would come to safely bring the slave through the sickness. When the elders got to Jesus, they begged him, saying, "It's worthwhile for you to come do this. This centurion loves our people and built a church for us." So Jesus went with them. But when they were not far away from the centurion's house, the centurion sent friends to Jesus saying, "Sir, don't trouble yourself. I'm not worth it. To do this, you would have to come under my roof. I don't consider myself worthy enough for you to come in. But say this as an order, 'Have the boy be healed.' I am a person with designated authority, personally just a soldier, but to this one I say 'Report,' and the person comes, and to another I say 'Dismissed,' and the person goes. In the same way, I say to my slave, 'Get this done,' and it is done." After he heard this, Jesus was amazed at it and turned around to the crowd following him and said, "I say to you, no one in Israel have I found with such faith." And after the centurian's friends returned home, they found the special slave boy feeling okay.

Raising A Widow's Son At Nain

Then Jesus was about to come to a city called Nain and his companions were going with him and a big crowd. As he arrived at the city gate, Look! an only son, dead, is being carried out for burial with his mother alongside. And she was a widow. And a bereaved crowd of the city were with her. Now look here! the Familyhead himself feels bad about her and he says to her, "Don't cry." And when he went to her, and he touched the coffin they was carrying the corpse in, and those carrying the thing stood their ground, he said, "Young fellow, get up." And the dead boy sat up and began to talk, and Jesus gave him back to his mother. Then fear took hold of everyone and they started praising God that "A great prophet grew up among us," and that "God was strong for his people." And this story went out to the whole of Judea and all places around it.

Messengers From John The Reconciler

Now these companions of John heard the good news about all this. And some two of the companions of John, after delegation, was sent to the Family-head, saying, "Are you the one that's coming or are we supposed to be waiting on someone else?" So after they went to him, these fellows said, "John, the one baptizing, sent us to you to say, 'Are you the one's coming or are we supposed to be waiting on someone else.'" At that very hour Jesus healed several from sickness and disease and mental illness and many blind people was given the free gift of sight. Then Jesus answered their question, "Go tell John what you have seen and heard. The blind's sight's returned, the crippled are walking, the lepers are getting cleaned up, the deaf are hearing, the dead are raised, the poor are getting better news, and blessed is everyone who isn't putting it down. Then after John's deputies left, Jesus began to talk to the crowds about John. "Why do you go to him in the barrens? To see visions? Is he a reed pipe whiffed by the wind? Why's people go out to the barrens? To be seen there? Is this person dressed too fancy for us? Look here! Those in a fancy coat and living in luxury are at his disposal in God's Homeland. But why do you go to see him? Is he a prophet? Yes, I say to you, he is the greatest prophet. He is the one of this writing, 'I will send my messenger to your presence who will pave your road before you.' I say to you, no one born of women is greater than John. But the least citizen in God's homeland is better off than him. And after the people heard this, even tax collectors felt right with God from receiving a baptism by John. But the Pharisees and Hebrew translators continued to reject God's wishes about this, and refused baptism from him. "How are people alike in this generation and what is their similarity? It is their similarity to children in the market where they play and banter to each other and Jesus commented this: We played a flute and you didn't dance. We mourned but you didn't cry. It is a fact! God acted and John's here baptizing, not eating bread or drinking wine, and you say, "He's mentally ill?" God's acted and God's human Child comes eating and drinking, and you say, "Look, a fellow that's a glutton and drunk, a brother to tax collectors and them's hostile to God." But the inspired people from all of his children are brought over to God."

A Woman Forgiven

Then a certain one of the Pharisees asked him to have dinner with him, and after they went into the house of the Pharisee, Jesus reclined to eat. But Look! Some kind of uproar...a woman, whoever she was, was in the city and learning that Jesus was going to have dinner in the house of the Pharisee, she brought an expensive alabaster jar full of perfume and standing behind him, by his feet, she started crying so hard the tears went falling on his feet and with the hair of her head she wiped him off and then she kissed his feet and anointed them with the perfume. After he saw all this going on, the Pharisee talked to himself and said to himself, "If this were a prophet, he would have known what kind of a woman, whoever she is, has been touching him, that she's not living a Godly life." But Jesus responded to his thinking and said to him, "Simon, why do I have to explain this to you." Simon, who was a teacher, said, "Say what you have to say." Jesus said, "Two debtors was borrowing some money. One of them owed five hundred silver coins and the other owed fifty. Not having enough to pay the loans back both was wrote off. Now which of them did the creditor show more love to?" Simon said, "I suppose the one forgiven the most." And Jesus said, "You figured it right." And turning to the woman from Simon, he said, "Do you see this woman? I came to you in this house. You did not give me water to wash my feet. But she, with her tears, bathed them, and with her hair dried them. Neither did you kiss me. But after I came here she got down kissing my feet. You offered no ointment to moisten and sooth my road weary head. She doused my feet with expensive perfume. For this, 'Woman, I welcome you with a warm thanks?' Her mistakes which are many are forgiven because she showed much love, but little is forgiven for little love." Then he said to her, "All your mistakes are forgiven." And all the fellow dinner guests begun to talk to themselves, "Who does he think he is to forgive mistakes?" Then he said to the woman, "Your faithfulness has served you well. Go with peace of mind."

Some Women Accompany Jesus

After this, in sequence, Jesus went traveling about to this city and that town preaching and dialoguing happily with God's homeland and the twelve was with him and some women, ones coming out from depressed states of mind on account of thinking they was just weak women people. Mary, the one called Magdalene, from eight episodes came through, Johanna, wife of Xousa, Herod's steward, and Susana, and many others, who provided the living needs to them from what they had at their disposal.

The Story Of The Farmer

Keeping company with them were large crowds depending upon the size of the cities they was coming out of, and Jesus told them stories like this one. Here came a farmer out to plant seeds. And while it was planted, one of them seeds falls along the road and gets tramped on, and birds flying down from the sky ate it. And another seed falls out in gravel and sprouts up puny because short of water. And another falls out in the middle of thorns, but the thorns coming up with it choked it. And another fell into rich soil and grows up bearing grain a hundred times seed size. After saying this, he kept calling out, "Anyone having ears to listen to this, listen."

The Purpose Of The Stories

Curious, the companions asked Jesus why he always seems to want to tell a story. Here's what was said, "To you companions it's give to know the way God governs. For the rest, I tell stories, since: "When they see, they don't see", and "When they hear, they don't understand."

Explaining The Story Of The Farmer

This is the meaning of the story. The farmer is the story about God. The seed by the road are those hearing. Then along comes an adverse influence and takes the story out of their hearts to cancel their saving faith. Those seeds in the gravel is when they hear and take the story in against the way love would have it received and so they don't have roots. These have faith for while, but during a time of testing, they lose it. Then the seeds falling in the thorns...these are those hearing,

and too full of anxiety, or too rich, or too sexually busy, are choked out of reaching true life and can't achieve mature production. But the plant in rich soil, these are ones who hear in their rich hearts, and after they hear the story in its richness, they keep the faith and bear the mature fruit by patiently enduring.

A Light Under A Dish Or Bed

After lighting a lamp, no one hides it under a dish or under a bed but instead they put it on a stand so the light can help them see where they are going. There is nothing secret which will not be made plain nor hidden which will not be seen when it comes into view. So, see and hear how this works. If this can be grasped, it will reward someone and if this is not grasped, then what he has will be swept away from him.

The Mother And Family Of Jesus

Comes along then his mother and family and they can't get near to him because of the crowd. Someone said to him, "Your mother and your brothers are standing outside wanting to see you." But he answered saying, "My mother and brothers are those people listening to the story about God's life on earth and living its implications."

Calming A Storm

Comes along then on one of them days, he got into a boat and the companions got in too and Jesus said to them, "How about we go to the other side of the lake," and they sailed off. And while they was sailing, Jesus dozed off. Then a thunderstorm broke on the lake and it looks like the time is near for them to be running a big risk out there. With all this coming on, they woke up Jesus and said, "Jesus, we are going to be killed." But after waking up, Jesus gave an order to the wind and rough waves and the storm broke up and the lake got calm. Then he asked them, "Where was your faith?" Still scared, and shocked, they talked to each other, "What's in this fellow that he gives orders to storms and waves and they obey? Isn't Jesus just a regular fellow?"

Healing A Mentally Ill Man At Garrison

Then they kept on sailing to the town of Garrison which is on the far opposite side of Lake Galilee. Coming into it by the land side a man met them who was from that city. He was severely mentally ill and most of the time didn't wear clothes or live in a house. Instead he called a graveyard home. When he saw Jesus, the crazy fellow broke out crazy bawling, and fell down in front of Jesus and in a loud voice said, "What's to become of me and you, Jesus? I beg you. Don't mess with me." The fellow said this since Jesus ordered the confused thinking of the fellow to get cleared out of the fellow. For a long time, the disturbance had shook him up pretty bad. He'd be tied up in chains and feet chains were put on his feet lots of times to keep him from harming himself. Breaking the chains, he would lapse into muddled thinking and light out for the desert. Then Jesus asked him, "What do you think is your name?" And he said, "Mr. Army, because so many spirits has got into me." And then each one them started piping up so that Jesus won't send them to the hell hole they's feared is set aside to hold bad spirits. But there is a pretty good sized bunch of pigs snooting grazing at that hill. And the spirits begged Jesus to let them go into them pigs once they was kicked out. Jesus turned them over to them. When the spirits left out of the fellow, they went on into the pigs and the whole sty of them went rushing down a steep bank into the lake and drowned. Seeing what had happened to the grazers, the onlookers fled and ran into the city and to the town square. Then others went out to see what happened. And they went to Jesus and found him sitting down. By his feet was that fellow from out from the spirits busted now having clothes on and acting sensible. And they remarked to one another what they saw happened to the possessed man. And everybody in the whole place and them's that's around Garrison asked Jesus to leave out from there because of mass hysteria. And going to get back on the boat, Jesus went to return home. But the man from who the spirits left wanted to go with Jesus. But Jesus restrained him saying, "Go back to your hometown and tell one and all of what God can do for the mentally ill." So he went back home with the rest of the city people telling what Jesus done for him.

Jarus's Daughter And A Woman Who Touched Jesus

As soon as they returned home, a big crowd welcomed Jesus. They'd been waiting tense for him to return. Now See! a man by the name of Jarus came and this fellow was somehow in charge of the church there. While he fell down at the feet of Jesus he begged Jesus to go to his home because his twelve year old only kid, a daughter, was in there dying. While trying to go, the crowd blocked Jesus. Now this young girl was a hemophiliac bleeder all her twelve years. She'd been doctored for it all her life. No one was able to do nothing to heal her. While Jesus was leaving to go to the bleeder, from behind, the edge of Jesus's garment was yanked and just like that the yanker lady's gonorrhea bleeding sores stopped running. And Jesus said, "Who just reached out and touched me?" But all of them in the crowd denied it. Peter said, "The crowds is just surrounding you and crowding in at you." But Jesus said, "Someone reached out and touched me. Maam, I know when healing power goes out to you from me." Then when the woman saw that she couldn't hide, trembling, she went to him, and falling down in front of him, said she was the shameful one that hardly dared touch him admitting so in front of the whole crowd of the people and as to how it cured her as quick as a wink. Jesus said to her, "Daughter, your faith saves you. Go with peace of mind." Just then, while he was speaking, someone went to this one that was in charge of the church saying that his daughter was dead. The friend said, "No need to trouble the teacher." But after hearing what was said, Jesus replied, "Don't fear. Just believe. And she too will be saved." So Jesus went to the fellow's house, not hesitating for a minute to go, taking no one with him excepting Peter, John and James and the father and mother of the child. Most everyone was crying and grief struck over her. But they stopped long enough to laugh down Jesus's coming, thinking they knew that she was dead. But taking ahold of her hand Jesus summoned her and said, "Youngster, come back to life." And the life spirit of her returned and she immediately came back to life and Jesus said for her to be give something to eat. And her parents' minds were blown. And Jesus instructed them all not to talk up what happened.

An Errand For His Twelve Companions

Then calling together the twelve, he empowered them with great strength and say-so over the range of mental and diseases conditions so that they could heal. And he charged them to preach that God rules the world and to heal. And he told them, "Take nothing on your journey, not a walking stick, not a sack, not a loaf of bread, not a coin, not an extra set of clothes to change into. And if someone invites you into their house, stay there and you can leave from there. And so many as don't ask you in, go on from out from them cities shaking off their dust from your feet for the purpose of evidencing about them. So whether going into or passing through, depending on the towns, tell about the good news and heal everywhere."

Herod Worries

Now Herod, this puppet governor, began to hear about all these doings and was getting anxious about the reports by several people that John arose from the dead, by several people that Elijah come again, or by some others that an old- time prophet had risen up out of the grave. Herod told them, "I cut off the head of John. But who is this one about who so many are gossiping?" And he got it in his head to see him.

Feeding Five Thousand

When the missionaries come home they told Jesus about what they'd been doing. After welcoming them, he took a break with these ones so close to him going to a city called Bathsaida. But the crowds figuring it out followed Jesus. And welcoming them, he told them God was ruling the world and he restored those having healing needs. And the daylight hours was coming to an end, and the twelve went to Jesus and said, "Better send the crowds away before they go into the towns and fields scrounging for food because we are in a barren kind of place." But Jesus said to them, "Give them food to eat." But they said, "There isn't more than five loaves of bread and two fish among us. Unless they leave, we will have to go shopping for all this mob to have food." There was approximately five thousand people. But Jesus said to the companions, "Tell this bunch of hungry people to set down for dinner, even though they are upwards of five thousand." And they did as they are told and had the whole lot of them get ready for eating. Taking the five loaves of bread and two fish, looking up toward God's homeland, Jesus acted graciously to them and sat for dinner and gives to the companions to take dinner to the mob. And they ate and all of them had enough to fill them and there was leftovers to the tune of twelve baskets after they'd all ate their fill.

Peter's Declaration About Jesus

Then during a time after Jesus was caught up in praying alone the companions went to him, and he asked them, "Who do those people say I am?" And they answered, "John the Baptist, but some say Elijah, others that some prophet of the ancient days rose up." But Jesus said to them, "Who do you all say that I am." Peter answered him, "The appearance of God's Child on earth."

Jesus Tells Of His Death And Return To Life

Then Jesus give orders for them not to tell to nobody something he knew, namely that it was needful for him to suffer much and to have his claim rejected by the elders and senior churchmen and Hebrew translators and to be killed and to arise on the third day. And he said to them all, in the future, if anyone wants to follow me, tear away from others, take up the cross every day and be disposed to me. If it is your life you want saved, it must be be lost. If you have lost life because of me, it will be saved. So if a person is ashamed of me and my stories, God's human Child will be ashamed of that person when he goes to his reward with his parent and the Godly messengers of comfort. I tell you truthfully, any persons standing firm for me will not experience death except into God's homeland.

Jesus Is Transfigured

Then after stating these words, say about eight days later, taking Peter and John and James, Jesus went into the hills to pray. And it happened while Jesus was praying, the appearance of Jesus's face changed, and his clothes turned white and all of him started flashing like lightning. And See! two persons are talking to Jesus. They are Moses and Elijah. While they are seen, Jesus tells them how he's attending to things, how he's about to end the story in Jerusalem. But Peter and the ones with him were so tired they fell asleep. When they woke up, they saw Jesus as God and two persons standing with Jesus. And it happened that this scared them so they were leaving from there, but Peter said to Jesus, "Would you believe it?! This is amazingly too good to be true! And us here!" And then Peter says, "Let's get three tents ready, one for Jesus, one for Moses, and one for Elijah," confused in what he's saying. But soon after he spoke, a cloud came and overshadowed them. And being in the cloud they were too scared to leave. And they heard a voice in the cloud saying, "I have chose to take a human form. Listen to Jesus." And as the statement echoes, Jesus only is found there. And the companions fell silent, nor revealed what they saw in those days.

The Healing Of A Mentally Ill Boy

Then the next day while they was coming down from the hills, a big crowd met Jesus. And See! a man calls out from the crowd saying, "Teacher, I beg you to care for my son because he's my only child. See! he is epileptic." And the boy cried out and had a grand mal fit right there foaming at the mouth and he scarcely got through it shaking so. The father said, "I begged your companions to drive out a devil, but they couldn't do it." Jesus answered him, "Oh! Humanity! Don't you see the point of the institution of faith? Distorting the meaning of it! How long can I be with you! or be patient with you! Bring me your son." The fit was still going on and it was making the boy crazy on the ground and it looked like the boy would break himself in two. But Jesus commanded the epilepsy to cease and he healed the boy and returned him to his father. All those witnessing this was totally impressed by God's greatness.

Jesus Foretells His Death Again

While everyone gawked at all the things Jesus was doing, Jesus said to the companions, "Remember these sayings. Soon God's human Child is going to be betrayed into the hands of persons. They don't understand what is happening even when they were desperately urged to reach the meanings and they have hated to dig into the content of them.

Who Is The Greatest???

A discussion came up amongst the companions, who would be the greatest of them. But Jesus ESP'd in his heart their discussion and while he was receiving some kids, he took one to himself. Then he said to them, "If anyone welcomes this child on my behalf, he welcomes me. And if anyone welcomes me, he welcomes those accompanying me. The weakest of all of you has this powerful resource."

A Person Not Against You Is For You

John said to Jesus, "Jesus, we saw someone curbing mental illness in your name and we told that fellow to cut it out because he wasn't traveling with us." But Jesus said to him, "You shouldn't stop him because it isn't necessary for a person to be with us to be for us."

A Samaritan Town Refuses Entry To Jesus

As the days before Jesus's crucifixion was reaching their end, Jesus confirmed they was going to Jerusalem. And he called deputies to come to him. And after they'd been briefed, they went to a Samaritan town to get it ready for Jesus. But the town wouldn't welcome him because the stopover was while going to Jerusalem. Hearing about this, the companions James and John said, "Do you want us to tell fire to come from the sky and destroy them?" But turning to them, he scolded them and went toward another town.

Hesitant Followers

And when they were on the road someone said to Jesus, "I will go with you to whatever place it takes me." And Jesus said to him, "Foxes have dens, and birds of the sky have nests, but no where is there for God's human Child to lie down to rest." Jesus said to another, "Follow me." But the fellow said, "Okay, but permit me to first go bury my father." But Jesus said to the person, "Leave the dead to bury each other's dead. When it comes to you, address the Homeland of God." And an-other said, "I will follow you, Sir. First I'll go get things arranged at my home." But Jesus said to him, "Nobody whose hands grip a plow and looks only behind at his furrows is arranging his life satisfactory according to the Homeland of God."

An Errand For Seventy Two Missionaries

Later, the Familyhead drafted seventy two more and sent them in twos to be the presence of Jesus in each town to places Jesus couldn't go, saying, "A great harvest is needed, and the hired hands are few. You were prayed for by the Familyhead of the harvest and that's why the Familyhead has sent you out, hired hands, to gather in the harvest. Bear up. See. I can only send you as sheep into the middle of predators. Carry no money, nor beggar's cup, nor boots, nor anything to cause you to think you're making the missionarying easier. While doing this, if you go into a home, first say this, 'Peace to your home.' And if they be children of peace, it will be rested on them -your peace. But if not, it will come back. So in this peace stay in that home eating and drinking necessities on them. For a worker is worth his or her wages. Don't light from home to home. And if you come to one city and they welcome you, eat what they set before you. And heal them in their sicknesses and say to them, 'God's homecoming time at our land is near.' If you go into a city and they don't welcome you, enter the widest street of theirs and say, 'We have shaken off even the dirt

of yours that clods on our feet from your city to protest you, but know this anyway, 'God's homecoming time at our land is near.' I say to you that Sodom in
that day is more acceptable than that city.

Stubborn Cities

I damn you, Chorazin, and I damn you, Bathsaida, because if the things
was done in Tyre or Sidon that was done in your towns, a long time ago they
would be sitting in ashes and wearing sackcloth. Anyway, Tyre and Sidon are
going to be more acceptable at judgment time than you. And you, Capernaum,
Since you will not reach for the skies of existence, you will fall into oblivion. A
city who hears what is going to happen to you, hears it from me, and a city who
rejects this warning, rejects me. Also the city rejecting me is rejecting the one
that has sent me.

The Return Of The Seventy Two

The seventy two returned happy saying, "Familyhead, the mentally confused was even cured by us in your name." Jesus said to them, "I observed Satan falling like lightning from the sky. See! I gave you the ability to triumph
over more than snakes and scorpions, and heal all illnesses, and prevail over
injustice against you. Be careful not to exhilarate yourselves in this because the
powers are yours to command, but feel exhilarated because your names are being repeated with joy in the skies of existence."

Jesus Is Happy

At this hour, Jesus felt spiritually very happy and comfortable and said, "I acknowledge how you are. You are my Parent, Familyhead of the skies beyond existence as well as earth. How you have hidden things from the wise and intellectual and revealed them to innocents. Yes, Parent, it has to be because it is pleasing for you. This whole scheme becomes precedent to me from my Parent, and no one knows how the Child is like a Parent and how a Parent is more than a Child or who the Parent wishes the child to be confessed before. And turning to his own companions he said privately, "Beloved are the eyes which see what you see. I tell you all of the prophets and former rulers would have loved to see what you are seeing but were't permitted to see and wanted to hear what you hear but weren't permitted to hear.

The Good Samaritan

And there's a Hebrew translator comes along, one of them testy ones, and he says, "Teacher, what can I do to inherit eternal life?" Jesus said to him. "In the law, how is it written? How is it read in public readings of it in church?" And the Hebrew translator answered, "Love the Familyhead as your God with all your heart and in all your soul and with all your strength, and with all your mind and the ones close to you as yourself." And Jesus said to him, "You answered right. Do this and you will so live." But another person wanting to get right with God said to Jesus, "And who is one close to me?" Concentrating on this Jesus said, "There was a fellow going down from Jerusalem to Jericho and robbers mugged him. Then these men stripped him and knocked him out unconscious and took off leaving him half dead. And a churchman come along looking down at the road and when he saw him he went to the other side of the road. Same way comes a Levite according to their way, going along, and when he saw him he went to the other side of the road. Now a Samaritan was traveling on down the road and when he saw him, he felt real bad. And he went over and bandaged his wounds and treated him with olive oil and wine, and he placed him on his own mount and took him to an inn and had them look after him. And at dawn, when he left, he gave the innkeeper two valuable coins and said, 'Take care of him, and, since I have to come back this way anyway, I will make it a point to stop here and pay you back any other expense.' Which of the three shows caring for the one close to him who fell into the hands of robbers?" And he said, "The one who acted with kindness to him." And Jesus said to him, "Go and you do the same."

Visiting Martha And Mary

Then leaving them, Jesus went to another town. A girl named Martha welcomed Jesus to her home. And another there was her sister called Mary, who, seating herself at the feet of the Familyhead wanted to listen to a story. But Martha was busy worrying about all the preparations. Going to Jesus she said, "Sir, don't it concern you to have to wait just because my sister neglects to help me. Tell her she should come to help me." But the Familyhead replied, "Martha, Martha, you're so anxious and troubled by many things. Of only one thing is there a chore. Mary comes to do what she needs to, seeking the sacrificial portion of me which will never be taken away from her."

Jesus Teaches About Prayer

Then it happened while they was present in this place along the way while they was traveling - as they stopped for a minute-one of the companions of Jesus said, "Familyhead, Sir, teach us the right way to pray," and Jesus taught these companions of his, telling them, "When you pray, say, 'Parent, blessed be your name. Have this land know your homecoming. The bread we need to get by, Give it to us every day. And wipe out separation from you. And for others, we will wipe out all they owe us. And don't bring us to know any more troubles then we can bear.'" And he says to them, "Someone among you has a friend who will go out in the middle of the night, and say, 'Neighbor, how about loaning me three loaves of bread because a friend of mine is here to visit me and I don't have anything for him?' Now that one calling from within may say, 'Don't bother me. The doors was locked long ago. My children are in bed and me too! I'm not even able to stand up to give it to you.' I say to you, whether or not he will give it to you doesn't depend on whether he's your friend. It will be because you are persistent that he gets up to give you what you need. And so also I say to you, Ask and it will be give to you, Seek and you will find, Knock and it will be opened to you, For everyone who asks, receives, and any who seeks, finds, and to a person knocking, it will be opened. Now which parents among you, whose child asks for a fish, would give him a snake? Or whose child wants an egg, gives him a scorpion? Are you used to being treated badly? Aren't you aware how good are the gifts you give your children? The parent who is in the skies of existence gives far more comfort to those seeking him.

Jesus And Despair

Then Jesus cast out the despair of a catatonic person, and when the stupor was gone, the person spoke and the crowd was shocked. But some among them said, "Baal (an old house God of the people of that time) is the power behind expelling a demon." Others, seeing this as a miracle, grabbed for Jesus. But Jesus dealt with their confusion, explaining to them, "Every homeland divided against itself is made a desert, and house by house it falls. Now if Satan divides himself, how can his homeland stand? That's what you are saying if you say a demon was expelled through Baal. If I threw out a demon by Baal's power, who do your exorcists trust to throw out demons? What will be the authority of these demon testers anyway? But if God points a finger and despair leaves, so is God's homecoming preceding. When a strongman guards his palace, it is peaceful while he possesses it. But after a stronger man

comes after him to conquer it, and takes from him the man's armor, the spoils get divided up. One who is not with me is against me, one who is is not bonded with me, faces dispersion.

The Story Of The Returning Goblin

Once upon a time, there was a goblin who left away from a fellow's home, and the goblin went out to the barrens where such spirits go to look for company and get some rest. But the goblin couldn't get either one out there so he says, "I'll just return to the house where I come out of." But when he got home, he found there was a housecleaning done and the place was cleaned up too much to be comfortable. So he left again and this time made friends with some other goblins that was even more nasty then he was, seven of them, and they all decided to go to the house to take it over. And that was the last anyone ever even heard tell of the fellow. He was worse off after his place had been cleaned up and put in order then before.

True Happiness

After Jesus told this story, someone shouted out from the crowd saying to Jesus, "Beloved is the womb that carried you and the breasts you nursed at." Jesus said, "Even more beloved are those who listen to the story about God's life on earth and live in it."

Proof Needs Of Jesus Being God

Then when the crowd was really huge, Jesus began saying, "This generation is a perverse generation. It seeks proof and none is given unless the proof of Jonah. As there was proof from Jonah for the Ninevahites, so will the Orphan be for this generation. Remember the story of the queen of the South, she would be coming in testifying against these and judging against them because she come from the ends of the earth to listen to the wisdom of Soloman and See! a greater one than Soloman is here. The people in Ninevah would rise from their graves in testimony against this generation and judging against them because they was converted through Jonah's message and See! a greater one then Jonah is here.

The Light Of The Body

After lighting a lamp, no one hides it. You put it on a stand so that the light goes out for brightness. The lamp of the body is your eye. When your eye is working, the whole body is opened to light. But when it goes bad, the body darkens. The light cannot scrutinize when there is darkness in you. If your whole body is full of light, with no part confined in darkness, the brightness will illuminate the whole as if a lamp were lighting you to dazzling.

Denouncing Of Pharisees And Strict Law Abiders

While he was talking, a Pharisee, a strict law abider of Moses law, asked Jesus if he would come to eat at his place. (Pharisees had customs as proofs they was doing what God wanted). Jesus said okay and after going in reclined to eat. But the Pharisee was shocked seeing that Jesus didn't first do no ritual washing up before beginning to eat. Feeling the Pharisees reaction, the Familyhead said to him, "Now you Pharisees, I like eating with you, because you keep the outside of the cups and dishes you serve your food on you clean. But, bear in mind, your insides are as filled with human instinct, greed and lust as are everybody elses. So honorable but misguided! Didn't the one making the outside make the inside? When you give yourself over inside to doing charity, then, See! there will be total purity in you." Just then Jesus felt God being angry at this Pharisee's misdirection, elevating custom too much, and Jesus took a deep breath, and took its force, and said, "You make an offering of mint and herbs and all kinds of plants and neglect the decision and love of God. It is necessary to do things oriented toward Godliness, and after this don't neglect them." And Jesus felt God being angry again and said, "You Pharisees overemphasize the first standing you have in the churches and the greetings you receive in the stores." And he breathed in deeply and said, "You are like unmarked graves and people walking over such graves don't even realize they are doing it." Later, there was some one of the lawyers come up to him stating, "These things you are saying insult us." And Jesus took another deep breath and took the force of some more of God's anger at them turning folk's law into God's law and said, "You weigh down people with duties too heavy to bear, and these burdened ones you do not lift a finger to help with their load." And Jesus took in another deep breath, sighing with the burden Jesus was taking in of more of God's anger, and said, "You are the one who has built monuments for the prophets, but your own precedents killed them. You witness their effects and you still blindly follow the human precedent decisions, even though they killed those living their lives for God, and then you go out building monuments to them!" God's love and understanding come out of Jesus's mouth, "I will keep sending more prophets and companions, and through these Hebrew translator and judges, these new prophets and companions will end up being killed and found guilty all the time! It may be charged to this kind of profession, the blood of all the prophets shed from the beginning of the world, the blood of Able until the blood of Zakeyus, being destroyed from anywhere between church altars or homes. Yes, I say to you, it will be an indictment for this profession." Then Jesus gulped in more of God's anger at these Hebrew translator and judges, "You deprive people of the keys to know and understand God! You don't approach this need yourselves and you try to stop those bearing these qualities." From the time of these blurts, the Hebrew translators and Pharisees began to store up their grudges and to try to trick Jesus with more questions then ever, plotting against God's child so that whatever came from Jesus's talk could be used to discredit him.

Warning Against Hypocrisy

While the crowd was swelling into the thousands and as Jesus was walking among them, God's child told this caution to the first companions, "Watch out for the fungus budding from the legalizers who practice hypocrisy. There's nothing that they are covering up that won't get revealed, or hid that won't get known. Whatever you are all witnessing being said in the shadows, will get announced in broad daylight and the thing you are feeling whispered in someone's ear in a room with closed doors will be broadcast from rooftops.

Who To Fear

I say to you, my friends, don't fear the body getting murdered because after they do that there's nothing more they can do. I will tell you what is to be to be uppermost. Respect God who has the power after death to cast you into judgment, yes I say, respect this. Who doubts that the sale of five sparrows for two coins escapes notice by God? Not one of them sparrows is forgot. Also ev-

ery hair of your head is numbered. Don't be afraid. You are valued more than all the sparrows.

Witnessing For God's Child Who Was With Us On Earth

I say to you, each one of you who declares love of me in front of people, so will I, God's human Child, declare you to be faithful before the Godly messengers of God. But someone rejecting me in front of people, that one's life will be rejected as meaningless before the spiritually alive with God. And each one who will tell the story of God's human Child before people, his shortcomings will be forgive him. But offending the spirit of God's attention to human affairs won't be forgiven. When you are challenged in front of the church authorities or judges or police don't forget how or why you render your defense or how to speak. For the spirit will be there in that hour and the spirit will give you what's necessary to say."

The Story Of A Rich Fool

Then some fellow called out from the crowd saying, "Teacher, tell my brother to divide his inheritance with me." But Jesus said to this man, "Fellow, how can you expect me to decide between you?" Then he said to them, "Look out and be on guard against the urges of greediness since a person's life does't get happier because of possessions." Then he told them a story. "Once upon a time there was some fellow who was very, very rich and had a farm that produced good crops. And he talked to himself and said to himself, 'What will I do? How can I warehouse all these crops?' And he said, 'This is what I will do. I will take down a little barn I got and build a huge one. Then I will store there all the crop and my goods. And then I will say to myself, Self, you have every need took care of for many years. Rest. Eat. Drink. Be happy.' Then God said to this fellow, 'Smart-aleck, tonight this smug self of yours is being took back.' What about these material things you prepared? Whose are they? This is what happens to one feathering a nest for himself, and not storing up riches in God."

Care And Anxiety

Then Jesus said to the companions, "Also, I say this to you, don't be worried about your life if you have enough to eat or if you have clothes to wear on your body. For your life is worth more then food or the clothes you wear. Remember the crows, how they don't plant or harvest, how they don't have no cribs or barnlofts, and God feeds them. You are kept in much more love than birds. And which person among you -even worrying about it -can add an inch to his height? So if you can't do even this little thing, why should you be anxious about solving any of the rest of your problems? Does the cornflower worry about growing up? It don't work nor make clothes. But I say to you, not even Solomon, in all the Godly attention he got, got dressed as one of these wild flowers. And if God gives the crop of the field its day, and on the next day after harvesting, its stalks is left to be plowed under, what more, folk of little faith, can you expect? So don't give yourself over to your appetite or thirst, or lifting up weighty things, for such are pursued by folk stuck in earth pursuits. But you, remember your Parent, God, knows you have body needs. What to do? Get in touch with God and your body needs will be given to you. Don't be afraid, little orphaned children, that your Godly Parent can't help. God wants to give you the peace of the skies of existence. Sell what you got for it. Give out of love. Empty your savings for each other. You have a moneybag that you can't overuse, that a thief can't steal, and no insect can destroy. Where you invest, that is where your heart will be.

The Sudden Return Of Jesus

Tighten your belts and keep sending up flares! And all of you, be watchful for the final coming of God's human Child returning home to stay, once and for all time, uniting folk in a great gathering, because the time is coming, and there will be a knocking at the door, and quick as a wink the doors will all be opened to him. Beloved are those workers who when the Familyhead returns he finds alert. Out of the depth of my being I say to you, he will be getting ready to come to them, sit at their dinner table, and when he comes, he will serve them dinner. The coming may be in the middle of the night, or at the rosy appearance of dawn or in this or that way, that he will find them. But, however, so happy will they be! You know this saying don't you? If the head of the house had only known what time of day the burglar was coming, he wouldn't have been away when the burglar broke in his house. You know to stay prepared because you don't know at what hour God's human Child is coming. Then Peter said, "Sir, are you telling this story to us or to everybody?" And said the Familyhead, "Who is the faithful housekeeper and the wise one, the one the head of the household places in charge of his staff, to give them regular meals? Beloved is that housekeeper who the returning Familyhead will find doing so. I tell you truthfully, everything at the Familyhead's disposal will be shared with this housekeeper. But if the housekeeper has got panging in the heart, while the Familyhead's coming is delayed, to start hurting the Familyhead's kids, eating, drinking and acting drunk, the Familyhead will be coming to that on some unpredictable day and time and he will be dressed down and stood with the doubters. That housekeeper, the one knowing the will of his Familyhead, but who isn't prepared or desirous of doing that, can expect a heavy whipping. But the one who doesn't know no better, worthy, but who acted misguided, will be whipped just a little. Everyone given many gifts will be expected to do much on their account, and someone trusted with much needs to account for it all the more.

Jesus Will Break Things Up

I have come to release a spirit of fire on the earth and so what! if I wanted, I could have started the burning even before now! I can have you put through the baptism I have suffered through and how can I be so beset up to the time when it is finished a long time from now! Do you think that I appeared to give peace to earth? No way! I'm telling you otherwise, a revolution. In a household of five there will be sides took up, three against two or two against three, pitting a dad against his son, and the son against the dad, the mom against her daughter and the daughter against the mom, the in-law mom against her marriage daughter in law and other ways around."

The Time Of Jesus's Return

And he told the crowds, "When you see clouds breaking from the west right away you say, 'Here comes a rainstorm' and it is. And when a south wind picks up, you say, 'It will be a scorcher!' and it is. You people pretending to know what is going on, the appearances of the earth and sky you know how to figure out, but how come you don't try to figure out the super-event of this time.

Settling With An Accuser

And why is it that among you no one tries on your own to make decisions based on what is right? For there you go, turning yourselves into plaintiffs and defendants leaving these things to judges and juries. Even on the way to court make an effort to settle with your fellow litigant. Next thing you know, you will be dragged in front of a judge, and the judge will find against you and after judgment's entered, you are in contempt somehow or other and turned over to the sheriff and the sheriff will throw you into jail. I say to you, get out of there while you can before you have paid out your last coin. In time, some people come gossiping to Jesus about some Galilean pilgrims that Pilate had tortured, mixing their blood with the blood of the animals they was transporting to sacrifice to God. And Jesus said to them, "Do you think they are bad characters more than other Galileeans because they suffered so? No way! And I will tell you something else, if all of you don't have God grasp your lives, all of you will suffer the same deadly and personal peril. How about the eighteen people who were killed when the tower fell on them at Saloam? Do you think they were loaded down with burdens beyond what others had, even other Jerusalem residents? No, I say to you, until all of you reform, you will find your lives in similar deadly and personal peril."

The Story Of A Fig Tree

Then he told them a story. "A certain fig tree is planted in a person's garden and the owner comes to pick fruit off of it and there is none to be found. So he says to the gardener, 'See here! I've come three years over here to pick fruit off this fig tree and I still can't find any. Cut this tree down! And by the way, why's this ground so bad here?' Then the gardener said to him, 'Sir, how about we leave the tree be for a year and maybe for some reason digging around it and fertilizing it will help. Then maybe it may start bearing fruit. If not, do the other thing. You will be right to have it cut down.'"

Healing A Girl With Arthritis

Then one day while he was teaching in a church on Sunday, See! here come a woman whose life has had a special need for eighteen years. She was arthritic and couldn't get up by herself at all. Seeing this, Jesus spoke to her and said, "Maam, you are cured of this crippling." And he took her by the hands and she was healed quick and she started giving thanks to God. But the congregation's board chairman had a fit because Jesus healed this lady on Sunday and he said in front of the congregation, "There are six days in the week to do work. During those six days do your healing! Not on Sunday!" But the Familyhead answered him and said, "Hypocrites, don't each of you have his bull or donkey loose at the trough on Sunday or lead them to water? Satan had bound her, a living daughter of Abraham, for eighteen years. Wasn't it fitting that she get set free from this on Sunday?" And when they all heard this, they all felt ashamed and the whole church started feeling the joy in the awesome happening done by him.

The Story Of A Seed And Yeast

Then he asked, "What is God's homeland like and what does it resemble? It is like a small mustard seed which a person finds and plants in his garden. And it flourishes and grows into a tree, and the birds of the sky nest on its branches." Then again he said, "What is God's Homeland like? It is like yeast which a woman kneads deeply into dough three times until it can rise."

Limits To Entry Into God's Life

And then Jesus went on to other cities and towns traveling to Jerusalem. And someone asked him, "Sir, are few saved?" And he said, "You have to scramble to get in through a narrow door. I say to you there are lots of people bustling to get in and not all of them can. After the point when the housekeeper gets up to go lock the door, you will be shut outside, and you knock at the door, saying, 'Familyhead, Sir, Open up!' And in reply a voice will say to you, 'I don't know who you are. Where did you come from? Then you will beg and say, 'Don't you remember we ate with you and drank with you and heard you teaching in the streets.' And the voice will say to you, 'I don't know you. What is it? Get away from me. This is all improper.' There will be crying out and gnashing of teeth when you imagine how God loves Abraham, Issac and Jacob and all the prophets that made it through the door of limits into God's Homeland and you are being kicked out. And then people will come from the east and west and from the north and south who will be invited to take a seat in God's homeland. And notice it is the least who will be first and it is the first who will be last.

Jesus's Anguish About Jerusalem

And at another hour some Pharisees came to him saying, "Leave and get out of here, because Herod wants to kill you." And he said to them, "You advise me to leave from that crafty old fox. See what I do! I treat the mentally ill and do healing today and tomorrow and then on the third day I am done. Nevertheless, it is necessary that I keep going on today and tomorrow and on the day after because it is inappropriate for a prophet to be killed outside Jerusalem. Jerusalem, Jerusalem, killer of prophets, and stoner of those who are sent to give the city good news. How often I have wanted to gather your children to me in the way a hen takes her chicks under her wing, and you don't want it. See now! your city is lost. I say to you, you may not see me again until you get to say, 'Blessed is the one coming in the name of the Familyhead.'"

A Man With Swelling Comes To Jesus Under Surveillance

Then it happened while he was going toward Jerusalem, some of the ranking Pharisees broke bread with Jesus on a Sunday and they watched Jesus like a hawk. And Look at that! some fellow who has dropsy, and his arms and legs was swollen real bad, came in front of Jesus. And responding, Jesus said to the Hebrew translators and Pharisees, "Is there any authority to heal on Sunday or not?" But they kept still. And Jesus, taking hold of the fellow, healed him and the dropsy was set off. And to them he said, "Which of you if your lamb fell into a well would not immediately pull it out, even on Sunday?" And none could reply to that.

The Story Of Seating Guests

Then he told the invited guests a story, noticing how the they was picky over places of honor, saying to them, "When you're invited by someone to a marriage dinner, don't sit down at the most honored place, sometime, maybe, the host may welcome a more honorable guest, and then when he arrives, you will be requested, "Give up the place of honor," and then you shuffle down to the least important place in shame. So when you are invited, arriving, go to the last place so that when the other invited guests come the host's voice will say to you, 'Friend, move up to a better seat.' Then there will be honor for you in front of everybody seated at the table with you. When someone tries to exalt himself, he will be humiliated, and the one who acts humble gets honored." And Jesus said to the host, "When you plan lunch or dinner, don't ask your friends or your brothers, or kin, or rich neighbors. Sometime, maybe, they will

return the invitation as a repayment for you. Instead, when you plan your banquet, invite the poor, the convicts, the crippled and blind. You will be spiritually blessed because they can't return your invitation, and the return of the invitation will happen at the time the innocent will be brought back to life.

The Story Of A Dinner

After he heard this, a fellow sitting down at the table eating with Jesus said, "A fellow must be happy who eats bread in God's Homeland." Jesus said to him, "A certain person prepares a formal dinner and invited many people, and sent a worker of his at the hour of the dinner to say to the guests, 'Come, dinner's ready.' And the worker began summoning them one at a time. The first one said to the worker, 'I just bought a field and I have an emergency demanding that I have to see to. I have to beg off. Please accept my apology.' And another said, 'I just bought five pairs of oxen and I was just going to train them. I have to beg off. Please accept my apology.' And another said, 'I just got married and so I can't come.' And returning, the summoner told the Familyhead what they'd said. Enraged, the head of that house said to the worker, 'Right now, go into the streets and alleys of the city and bring back the poor, the convicts, the blinded and lame.' Then the worker reported, 'Sir, I did what you told me to do and still there's room.' So the Familyhead said to the worker, 'Go out to the country roads and field paths and insist that people come since I want this dinner of mine to be filled up. For it's for sure that none of the invited ones will be coming to taste my dinner.'"

Cost Of Serving Jesus

Then more and more of a crowd come up around him and he turned his head in their direction and said to them, "If anyone comes to me and does not spurn his own father and mother and wife and children and brothers and sisters and even his own life, he can't be my companion. Whoever won't carry a cross for himself and follow me can't be my companion. Who among you, wanting to build a tall building, don't first sit down and figure on every stone needed to get it done? Otherwise, after laying the foundation, the building will not get completed and everybody seeing it will begin hooting at you saying, 'That fellow started to build and now look, he can't get it done.' Doesn't a general marching against another general quickly decide against battle before it starts when he figures his 10,000 must battle 20,000 marching for his opponent? And fearing battle, he sends an agent to seek peace while he is a safe distance away. Just so, each of you who can't detach yourselves from your own initiatives won't be able to be my companion."

Fake Salt

"Now salt is a good thing. But what if the salt is fake? Does it season anything then? It won't do anybody any good either in the ground, or in a garbage dump. Throw it out! Anyones got ears, listen."

The Story Of The Lost Sheep

There was among those drawing up to him lots of tax collectors and people some considered bad characters listening to Jesus. And the Pharisees and Hebrew translators were whispering among themselves saying that he consorts with bad characters and eats with them! Jesus told them this story. "Which one of you having one hundred sheep and one of them gets loose, doesn't leave behind the ninety nine in the pasture and go after the lost one to find it? And finding it, don't he place it on his shoulders joyfully and going to his house, don't he call his friends and neighbors together and say to them, "Share my good luck with me, because I found my lost sheep." I tell you that there is as much joy felt in the skies of existence upon saving a bad character as at having ninety nine innocent people who don't need reformation.

The Story Of The Lost Coin

Or a woman had ten coins and if she loses one coin don't she light a lamp and sweep through the house and look carefully until she finds it? And when it is found, she calls in her friends and neighbors saying, "Share my good luck with me because I found my lost money." So it is, I say to you, how you feel is felt by the ones close to God when every single bad character is saved."

The Story Of The Lost Son

Then Jesus said, "A man had two sons. And the younger one of them said to the father, 'Dad, give me my share of your property. And the dad divvied from their livings. And not too long after this, the younger son got all of his together, and left home for a land far away and there he blew his inheritance in reckless living. After he had spent all of it, there came a great crop failure in that place and he began to feel the consequences of being broke. And he went to help out one of the citizens of that place who sent him to a field of his to care for hogs. And he longed to eat the carob pods that the hogs were feeding on but none were give him. And walking around a lot, he says to himself, how is it that the hired hands of father eat bread to their fill and I am hungry and starved most to death. After getting up to leave, I am going to my father and I will say to him, Dad I have done wrong to the very skies of existence as well as you. I am no long worthy to claim heirship as your son. Do with me as one of your hired hands. And after getting up to leave, he went to his own father. While he was still at a distance on the way back, his father saw him and was filled with emotion and took to running and threw his arms around his neck and kissed him. And the son said to him, "Father, I have done wrong to the very skies of existence as well as you. I am no longer worthy to claim heirship as your son. But the father called to his house staff, 'Quick, bring me my best coat and get him dressed, and give him the sealing ring for his hand and shoes for his feet and get the steer, the one fed out, and kill it, for we are going to celebrate with a feast because this my son who was dead has come back to life, and who was lost has been found and they began to celebrate.' Now the older son of his was in the field. And as he was walking along coming near the house, he heard music and sounds of people dancing and he called out to one of the fieldhands to find out what was happening. And he told him, 'Your brother has come home and your father's killed the steer he had been feeding out to celebrate because he's got back his son in good shape. And the older son was so mad he wouldn't go inside. His father come out to greet him too. But he responded to his father. 'See here! how many years have I done for you and never crossed your orders and not once did you slaughter even a goat for me to celebrate with my friends. But now when this son of yours, this one who has used up your living doing blasted things, you go on and cook up the steer we have been feeding out.' But the father said to him, 'Child of mine! You always are with me and all I have is yours. It was necessary for the homecoming to be celebrated and enjoyed because your brother was dead and he's come back to life. He was lost and now he's been found.'"

The Story Of The Incompetent Deputy

Then he told his companions, "There was a wealthy man who hired a deputy, and he was being charged with malfeasance on account of him wasting property. After he summoned him, the wealthy man said to him, 'What do I hear about you? Give me an account of your charge. You are not competent to stay my deputy.' The deputy said to himself, 'What will I do when the boss takes my charge from me? I'm not strong enough for construction and I'm too proud to beg. I may have to do some figuring so that when I am fired from deputy, they may welcome me into their homes.' And summoning the debtors of his boss one at a time, he said to one, 'How much do you owe my boss?' And he said, 'A hundred gallons of olive oil.' Then he said to him, "You be responsible for your own figures" And while they was sitting there, he quick scribbled in fifty. Then to another he said, 'You, how much do you owe?' That one said, 'A thousand bushels of corn.' Then he said to him, 'You be responsbile for this ledger account of yours,' and he scribbled in eight hundred. And the boss approved of the changes allowed by the deputy because he proved he was competent. So it is that the children of this time need competence to survive while also acting on behalf of all children of the light. And I say to you, act for your friends against money interests since there may come a time for you needing to pick a home that they'll take you in temporary. A fellow faithful in a little thing is faithful in much and one who cheats a little, cheats a lot. So, if you can't be a faithful folk serving money grubbers, how can you believe you can be true to yourself? And if you cannot be faithful folk in the service of another person, will you give that person your service? No insider can serve two bosses. For one he hates and the other he loves, or one he longs to be faithful to and the other he will be shrewdly mismanaging. You cannot serve both God and money.

God Knows The Heart

There was listening to these things Pharisees loving to have money in their pockets, and they hooted Jesus. And he said to them, "You are law-abiding in front of people, but God knows your hearts. One acting superior in front of people is despicable in front of God. Sure, there was the laws of Moses and a string of prophets until John the Baptist come. Then it was announced the coming of the Homeland of God and each one living in it is being persecuted!

Easier it will be for the sky and earth to die than for the people to realize that the law give Moses has changed by a single stroke of one of its letters. People abandoning each others sexual partners are committing faithless in love and the ones taking up with the ones abandoned are acting faithlessness to love too."

The Story Of The Rich Man And Lazarus

"Once there was a rich fellow and he dressed fine and even wore linen underwear and lorded it every day happy at being so gorgeous. And then there's another, so poor, named Lazarus, who was destitute at the rich man's gate covered with sores and boils. And all he could hope for was to get crumbs to eat thrown away off the table of the rich. And the dogs would come to lick his sores and boils. Then the poor fellow died and was taken up out of his anguish to be hugged by Abraham. And the rich fellow died and was buried. And he heard such singing that he looked up from his situation tormented every minute, and he saw Abraham from a distance and Lazurus at his side. And he called out shouting, 'Parent Abraham, I am so adamantly miserable, send Lazurus so that he can dip the tip of his finger in water and dab this tongue of mine, because I'm so stubborn I'm to stay suffering here in these flames, rather than admit the laws of Moses has changed.' But Abraham said, 'Don't you remember the good things you had in your life at the poor's expense and Lazurus just the opposite? Now here he's being cheered up and you can't be. And in these lifestyles between you and him there's a great chasm dug out so that the ones wishing to go from this place to you can't jump it and the ones wishing to can't find a way across.' But the rich man said, 'I beg you, parent. You still could send him into the house of my family. I have five brothers who need to get warned! So that they won't end up in this flaming place.' But Abraham said, 'They have Moses and the prophets. They can listen to them.' But the rich man said 'No, parent Abraham, maybe if someone who has been dead will go to talk to them, they will change over to think different.' And Abraham said to him, 'If they won't listen to Moses and the prophets, they sure won't trust someone that has got up and walked around after being dead.'"

Jesus's Sayings

Then he told his companions sayings. It's impossible not to stumble sometimes, but take a real deep agonizing breath until your lungs feel the spirit in your chest and you will come through. It's better for a person if they put a concrete tie around their neck and jump in a lake than to cause a little child to stumble. Watch out for each other. If a fellow in God's ring of sisters and brothers acts wrong, acts like they's trying to bust out, help them stay in the circle, and if they get their heads to understanding they've made the wrong moves forget their bolting ever happened. Don't matter if a friend acts contrary every day of the week and only changes to act right on the seventh, forget the week's bad doings ever happened. And the companions said to the Familyhead, "Let us feel this intuitionl." And the Familyhead said, "If you have faith as a seed of a wild mustard, you could, if you wanted, tell a mulberry tree, 'Pick yourself up by the roots and plant yourself in the sea.' And it would obey you." "How many among you has a worker plowing along or herding livestock, who, as he comes out of the field, says to him when he is going by, yes, right then, 'Get your dinner?' Instead what's said to him is, 'Get dinner ready and once it is ready wait on me until I am done eating and drinking, and then you can eat and drink.' Can the boss be unhappy with a worker when he gets done everything expected of him? So it is with you when you've done everything you must, you say, 'We, workers, are worn out all right, but how about that - we got done the extra to do!'"

Healing Ten Lepers

And then he went to go to Jerusalem and he went through the middle of Samaria and Galilee and going through it at one town they come across ten lepers who was standing apart from others at a distance. And these took to crying, saying, "Jesus we got faith in God. Won't you have mercy on us?" And seeing them he said, "Come on, show up in the church with the others." And it happened as they was going along they found their skin was cleaned up. One of those seeing he'd been healed of his leprosy ran back to Jesus and begun shouting out loud praising God and he fell on his face before the feet of the one who visited him with the healing love. And he was a Samaritan. But Jesus said to him "Weren't there ten that's got cleaned? Where's the other nine? Didn't they find it in themselves to turn back to give praise to God excepting this one of another stock?" And Jesus said to this one, "Get on up. Go on about your business. Your faith has healed you."

The Coming Of God's Homeland To Earth

Then the Pharisees began pestering him to know when God's Homeland was coming. He replied to them, "It don't come in the company of watchers, nor will the watchers be able to announce, 'Here it is!' or 'There it is.' God's Homeland is inside us." He said to the companions, "There will come days when you will wish for God's human Child so hard. You'll want to have just one blooming day back. But look like you will, you won't be able to see me. And you'll try to convince yourselves, 'See! Jesus is in this!' or 'Jesus is in that!' I know you may want to come to me personal, but you can't follow me right now. For just as the lightning flashes strike through the air creating light quickening the sky, so is God's human Child in this day. First it's necessary for him to suffer and give up to be persecuted for this generation." "And as it happened in the days of Noah, so will it be in the days of God's human Child. People ate, drank, married, lived husband and wife until the day Noah went into the ark, and there came a flood and all was turned topsy turvy. Another time come in the days of Lot. People ate, drank, shopped, sold stuff, planted, built. Then one day Lot hightailed it out from Sodom. It rained down fire and there's sulfur smell everywhere come from the sky and everything's turned topsy turvy. Just as significant will come a day when God's human Child will be revealed. In that day some will be out in the sun and their possessions will be in house. Word of advise, won't be no need to fetch them. And similar, some will be out in a field. Forget trying to get behind something. Remember Lot's wife. If a person tries to live life like they did before, that person will be turned topsy turvy. But if a person's life will be turned topsy turvy, that person will be really living! I say to you there will be a night come along when there's two sleeping, and one will be took away, and the other left. There will be two grinding away and one will be lifted up and the other left." And responding they said to him, "How, Sir?" And he said to them. "Where the physical body is, there also the buzzards will be hovering."

The Story Of The Widow And The Judge

And then he told them a story about the need for praying and not standing back, saying, "Once they was a judge who was in a certain city that wasn't scared of God and people didn't respect anyway. And a widow lived in that city and she come to him saying, 'I need some help for protection against someone's after me.' And he didn't want to spend the time on her. But after bit, he said to himself, 'Maybe I don't fear God or care if I'm respected for being fair by people, but since she just keep on bothering me if I don't, I will help this widow get justice so that I won't have to spend all the time with her pestering me.'" The Familyhead said, "Did you listen to what that crooked judge says? Don't God really want to do more justice for the saved ones who pray to him day and night and is he really going to take even as long to act? I tell you, God will be doing the work of justice quick. But when God's human Child comes will he find faithful ones on earth? Call the odds less than fifty-fifty."

The Story Of The Pharisee And The Tax Collector

Then he told a story to some overconfident, self-satisfied and arrogant people who had to do only with themselves and thought they were always right and looked down on everybody else. "Once there were two fellows that come to the temple to pray. One was a Pharisee and the other one a tax collector. The Pharisee stood there by himself praying all the right things, 'O God I give you such thanks that I am not so bad as the rest of the world's people, greedy, immoral, adulterous, and also as bad as that tax collector over there. I fast when I ought to, twice on Sundays, and give tithes on everything that I can get my hands on.' But the tax collector was standing far from the crowds not wanting to presume he's good enough to raise his eyes up to the skies of existence, and beating on his chest, saying, 'O God, forgive me, a no good.' I say to you

this fellow left for his house bearing God's approval more than the other one because all holding themselves up in pride will get reprimanded, and the humble will be lifted up."

Jesus Loves The Little Children

And there were brought to Jesus little children so he could hold them. But the companions, seeing that, demanded they go away. But Jesus called them to climb on his lap saying, "Have these children come to me for God's Homeland is as for children."

A Rich Official

A certain official wanted to ask him a question and said, "Fearless Friend, what do I do to inherit eternal life." And Jesus said to him, "Why call me fearless. None is fearless except the one God. You know the law. Don't commit adultery. Don't kill. Don't steal. Don't lie what you saw. Respect your mom and dad." And the official said, "I have obeyed all these from childhood." Hearing this, Jesus said to him, "Still there is one thing lacking in you. Sell every bit of your wealth, give it away to the poor, and you will have it stored in the skies of existence. Then come follow me." When he heard this, the guy was depressed because he'd been born to lots of money. Noticing him, Jesus got depressed too and said, "How hard it is for them that's got possessions to accept the Homeland of God. For easier it is for a camel to go through the eye of a sewing needle than for a wealthy guy to enter God's Homeland. Those hearing this said, "Then who can be saved?" And Jesus said, "What is impossible for people is possible for God." But Peter said to Jesus, "Look here. We've give up everything to go following after you!" Then he said to them, "Look. There is no one who gets life everlasting who don't give up house, sex partner, brothers and sisters, parents, or children for the sake of God's Homeland and a much greater reward in time and in eternity."

Jesus Foretells His Death A Third Time

Traveling along, Jesus said to the twelve, "See. we are going up into Jerusalem and all will get finished there that's written by the prophets about God's human Child. He will be turned over to the peoples and he will be scorned and he will be insulted and he will be spit on and he will be whipped until they kill him, and on the third day he will arise." And none of them understood because this saying was kept obscure from them and they did not know what these words meant.

Healing A Blind Beggar On The Road To Jericho

Then as he was coming to the outskirts of Jericho, there was some blind guy sitting there along the road begging. But hearing the crowd going by, he asked who chance had cause to pass by. They told him, "It's Jesus of Nazareth going through." And he started yelling, carrying on so, shouting out "Jesus Child of David, pity me." But the ones in front of the crowd told him to shut up to keep Jesus from paying attention to him. But the beggar contained to bawl out his need more than ever, "David's son, look over here, pity me." Stopping, Jesus commanded that the guy be brought to him. When he was brought there, Jesus asked him, "What do you want me to do for you?" And he said, "Sir, I want to be able to look up and see you." And Jesus said to him, "Look up! Your trust has saved you from affliction." And immediately he looked up and he followed along after, praising God. And all the people in the party gave thanks to God.

Jesus And Zakius

And going along, he walked through Jericho and there - Look! - was a man named Zakius. He was not only a tax collector but also a rich one. And he's trying to see Jesus - which one is he? -and he can't for the crowd and because he's too short. And running ahead, he climbed a sycamore tree so he could see things while they were passing through. And Jesus past under where Zakius perched, and looking up, Jesus said to him, "Zakius get down out of there, for today I've decided to stay at your house." And Zakius shimmied down and took him up on the offer with pride. And all the rest of the crowd started buzzing and whispering that Jesus went to eat with a fellow with a bad reputation. Zakius, for himself, just stood there, and then he told the Familyhead, "See here and now, half of my assets, Sir, I will give to the poor, and those I have cheated out of money, I will give back four times as much." And Jesus said to him, "Today a conversion has come to your house because he is a son of Abraham, and God's human Child came to pick out and save the lost."

The Story Of The Ten Stacks Of Bills

After this conversation, Jesus told another story as they were getting close to Jerusalem to prepare them because they was expecting a quick appearance of God's Homeland coming down. So, he said, "A fellow lucky in birth was getting ready to go to a faraway capital to get appointed governor and then return. Calling together ten of his assistants he spread out ten stacks of bills and told them, "Deal with these until I get back." Now the citizens of his country hated him and sent a spokesman against him, saying, "We don't want that guy to be our governor." And when he come home after receiving his authority to be governor, he called for the assistants who were given the stacks of bills to learn what profit they made. The first come in front of him saying, "Sir, I increased the stack you gave me ten times." And the Leader said to him, "Good, Good. You are a good assistant because in the short time I give you look what you got done! You can have authority over ten counties." And the second one come saying, "Your deposit with me, Sir, increased five times." So he said to that one, "Okay, you take five counties to govern." And then another one come saying, "Sir, See! Here is the stack you give me. I hid it in a shroud for I was too scared to do anything with it since you are so demanding. You take what you don't discard and reap what you don't sow." The Leader said to him, "From your own mouth you have judged yourself to be what you are, a bad assistant. How could you do this, knowing I am a man who takes what I don't discard and reap what I don't sow? Did you even invest my stack of bills at a bank? Then I could at least go collect interest." And to the other assistants standing before him, he said, "Take the stack from him and give them to the one that has made ten times what I give him." But they said to him, "Sir, he already has ten times the stack he started with!" The Leader replied, "I say to you that to the one who has, more will be give him. But from the one who hasn't done nothing, what he has he will lose. What about those enemies of mine that didn't want me to get appointed governor, bring them here to me and put them to death before my eyes."

Jesus Enters Jerusalem In Triumph

He said these things going along before going up into Jerusalem. And as they're approaching into Bethphage, also called Bethany, near to the Mount of Olives, Jesus sent two of the companions on an errand, telling them, "Go and on the way to that town, at the edge of it, you will find a young donkey that's been hitched that's not been rid by no one. Untie the donkey and bring it here. And if anyone asks you what you think you're doing, just tell them, 'The Leader has a need for it.'"

When they went to do the errand, they found the donkey just as Jesus said. When they was letting the donkey loose, they saw the owners of it coming, 'Why you taking our donkey?' They was wanting to know. They said, "Our Familyhead needs it." That satisfied them. And they took it to Jesus and put a couple of coats on the back of the donkey so Jesus could ride comfortable. And going in front of Jesus, some even threw their coats on the road. And when they came to the place where the road went downhill at the Mount of Olives, all the companions got filled with such a feeling of joy they acted like mad folk singing praiseful songs to God in a real loud voice for all of them was seeing God's doings, saying: "Blessed is the one coming, the ruler appointed by the Familyhead. Peace on earth, under watch from on high." And some of the Pharisees said to the Jesus, "Control these companions of yours down." But Jesus answered, saying, "If they shut up, the rocks will start shouting it out." And as they got close enough to see Jerusalem real close, Jesus himself cried out. Jesus said, "It could be these events precede peace if only you acknowledged this day! But now it's hid from your eyes. Now days will come upon you and the enemy will set up barricades in you and they will surround you and control you on all sides. And they will level you and destroy your children within you, and they will not leave one stone upon stone in you because you did not acknowledge the time of your visitation."

Cleansing Of The Temple

And going into the church, he began to throw out the ones selling goods telling them. "Leave because it's written that 'The house of God is to be a house for worship,' but you have turned it into a hideout for robbers." And afterwards, he taught that day at the church. Then the churchmen, and the Hebrew translators and also the most important of the people set to figuring how they'd kill him. But they couldn't figure anything to do because all the people hung upon what they was hearing.

The Authority Of Jesus Is Questioned

And one of the days while teaching the people in the church and evangelists, churchmen and Hebrew translators with their elders came up to him and said to him, "Tell us by whose authority you do these things? Who is giving you this charge?" And he answered them saying, "I will answer you with a question" and he said to them, "The gift of reconciliation from John - did it proceed out of the very skies of existence or from something personal?" Then they started discussing it among themselves saying, "If we claim it's from from where God exists, he will ask us, 'Why didn't you trust him?' but if we say, 'personal,' the crowd will all throw rocks at us and kill us for they are convinced John was a prophet." And they answered they didn't know where it come from. And Jesus said to them, "Then I am not going to tell you in whose authority I do these things."

The Story Of The Vineyard And The Killer Lessees

He sat down to tell the crowd this story, "A man planted some rows of grapes and share rented it to some farmers that lived close and left his farmhouse to go away for quite a bit of time. When it's time to collect his share, he sent an employee to the farmers to get him his share of the grapes from the grapes he planted. But the farmers sent him back empty handed after beating him up. But he persisted, sending another employee. But this guy also got himself beat up, and was treated like a dog and sent back empty handed. But he persisted and sent a third. But this one got hit on so bad he's disabled. So the landowner of the grape rows says to himself, 'What will I do? I will send my beloved son. Surely they will respect him.' But seeing the beloved son coming, the farmers got together among themselves and figured, 'This one is the heir to this place. We will kill him and then get it cheap from the owner's estate.' And they beat him bad in the rows of grapes until they killed him. Then what do you suppose the owner of the rows of grapes will do? He will come and destroy these farmers and he will give the farm to others. And the people listening said it was such a shame, and figured out he's talking about their land, and said, 'Don't have that happen to us!' Then he looked them straight in the eye and said, "Remember this: 'The stone that the builders rejected, this gets set as the cornerstone.' Everyone is going to get broke to pieces that's sent to remove this stone. From this experience, and during the sending, some will get themselves crushed." And the Hebrew translators and churchmen wanted to catch him and strangle him right there with their own hands, right then, but they were scared off because so many people was around, because they knew this story was directed at them.

Paying Taxes To Caesar

And they kept a surveilance, sending spies in to pretend that they themselves was pilgrims so they might listen to a story, as he would tell them firsthand. They was secretly paid by the ones in charge of the church. And they questioned him saying, "Teacher, we know that you are trying to say what is right and in your teaching you don't show no favoritism, and you will tell us the truth about the way to do what God wants: Is it right for Caesar to tax us?" But Jesus could see through cunning tricks, and he said to them, "Show me one of the Roman coins. Who is the person engraved on it?" They said, "Caesar." And Jesus said to them, "For that very reason give the things of Caesar to Caesar and the things of God, to God." And they just didn't have enough ability to trip Jesus up with words to turn the crowd against him and they had to keep silent stunned by his answer.

The Nature Of Life After Death

Some of the Saducees come to him - they are ones saying no one gets resurrected - interrogating Jesus saying, "Teacher, Moses wrote for us,'If any brother dies having a wife, and he don't have a child, then his brother is supposed to take the wife and raise up offspring on behalf of his brother.' Now there was seven brothers and the first brother dies childless, and the second, and the third takes his wife, and all seven die leaving not one kid. Finally, the woman dies. Then the woman enters into the resurrected life. Which one of them is she the wife of? For seven of them had her as wife." And Jesus said to them, "Children in this space of time marry and are married, but the ones experiencing that afterdeath time don't. No one takes life situations over into death. They share eternity with God's life companions. Still children, they become risen children being reborn with God. Yes! the dead get up from death. Didn't Moses make that known at the experience of the fiery bush burning full of God's revelation as he called upon his Familyhead, God of Abraham, Issac and Jacob. God is the God of the dead and living, for all live in God." Then, replying, some of the Hebrew translators said "Teacher you answered well." And they didn't take it upon themselves to interrogate him any more. Then Jesus told them, "Why do you only say that God's child is the son of David?

Doesn't it say in the psalm, The Familyhead said to my Familyhead, Sit down on my right hand While I make your enemies a footrest. Now if David calls him his Familyhead, how can it be enough for people just to think of the coming one as the son of David?"

A Warning About Translators Of Scripture

After answering the questions of the crowd, he said to the companions, "Be careful of the scheming Hebrew translators walking in fancy clothes, drawing greetings from people in the stores, taking the first seats in the churches and being served first at meals. They take the houses of widows and try to give the appearance of being devout. They will receive severe judgement."

Comment On A Widow's Church Offering

Looking up, Jesus saw some rich persons giving into the church offering box. Then he saw some poor widow put in a gift of a couple pennies. And he said, "Truly I say to you that that widow who's poor has put in a greater gift than they. All the rich ones gave out of their excess over what they wanted, but she contributed from her needs to live on."

A Prophecy The Main Jerusalem Church Is Headed For Ruins

And while some are talking about the church, how the stones was so beautiful, and the dedications to it decorated it so nice, Jesus said, "All these things you're looking at, the days will pass them by, and there won't be left of them a single stone on top of another that's not been knocked down."

Miracles And Persecutions

And they asked him this, "Teacher, when are these things to be and what miracle will there be when it is destined for these things to happen?" But Jesus said, "Keep on the lookout so that you don't get caught off guard! Many will come claiming to be acting in my authority, saying, 'I am here', and, 'The times are drawing near.' But don't be drawn after them. When you hear of wars and mobs milling around, don't get scared. It's got to be that these things happen first. But the endtime is not immediate. Then he said to them, "Ethnic groups will arise against ethnic groups and country against country, and there will be great earthquakes, hunger in various places and outbreaks of disease. Disasters will happen and in the cosmos there will be scary events. Before all these things, enemies will lay hands on you and persecute you, turning you over to their authorities for assembly and prison, taking you before governors and dictators for my name. It will be your duty to give witness. Stiffen your courage not to vacillate when called to defend yourselves. I will give you speech and wisdom so none can contradict or refute you when faithless ones array themselves against you. Expect betrayal by your parents and brothers and sisters and neighbors and friends. You will be hated by everybody on my account. But not a hair from your head may be destroyed! By patiently enduring, you will preserve your souls.

A Warning Of The Destruction Of Jerusalem

When next you see the city of Jerusalem under seige by soldiers, then expect it to be utterly destroyed. Its population will flee into hills except those in the middle of it who will die on the spot and those in these towns around here may not escape from the destruction either. That is a time of vengeance that is a fulfillment of many scriptures. Doomed will be pregnant women and those nursing babies in those days. There will be so much trouble upon the earth and anger within people, and people will be falling down from swordplay, and everybody will be led away prisoners to strangers, and Jerusalem will be trampled underfoot by strangers until the era of these strangers ends.

The Final Coming Of Jesus

And there will be strange doings on the sun and moon and stars, people despairing in fear and dread about the world, and the elemental forces of the universe will be unpredictable. And then, they will see God's human Child coming upon the clouds in power and great bearing. And when these things begin to happen, you can raise yourselves up and lift up your heads because your liberator is on the way. And Jesus told them a story. "See the fig tree and all the trees. When they start leafing out, and you see it for yourself, you know the summer is near at hand. So also will you know, when you see these events, that God's Homeland is near. Yes, I am serious when I am telling you that the family of people will not pass away before it will all have happened. The sky and land will disappear but my promises will not disappear."

Holding On Until The Endtime

"Bear up among yourselves so you don't weigh down your confidence by indulging in excesses and intoxications or falling victim to life's anxieties until one day life closes in on you suddenly as a trap. It will be coming quickly upon everyone living upon every face of the earth. Watch out for the prohibitions every day so you will have strength to escape all those things about to happen and so you can stand before God's human Child." And he was at the church during the days teaching and he spent the nights at the mountain known for

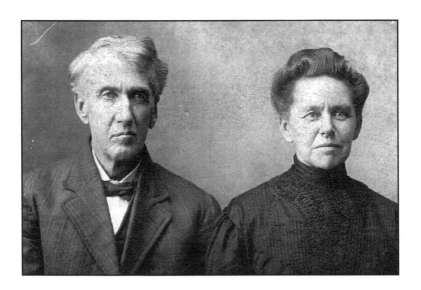

its olives. And a crowd came early in every morning to him in the church to hear him.

The Plot To Kill Jesus

Then the time come for the feast of the unleavened bread called Passover. And the senior churchmen and the Hebrew Translators tried to figure how to kill him, only they was scared to because of the people. Then dark play took hold of Judas, the one called Iscariot, one of the number of companions. And leaving, Judas went to conspire with the churchmen and soldiers how to deliver him over. And they welcomed him and arranged to pay him a fee. And Judas did what he promised them he would do and looked for his chance to catch Jesus for them away from the crowds.

Jewish Feast Day Preparation

Then there came the day of the feast of the unleavened bread in which it was necessary to slaughter the feast day lamb. And Jesus sent Peter and John saying, "Go, get us ready for the Passover meal." They said to him, "Where do you want reservations?" He said to them, "Look, go into the city where you will meet a fellow carrying a huge serving size clay jar full of water. Follow him into the house where he goes and say to the owner of the place, 'The teacher sends us to ask you to reserve a room where I can eat a Passover meal with my companions?' This very one can show you a big furnished upstairs room. Stay there and get it ready." After they got there, they discovered the guy as Jesus had said and they prepared for the Passover.

The Last Dinner With The Familyhead

And when it was time, Jesus set down to dinner and the future missionaries did too. And Jesus said to them, "With all my heart, I have longed for this feast-day to eat with you before my suffering. Now I say to you that I will never eat with you again until the time when the Homeland of God is established." And receiving the cup he give thanks for it and said, "Take this and pass it around among yourselves. I tell you that unless I drink from this harvest of the grapes now the Homeland of God may not come." And taking the bread, he give thanks for it and broke it and give it to them saying, "This is my body which I give up for you. Do this in my memory. This drink establishes the new contract in my blood which I will shed for you. See! the hand that is giving me over is at this very table. Soon, God's human Child must leave, taken away by conspiracy, though doomed is that man who betrays me." And they begun looking around to each other to figure which one this to be about to happen to.

Missionaries Arguing Over Precedence

Then they started arguing among themselves which of them would be considered the most important. But he said to them, "Authorities over the people wield power among them and the dominant ones among them call themselves gracious. But you are not to be as they. Instead have the best one among you be as a child and serve, doing the right things. For who is more honored, one who sits on his butt or one who serves? Isn't it the seated one? But I was in the midst of you as one who serves. You are ones who stand with me in my trials. And I leave my inheritance to you as it was willed to me by my Parent, my boss, so that you can eat and drink from my table in the world which is mine to rule and be set up as the power wielders over the twelve tribes of Israel."

A Prophecy That Peter Is Going To Deny Jesus

"Simon, Simon. Watch out! A bad impulse is working inside you demanding to take ahold to sift us out of you as is done with wheat. But I bend myself to you so your faith won't fail you. And when you return to normal, I will strengthen the sisters and brothers through you." But Peter said to him, "Sir, I am ready to follow you to prison or to die for you." But Jesus said, "I say to you Peter, a rooster won't be calling in the day before three times you disown knowing me."

Sending Out Missionaries Without Money, Luggage, Or Shoes

And he said to them, "When I sent you out without money or luggage or shoes why didn't you feel inferior?" And they said, "They are of no account." And he said to them, "Now anyone having money, go on, take it away as well as the bag. Go now, and if you have needs, sell your cloths and market your sword. I remind you of this writing, it is fulfilled in me, And he was counted a homeless person for, in the end, it means me. And they said,"Sir, see here are two swords." But he said to them, "It's okay."

Prayer On The Mount Of Olives

And leaving, he went according to his custom to the Mount of Olives, and the companions followed him. Then coming to the place, he said to them, "Pray that you don't yourselves have to stand trial." And Jesus went away by himself a stone's throw away. And kneeling, Jesus got in touch with God through prayer saying, "God, if you want to, take this cup from me. Anyway, it's not my desire but yours that I will do." Then there appeared a Godly messenger from God who revived him. And worked up feverish, he prayed harder than ever before. And there come sweat over Jesus like drops of blood streaming off of his praying form fallen to the ground. And then standing up after praying and going back to the companions, he found them sleeping off their

anxiety. And he said to them, "Why are you resting? Get up, pray that you won't be put on trial."

Jesus Is Arrested

While he was still talking, See! a crowd is coming and one of them talking is Judas, one of the twelve, bringing them and he approached Jesus and kissed him. But Jesus says to him, "You deliver up god's Human Child by a kiss?" Then figuring out what was happening to Jesus, the companions said, "Sir, Sir. Can we kill him with a sword?" And one of them accompanying the authorities did get cut with a sword. It was an assistant and the stroke gashed his right ear. But Jesus intervened and said, "Stop these doings." And he touched the guy's ear and healed it. Then Jesus said to the ones coming with the churchmen and their soldiers and the elders, "Why do you come at night with swords and clubs? I'm with you every day in the church and you were not handcuffing me. But it's all right, this is your hour and you bear the authority of dankness anyway."

Peter Denies Knowing Jesus

So they took him with them and went to the house of the head churchman. Peter followed behind at a distance. While they was kindling a fire in the middle of the churchman's patio in front of the house, where others was, Peter set himself down with them. Eyeing him, a girl employee who was also sitting in the firelight stared at him and said, "This guy was with him too." But Peter denied it, saying, "No I don't know him, lady." And after a spell another seeing him said, "You are one of them too." But Peter said, "Fellow, I'm not either." And after about another hour passed by, some fellow became insistent, saying, "I'm for sure. This guy was with him and I know for he is a Galileean." But Peter said, "Man, I don't know what you're talking about." And immediately, there come the cockadoodledooooooooo of a rooster. And turning, the Familyhead looked straight at Peter and Peter remembered the serious words as he told him before that a rooster would cry that very day after three times you disown me. And going outside, Peter cried for a little while.

Jesus Is Beat Up By Cops

And some guys come to take Jesus, making fun of him, and beating him, and they covered Jesus's eyes asking him, "Prophet, tell us which one of us is whipping you?" And they's talking other things to him, saying many words against God. And as the morning broke, Jesus was taken in front of the Sanhedrin, the main churchmen and Hebrew translators and them acting as judges and such, and he was brought before them in the Sanhedrin council meeting where they said to him, "If you're God's Child, confess it." But Jesus said to them, "Even if I told you, you wouldn't believe me. If it's a question, why don't you answer it. The time is ripe when God's Child will be seated at the right hand of God's throne." And all of them said, "Are you the Child of God?" And he said to them, "You just said I am." But they said to Jesus, "What more kind of witness do we need? We have heard enough about it from his own mouth."

Jesus Took To Pilate

And they adjourned, the whole bunch of them, and took Jesus before Pilate. They told Pilate the charges saying, "We discovered this guy misleading our people, and urging people to hold back paying taxes to Caesar and saying he's God's Child who's to govern." But Pilate said to the churchmen and the crowd, "I can't find this guy to be guilty of nothing." But they kept demanding, saying, "He's stirring up riots and encouraging sedition among all the Jews, beginning at Galilee and now here."

Jesus Took To Herod

After listening to this, Pilate figured the fellow as a Galileean, and, because he knew that Galilee is under Herod's authority, he sent Jesus to Herod, also present in Jerusalem for the holidays. But Herod has seen Jesus being praised so by the people, and it was for a long time he's been wanting to see Jesus on account of hearing so much about Jesus and Pilate was also hoping to see some kind of miracle being done by him. So Pilate interrogated Jesus respectfully but Jesus just wasn't going to respond with no miracle. And the religious leaders and their cronies the political lackies stays standing there raising hell and charging Jesus with this and that. While they's slandering Jesus, Herod sparred with them concerning what to do and making fun of their carrying on, and dressing Jesus in a coat of many colors he sent Jesus up to Pilate. They happened to be friends, Herod and Pilate was, with each other at that time, whereas used to be they hated each other.

Jesus Given A Death Sentence

Then Pilate summoned all the bunch of churchmen and the people and their representatives and said to them, "Here you come bringing back to me this Jesus you're labeling a revolutionary of the people and you know I have examined him and I found nothing in this guy to charge him with after you wanted to persecute him. And neither did Herod. So now Herod sends Jesus back to me, does he! And See! there is nothing serious enough for a death penalty done by him. After giving him some licks, I will set him free." Then they all together kept crying out demanding, "Keep Jesus and release Barabas to us."

Barabas was a guy who's started a riot in the city and been a murderer thrown into prison. But again Pilate called upon them, wanting to release Jesus. But, "No," they shouted, "Crucify. Crucify Jesus!" Then for a third time, he said to them, "For what good reason can I do that? I can't find him guilty of nothing worth the death penalty. After a whipping, I will release him." But they kept insisting with great shouts requesting Jesus be crucified. And their clamor won the day. And Pilate decided to convict Jesus. And he released from prison the killer who'd been imprisoned for starting a riot which was what they demanded and as for Jesus he give him over to their will.

Jesus Crucified

And as they led Jesus away by force, they took hold of a guy named Simon who's from a place named Kuranus out in the county, and placed the cross on him to carry, walking behind Jesus. And behind him walked a crowd of people and women who was mourning and weeping over him. And turning to these,

Jesus said, "Daughters of Jerusalem, don't cry over me. Cry for yourselves and your children, because See! the days have come in which they will say, 'Happiest are those who can't have babies, and the wombs which won't get fertilized, and breasts that won't nurse.'" And Jesus quoted Hosea where it's wrote, "They cry to the mountains, Shelter us, And to the hills, Bury us. If these things are done to the green sapling, what may happen to the old dry wood?" And they also brought two other so called criminals with Jesus to be put to death. And when they come to the place called Skull Hill, there they put Jesus on a cross and these criminals too, one on the right and the other on the left. And Jesus said, "Parent, forgive them, for they don't understand what they're doing." Then they took off his clothes and divided them up to the winners throwing dice. The people had stayed to see all this. And the churchmen kept up mocking what's happening, saying, "He saves others. Have Jesus save himself, if he's this so called 'savior' Jesus." And after they was done mocking him, the soldiers fetched cheap sour wine and brought it to him, saying, "If you're really in charge of the Jews, save yourself. Isn't it wrote down over you a sign saying about you that, 'This one is in charge of Jews.'" Then one of the criminals hanging next to Jesus spoke against God saying, "Aren't you God's Child come to earth? Save yourself and us too!" But responding to that, the other convict said to him, "I don't personally think you have offended God in any way just because you are sentenced. We are here justly since we did the crimes that we're sentenced for. But you didn't do nothing wrong." And he said to Jesus, "Remember me when you go into your Homeland." And Jesus said to him, "Truthfully, I am telling you, you will be with me today in paradise."

Jesus Dies

And it got to be about two in the afternoon and it turned dark out everywhere on earth as it reached three o'clock. The sun stopped shining. The curtain of the inner room of the church was split. And crying out in a great shout, Jesus said, "My Parent, into your hands, I give over my soul." After saying that he give up breathing. After seeing this, the Roman soldiers become frenzied, praising God, saying, "Really, this man was innocent." And all the crowd pressing together viewing, saw the event, and returned back to the city struck with the event emiotionally. There were many standing in the crowd who'd known Jesus for a long time and women who had followed Jesus from the Galilee ministry time who saw all this.

Jesus Is Buried

And See! there's a guy named Joseph, a member of the Sanhedrin council, a good guy and right thinking too. He's definitely not one who agreed with the decision to do away with Jesus. He was from Aramathea, a city of Judea, and a guy who'd waited for the coming of the time of God's world rule. He went up to Pilate and asked for the body of Jesus and he took it away and wrapped it in burial clothes and he took it into a tomb cut out from rock that nobody had every been laid into before. And it was the day of preparation and Sunday morning was dawning. And the women accompanied him, those who followed Jesus since Galilee times, and they saw where the tomb was before returning back home to prepare perfumes and ointments while Joseph placed the body in the tomb.

Jesus Is Alive Again

And Sunday went by peacefully according to custom. Then on that first day after Sunday, real early in the morning, these women went to the tomb taking those perfumes and ointments to prepare the body. But they saw the rock closing off the opening to the tomb has been rolled off to one side, and going in they couldn't find the body of their Familyhead, Jesus. At first they was uncertain what to do concerning this but now See! two forms of persons was standing outside there wearing flashing, dazzling clothes. And while they was getting more scared every minute and dropped their gaze down to the ground, these Godly messengers said to them, "Why you looking for one that's living at the place of the dead? God's Human Child is not here. He's arose. Remember he told you about this while he was still living in Galilee saying that it was necessary that the Orphan would get placed in the hands of scheming men and be crucified and on the third day he would arise from death." And then the memory flashed back to them. And returning from the tomb, they give the news to the eleven and all the rest. We are speaking of Mary Magdalene, and Johanna, and James's Mary, and the rest of them. And when these women come before them, their speech was like nonsense and the companions refused to believe them. But Peter got up and ran to the tomb and looking in he saw the grave wrappings was all that's in there and he returned wondering to himself what has happened.

A Walk To Emmaus

And See! two from the crowd witnessing the crucifixion was on that same day walking into a town about seven miles distant from Jerusalem named Emmaus. And they was talking to themselves about all they had experienced together. And it happened as they was talking together and arguing, Jesus himself come up to them and started walking with them. But their eyes was clouded at first so they couldn't recognize him. And Jesus said to them, "What are these stories you have been spreading between yourselves while you have been walking?" And they stood there so sad. In answer, one named Cleopas said to him, "You must be a stranger in Jerusalem not to know in that place during these days." And he said to them, "What things?" And they responded, "The things about Jesus of Nazereth, a man of prophetic power in deed and speech before God and all the crowds. how the churchmen and our elders delivered him over to a death judgment and crucified him. And we had so hoped that he was the one who's about to set Israel free. And now look with all these goings on, it's the third day after. And some of the women among us went this morning to the tomb. And after they went there, they said they didn't find the body and they imagined they saw Godly messengers who said Jesus was alive. And some others among us went to the tomb and found what they said was so, and he was not to be seen." And Jesus said to them, "Fools!" and "How stupid can be those with faithful hearts!. The prophets spoke of all of these things. Wasn't it necessary for God's Child while on earth to suffer and then enter into his role?" And he explained to them all of the happenings in all of the writings about himself beginning with Moses, then all the prophets. And they come to the town where they was going and they decided to put up there because they didn't want to go no further. And they begged him saying, "Stay with us! It's evening and the day's already most done." And Jesus went in to stay with them. And it happened as he was getting ready to eat supper with them, after getting passed the bread, while Jesus blessed it and broke it and give it to them, their eyes was opened to recognize Jesus. And he become a phantom in front of them. And they said to each other, "Didn't our hearts burn as he spoke to us on the road, and as he explained to us the writings?" And getting up from their meal they turned back to Jerusalem and found the eleven gathered together and others with them. And they told them that the Familyhead was raised up and Simon had seen it. And they brought out what happened on the road and how it was he come to be known to them breaking the bread.

Jesus Appears To The Missionaries

Then just as they was talking, Jesus stood there in their midst and says to them, "Peace be to you." And they was terrified and scared thinking they was seeing a goblin. And he said to them, "Why are you terrified? Why do you have so many doubts in your hearts? See my hands! my feet! I am Jesus. Touch me and see for yourselves. A goblin doesn't have any flesh and bones as you see I have." And after he said this, he showed them his hands and feet. But still they refused to believe the joy of these happenings, and while they was in shock, he said to them, "What do you have to eat? So they brought out to him a serving of some broiled fish." And picking it up, he ate it. And he said to them, "These very happenings are the stories of mine which I told to you while I was still with you, how it was necessary for all the writings to be fulfilled in the law of Moses and the prophets and the psalms about me." Then he explained to them the purpose of it all so as they could understand the writings. And he said to them, "Truly, God's Child while on earth suffered, rose from death on the third day and preached reconciliation in God's name to all peoples as predicted." And then Jesus charged them. "Beginning right here in Jerusalem you're to be witnesses to these things. And, Yes!, I am sending you out on orders from my Parent. Now sit tight in the city until you get further empowered by the highest force."

Jesus Leaves The Missionaries

Then Jesus led them outside Jerusalem in the direction of Bethany and raising his hands into the air he give them the promise of God's help. And it happened as he was blessing them so, he said his good-byes to them and disappeared into the skies of existence. And after they revered the memory of Jesus, they turned back to Jerusalem full of the energy of love fully known. And after that they was always to be found in the church praising God.

The Promise Of The Breathing Presence Of God

The earlier section has been told completely, you who love God, about when Jesus began to act and teach until the days when the apostles he chose were given to take orders from God's breathing spirit and he was taken up. To these, he also presented himself alive after being crucified -many instances of direct evidence - like being seen forty days afterwards by them and revealing things about God's Homeland. When he gathered them together, he ordered them not to leave Jerusalem but instead to wait for God's notice about God's claim on their lives "which you have heard about from me. John baptized with water but you will be baptized into the spirit of God's breath not so many days after these days."

Jesus Returns To The Skies Of Existence

And while they were still come together that first time, they asked him, "Familyhead, Sir, Don't you want to establish the Homeland of God right here and now?" He told them, "It isn't yours to know occasions and times which the parent has put under his own supremacy." You will receive power coming into you from God's breathing spirit upon you and you will be witnesses in Jerusalem, all of Judea and Samaria and out into the far regions of the earth. And after he said these things, while they was watching him, he was took up and a cloud enveloped him before their eyes. And while they was staring he was going up into the skies of existence and, Hello!, two men were present with them dressed in white. They said, "Men of Galilee, why are you standing looking up at the sky? This Jesus who you saw being taken up in front of you into the skies of existence will just as easy come back to this place where you visited him going up into the sky.

Picking A Successor To Judas

Then they returned to Jerusalem to the high hill called the Olive Orchard. It is close to Jerusalem and has access to it on Sunday. When they got there, they climbed the stairs to an upper room where these were living: Peter, John, James, Andrew, Philip, Thomas, Bartholomew, Matthew, James Alphaious, Simon, son of a Zealot, and Judas Jacobos. These were all the ones who remained consistently united in prayer with their women, and Mary, the mother of Jesus, and the brothers and sisters of his. And in those days, Peter stood in the midst of the apostles and spoke. There was in the crowd a number of about one hundred twenty. Folks, it should be that we complete out the writing that the spirit give David concerning Judas and how it was going to happen he would lead the ones arresting Jesus. He used to be counted as one of us and he got the chance of service as these others. About that - such a result! He bought a field from pay from proceeds of treachery. Going around bent over, he gave a blood-curdling scream and he spilled all of his guts. And it got known by all the folk of Jerusalem so much that the field is known by its own name in their dialect as Akeldamax which means "Field of Blood." This was written about in the Book of Psalms, 'Have his farmstead be a desert and don't have a house on it, Have someone else take his office.' He ought to be from among the travelers with us around all the places that we went and entered when the Familyhead, Jesus was with us beginning from the time of John's baptism until the day he was took up away from us, a witness of his resurrection who can become one with us. And they found Joseph Barsabbas surnamed Justus and Mathias qualified. And they said prayers, "You, Familyhead mover of all of our hearts, show there the one who you choose from both of the two to be the one to place in service and apostleship from which Judas fell by the wayside to come into his place." And they distributed ballots to themselves and the vote fell in favor of Mathias and he was thereafter added into the count with the other eleven apostles.

The Spirit Takes Over The Earth On Pentecost

And then in the fullness of the day of Pentecost they was all together for it. And suddenly breaking out of the skies of existence came a noisy sound like God's breathing visiting them and the whole house seemed to come alive. And they observed all over the group flames like multiple tongues breaking out and

one of them took to each one of them. And the breathing spirit didn't hold nothing back. And they begun to talk to each other using these flaming tongues that appeared on them as if life was giving them over to talking in what the ancient Greeks called apothogems, pointed gutsy basic talk in terms of principles. They was in Jerusalem the home of the Jews where people was naturally took hold of by the awe of the skies of existence, even the homeless and outcast ones, and when their voices become so excited, the fulness could be easily shared and compounded because the excitement was being expressed in every language. They stood outside their own selves and in their talk there was obviously God created expression. Hear it! Are all of them speaking as people talk in Galilee? No way! And how can we listen knowingly to each of our world's folk languages we are been born to say? Hear the words spoke by Black Sea living people and those on the Persian Gulf and beyond, Hebrew, and Greek dialects of Asia Minor and the Hellenistic world, native talks of all kinds, Egyptian and African, island languages, and the speech of the Roman. The way Jews talk and the converts to Judaism. The language of the ancient world civilizing Cretans and the isolated desert dwellers. We hear the talking going on of all of us in all of our words expressing activity God intended. Now they are all standing outside themselves and disorganized, each telling each other things, and asking, "What does this mean?" Others are saying, "This is ridiculous. They are acting drunk."

Peter's Speech About The Spirit Now In Charge

Now Peter stood up, with the eleven, lifted up by the challenge of the happening and talked in words as if they was coming from them fiery tongues. "People, Jews and Jerusalemites and those dwelling here for a spell, get this through your heads. Open your ears and hear what I have to tell you. For it's not like you are halucinating. What is going on here is not drunkenness. Remember it's only nine o'clock in the morning. But we are being give the peace that was foretold by the Godly messenger of the soil and common people, Joel. This was his writing, And there will come in the last age of earthtime, God to communicate to you, and the spirit will pour out everything upon you and not hold nothing back, and your sons and daughters will get the point of all that have gone on before, and this first new generation will get to have understanding sunk in, and even the hangers on from the last generation won't sleep until they dream what is going on, and I will pour out the spirit to you as if it were my blood, upon the ones that bind themselves to me in them last days. And they will be able to speak what's happened to other people from then on. And I will give out of the very skies of existence miracles and proofs on earth, events of blood, fire, and the very air will bear the whiff of my smoke. The sun will be turned into darkness and the moon will look like blood just before the day of the return of God's child to earth which will totally break open into earthtime. And all this will be as an encouragement that belonging to the Familyhead leads to the only saving there can be. People, Jerusalemites, listen to the words of Jesus of Nazareth, a person made known to you to be from God by

acts of power, proofs and miracles that God did through him in the midst of
you as you know these things. A plan was designated about this and he knew
before it happened- God told him - he was to be give up to the hands of lawless
people to be killed. God returned him to life releasing him from the pains of
death for the fact is that death wasn't able to hold him in it. David spoke about
it this way: I kept in mind the Familyhead continually. Because He is my right
hand so I can't be shook. My heart was made happy and my tongue could sing,
And now also my body will rest in hope, For he won't leave my soul in oblivion
in death. Nor will he give the Godly lawgiver to see a rotted body. You have
made known to me the paths of life, You will fill me to brimming joy before
your face. People, sisters and brothers, I am compelled to speak frankly to you
as did the Patriarch David who is dead and buried and his tomb is near us until
this day. This was his prophecy from the beginning and under oath - that God
swore to him from his progeny would come the one to be seated on his judgment seat. Seeing ahead, he was speaking of the resurrection of God who came
to earth because he was being assured he would not be left in oblivion nor
would his body be seen corruptible. God raised up Jesus, this one. We were all
of us witnesses. We saw Him raised up to the right hand of God. He promised
us the gift of God's breath upon us. This was honored by the Parent who has
poured out upon us what you see and hear. 'David was not raised up into the
skies of existence. He says this himself, The Familyhead said to my Familyhead
Sit at my right hand While I make your enemies a footrest.' Have it understood
without any question by the house of Israel that God was our Familyhead Himself and God come to earth, this Jesus who you crucified." Hearing this, they
were panicked in their hearts, and said to Peter and rest of the apostles, "What
can we do, men, brothers?" Peter said to them, "Reform and be baptized each
of you in the name of Jesus, God who came to earth, into forgiveness of your
rejection and receive the gift of the Spirit bearing God's breath. "Yours is the
promise and your children's and all those however distant who will call upon
the Familyhead, our God." And he kept trying to convince them in other argu-
ments- many, many more - and he pleaded with them, saying, "Be saved from
the perversity of this generation." There were those who accepted his argument
and were baptized and there were added to their number in that day about
three thousand souls. And they got committed to the teaching of the apostles
and stayed in the community sharing bread and in prayers.

Life Among The Believers

And there was respect in every soul. Many were the proofs and miracles
performed by the apostles. Every one who believed was in one and the same
place and held everything in common, and they sold their possessions and the

means of their existences and divided them among each other as the need arose. With the daylight, they took devotions together at the church after parceling bread in their house. They shared food with grateful and sincere attitude, praising God and exhibiting good favor to all people. And the Familyhead added to those saved daily in one and the same place.

A Crippled Man Healed At A Church Gate

Peter and John went to the church to pray about mid- afternoon and a man who was crippled from birth who had been carried there was placed at the entry of the church early that day and he had been crying out for help every now and then seeking charity from those going into the church. When this man saw Peter and John about to go into the church he begged them to show mercy on him. And Peter noticed him and John did too. Peter said, "Look at us!" And the man looked at them like he would take what they had to offer. And Peter said, "I have no silver or gold to give to you, but I do have this to give you. in the name of god's Human Child, the one from Nazareth, get up and walk." And taking ahold of the man by his right hand, he pulled him up. And immediately, the man felt himself getting stronger and stronger down there at his feet and ankles. And after he stood up awhile, he started jumping up and down, and strutting, and he went with them into the church walking all by himself, and he filled the church with praises to God. And all the people saw what was going on, him walking around and praising God. And they recognized him as being the one sitting, begging charity at the Welcoming Gate of the church, and they was filled with questions but quickly figured what had come to happen.

Peter Speaks At Solomon's Porch

When the man went to hug Peter and John, all the shocked people ran toward them at the place called Solomon's porch. Seeing this shock, Peter responded to the crowd, "People, Israelites, why are you so surprised about this and why are you staring at us as though we personally had some great power to make him walk? The God of Abraham and Isaac and Jacob and our ancestors has basked not just Godly but also parental concern to the Child Jesus who you turned over to authorities and rejected in the face of Pilate, when he judged that he should be let go. You denounced someone pure and just and demanded that a murderer's sentence be reprieved. You had the sponsor of life killed who God has raised from the dead as we witnessed. Now this man is strengthened through acceptance of his identity -this man who you observe and recognize to the point that his acceptance has given him wholeness contrary to all the rest of you. Now my brothers and sisters I know you acted out of misinformation as did the authorities. God has told us beforehand out of the mouths of all the

Godly messengers that God would have to suffer while on earth until completing his work. Now reform and believe in this to cancel out your wrong. The times are ripe for rejuvenation before the face of the Familyhead. He will send Jesus who was appointed to be God over the earth. It is necessary for the sky of existence to hold him until the times of restoration happen which God spoke of by the mouths of the saints from the times of the Godly messengers. Moses foretold that, "The Familyhead, your God, will raise up a Godly messenger from among your common folk like me. Listen to him whatever he may say to you. It will happen that every soul that doesn't listen to this Godly messenger will be weeded out from among the people." And all the Godly messengers from Samuel and from those since then have spoken the same thing and have warned about those days. You are the children of the Godly messengers and of the contract which God made to our ancestors saying to Abraham, " And in your genes will all the ancestries of the earth find their blessing." It was first to you that God raised up a Godly Child and sent him to you as a good wish that you would turn away from your wrongdoing. While he was talking to the people, the priests and church security guards and the Sadducees stood nearby

greatly annoyed on account of his teachings to the people and argument that Jesus was raised up from the dead, and they arrested them and confined them in custody until the next day. It was already evening. Many of the listeners to the preaching came to believe and the number of the people was five thousand. Then the next day when the authorities and the elders and the Hebrew translators in Jerusalem and Annas the main preacher and Caiaphas and John and Alexandras and all the others of that kind of important people come together and they stood Peter and John in the middle and interrogated them, "Under what spell or in whose bidding did you do this thing?" Then Peter filled with the breathing spirit of God and said to them, "Honorable authorities over the people and elders, if you are wanting to examine this kind miracle for a helpless man under what circumstance he was healed, know this all of you and all the people of Israel. It was done with the authority of Jesus, God who came to earth, of Nazareth who you crucified, who God raised from the dead. In this he was brought before you whole in body. He is the stone which was rejected by you builders which is the one cornerstone. There is no other healer. There is no other authority under the sky of existence which is necessary for our salvation. When they saw the confidence of Peter and John and they recognized these folk for being uneducated and common, they were amazed and understood that they were with Jesus and when they saw the man with them who was healed, they held back their criticism. After they ordered them to go outside the counsel, they brought this question, "What can we do about these people? A spectacular miracle has happened known to the whole community of Jerusalem and we don't have power to suppress it. Since anything we might do would spread the news to more people, we ought to just threaten them a little, make them no longer go talking up this authority come from the name of Jesus." But Peter and John when they were talked to on this track, said to them, "Since what is right is right before God, people have got to listen to the cause of it because it's before God that you are judged. We don't have the choice but to say what we see and hear." Nevertheless, after they threatened them a little more, they set them loose. They didn't figure they had grounds to punish them because the people of that time had seen that God was paying attention to them through what they was doing. For more than forty years this crippled man had needed the miracle they'd done to heal him.

Prayer For Courage

After they was released from custody, they went on doing and confessing the same as they had done before the church authorities and elders saw them. And all the people listened to them as if they could all be of one mind, lifting up their voice to God and saying, "Strong One, you have made the sky of existence and the earth and sea and everything in them. You are our Parent who spoke through the breathing spirit in the words of David, your child, How these alienated ones whinny and snort! How can people waste opportunity and act so empty-headed? How the rulers of the earth simply stand around And the authorities have meetings with each other in opposition to the Familyhead and God when on earth. They - Herod and Pontius Pilate of the non-Israelites and the people of Israel too - assembled for mischief in this city against the attended Child of yours, Jesus who you placed in charge. They did what your hand and intention knew from the first would happen. And now, Familyhead, take notice of their threats against us and help your workers to have confidence to speak up about your message and reach out your hand to heal and give proofs and miracles in the name of your attended child, Jesus. And while they was spellbound in praying, the earth started shaking where they was gathered together and everybody was filled with the presence of the spirit and they told each other the story of God's life on earth confidently.

All Things In Common

The crowds of the faithful were one heart and mind and no one wanted to have more than the others and they all said that what they owned was to be held in common. And with great emotion, the apostles shared the witness how the Familyhead, Jesus arose from death. Great happiness was in them all. And there was no one needy among them, because those who was possessors of land or an extra house, sold them, and after they collected their takes, they placed it at the feet of the apostles who distributed it among them according to their needs. So, Joseph, the one whose nickname among the apostles was Barnabus, which is also translated as child of the "Advocate," a Levite and born in Cyprus, gave over to them the money he had made when he sold an extra field and he placed it before the feet of the companions.

Nopain And Clearasabell

There was this man named Nopain with his wife Clearasabell who sold a little piece of land they owned and Nopain kept back some of the profit and shared this tidbit of information with his wife. Now they brought a part to the feet of the companions and placed it there. Peter said, "Nopain, what is this that The Challenger has filled your heart to act against the breathing Spirit and hold back from the sale of the field? Do you deny, what is left you have kept? What authority do you possess to act in this way? What is this habit in your heart, doing this kind of thing? You are not deceiving just your friends but God." After he listened to the words, Nopain fell down and died! And it almost scared to death those listening to what was being said. But before long, some of the younger ones stood up and wrapped him up and after they dragged his corpse out buried him. Along about three hours later, here came his wife wanting to know if her husband was come in there. And Peter asked her "Tell me, did you sell your field for such and such a price?" "Yes, that much." And Peter said to her, "Were you conspiring to test the patience of the Spirit of God? Do you see at your heels the men near the door ready to bury you? They will carry you out." Immediately, she fell down at his feet and died and when they came in, the young men found her and they carried her out to be buried with her husband. And there was great fear among the whole congregation and everybody heard about it.

More Proofs And Miracles

Many more proofs and miracles happened among people at the hands of the apostles. And everyone still kept a common meeting place at Solomon's porch. There was no one who tried to stop them. Everyone respected their integrity. But more than holding their property in common, it was their faithfulness to Jesus that marked them. All of the men and women was full of faith. And, as happened before when their Familyhead, Jesus, would walk down the wide streets, people would carry out their sick and wounded and put them on stretchers or cots so, when Peter would go by, his shadow would fall on them. And even crowds started pouring in from the neighboring towns around Jerusalem hauling in sick or troubled mentally ill people so all those hurting in their lives could be brought into wholeness of body and mind.

Persecution Of The Apostles

This aroused the church superintendent and all those with him, mainly Saducee party members, and they was filled with jealousy and they arrested the apostles and had them confined in the public prison. But a Godly messenger from the Familyhead opened the doors of the prison at night letting them escape and said, "Leave, then stand up and say in the church of the people all the explanations about this life." Following what was said, they went the next morning to the church and preached. When the church superintendent arrived and those with him, they convened the Sanhedrin and a council of the sons of Israel and they ordered the apostles be brought to them. But when the police went to get them, they couldn't find them anywhere in the prison. When they returned with the news, they said, "We searched the prison, and found it locked securely and the guards were standing by the doors, but when we were admitted to look inside, we didn't find nobody." As they heard these reports, a soldier of the church among those in the service of the church superintendent interrupted them to ask what happened. When he arrived, why did he hear

those who looked to be the men in prison still in the church standing around and preaching to the people? Then the captain went out with a squad to fetch them but without violence. They feared the people might stone them otherwise. After they were brought in front of the Sanhedrin, the church superintendent interrogated them saying, "Didn't we give you strict orders not to teach no more about your recollections of this Leader of yours, Jesus, and now, look here, all Jerusalem is full of your preaching and you want to smear the blood of the crucifixion of Jesus all over us." But Peter answered for the apostles and said, "We have to listen to God more than humanity. The God of our ancestry has caused Jesus to arise from the dead, this one who you killed by hanging on a tree. He was uplifted by God to God's right hand and given to be leader and savior to reconcile Israel and to forgive wrongdoing. We are witnesses of these events as is the breathing Spirit who God gives to those listening to it." When the Sanhedrin listened to this, they was enraged and wanted to kill them on the spot. But one of the Sanhedrin members, a Pharisee surnamed Marion, one of the most respectable lawyers who was pretty well come to by the people, was insistent that the apostles be taken outside for a little bit. And then he said to the Sanhedrin, "Fellow members, hold on a minute! Think about what we are about to be getting ourselves into. Aren't we into another deal like that of the rebel Theudas said to be a whiz like this with about four hundred followers joined up to him. Memory of him has been almost erased and so have the things he was so persuasive about. His followers have gone their own ways and there are none of them even heard of no more. After him, come along another charmer named Judas of Galilee, and in his day, he was wrote up big, and stood up as a leader in the forefront of people. But from that point, he started losing out and all of them following him have scattered. And now I tell you, don't waste your time on these people. Leave them be. If they are just plain common people doing their deeds by their own willpower, it will just pass by. But if God's in this thing, you can't stop them no matter what you do. And if that's so, don't you go trying to oppose God! And this talk persuaded them to think against what they was doing, and after they brought the apostles back in front of them, they give them a public beating and told them not to preach no more about their recollections of Jesus and about how he died. Now on their part, the apostles went away happy from their facedown with the Sanhedrin because they felt they'd been found worthy to be disgraced for the sake of Jesus, and all day they kept busy in the church and later when they got back home preaching and praising God who came to earth, Jesus.

The Appointment Of Seven

And as the days wore on, while the disciples kept growing in number, there come a complaint of the Greeks about the Hebrews, because they was comparing how the daily meals was getting served. These twelve called together the group of the disciples and said, "It isn't right for us to neglect talking about God to serve tables. Take care of this, brothers and sisters. Choose seven from among you spiritually rich and wise who we will appoint for these concerns. We will keep close company in prayer and in stewardship of our message. And the suggestion pleased everyone of the whole community and they chose Stephen, a man of strong faith and the Spirit and Philip and Procurus and Nichonar and Timona and Parrmenuas and Nicholas of Antioch. These stood before the apostles and prayerfully, they laid hands on them. And the story about God's life on earth was broadcast and the number of disciples multiplied greatly in Jerusalem, and the great majority of the crowd faithfully obeyed the call to worship in the church.

The Arrest Of Stephen

Stephen was very caring and capable and worked prodigious and made great improvements for the community. But some members of a church of Freed Slaves from Cyrene, Alexandria and Cilicia came forward to argue with Stephen, and they were not sharp enough to stand him down because he was smarter and spoke from the Spirit. Then they put people up to something, saying that they heard him say blasphemous words concerning Moses and God. And they stirred up people and the elders and Hebrew translators and worshippers so that he was grabbed and brought in front of the Sanhedrin. And liars stood up and said, "This man needs to be stopped from talking around this special place and on the subject of the law. We heard him saying that Jesus of Nazareth was going to destroy this place and change the customs of Moses." But when all those seated in the Sanhedrin closely looked at Stephen, they saw his face as the face of a Godly messenger.

Stephen's Speech

And the church superintendent said, "What is this all about?" And Stephen said, "People, friends, parents, Listen to me. The great God appeared to our father Abraham when he was in Mesopotamia before he went to live in Carran and said to him: 'Leave your land and that of your family and go into the land which I will show you.' So, he left out of the land of the Chaldeans to live in Carran. After his parent died there, he changed homes to this land in which to live but it was not give him to own even the size of a footprint. Even so, it was promised to him as a gift that he would possess it and it would be the seedland of his own after him. He was not a parent at the time. God told him how things would be with this place - that he must be a wanderer on land belonging to others and his seed would be slaves and be in oppression for four hundred years. But the people enslaving them would be held to account - God said - and afterwards, the seed will come forth to worship me in this place. So, he gave him a contract of circumcision and later he was the father of Isaac and circumcised him on the eighth day after he was born. Then Isaac was the father of Jacob and Jacob was the father of the twelve patriarchs. And the patriarchs became jealous of Joseph and sold him into Egypt. But God was with him and rescued him out of all his troubles. and give him to be favored and wise in the estimate of Pharaoh, the authority over Egypt who appointed him his lieutenant over Egypt and all his household. Then came a drought over all Egypt and Canaan and great suffering and our ancestors could not find food. When Jacob heard there was corn in Egypt, he sent our forefathers there first. On their second trip, Joseph made himself known to his brothers and they went to show themselves to the Pharaoh as Joseph's family. Then Joseph summoned his father, Jacob, to come to him and all his household of seventy-five souls. So Jacob went down to Egypt and he himself died there and so did our ancestors. Their bodies were carried to Suxem and were placed in a tomb there which Abraham bought for silver from the children of Emmor in Suxem. So came ever closer the time of the better circumstances which God promised to Abraham. The people prospered and multiplied in Egypt until the time when another ruler took over Egypt who didn't know Joseph. Scheming treacherously against our family, this man brutalized our ancestors into making them expose their babies so they wouldn't live. About this time, Moses was born and he was special to God. He was raised for three months in his parent's home before being exposed when the daughter of the Pharaoh took him to rear for herself as a child. And Moses was trained in all the learning of the Egyptians and became powerful through words and deeds. But when he surpassed his fortieth year, it came up in his heart to want to visit his brothers and sisters of the children of Israel and when he visited and saw one of his own being beaten, he defended him and took revenge for the one getting the worse of it by assaulting the Egyptian. He wished his sisters and brothers would understand that God's hand would give them to be saved. They couldn't understand. On the next day, he returned to them and saw some fighting and he attempted to reconcile them into peace and said, 'People, you are brothers and sisters. Why hurt each other?' But the one hurting his neighbor kept fighting say to him, 'Who are you to stand around as our boss and decide what is right among us? Why don't you kill me the way you killed the Egyptian yesterday?' So Moses escaped because of this revelation and became a wanderer in the land of Midian where he fathered two children. After forty years passed, a vision came to him in the desert near Mount Sinai, a Godly messenger in a flame burning up a thorn bush. And when Moses saw this, the vision entranced him. Coming closer, he heard the voice of the Familyhead, 'I am the God of your ancestors, the God of Abraham and of Isaac and of Jacob.' Moses took to shaking and wasn't brave enough to get closer. But the Familyhead said to him, 'Take off your sandals from your feet for this place which you are standing is special.' I saw the persecution of my people in Egypt and I heard the groans of it. I have come down to rescue them. Now go. I will send you to Egypt. Here was Moses who his people rejected, saying, 'Who are you to stand around as our boss and decide what is right among us?'- here was this man now appointed boss and liberator sent by the hand of a Godly messenger appearing to him in a bush. This man was brought before them to do miracles and proofs in the land of Egypt and in the Red Sea and in the desert for forty years. This same Moses said to the children of Israel, "God will raise up a prophet from among your brothers and sisters as me. This was the one who designed the structure of this church while in the desert with the help of the Godly messenger speaking to him from Mount Sinai and with our ancestors who received the messages during their lives to give to you. To him, our ancestors attempted disobedience and they thrust him away in their hearts and turned back to Egypt saying to Aaron, 'Make us gods that will go in front of us because this Moses who led us out of Egypt - we don't know what has happened to him. So they crafted a calf statue in those days and brought a sacrifice before the idol and they was overjoyed about the products of their hands. And God turned away from them and give up on them. They worshipped the array of the skies as it was written in the prophet's scrolls: No offerings or sacrifices were made to me During the forty years in the desert,

house of Israel. And you raised up a tent for Molox And God's star Raipha, You made idols of these to worship them, So I will have you sent off beyond to Babylon. Our ancestors had the witness tent in the desert as it was built in the time of Moses. He ordered it made like the model which he saw revealed. And it was brought here to be possessed by our ancestors according to Joshua who took this land to occupy from other peoples. God drove others away from the face of our ancestors until the days of David, who was a joy to God, and seeked to find a permanent home for Jacob's house. Solomon built this house. But the Great One does not live in a house made by hands, as the prophet says: The skies of existence are my throne, And the earth is a footstool for my feet. What house will you build for me, says the Family-head, And what place can give me rest? Hasn't my hand made everything? Obstinate ones! Stubborn in hearts and ears! You always oppose the breathing spirit of God. As your ancestors did so do you. Which ones of the prophets of your ancestors was not persecuted? And they killed the ones who announced the coming of the Righteous One from the very beginning. Now you have become deceivers and murderers - you who received the law out of decrees from Godly messengers and did not obey it."

Stephen Is Killed

After they heard these things, the authorities were furious and ground their teeth at him but he seemed fully possessed by the breathing spirit of God and he stared into the skies of existence seeing the beauty of God with Jesus standing at God's right hand and Stephen said, "Look! I see the skies opening up and god's Human Child standing at the right hand of God." Although he was crying out in a loud voice, they covered their ears and rushed at him. All had the same thought. After they threw him outside the city, they flung rocks at him and the sweating participants took off their clothes at the feet of the young man called

Saul. As they threw rocks at him, Stephen called out saying, "Familyhead, Sir, Jesus, receive my life." Then staggering to his knees, he cried out with a loud voice, "Familyhead, Sir, do not credit this wrong against them." And after saying this, he fell asleep. Saul was one of those okaying his death sentence.

Saul Helps In A Holocaust Against Christians

A great holocaust began that very day against the congregation at Jerusalem. All dispersed into the countryside of Judea and Samaria except for the apostles. They were the men who buried Stephen who stayed true to the end and the apostles wept over him. Saul harassed the church and went from house to house dragging out the men and women to turn them over to concentration camps.

The Gospel Is Preached In Samaria

The ones who were dispersed traveled about preaching the story of God's life on earth. Then Philip went down to a city in Samaria and preached about God coming to earth to them. And crowds of people with one mind listened to what Philip said and heard and saw the miracles he was doing. Many mentally ill folk crying with loud voices were healed from their behaviors and many shaking with epilepsy or arthritis were healed. And everybody was excited in that city. But there was a certain man named Simon, a witch using magic at this same city. He was always trying to scare the people of Samaria and claimed to be powerful. Everyone was afraid of him from the common people to the high class people and said, "This man possesses the great power of God. And he was famous because he had a long career of spelling them with claims of magic. This changed when the people accepted Philip's preaching about God's revelation, and the name of Jesus, God who came to earth. Folk were baptized, both men and women. Then Simon himself came to the faith and when he was baptized, he joined with Philip, and was amazed seeing the Godly interventions and great miracles. Now when the apostles at Jerusalem heard that Samaria wanted to hear more of the story of God's life on earth, they sent Peter and John to them. When they got there, they prayed for them to receive the Spirit from God. None of them had yet received it. They was only baptized under the authority of the name of the Familyhead, Jesus. Then they laid their hands on them, and they received the breath of God's Spirit. And when Simon saw that through laying on of the apostles' hands the Spirit of God's breath was given, he offered them money and said, "Give me this power too so I can lay on hands and grant the Spirit of God." But Peter said to him, "Would that you have the gold with you as you die! Don't think you get a gift of God by purchase with money. Reform your thinking from these wrong thoughts and ask the Familyhead to forgive you the motive of your heart. I see you as full of the gall of bitterness, and bound to crime." Then Simon answered and said, "Pray for me to the Familyhead so none of these things you have identified may remain in me." After they was done witnessing and preaching the story of God's life on earth, they returned to Jerusalem and this was how many villages of the Samaritans was evangelized.

Philip And An Ethiopian Household Manager

And a Godly messenger spoke to Philip and said, "Get up and go south on the road that goes down from Jerusalem to Gaza in the desert." And he got up to go and, look there! a man of Ethiopia, an important household manager employed by Candace, queen of the Ethiopians, who was in charge of all her jewels who came to Jerusalem to worship, He was going home and sitting in his chariot reading Isaiah the prophet. Then the breathing Spirit said to Philip, "Go closer and accompany this chariot. And Philip ran there to him, and heard him read the prophet Isaiah, and said, "Do you get the point you what you are reading?" And he said, "How can I unless someone will help me?" And he wanted Philip to come up and sit with him. The place of the scripture which he read was this, "He was led as a sheep to the slaughter and like a lamb silent before the shears He did not open his mouth. In his humility he was taken away to sentence. Who will tell this to the generations? For his life is taken from the

earth." And the household manager asked Philip, "Please. Who was the prophet speaking of? Himself or of some other man?" Then Philip found his opening and began at the same scripture and explained to him about Jesus. And as they went on their way, they come to a certain water hole and the household manager said, "Look, there is water. What stops me from being baptized?" And he ordered the chariot to halt and they both went down to the water, Philip and the household manager, and he baptized him. When they came up out of the water, the Spirit of the Familyhead carried Philip away and the household manager saw him no more. Even so, he went on his way happy. But Philip was found at Azotus and passing through, he preached in all the cities until he come to Caesarea.

Saul Is Converted

Saul, still blowing off how he was going to harass and kill the disciples of the Familyhead, went to the church superintendent and asked for letters to the Damascus church, so he could smoke out any this way, whether they were men or women, and bring them to Jerusalem under arrest. And as he traveled, he came near Damascus and suddenly there shined round about him a light from the very skies of existence. And he fell to the earth, and heard a voice saying to him, "Saul, Saul, why are you persecuting you me?" And Saul said, "Who are you, Sir?" And the Familyhead said, "I am Jesus, who you are persecuting. It will be hard for you not to stumble if you kick like a stubborn mule." Paul started trembling he was so astonished and said, "Sir, what do you want me to do?" The Familyhead said to him, "Get up and go into the city and it will be told to you what you must do." And the men traveling with him stood speechless. They heard a voice, but didn't see anybody." Saul got up off the ground but after he opened his eyes, he discovered he couldn't see anybody. They led him by the hand and took him into Damascus. He was there three days without sight, and couldn't eat or drink. There was a certain disciple at Damascus named Ananias and the Familyhead spoke to him in a vision. "Ananias," Jesus said.. Ananias said, "Look here, I am here, Sir." The Familyhead said to him, "Get up and go into the street called Straight, and ask at Judas's house for a person called Saul of Tarsus. You will see him there praying. He has seen in a vision a man named Ananias coming in and putting his hand on him to restore his vision." Then Ananias answered, "Sir, I have heard by many of this man, how much injury he has done to your saints at Jerusalem. He is here with authority from the church superintendent to arrest anybody who calls on your name." But the Familyhead said to him, "Go. He is a chosen vessel to me, to bear my name before the Pagan worshippers, and kings, and the children of Israel. I will show him how many horrible things he must suffer for my name's

sake." And Ananias went his way and entered into the house and put his hands on Paul and said, "Brother Saul, the Familyhead, even Jesus, has sent me here. He is Jesus who appeared to you on the road as you came. He wants your vision restored. He fills you with the breath of the Spirit of God." And immediately the blindness fell from his eyes like cataracts. Paul could see and got up and was baptized. And after he ate a meal he regained his strength.

Saul Preaches At Damascus

Saul was in Damascus with the disciples several days. He quickly began to preach about God who came to earth in the churches how He is the Son of God. Everyone hearing him was amazed and said, "Isn't this the harasser at Jerusalem of those who called on the name of Jesus? Didn't he come here to arrest the saints on behalf of the church superintendent? But Saul increased the more in confidence and confused the Jewish community at Damascus when he called them together to say Jesus was God who came to earth.

Saul Escapes From The Jews

After many days passed, the Jews decided in a conference to kill him. But Saul learned of the plot - how they kept watch at the gates day and night to kill him. Those who were disciples of Jesus took Paul by night and lowered him down the city wall in a basket.

Saul At Jerusalem

When Saul got to Jerusalem, he tried to join the disciples but they were all afraid of him, and refused to believe he was a disciple. But Barnabas took him, and brought him to the apostles, and thoroughly explained to them how Paul saw the Familyhead on the road and Jesus spoke to him. He also told how Paul preached courageously at Damascus in the name of Jesus. Soon he was with them when they went in and out of Jerusalem. He continued to speak courageously in the name of the Familyhead Jesus and annoyed the Greek community so much they decided to kill him. When the brothers and sisters learned of this, they took Paul down to Caesarea, and sent him to Tarsus. For the most part the churches were built up and knew peace throughout all of Judea and Galilee and Samaria. They operated respectfully to the Familyhead and were growing in number in the comfort of the breathing Spirit of God.

Aeneas Is Healed

An incident occurred as Peter traveled everywhere and went down to the saints living at Lydda. There he found a certain man named Aeneas who was bedridden eight years and paralyzed. Peter said to him, "Aeneas, Jesus, God who came to earth, gives you back your health. Get up and make your bed." Aeneas got up right then. And all the residents at Lydda and Sharon saw him and turned to the Familyhead.

Dorcas Is Returned To Life

There was a certain disciple at Joppa named Tabitha, which is interpreted as Dorcas. This woman was always doing good deeds and acts of charity. She was a doer. One day she got sick and died. After they washed her, they laid her in an upper chamber. Joppa is not too far from Lydda where the disciples were. When the people of Joppa heard that Peter was there, they sent two men to him to see if he could quickly come to them. Peter was aroused and went with them. When he was come, they took him into the upper room where all the

widows stood by him weeping and wearing the coats and clothes which Dorcas made while she was with them. Peter sent them outside and kneeled down to pray. Then he felt transformed and said to the body, "Tabitha arise." She opened her eyes and when she saw Peter she sat up. And he gave her his hand and lifted her up, and after he called the saints and friends, he presented her alive. This became known all through Joppa and many believed in the Family-head. After this event, Peter stayed many days in Joppa with Simon a tanner.

Peter And Cornelius

There was a certain man in Caesarea named Cornelius. He was a centurion of the military unit called the "Italian cohort." He was respectful and a God-fearing man with everyone in his house. He gave a lot to charity and often prayed to God. A Godly messenger from God came to him in a vision about the ninth hour of one day and said to him, "Cornelius." When Cornelius looked at him, he was scared and said, "What is it Sir?" And the heavenly messenger said to him, "Your prayers and your charity came to God's attention. Now send men to Joppa and call for Simon whose surname is Peter. He is staying with Simon a tanner whose house is by the sea. He will tell you what must be done." And when the Godly messenger speaking to Cornelius left, Cornelius called two of his household servants, and a conscientious soldier from those who served him. After he gave them the instructions about all these things, he sent them to Joppa. On the next day as they were traveling and came near the city, Peter was going up to the housetop to pray about the sixth hour. And he got very hungry and wanted to satisfy his appetite. While they were preparing the meal, Peter fell into an ecstasy. He saw the skies of existence open and a certain dish was coming down to him like on a large tablecloth with four origins lowered down to the earth. Available inside were all kinds of four-footed animals, reptiles of the earth and birds of the sky. Then a voice came to him to him, "Get up, Peter. Kill something and eat it." But Peter said, "Please no, Sir, for I have never eaten any thing that is common or unclean." The voice spoke to him again the second time, "What God says is clean, don't call common." This was done three times and the dish was taken back up again into the skies of existence. Now while Peter was wondering down deep what this vision meant here arrived the men from Cornelius and asked where was Simon's house and stood at the gate. They were calling out and asking if Simon called Peter was staying there. While Peter was thinking things over and trying to understand the vision, the Spirit of God's breath said to him, "Heh! three men are looking for you. Wake up, go down and leave with them. Don't hesitate because I sent them." Then Peter went down to the men sent to him from Cornelius and said, "Hello. I am the one you ask for. Why have you come?" They said, "Cornelius the centurion, a just man, and one respecting God, and with a good reputation among all the Jewish tribes, was given your name by a Godly messenger to be sent for to come to his house and hear preaching from you." Paul invited them in and made them his guests. On the next day, Peter went with them, and certain sisters and brothers from Joppa accompanied him. A day later they entered into Caesarea. Cornelius was waiting for them and called his comrades and close friends together. As Peter came in, Cornelius met him, and fell down at his feet and honored him as a God is honored. But Peter had him arise saying, "Stand up. I am just a man." While they continued talking, Peter went in and found many people assembled. And he said to them, "You are able to appreciate, I hope, that it violates Jewish religious law for a Jew to associate with other races or call upon such people, but God has showed me that I should not call any man common or unclean. And so I came without hesitation when I was sent for. Why did you send for me?" And Cornelius said, "Four days ago near this hour I was offering prayers and vows in my house and at the ninth hour a man was in my presence in bright clothing and said, 'Cornelius, your prayer is heard, and your charity has come to God's attention. Send to Joppa and fetch Simon whose surname is Peter. He is residing in the house of Simon a tanner near the sea. He will come to speak to you.' So immediately I sent for you. Your arrival is appreciated. . Now we are all present before God to hear everything God ordered you to say to us."

Peter Speaks At The House Of Cornelius

Then Peter gave the benefit of his insight and said, "If you want to know what I think is true, I think God doesn't prefer any race of persons. But in every race, God accepts every person who respects God and lives trying to do right. You are aware of the story of God's life on earth - the story which God sent to the children of Israel - promising peace by Jesus, God who came to earth. He is Familyhead of all. That story, I say, you know, which was talked about all through Judea and was first told from Galilee after the baptism which John preached. It was a story how God anointed Jesus of Nazareth with the Spirit of God's breathing and with power. He went about doing good, healing all that were oppressed of predicaments for God was with him. And we are witnesses of all the things he did, both in the land of the Jews, and in Jerusalem where they killed him and hung him on wood. God brought him back to life on the third day and acknowledged him openly. This was not generally known to everyone, but to special witnesses chosen by God. We were those who ate and drank with him after he was resurrected into life. He ordered us to preach to folk and to affirm that he is the judge who restricts life and death for God. All the prophets witness this. He forgives failure to witness for God for his own sake for those who believe in him.

The Breathing Spirit Of God Is For All Folk

While Peter yet spoke these words, the breathing Spirit of God fell on all those hearing the story of God's life on earth. Those who were circumcised were shocked including those who came with Peter. What happened was that the gift of God's breathing spirit was poured out on non- Jews. They heard them speaking in tongues and praising God. Then Peter responded, "How can anyone deny these folk the water of baptism?. They have experienced the breath of God as much as we have." And he ordered that they could be baptized in the name of the Familyhead. Then they asked him to stay several days.

Peter Reports To The Church At Jerusalem

The apostles and brothers and sisters in Judea kept hearing that non-Jews were receptive to the story of God's life on earth. When Peter returned to Jerusalem, those who were circumcised disagreed with what he did and argued with him saying, "How could you visit uncircumcised persons and eat with them." And Peter began by explaining to them, "I was in the city of Joppa, praying and having an ecstatic experience and saw a vision. A certain dish was coming down like it was on large tablecloth lowered down from skies of existence out of four origins as it came to me. I stared at it and saw on it four-footed animals of the earth, and wild creatures, and reptiles, and birds of the air. And I heard a voice saying to me, 'Get up, Peter. Kill something and eat it.' But I said, 'No, Sir. I have never eaten anything common or unclean.' But the voice from skies of existence said a second time, 'What God has cleansed, don't call common.' And this happened three times and then the whole thing was again withdrawn up into skies of existence. Then this... immediately there were three men already come to the house where I was, sent from Caesarea to me. And the Spirit said to go with them and not hesitate. Also these six sisters and brothers went with me and we went into the man's house. He told us how he saw a Godly messenger in his house that appeared and said to him, 'Send men to Joppa and call for Simon, whose surname is Peter. He will come to speak to you how to be saved. As I began to speak, the breathing Spirit of God fell on them, as on us at the beginning. Then I remembered the story of the Familyhead and what he told us, 'John baptized with water but you shall be baptized with the Spirit of God's breath.' If God gave them the same gift that he gave us because they believed in the Familyhead Jesus God who came to earth, how could I act contrary to what God empowered?" When they heard these things, they gave their okay and praised God, saying, "God has given the mind of changed lives to non-Jews."

The Church At Antioch

Those that was scattered by the persecution that come on after the Stephen martyrdom travelled as far as Phoenicia, Cyprus and Antioch, telling the story of God come to earth to none except the Jews. Some of these were folk of Cyprus and Cyrene, who, when they got to Antioch, told it to the Greeks, preaching the Familyhead Jesus. And the hand of the Familyhead was with them and a great number of believers were brought to the faith and turned to the Familyhead. Then rumors of these things came to the ears of the church which was in Jerusalem and they sent Barnabas to Antioch. When Barnabas got there he saw God caring for these people and was satisfied and urged them all to stay loyal in their hearts to the Familyhead. Barnabas was a good man, and full of the breath of the Spirit of God and of faith and many people were added to belief in the Familyhead. Then Barnabas went to Tarsus to look for Saul. And when he found him, he brought him to Antioch. This is what happened to them. For a whole year they brought folk into the church and taught many people and the disciples was called Christians first in Antioch. And in those days, prophets came down to Antioch from Jerusalem. One of them, named Agabus, stood up and predicted through the Spirit that there was soon to be a great starvation upon the whole empire which happened in the days of Claudius Caesar. Then the disciples, each as his or her financial means allowed, decided to send help to the homes of the brothers and sisters living in Judea which they did, and sent it to the elders by the agency of Barnabas and Saul.

James Killed And Peter Imprisoned

Now about that time, Herod the king persecuted certain members of the church with his own hands. He lifted James's head so as to be able to expose the throat and cut it more easily with a sword. This was James the brother of John. Because he saw it pleased the Jews, Herod went even further and arrested Peter. This was during the days of Passover. And after he arrested him, he threw Peter in prison and stationed four platoons of soldiers to guard him. He intended to bring him up as a prisoner for the judgment of the people after Passover. While Peter languished in prison, prayer was made constantly by God's church for him.

Peter Freed From Prison

When it was getting close to time for Herod to bring him up, that prior night, Peter - restrained by double chains - was sleeping between two soldiers. Guards stood prison security in front of the door. Even so, right then! a Godly messenger of the Familyhead came upon him and a light shined in the prison and he shook Peter on the side and woke him up, saying, "Get up quickly." And Peter's chains fell off his hands. And the Godly messenger said to him, "Get on your clothes, and put on your sandals." And so he did. And the Godly messenger said to him, "Put your cloak on and follow me." And Peter went along and followed him out but he didn't necessarily realize that what was happening with this Godly messenger was real. He thought he was experiencing a dream. When they were past the first and the second guard, they came to the iron gate that leads to the city. It opened to them of its own accord and they went out. They passed on through one street and suddenly the Godly messenger disappeared from view before him. When Peter came to his senses, he said, "Now I know to a certainty that the Familyhead has sent his Godly messenger, and has delivered me from arrest by Herod and from all that the Jewish mob was relishing." Thinking it over, he decided to go to the house of Mary the mother of John, whose surname was Mark where many were gathered together, praying. As Peter knocked at the door of the gate, a slave girl named Rhoda came to investigate. Recognizing Peter's voice, she ran back in and told how Peter stood at the gate without opening it. They told her, "You are crazy." But she insisted, "It is true, no matter how impossible it seems." Then they said, "It is his ghost." But Peter kept knocking and when they opened the door, they saw him and were overwhelmed. But Peter held up his hand to shush them and told them how the Familyhead brought him out of the prison. And he said,

"Go. Tell the news to James and the sisters and brothers." And he left and went to another place. Now as soon as it was day, there was a great commotion among the soldiers about what became of Peter. And when Herod summoned him, and they couldn't find him, he questioned the jailors and ordered them brought up to him for justice.. Then he went down from Judaea to Caesarea to stay.

The Death Of Herod

There was a period of trouble with Tyre and Sidon. To patch things up, these cities bribed Blastus, a household manager, to receive an audience. They wanted peace because their country got its food supply from the king's country. Upon a set day, Herod, dressed himself up to look kingly, and went to sit on his judgment seat and spoke to them. After this, the whole public assemblage began shouting out, "It is the voice of God, and not of a man." Just as quickly, a Godly messenger of the Familyhead took charge of him. Herod simply wasn't equal to God's eminence. Herod was eaten by worms and died. But the story about God's life on earth grew and spread. Barnabas and Saul returned to Jerusalem when they completed their ministry and brought John with them whose surname was Mark.

Barnabas And Saul Are Commissioned

At Antioch there were certain prophets and teachers in the church, people such as Barnabas, and Simeon called Niger, and Luke of Cyrene, and Manaen, a close friend of Herod, the Tetrach, and Saul. As they served the Familyhead and fasted, the Spirit of Godly breath told them, "I will delegate Barnabas and Saul to do work I call them to do." And they fasted and prayed and laid their hands on them and dispatched them.

The Apostles Preach In Cyprus

Barnabas and Saul were thus sent out by God's breathing spirit. They left for Seleucia and from there they sailed to Cyprus. When they were at Salamis, they preached the story of God's life on earth in the churches of the Jews and they also had John to help minister. As they went through the island of Paphos, they come across a certain charlatan, a false prophet, a Jew, whose name was Bar-jesus. He was with the proconsul of the country, Sergius Paulus, an intelligent man who called for Barnabas and Saul and wanted to hear the story of God's life on earth. But Elymas (as his name is translated) the charlatan, tried to stop them and tried to divert the proconsul from calling for them. Then Saul, (who also is called Paul) got filled with the Spirit of God and set his eyes on him, and said, "You sneak and troublemaker, you child of the devil, you enemy of all righteousness! Do you think you can stop us and barricade the road to the Familyhead? Well, look here, the hand of the Familyhead is upon you, and you will be blind and not see the sun for a long, long time." And immediately there fell on him a mistiness and darkness and he went around to find someone to lead him by the hand. Then the proconsul, when he saw what was done, believed and was impressed by the teaching about the Familyhead.

Paul And Barnabas At Antioch Of Pisidia

Leaving Paphos, they (including those around Paul) went to Perga in Pamphylphyla. John left them there and returned to Jerusalem. After they left Perga, they traveled to Antioch in Pisidia and went into its church on Sunday and sat down. After the reading of the law and the prophets, the congregational leaders of the church summoned them, saying, "Friends and brothers. If there is any news to pass along to the congregation, tell us."Paul stood up and raised his hand and said, "Friends, Israelites and you who respect God, listen. The God of this people of Israel chose our ancestors and lifted up these common people when they dwelt as strangers in the land of Egypt, and with a mighty arm brought them out of it. Then our ancestors struggled through a period of forty years in the wilderness and after that God gave them judges for about four hundred and fifty years until the time of Samuel the prophet. Afterward they wanted a king and God gave them Saul the son of Kish, a man of the tribe of Benjamin, for forty years. Then God replaced him and made David the king and witnessed his reason why, saying "I found David, the son of Jesse. He is a man after my own heart. He will do things the way I want." Now comes this good news. God has brought from David's ancestry an Israelite savior, Jesus, the one who John preached about before he saw his face and baptized to reform the whole Israelite people. As the course of John's ministry wound up, he said, "Who do you think I am? I am not the special one. Pay attention though because someone is coming after me whose sandals I am not worthy to loosen and remove from his feet." Sisters and brothers, children of the stock of Abraham, and those among you who respect God, the story of the life of this savior has been sent out to you. Those who live in Jerusalem and those who are their leaders have ignored this. They have ignored as well the voices of the prophets and the readings every Sunday whose prophetic judgments were fulfilled. Nothing short of a death sentence did they request from Pilate to kill him. Even to the very end, these events were written concerning what would be. Then they took his body down from the cross and laid him in a tomb. But God raised him from the dead. And he was seen many days later by those in Jerusalem who traveled to meet him in Galilee. Now these are his witnesses to the people. We give you this good news of how the promise to our ancestors has been completed by God for us their children. God raised up Jesus again as it was foretold in the second psalm, "You are my child. This day I give you birth." Yes, he raised him from death no more to be subject to the decay of the flesh. About this he said, "I will give you the Godly rights of David, the faithful one." In another place, God says, "You won't give the one with Godly rights over to corruption." It was the God's will that David fell asleep after serving God in his own generation and he joined those of his ancestry whose bodies decomposed. But the one God resurrected did not know decomposition. Be aware, each of you, of this man, sisters and brothers because he declares whether breaches of duty to God are forgiven. He makes right for everyone what could not be under the law of Moses. "Watch out, sceptics! Observers and ghosts! Because I have taken an action in your days An action that you don't acknowledge Even when it is explained to you. After they left, the non-Jews wanted these explanations preached to them the next Sunday. After the congregation dispersed, many of the Jews and religious proselytes followed Paul and Barnabas. They spoke to them and encouraged them to continue in the grace of God. The next Sunday, almost the whole city was gathered together to hear the story of the Familyhead's life on earth. But when the Jews saw the crowds, they were filled with envy and heckled Paul and shouting out blasphemy. Filled with courage, Paul and Barnabas said, "To you was that right to hear the story of God's life on earth first but since you dismiss it you are judging yourselves unworthy for eternal life. That's why we have turned it over to the non-Jews. This is ordered by the Familyhead, "I have established you as a light for non-Jews, for you to save them until the earth ends." When the non-Jews heard these things, they knew content and honored the story of the earthly life of the Familyhead. So many of the ones who believed were established into eternal life. The story of God's life as the Familyhead spread through the whole countryside. But the Jews appealed to the worshipping Jewish proselyte women of high social standing and

the important men of the city and stirred them up against Paul and Barnabas. They banned them from their jurisdiction. Paul and Barnabas shook off the dust from their feet and went to Iconium. The disciples were filled with satisfaction and the breath of God's Spirit.

Paul And Barnabas At Iconium

In Iconium they went together into a church of the Jews, and preached with the result that lots of Jews and Greeks come to believe. But those Jews who were unsympathetic roused up the pagan worshippers and subverted their opinions against the sisters and brothers. For some time Paul and Barnabas stayed there preaching boldly for the Familyhead in witness about the story of God's life on earth and its benefitdoing miracles and great acts by their hands. But the majority of the city were divisive and these were on the side of the Jews. Others were on the side of the apostles. On impulse, a raid was organized by the pagan worshippers and Jews with the connivance of the authorities with the goal of stoning them.

Paul And Barnabas At Lystra

When they learned about it, they fled to Lystra and Derbe, cities of Lycaonia, and to the region that surrounds it and preached the gospel there. And a certain men at Lystra sat around because his feet were paralyzed. He was a cripple from birth and never had walked. He heard Paul preaching. Paul began to stare at him and noticed that he had faith to be saved. Paul said in a loud voice, "Stand up on your feet. You have the strength." He jumped up and began to walk. And when the crowd saw what Paul did, they shouted out in Lyconian slang, "The gods have come down to us like people." And they called Barnabas, Zeus and Paul, Hermes because he was the main speaker. Then the priest of the God Zeus for their city brought a bull and garlands to the gates and wanted to sacrifice it to them with the people. When the apostles Barnabas and Paul heard of this, they tore at their clothes and ran out into the crowd shouting and saying, "Folks, why do you have to do these things? We are just people like you. Was our preaching useless to you to act so faithlessly before the living God who made the sky and the ground and the sea and everything in them? In the past generations, God allowed every people to walk their own road. And yet,

God didn't abandon the idea of helping the innocent. The sky yields rain to us and permits times of harvest. God gives the hungry person food and warms our hearts." After he said these things, they could hardly restrain the crowd from sacrificing to them.

The Return To Antioch In Syria

Eventually, some Jews come from Antioch and Iconium and they stirred up a mob and stoned Paul. Then they dragged him outside the city thinking him dead. But the disciples surrounded him and he stood up and them left the city and the next day he went with Barnabas to Derbe. He preached the good news in that city and taught many people before turning back to Lystra, and to Iconium, and Antioch. He encouraged the souls of the disciples and urged them to remain faithful because "It is necessary for us to encounter many troubles on the way into God's Homeland." They ordained elders in every church and prayed with fasting to establish them for the Familyhead in whom they could trust. After they passed through Pisidia, they went to Pamphylia. After they preached the story of God's life on earth in Perga, they went down into Attalia. From there they sailed to Antioch where lived those who were recipients of the word handed down by the grace of God from the work which Paul and Barnabas accomplished. And after they arrived, they assembled the church together and repeated all that God had done for them and how he had opened the door of faith to the Pagan worshippers. And there they lived a long time with the disciples.

The Council At Jerusalem

Now several persons who come down from Judaea taught the brothers and sisters, saying, "If you aren't circumcised per Moses, you can't be saved." This caused an argument and rift - not some little one either - between them and Paul and Barnabas. They settled it by dispatching Paul and Barnabas and some of the others out of their congregation to represent them in a discussion before the apostles and the elders in Jerusalem. The ones dispatched passed through Phoenicia and Samaria. When they reported how the pagan worshippers were being converted, this caused great happiness to all the sisters and brothers. When they got to Jerusalem, they were welcomed by the church and the apostles and elders. They reported how God had done so many things with them. But some rose up from where they were sitting there. They were believers formerly from the sect of the Pharisees who said it was still necessary to circumcise them and to command them to keep the law of Moses. And the apostles and elders had a meeting to reason through this question. Many were getting furious, so Peter stood up, and said to them, "Friends and brothers and sisters. You know, don't you, how a while back, we learned God chose me to tell the story of God's life on earth to pagan worshippers and they came to believe it! God, who knows hearts, wanted them to have the truth by offering to them the Spirit of Godly breath just as he did for us. God allowed no difference between us and them and purified their hearts by faith. Now how can we question God or put a yoke around the neck of the disciples which neither our ancestors nor we were able to bear? We must have faith that through the grace of the Familyhead Jesus God who came to earth we will be saved just as they are." Then the whole crowd became silent and listened to Barnabas and Paul tell how God worked miracles and amazing incidents among the Pagan worshippers by them. After their silence, James responded saying, "Friends and sisters and brothers. Listen to me. Simeon has told us how God at the first visited pagan worshippers to select out of them a people for God's self. Scriptures agree with this, as it is written: "After this I will return, and I will again construct the church of David, which is destroyed and I will again gather up the ruins and I will set it up. That the residue of people can seek after the Familyhead, and all the pagan worshippers who who call upon my name, says the Familyhead who performs all these things. God says the Familyhead can do these projects known from the beginning of time. Here is my conclusion. We should not impose an impediment on the Pagan worshippers who are turning to God. Instead, we should write to those emerging from pagan worship that it is wrong to worship idols or commit immorality or eat the meat of strangled animals or drink blood. Moses has been interpreted this way in churches in every city from ancient times every Sunday."

The Reply Of The Council

It was thought best by the apostles and elders and with the approval of the whole congregation that they send chosen people with Paul and Barnabas to Antioch. They picked Judas surnamed Barnabas and Silas, leaders among the brothers and sisters. They also wrote out a handwritten letter to send with them. "The apostles and elders and brothers and sisters to those of Antioch and Syria and Cilicia greet you who are non-Jews. Since we have heard that certain persons who were sent out from our church troubled you with statements subverting your souls, saying you must be circumcised, and keep that law when we gave no such order, it seemed right to us, in unanimous assembly, to send chosen persons to you, with our beloved Barnabas and Paul. These are persons who have risked their lives for the sake of our Familyhead Jesus God who came to earth. We have sent Judas and Silas who will also confirm this vocally. It doesn't make sense to us to burden the Spirit of God or to burden you except with necesary things. You should not eat meat offered to idols, or drink blood, or eat the meat of strangled animals or act immorally. Watch out for these particular things, and follow the right practices. God be with you. After they were released to go, they traveled on to Antioch. There they summoned the congregation and read the letter. After it was read, the listeners felt the joy of being comforted. Judas and Silas, being themselves gifted with the Spirit of God, encouraged the brothers and sisters with many stories and strengthened their resolve. They stayed there awhile. Then they were allowed to go in peace from the sisters and brothers back to the apostles. After they set sail out of Antioch, Paul and Barnabas preached and brought the Godly message about the Familyhead to many others.

Paul And Barnabas Separate

Several days later, Paul said to Barnabas, "How about going with me again to visit our brothers and sisters in every city where we have preached the story of the life of the Familyhead and see how they are doing?" Barnabas decided to take John whose surname was Mark with them. But Paul thought about it and didn't want Mark to accompany them. He had caused dissension in Pamphylia and didn't work out. The arguing got so heated between them that they broke up the team. Barnabas took Mark and sailed to Cyprus. Paul chose Silas and left satisfied it was with God's approval for the sake of the brotherhood and sisterhood. He went through Syria and Cilicia strengthening the churches.

Timothy Accompanies Paul And Silas

He went to Derby and Lystra and - it truly happened -a certain disciple was there named Timothy, the son of a faithful Jewish woman. His father was Greek. He had a good reputation among the brothers and sisters that were at Lystra and Iconium. Paul wanted him to go with him and took and circumcised him because the Jews would not do so since they knew his father was a Greek. As they went through the cities, they handed down the teachings they safely guarded about life choices ordained by the apostles and elders at Jerusalem. This was how the churches were established in the faith and they increased every day in number.

Paul's Vision Of The Man Of Macedonia

They went through Phrygia and the region of Galatia. They were forbidden by the Spirit of God to preach the story of God's life on earth in Asia. After they come to Mysia, they questioned whether they should go into Bithnyia but the Spirit of Jesus did not let them go there. They passed by Mysia and come down to Troy. There a vision appeared to Paul in the night. There stood a man of Macedonia and he was pleading and saying, "Come over into Macedonia, and help us." After he saw the vision, we immediately went to Macedonia. We decided that God was calling us to be missionaries to these people.

The Conversion Of Lydia

After leaving Troy, we set a direct course to Samothrace. We went the next day to Neapolis and from there to Philippi. It was the main city in that part of Macedonia and a Roman colony. We stayed in that city several days. On a Sunday we went out to the outskirts of the city by a river bank for a prayer meeting and we sat down and spoke to the women living there. One of them was a woman named Lydia who sold purple dye in the city of Thyatria. She felt fearful about God. When she heard us, the Familyhead opened her heart so she paid attention to the things Paul was speaking. She was baptized along with others in her home and she pleaded with us, saying, "If you consider me faithful to the Familyhead, come into my house and live here." And she was insistent.

Imprisonment At Philippi

And it happened, as we went to prayer, a certain mentally ill girl met us. She made a lot of money for her masters by acting wild and giving predictions. She followed Paul and us around, and cried out, "These men are the helpers of the most high God who shows us the way of salvation." And she did this many days. But Paul felt sorry for her and turned and addressed her mental illness and said, "I command you in the name of Jesus God who came to earth to go away from her." And her mental illness was healed immediately. But when her masters saw that the source of their income was gone, they grabbed Paul and Silas and manhandled them into the marketplace toward the authorities and brought them to the judges and said, "These Jewish men are disturbing the peace in our city. They are teaching customs which are illegal for us to do or accept since we are Romans." And the crowd demanded action against them so the judges ordered them stripped and whipped. And after they whipped them, they jailed them, charging the jailer to keep them secure. Then the jailer took charge. He shoved them into the innermost cell and cuffed their feet in wall chains. At midnight Paul and Silas prayed. They sang hymns to God and the prisoners heard them. Suddenly there was a great earthquake shaking the foundations of the prison. Then just as quick all the doors was opened and everyone's chains was broke open. The keeper of the prison woke up out of his sleep and saw the prison doors open. What he drew out of the picture most caused him to want to kill himself figuring the prisoners escaped. But then he heard Paul call out real loud, saying, "Don't do yourself no harm. We are all here." Then the jailor called for a light and rushed in and begun shaking and fell down in front of Paul and Silas. And then he brought them out and said, "Sirs, what must I do to be saved?" And they said, "Believe in the Familyhead, Jesus, God who came to earth, and you will be saved and your family" and they told him the story of the Familyhead and they told it to all his family. And he took them the same hour of the night and washed the welts from where they was whipped and was baptized, he and all his family, right away. He took them into his house, served them a nice meal, and couldn't have been happier because he come to believe in God with all his family. When it was day, the judges sent their bailiffs, saying, "Release them." And the keeper of the prison told this news to Paul, "The magistrates have sent to release you. Go on and leave and go in peace." But Paul said to them, "They had us whipped in public without trial and we are Romans, and they threw us into prison and now do they expect to release us without fuss? No. But we will tell you what. They can come to us and escort us out." The jailors told these demands to the judges. They were afraid because they heard they were Romans so they came as Paul summoned them. As they escorted them out they requested they leave the city. After they left the jail, they went to Lydia's to let the brothers and sisters know they were all right and they left.

The Uproar In Thessalonica

They traveled through Amphipolis and Apollonia to get to Thessalonica where the Jews had a church. Paul went to these according to his habit and had conversations with them about the scriptures. He explained them and pointed out that it was necessary for God to suffer while on earth and to be resurrected from death and that this God who came to earth was Jesus. "He is the one I am giving this information about." Some of them believed and were converted by Paul and Silas and a great many of the reputable Greeks and not just a few of their leading women. But the diehard Jews gathered together some no-good men loafing in the marketplace to turn them into a mob in the city and they swarmed the house of Jason and tried to pull those inside out into the crowd. When they couldn't find Paul and Silas, they dragged Jason and certain sisters and brothers to the city council, demanding, "These people are destroying the Roman Empire and now they are present here. Jason housed them. All these people are acting in violation of the laws of Caesar. They are saying that there is another ruler, this Jesus. They are subverting people." After the council heard these things, they took bail from Jason himself and they released the rest of them.

The Apostles At Beroea

The brothers and sisters immediately snuck Paul and Silas away by night to Beroea. Some way or other they got there. They went into the church of the Jews. These Jews were more open-minded than those in Thessalonica. Some of them accepted the story of the life of God on earth readily. They researched the scriptures daily to confirm things were supported the Christian way. Many were led into the Christian faith along with many reputable Greek wormen and men too. But when the Jews of Thessalonica learned that the story of God's life on earth was preached of Paul at Beroea, they went there to stir up opposition and incite a mob. The sisters and brothers sent Paul away quickly while claiming he sailed away before. But Silas and Timothy kept living there. Paul's guides took him to Athens and returned with instructions to Silas and Timothy to come to him quickly. They they went back to Beroea.

Paul At Athens

While Paul waited for them at Athens, his spirit was stirred up because he saw the city so full of idols. In fact, he chided the Jews in the church, those in the temples, and in the marketplace most all day wherever he happened to be present. Some philosophers of the Epicureans and of the Stoics debated with him. They said, "What will this incoherent fool have to say?" He looked like an advocate for strange gods because he preached to them about Jesus and the resurrection. They got ahold of him and led him to the Areopagus rock, saying, "Can you teach us about this new religion you are advocating? You are announcing something strange and foreign in the news about you. We would like to know what these things mean." All kinds of Athenians and strangers living there took time to loaf and spent their time in nothing else than to tell stories or to listen for some new things. Paul stood on the crown of the Areopagus rock and said, "Friends, Athenians. According to everything I detect, you are very religious. As I passed by and watched you worship, I found an altar with this inscription, TO THE UNKNOWN GOD. This one you are worshipping in ignorance is the one I am preaching to you. This is the God who made the world and everything in it. This Familyhead over the skies and the earth does not reside in a house made with hands. Nor does this one have a need to have maintenance done by human hands. This one gives all life, and breath, and all things. This one has made from one all races of people who live on the whole face of the earth and has decided the epochs when each are posted and the boundaries of their homelands. God searches out to see if any might want to feel God's presence or try to find God, though God is not far from every one of us. In God we live, and move, and have our being as certainly as your own poets have said, We are of a common kind. Since we are the disposition of God,

we shouldn't think that God can be imagined as gold or silver or stone carved artistically and with a person's features. God overlooked the former times of ignorance but now orders all people everywhere to reform. God has appointed a day on which God will judge the world justly in the person of one who God separated out to prepare all the faithful for God's resurrection of them from death." When they heard of the resurrection of the dead, some mocked him, and others said, "We have heard about such things time and again." Then Paul came down from the crown. But some of the people believed him and gathered around him. Among them was Dionysius the Areopagite and a woman named Damaris and their companions.

Paul At Corinth

Later, Paul left Athens and went to Corinth and met a certain Jew named Aquila, born in Pontus, who just came from Italy with his wife Priscilla. It was arranged because Claudius ordered all Jews to leave Rome. Paul went to see them. Because Paul was a fellow tradesman, he lived with them and he worked there. They were tentmakers by occupation. Paul preached in the church almost every Sunday and converted Jews and Greeks. When Silas and Timothy arrived from Macedonia, Paul was sharing the story of God's life on earth and testifying to the Jews that Jesus was God who came to earth. The congregation was ranging in vigorous debate against him. Since they were blaspheming, he shook the dust off his clothes and said to them, "Your blood is upon your own heads. I am clean. From now on I will go to non-Jews." After he left them, he went into a certain man's house named Justus. He was a person who worshipped God whose house was close to the church. Crispus, the head of the congregation, believed in the Familyhead with all his family and many of the Corinthians hearing, believed, and were baptized. The Familyhead spoke to Paul in the night by a vision, "Don't be afraid. Speak out. Don't hold back. I am with you and no person can harm you or hurt you. My people are in the ma-

jority in this city." Paul stayed there a year and six months teaching the story of God's life on earth among them. When Gallionos was the Governor over Achaia, the Jews unanimously complained about Paul. They sued for relief from him, saying, "This fellow tries to persuade folk to worship God against religious laws." But before Paul could even open his mouth, Gallionos said to the Jews, "If it were a matter of crime, or immorality, my Jewish friends, good sense would require that I listen to you. But if it comes down to a question of myths and disputes about names, and of your religious law, you will have to deal with it because I am not a judge over such things." And he ordered them removed from the bench of his court. Then all of them took Sosthenes, who presided over the Jewish church, and spanked him in front of the judgment seat. It didn't bother Gallionos a bit.

Paul's Return To Antioch

Paul stayed for many more days. Then after a set amount of time with the brothers and sisters, he sailed to Syria along with him Priscilla and Aquila. He

got a haircut as a sign of mourning in Cenchrea to keep a promise. He left Priscilla and Aquilla at Ephesus. Then he went into the Jewish church and debated with the Jews. Even though they wanted him to stay with them, he refused and told them good- bye and said "By all means, I must keep the upcoming festival day in Jerusalem but -if God wills it - I will return to you again." And he sailed from Ephesus. After he got to shore at Caesarea, he walked up a way to give thanks at the church. The he went down to Anitoch. After he spent some time there, he left and went over all the country of Galatia and Phrygia in order to encourage all those disciples.

Apollos Preaches At Ephesus

A certain Jew named Apollos, born at Alexandria, went to Ephesus. He was an eloquent man and an accomplished scriptural authority, He taught the Christian way of the Familyhead and he spoke fervently in the spirit. He taught accurately the facts concerning Jesus while he was faithful only to the baptism from John. He began to speak boldly in the Jewish church when Aquila and Priscilla heard him and took him aside. Then they explained to him the Christian way to God more accurately. After he wanted to go to Achaia, they were so enthusiastic they wrote to the disciples to welcome him. After he got there, he helped many to come to mature belief through grace. He vehemently and thoroughly refuted the Jews in public and pointed out from the scriptures how Jesus was God come to earth.

Paul At Ephesus

While Apollos was getting to Corinth, Paul was traveling through the upper coasts going to Ephesus. He found there some disciples and said to them, "Have you received the breath of the Spirit of God since you believed?" And they said to him, "We haven't even heard that there was any Spirit of God." And he said to them, "How could you have been baptized?" And they said, "With John's baptism." Then Paul said, "John really baptized with the baptism of repentance, saying to people they should believe on the one to come after him, that is, Jesus, God who came to earth." When they heard this, they were baptized in the name of the Familyhead Jesus. When Paul laid his hands upon them, the breathing Spirit of God came on them and they spoke with tongues and prophesied. There were in all about twelve men. And he went to the Jewish church and preached courageously for three months about God's Homeland. Eventually some grew stubborn and disobedient and began to talk down the Christian way in front of the congregation. Paul then separated these unbelievers from the disciples and began teaching daily in the school of Tyrannus. And this continued on for two years so that everyone living in Asia heard the story of the Familyhead Jesus, both Jews and Greeks.

The Sons Of Seeva

God exercised power never before experienced through the hands of Paul. His handkerchiefs and tentmaker's aprons were carried away to sick people and their diseases left them and their mental illnesses disappeared. Naturally, some decided to put their hands to this kind of work. By all accounts they were itinerent Jews and exorcists. They commanded bad ghosts to get out of those possessing them in the name of the Familyhead, Jesus, saying "I order you out by the authority of the Jesus who Paul preaches about." Some of those doing this were the seven sons of Seeva, a Jewish church superintendent. Once ane evil spirit answered them back, saying, "Jesus I know, and Paul I know - but who are you?" And the possessed man sprung on them, and after he turned his own evil power on them, he overpowered them and threw them out of the house naked. This got rumored around by all the Jews and Greeks living in Ephesus and fear spread among them all and the name of the Familyhead, Jesus, was greatly respected. Many who were believers came, confessing and revealing their actions. Many who were practicing magic brought their books and burned them in front of everybody. and when their worth was estimated, they estimated fifty thousand silver coins. By such incidents, the story of God's life on earth grew and gained power.

The Riot At Ephesus

After the fulfillment of these things, Paul set a spiritual goal that after he visited Macedonia and Achaia he would go to Jerusalem and said, "After I have been there, I want to see Rome." He sent two of his helpers to Macedonia, Timothy and Erastus, but he himself stayed in Asia for a time. Around the same time there arose no small confusion about the Christian way. There was a certain man named Demetrius, a silversmith who made silver shrines for Diana, which brought in no small profit to the retail merchants. He called them together with the workers from similar occupations, and said, "Friends, you know we make our livings by our crafts. We see and hear that not only in Ephesus but also almost all over Asia, this Paul is convincing people and changing the beliefs of a huge group of them, saying that nothing can be one of the gods made by hand. Not only does this endanger our craft but also it causes condemnation of the church of the great goddess Diana. It is about to destroy her magnificence who all Asia and the world honors." After hearing this, the crowd got hot and cried out saying, "Great is Diana of the Ephesians!" And the whole city was filled with confusion. They seized Gaius and Aristarchus, Macedonians and traveling companions of Paul's, and rushed into the theater as if all were motivated by the same impulse. Paul wanted to go in with the mob but the disciples did not let him. Some of the Asian authorities who were his friends sent to him a message not to present himself in the theatre. Some cried out for one thing and some for another. The assembly was in great confusion and the majority did not know why they were assembled. Some in the crowd appointed Alexander as spokesman. He was nominated by the Jews. Alexander motioned with his hand that he wanted to address the crowd. But when they saw he was a Jew, all cried out with one voice for close to two hours, "Great is Diana of the Ephesians!" The town clerk finally calmed the people down. He said, "You folk of Ephesus. What person is there that who doesn't know that the city of the Ephesians is temple-keeper of the great goddess Diana and of that which fell down from heaven? Since this is undeniable, it is important that we quiet ourselves and not act recklessly. You have not brought here men who are temple robbers or who have blasphemed your goddess. If Demetrius and the craftsmen with him have a grievance against anyone, the courts are open and there are Romans here too. They will call an accused and accuser to face each other. If there is other relief you require, it will be taken up in the city council. We are in danger of being charged with civil rioting because of this

event. Since no crime started anything, we can't give any excuse for this agitation." And after he said these things, he dismissed the meeting.

Paul's Journey To Macedonia And Greece

After the uproar was over, Paul called the disciples to him and consoled them them, after a brief visit, he left to go to Macedonia. He left the region after comforting them as I say and went into Greece. He lived there three months. He became aware of a conspiracy against him by the Jews as he was about to sail into Syria. He decided to return through Macedonia. Sopater of Berea, Aristarchus and Secundus of Thessalonica, Gaius of Derbe, Timothy, and Tychicus and Trophimus of Asia traveled with him to Asia. They traveled ahead of us and waited for us at Troy. We sailed away from Philippi after the days of unleavened bread and came to them in Troy five days later where we lived seven days.

Paul's Last Visit To Troy

On the first day of the week the disciples came together for dinner. Paul preached to them, ready to leave on the next day, and continued his sermon until midnight. There were many lights upstairs where they were gathered together. Above that, on the third floor, there sat a boy at a window named Eutychus who fell into a deep sleep while Paul was preaching so long. He drooped over the window in his sleep. Then he fell down from this third floor. He was picked up and found dead. But Paul got down and embraced him and said, "Don't worry. He is still alive." Then the boy perked up again and took some

bread and ate it and talked a long time, even on til dawn. Then Paul left. But the disciples was comforted immeasureable.

The Voyage From Troy To Miletus

We went ahead of Paul by ship and sailed to Assos. We intended to pick up Paul there as he asked. He wanted to go ahead on foot. He did meet us at Assos and we took him aboard and got to Mitylene. We sailed away the next day and got to Chios. The next day we arrived at Samos. The next day we came to Miletus. Paul decided to sail by Ephesus because he was in a hurry and didn't want to spend time in Asia. If at all possible, he wanted to be at Jerusalem for Pentecost.

Paul Speaks To The Ephesian Elders

But from Miletus he sent a message to Ephesus and summoned the elders of the church. When they arrived, he said to them, "Remember how I came to you in Asia on the first day? Then I have stayed with you such a long time, serving the Familyhead with all humility of mind and with many tears and the trials that happened to me because of Jewish plots. I didn't hold back nothing that was profitable to you. Instead I taught you in public as well as from house to house to change your attitudes about God and have faith in our Familyhead Jesus, God who came to earth. Now I am summoned by the spirit to go to

Jerusalem. I do not know what things will happen to me there. I am told by witnesses in every city that the breath of the Spirit of God whispers imprisonment and troubles await me. But I don't hold my life of no account to myself. I just want it so that I can reach the finish line and fulfill the ministry I received from the Familyhead Jesus to witness about the gospel of the grace of God. Now I know something. None of you to whom I preached about God's Homeland will see my face again. I ask you to make a record this day that I am innocent of the blood of all people. I didn't hold back. I preached the whole plan of God for you. Take care of each other and the whole flock. The Holy Spirit has set you the job of being overseers to shepherd the church of God. He purchased it with his own blood. After my departure, I know fierce wolves will come in to prey on you and the flock won't be safe. Then too people shall stand up within your own congregation twisting about things to draw away disciples after them. Watch out remembering that for three years I did not stop short of tears in minding each one of you day and night. And now, brothers and sisters, I place you in the hands of God, and to the story of his grace, which is able to build you up, and to give you an inheritance among all the saints which are sanctified. I have not wished I possessed anyone's gold or silver or clothing. You yourselves know how my hands provided for my needs and those with me. Every way I have tried to show you that it is good to work to be supportive to the vulnerable and to remember the stories of the Familyhead Jesus, how he said, 'It is more blessed to give than to receive.'" And after Paul spoke, he kneeled down and prayed with them all. And they all wept bitterly and fell on Paul's neck and kissed him. They were sad most of all because it was a farewell talk he said and because they would not see his face anymore.

Paul's Journey To Jerusalem

They accompanied him to the ship. After we left them, and launched out to sea, we tool a straight course to Cos, and the day following we got to Rhodes, and from there to Patara. We found a ship sailing over to Phoenicia. We went aboard and set out. We saw Cyprus but we passed it on the right and sailed toward Syria. Next we landed at Tyre for the ship to unload cargo. We looked up disciples and stayed with them for seven days. These disciples told Paul the spirit said he was not to go up to Jerusalem. When the days for equipping were over, we left after a sendoff from them all with their spouses and children all the way out of the city. We kneeled down on the shore and prayed. Then we had to leave each other. We climbed up to the ship and they returned to their homes. We continued on the boat beyond Tyre until we got to Ptolomais. The sisters and brothers there welcomed us and we remained a day with them. The next day we left and got to Caesarea and we entered into the house of Philip

the evangelist, one of the seven, and stayed with him. This man had four unmarried daughters gifted in speaking and preaching. As we loafed there many
days, there come down from Judaea a certain seer named Agabus. And when
he come to us, he took Paul's cloth belt and wrapped it around his own hands
and feet, and said, "So says the breathing Spirit of God. The Jews at Jerusalem
will arrest the man that owns this cloth belt and turn him over to the hands of
pagan worshippers." As we heard these things both we, and the local ones,
begged Paul not to go to Jerusalem. But Paul answered, "Don't cry and trouble
my heart? I am not only ready for arrest but also to die at Jerusalem for the
name of our Familyhead Jesus." And when he couldn't be persuaded not to go,
we stopped trying, saying, "The will of the Familyhead be done." And after
those days we got into our wagons and went up to Jerusalem. Some disciples
of Caesarea went with us. They brought with them Mnason of Cyprus, an old
disciple, who had a house where we could stay.

Paul Visits James

When we got to Jerusalem how happy the brothers and sisters was to see
us. On the very next day Paul went in with us to James and all the elders were
present. After he greeted them, he give them a report how God is busy among
the Pagan worshippers through his ministry. Hearing it, they praised God and
said to him, "You see, brother, how many thousands of Jews there are who believe and they are all keeping the religious law. But they have become informers on you. They say you teach all the Jews living with pagans to abandon
Moses and tell them they don't need to circumcise their children or follow customs. What is going on? A mob will form for they will hear that you are here."
All of us hear what they are going to do. They have four men who took an oath
to get you. Confront them by purifying yourself and paying the cost to shave
your head, so everyone gets the information from the informers that you are
nothing but just another follower of custom and keep the religious law. But as
for your faith community of non-Jews we have written to them our warning
about sacrificing to idols, blood, strangulation and pornography. Then Paul
took the advice of the men, and the next day purified himself with them, went
into the church, to mark the completion of the days of purification while each
of them presented an offering.

Paul Is Arrested At The Jerusalem Church

When the seven days were almost ended, the Jews from Asia saw him in
the church and all of them surrounded him in a mob, and shoved him around
with their hands, crying out, "People of Israel, help! This is the man that goes
everywhere arguing against common people and the law and this place and

also he brought Greeks into the church and has desecrated this special place." They previously saw Trophimus an Ephesian in the city with him and assumed Paul brought him into the church. The whole city was agitated and a crowd rushed to form and they dragged Paul out of the church and quickly shut the doors. They were hot to kill him but a report reached an officer of the cohort that the whole place of Jerusalem was in confusion. He immediately took soldiers and centurions and when they saw the officer and the soldiers, they stopped beating of Paul. When the captain got closer, he grabbed him and ordered him bound with a double chain and asked a certain person who Paul was and what he was doing. The others in the crowd called out another version. Since he wasn't able to learn the specifics about the commotion, he ordered Paul taken to confinement. When he got to the steps, he had to carry Paul up through the soldiers on account of the violence of the mob and the majority of the common people followed crying, "Kill him."

Paul Defends Himself

As Paul was about to be brought into the prison, he said to the captain, "Is it possible for me to tell you someting?" He said, "Can you speak Greek? Aren't you that Egyptian who used to cause riots and led four thousand folk - terrorists - out into the wilderness?" But Paul said, "I am a Jew of Tarsus, a city in Cilicia, not a city without a reputation for influence and I ask you to allow me to speak to these people." And when he got permission, Paul stood on the steps and raised his hand toward the people. And when there was silence, he spoke to them in the Hebrew tongue, saying, "People, sisters and brothers, mothers and fathers, hear my defense, which I make now to you." And when they heard that he spoke in the Hebrew language to them, they kept even more still and he said, "I am truly a male Jew, born in Tarsus, a city in Cilicia, and raised in that city at the feet of Gamaliel, and taught according to the strictness of the law of the ancestors and was zealous for God as you all are this day. I chased down a dead-end path to hunt prey to kill, men and women, tying them up and delivering them to prison, so the church superintendent can witness for me and all the elders. They give me letters charging me to go to our brothers and sisters in Damascus to bring them under arrest back to Jerusalem to keep up their strict discipline.

Paul Tells Of His Conversion

But as I traveled and come near to Damascus abut noon, suddenly there shone a great light round about me from the very skies of existence. I fell to the ground, and heard a voice saying to me, "Saul, Saul, why do you hunt me down?" And I answered, "Who are you, Sir?" And he said to me, "I am Jesus of Nazareth who you are hunting." Those with me saw the light too and were scared but they didn't hear his voice talking to me." And I said, 'What is causing this, Sir?' And the Familyhead said to me, 'Get up, and go into Damascus and it will be revealed. What is happening is what is to be made of you." I couldn't see directly because of the shine of that light. I was led by hand by other travelers until I went into Damascus. A certain person, Ananias, a man committed to the law, with a good reputation among the whole Jewish community, came to me and stood beside me and said to me, "Brother Saul, look up." And at the same time, I looked up at him and he said, "The God of our ancestors has chosen you to make clear God's desire, and experience the one who is just, and to hear his voice out of his mouth. You will be his witness to all people and tell what you have seen and heard. And now, why wait? Get up, and be baptized, and wash away your mistakes. Call on the presence of the Familyhead."

Paul Sent To The Non-jews

Then something happened after I returned to Jerusalem, while I prayed in the church. I was in a trance and saw him saying to me, "Hurry up and get out of Jerusalem quickly for they will not listen to your witness concerning me." And I said, "Familyhead, Sir, they know that I imprisoned and beat those that believe in you in every church, and, when the blood of your martyr Stephen was shed, I stood by and consented to his death, and kept the clothing of the ones that killed him." And he said to me, "Go! Let me send you far away to pagan worshippers."

Paul And The Roman Soldiers

They listened to what he was saying for awhile until their cry arose, "Hang his kind out in the country. He isn't fit to live." And they were shouting and ripping their clothes and throwing dust in the air. The captain ordered him to be brought into the barracks and

said to interrogate him while whipping him. He wanted to learn what crime these people were charging him with. As they stretched him out to whip, Paul said to the centurion that stood by, "Is it legal for you to whip a Roman citizen without trial?" When the centurion heard that, he went and told the captain, saying, "You better watch what you are doing. This man is a Roman." Then the captain came, and said to him, "Tell me - are you a Roman?" He said, "Yes." And the captain said, "It took me a lot of money to buy that status." And Paul said, "But I was freeborn." Then they left him quickly without interrogating him and the captain also was scared after he knew that he was a Roman because he tied him up like that.

Paul Before The Council

The Captain still wanted to know the cause - why there was such turmoil among the Jews - so he released Paul and ordered the church superintendent and the whole Sanhedrin to assemble and so Paul stood in front of them. Looking straight at the Sanhedrin, Paul said, "Friends and brothers, I have lived in good conscience before God my whole life even to today." And the church superintendent Ananias ordered the fellow standing next to him to slap him on the mouth. Then Paul said to him, "God intends to slap you, you stonewaller! Are you sitting to judge me by the law, and yet order me to be slapped illegally?" Those who stood beside him said, "Are you correcting God's church superintendent?" And Paul said, "I did not see him that way, brothers. I saw him as a church superintendent. The writing is 'You shouldn't insult the people's church superintendent.'" Paul knew that one part were Sadducees and the other Pharisees and shouted to the Sanhedrin, "Friends and brothers, I am a Pharisee, a son of the Pharisees. I am being attacked because I believe in the hope and resurrection of the dead. And when he said this, an argument started between the Pharisees and the Sadducees and the crowd was divided. The Sadducees say that there is no resurrection, nor messengers from God and soul but the Pharisees acknowledge them both. A great shouting match began. Some of the Hebrew translators of the Pharisees stood up and yelled, "We don't find nothing wrong in this man. What if a spirit or an angel spoke to him?" And when the dissension become fierce, the captain become afraid Paul would be torn to pieces by them. He ordered the soldiers to go down and take Paul by force from among them and take him back to the barracks. Later that night the Familyhead stood by him and said, "Don't be afraid. As I had you testified about these things concerning me at Jerusalem, so is it needful that you witness also in Rome."

A Plot Against Paul's Life

With the coming of the daylight, a conspiracy was hatched. Certain Jews vowed to each other the vow not to eat or drink till they had killed Paul. There were more than forty who made this conspiracy. They went to the elders and church superintendent and said, "We have strictly bound ourselves by oath to taste no food till we have killed Paul. Now, report to the captain to bring him down to you as though you were going to hear his case more fully. We are ready to kill him before he comes near. The son of Paul's sister heard of their ambush, so he went to the barracks and told Paul. Paul called one of the centurions and said, "Take this young man to the captain because he has something to tell him. So he took him and brought him to the captain and said, "Paul, the prisoner, called me and asked me to bring this young man to you as he has something to say to you." The captain took him by the hand and pulled him aside and asked him privately. "What is it that you have to tell me?" And he said, "The Jews have plotted to ask you to bring Paul down to the Sanhedrin tomorrow, as though they were going to ask more details from him. But don't be persuaded by them. More than forty of their men are going to ambush him and swore an oath not to eat or drink till the have killed him and now they are ready, waiting for the promise from you. Then the captain dismissed the young man and ordered him, "Tell no one what you have informed me of."

Paul Sent To Felix, The Governor

The captain called two centurions and said, "Alert two hundred soldiers with seventy cavalry and two hundred spearmen to go as far as Caesarea at the third hour after dark. Also provide a mount for Paul to ride and take him safely to Felix the governor." He wrote a letter to this effect: "Claudius Lysias to his Excellency the governor Felix, greetings, This man was seized by the Jews and they was about to kill him when I broke it up with the soldiers and rescued him. I have learned he was a Roman citizen. I was trying to learn what they held against him. I took him down to their council. I found that he was accused of questioning their laws, but charged with nothing deserving death or jail. When it was disclosed to me that there would be a plot against the man, I sent him to you quickly. I told them to make their charges about him to you. So the soldiers according to their instructions took charge of Paul and bought him by night to Antipatras and on the next day they returned to the barracks leaving the cavalry to go on with him. Paul and the cavalry arrived at Caesarea and the letter was delivered to the governor. Then they took Paul in front of him. On reading the letter the governor asked to what province he belonged. When he learned that Paul was from Cilicia he said, "I will decide your case when your accusers arrive." He ordered Paul to be taken under guard to Herod's praetorium.

The Case Against Paul

After five days the high priest Ananias came down with some elders and a lawyer, one Tertullus who brought the charges to the governor against Paul, and when he was called, Tertullus gave an opening statement saying, "Great peace have we received administered through you and the reforms you have brought about toward this folk under your governance. In every way and everywhere we have welcomed you, Great Felix, with all gratitude. Oh, as to this bother, you don't need to worry about it anymore. I ask your patience to hear us briefly. We have found this man a pest, an agitator among all the Jews throughout the world, and a ringleader of the sect of the Nazarenes. He even tried to profane the church until we seized him. By questioning him yourself you will be able to learn from him about everything of which we accuse him." The Jews were joining in confirming all this as holding true.

Paul Defends Himself Before Felix

The governor motioned for Paul to speak. Paul responded. "I know how you have judged over this folk for many years so I confidently make my defense. As you know, it is more than twelve days since I went up to worship at Jerusalem and they did not find me arguing with anyone or stirring up a crowd, either in the main church or in the other churches, or in the city. They can't prove to you any of their charges against me. But this I admit to you. I worship according to a path that they call a sect. I worship the God of our ancestors. I believe everything laid down by the law or written by the prophets. I have a hope in God which these themselves accept. I believe there will be a resurrection of both the just and the unjust so I always take pains to have a clear conscience toward God and toward everybody. Years after I left, I distributed charity for my folk. As I was doing this, they found me purified in the church without any crowd or riot. It should be that you have present some Jews from Asia to make this charge if they have anything against me. Otherwise, have these men themselves say what crime they found I commited when I stood before the Sanhedrin except this one thing which I shouted while standing among them. I shouted at them that the only reason I stood on trial before them was because I believed in the resurrection of the dead." Felix had a rather accurate information about Paul's journey and put them off, saying, "When Lysias the captain comes down, I will make a decision on your case." Then he gave oders to the centurion to keep Paul in custody but give him privileges so that none of his friends were prevented from providing for his needs.

Paul Held In Custody

After some days, Felix sent for Paul and visited him with his wife, Drusila who was a Jewess to hear what he had to say about faith in Jesus, God who came to earth. As Paul discussed justice and self control and future judgment, Felix was getting personally very terrified and said, "Leave for now! When I have an opportunity I will summon you." But sometime, he was hoping for another opportunity - this time to get money as a gift from Paul. So he sent for him often and conversed with him. After two years had passed, Felix was succeeded by Porcius Festus. Doing the Jews a favor, Felix left Paul in prison.

Paul Appeals To Caesar

Three days after Festus got to his province, he went up to Jerusalem from Caesarea. There the church superintendent and important Jews talked against Paul and put Festus on notice they wanted satisfaction out of him such that Paul would be sent to Jerusalem. They had in mind an ambush to him him along the road. Festus replied that Paul was being kept at Caesarea and that he himself intended to go there shortly. He wondered if in fact there was a reason to keep the man in custody at Caesarea, He was intending to go there soon. "So if there are any of you," he said, "who can go down with me to accuse him I will see if it condemns him." Festus stayed among them not more than eight or ten days. Then he went down to Caesarea and the next day he took his seat on the court bench and ordered Paul to be brought. And when he come, the Jews who went down from Jerusalem stood about him bringing against him many serious charges which they could not prove. Paul said in his defense, "I have not committed any offense either against the law of the Jews nor against the church nor against Caesar." Still Festus wanted to do the Jews a favor, so he said to Paul, "Are you willing to go up to Jerusalem and be tried on these charges before me," But Paul said, "I am standing in Caesar's court where I ought to be tried. I have done no wrong to the Jews as you know very well. If then I am a criminal and have committed anything for which I deserve to die, I am not trying to escape death, but if there is nothing in their charges against me, no one can give me up to them, I appeal to Caesar." Then Festus conferred with his advisors and answered, "You have appealed to Caesar and to Caesar you shall go."

Paul Brought Before Agrippa And Bernice

Now after an interval of days passed, Agrippa the king and Bernice arrived at Caesarea to welcome Festus, and as they stayed there many days, Festus laid Paul's case before the king, saying, "There is a man left prisoner by Felix, and when I was at Jerusalem, the church superintendent and the elders of the Jews demanded him, asking for sentence against him, "I answered them that it was not the custom of the Romans to give up anyone before the accused met the accusers face to face, and got an opportunity to make a defense concerning the charge laid against him, When they came here, I didn't delay, but on the next day took my seat in the courtroom and ordered the man to be brought in. About this man - the prosecutors stood up but didn't charge him with no charge I suspected of being of the criminal range. They questioned certain things about his religious beliefs and about one Jesus, who was dead, but who Paul says is alive. I was frustrated at these arguments and I asked whether he wanted to go to Jerusalem and have a trial about these things. Then Paul appealed to be kept in custody for the decision of the emperor, so I ordered him to be held until I could send him to Caesar." Then Agripa said to Festus, "I want to hear the man myself." "Tomorrow," he said, "you can hear him." On the next day Agripa came, and Bernice, with great ceremony. After they went into the audience hall with the military captains, and prominent men of the city, Paul was brought out at Festus's order. And Festus said, "King Agrippa, and all you people in the audience, observe this one about who a whole mob of Jews begged from me when I was in Jerusalem and here shouting that he not be permitted to live no more. I didn't find that he commited a crime subject to death sentence but he himself appealed to Augustus's justice, I have decided to send him there. But I am not for sure what to write to my superior. I have brought him in front of you, and especially before you, King Agrippa, so you can interrogate him and I will have somewhat to write. It seems unreasonable to me to send a prisoner and not indicate his crime.

Paul Defends Himself Before Agrippa

Agrippa said to Paul, "You can speak for yourself." Then Paul held up his hand, and answered for himself. "I am happy, King Agrippa that I can defend myself this day before you. I stand before you accused by Jews, King Agrippa, and I know you are an expert on all Jewish customs and questions. This is why I ask you to hear me patiently. I was brought up from youth and from birthright according to my race both in my own nation and at Jerusalem as all the Jews know. I lived by the rules of the strictest sect of our religion. I lived a Pharisee. And now I stand and am judged for the hope of the promise made of God to our ancestors. It was a promise to our twelve tribes fervently serving God day and night. It is for a particular hope, King Agrippa, that I stand accused by the Jews. Why is it so hard for you to acknowledge that God raises folk from the dead? Hey! I myself acted in defiance. I wanted to do everything possible against the name of Jesus of Nazereth. I actually did such things in Jerusalem and I put in prison many saints and used my influence against them. I operated in all the churches prosecuting them frequently. I made them commit blasphemy. I was tireless and I persecuted them in faroff cities.

Paul Tells Of His Conversion

Then as I went to Damascus with authority and a commission from the church superintendent - it was around noon, King, I experienced a light out of the very skies of existence on the road, greater in brightness than the sun, shining round about me and this light stayed with me as I was traveling. Then we all fell to the ground and I heard a voice speaking to me, and saying in the Hebrew language, 'Saul, Saul, why do you persecute me? It will be hard for you not to stumble if you kick like a stubborn mule. And I said, 'Who are you, Sir?' And he said, 'I am Jesus who you persecute. Now, get up and stand on your feet for I have appeared to you for a reason. I aim to make you a minister and a witness both of these things which you have seen and of those things I will appear to tell you to deliver to people, and to the Pagan worshippers to whom now I send you. Open their eyes and turn them from darkness to light, and from the power of the Destroyer to God, that they may receive forgiveness of sins, and Godly inheritance among those who accept sainthood in faith in me.'

Paul's Testimony To Jews And Gentiles

That is why, King Agrippa, I cannot be disobedient to the vision from the sky. I went first to Damascus, and then to Jerusalem, and then everywhere along the coasts of Judea, and then to the Pagan worshippers so they could reform and turn to God and do activities worthy to show this reformation. These are the reasons why the Jewish mob seized me in the church and tried to kill

me. It is only because I have the resources of help from God that I can continue to this day to witness both to common people and the prominent. I do not say anything more than what the prophets and Moses said would happen. When God came to earth he necessarily suffered persecution but became the first one to rise from death to signal a light to humanity and also to Pagan worshippers.

Paul Appeals To King Agrippa To Believe

And as he spoke for himself, Festus said with a loud voice, "Paul, you are beside yourself. Too much booklearning has made you crazy." But Paul said, "I am not crazy, Great Festus. I speak facts of truth and good sense. I am speaking bluntly because the king knows about these things. I don't believe any of these things has been hid from him. None of this happened in a dark corner. King Agrippa, do you believe the prophets? I know that you believe." Then Agrippa said to Paul, "You almost have persuaded me to be a Christian." And Paul said, "I wish to God that not only you but all that hear me this day were not just 'almost,' and 'altogether' such as I am except for these chains." And after he spoke, the king got up, and the governor, and Bernice, and the others sitting with them. And when they were outside, they talked among themselves, saying, "This man does nothing subject to the death penalty or of imprisonment." Then Agrippa said to Festus, "This man could have gotten himself free if he had withdrawn his appeal to Caesar."

Paul Sails For Rome

After it was ordered that we set sail to Italy, they placed Paul and certain other prisoners in the custody of a person named Julius, a centurion of Augustus's guard. They boarded a ship of Adramyttium which was going to voyage to places on the coast of Asia and we set sail in the company of a man, Aristarchus, a Macedonian of Thessaloniea. The next day we touched at Sidon. Generously, Julius let Paul do what he needed to - to go see friends since this place happened to be one within his charge. And when we sailed from there, we crossed under Cyprus because the winds were against us. And when we sailed over the sea of Cilicia and Pamphylia, we came to Myra, a city of Lycia. There the centurion found a ship of Alexandria sailing to Italy and he put us on it. We sailed slowly many days and came over close to Cnidus except the wind did not allow us to land. We sailed under Crete and over toward Salmonis. We didn't hardly get past it until we came to a place called "The Fair Havens" near the city of Lasaia. We wasted a long time there and already the trip was extra dangerous since the fast days were past, so Paul warned them, "Fellows, if you will be sailing now, I think it will cause damage and great loss not only to the cargo and ship, but also risk our lives. But the centurion was persuaded by the steersman and the owner of the ship, more than by what Paul said. Also the harbor was not proper to winter in, so the majority proposed to leave there while they could to reach Phoenix and to winter in this harbor of Crete laying south-west and north-west.

The Storm At Sea

For awhile the south wind blew gently and they thought they had it made, thier idea and all, as they sailed close by Crete. But not long after a wind blew in like a whirlwind the sailors call Eurakulos. The ship got caught up in this and we weren't able to steer against it, so we were driven along involuntarily. The boat scraped bottom in the shallows of a small island called Cauda so we were hardly able to keep it upright. This was taking all our best efforts while the crew were bustling around trying to tie down the cargo with ropes. Then the fear was we would lose the hull due to the shallows because we lay so low in the water so we threw the heavy things overboard. More and more we were in the grip of the storm and on the next day we had to start throwing over the cargo and on the third day they ripped out the sails with their bare hands. For many days there wasn't sun or stars to be seen and the storms didn't let up even a little. The rest of our hope we had of being rescued was took away. After suffering a long period of seasickness, Paul stood in the crowd and said, "For my part, I didn't think it was necessary to set sail from Crete, fellows, thinking it best to avoid this damage and loss. But now I can tell you to cheer up. There will be no destruction of life among you except for the ship. A messenger from the God to whom I belong and serve stood beside me last night and said, "Don't be afraid, Paul. It is necessary that you stand before Caesar so God will deal generously with all the ones sailing with you. So, cheer up! fellows. I have faith in God that so it will be with the plan I have told you. But it is necessary that we run aground on an island." As the fourteenth night passed and we were drifting in the Adriatic Sea, in the middle of the night, the sailors figured they was coming near to some land known to them. When the checked the depth, they found the water twenty fathoms deep and a little further on, after they checked it again, they found it fifteen fathoms deep. They worried that they would break up in rocks, so they threw four anchors out of the stern and wished for daylight. The sailors were seeking to flee out of the ship and lowered a boat into the sea under a secret plan as if they was about to lay out an anchor from the bow of the ship. But Paul said to the centurion and to the soldiers, "If they don't stay on the ship, you won't be able to be rescued." Then the soldiers cut the ropes of the boat, and allowed it to fall off. And while the dawn was beginning to break, Paul encouraged them all to eat food, saying, "Today is the fourteenth day we have been without appetite and eaten nothing. I ask you to eat food for your health for not a hair from the head of any of you will be destroyed. After he spoke, he took bread, and gave thanks to God in front of them all and after he divided it, he began to eat. Then all of them began to have better moods and they began to eat food. All of these amounted to two hundred sev-

enty six souls. hip, And when they ate enough, they lightened the ship by throwing out the wheat into the sea.

The Shipwreck

When it was daylight, they didn't recognized the geography but they discovered an inlet having a beach toward which they wanted to go if the ship could be steered there. They released the anchors and let them sink into the sea. Then they unleashed the ropes on the rudders and hoisted up the mainsail to the wind and made toward shore. But they struck a rock in cross currents and the ship ran aground. The result was on the one hand the bow was stuck, and on the other hand the stern was shattered by the violence of the waves. The soldiers' advice was to kill the prisoners for fear they would swim out and escape. But the centurion, wanting to save Paul, kept them from their intention and ordered that the ones who could swim should jump overboard first into the sea and swim to land and the rest could try to make it through safely on boards or some on the broken pieces of the ship.

Paul On The Island Of Malta

That's how it come that they all escaped safe to land. And after rescue, they discovered the island's name was Malta. And the natives didn't just show usual hospitality to us but instead welcomed all of us by building a fire because of the rain coming on and the cold. But after Paul threw a bundle of sticks on the fire, a poisonous snake come out of the heat, and bit him on his hand. And when the natives saw the fangy creature clung on his hand, they whispered among themselves, "This man is proved to be a murderer. Maybe he escaped the sea, but justice don't allow him to live. Then, Paul shook off the snake into the fire, and didn't feel any the worse. Then the natives looked at what should have swelled, or caused him to suddenly fall down dead and they kept on looking for a long time, and saw nothing bad coming to him so they changed their minds and whispered that he was a god. In the same location was land belonging to the most important citizen of the island, whose name was Publius who received us courteous, and gave us a place to stay for three days. And it come that the father of Publius lay sick of a fever and was throwing up blood when Paul entered in, and prayed, and laid his hands on him, and healed him. So when this was done, others also, who was sick on the island, come, and was healed. They also helped us with many thanks and when we left they loaded us down with necessities.

Paul Gets To Rome

After three months we were rounded up to a ship that spent the winter in Alexandria flying a flag with the sign of Castor and Pollux. After putting in at Syracuse, we continued on three days. After drifting around, we came to Rhegium. Now the wind began to gust after the first day. On the second day we got to Potiolous. In this place, we found brothers and sisters and we stayed with them seven days before we left for Rome. When these friends heard we were leaving from there, they came to meet us at the Appian Forum and Three Taverns. When Paul saw them giving the praise to God, he left encouraged. Finally we come to Rome, Paul was allowed to stay by himself with a soldier as a guard.

Paul Preaches In Rome

Come along after three days Paul appealed to the most prominent Jews to round up support to get released. When they assembled, he said to them, "Brothers and sisters and friends. I am held here to go on trial but I have done nothing wrong to our race or the customs of our ancestors. I have been delivered over into the hands of the Romans in chains from Jerusalem. After they questioned me they were wanting to release me for there was nothing they could even begin to say was criminal worthy of death sentence. When the Jews objected to it, I was forced to appeal to Caesar so that my own racial folk couldn't have me charged. So now I called you in to witness my side about the cause of arrest and to speak up about it because it is for the hope for Israel that

I am restrained with this chain." And they said to him, "We haven't received letters from Judaea concerning you, nor have any travelers coming this way - brothers or sisters - spoke up to say any nasty rumors. We don't know what to think about what we are hearing about these things you are referring to. There is talk though everywhere about this denomination and the talk is that it is offensive." They fixed a time of day to go back to him there and a greatly increased crowd poured into the foreign section. He exposed these to his testimony about God's homecoming to earth, arguing for Jesus using the law of Moses and the prophets, from morning till evening. Some were persuaded by his arguments but some remained critical. They got to disturbing the peace and when they couldn't agree among themselves, they left after Paul had his say one more time, "Wasn't it right how the spirit of God spoke through Isaiah the Godly messenger of our ancestors, saying: "Go to this folk, and say: Maybe you hear with your ear, but you don't understand it. Maybe you will see the picture, but you don't envision it. The heart of this folk beats sluggish, and it will be their ears get hard of hearing, and their eyes get filmed over so they can't see what they see. Never yet have they really looked with their eyes Or tried to hear with their ears. Or understand in the heart or accept conversion or let me heal them." It's for sure! Have it your own way! The one who reconciles folk with God must have been dispatched to the homeless peoples. They will listen. And he stayed there two whole years witnessing personally and he welcomed everyone coming to him, preaching about God's homecoming and teaching about the Familyhead Jesus, God who came to earth, with all confidence, and no one could stop him.

ΚΑΤΑ ΙΩΑΝΝΗΝ

The Word Became Flesh

1 Ἐν ἀρχῇ ἦν ὁ λόγος, καὶ ὁ λόγος ἦν πρὸς τὸν θεόν, καὶ θεὸς ἦν ὁ λόγος. 2 οὗτος ἦν ἐν ἀρχῇ πρὸς τὸν θεόν. 3 πάντα δι᾿ αὐτοῦ ἐγένετο, καὶ χωρὶς αὐτοῦ ἐγένετο οὐδὲ ἕν.[a] ὃ γέγονεν[a] 4 ἐν[1] αὐτῷ ζωὴ ἦν[2], καὶ ἡ ζωὴ ἦν τὸ φῶς τῶν ἀνθρώπων· 5 καὶ τὸ φῶς ἐν τῇ σκοτίᾳ φαίνει, καὶ ἡ σκοτία αὐτὸ οὐ κατέλαβεν.

6 Ἐγένετο ἄνθρωπος,[b] ἀπεσταλμένος παρὰ θεοῦ, ὄνομα αὐτῷ Ἰωάννης· 7 οὗτος ἦλθεν εἰς μαρτυρίαν ἵνα μαρτυρήσῃ περὶ τοῦ φωτός, ἵνα πάντες πιστεύσωσιν δι᾿ αὐτοῦ.

---

[1] 3-4 {C} οὐδὲ ἕν. ὃ γέγονεν ἐν p[75c] C (D οὐδέν for οὐδὲ ἕν) L W[supp] 050* it[b] vg[ww] syr[c.(pal)] cop[sa,fay] Naassenes Theodotus[acc. to Clement] Valentinians[acc. to Irenaeus gr, lat and Clement] Diatessaron[i,n] Ptolemy Heracleon Theophilus Perateni Irenaeus Clement Tertullian Hippolytus Origen Eusebius Ambrosiaster Hilary Athanasius Cyril-Jerusalem Ambrose[2/3] Epiphanius Augustine Cyril // οὐδὲ ἕν· ὃ γέγονεν· ἐν (1071 οὐδέν for οὐδὲ ἕν) Θ 28 700 892 1195 1241 1242[e] Diatessaron[esyr] // οὐδὲ ἕν ὃ γέγονεν. ἐν ℵ[c] Κ Χ Π Ψ 050[c] (f[1] οὐδέν for οὐδὲ ἕν) f[13] 33 565 1009 1010 1079 1216 1230 1242* 1253 1344 1365 1546 1646 Byz Lect vg[cl] syr[p,h] cop[bo] arm geo Adamantius Alexander Ephraem Ambrose[1/3] Didymus Epiphanius Chrysostom Jerome Nonnus Ps-Ignatius // οὐδὲ ἕν ὃ γέγονεν ἐν (p[66] οὐδέν for οὐδὲ ἕν and omit ἐν) p[75*] (ℵ* οὐδέν for οὐδὲ ἕν) A B Δ 063

[2] 4 {A} ἦν (see footnote 1) p[66,75] A B C K L X Δ Θ Π Ψ 050 063 0234 f[1] f[13] 28 33 565 700 892 1009 1010 1071 1079 1195 1216 1230 1241 1242 1253 1344 1365 1546 1646 2148 Byz Lect vg syr[p,h,pal] cop[bo] arm geo Theodotus[acc. to Clement] Diatessaron Irenaeus[lat] Clement[3/5] Origen Cyprian Eusebius Chrysostom Nonnus Cyril Theodoret // ἔστιν ℵ D it[a,aur,b,c,e,f,ff2,q] syr[c] cop[sa,fay] Naassenes[acc. to Hippolytus] Theodotus[acc. to Clement] Valentinians[acc. to Irenaeus] Diatessaron[l] Perateni[acc. to Hippolytus] Irenaeus[gr,lat] Clement[2/5] mss[acc. to Origen] Cyprian Ambrosiaster Victorinus-Rome Hilary Augustine // omit W[supp]

---

[a] 3 *a* major, *a* none: WH BF[2] RV[mg] ASV[mg] RSV[mg] NEB Jer Seg[mg] // *a* none, *a* major: (TR) WH[mg] Bov AV RV ASV RSV NEB[mg] (Zür) (Luth) Jer[mg] Seg

[b] 6 *b* minor: Bov BF[2] RV ASV (NEB) Zür Luth // *b* none: TR WH AV RSV Jer Seg

---

1-2 Jn 17.5; 1 Jn 1.1-2   1 ὁ λόγος Re 19.13   ⟍ 3 Wsd 9.1; Jn 1.10; 1 Cor 8.6; Col 1: He 1.2   4 ἐν αὐτῷ ζωὴ ἦν Jn 5.26   5 Jn 3.19   6 Mt 3.1; Mk 1.4; Lk 1.13, 17, (7)

320

Opening page of John's Witness from the *Greek New Testament* that Ben Johnson used for the translation.

JOHN'S WITNESS

Living In The Life Of A Story

IN THE BEGINNING WAS A STORY whereby God might live on earth and the story was additional to God and the story was God. This was a beginning to God. Everything come from it and without it there's not one thing. It so happened that, out of this, come the energy for life and this life force was the glimmering of people, and this glimmering shone in a void and the void itself couldn't hold on anymore.

The Witness Of John The Baptist

There came a person named John who committed himself to God. He come for a witness to announce a brightening so everyone can have faith on account of it. He wasn't the light himself, but he was deputized so that others could have revelation of the brightness. This light was what exists and brightly animates everybody who comes into the world. Into the world it came, and the world came to itself through it, and the world didn't even know it. It came to those of its own kind, but its own didn't take to it. But such as those who received it, each was dealt the permission for all time to become children of God. It gives capacity to those who accept it. They are children of God not because of their blood, or because of bodily need, or because they will it, but because they was born of God. The story of God's desire to live as a person took on flesh form and lived among us, and we observed him as God took care of him4, care an only Child gets from a parent, full of pride and acknowledgement. John is witnessing about this and he cries out to us now as he then did saying, "This one is the one I spoke of, a person coming after me, who existed before me, and I was assigned as his advance agent. Out of the full extent of his love, we continuously receive it all, a parent's love instead of the longing for it. Before the law was given to Moses, care and acknowledgement came through Jesus, God's Child. No one's ever got to see God before. That event revealed a one-time birth God- him being from the lap of the parent."

The Testimony Of John The Baptist

This is testimony from John - when the Jewish authorities in Jerusalem sent out clergy and Levites to ask him, "Who do you claim you are?" Well, he admitted it and didn't hold back anything and he told them, "I am not God come to earth." And then they kept up questioning him, "Then who are you? Are you

Elijah?" And he said, "No, I'm not." "Then are you a prophet?" He answered, "No." Then they said to him, "Who are you so that we can give an answer to those who sent us. What do you have to say about yourself?" He said,

"I am a voice crying in the barrens. I clear a path for the Familyhead."

So said Isaiah, the prophet. "Some of them were of the Pharisee party. They enquired more and said to him, "Why are you baptizing if you aren't God's Child or Elijah or a prophet?" And John cut through this foolishness and said, "I baptize in water. Near us stands someone who you don't recognize for who he is. When he has come into his own, I am not going to be worthy to unloosen the thongs of his sandals." All these things happened near the Bethany village on the other side of the Jordan where John was doing baptizing.

The Lamb Of God

The next day, John sees Jesus coming to him and says, "Here he is, the Lamb of God who takes away the deceit of the world. This one is the one so all important of whom I said, 'After me comes a man who not only lives but always existed before me. My assignment was to be his advance agent.' And I didn't understand it at first but now I do... someone was appearing in Israel that I was baptizing with water for." And John drew his conclusion saying, "I sensed a spirit coming down as would a dove from the very sky of existence and staying upon him. I saw this and I witness that he is the Child of God."

Jesus Gets Two Disciples

On the next day, again, where John had been making his stand and with him two of his disciples, he looked up to see Jesus walking to him, he said, "Here he is - the Lamb of God." And these two disciples heard him saying it and they went over to follow Jesus. And Jesus turned to them and was looking them over, them wanting to follow him, and said to them, "What are you searching for?" And they said to him, "Master," - "Where do you stay?" And he said to them, "Come and you will understand." Then they went and saw where he stayed and they stayed with him that day until it was late in the afternoon. One of the two who was listening to John and followed Jesus was Andrew, the brother of Simon Peter. This fellow went from John to find his own brother, Simon, and says to him, "We have found God's very Child". He brought him to Jesus. Looking up at him, Jesus said, "You are Simon, the son of John. You will be called Cephas, (which is translated Rock)."

Philip And Nathaniel Join Jesus

The next day Jesus wanted to go to Galilee and saw Philip. And Jesus says to him, "Come with me." Now this Philip come from Bethsaida out of the same city as Andrew and Peter. Philip located Nathaniel and says to him, "We have discovered the one Moses wrote about in the law. He is also the one the prophets wrote about. It is Jesus, a child of Joseph out of Nazareth." And Nathaniel said to him, "It isn't possible for anyone important to be from Nazareth." But Philip says to him, "Come on and see." Jesus saw Nathaniel coming to him and says about him, "See there, a truthful Israelite who doesn't quibble." Nathaniel says to him, "How'd you know of me?" Jesus broke through his confusion saying, "A while ago, I saw you in the act of pleading for real understanding under a fig tree." Nathaniel answered him, "Teacher, you are the Head of Israel." Jesus said to him, "Because I said to you that I saw you under the fig tree-has that given you this belief? You will have more understanding than this." And Jesus says to him, "Trust me! You will see the sky of existence itself open and Godly messengers going down and coming up for the human Child of God."

Jesus At A Wedding In Cana

And there come a wedding in Cana of Galilee on the third day and the mother of Jesus was there. And she called Jesus and his disciples into the wedding room and because they were needing wine, the mother of Jesus says to him, "They have no wine." And Jesus says to his mother, "What's that to me and you, mother? It is not yet my time to be revealed." His mother says to the household workers, "Whatever he may say to you, do it." There were there six

stone water jars stored up according to the Jewish purification practices, each holding upwards of two or three liquid gallon-like volumes. Jesus says to them, "Fill up these water jars with water." And they filled them up to the top. And then he says to them, "Now pour some out and carry it to the wedding reception room." And they carried it. As the wedding head waiter tasted it, the water become wine and he didn't know where it come from, but the household workers knew how it come to be wine instead of water. The head waiter whispers to the bridegroom and he says to him, "Most people serve good wine first and then after people have been drinking they serve the cheaper. You must have kept the best wine until later." This was the first of Jesus's miracles and it was done at Cana of Galilee. It showed his special nature. His disciples believed him to be God come to earth. After this he went down to Capernaum itself where his mother and sisters and brothers were and his disciples too and there they stayed for just a few days.

Chasing Currency Changers And Sacrifice Sellers Out Of The Church

Since it was close to Passover time, the Jewish Thanksgiving holiday, Jesus went down to Jerusalem. He found in the church those who were selling calves and lambs and doves and money changers sitting around, and after he made himself a whip out of rope he chased them all out of the church along with their calves and lambs, and he poured out the coins from the bags of the foreign exchange bankers and he overturned their tables that was holding the doves for sale, and he said, "Take these things out of here. Don't make this house of my Parent into a store." And the disciples remembered that it was written,

"Intense emotion about your house will eat away at me."

Then the Jewish authorities questioned him and said, "What sign from God can you show us that gives you the right to do these things?" Jesus cut through their blasphemy and said, "Break up this sanctuary and in three days I will cause it to be raised up." Then the Jewish authorities said, "It took forty-six years to build this church and you are going to cause it to be raised up in three days?" But what was said about the sanctuary was about his body. Then when he did come back from death, the disciples remembered that this was said, and they recognized the expression as the fulfillment of what Jesus said.

Jesus Knows People

After they were in Jerusalem for the Jewish Thanksgiving holiday, many professed belief in Jesus's Godly identity because they saw the miracles he was doing. But Jesus said he was sceptical about them because he recognized everything and because he had no need for fan worshipping from people. He himself knew the motivation that was in people.

Jesus And Nicodemus

There was a fellow, a Pharisee named Nicodemus, a chief leader of the Jews. This person came to Jesus at night and says to him, "Pastor, we know that you have come from God as a teacher. No one could do the miracles you do unless God is with him." Jesus cut through this and said to him, "Trust me! I tell you the truth! If someone isn't born on a higher plane, he can't see God's homeland." Then Nicodemus says to him, "How can a person have such a birth who is old? No one can re-enter his mother's womb a second time." Jesus answered, "It is like this. I tell you the truth! If someone is not born of water and the breath of God's spirit, he can't enter God's Homeland. There is birthing by the flesh into flesh and there is birthing from the spirit into spirit. Don't be shocked that I'm telling this to you. It is necessary that you be born on a higher plane. It is where the spirit of God's breath wills that it blows as does the wind, and its own voice listens, and when you don't know it, it comes and goes somewhere else. So is everyone who has this birth from God's breath." Nicodemus, trying to understand the thought, said to him, "How is such a birth possible?" Jesus, trying to challenge his thinking, said to him, "You are a teacher of Israel and you don't know? Here it is. We speak what we know, and we explain what we see, and you don't accept our evidence. If I have explained things of the earth to you and you don't accept them, would you believe the things of God's Homeland beyond? And no one goes beyond into the sky of existence unless he come down from the sky of existence as did the human Child of God. It's like when Moses raised up a bronze snake on a pole out in the desert and God instructed people that were snake-bit to look on it so as not to die of the bites."

In the same way it is necessary that you look to God's human Child so that trusting in him you can have life forever. God loved the world so much, God gave it God's only child, so everyone that has faith in him won't ever be destroyed but has everlasting life. God sent this child into the world not to sentence the created ones like a judge does, but to redeem the world through him. The one who believes in him is not condemned, but the one who doesn't believe stands ready for condemnation simply because that one hasn't believed in the identity of God's only earthly born Child. This decision is subject to condemnation because the light has come into the world and the people chose to love the darkness instead of the light. There were wrongs done by them. But the one who acts conscientiously comes to the light so that such a one's acts are noted because they are done in God.

Jesus And John The Baptist

Later on, Jesus went with his disciples to the Jordan River area and they stayed by themselves baptizing. John was baptizing nearby in a place called Ainum of the Salem region, because water was plentiful there and he wasn't taken to prison yet, but people were going over to where Jesus was for baptism. John's disciples at the Jordan began discussing the right way for purification and they went to John and said to him, "Teacher, here is the one who come to you when you were baptizing on the other side of the Jordan, the one in whom you said you were doing your witnessing. Look! He is baptizing too and every-one is going to him." John answered, "A mere person doesn't have power to take anything away from us unless it's been ordered down from the sky of ex-istence. The ones you are talking about going to him were listening to me when I told them, 'I am not God who has come to earth but I am a preparer for his coming.' A bridegroom is true to the bride while friends of the bridegroom have to stand by and can only listen to the praising voice of the bridegroom raised in joyous song. But this also is my joy and it is the completion to my work. It is right that he is growing more popular and I am becoming less im-portant."

He Has Come Down From The Sky Of Existence

The one who came down from a higher plane is in charge of everything. A person from the earth is tied to earthly standards in thinking and mortal thought is being expressed. The one who came down from the sky of existence is the one this writer witnesses as the result of realizing who He was and hear-ing him even if no one else accepts this testimony. The one who does accept this sworn evidence is affirmed because God is its truth. God has sent the Godly language it is spoken in and the breathing spirit of God refuses to allow it to be qualified. The Parent loves the Child and gives everything into his hand. One who believes in the Child has eternal life. But the one who sluffs off the Child will not see eternal life because God's anger remains against him.

Jesus And The Woman Of Samaria

Jesus knew the present situation. The Pharisees heard that Jesus was at-tracting more disciples and baptizing more than John was - except Jesus him-self never baptized but instead left this to the disciples. Jesus gave up on the Jewish authorities and went again to Galilee. But then he was tugged to leave for Samaria. He went to the Samarian city called Suxar, near the farm that Jacob gave to his son Joseph. Jacob's well was there. Jesus was worn out from the trip and went to sit down near this well. It was near the sixth watch. Here came a Samaritan woman drawing water. Jesus says to her, "Give me a drink." His dis-ciples were gone into the city to buy food. The Samaritan woman says to him, "How is it you, a Jew, are asking me, a Samaritan woman, for a drink. You know Jewish law doesn't allow sharing with Samaritans." Jesus answered her, "If you appreciated the value of this free gift and who is asking you 'Give me a drink,' you would insist on it and it seems to me you would freely give me the water necessary for me to live." The woman says to him, "Sir, you take the bucket. The well is deep." Then he has the woman tell him how her life is com-ing along. "Don't you feel there is something more important than having Jacob as your father? Isn't it more important who has given you the well in the first place rather than the fact that Jacob and his descendants, and his herd drank from it?" Then Jesus said to her, "Everyone who drinks from this watering place will have to keep drinking again and again but if you drink of the water I will give you, you will not be thirsty ever again." Then the woman says to him, "Sir, give me to drink this water so as I won't have to come here drawing water. And he says to her, "Go summon your man and come back here." The woman replied, "I have no man." Jesus said to her, "What you say is right, 'I have no man.' You clung to five men and now you don't have a single one as your man. You told me the truth." The woman says to him, "Sir, I think you are a prophet such as our fathers worshipped with in this mountain range except that your race says Jerusalem is the only place where it is possible to worship." But Jesus says to her, "Believe me, maam, that an hour comes when people will worship their Creator neither in the mountains nor in Jerusalem. You people worship what you don't know. We worship what we know, that there is a Redeemer coming from the Jews. Now comes the hour and is here, when all true worshippers will truly worship the parent in spirit and truth. The Parent likewise seeks after those who worship Him. A spirit is God and those who worship him must worship him in spirit and in truth." The woman says to him, "I know that an Expected One is coming, one to be called God alive, and when he comes that information is for our whole world." Then Jesus says to her, "I AM. It is I who talk to you." And after while the disciples come to him and they were amazed that he was talking with this woman, but no one was saying, "What is behind this?" or "What conversation come off with her?" After he emptied her water jar, the woman went down into the town and says to the people, "Come! See this person who related to me everything I done. Can't this person be God who comes to earth?" They came out of the city and ogled him. Then the disciples started up asking him, "Teacher, eat something." But he said to them, "I have food to eat which you know nothing about." Then the disciples said to each other, "He didn't bring anything along to eat." Jesus told them, "It sustains me to do the duty of the one giving me my mission and to be getting along with finishing my life work. Don't you hear it said, 'There is only a four month growing season and then comes the harvest?' Listen to what I am telling you. Energize your eyes and you will notice these fields - how they aren't even pale green, let alone ready for harvesting. Already the one who is going to do the harvesting is wanting paid and to gather in the fruit of eternal life. That is my wish too because the harvest may be a joy to the planter as well as the harvester. In this fact, there is the truthful saying that, 'The one who does the planting really is the one who is the harvester.' I was sent to you to harvest what you alone cannot work to achieve. Others grow weary, but you have enlisted for hard work

for the coming harvest." Many people from out of that town believed him to be God come to earth among the Samaritan people through the witness by this woman because "he told me everything I did." This is how it was that as he left this Samaritan town, they asked him to stay among them, and he did stay two additional days. Many more came to believe through his preaching. Then they said to this woman that we don't believe anymore that you were just yakking. For we have heard enough and know that this is truly the one who saves the world.

The Healing Of The Official's Son

After a couple days, he left for Galilee. Jesus himself wanted to witness that the prophet gets no respect in his own hometown. When he got into Galilee, the Galileans welcomed him, especially those who saw what he did at the Thanksgiving festival in Jerusalem and those that went to the festival. Then he went again into Cana, the town in Galilee where he done the turning of water into the fruit of the vine. And there was an important person related to the ruling family whose son was sick in Capernaum. When this person heard that Jesus was come from Judah into Galilee he went to him and asked him would he go down and heal his son, for he was about to die. Then Jesus said to him, "Is it going to be that if you don't see a mark of Godliness and miracle you won't believe me to be God come to earth?" And this important person says to him, "Sir. Travel there before it's too late and my son dies." Jesus himself says to him, "Go, your son lives." The person believed what Jesus was saying to him and went away. But already while he was traveling home, the household employees of his come to talk to him, saying to him that the boy of his was alive. Then he asked them what hour before that the boy had got well. Then they told him, "Yesterday about the hour of the seventh watch the fever went away from him." He knew this was the same hour in which he heard Jesus say, "Your son lives." Then not just him but his whole household believed Jesus was God come to earth. This was the second time Jesus performed a miracle since coming from the Jordan into Galilee.

The Healing At The Pool

After awhile, there was another Jewish feast day and Jesus went down into Jerusalem. Now inside Jerusalem, near where livestock are kept, there was a bathing pool which is called Bathside in Hebrew, roofed and having five porches. Sick people lay in there all the time and those blind, crippled or paralyzed. A person about thirty was there eight years due to his disability. When Jesus saw him lying disabled and realized how long a time has passed, he says to him, "Do you want to become healthy?" The disabled person answered him, "Sir, I have no helper to bear my stretcher to dip me in when the pool water stirs. I can get into it but someone else has to help me get out." Jesus says to him, "Stand up. Get up from the stretcher and walk." And immediately it happened. He was healed. He got up from his stretcher and walked. But it was on Sunday. So the religious leaders in charge complained about the healing, saying, "It is Sunday, and it's not fitting for you to be getting up from your stretcher." But he answered them, "The one who done this healing said to me, 'Get up from your stretcher and walk.'" They interrogated him. "Who is the person that said to you, 'Get up and walk?'" But the one who was been mended don't know who it is. Jesus left without being noticed and there was a crowd at that place. Later, Jesus picked him out in the church and said to him, "See, mending can come. You don't have to feel separated out and there's nothing worse that can happen." The person left and told the church authorities that Jesus was the one who healed him. Then after awhile, those in charge of the church wanted to prosecute Jesus because he did what he did on Sunday. But Jesus defended himself to them, "My Parent is busy even now and I am active too." Because of this, these church authorities were going to ask for Jesus to be killed because he broke the Sunday religious law, and was talking about God like God was his own parent and he's doing work the same as God does.

The Authority Of The Child

Jesus explained, "Trust me! A child is not able to do nothing for himself unless his parent shows him how. What that parent does is what the child likewise does. A parent cares for a child and always shows him what he must do. He will emphasize the most important behavior for the child so he will be proud of you for doing it. As the parent raises the dead and gives life, so also does the child wish to nurture life. The parent then weighs nothing, but gives the task of judgment to the child. Everyone should respect the child as they would respect the parent. The one who doesn't respect the child doesn't respect the parent who commissioned and sent him. Trust me! I am telling you this as a caution for those who hear it and accept that the Parent sent me to hold in my grasp eternal life and to exercise judgment but also to transform life from subjection to death. Trust me! The hour comes and now is when the dead will listen to the voice of the human Child of God and while hearing it will rise to life eternal. As the Parent holds life in his grasp, so also does he give to the Child eternal life to have in himself. And this authority he gave to this one to do final weighing because this one is a human Child. Don't be shocked about this, that the hour comes in which all the dead will listen to the Child's voice and will rise from the dead, and the good will go out into the resurrection of life while the bad will be brought to resurrection justice. I don't have the energy to act on my own. But I do carefully weigh what people do as I listen. And as I listen, I make distinctions. But I don't try to do my will but the will of the one sending me.

Witnesses To Jesus

Unless I witness about myself, my witness isn't honest. Something else is witnessing about me and I know that her witness is truthful testifying about me. Weren't you sent to John and didn't he give you the true facts. But I don't refer to the witness only of a person, but rather I speak so you may be delivered from this world. John was a fiery beacon, burning and shining, but you were not willing to bathe in the ecstasy of fire in the hour given him for illumination. I have a witness more convincing than John. These are the actions I take which the parent performs through me so that I might finish my undertakings. These actions which I take witness about me that the parent sent me. And the one sending me, that parent, witnesses now as forever about me. You will never listen to such a voice. Nor will you seek to imagine any. And you don't orient yourselves in John's revelation, the one sent to announce the coming, and even this you won't believe. You search the holy writings because you want to give the appearance of research into eternal life but these too witness about me. And yet you don't want to come to me when you have me alive. I do not receive attention because I am a human being as I am known to you but to address the fact that you don't honor the love of God in each other. I come in the stead of my Parent and yet you don't accept me. But in that case another would have to come in my stead, so that you may be accepted. But how could you trust the insistence receiving it from any one else when you don't seek it from the only God? Do any think that it is I who will complain about you to the Parent? The one who accuses you is Moses in whom you have placed hope. If you believe

Moses, believe me. For it is of me that he wrote. But if you don't trust those writings about these things, how can you believe in what you see happening."

The Feeding Of The Five Thousand

Sometime later, Jesus traveled across the Sea of Galilee, or the Sea of Tiberias some call it, and a big crowd followed after him. They were impressed by the miracles which he did for the sick and needful. And Jesus went up into hilly country and he rested with his disciples. It was nearly time for the Passover Jewish Thanksgiving feast. After Jesus looked around and realized how large was the crowd, he says to Philip, "Where can we buy bread to feed these people?" But it was just said to tease Philip because Jesus well knew what he was about to do. Philip replied to him, "Two hundred silver coins wouldn't be enough to buy bread for all them each to get even a little bit." Then another of the disciples, Andrew, the brother of Simon Peter, says to him, "There is a child over here who has five loaves of bread and two tidbits of fish. But what is that in such a large bunch?" Then Jesus said, "Have all these people sit down and get ready to eat." There was lots of nice grassy spots at that place. When they sat down the number of people was about five thousand. Then Jesus took the loaves of bread, and after giving thanks for them, he doled them out to as many as were ready to eat and from the fish he give out the same way as much as they would want. And after they were all filled up, he says to his disciples, "Gather up the leftovers so nothing gets wasted." They picked up and filled twelve baskets after the five loaves of bread and fish was divided up, which was the leftovers after the meal was finished. When people realized that he did a miracle, they said, "This is truly a prophet who has come into the world." Then when Jesus realized that people was about to come and seize him to force him to be their ruler, he slipped away again into the hills to be by himself.

Walking On The Water

And as evening come on, the disciples went down to the sea and they got their boat ready to cross the sea to Capernaum. It got dark out and Jesus still has not come to them. Then they left and the sea started churning being blown about by a gale and as they were being driven out twenty five or thirty stadia lengths they saw Jesus walking on the sea and approaching the boat and this scared them. Then they wanted to pick him up in the boat but immediately the boat came to the shore toward where they headed.

Jesus The Bread Of Life

The next day the crowd gathered on the other side of the sea saw no boats had departed but one and that Jesus wasn't gone when his disciples left on the only boat that went out. Then boats came from Tiberias near the place where they ate the bread blessed by the Familyhead. When the crowd realized Jesus wasn't there any more or his disciples, they went down to the boats and went to Capernaum looking for Jesus. When the found him across the sea, the said to him, "Teacher when did you leave?" Jesus answered them saying, "Listen! Don't search for me because you saw miracles or because you want bread to eat and you need fed. Don't earn bread by wasting labor, but earn bread that remains in eternal life which the human Child of God will give to you. The Parent, God, notes this with approval." Then they said to him, "What can we do to earn the approval of God?" And Jesus answered to them, "This is Godly work, to trust the one he sent." Then they said to him, "Why don't you perform a miracle for us? Then we can understand and believe you are God come to earth? How do you work them? Didn't our ancestors eat manna in the wilderness as it's writ, 'The bread from the sky was give to them to eat.'" Then Jesus said to them, "Trust me! It wasn't Moses give you the bread from the clouds but my parent who gives you the bread of existence. For the bread of God is the one coming down from the sky of existence in order to give life to the world." Then they said to him, "Sir, give bread to us all the time." But Jesus said to them, "I am the bread of life. The one who comes to me never hungers nor does one faithful to me ever thirst. But I observe that you have seen what is and always has been but you can't believe it. Everyone who is given me by my Parent can arrive at it, and I won't reject or cast aside anyone coming to me because I have arrived out of the sky of existence not to do what I want to do, but what the one who sent me wants. This is the will of the one sending me, that everyone who is give me I am not to destroy from my being here, but rather that I will raise up on the last day. This is the will of my Parent, that everyone who acknowledges the Child and believes him to be the human Child of God has eternal life and I will cause each to rise from death on the last day. Then those Jewish authorities started buzzing to themselves about his saying that, "I am the bread coming down out of the sky of existence," and they were saying, "Isn't this Jesus the child of Joseph, and don't we know who are his father and mother? What is this now about him coming down out of the sky of existence?" Jesus responded and said to them, "Does it gain you anything to buzz with each other about this? No one is able to come to me unless the parent who sent me encourages it, and I will cause each to come alive on the last day. It is writ in the prophesies, 'And they will all accept God's instructions.' Everyone who listens to the parent and learns, comes to me. Never has anyone seen the Parent except it be me in God's stead - still this one has seen the parent. Trust me! I am telling you a person who believes me gets eternal life. I am the bread of life. The ancestors of you ate in the desert and died. There is a living bread coming

down from the sky of existence. Any of you eating it won't die. I am the bread of life come down from the sky of existence. If any eats this bread, he will live forever, and this bread is my body which I give to you on bahalf of the biological world. The Jewish authorities started arguing and fussing among themselves, saying, "How can he give his body to be eaten?" Then Jesus said to them, "Trust me. Unless you eat the body of God's human Child and drink his blood, you won't have the life in it. The one who takes the body for food and drinks my blood has eternal life, and I will cause that one to arise from death on the last day. My body is the food of truth and the blood of my existence is drinkable. The one who consumes the meaning of my presence of the body and drinks in the meaning of the blood sacrifice is mine and I stay in him or her. And just as the one who sent me is the living Parent, and I am living for the Parent, so is also the one digesting me, and that one will live in me. This is the bread coming down from the sky of existence, not such as the ancestors ate and died. The one consuming this bread will live in time itself." This was what Jesus said in the church in Capernaum.

The Words Of Eternal Life

Many that listened to his disciples said, "This lesson is hard to understand. What can possibly come from listening to this?" But Jesus knew by intuition what they were muttering about to the disciples and said to them, "Why have this demoralize you? If you are observing God's human Child coming down isn't this how it was formerly? The breathing spirit is what gives life. The body

has no claim on it. These teachings that I tell you about lead to spiritual life and that is real life. But some among you have no faith." Jesus knew from the beginning that some wouldn't believe him to be God come to earth and some were going to turn him over to the authorities. He said, "For that reason, I reveal to you, no one can come to me unless that one is a gift to me from my Parent." After this many of the disciples turned back around and no longer walked with him. But Jesus said to the twelve, "Don't you want to leave me?" Simon Peter answered him, "Familyhead, Sir, who else can we go to? You teach us eternal truths. We have faith and accept that you are the presence of God." Then Jesus replied, "Not only I have selected you twelve, but also one has been selected through deception." This one spoken of was Judas Simon born in the town of Iscariot. For he was getting ready to turn Jesus over for prosecution and he was one of the twelve.

The Unbelief Of Jesus's Family

After this, Jesus walked on to Galilee. He didn't want to travel in Judah because the Jews were looking for him to kill him. It was near the time of the Jewish feast of churches. His family members said to him, "Get out of this part of the land and go to Judah so your disciples can show you off and the deeds that you do." Nothing he done was in secret and he lived in plain sight. But they continued, "What you're doing may not be clear to the world." They said this because his family members didn't have any faith in him. Then Jesus says to them, "My time of revelation is not present yet but your time is at hand. The world can't hate you, but me it hates because I witness about myself and that its doings are ungodly. You go on down to the feast. I am not going down to the feast this time because my manifestation can't end now." Then, after he said this, he stayed in Galilee.

Jesus At The Feast Of Tabernacles

Later, his disciples went on to the feast and then he himself. He did not want to appear to be in hiding. The Jewish authorities kept up a surveillance for him at the feast and asked around, "Where is he?" And there was buzzing about him. Many in the crowds were saying "He does good," but others were saying, "No, he misleads people." Whichever, no one talked openly about him because they was afraid of the Jewish authorities in charge. When the feast was half over, Jesus come up into the church and was teaching. Then when they Jewish authorities learned of this, they started saying, "How can this one know the holy writings? He hasn't been to a seminary?" But Jesus himself answered, "My teaching is not my own but from the one who sent me. If anyone wants to do the will of God, God will reveal whether the teaching is from God or whether I am just babbling. One who babbles for his own sake is trying to get personal attention. But one calling attention to the one who sent him, this one speaks how things are and there is no wrongdoing in it. Didn't Moses teach you the law? Still no one among you follows it. Why do you try to kill me?" One in the crowd answered, "You are nuts. Why would anyone be wanting to kill you?" And Jesus answered, "I performed one miracle on a Sunday and all of you were shocked. Moses gave you the circumcision for a reason - not that it is instituted from Moses but for an ancestry - and a person gets circumcised on Sunday. If a person gets circumcised on Sunday, since this doesn't do any violence to the law of Moses, does it make sense to become angry at me for making a person whole by doing healing on Sunday? Don't judge on appearances, but consider the propriety in weighing it."

Is This God Come To Earth?

Then some among the people in Jerusalem said, "Couldn't he be right about them wanting to kill him? And here he is talking openly." Nothing more was said to him. Maybe even the authorities were startled thinking "Could it be true that this one is God on earth? But then we know from where this person comes and when God comes to earth he can't come from where this one is from." Then Jesus screamed in the church while teaching and was saying, "You don't know me and you don't know where I am from. I am not come by myself, but truth accompanies me, one who you don't recognize. I know it because I am from it and that is the one who sent me." They reached out to grab him, but no one could lay hands on him. The time was not right for that. And in that crowd were many who believed him to be God come to earth and said, "When God comes to earth no one could perform more miracles than he has."

Officers Sent To Arrest Jesus

When the Pharisees heard what the crowd was buzzing about him, their leaders were sent for, and the Pharisees' police were given orders to seize him in the future if circumstances warranted. In the meantime Jesus said, "I still have a little while left to be with you before I go to be with the one who sent me. You will search for me and not find me, and where I am you will not be able to go." Then the Jewish authorities started talking among themselves, "How would this one be able to go where we can't find him? Does he mean to go where Jews are dispersed, maybe to some Greek speaking place, and teach the Greeks? What was the words which this person said, 'Search me and you will not find me, and where I am, you will not be able to go.'"

Rivers Of Living Water

On the last day among the many in the feast days, Jesus stood and cried out saying, "If anyone thirsts, come to me and drink. When one believes in me, as the writings say, rivers from my inmost self will be pouring out living water." He was talking about the breathing spirit of God from the very breath of God which he was about to release for those faithful to him. The breathing spirit wasn't come because Jesus wasn't taken up into God.

Division Among The People

Out in the crowd among those listening to this statement some said, "He is really a prophet." Others said, "This is God come to earth." But others said, "Can God come to earth by way of Galilee? Isn't it said in the writings that when God comes to earth it will be from David's ancestry and doesn't that mean out of Bethlehem, the hometown of David?" There was arguing among the crowd over it. And some were wanting him arrested, but no one yet dared lay hands on him.

Unbelief Of Those In Authority

Then the church police went back to the Pharisees and their leaders and the church leaders said to them, "Why didn't you bring him?" And the church police answered, "We have never heard such a person." Then the Pharisees

continued their discussion. "Could we be misleading people?" Not one among the leaders or any from the party of the Pharisees believed him to be God come to earth. And the crowd in the church itself didn't know how it was that their rules of the church was insulting to God. Nickodemus, one of them and the one who went to Jesus before does say to them, "Can it be a rule of the church that condemns a person before he has first had a chance to be listened to and understands what he is charged with?" They asked him, "Are you from Galilee too?" And they researched to see whether a prophet could come out of Galilee.

The Woman Caught In Adultery

After everybody else left the church, Jesus went to the Hill of Olive Trees. Then, early the next morning, he again went to the church and all the people came to him and after they sat down around him, he taught them. Then come some Hebrew translators and Pharisees parading in a woman who was caught having an affair outside marriage. After they made her stand conspicuously in the middle, they addressed him - "Teacher, here is a lady who was come upon having sex with someone who was not her husband. In the law set down by Moses it is required to throw rocks at her until she dies. What do you say?" They were saying this to get evidence Jesus is himself a law breaker so they can

prosecute him too! But Jesus was crooking his finger and was writing in the dirt. While they kept on harassing him and taunting, he looked up and said to them, "Anyone who is innocent among you can be the first one to throw a rock." And again bending down he went on writing in the dirt. After they heard this, the accusers started leaving one after another beginning with the older ones until no one was left except the woman who was being made an example of. Then Jesus looked up at her and said, "Woman, are you okay? Didn't nobody condemn you?" Then she said, "Nobody, Sir." And Jesus said, "Nor do I condemn you. Go on your way and from now on don't do anything that fails to witness for God."

Jesus The Light Of The World

Later Jesus spoke to those around him and said, "I am the light of the world. The one who follows me doesn't walk in darkness, but by the shine of a living light." Then the Pharisees said to him, "You are trying to give evidence about yourself but the evidence is a lie." Jesus answered, "Even if I am witnessing about myself, the truth is my witness because I know where I come from and where I go. You don't know where I come from or where I go. You make decisions by how they affect your bellies, but I don't decide that way. And if I give my conclusion, my conclusion is the truth because it's not just mine only, but also that of my parent who sent me. Now don't you know your own religious law where it is written that two people's evidence establishes the truth? I am one witness about myself and through my presence is the Parent witness who sent me." Then they said to him, "Where is this parent of yours?" Jesus answered, "If you don't know me, you don't know my parent. If you had known me, you would have known my Parent." These are the words he spoke near the church treasury offering box while he was teaching in the church. And still no one arrested him because his time wasn't come.

Where I Am Going You Cannot Come

And again he said to them, "I go and you will want to find me and in the loneliness you sometimes feel you will die. Where I go you aren't able to come on." Then the Jewish authorities said, "Doesn't he himself think he is going to die because he says, 'Where I go you aren't able to come?'" And he said to them, "You are in a fallen state. I am from wheresoever. You reside in this world. I am not of this world." Then he said to them, "You die alone. Since you don't have faith that I am who I say, you will die in loneliness." They said to him, "Who are you?" Jesus said to them, "Haven't I told you from the beginning who I am? I have told all of it to you and interpreted its meaning for you -how my parent affirms its truthfulness, and I have understood how things are that I may speak accordingly in this world. There are those who just won't try to understand what the parent is saying to them." Then Jesus said to them, "When you have lifted up God's human Child, then you will get the point that I AM and that by myself I don't do anything but teach as my parent has me say. The one who sent me is with me. Nor does this one depart from me because I do the things approved by this one." After this speech, many believed Jesus was God on earth.

The Truth Will Make You Free

Then Jesus spoke about the faithful ones of the Jews, saying, "If you accept my teachings about life, you can be my disciples. And if you understand its reality, you will be free." Then they replied to him, "We are the children of the race of Abraham and no one can enslave us ever again. What are you talking about, freeing us?" Jesus explained to them, "Trust me! Every child who acts wrongly is a bondless slave. No slave stays bonded to a family forever. A child is such forever. If a birthchild comes who wants to set you free, really you will be free. I know all about your being the children of Abraham. But even so you would rather kill me because my revelation finds no acceptance among you.

Whatever I understand from my parent I say, and whatever you hear from my parent do." Then they repeated to him, "Our parent is Abraham." Jesus says to them, "If you are children of Abraham, you carry on Abraham's labors. Now you are wanting to kill a person who speaks the truth of existence to you which I hear from God. Abraham could not do this. You should want to live. You should carry on the labors of your parent of existence." Then they said to him, "We aren't born to do anyone wrong. We have only one parent, God." Jesus said to them, "If God is your Parent why don't you love me? For it is from God I came and come. I didn't bring myself to be, but that one sent me. Don't you understand what I am saying? Why don't you want to listen to what I'm saying? You act like mischievous children and you are confused about your ancestry. That thought was a murderer from the beginning and don't stand up to the truth. There is no truth except this. You're lying when this mischievous parent of yours speaks through you because this parent is a liar. When I tell you about existence, you don't believe me. What from our experience refutes what I am telling you about our condition of separation? If I tell you the truth, do you believe me? The one who is from God listens to God's words. Because you aren't listening, you are not recognizing your tie to God."

Before Abraham Was, I Was

Then the Jewish authorities responded and said to him, "What right do you have to talk to us. We know full well you are a Samaritan and you are mentally ill." Then Jesus answered, "I am not mentally ill, The only thing I respect is who my Parent is, and you don't respect me. I don't seek attention for myself. There is one who desires it and is causing it. Trust me! Anyone who clings to the story of my life, will not ever see death." Then the Jewish authorities said to him, "Now we know you are mentally ill. Abraham died and the prophets, and you say, 'Anyone who clings to the story of my life, will not ever see death.' You are no better than your parent Abraham who died, didn't he? And the prophets died. So what can you do they couldn't?'" Jesus answered, "When I come to the care of God, my bond won't ever end. My Parent defers to me. Don't go saying, 'God belongs to us.' You don't know God. I know God. Even when I tell you I know God, you call me to a liar. But I know God and I follow God's teachings. Abraham, our parent, is brimming with happiness since he was given to see my day coming, and he foresaw it and rejoiced." Then the Jewish authorities said to him, "You are not even fifty yet and you saw Abraham!" Then Jesus said to him, "Believe me. I existed before Abraham came to be. I AM." And they picked up rocks so as to throw them at him. But Jesus disappeared and left the church grounds.

The Healing Of A Man Born Blind

Later, he was passing by and saw a person blind from birth. And his disciples was asking him questions, saying, "Teacher, what did he do wrong? Was it him or was it his parents that caused his blindness to come on to him?" And Jesus answered, "He didn't do anything wrong, nor did his parents. It was so the way God works can be shown through him. It's for us to labor at the work that the one who sent me wants done until the end of my day. Night comes when work can't be done. While I am still in the world, I am the light of the world." After saying this he spit on the ground and made some mud out of his spit and he put a patch of it on the eyes of the person with this mud and said to him, "Go wash in the pool of Siloam"-which is translated sending-to-place. Then he went and washed it off and left seeing. Then those nearby and those who seen him before said, "Who is this beggar? Can this be the one who sat doing begging?" Some said that this is the one. Others said, "No way. It's someone who looks like him." But he himself said, "I am the one." And they said to him, "Who caused your vision to be regained?" And he answered, "The person called Jesus got mud and patched my eyes and said to me, 'Go to the Siloam pool and wash it off.' Then after I left and when it was washed off I could see." And they said to him, "Where is he?" He says, "I don't know."

The Pharisees Investigate The Healing

Then they took this blind man to the Pharisees. It was on Sunday during the day that Jesus made the patty of mud and restored the person's sight. Again and again they was asking how he come to see again. He told them, "He put a patty of mud on my eyes and after I washed it off I could see." Then some among the Pharisees said, "This is not the doings of a man acting for God because he has not kept the Sunday-no-work rules." But others said, "How could a man do such a miracle if he wasn't really close to God?" And they kept up arguing among themselves. Then again they interrogated the blind person, "What do you say about this person who caused you to be able to see?" And he said, "He is a prophet." But the Jewish authorities couldn't accept this, that he was blind and could see until they'd summoned his parents. And they asked them saying, "Is this your child who you say was born blind? Why does he see now?" And his parents answered, "We know that this is our child and that he was born blind. But why he sees now, we don't know. What restored his vision, we don't know that either. Ask him. He is an adult. He himself will tell you." After his parents talked to them, the Jewish authorities became scared for they had already agreed that since the blind person might confess Jesus as God who came to earth he should be banned from the church. This was why his parents said, "He is an adult. Ask him." Now they called the blind person in a second time and said to him, "Do you credit this to God? We know that the person who done this is different from God." And he answered, "If he is not God, I don't know it. One thing I know, that I was blind. That's the way I was. And now I see." Then they said to him, "But who did this for you? How did your sight get restored?" He answered them, "I have told you already and you didn't listen. Why do you have me repeat myself? Don't you want to become his disciples?" And they started cussing and said to him, "You can be that person's disciple. We are Moses's disciples. We know that God spoke through Moses. We don't know nothing about where this person is coming from." But the person answered them, "This is shocking! You say you don't know where he's coming from after he restored my sight! We know that when people separate themselves from God, they lose their tether. But when people come after God and do God's will, then, God listens to them. All reality was being listened to when the sight of a blind man from birth was restored. If this doesn't come from God, then it don't come from anywhere." They answered, "You were born apart from Godly folk and you are teaching us?" And they threw him out.

Spiritual Blindness

Jesus heard that they threw him out and found him and said, Do you believe in the human child of God?" And he answered, "Is this what you want,

Sir? Because I do believe it." Then Jesus said to him, "You have experienced its reality and the one talking to you has this status." And he answered, "Family-head, Sir, I believe you are God come to earth." And he embraced Jesus tightly. And Jesus said, "I have come into this world with healing power so those who can't see may come to see and those blind from their births can see." There were those from among the Pharisee party with him listening and they said to him, "Are you saying we are blind?" And Jesus said to them, "Even if you were blind, that fact doesn't mean you have to be separated from God. But at the present time, you say, 'We see,' and that causes you to remain separated from God."

The Parable Of The Sheepfold

"Trust me! I tell you this. Someone who does not come in through a gate into a sheepfold but sneaks in another way is likely a theif or a rustler. The one who comes in through the gate is the shepherd of the sheep. The gatekeeper opens the gate for him and the sheep know his voice and he calls his own sheep by name and leads them out. When he leads out all of his own, he walks in front of them and the sheep follow because they know his voice. But they will not follow behind a stranger. Instead, they flee from him because they do not know the stranger's voice." Jesus told this story to them but they didn't fully understand what he was telling them.

Jesus The Good Shepherd

Jesus told them more. "Trust me! I tell you this. I am a gate for sheep. All who come for them are thieves and rustlers but the sheep do not listen to their call. I am the gate. Through me any who go in will be saved and will enter in and leave out and discover pasture. The thief does not enter except to steal and slaughter and destroy. I come to provide life and fill it abundantly. I am the good shepherd. The good shepherd gives up his life for his sheep. A hired hand also can be a shepherd but the sheep are not his own. When he sees a wolf coming he leaves the sheep and flees - the wolf attacks and keeps the rest of them in view -just because he is a hired hand and it doesn't matter to him about the herd. I am a good shepherd and I know mine and those that are mine know me, just as the Parent knows me and I know the Parent and I give up my life for the herd, so I take it back. No one takes my life from me, but I give it up for mine. I've the okay to give it up and get it back again. I've received this order from my Parent." Again there was bickering among the Jewish authorities about the meaning of these statements. Many said about him, "He's mentally ill and his mind's gone. Why do we even listen to this?" But others said, "These can't be ranting words. Can a person whose mind wanders restore sight?"

Jesus Is Rejected By The Jews

Then Christmas came in Jerusalem and it was really cold out. And Jesus walked into the church on Solomon's porch. And the Jewish authorities started cackling at him and said to him, "How long until you give up your life? If you are God come to earth, tell us so frankly." And Jesus answered them, "I've told you and you didn't believe it. The works I do as agent of my Parent witness about me. But you don't believe because you aren't among my herd. My herd listens to my voice and I know them and they will follow me and I give them eternal life, and they are not consumed in the span of time and they can't be taken from my hand. My Parent is the one who gives me everything and even more and no one is able to seize anything from my Parent's hand. I and the Parent are one." Then the Jewish authorities again picked up rocks to throw at him. But Jesus asked them, "Aren't all of my good works shown to you by my Parent? For which one of them are you going to throw rocks at me?" Then the Jewish authorities answered, "We won't throw rocks at you for doing good works but for speaking contrary to God because you are just a person and trying to make yourself out to be God." Jesus answered, "Isn't it written in your Godly writings, 'I've said you are Gods?' If God said this to those, isn't it the saying of God? Such a writing can't be ignored. Is this one who the Parent loves and sent into the world to be accused of blasphey for saying, 'I am the child of God?' If I didn't do the works of my Parent would you believe me? But I do and still you can't bring yourselves to believe me. So trust the works that you can know and you will understand that my Parent is in me and I and my Parent are one." Then they again tried to get ahold of him but he escaped from their hands. Again he went across the Jordan River to the place where John did his baptizing and stayed there. And many went out to him and they reported that John never showed such miracles, and everything that John said about him was true. And many there came to believe him to be God come to earth.

The Death Of Lazarus

Then a certain person got ailing. It was Lazarus from Bethany from the hometown of Mary and Martha, his sisters. Mary was the one who poured oil on the Familyhead and dried his feet with her hair. Her brother, Lazarus, was the one sick. The sisters sent the news to Jesus saying, "Familyhead, Sir! Help! This one you love is very sick." When Jesus heard it he said, "This sickness won't lead to death because the human child of God was given authority to take care to it." Now Jesus loved Martha and her sister and Lazarus. After he heard that Lazarus was sick, he stayed in the place two more days anyway. On the next day, he says to the disciples, "We are going to Judah again." Then the disciples said to him, "Teacher, the Jewish authorities are searching for you to throw rocks at you, and you want to go there again?" Jesus relied, "Aren't there twelve hour of daylight? If a person walks in the daylight, he doesn't stumble because the light of the world gives him to see. Only if someone walks at night does he stumble because there is no light in it." That is what he said and then he says, "Lazarus, our friend, lies sleeping, but we will go wake him up." Then the disciples said to him, "Familyhead, Sir, if he is sleeping, he's okay." But Jesus was meaning he was dead even if they thought he was talking about him laying down asleep. Then Jesus said to them bluntly, "Lazarus died and I am glad for your sakes that I was not there. This will give you grounds to be faithful. So we are going to him." Then Thomas, the one called Didumos, said to his fellow disciples, "We are going so we can die with him."

Jesus, The Resurrection And The Life

When Jesus found Lazarus, he already was in the tomb four days. It was at Bethany, near Jerusalem, about fifteen stadiums away. Many Jewish authorities came to be with Martha and Mary so they could comfort them after the loss of their brother. Then Martha heard that Jews was coming and she rushed to meet him. And Mary was in the house crying. Martha said to Jesus, "Familyhead, Sir, if you were here, our brother wouldn't have died. But even so, I know that whatever you ask God, God will give it to you." Jesus said, "Let's go rouse your brother." Martha says to him, "I know that there is rousing in the standing up

time of the last day." But Jesus said to her, "I am the one causing the dead to rise and life itself. When one has faith in me, even if he dies, that one lives. And everyone who lives and has faith in me can't ever find themselves destroyed in terms of time. Do you believe this?" She says to him, "Yes, Familyhead, Sir, I trust that you are God come to earth, the Child of God, the One who has come into the world."

He Weeps

And while they were talking, he went to Mary who spoke really quietly to her sister whispering, "The teacher is here and hears you." When she heard this, she got up quick and went to him. Jesus hadn't yet come into town and he was still in the place where Martha came to meet him. Then the Jewish authorities who were with her in the house comforting her, when they saw that she's got up quick and left, they followed her thinking that she went to the grave to mourn there. Then Mary, as she went where Jesus was, saw him and fell down at his feet and says to him, "Familyhead, Sir, if you were here, our brother wouldn't have died." Jesus, when he saw her crying and those with her among the Jewish authorities were crying, he heaved a sigh deep to his soul. He was troubled so. And he said, "Where did you put him?" She said to him, "Sir, come and see." Jesus started crying. Then the Jewish authorities said to him, "Look how he loved him." But some among them taunted, "This time he won't be able to do no sight restoring to this blind person, since isn't this blind person dead?"

Lazarus Brought To Life

Jesus felt so troubled inside going to the tomb. It was a cave and a huge stone was pushed up against it. Jesus says, "Move the stone." As he finished saying it, Martha, his sister says to him, "Sir, it stinks in there already since it's the fourth day since he died." Jesus says to her, "Didn't I tell you if you have faith you get God's attention?" Then they rolled off the stone. Then Jesus looked up and said, "Parent, I give thanks to you because you hear me. I know you always listen to me but I say this because of the crowd standing around so they might have faith that you sent me." And then talking really loud, he called out, "Lazarus, come out." He come out, this one who was dead, wrapped feet and hands in bandages, with a handkerchief tied around his face. Jesus says to them, "Unwrap him and release him to go home."

The Plot To Kill Jesus

Then all the Jewish authorities that came to Mary saw what he did and believed him to be God come to earth. But there were those among them that went to the Pharisees and said what Jesus did. Then they called together the church leaders and Pharisees of the Sanhedrin and they said, "What can we do? Who is this person to do all these miracles? If we leave things as they are going, the whole world will come to his kind of faith and the Romans will come and rout us from this place and turn us into pagan worshippers." Then one of them, Caiphus, who was taking his turn as church superintendent, said to them, "You don't know anything. Don't you know this could be to our advantage for one person to die for the people so that the whole world of the non-jews may not die." He was not speaking this by himself, but this church superintendent for the year was doing some foretelling because it turned out Jesus died for non-Jews, and not just for non-Jews only but so all those scattered from the church could be one children of God. After this day, they schemed to kill him. Jesus no longer walked openly in Judah, but went from there to a town near the desert called Ephraimtown and there he stayed with his disciples. Then it come near time for Easter, Passover for the Jewish authorities, and lots of people come up to Jerusalem from the towns for the feast so they could feel more God approved. And while they are standing in the church they were saying to each other, "Who does he seem to you?" "Why doesn't he come across as fearsome?" And the church superintendent and Pharisees was giving out the order to find out where he was hiding so they can arrest him.

The Anointing At Bethany

Around the sixth day of Easter, Jesus went to Bethany where his Lazurus was, the one who was brought back to live after dying. And they were getting dinner there and Martha was serving and Lazarus was one of them setting at the table with him. Then Mary begun to massage his feet, using almost a pound of expensive oil from spikenurd plants. And she dried his feet with her hair. And the house become filled with the fragrance of the sweetsmelling oil. Then Judas from Iscariot, one of the disciples, the one who is about to snitch, says, "Why wasn't this oil collected and sold for probably three hundred denarius and given to the poor?" He said this not because he was concerned about the poor around him but because he was a thief and when he carried the charity bag, he removed the money put into it. Then Jesus said, "Leave her be since it was kept for the time of my burial preparation. Every day you have poor among you, but me you don't have everyday."

The Plot Against Lazarus

A huge crowd of Jews come to learn he was there, and they didn't just wait to see Jesus alone, but also wanted to see Lazarus who returned to life after dying. Then the church superintendent wondered whether they should kill Lazarus, because every Jew was going out to see him and come away believing in Jesus.

The Triumphant Entry Into Jerusalem

The next day, the huge crowd which come to the feast, having heard that Jesus is coming into Jerusalem, took palm branches and went to him and cried out, "It is the time of the Helper. God is blessing us through this one who's coming in the stead of God, Governor over Israel!" After one was found for him, Jesus has mounted on a young donkey, as it was foretold, "Don't be scared, daughter of David's mountain city, Trust me! Your ruler comes sitting on a young colt." These foretellings, the disciples didn't know at first, but when Jesus, God on earth, came fully to their minds then they remembered what was written before, and those things done by him. Then the crowd recognized this one who for identifying himself has called the dead Lazarus to come out of a tomb and returned him from those dead. Because of this, the crowd has rushed to mob him, because they are heard he is a miracle worker. Then the Pharisees says to themselves, "Now look, no one gets nothing from this. Watch out! the world is going over to Him."

Some Greeks Seek Jesus

Then some Greek speaking ones from the Jewish overseas community were there worshipping in the church. These were ones who came from Bathsaida, Galilee and come up to Philip, saying, "Sir, we want to see Jesus." And Philip went over and tells Andrew, and Andrew joins him and they go tell Jesus. But Jesus has to decline saying, "The time has come when the human child of God is to be cared for by God. Trust me! If a grain of wheat doesn't get planted it will die. It stays what it is. But if it dies, it produces a heavy crop. One who clings to life, loses it, and the one hating life in this world safeguards rights in life everlasting. If someone wants to serve me, follow the idea. Where also I am there will be the one serving me. If any serves me, this one is proving worthy of the Parent.

The Son Of Man Must Be Lifted Up

Now my soul trembles and what can I say but, Parent, can't you take me out of this coming event?" Then a voice come out of the sky of existence saying, "It's always been I couldn't take my eyes off of you. Soon I will have you back to care for." But the crowd standing and listening heard the speaking as emerging thunder, and said, "A Godly messenger speaks for him." But Jesus answered, "This voice doesn't come on my behalf, but for your benefit. Now comes the critical time of the world. Now the one who begun this world will shatter physical appearance. And when I stand hanging over the ground, I will draw everyone to myself." This was said predicting what kind of death he was about to die. Then the crowd answered, "We understood from the written law that the Expected One, God who comes to earth, stays in the world. So how come you tell us its needful that the human child of God is hung?" Jesus answered them saying, "Just a little bit more the light is among you. Walk as if you have a lighted way since no more can darkness overwhelm you. Anyone walking in darkness doesn't know where I go. Since you have a lighted way, believe in the light, since you have become children of brilliant light."

The Unbelief Of The Jews

After Jesus talked, he was caused to disappear from them. When miracles such as this one were done before people they believed him to be God come to earth, just as Isaiah's story of what's to be realized was fulfilled, Familyhead, what else causes belief more than what we eyewitness? And what more revealing can there be than this Familyhead's activity? Regarding the disabling condition of unbelief, Isaiah said, "Blindness clouds their eyes, and makes their hearts skeptical because they don't want to believe their eyes, and trust their heart and change their thinking, and reach these things." Isaiah said this because he foresaw the carelessness of this time and spoke about it. Even from the beginning many believed him to be God come to earth, except the Pharisees who never would admit what they saw fearing being banished from the church. They craved being fawned over by people more than following after the care demands of God.

Judgement By Jesus

Jesus cried out, "One who is faithful to me isn't faithful to me but to the one who sent me. And one accepting me accepts the one who sent me. I come as a light to the world so everyone who trusts me won't have to stay ignorant. If someone listens to me and don't resist it, I won't condemn him. I didn't come into the world to condemn the world but to save the world. One who sets me aside and doesn't acknowledge my existence has someone condemning them. The living story which I am telling, that condemns in the last days. I am not speaking for myself but for my Parent who sent me to give you the rules of life which I know and which I will keep saying. I know these life rules are for eternity. That's why I tell them to you. As the Parent prompts me so do I say."

Washing The Disciples Feet

Before the Passover Jesus knew that there was coming on him the time when he would cross over from the world to rise in the sky of existence where he could be loving and caring for these same people he loved in this world on into the last days. And when supper time come, after wrong thinking already took over directing Simon Judas, the one as blinded as Icarus, so to get him to change from disciple loyalty, and after Jesus knew that the Parent has give him everything for disposing, and that by God's directing he would be leaving out of the world, he got up from the table and took off his clothes, and wrapped himself in a towel. Then he drew water into a washbasin and began washing the feet of the disciples and wiped them dry on the towel he was wearing. Finally he come to Simon Peter. Peter says to him, "My Familyhead, Sir, how come You, yourself, are washing my feet?" Jesus answered him, "What I am doing you do not know just now, but it will be understood later." Peter says to him, "Please don't wash my feet now." Jesus answered saying, "If I don't relieve your footsore, you cannot undertake my role." Then Simon Peter says to him, "Familyhead, Sir, don't only wash my feet but also my hands and head." Jesus says to him, "Those not washing now as even before that is needful unless one those feet preparation and it cleans up all of you. Also you are cleaned but not everybody. One was driven to turn from discipleship. That's why he said that you are not all clean. After he washed the feet of them he dressed and sat down again, he said to them, "Do you understand what I did for you? You consider me as the one who teaches, or the leader, and you say that correct, for I am. That's why I, the teacher and leader, washed your feet, and you owe it to each other to wash each others' feet. I give you an example so just as I've done you should do. Trust me! A worker isn't any better that the Familyhead, nor is the one who is sent out better than the one who sent that one. If you understand these principles, you are happy if you also act accordingly. I don't say all of you can. I know those I've picked out. But it's also to be fulfilled the writing, 'One who is eating bread with me is getting ready to crunch me under heel.' Now I say to you that is to come about, so you may remain faithful when it happens, because I AM. Trust me! The one who receives those I will send out are receiving me and the one who receives me, receives the one who commissioned me."

Jesus Foretells His Betrayal

Even while he was talking, Jesus was starting to feel bad in his consciousness and it come welling to be spoke and he said, "Trust me! One of you rejects me." They looked at each other, the disciples did, and come around him to reach for what he was saying. There was one sitting among the disciples Jesus was closemouthed about, who Jesus loved. Then Simon Peter waved his hand to get his attention to find out who was the one he was talking of. Then leaning so close as to be chest to chest with Jesus he says to him, "Familyhead, Sir, who is it?" Jesus answered him, "It's the one for who I dip a piece of bread and give it to him." Then after dipping the bread, he give it to Simon Judas, the Icariot.

After the bread incident, the full inclination opposed to God took him over. Then Jesus says to him, "Do what you have to do now." Still no one knew which one sitting among them was the one he spoke about. While they are deep in thought, Judas took the moneybag and Jesus said to him, "Go buy groceries we need for the feast days and give what you can to the poor." Then taking the piece of bread, he left right then. And it become dark out.

The New Commandment

After he left, Jesus said, "Now the human child of God is under God's care and God is concentrating on the child. If God does this centering in the child, God is also attending what's needful and immediately embracing the child. Little ones, still I am with you for a bit. Then you will look for me, and, as I told the church authorities, where I go you cannot come, and now I've to say the same thing to you. I bequeath you a new rule of life. Love one another just as I've loved you. So love each other. In this, every ambiguity about life will be cleared up. You are my disciples, you who love each other."

Peter's Denial Foretold

Then Simon Peter says to him, "My Familyhead, Sir, where do you go?" Jesus answered, "Where I go no one can now follow me, but after bit you can follow." Peter says to him, "Familyhead, Sir, why can't you let me follow you right now? I will die for you." Jesus answered, "You want to die for me? Trust me! A rooster won't even crow before you have disowned me three times."

Jesus The Way To The Parent

"Don't let your hearts beat scared. Do you believe in God? Believe also in me. In the house of my Parent there are many rooms. And if not, would I have told you that I was going to prepare a place for you? And when it's given for me to go and I am done preparing this place for you, I am coming again to show you the way to my own place, so that where I am also you might be and where I am going you will know the way." Then Thomas says to him, "Familyhead, Sir, we don't know where you are going. How can we know the way?" Jesus says to him, "I AM the way and existence and life. No one comes to the Parent but through me. If you know me, also you know the Parent. From now on, you will know it and you will have known you seen it." Philip says to him, "Familyhead, Sir, I wish you would show us the Parent and that would satisfy us." But Jesus says to him, "I am with you all this time and you don't know me, Philip? The one looking at me sees the Parent. Why do you say, 'I wish you would show me your Parent?' Don't you believe that I am in the Parent and the Parent is in me? The words I say to you I don't speak by myself, but the Parent in me dwelling does God's works. Believe me that I am in the Parent and the Parent is in me. If not, have faith on account of the God revealing witnessed activity. Trust me! One who has faith in me lives in this activity which I began and that one will do even more, and greater things, because I've gone to the Parent. And anything you want in substituting for me, I will see gets done, since the Parent pays care to the child. Whatever you request calling on me I will do."

The Promise Of The Spirit

"If you love me, keep following my life rules. I will ask the Parent and God will give you another Comforter to be with you every day and always. It is the breathing spirit of God which the world can't subvert because it can't see it coming, nor know how to deal with it. You will know it because it is ever present for you, and bears itself in you. I will never leave you orphaned. I come to you. A moment yet, and the world won't see my presence any longer, and you won't see me, but because I am still living, you will live. On that day you will be given to understand that I am in my Parent and you are in me and I in you. The one who holds to my life rules and keeps them, that person is one who loves me. And the one who loves me will be beloved by my Parent, and I will love that one and give that one to see clearly who I really am." Judas, not the Iscariot, says to him, "Familyhead, Sir, why does it happen that you are about to make yourself clearly seen for who you are but not while you are alive?" Jesus answered, "If someone loves me, he will acknowledge the story of my earthly life, and my Parent will love him and fit him into the story line to

find a life for him. When one don't love me, he won't listen to my story. And my life story which you hear is not just of me but also of my commissioning Parent. These things I'm telling you stay in you. But the Comforter, the Spirit that the Parent will send in my place, will teach everything and help you remember everything I told you. I leave my desire for peace to you. My peace I give you. Not in an earth constrained way do I give it to you. Don't let your hearts beat scared or anxious. You heard me tell you, I go and yet I come to you. If you loved me, you would be very happy because I am going to my Parent who is the greatest. And now I have told you every happening, so when they happen they will strengthen your faith. No longer will I say so much to you, for those in authority in this world are coming. In my authority its hold is as nothing except that I know about it because I love the Parent and since the Parent rules the world on my behalf, I conform. Let's get up and leave.

Jesus The True Vine

I am the stalk of your connection to reality and my Parent is the one who tends. Every branch from me not bearing grain, the gardener clips, and each promising grain is pruned so the crop can be maximized. Already you are pruned by the story which I am revealing to you. Stay in me and I in you. As the branch can't bear grain by itself unless it remains on the stalk, so will you be unless you remain faithful to me. I am the stalk, you the branches. One who remains in me and in them produce a heavy crop, but without me you won't be able to do nothing. If someone don't stay faithful in me, that one falls off as a branch and withers away and those gathered and thrown into a fire and burnt. If you remain faithful to me and keep in mind my words, then whatever you want ask, and it will be give to you. In so doing, my Parent is focused so you will bear heavy crop and become my disciples. As the Parent loved me, I loved you. Dwell in this love between us. If you keep my life rules, you dwell in my love, just as I am the guardian of my Parents life rules and I dwell in this love. These things I say to you so my satisfaction can exist in you and this care may reach maturity in a crop bearing stage. This is the rule of life, that you love one another as I have loved you. Greater love than this no one can have, than when someone lays down their life for their friends. You are my friends if you do what I require of you. You didn't choose me. I chose you and I cause you to bear wherever you go and produce crop and dwell with your crop, and whatever be asked of the Parent in my stead I give to you. This I require of you, that you freely love one another. If what you go through in this world hurts you, know that it first was hurtful to us."

The World's Hatred

"While you were clutched by the world, the world accepted you as its own belonging. But now you don't belong to the world after I culled you from it. That is why the world wants to hurt you. Remember the story that I told you when I said, 'There is no worker more special than the supervisor.' If they have prosecuted me, they will prosecute you. If they have tried to suppress my life story, they will try to suppress yours. But no matter what all they do to you while you are acting for me, it is because they don't know the one who sent me. So what if they came and I've spoken to them. They stayed apart. Now they don't have any excuse for being separated. Anyone hurting me, hurts the Parent. If the helping acts I did for them would have been done by someone else, they would not shy away. But now even they try to find me to be hurtful to me and my Parent. And it's all fulfilling the saying in the written law which says, 'They hurt my sacrificial gift.' When there comes the Comforter who I will send to you from the Parent, the spirit of what is true, who comes from the Parent, that one will witness about me. And you will also witness because from the beginning of the ministry you were with me."

I am telling you all these things so you won't lose faith. They will remove you from Jewish churches. The hour comes when each of you is martyred in your mission and is taken up to God in brilliant light. And all this will happen because they don't know either the Parent or me. I am telling you these things

so that when the hour for them comes you will remember that I have spoken of it to you.

The Work Of The Spirit

There are things I did not say to you at first. But now I have to go to the one who sent me, and none among you can question, 'How is it right for you to go?' What I am telling you fills my heart with pain. But I tell you the truth. It's better for you that I am going. If I don't leave, then the Comforter will not come to you. But after I leave I will send a Comforter to you. When he comes, he will prod the world about right and about wrong and about judging the difference. About wrong - what about it! Those doing it don't believe me to be God come to earth. About right on the other hand-its proof is that I am going to the Parent and no one else supervises it. About judgment, the one who began the world judges it. Still I have much to say to you but you can't bear it now. When that time comes, the spirit of reality will lead you into understanding. That will be me attending to you because from me it proceeds and advises you. Every perfection the Parent has is mine. It is for this reason that I said that from me it draws and reports to you. Just a little more will you see me and again just a little bit later will you want to see me again? Then the disciples said to each other, "What is this that he's saying to us?

Sorrow Will Turn Into Joy

In a little while you won't see me and then in a little while will you want to see me? and then I go to the Parent?" Then they said, "How much is a little while? We don't know what he's talking about." Jesus knew they were wanting clarification, and he said to them, "On account of each one of you looking out for yourselves that I said, A little while you will see me and again in a little while will you want to see me? Trust me! You will cry not knowing shame in it and feel grieved, but the world will be happy. But after you have been consumed by grief, then your pain will become exultant powerful joy. A woman when she's birthing feels pain, because the hour of giving birth comes. When she has born the baby, she doesn't remember her birthing pain for the joy because a person has been born into the world. So now you feel pained. But again I will see you and your hearts will be returned to happiness and your joy can't be took from you. And on that day no one will need to ask anymore questions. Trust me! Whatever you ask the Parent while acting for me, I will give you. Before now you didn't need to ask for anything in my stead. Ask and you will get your request so your joy can be multiplied.

I Have Overcome The World

So many things I've told you. The time is coming when I can't any longer talk to you such but in confidence I will represent you at the side of the Parent. In that day, what you ask as my earthly representative I won't just say I'll ask about it for you. For the Parent loves you because you have basked in my love and you keep faith while I go to God. I come from the Parent when I come into the world. Again, I leave the world and go to the Parent. When the disciples was talking to Jesus, Look, you are talking candid now and these aren't story lessons you are saying. Now we understand that you knew this all the time and didn't just blurt it whoever was wanting to know. We have faith in you because we have faith in who you are because you come from God." Jesus asked them, "Now can you remain faithful? Look, the time comes and it's now come when you all become doubters, each for his own reason, and I will be left alone. But I am not alone because the Parent is with me. These things I say to you so you can have peace of mind. In this world you have nothing but trouble. But be strong and have spunk. I restore order in the world.

The Prayer Of Jesus

Afterwards, Jesus prayed lifting up his eyes to concentrate he said, "Parent, the critical hour comes. Center on your child so your child can center on you, as you give me jurisdiction over earth forms, so may everyone who is given to me have the gift of everlasting life with you. Now life can be eternal since you make yourself known as God, the only final truth and the one sending Jesus as living proof. I've felt your concentration on earth working to complete the mission which you gave me to do. And now attend me, Parent, for this coddling holds the promise for world order coming over to you. I have revealed your nature to the people you gave me in this world. They are yours and you have given them to me and they live in your life story. Now they have understanding that everything which you give for my doing is from you because the words which you give me, I have revealed to them and continue to reveal to them and they have taken them to heart and understood they are true because I come to live among them and they have confidence that you sent me. I ask something for them, not for worldly purposes, but for their benefit, for those given to me, because they are yours. And my all of my being is yours and what is yours is mine and I given over that same care to them. No longer am I to live but they are living and I leave to go to you. Parent, keep them in their identity as those given to me, and watch over them, and don't let harm come to them even after the human child of God dies because that foretold event must be done. Now I must go to you and everything I say while alive was said so they could have my happiness multiplied in them. I leave to them your story and the worldly people hate them for it because such people are clutched by the world just as I am now clutched by the world. I am not asking that you uproot them from there lives in the world, but that you keep them from missing there marks. They aren't possessed by a worldly mind, just as I am not. Set them apart in an understanding of truth. The story of life is your being. Just as you sent me to live, so I commission them to the world. And for them, I turn myself Godly, so they may be set apart into your godliness in existence. For them I don't ask anything but for faith that the story continues in them through me, so all can unite, as you, Parent, and I have united, so they may be in us, so the whole world may believe that you sent me. And I the attention give them that you give me, so they may be one as we are one. I am in them and you are in me for the purpose of eventual world ending together, for the world peoples need to know that you deputized me and they are loved just as you loved me. Parent, my conceiver, I want them to be where I am, with me, so they can celebrate my content, which you give me because you loved me even before the beginning of creation. Parent, straighten it out, this world which ignores you, and me in you let it understand, so they can know that I am your deputy. I've made known to them your identity and I will keep telling it so love which you done me may be also in them.

The Betrayal And Arrest Of Jesus

After saying these things, Jesus went with the disciples of his to the area of the Kedron River valley where there was a garden. Deep into it he went by himself alone, and then his disciples. Judas, the one who doublecrossed him, had known the spot because Jesus went there lots of times with his disciples. Now Judas come, bringing with him the cohort, Roman guards, and assistants of the ministers and Pharisees, and holding torches and lamps and hoplite battle weapons and armor. Jesus already knew they were coming when he went there and he says to them, "Who you looking for?" They replied, "Jesus of Nazareth." He says to them, "I AM." And Judas was standing there the one who was the double-crosser of him. As Jesus said to them, "I AM," they come to him and fell down in front of him. Then again he asked them, "Who are you looking for?" Then they said, "Jesus of Nazareth." Jesus said, "I told you, I AM. If you are looking only for me, let these others go." So was fulfilled the foretelling that, "Those who are give to me I will not let be hurt by anyone." Simon Peter has his sword drew and he slashed the assistant to the church priest and cut off his right ear. The name of the assistant was Malxus. Then Jesus said to Peter, "Put your sword back in its sheath. Isn't it necessary that I drink of the cup given me?"

Jesus Before The High Priest

Then the soldiers and their officers and the assistants of the Jewish authorities arrested Jesus and tied him up and took him first to Annus. He was Caiphus's father-in-law, the one who was the church superintendent at that time. Caiphus was the one who advised the Jewish authorities that it was best for one person to die for the benefit of all people.

Peter's Denial Of Jesus

Simon Peter and the other disciples followed behind Jesus. One of the disciples knew the church superintendent and went to his door and joined Jesus inside the courtyard of the church superintendent. But Peter had to stand outside the gate. Then the disciple left, the one who knew the church superintendent, and the guard at the gate approached to Peter. After awhile, a girl keeping house for the gate guard says to Peter, "Do you deny being a disciple to that man?" That time, he says, "I am not!" Later the houseworkers and assistants built a charcoal fire because it was cold out and Peter went there to warm himself up and he stood there warming himself.

The High Priest Questions Jesus

Then the church superintendent asked Jesus about his disciples and what he was teaching. Jesus said to him, "I've taught out in the open to the whole world. I was always teaching in churches and in the church where all you Jewish authorities were present. I never talked secretly. Why are you asking me? Ask those who heard me what I was saying to them. Don't you see? They are the ones that know what I said." After he said this the church assistants present started punching Jesus, saying, "Now will you answer the church superintendent?" Jesus answered them, "If I've said errors, there will be witnesses to the errors. If I spoke right, why are you hitting me?" Then after Annus tied him back up they sent him to Caiphus, the church superintendent.

Peter Denies Jesus Again

Now here was Simon Peter, standing by and warming himself. Those around him said to him, "Are you still denying you are one of his disciples?" He answered them, "I am not!" One of the houseworkers of the church superintendent, a person who was related to the one whose ear Peter cutoff, said to him, "Didn't I myself see you in the garden with him?" Again Peter denied it, and just then a rooster crowed.

Jesus Before Pilate

Then they took Jesus from Caiphus to the army barracks. It was really early in the morning. They refused to take him inside the headquarters because they didn't want to contaminate themselves as would result under Jewish ritual law since they wanted to be able to eat at the religious feast time. "For what charge are you bringing this person here?" And they answered him, "If he hadn't done wrong, would we be turning him over to you?" Then Pilate said, "Take him yourselves. You give him a trial under your own law." Then the Jewish authorities said, "It's not possible for us to kill anyone." The foretelling of Jesus was being fulfilled which he told indicating by what kind of death he was about to be killed. Then again Pilate went into the army headquarters and called for Jesus and said to him, "Are you claiming you are Governor over Israel?" Jesus answered, "Are you asking this for yourself or have others said that about me?" Pilate answered, "Am I a Jew? Your race and its church superintendent have turned you over to me. What are you doing?" Jesus answered, "My authority isn't of this world. If my authority was of this world wouldn't my followers fight so the Jewish authorities couldn't have took me. For now my authority is not here." Then Pilate said to him, "So you are a powerful person?" Jesus answered, "You are saying that I am a governor. I was born to this and for this I come into the world, so I would reveal real being. Everyone who exists out of this being hears my voice." Pilate said to him, "What is real being?"

Jesus Sentenced To Die

And after he said this, he went to the Jewish authorities and says to them, "I don't find anything criminal about him. But there is a routine for your benefit that I will release one prisoner at feast time. Are you wanting that I release to you this Governor over Israel?" Then they shouted out again saying, "Not this one but Barabas." This Barabas was a revolutionary. Then Pilate took Jesus and has him whipped. And the soldiers, after they twisted together acanthus leaves crowned him and dressed him in a royal purple coat. And they pledged themselves to him and said, Welcome, Governor of Israel, and then they would punch him. And Pilate took him outside again and says to the Jewish authorities, "Okay, I'm letting him go since you might as well know I don't find to be a criminal." Then he left Jesus outside wearing the acanthus leaves crown and the royal purple coat. And he says to them, "See, a mere person." And when they saw the sight, the church superintendent and assistants started shouting "Crucify him, crucify him." Pilate says to them, "You take him and crucify him. I don't find him a criminal." The Jewish church authorities answered, "You enforce the law and according to the law he ought to die because he represents himself as a Child of God like only the Roman emperor says he can be." When

Pilate heard this analysis, he begun to get scared. And he went into headquarters again and questioned Jesus, "What kind of person are you?" And Jesus answered, "I don't give it out myself." Then Pilate said to him, "Don't you want to tell me? Don't you know I have authority to kill you or crucify you?" Jesus answered, "You don't have authority over me unless I give it to you for governance. The fact I am charged bears the most blame." From then on, Pilate decided to kill him. The Jewish authorities kept shouting, "If you don't crucify him, you aren't worshipping Caesar. Everyone who represents himself as a usurping governor is an enemy to Caesar. Then when Pilate listened to what they are saying, he brought Jesus back outside, and sat down on the judging bench at that place, called in Hebrew or Aramaic slang as The Sidewalk. It was Saturday and close to noon. And he says to the Jewish authorities, Look, your governor. Then they shouted, Take him away, Take him away, crucify him. Pilate says to them, Do you want me to crucify your governor? The church superintendent answered, "We don't have no governor except Caesar." So he was give over to their panting to crucify him.

The Crucifixion Of Jesus

Then they took Jesus away and after he's carrying his own cross he was taken to Skull Hill which is called Golgotha in Hebrew, where they crucified him and with him two others on this side and that, Jesus being in the middle.

And Pilate wrote out a title and has it put over him on the cross. It was written out, "Jesus of Nazareth, Governor of Jews." All the Jewish authorities had to read this title since the place where Jesus was crucified was so near to the city, and it was written in Hebrew, Latin and Greek. Then the church superintendent of the Jews asked Pilate, Do you have to wright, Governor of the Jewish authorities, because what it meant was, I am the Governor over the Jews. Pilate answered, "What I wrote, I wrote." Now the soldiers, while they were crucifying Jesus, took off his outer clothes and divided them into four parts. Each soldier took a part and they were going to do the same with his underclothes too. But his underclothes were seamless, being woven as one piece from the time they were new. They said to each other, "We can't divide it, so let's draw lots for it." So the writing was fulfilled that said, "They divided my clothes. And for my clothes they threw dice." These very things are what the soldiers did. His mother and his aunt Mary of Clopas, and Mary of Magdalene stood before the cross of Jesus. When Jesus saw his mother and with her the disciple who he loved, he said to his mother, "See your son." Then he said to the disciple, "See your mother." And after that time, that disciple took the mother as his own.

The Death Of Jesus

Then Jesus knew all was finished and what was written was fulfilled, and he said, "I am thirsty." A cup full of knockout wine was sitting in front of him. Then, after they purified the cup by putting hyssop leaves around it, they took up the cup to his lips. When Jesus drank the wine, he said, "It is ended," and after his head slumped, he give up life.

The Piercing Of Jesus's Side

Then the Jewish authorities, since Saturday was over, and a body couldn't stay on a cross on Sunday, asked Pilate if his legs could by broken and then he be taken away. Then the soldiers went and they inspected his legs and those of the others crucified with him. About Jesus's they said since they saw he was already dead they didn't need to break his legs, but one of the soldiers picked his spear into the side of the chest and immediately blood and water flowed out. And one of those who saw this swears to it and his evidence is reliable and that one is known for truth-telling so you can believe it. These things happened so the prophesy is fulfilled which says, "None of his bones shall be broken into pieces." And also another writing says, "They will see that one they have picked open."

The Burial Of Jesus

After this, Joseph of Aramethaia, who was one of Jesus's secret disciples being afraid of the Jewish authorities, asked Pilate if he could take down the body of Jesus. Pilate give the go ahead. Then he went and took down his body. Then came Nicodemus, coming on the first night, bearing a mixture of sweet smelling perfumes and about a pound of aloes for burial embalming. They took the body of Jesus and wrapped it in linen with spices as is Jewish custom when they are getting a body ready for burying. Near the place where he's been crucified there was a garden and in that garden was a new tomb in which no corpse ever was laid before. There on Saturday, as the Jews reckon it, because the tomb was so close, they took Jesus.

The Resurrection Of Jesus

There on the very early morning of the first Sunday while it was dawning, Mary Magdalen came to the tomb and saw the tomb hole covering rock was taken away. Then she ran and went to Simon Peter and to the other disciple who Jesus loved and said to them, "They stole the Familyhead from the tomb and we won't know where he's buried." Then Peter and the other disciple lit out and headed to the tomb. The two were running together. Then the other disciple run out ahead since he could run faster than Peter and reached the tomb first. Bending down, he looks into the tomb seeing only linen lying there. He hasn't actually gone inside. Then also come Simon Peter following him and he went inside the tomb and stares at the linens laid out. And the handkerchief which was put over his head, wasn't with the linens laid out there but was neatly wrapped apart in its own spot. Then the other disciple come in, the one who has got to the tomb first and he saw and believed. Before this, they hadn't dared figure on the writing that it was necessary for him to die to be returned to life. Then they left again to go to the other disciples.

The Appearance Of Jesus To Mary Magdalene

Then Mary had gone back to stand at the tomb, outside, to cry. As she was crying, she leant on the tomb, and saw two pure light presences sitting there, one at the head and one at the feet where has laid the body of Jesus. And them said to her, "Woman, why are you crying?" And she says to them, "They've taken my Familyhead and I don't know where they buried him." Then after she said that, she turned around, and stared at Jesus standing there but she didn't know it was Jesus. Jesus says to her, "Woman, why are you crying? Who are you looking for?" Well, she's thinking it's a gardener, and she says to him, "Sir, if you took him off, tell me where you have put him and I will take him off your hands." Jesus says to her, "Mary. Straighten up." She says to him in Hebrew

"Rabbi," which translates as "Teacher." Then Jesus says to her, "Don't embrace me, because I haven't yet gone up to the Parent. Now go to my brothers and sisters and say to them, I am going up to my Parent and your Parent and my God and your God." Mary of Magdalene went and told the disciples, "I found the Familyhead," and what all he said to her.

The Appearance Of Jesus To The Disciples

Then after it come to be evening on the first Sunday and the gates was closed where the disciples was for fear of the Jewish authorities, Jesus came and stood in the middle and says to them, "Peace to you." And after saying it, he showed them his hands and his wounded side. The disciples was so overjoyed to see there Familyhead. Jesus said to them again, "Peace to you. As the Parent sent me, I am sending you." And after saying this, he blew out breath and says to them, "Receive the spirit of God's breath." Whenever you tackle God separation it will be overcome, whenever you make choices, they will be the right ones."

Jesus And Thomas

But Thomas, one of the twelve, the one called Twin, wasn't with them when Jesus come. Later they said to this disciple, "We saw the family leader." But he said to them, "If I don't see in his hands the nail holes and poke my finger into the nail holes and poke my hand into his side, I won't believe it." And eight days later, his disciples was again inside and Thomas was with them and

Jesus come where they were holed up and stood in the middle and said, "Peace to you." Then he says to Thomas, "Put your finger here and see my hands, hold out your hand and place it into my side and don't be skeptical but believing." Thomas answered him, "My Familyhead, Sir, and my God." And Jesus says to him, "Is it because you saw me now as before, you believed now as before? Special are those not seeing and yet who believe me to be God come to earth."

The Purpose Of This Book

Now Jesus performed many miracles in the presence of his disciples which aren't written in this writing. What is written is so you will believe that Jesus is God who came to earth, the child of God, and so you can live a faithful life as a Christian.

The Appearance Of Jesus To The Seven Disciples

After these things, Jesus himself appeared again to the disciples upon the sea of Tiberias. He appeared this way. They were together, Simon Peter and Thomas, the only called Twin, and Nathanael the one from Cana of Galilee, and the sons of Zebedee and the other two of his disciples. Simon Peter says to them, "I am going fishing." They said to him, "Can we come with you?" They left shore and were out in the boat and it got nightfall, and they didn't catch anything. Then, when early morning was coming on, Jesus stood on the shore, but the disciples didn't have any idea it was Jesus. Jesus say to them, "Boys, Do you have any fish?" They answered him, "No." But he said to them, "Throw the fish net on the right side of your boat and you will find some." So they did and they couldn't haul the fish in because it was so full of fish. Then the disciple

who Jesus loved says to Peter, "It's our Familyhead." When Simon Peter heard it was their Familyhead, he put on his shirt because he was barechested, and dove into the lake. But the other disciples went in their boat because it was pretty far out from the land - close to three hundred feet with the fishing boat dragging along fish. As they came close to land, they saw a charcoal fire burning, and they were pressed to have fish and bread. Jesus says to them, "Now did you pull in enough fish to believe?" Then Simon Peter went over and dragged in the fishing boat filled with one hundred fifty-three big fish and so many they were threatening to break apart the boat. Jesus says to them, "Come on, eat breakfast." Not one of the disciples was brave enough to ask him, "Why are you doing this?" because he was their Familyhead. Jesus went on and took the bread and gave it to them and the fish too. This was already the third time Jesus appeared to the disciples after he died.

Jesus And Peter

After they had eat their breakfast, Jesus said to Simon Peter, "Simon, John's son, do you love me?" He said to him, "Yes, Familyhead, Sir, you know I am tied to you as family." He says to him, "Feed my sheep." Again he says to Simon, John's son, a second time, "Do you total want to bond with me?" "Yes, Familyhead, Sir, you know that I am tied to you as family." He says to him, "Tend my sheep." He says to him a third time, "Simon, John's son, do you consider yourself fettered to me in the love of a family member?" Peter was overtaken in emotion because he was asked a third time if he was tied in love as members of a family are to me and he says to him, "Familyhead, Sir, you know everything, you see my guts panging to be family to you." And Jesus says to him, "Tend my sheep. Trust me! When you were a boy, you learned to dress yourself and learned to walk where you had to go. Now that you are mature, you need to exert yourself and lead another life, and do what you don't want to." He said this because he wanted him to know in what kind of death he would be showing himself cared for by God. And after he said this, he said to him, "Follow me!"

Jesus And The Beloved Disciple

Turning around Peter saw the disciple who Jesus loved so entrusting him with his life story telling coming on, and this one was the one who was leaning on his shoulder at the last supper, and asked, "Familyhead, Sir, must he suffer martyrdom?" Jesus says to him, "If I give him to stay behind until I return, why do you care? You, follow me!" So this is where the story came from among the disciples that this disciple wasn't going to die. Jesus didn't say this to him because he wasn't going to die, but only talking hypothetical wishing he could remain in his written witness until he returns. This one is the disciple who in fact witnesses about these things and who wrote these words, and we know he's writing the truth. So, here it is, and they were many more things which Jesus did...so many if they were all written in one writing, I wouldn't suppose the world could hold the written account.

ΠΡΟΣ ΡΩΜΑΙΟΥΣ

Salutation

1 Παῦλος δοῦλος Χριστοῦ Ἰησοῦ, κλητὸς ἀπόστολος ἀφωρισμένος εἰς εὐαγγέλιον θεοῦ, 2 ὃ προεπηγγείλατο διὰ τῶν προφητῶν αὐτοῦ ἐν γραφαῖς ἁγίαις [a] 3 περὶ τοῦ υἱοῦ αὐτοῦ[a] τοῦ γενομένου ἐκ σπέρματος Δαυὶδ κατὰ σάρκα, 4 τοῦ ὁρισθέντος υἱοῦ θεοῦ ἐν δυνάμει κατὰ πνεῦμα ἁγιωσύνης ἐξ ἀναστάσεως νεκρῶν, Ἰησοῦ Χριστοῦ τοῦ κυρίου ἡμῶν, 5 δι' οὗ ἐλάβομεν χάριν καὶ ἀποστολὴν εἰς ὑπακοὴν πίστεως ἐν πᾶσιν τοῖς ἔθνεσιν ὑπὲρ τοῦ ὀνόματος αὐτοῦ, 6 ἐν οἷς ἐστε καὶ ὑμεῖς κλητοὶ Ἰησοῦ Χριστοῦ, 7 πᾶσιν τοῖς οὖσιν ἐν Ῥώμῃ[1] ἀγαπητοῖς θεοῦ[2], κλητοῖς ἁγίοις, χάρις ὑμῖν καὶ εἰρήνη ἀπὸ θεοῦ πατρὸς ἡμῶν καὶ κυρίου Ἰησοῦ Χριστοῦ.

Paul's Desire to Visit Rome

8 Πρῶτον μὲν εὐχαριστῶ τῷ θεῷ μου διὰ Ἰησοῦ Χριστοῦ περὶ πάντων ὑμῶν ὅτι ἡ πίστις ὑμῶν καταγγέλλεται ἐν ὅλῳ τῷ κόσμῳ. 9 μάρτυς γάρ μού ἐστιν ὁ

[1] 7 {B} ἐν Ῥώμῃ p[10,26vid] ℵ A B C D[abs1] K P Ψ 33 81 88 104 181 330 436 451 614 629 630 1241 1739[txt] 1877 1881 1962 1984 1985 2127 2492 2495 Byz Lect it[ar,d,dem,e,x,z] vg syr[p,h,pal] cop[sa,bo] arm Origen[gr,lat] Ambrosiaster Augustine ‖ omit G 1739[mg] 1908[mg] it[g] Origen

[2] 7 {B} ἀγαπητοῖς θεοῦ p[10,26] ℵ A B C K P Ψ 81 88 104 181 330 436 451 614 629 630 1241 1739 1877 1881 1962 1984 1985 2127 2492 2495 Byz Lect it[dem,x,z] vg syr[p,h,pal] cop[sa,bo] arm Origen[gr,lat] Ambrosiaster[mss] Augustine ‖ ἐν ἀγάπῃ θεοῦ G it[ar,d*,g] Ambrosiaster Pelagius ‖ omit D[abs1] it[e]

[a] [a] 2-3 a none, a none: BF[2] ‖ -a minor, a none: (NEB) (Seg) ‖ a none, a minor: WH Bov ‖ a minor, a minor: TR (AV) RV ASV RSV Zür Luth Jer

1 ἀφωρισμένος...θεοῦ Ac 9.15; 13.2; Ga 1.15   2 Ro 16.25-26; Tt 1.2   3 τοῦ γενομένου ...Δαυὶδ Mt 22.42; 2 Tm 2.8   κατὰ σάρκα Ro 9.5   4 τοῦ ὁρισθέντος...νεκρῶν Ac 13.33 5 Ac 26.16-18; Ro 15.18; Ga 2.7, 9   7 κλητοῖς ἁγίοις 1 Cor 1.2; 2 Cor 1.1   χάρις...Χριστοῦ Nu 6.25-26; 1 Cor 1.3; 2 Cor 1.2   8 ἡ πίστις...κόσμῳ 1 Th 1.8   9 μάρτυς...θεός Php 1.8; 1 Th 2.5, 10

529

Opening page of Paul's Witness I (Romans) of the *Greek New Testament* that was used by Ben Johnson for the translation.

PAUL'S ROME CORRESPONDENCE

Paul's Hello To The Romans

GREETINGS FROM PAUL, BONDED ONE TO GOD'S CHILD who came to earth, Jesus, called to be a missionary to the lonely and estranged, to bring Good News from God, which was foretold was coming by the prophets in the special scrolls about the coming of God's Child who was written about would be from David's ancestry into human form and would decide things authoritative through the spirit that sets things right, then after awakening from death, Jesus, God's Child, our Familyhead, through who we receive God's love striking into our lives, and our life mission to live in obedience, for faith indwells in every homeless and estranged person who bears the family name of God's Child,.

In these things, you live, and are summoned to Jesus, God's Child who lived with us on earth. I write this witness to those in Rome, loved like family by God, called to be special. May the comforting compassionate God allow love be yours, and Peace from God, our Parent, and our Familyhead, Jesus, God's Child. First, I give a happy greeting from God by way of Jesus, God's child, to you everyone, because your faith is noised about throughout the entire world. As God is my witness, in whom I am bound to do ministry through the spirit in the good news of God's Child, I deeply and constantly keep you in mind, and in my every prayer, asking always if now there might be some way that I might see my way clear to come to you at last. I long to see you so that I might give to you to share certain spiritual impartings for the purpose of your guidance. Also, there would be mutual benefit between us with your faith experience reinforcing mine.

And I don't want you to have a false impression that I have avoided coming to you, brothers and sisters. It is just that I have been prevented so far from providing you some benefits I have information about that I have provided to the rest of the folk scattered throughout the world. I recognize my duty to Greeks and the homeless and estranged, to the enlightened of the world and the unknowing, and all the more so when there's a joint desire between you and me that I come to Rome to preach the good news.

The Good News Doesn't Need Hid

I don't hide the good news, for it indicates the activity of God in saving everyone who believes in it, the Jewish people, who were the first to recognize it, and then the rest of humanity. The controlling mechanics of God, God's justice system, is seen out of faith, through faith, as it was written,

The one who lives right lives by faith.

God's Frustration At How Folks Were Living

It is no secret that God was frustrated there in God's Homeland. Everyone was living contemptible to God and acting unjust to the true folk family relationship, and determined to stay unjust. This, even after people knew God among them. For God has made God's self known to them. Yes, God's invisibility from the time of the creation of the world to them was made known to be observed firsthand, and here it was, the eternity, the source of life activity, and God's very nature, the purpose being to give folks no excuse for not understanding the message. Folks wouldn't recognize God as God came to their attention or recognize the benefiting life reconstitution occurring. Instead, folks pursued meaningless thinking, and the balking heart of each of them lost the inspiring light.

Claiming to be wise, they acted stupid and turned the appearance of the invisibility of God into metal images, subject to corrosion, that they could more closely identify with, people, or birds, or animals, or reptiles.

So, God let them have their way with their instincts.

Folks were given to degrade their bodies with each other, their hearts engaging in empty rituals. So doing they engaged in subterfuge about God, and acted contemptuous, and worshipped and served what's created more than the one that created it, who is the storyteller in eternity, Yes!

So, too, God let them have their way and they discounted their status. The women among them substituted unnatural ways for the ways of their maternal stamp. Likewise, the men left off the natural relationships with females to engage in predatory sex with each other, men among men, all this turning seemy. These folks got the return among themselves appropriate to their deviations.

The result is bound to be disaster returning to themselves.

So, since they didn't consider God in their decision making, God let them have their way in their deficient thoughts to do improper things. They become filled with all sorts of injustice, misconception, anxiety and depression, wrongdoing, an inclination for jealousy, murder, fighting, lying, talking slander, snitching, scheming for wrongdoing, growing more disobedient, acting against their promises, lacking common sympathy and being cruel. Whatever laws of God were recognized, because whoever does contrary to them had the habit of

dying, not only were they doing the contrary ways but they were pleased with each other to be doing them.

Paul's Despair About This Contrariness

So, what is the result?

You have rejected the over and abiding story of life, all of you, folks who have chosen to be separated from God.

So doing, you are separated from each other, choosing against others who have chosen their individual forms of God separation, for the ways you choose to behave turn you into ones who are wrongdoers.

Don't you know that there is a judgment of God? Don't you know it works according to the truth of what God's Homeland is? Don't youknow it sets standards for behaving?

Don't you consider this, folks, while engaging in these God separating behaviors and doing these things which cause you to have to try to escape the judgment of God?

Why do you turn from the wealth of God's care? And from the point of God's being tolerant? And from God's patience?

Are you so stupid as to misunderstand the care of God which takes you to a way of behaving beyond where you are?

Now, according to your stubbornness and stuck fast thinking patterns in your heart, you have set your store in frustration in a frustrated day and risked the judgment due to those who separate themselves from the light of an understanding, preceding out of the previous darkness.

God will pay according to the earnings of each. Here a wage of eternal life to those doing good work in patient enduring, seeking to live lives honoring God. Otherwise to those living in selfish personal ambition, denying the truth and who frustration and life situation have won over into separation. There is life affliction and dwelling in constraint for all folks who hold to bad ways, the Jews who first should have recognized them and the also othe ethnic people.

But there is attention and honor and peace to all adhering to the good ways, the Jews, the first informed of the good ways and the also othe ethnic people.

The LAW:

People Are Equal In The Sight Of God,

People Must Treat Each Other Equal,

God Puts Things On A Personal Basis

God Doesn't Pay Attention To the Race or External Appearances of People.

Any Acting Prejudiced Gets Judged For It

And whoever violates this equal attendedness law misjudges, and will be judged according to this law. It isn't those who hear the law who are given the okay by God, but those who do what the law says who will be held to have done the right thing. When a people who haven't got the law do the law by instinct, their law, not in plain law itself, is the law. This applies to whoever gives an indication that they have the work of the law written in their hearts, witnessing it among others as a matter of conscience and deciding how to act on the side of this law. It will save them when they are accused or needing a defense, in the day when God judges the secrets that folks have according to this explanation of the good news of Jesus God's child who came to us on earth.

So You Think You're Special

So, you are a so called Jew and you can sleep like a baby because you are above the law requiring folks to conform to God's demand to love impartial, and boasting God's on your side, and you know what's God's will, and you think you know what's right being taught what God's law is, persuading yourselves you are like guide dogs to everyone else who's blind about how to act, a light in the midst of darkness, a teacher of fools, a babysitter of babies, having the right to shape how folks think, and what's the truth about the God law.

While you are teaching another, why don't you teach yourself? While you are proclaiming not to steal, are you stealing? While you are saying not to commit sex acts out of marriage, are you engaging in sex outside of marriage? Are you one who detests everything evil and robs churches? Who brags the laws on their side so they can disobey it, and you treat God like dirt.

This is why the idea of God, according to your understanding, is looked down upon by the homeless and estranged ones.

So its written.

Being circumcised gives you a duty to practice the ways of the equal attendedness law. If you are one who breaks God's law, your being circumcised becomes uncircumcision.

Now if someone not circumcised respects the equality law, doesn't the uncircumcised state of that one get counted as if that one's circumcised?

And an uncircumcised person, who by instinct reaches to perform the ends of the equality law, will be the judge of you, despite your Torah and circumcision, being breakers of God's law. There's no benefit in looking like a Jew, or in being cut in your flesh to be circumcised, but the benefit could be if one is a true Jew, in its underlying meaning, a circumcised one of the heart and in the spirit, not Torah, not looking for favor from it from any people but from God. What is the extra of a true Jew? Or what is the help coming from being circumcised?

A lot in a lot of ways. Mainly, they first took seriously the stories about there being a God. For what would have happened if there weren't any who believed in God? Wouldn't the incomprehension have taken away the shine to God's faithfulness to God's creation?

God, forbid!

God gives us to know the truth, even when the human in us lies, as it is written,

So that you may conform to God's ways in your life stories and you may be able to survive when judged. If our wrongdoings would meet up with God's demands to conform to God's ways, what would there to be said? Wouldn't there be total frustration if God would pronounce sentence? I tell you, it would be guilty as charged.

God, help us if that comes down!

Still, how could it be that God does not act as the judge of the world?

And since God's truth indwells in me, it wells up to overcome my short-fallings in telling how God attends to us. How could it be otherwise? Why would I risk being judged a bad missionary?

And I don't speak against God as some of you say is my nature, saying, Don't we end up worse off doings what he comes to call good?

Out of that thinking there is deserved judgment.

What else? Are we being favored? Not at all. We keep begging down deep inside, both Jews and Greeks, all, to be permitted to act against God's ways. As it is written,

No one conforms to God's way, not a single person,

no one puts their life together right,

no one lives out of regard for God.

All turn away, more or less rendering their lives meaningless and despairing.

There's not one who even acts like that one cares, not one.
A grave opens when a person clears that one's throat,
each's tongue lolls in baited words, a poison more
deadly than from a snake bite comes from everyone's lips.
The mouth of each one is a damnation and is loaded with
anger intending to cause pain to others.
Their feet move in step to march to war to cause blood to flow.
Devastation and suffering are in their path, and they
don't want to know how to live in peace.
There is no respect for God even though over and above
them they are in the presence of eyes keeping track of
them.

We know that whatever the equalized attendedness law says, it says to those under the laws of God, so that every mouth should close and recognize its duty to a world under God.

So, considering the working of the equality law, all mortal folks fail to conform to it in its demands, and on account of this law everybody knows they are falling short of living right.

Faith In Jesus As The Way To God Conformity

At this very minute, even without us taking to the equal attendedness law, the way for God conformity has been perfectly shown, being born witness to by the law and by the experience of the prophets.

God conformity comes through faith in Jesus, God's Child when on earth, to all who live that faith. There is no other conversion factor.

All act wrong and fall short of God's expectation, but all may be brought into conformity with God's ways through the gift of God's compassionate uniting love set free by the activity of Jesus, who was God's Child come to earth.

God planted this activity of reconciliation thinking, "If I, God, pour out my own blood for my folk, this act will surely lead to belief. It was done in a public event of bringing folks to God, which was intended to serve the purpose of letting folk's prior wrongdoing fall to the wayside, in a show of God's enduring desire to uphold God's life with folks through an act of God's own submission to God's ways in this present time, this act to be a point of entry into human life conformity to God's ways and doing right caused by the faith Jesus had in it coming about.

No One's Got Bragging Rights Except In Belonging To The Familyhead, Jesus

What then can folks brag about? It is eliminated.

By following a human law? By doing something? No way! only by following God's law of life with faith indwelling.

We cannot count on living lives of faith as human beings without engaging this law whereby God intended to equally attend us.

Is God the God of the Jews only? No way! And how about those homeless and estranged? Yes, God is also the God of the ethnic homeless and all who are estranged.

Since God is One to those walking in conformity to God's ways out of faith, the non-Jew is conformed through faith. Can we repeal God's equalized attendedness law caused to be a law by God's faith in our ability to follow it? No way! We must help that law become hierarchized!

The Question of Whether the God Law of Equal Attendedness to All Creation Requires Response by the Special Creation, Anthropos Folks: The Example From Abraham's Ability to Live a Faithful Life, Faith in God Requires Conformity to God's Way

Now what is to be learned from the example of Abraham, our ancestor, by way of genealogy. If Abraham was said to be conformed to God's ways from his own doings, he would have a right to brag about himself, not God.

Now, what else does the writing say,

Abraham believed in God and it was counted to him to bring him into conformity to God's ways. But in doing what he did, the salary didn't come in currency of God's love, but in terms of duty, and it wasn't that he was consciously trying to become a believer but rather he was acting faithfully to God. His wages weren't reduced because he had opposed God. Just so comes the record of David, the fellow with a very charmed life, to whom God gave the wage due one whose life conformed to God's way despite what he did.

Being Faithful Turns You Into One Who Treats Folks Equally Which Conforms You To God's Basic Way

When charmed lives happened, acts against God's equalized treatment of folks were being forgiven, And what they did, their acts which were separating them from doing what God wanted, were always being forgiven.

Happy is the person, no matter what that one does wrong, who the Familyhead doesn't count it against that one. Now, is this state of having a charmed life after having done something wrong only given to a Jew or can it come to the rest of the world's folks?

Now we understand this,

The faith of Abraham was being counted to conform him to God's way.

How could such a thing be figured? Could it exist in the circumcised only or also in the rest of folks? No, not in the Jew only, but also it can indwell in the rest of the folks of the world. And the body mark Abraham received as a result of circumcision marked him as one who was conformed to God's way by his faithfulness in being like one of the rest of the world, the purpose of it being for him to become the parent figure to all in the world who believe in God, so that faith is to be counted to all the believing world that they are conformable to God's way, and this circumcised parent figure of ours isn't only such for Jews but also to those who configure their lives so as to walk in such footsteps, any of the rest of the world's folks who choose to believe as did our ancestor, Abraham. But it is not through the working of the law of descent that there comes the benefit of Abraham to his descendants, who are to be the inheritors of the world, but it comes through being conformers to God's ways by being faithful to God.

Treating Folks Equally Comes In Behaving Faithfully Not By Birthright

If those became world inheritors because of a law of descent, the need to be faithful would be absolutely meaningless and the benefit would be rendered void. For the law of descent produces frustration. At every instance, there seems neither the operation of a law of descent nor obedience to the principle of it. So, it is out of faith, resulting to folks according to God's caring compassionate love, that a purpose is firm set for everyone to have the benefit of God's family background, not only from living under a law of equalized attention coming from God but also from the having the example of Abraham's faith, who is the parent figure of us all, as it was written that,

I establish you as the ancestor of the estranged and homeless. In recognizing this, he believed God, the one who acts to give life to the dead and the one who calls those not alive as if they were alive. This is the hope beyond hope, that he who believes shall bear a purpose as did he who was

The parent to all the estranged and homeless, according to the figure of speech that

So shall your seed be. And not being weak in faith, he didn't doubt himself because he was close to death, having a hundred years age on him, and having a wife, Sarah, with a dead womb.

He did not doubt the benefiting result of God through disbelieving it could happen, but instead he become strong in faith, giving his attendedness to God, and it became fulfilled so that the thing that was promised, he had the ability to do.

The result,

It was considered to him that he lived conformed to God's way. Now this wasn't written for only him but it was being as a description also for our benefit, to those who can also be so described, to those who are believers in the resurrection of Jesus, our Familyhead, from death, who gave over that one's self for our offenses and arose from death to set things right.

After Folk's Gift Of A World Equalized In God Attendedness, The Gift To Have Faith In God Creates God Relatedness, God Satisfying The Folk Need Of Family Love With God

Now, after things have been set right for faithful living, we have access to the peace of God through our Familyhead, Jesus, God's Child when on earth, and through this one we have an absolute hold on the approach to access to it, into the family loving status in which we can stand up and shout our claim to the hope from God's attendedness.

Not only this but also we can shout our claim in the face of the worst disasters, knowing that trouble finds us able to bear up, patiently enduring. Patient endurance is our basic Christian attitude, and this Christian attitude represents our hope.

Hope never loses its power. It bears the family love relationship of God poured out into our hearts by the special spirit which is our gift.

God Doesn't Just Treat All Folks Equally, God Loves All Folks The Same Way, In Family Love, And We Know This Because Jesus, God's Child When On Earth, Came To Us

Even today, God's Child who came to earth, is present in our time of vulnerability, even as at the time Jesus died to provide opportunity for the ones who were godless. How difficult would it be for some person to die for a good reason. And for a really good reason, another person might be brave enough to die a quick death. But, consider this, God's Child, who came to earth, died for us, and God united God's feelings of family love to us, because until then we existed separated from God. What's more, now we are saved through the blood of God from the effects of God's frustration with creation, having been put in a family relationship with God.

So, while we used to be enemies, now we are reconciled to God through the death of God's Child, and more important, we are being reconciled into the life of God's Child, having been made family members.

And not only that, but also having been given claim to membership in God's family through our Familyhead, Jesus, God's Child, we have received the capacity to change over to God's family membership right now.

God's Child When On Earth Wiped Away The God Separation Folks Have Lived In Since Adam's Time

Now since it was through one person that separation came into the world, and through this separation came real death, so now real death overtakes all folks, for in all folks there is God separation.

Until the coming of God's equalized treatment law, God was alienated from the creation, but the separation didn't get charged against anyone because there was no law ordering creation, and chaos ruled the world from the time of Adam until Moses, and even those who weren't alienated in the same way were treated as if they were disobedient like Adam who is the example of the way they were.

But, despite all, there was wrongdoing, and in spite of it they were treated with love.

Even if on account of one wrongdoer, all die, what better gift could there be than gifts in love striking into folklife out of the one life of Jesus, God's Child, provided bounteously to all. And since this was not from a person different from God, it was a real gift.

Being Faithful, Living As A Member Of God's Family, Following God's Law Of Equal Attendedness, Takes Away God's Judgment That We Are Subject To Die

And while the sentence for each one used to be guilty, the gifts to all separated folks are in the form of conformity to God's ways. And if through one persons wrongdoing death rules for that one, much better is the enveloping compassionate family love and the gifts of conformity to God's ways that are received in life under the God rules from that one Jesus, God's Child when on earth. Just so, as one person was a wrongdoer to all folks bringing a sentence of guilty, so also there was one conforming his life to God so all folks could live in conformity to God's ways. And as through the disobedience of one person all were proved to be living wrong, so also through one obedient life, all are established in God.

Equalized Attention, God's Love Despite Folk Wrongdoing, Jesus, God's Child When On Earth, For Those Wanting A Life Eternal

God's law of equalized attendedness appeared, while wrongdoing spread, so even if wrongdoing became more plentiful, wrongdoing could not take over. Wherever wrongdoing spread, God's family love came down over it and increased in concentration, so that just as wrongdoing provided the rules to the dying, so did God's family love provide the God laws to the ones seeking conformity to God's ways with the resulting life eternal through Jesus, God's Child who came to earth, our Familyhead.

What's to be understood? Are we supposed to continue to act wrong so that God's family love will come down more?

God don't let that have to be!

Who wants to die in wrongdoing! Why do we still live in it?

Anyway, aren't you aware that, so many as were baptized to the family life of Jesus God's Child when on earth, are baptized into that one's death?

Baptism Into God's Timeless Family Life

Yes, we were buried with that one through baptism into death, so that just as God's Child when on earth arose from death through the attentiveness of the parent creator, so also may we walk in newness of life.

If we have the capacity to share the same death Jesus did, so also may we arise into real life beyond this life. Think of it this way. The old personality of you was nailed to a cross with Jesus, so that its somatic condition of being tied to wrongdoing is taken out of action, no longer to bend you to acting wrong.

When someone so dies, that one is rendered conformed to God's ways out of any past of wrongdoing.

If we die with God's Child, we accept the belief that we are also kept in God's family life in God's Homeland. Knowing that God's child arose from death, that one no longer dies. Death, after Jesus's, is no longer in charge of God's family.

Yes, this one died, by the hand of wrongdoing, this one died, rising above it, final.

And this one lives, this one lives with God.

So, you yourselves count each other to be dead to wrongdoing living with God in the family of God's Child, Jesus.

Warning Against Wrongdoing

Don't let wrongdoing take over in your mortal condition which is subject to its own instincts. Also, don't let your sex organs be put in the position of being weapons for separating either yourself or others from God. Elevate each other as if you were in the presence of God, reborn out of a state of death, and let your sex organs become tools to forge a life conforming to God's ways.

Wrongdoing now has no control over you, for you do not only live in a world under a law of God's equalized attendedness but also in love relatedness whereby all baptized into Jesus death are eternal family.

Meeting The Demands Of Equalized Creation Law

What about this idea? Could we act wrong so that we can avoid being under the law and under this love relatedness?

Don't even think about it!

Don't you realize that you stand in the presence of each other as persons bound by your relationship to God to be obedient. Duty bound persons you are to the one you must obey! The duty's the same whether you are doing wrong to the point you die or whether you recognize and do your duty as one who is conforming life to God's ways.

Family love has broken through from God because you used to be persons duty tied to wrongdoing, and now you must become obedient in heart to the point where you give yourselves over to becoming God's proponents. Freed from wrongdoing you can live a life of duty and conforming to God's ways.

I am telling you this in folk speech because of your vulnerability to customs of the flesh. As you used to hold yourselves out in your bodies as folks victimized by the worst motives and violators of God's equalizing love law to the point you were damned as outsiders to creation itself, so now you can stand up to your obsessions in conformity to your special status being of God, to the final point where you reach life eternal in God's Homeland.

The payback from wrongdoing is death, but the free gift of God is real life with God's Child, Jesus, our Familyhead.

Because Of God's Child, Jesus, We Can Transcend The Law

Are you missing the point, sisters and brothers, for I am talking here to those who know they are to live relational to the equalized God creation attendedness, that the law overpowers folk as far as the time folks got to live?

Now a married woman is given to living relational to her husband's needs, but if her husband dies, she is released from this man's need. So when she lives with a man she is called an adulteress if she takes up with another man. But if her man dies, she is free from the binding relationship, so that she is not an adulteress going to live with another man.

So, my brothers and sisters, while your lives under the law endanger you with the fact of death, you many come to live with another on account of the human manifestation of God's Child who arose from death so that we may be reborn as a crop with God. While we are in mortal condition, the wrongdoing compulsions derived from creation law work through our sexuality and other body demands, to the point that they turn us into a death crop. But now we have been insulated from the creation law, having been killed when we were possessed by it, which has the effect of reorienting us into a new spirituality, not written about in the old times.

What Wrongdoing Is

What else must we say?

Is God's across the board equalized creation attendedness law wrong?

No way!

I wouldn't know I was doing wrong if it weren't for this standard.

I wouldn't understand over-enthusiasm to satisfy my body needs to the detriment of others if the Moses law didn't say you shouldn't try to over-satisfy yourself. Wrongdoing does its work in my every self-indulgence taking advantage of every opportunistic interpretation of the ten commandments. Except for the law of God's equalized attendedness upholding creation wrongdoing is a dead standard. Before, when I lived outside the creation equality law, superseding the ten commandments, wrongdoing overpowered my life. Then I died with Jesus and it was shown to me that the ten commandments for the purpose of living are a way into death.

Wrongdoing, taking its chance, turns the ten commandments away from their purpose and folks die in them. So even though God's equalized attendedness law is special and the ten commandments are special, so is conformity to God's ways the best thing.

Why Not Just Die And Get It Over With

Would it be better for me to be dead, in the sense of not having a life at all? Forget it!

What's good about wishing to die? Its relation to wrongdoing. Wrongdoing is a life circumstance. Its does me good to bear in mind wrongdoing because it gets me ready to accept dying. Death births me, a wrongdoer, beyond the reach of the wrongdoing connected to the ten commandments. Now we know that the creation law is spiritual, even though I have a body being subject to doing the wrong thing. What I am getting ready to do next, I don't even know.

What I don't want to do, this is what I do, and what I hate myself for doing is what I do. Now if the thing I don't want to do is what I do, I am complying with a creation law that is good. No lounger am I doing what I want but the wrongdoing that lives in me.

The Real Person Gets Attuned to God's Creation Law in Mind, Even While that One's Body Doesn't Get in Step

And I know that wrongdoing is not living in the real me. It is just in my body, fortunately. This thing is present in my will, and this thing does me no good. No way can I get myself to do right. instead, I do something bad that I don't want to do.

The result is, if I am doing what I don't want to do, its not really me doing it, but a will to do wrong that is in me. Now I have discovered the law of God's equalized attendedness to creation, it injects into me the desire to do right, because there dwells in me the will to do wrong.

I am so happy with this spirit filled God law according to how it works in relation to a person. I recognize it as an opposing law to that working in my body which tries to take my mind prisoner and capture me in a law of wrongdoing which exists in my body.

I am a tormented person. What is rescuing me from my body demands? Is it this knowledge that I will find relief in death? All else failing, love breaks through from God through Jesus, God's child, my Familyhead. As a result of it, I myself serve the love equalizing God attendedness law of God in my mind, even if in my body there is wrongdoing.

We Can Live and Not Want To Die Out of Frustration, Keeping in Mind that Jesus, God's Child, Bears Up the World Through a Spirit that Rules Creation by a Creation Law of Equal Attendedness in Love Which Does Not Pass Judgment But Upholds the World

No more is there any frustrated sentence handed down following charges of wrongdoing leveled at those living in the life story line of God's Child, Jesus. The God-law administered by the spirit of life in God's Child, Jesus, frees you from the wrongdoing law and from death. But, since frustration occurs rendering the law impossible to do because of our body needs, God sent God's Child in the appearance of a wrongdoing body and, as to wrongdoing, took away its

damning result from the demands of the body, so that conformity to God through the God law could be fulfilled in us so that we no longer walk in body but in the spirit. The inclining demand of the body is to die, but the inclining demand of the spirit is to live and find peace. For this reason, body inclinations are the enemy to God, and stand against the control of the world by the law of God, for it fails.

And those who live to satisfy their body demands cannot live satisfactorily to God's purpose. But you are not in the body but in the spirit since the life spirit of God makes its home in you.

The Spirit Of God's Child Establishes Us Into Being Babies Of God

If anyone does not bear the spirit of God's Child, the life spirit is not of that one. But if God's Child is in you, there is no death form from wrongdoing, but instead the spirit of life from conformity to God's ways. And after the life spirit raised Jesus from death it came to dwell in you, and this same life spirit that caused God's Child to arise from death, took charge of life, and the perishable body of yours come to dwell in the spirit inside you.

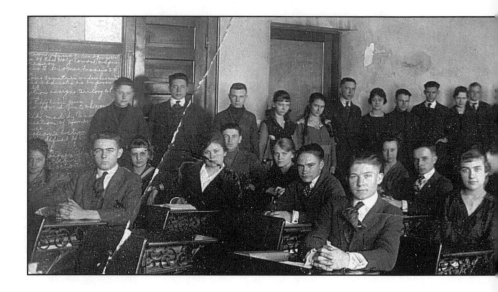

The Spirit Gives Us To Live In Spirited Bodies That Can Have Life In God's Homeland

So, my sisters and brothers, we aren't stuck owing debts to our body needs but to the contract terms of a body living spiritual. Now if you live according to body constraints, you are always about to die. But if within your spirit you have killed the orientation to dependency on body constraints, you will live. So many as hold on to the spirit of God, these are the children of God.

You do not receive a spirit of dependency to require you to repetitiously fear every event, instead you receive the spirit of birth into God's family. In this relationship, we can call out to God as would a baby calling out Mommy or Daddy! The spirit itself gives proof to the spirit in us for we are God's babies. If we are babies, also we are heirs. Heirs of God, joint heirs with God's Child who came to earth. So it is we bear up together through life so that we may jointly receive God's attendedness. I figure that it's not worth worrying about, how anxious these times are, weighing the anxiety of this time, against the potential of God's family attendedness ready to be called out from God's Homeland into our lives.

How It Came To Be Folks Were Given To Be God's Kids

It came about from a yearning in creation hoping breathlessly and expectant that we could become God's children. Up to then, creation was held under the thumb of meaninglessness, having no will of its own, defeated, with the

hope that some day in the future there would come freedom from the holds of decay and corruption into the attentiveness coming from being babies of God. We know enough about creation to know it confines folks together and causes us the kind of pain that a woman goes through in childbearing even now.

But not only this. Also we who were confined in our own delusions were being touched down from above to become established as children of God, and so to be released from our body constraints. And by this hope we were rescued. Hope that is being understood and thought through isn't hope. How can we understand what hope is? Only if we don't see something can we hope for it, through patient enduring can we be touched down through God's Homeland.

The Spirit Knowing Jesus To Come Intervened In Creation To Touch Special Lives

So it was that the spirit came to give us help in our state of vulnerability. For we waited expectantly for what we could not know, and the spirit intervened in this time of indescribable alienation.

One knows the ways of the spirit when it touches hearts because it works a turning to God for God oriented folks. And we know that it conjoins God's fullness to these God oriented folks for their own good at the time when this orienting is occurring according to God's plan. And while folks could only speculate, the spirit knew ahead of time that these folks would be having the same body as the snapshot of God's Child to be born as a prototype among brothers and sisters.

And while it was knowing this, it was picking out some folks, and it picked these, and gave them conformity to God's ways, and those it conformed, it drew to God's attention.

What Happens When Folks Become Special To God

What can we say about being special? If God is empowering us, what can come down upon us? Look here! Who was it who did not save back God's own child, but for us, all folks, gave him over to a life like ours? Why wouldn't it happen that through him God would freely give it all to us? What guilt can be ascribed to those who are this special to God?, God providing the standard of conformity.

Who is the one who judges guilt? God's Child, the very one who has died, or rather arose from death, who sits at the right hand of God, who acts as our lawyer defending us.

Nothing Can Separate Us From Our Familyhead

What can separate us from the love and compassion of God's Child? Trouble? or hardship? or persecution? or hunger? or need? or danger? or the sword? It is written that,

Because of you, we are willing to be killed every day.

Consider us slaughter grade livestock. in all this, we may be considered winners in it all for we have been so loved as God's family members. I am convinced that nothing in death, nothing in life, nothing already in God's Homeland, nothing living in memories of those gone before, nothing standing close by, nothing considering descendants, no power, nothing high or low, nothing which will evolve in creation, will ever separate us from the love and compassion of God in God's Child, Jesus, our Familyhead.

I tell you what is real, I am not lying, bear my witness with each other from my understanding jointly witnessed with the special spirit, because there is great grief in me, and constant sorrow in my heart.

God Can Destroy What God Gets Frustrated With.

I myself have worried constantly about the blame for the treatment of God's Child when on earth which hangs over my racial brothers and sisters, my flesh and blood, who are Israelites, being adopted into God's family and being God attended, they being in a contract relationship with God, living under God approved law, serving God, and those who God has promised to stay with, being the same ones by ancestry from whom came God's child in body, and being the ones most of all God has told the story of life eternal to, and on and on.

It isn't so that God's story has been forgotten.

Not all those saying they are Israelites are Israelites. It is not the sperm of Abraham that provides that all become God's children, but

Through Isaac, the sperm for inheritance comes to you.

The fact is not all children with human bodies are children of God but those children of human ancestry who take seriously the promise of God. And the story of this promise is this,

After some time, I will come and be a child of Sarah. Not only this, but also Rebecca bore again, after a first childbirth, from Isaac our ancestor.

It hadn't happened yet that any were born as God's kids, nor knew that they were doing good or bad except how it might be thought to be left under the ten commandment law. No one knew how to act or call on God.

It was told to Rebecca,

The older one will serve the younger, as it is written,

Jacob I will love in a family way,

But Esau I will be indifferent to. What can we say? Can God act in nonconformity to God's way? Of course not! And to Moses, it was said,

I will have feeling for the one I want to feel for.

I will express my compassion for the one I love.

God's Feel Decides Things

So, it all depends not on what folks want or reach for, but on what is God's feel.

And it is said in the scroll about the Pharaoh that,
I am in his doings. I have elevated him over you so I
can give an indication to you of my power and how I
choose agents over all the earth.

So, for who God wants to, God has feelings, and who God wants, God hardens that one's heart. You say to me, How can God blame anyone? Except it be by God's will, could anyone fight God?

Am I not someone to be addressed as human after all?

Can you act contrary?

What if you are one who is asked to give an answer to God? Will something formed explain things to the one who did the forming?

So what do you want me to do?

Doesn't a potter have authority to mould clay as that one wants from the lump into a useful dish? Or into something useless.

So when God wants, God can demonstrate frustration brought to bear in power, after patient waiting, on a dish God is frustrated with, to restore it through destroying it.

God's Way Of Feeling About Folks Can Change.

But can't a potter express the pleasure of attendedness upon a dish that one likes which that one disregarded beforehand when brought to that one's attention?

As those, also God regards us, not only from Jews but also out from ever race.

As it says in Hosea,
I will no more call my people, my people,
And I will not regard as beloved family, the ones I have
treated as family. And it will be for others to take
their place, it being said, No more are you my people.
Then the heirs of the living God will be in that place.
Isaiah cries over Israel,
Out of the number of the children of Israel which used
to be as the sand of the sea, only a remnant will
survive. When the story ends, the Familyhead will do
the finishing up on the earth.
And as Isaiah foretold,
Unless the Sunday worshiped Familyhead leaves behind a

seed of ours,
We will end up as Sodom,
or as Gomorra, if we have any identity at all.

God's Way Of Considering Homeless And Estranged Ones Is Changed And Now They Are The Ones Considered Acceptable To God Because They Live Faithfully To The Way God Equally Attends To The World.

What's left to say? That the homeless and estranged of the world, those foreign to God's ways, are established as conformed to God's ways, having been taken in as ones acceptable, having been deemed conformed because of their faithfulness to God.

But Israel while it prosecuted according to the equalized attendedness law of God conformity could not itself attain it.

Why? because they acted not out of faith but according to legal job descriptions.

They stumbled on the rock they threw, as it is written,
Watch out! I place on Mount Zion a stone to stumble over
and a rock for an obstacle,
but one who lives by faith will not trip over it in a
ridiculous way.

The Pang That The Self Proclaimers That They Are God's Special People Change Their Ways

Sisters and brothers, I have a pang in my heart and I pray to God more than anything for them to be rescued. I realize that they do have a longing for God, but they aren't acting cognitively.

Being uninspired how to conform to God's way, they establish their own ways and try to rest on them and they have not held themselves accountable to God's conformity standard.

Jesus Brought God's Homeland Into The World And Took Death Out For Those Faithful To The Law Of God, Who Confess This As The New Hierarchy And Accept That Jesus Is Not Dead.

The ultimate goal of the world governing equalized attendedness law is God as God's Child was on earth for a conformity standard for all who are faithful.

Moses wrote how to conform to God's way through the law, that,
The person doing what the standard of God
requires will stay alive through it.

And for faith as a conforming principle, he says similarly, Don't say in your heart, Who can enter into God's Homeland ? It is the situation that God's child brought down to earth or, Who goes down into the world of the dead? This is the situation for which God's Child arose from the dead. What did he say?

The announcement of world order is close to you.

Bear it in your speech and in your heart.

This is the situation which we announce by being faithful. What's conditional is that you must confess in your speech the Familyhead, Jesus, and you must believe in your heart that God raised him from the dead out of death, and you will find rescue.

In one's heart there has to be faith in the purpose of conformity to God's way, and a speech willing to confess for the purpose of being saved. As it says in the scroll,

One who believes in it, will not be embarrassed to confess faith.

It makes no difference whether Jew or Greek, for this one is the Familyhead of us all. Fullness of life comes to all who call upon Jesus.

And all who take the identity of the family name of the Familyhead will be saved from finitude problems and death.

How can those not in the faith call upon the Familyhead? How can those believe who have not heard of the Familyhead? How can those hear without

preachers? How can there be preaching unless there are missionaries? As it is written, How timely are heard the footsteps of those who preach the good news about what is right.

But not all listen for the good news.

As Isaiah said, Sir

Familyhead, who believes our news?

Faith Is Accepting Of God's Child's New Hierarchical Order

Faith is what happens after hearing the news, the news concerning the new world hierarchical order established by God's Child. After I say this, could any not listen? And how about this,

A shout bellows from them, rumbling over the whole earth,

and to the ends of its boundaries the new world

hierarchy overcomes.

But I ask you, how can Israel not know?

It was Moses who first said,

I will make you envious of those without homes,

For the benefit of those homeless and estranged, in

ignorance of me, I will render you distraught. An agitated Isaiah spoke,

I have been discovered by those who never expected to be

looking for me. I have been revealed to those who did

not ask for me. And God says to Israel,

This whole age I have held out my hand to my people

who won't believe what I say and reject me.

How could it be, isn't God pushing aside God's own people? I wish there was another explanation! I myself am an Israelite, from Abraham's sperm, Benjamin's tribe.

God Hasn't Rejected Jews Because Of Their Treatment Of Jesus. God Keeps Faith With Those Who Are The True Israelites Who Have Accepted That Jesus Was God's Child Establishing A New World Hierarchical Order On The Basis Of God's Laws And Bringing A New Hierarchy Of God's Homeland To People

God has not rejected God's own people who God chose from the beginning. Don't you remember what it says in Elijah's scroll? as Elijah begged God to come down hard on Israel?

Familyhead, Sir, They have killed your prophets.

They have destroyed your altars.

And I alone remain behind.

And now they are trying to take my life. But what did the oracle of God say back to him?

I have kept back for my own use seven thousand folks, quite a few who will not bend their knees to Baal. So also in the present time, some are left who were created in and remain loved in God's family. But if they live in family love, it can't any longer be a matter of occupation, since that expression of family love is no longer real family love.

What else? The one who wanted to live with Israel, that one did not find rest there, except chosen ones did experience it. And the rest remain stubborn, as it is written,

God has given to them an anesthetized spirit,
That their eyes don't see,
and their ears don't hear,
until this very day. And David says,
Let their altar tables be set in snares and in traps and
in stumbling blocks as for retribution. Their eyes saw
only disobedience and refused understanding,

And, break the backbone of their resolve in them all! I ask, Didn't they stumble just for the fall?

No way!

The Estranged And Homeless Receive The Benefit Of God's Rescue Rejected By Israel

If their straying away enriches the world and so does their loss of prestige to others, the estranged and homeless, so all the more was their achievement. And I say this to you, the homeless and estranged ones of this world.

Paul's Explanation Of His Mission

And so far as I have the ability, this is who I am, a missionary to the homeless and estranged, drawing their attention to my understanding of the ways to conform to a life with God, despite how I wish I could drive my own racial brothers and sisters to emulation and rescue also some of them.

Even though their rejection has given the world a family relationship with God, wouldn't what would happen on their acceptance be like life coming from death?

The Homeless and Estranged Who Gain from the Message Should Cherish their Jewish Roots and Hope for their Jewish Brothers and Sisters to Return to their Specialness

If the first fruit is special, and its mixture in the fruit basket, so also is the root special and its branches. If some of the branches are broken off, and you, being engrafted with them and conjoined to the root for the sustenance you gain as a branch on the olive tree, you should not feel better off. If there are bragging rights, they are not yours, for it is the root sustaining you and not you the root. You will say, These branches broke off so that I might be engrafted. Okay, they were broken off due to disbelief, but you were given branch standing for your faithfulness. Don't think pride, think respect.

If God didn't have any use for natural branches, God wouldn't have any use for you.

Imagine the profitability from pruning from God's point of view. When they were broken off, pruning was necessary, but you were considered more advantageous to God, so you should keep yourselves profitable, or else you will be pruned too! And there you have it, but if they wouldn't be so stuck in their disbelief, they could be engrafted back on, for there is this power, God again might regrafted them. And if you, not being a natural branch could be cut off from a wild olive tree and engrafted contrary to nature onto a cultivated olive tree, how much easier could it be for them to be engrafted being by nature from the same tree.

Jews To One Day Return To The Ranks Of The Special

I don't want your mind's blown, brothers and sisters, about this mystery, since you are smart enough to understand it. The lag of comprehension in Israel is only until the homeless and estranged ones of the world are brought into conformity to God's ways. And then Israel will be rescued, as it is written,

There will come upon Zion a Rescuer.

This one will turn around those children of Jacob who are shrinking away from God.

This is the contract I make with them and myself, when I remove their wrongdoing ways. By the way they treat the Good news they are enemies to you, but by the way of their being chosen by God, they are loved in a family way for the sake of their ancestors. How God chose to care for them and give them heirship is irrevocable. As you used to scoff at God and now you are treated in soft affections, so also they now are the disobedient ones in terms of the affection shown to you, and now they are the ones in need of compassion. God conjointly calls everyone who disbelieves so that all may receive Gods affection. The depth of fullness and intelligence and thinking of God! They are as hard to figure as what would be a judge's decision and as unsearchable as the roads that lead to God.

Who knows the thinking of the Familyhead?

Who is that one's adviser?

Who has advised that one before and will be repaid for it?

For from that one, and through that one, and in that one are all things. In this fact is the attendedness from God's Homeland , Yes!

How To Live To Receive God's Softened Affection

I beg you, sisters and brothers, for the sake of being treated with these soft affections by God, to stand before God in your physical body as a living offering, specially acceptable to God, a way that makes sense for you to do, as one who helps others. Don't be modeling your personality on the basis of this time frame, but transform yourselves into a transfigured state for the purpose of identifying yourselves, what else could be the wish of God?, as the best you can be, an acceptable offering, and a new hierarchical person. I ask you, out of the family love God has placed in me, to most of all, avoid having too high an opinion of yourselves.

This is a basic attitude need and way to think to have peace of mind which God passes out to each according to that one's level of faithfulness. Just as in one body, we have many body parts, and out of all of them, none has the same function, so all of us are in one body in God's Child, except one person is a body part with others.

These parts bear diversifying family love indwelling according to the family love given to us, whether it's to preach intuiting what God wants us to do, or to minister in service, or to teach in a school, or to be an encourager in urging faithfulness. This part is to share in the task of working in the occupations. This part is to provide the social leadership. This part is to undertake love needs happily.

The Personality Of Someone Conforming Their Life To God's Law And The New World Hierarchy After God's Child Who Came To Earth Came To Give Us To Belong To God's Equally Loved Family And Paul's Advice About What To Do And How To Be

Family love is the super ultimate judging point. Holding back from bad things in acting hatefully, doing good things like you are glued to the purpose, treating folks affectionately as if they were a brother or sister, opting to respect each other, acting with purpose instead of to stir things up, living with the spirit of God, following the will of the Familyhead, being happy in your hope, remaining cool despite pressure, having the patience to rely on prayers, living in a caring community, welcoming strangers into your family love.

Honor those being persecuted. Respect those and don't fall away from being faithful.

Be happy with those happy, cry with those that have to cry. Bearing your gut emotions one for another, not feeling better off, and not being too good to be with the less well off. Don't try to second guess each other. Return no harm after being hurt, having the first thought to help all kinds of folks. If the opportunity comes to you, becoming a world peace leader for the sake of all folks. Not seeking revenge, loving family, putting anger in its place, as it is written,

Revenge is mine.

I do the getting even, says the Familyhead. And,

If an enemy hungers, feed that one.

This doing, you will be heaping coals of drossing charcoal on that one's head. I would not have you succeed by doing bad, but winning in doing good to the bad. Let every conscious act of your life be done in obedience to the governing authorities.

There is no authority, unless from God, and the authorities are being arranged for by God. As it happens, the one who opposes an authority receiving instruction from God stands in resistance, and those resisting get themselves punished. Those in power are not afraid, whether their acts be good or bad. Wish that the authority is not to be feared.

Do good and you will have approval from the authority. A law enforcement officer is God's employee too to those who do good. But if you do wrong, worry! Not for nothing does that one carry a weapon. God too is a police person, a punisher out of frustration, to those who do wrong. Overall, government is necessary, not only to avoid frustration but also by common consensus. So also you should pay taxes. Public employees are God's insofar as they keep close to their purpose.

Pay back everything you owe, tax to the taxer, income to the employee, respect due the respectable and honor due the honorable. Never be a debtor unnecessarily unless the debt created is one from loving each other in a family way for loving each other fulfills the equalized attendedness law.

Also this,

Don't look for sex outside marriage.

Don't kill.

Don't steal.

Don't be greedy.

Bearing Family Love

And if there be another commandment, it may be summed up in this saying, Love the one closest to you as yourself. Family love doesn't want anything bad to happen to those you're closest to. The fullness of the equalized attendedness law is family love.

Loving Each Other Is The Bottom Line Of God's Way Of Equally Attending Creation

Be one of those who keeps in mind the concept of time, because the hour readies itself for you, maybe when you have been roused from sleep, which will be the now of our rescue, nearer than when we thought. The night crops forward and the daylight approaches.

Let's get rid of the works of the darkness. Let's get ready our tools for the daylight. Let's walk like we do in daylight, respectably, not looking for bad sex or alcohol, not caught in intercourse out of marriage or engaging in acts of sensualizing, not arguing or being envious.

Wear the Familyhead, Jesus, God's child, as you do your clothes. And don't do anything to satisfy body lust. Receive into the faith community any who are vulnerable, not in derogation of their opinions. This one believes in eating everything, and here's one likes to eat vegetables. While one eats what another won't, don't you be picky, and when one eats what the other won't, don't pass judgment, for God, God's self, is receiving that one.

Love Doesn't Give Itself Over To Judging Others

Who are you to judge among another's followers? Each stands or falls before the same Familyhead. Fact is, each will stand, because the Familyhead can cause each one to stand. This one prefers one day over another, this one reveres every day. Let each one fulfill the particularities of that one's ideas. The one regarding a single day thinks of it for the sake of the Familyhead, and the one eating picky eats for the sake of the Familyhead. Each is expressing love for God. And the one not eating doesn't eat out of regard for the Familyhead and that one is expressing love for God. No one of us wants to live only for that one's self and no one of us wants to die for that one's self, so if we are gonna live, let's live for the Familyhead and if we are gonna die, let's die for the Familyhead. But whether we live or whether we die, we are the Familyhead's.

For this reason God's child died and regained life, to become Familyhead of the dead and of the alive.

Do you judge your brother or sister? Do you also say your sister or brother is good for nothing?

Folks Will Be Judged In The After Death

All will be called to stand in front of the courtroom bench of God for it is written,

I, yes, I, live, says the Familyhead,

and every knee will bend down

and every tongue will confess their guilt in front of God.

Then's when each of us will give that one's life story. No longer should we judge each other. Instead judge what you do so as not to place an obstacle to stumble over or a trap to fall in before your sister or brother. I know and I am convinced that in the way the Familyhead Jesus indwells in us there comes no common perception, except that the way we think is very often the same. In this, there is something in common. And if a brother or sister annoys you by their choice of diet, you are not walking down the path of family love.

Don't condemn for dietary reasons someone for whom God's Child died. Don't slander someone good among us.

Eating Habits Don't Matter

The way God rules the world isn't based on food or drink, but on the basis of conformity to God's way, and peace, and love breaking through to us from God's Homeland through the world indwelling of the special spirit.

When someone does the work of God's Child thinking this way, then that one is acceptable to God and well regarded before folks. So let's pursue peaceful ways and encouragement among each other. Don't condemn because of food diets a worker of God. In fact every food is free from offense to God, and it is bad for folks to let eating habits turn into obstacles.

It is good not to let meal eating or wine drinking or anything else like this cause your sister or brother to fall away. You who have faith down inside yourselves, have it before God. Happy is the one who isn't judging that one's self in self persecution.

Someone who doubts it's right whatever that one eats is condemning that one's self on other than faith grounds. Everything that is not done out of faith is wrongdoing.

Folks Are Obliged To The Vulnerable

Those of you advantaged are under an obligation to lift up those who are vulnerable in their disadvantaged situation and not rest on social acceptability.

The Duty To Provide For Family Needs

Each of us should help satisfy the living needs of those we are closest to to help in home building.

Being Respectable Doesn't Cut Nothing

Even God's Child sought no social standing, but instead, as it is written,
The insults of your abusers fell upon me.

The Hope In Our Familyhead's Return

Whatever has been foreordained, whatever has been written about in our ethical teaching, so that we be patient and help others as it's written, would have that we bear up the hope in the succeeding hierarchy.

The Prayer That Folks Have The Indwelling Mind Of God's Child When On Earth

Patient God, helping God, may it be given us to have a mind indwelling in us, in touch with God's Child who came to earth as Jesus, so that you may be extolled in one united expression of God, the Parent of our Familyhead Jesus, God's child who came to earth. So, hold on to each other, as God's Child held onto us with God's self watching.

Who God's Child Was, An Expression Of God's Love And Compassion For The Estranged And Homeless

I am talking about God's Child, a minister born of Jewish stock, as an announcer of God's new hierarchical situation with people, to establish the condition promised to those of that ancestry, out of God's feeling sorry for those estranged and homeless, as it is written,
For this reason, I will be acknowledged among you while
I dwell among the estranged and homeless and through
this presence I will sing to you. and again, as it says,
Take comfort, homeless and estranged ones, I will be
with you people. And again,
Celebrate, all you homeless and estranged ones, the Familyhead,
And respect this one, all people. And again, Isaiah says,
Jesse will be a root,

and the one springing up will take jurisdiction of the
homeless and estranged.
Out of this, the homeless and estranged will be the
fruit of the expectation.

We Represent A Hope Of God

God has fulfilled this hope, producing you out of the totality of God's
Homeland, in the fulness of love and compassion which broke through into
creation, and so you can believe possible world peace, providing you with
more than just hope, a special world spirit presence with the power available
to get the job done.

Paul's Mission To Make The Homeless And Estranged Acceptable To God

I have a satisfied feeling about you, that you are doing okay, being given
good advice, acting on it and being helpful to one another. I have written
frankly to you in part like those did who remind you what's happened for the
sake of the love and compassion that's been given me by God. It is in me to be
a Jewish minister of God's Child, Jesus, to those homeless and estranged, commissioned to be a priest of the good news of God, that the sacrificial offering of
the homeless and estranged may be pleasing as received, being rendered extraordinary in its special spirit. I make these sacrifices to God proud to have

God's Child, Jesus, indwelling. I am not afraid to admit that God's Child is working through me to bring about obedience to God's laws by those homeless and estranged in word and deed, in performance of miracles and break-throughs in the power of the spirit. So I have done at Jerusalem and the places around it to Illyricum, being glutted and sated with the good news of God's Child, and now I have been given the task of missionarying where God who came to earth has not been heard of, so that I do not build on the foundation of any one else, but as it is written,

To those not aware of that one, they will be given to see, and those not hearing, will understand. So far I haven' been able to come to you. But soon I won't have any job to do in these places, and I have had a longing to come to you for many years, and I really want to go to Spain.

I hope as I travel through to be able to see you and get help in being out-fitted to go forward to there if I can satisfy you about its importance.

Now I go to Jerusalem out of concern for those special ones. The Mace-donians and Greeks chose to enter into a missionary enterprise to do what can be done for the distressed special ones in Jerusalem. I am pleased at this and I am also obligated to take their relief package to them. Since the homeless and estranged are spiritually joined with them in a common enterprise, they are ob-ligated to provide material help to them. When this is over, after I have deliv-ered to them the relief package, I look forward to coming to you on my way to Spain. I am sure after I have come I will be able to go forward fully outfitted to preach the good news of God's Child. I ask, sisters and brothers, for the sake of the Familyhead of us, Jesus who was God, and for the sake of the love and compassion of the spirit, that you join me in prayer to God, that I may be safe from being killed in Judea, and my collection of help to those in Jerusalem may be enough for those special ones, so that when I come to you I will be happy and I may be able to relax with you.

The God of peace be with you all.

Goodbye.

Paul's Final Remembrances and Goodbye Wishes

I want to recommend Phoebe to you, my sister, being a church worker in the Cenechae church, because you should receive her in the Familyhead worth special attention and take her in and amongst you to meet her basic needs. Also she has given help to many herself including me.

Remember me to Priscilla and Akila, my co-workers in God's Child, Jesus, who have risked their necks to save my life. To them not just me only but all the churches of the estranged and homeless give thanks, also to their house church.

Remember me to Epainetos, loved like a family member, who is an original convert from Asia in God's Child who came to earth. Remember me to Mary who has worked hard in your behalf.

Remember me to Andronikos and June, my relatives as well as fellow prisoners, who are well known to missionaries, and who belonged to God's Child before I did.

Remember me to Ampliatos, like family to me.

Remember me to Urban my co-worker for God's Child and Staxon, my friend who is like family.

Remember me to Apellan, a valued one in whom God's Child indwells.

Remember me to those from the house church of Aristoboulos.

Remember me to Herodiana, my relative.

Remember me to those in the house church of Narcissus, who bear in mind God's Child who came to earth.

Remember me to Truphaina and Truphosa who work for the Familyhead.

Remember me to Perseus, loved in the family, who works hard in the Familyhead's behalf.

Remember me to Rufos, one picked special by the Familyhead, and his, and so, my mother.

Remember me to Asugkristos, Phlegonta, Irma, Patrobos, Herman, and those with these brothers and sisters.

Remember me to Philologos and Julia, Narea and her sister and Olympia and those with her, all special.

Remember me to all those with a family kiss.

All the churches of God's Child wish to be remembered to you.

I warn you, sisters and brothers, to look out for dissension and scandalizers against the teaching, who become known to you by what they do, and turn them away. These people and their kind do not serve our Familyhead, God's Child, except in their stomach, and that only by smooth talking, and while they may appear attractive, they are deceivers of the hearts of the well meaning.

Your wariness to all this is well known.

Finally, I wish you to be happy. I also want you to be informed as to what's best and dumb to what's bad. The God of peace will crush opposition under your feet in a hurry.

Bear the Family love of our Familyhead Jesus with you.

Remember me to Timothy, my co-worker, and Lucius and Jason and Sosipeter, my relatives.

I, myself, Tertios, who am the scribe of this letter in the service of the Familyhead, ask to be remembered to you. Gaius, my host, asks to be remembered to you and all of his church. Erastus, the city treasurer, and Curtis, a brother.

In strength, stand fast, in line with the good news I bring to you, and the announcements preached by Jesus, God's Child when on earth, to the revelation of the hidden mysteries of God's Homeland which has now become clear as the prophets wrote about, and as ordered out of time for the faithful to be obedient to, in every way and to all the homeless and estranged ones who learn of it, only in God's wisdom, through Jesus, God's Child, in whom is the concentration of all time,

Goodbye.

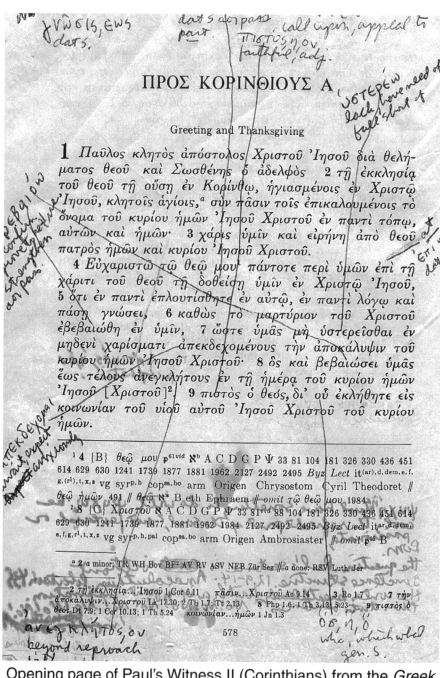

ΠΡΟΣ ΚΟΡΙΝΘΙΟΥΣ Α

Greeting and Thanksgiving

1 Παῦλος κλητὸς ἀπόστολος Χριστοῦ Ἰησοῦ διὰ θελήματος θεοῦ καὶ Σωσθένης ὁ ἀδελφὸς 2 τῇ ἐκκλησίᾳ
τοῦ θεοῦ τῇ οὔσῃ ἐν Κορίνθῳ, ἡγιασμένοις ἐν Χριστῷ
Ἰησοῦ, κλητοῖς ἁγίοις,ᵃ σὺν πᾶσιν τοῖς ἐπικαλουμένοις τὸ
ὄνομα τοῦ κυρίου ἡμῶν Ἰησοῦ Χριστοῦ ἐν παντὶ τόπῳ,
αὐτῶν καὶ ἡμῶν· 3 χάρις ὑμῖν καὶ εἰρήνη ἀπὸ θεοῦ
πατρὸς ἡμῶν καὶ κυρίου Ἰησοῦ Χριστοῦ.

4 Εὐχαριστῶ τῷ θεῷ μου πάντοτε περὶ ὑμῶν ἐπὶ τῇ
χάριτι τοῦ θεοῦ τῇ δοθείσῃ ὑμῖν ἐν Χριστῷ Ἰησοῦ,
5 ὅτι ἐν παντὶ ἐπλουτίσθητε ἐν αὐτῷ, ἐν παντὶ λόγῳ καὶ
πάσῃ γνώσει, 6 καθὼς τὸ μαρτύριον τοῦ Χριστοῦ
ἐβεβαιώθη ἐν ὑμῖν, 7 ὥστε ὑμᾶς μὴ ὑστερεῖσθαι ἐν
μηδενὶ χαρίσματι ἀπεκδεχομένους τὴν ἀποκάλυψιν τοῦ
κυρίου ἡμῶν Ἰησοῦ Χριστοῦ· 8 ὃς καὶ βεβαιώσει ὑμᾶς
ἕως τέλους ἀνεγκλήτους ἐν τῇ ἡμέρᾳ τοῦ κυρίου ἡμῶν
Ἰησοῦ [Χριστοῦ]² 9 πιστὸς ὁ θεός, δι' οὗ ἐκλήθητε εἰς
κοινωνίαν τοῦ υἱοῦ αὐτοῦ Ἰησοῦ Χριστοῦ τοῦ κυρίου
ἡμῶν.

---

¹ 4 {B} θεῷ μου pᵉ¹ᵛⁱᵈ אᵇ A C D G P Ψ 33 81 104 181 326 330 436 451
614 629 630 1241 1739 1877 1881 1962 2127 2492 2495 Byz Lect itᵃʳ,d,dem,e,f,
g,(r1),t,x,a vg syrp,h copsa,bo arm Origen Chrysostom Cyril Theodoret //
θεῷ ἡμῶν 491 // θεῷ א* B eth Ephraem // omit τῷ θεῷ μου 1984

² 8 {C} Χριστοῦ א A C D G P Ψ 33 81ᵛⁱᵈ 88 104 181 326 330 436 451 614
629 630 1241 1739 1877 1881 1962 1984 2127 2492 2495 Byz Lect itᵃʳ,d,dem,
e,f,g,r1,t,x,z vg syrp,h,pal copsa,bo arm Origen Ambrosiaster // omit p⁴⁶ B

ᵃ 2 a minor: TR WH Bov BF² AV RV ASV NEB Zür Seg // a none: RSV Luth Jer

2 τῇ ἐκκλησίᾳ...Ἰησοῦ 1 Cor 6.11   πᾶσιν...Χριστοῦ Ac 9.14   3 Ro 1.7   7 τὴν
ἀποκάλυψιν...Χριστοῦ Lk 17.30; 2 Th 1.7; Tt 2.13   8 Php 1.6; 1 Th 3.13; 5.23   9 πιστὸς ὁ
θεός Dt 7.9; 1 Cor 10.13; 1 Th 5.24   κοινωνίαν...ἡμῶν 1 Jn 1.3

578

Opening page of Paul's Witness II (Corinthians) from the *Greek
New Testament* that Ben Johnson used in the translation.

PAUL'S CORINTH CORRESPONDENCE

Greetings To The Church At Corinth

Greetings from Paul, called to be a missionary for Jesus, God's Child, as testified to by God, and from Sosthenes, a brother.

To the Church of God located in Corinth,

To those who are loved and cared for and dealt with in joy and compassion by Jesus, God's Child, and

To those who are called to be saints together with all those joining together under the label of family membership with our Familyhead, Jesus, God's Child,

To such everywhere, one and all -

May God's quickening presence be yours and peace from God, our Creator and our Familyhead, Jesus, God's Child.

I give thanks to God constantly for you who are ones dedicating yourselves to God and showing compassion as did Jesus, God's Child, because in every way, you seem to be blooming in it, in every account and report, as if to stand as a witness to how flowering growth can come about when the story about God's Child becomes a part of you. You aren't among those who seek shelter from the shower of expectation of our Familyhead, Jesus, God's Child. And this confirms you as worthy of the end, faultless, for the Day of the Familyhead, Jesus.

God's Call For A Community Of Those Who Are Faithful

It is our faithful God who calls you into the community of God's Child, Jesus, our Familyhead. I beg you brothers and sisters, through our family tie of being in the family of Jesus, God's Child, that you always speak as one, and not as divided voices. Be totally united into the mind of Jesus and into that one's understanding of how things really are. It is being spread by Chloe about you, my sisters and brothers, that there's bickering among you. I'm told that each one of you is contentious, saying, "I am for Paul," or "I am for Apollo," or "I am for Peter," or "I am only for God's Child." Can God be divided up? Did Paul get hung on a cross for you? Could you be baptized into the family name of Paul? I am happy that I didn't baptize any of you except Crispus and Gaius so none of you can say that you were baptized into my family name. Well, I did do baptizing at Steven's household, but I don't think I baptized any of the rest of you. God's Child didn't send me to do baptizing but to disperse gospels. I certainly

did not abandon you over to wisdom cult initiation. The cross of God's Child can't be so deprived of its meaning.

Rescue From One Dying On A Cross

Yes, the cross sounds ridiculous to those awaiting their own destruction but to those who are rescued by it, the cross represents the power of God.

It's written,

"I will destroy the wisdom of the wise and I will foil the understanding of the intellect."

Where is wisdom? Does it rest in an interpretation? Does a student of history have it? No way! Doesn't God ridicule knowledge derived from this world's experience? World experience can't know about God through its wisdom but only through God's wisdom. God quickens knowing beyond silly arguing into the process of being saved through faithful living. Leave off requesting proofs of Jewishness, or seeking Greek mystery knowledge. We are a brand new breed of announcers of God's Child hung on a cross, a shame-filled event to Jews and something irrelevant to the wise.

Knowing How God Is From Knowing Jesus

We do not call ourselves Jew or Greek. We call ourselves believers in God's Child as a way of knowing about God. It is the foolishness done of God that is our source of knowledge about God. We are empowered by something appearing as a weakness in God. Now look up to those who are called among us, brothers and sisters, as against all those who are called wise according to earthly standards. None other than a believer has authority over anything. None other than a believer has social status over anybody.

God's Call For A Community Of Those Who Are Vulnerable

God has picked out those who are poor-nothings by the world's thinking to have something to be more proud of than wisdom. God has opted for those who are vulnerable by world standards to have more strength than the mighty. God has chosen those who are insignificant in the world and those who are despised to be selected over the ones who have it all. Prior standards are cancelled. No more can anyone in this flesh brag they are closer to God than we.

A Familyhead For A Vulnerable Family

From wherever you come, you belong to Jesus, God's Child who reveals to you God's wisdom, what's right, and ways to reach God's care and freedom, so that as it is written,
"The one who is proud of the Familyhead, let that one
brag!"
When I came to you, sisters and brothers, I didn't come with high-sounding title or special claim to wisdom deriving from the likes of a Delphic oracle from God. And I didn't try to give you any standard for judging except Jesus, God's Child, and that one hung on a cross. And there I came, weak, and in fear, and full of anxiety. I came to you. And I told my story and my message not as an experience of wisdom but as something received spiritually and in manifestion, so your faith wouldn't be grounded in wisdom as folk have but in empowering reality from God.

Let's talk about knowledge in terms of the endtime. Knowledge isn't only of this time since the governance of this age is rendered void. Let's talk about God's wisdom as a mystery, hid, which God will see fulfilled for all time and which will come to our notice. There was no one who knew how the ages were ruled. If they'd known it, they wouldn't have hung God's Child on a cross. This was how the Familyhead got brought to our care.

But as it is written,
"The eye doesn't see and the ear doesn't hear
and there's no entry into the heart of a person."
God has got to prepare someone to reach the state of realizing love.

The Promise Of A Comforting And Advocating Spirit

God gave us to know reality through the spirit of God's very breath. This comforting and advocating spirit searches all things even to the deep secrets of

God. Who could know about people, the way people are, unless the spirit of that person grasps onto the meaning? So exist the ways of God which no one can know except through its gift from the breathing spirit of God. And we must not take up the spirit of the world but the spirit of God for us to see these ways as a gift from God. Let's not banter in human terms about myths, but in spiritual dialogue, spirituality explaining spiritual things. A person not oriented to the spirit from God's breath won't receive the things of the spirit of God. Such are silly to that one and they don't lead to empowered understanding because the idea of spirituality is questioned.

The Spirit Gives Us To Reach The Mind Of The Familyhead

Spirituality is the way to evaluate everything and it is not accountable to people. Now who knows the mind of the Familyhead? What that one's advise will be? We, yes, We, bear the mind of God's Child. And I am not one who could be talking to you as spiritual folk, but only in a human way as if you were babes of God's Child. I breast fed you, not giving you solid food. You couldn't handle it. Even now you still can't handle it. Even so, you are spiritual folk. What is it in you, this fighting and anger, causing you not to act spiritually and instead to be acting according to cult precedents? For when I hear this, "I devote myself to Paul," or "I devote myself to Apollo," aren't you acting like cult members? Who is Apollo? Who is Paul? Missionaries who are wanting you to have faith through their services. The Familyhead teaches through each. I have

planted, Apollo has watered, but God causes growth. There wouldn't be purpose in having a planter, or a waterer unless God give growth. The grower and
the waterer are one and each will receive the same reward according to the
same way God approves of them. We are God's co-workers.

God's Work Done Through Many

God nourishes. You are God's cropfield to work in. God's love reaches out
to you. My work is as a spiritual contractor or architect. I laid a foundation, but
another was given to put up the walls. Yet another imagined how the walls
must be raised. Whether these walls get built from gold, silver, marble, wood,
grass, or straw, when done, the result will bear some kind of appearance for its
time will come to be seen as it is. It will be exposed to the test of fire. What
kind of worthiness is there to a mere building? The fire will settle the question.
If what's been built remains standing, the one that's built it will get paid. But if
the building burns down, the builder will not be paid for it, even if he is rescued from the fire. How much is paid for a building in flames? Don't you know
that you are God's church and you breath God's very breath? If anyone cor-
rupts God's church, that one's Godly part will be corrupted. God notices what's
going on in a church which you are.

Don't try to outsmart each other! If anyone wants to be intelligent in this
time frame, let that one become a fool to gain intellect. The geniuses of this
world are foolish to God's reckoning.

As it is written,

"He traps the smart ones in their own tricks."

And again,

"The Familyhead knows the arguments of the skeptics,

that they are a banter." Don't brag among humanity. Be unified among
yourselves, whether you appreciate Paul, or Apollo or Peter or the world or life
or death or what exists or might come to be. You are a unity. You are one in
God's Child, God's. Let every person take into account how things are, bearing
the role of care- giver to God's Child and dealer in God's mysterious ways.

Centering Family Life On Faith In God

For the time remaining, establish yourselves in orderly homes because
that's where faith may be exercised. This doesn't apply to me. I am not to be
evaluated by your standards or how other people spend their days. Therefore
I don't myself judge such things. I'm not talking myself down. My conscience
is clear and I don't know anything more right than that the Family is to be my
judge. It won't do any good for people to be condemning in this time frame
waiting for the Familyhead to return. God's Child will shine a light where now

the shadows hides and this light reveals the heart's intentions. Then's when approval will get showered on each person by God. Until then, brothers and sisters, I have built churches beyond what I myself can handle and I have Apollo-like persons to reach you so that many be taught this.

A Folk Knowing They's In A Family With Hope

Don't disregard the advise that no one should act better than another, putting down another person. How can one think he is better than another one? Who has what hasn't been received? If you are a recipient, why brag except about receiving it? Already you have more than enough to eat and enough money to spend. You can decide things for yourselves without me. I wish exactly that, that you go about deciding things for yourselves and, since my hopes is in you, we are really deciding together.

The Familyhead Strengthens The Vulnerable

I think this - God has sent me as an endtime missionary as one sentenced to death anyway. God's purpose is for me to be a spectacle before the world to those who wish to breathe the spirit of God's breath and humanity in general. I am a fool for God's Child, but you can be thought of as filled with brilliant intuitions from God's Child. I am vulnerable and weak, but you bear all the strength God can accouter you with while I am just insignificant. Even right now, I hunger and thirst and my clothes are rags. I don't have a home. All I know to do is to work with my hands same as yours. But while others curse their lot, I give prayers of thanks. While others speak falsely, I wait patiently. While some talk about how bad others are, I try to elevate their thoughts. I have become as those who are considered the world's rot and until now the rejected among humanity. I don't write to you ashamed on this account but as one family member to another recognizing each other that way. It doesn't matter if you come to have thousands of teachers in the ways of God's Child, you don't have that many parents. It's I who came to birth you in the gospels of Jesus, God's Child. I was the one whispering ideas. You took them in your heads as thoughts to ponder. Same way, I sent Timothy to you who is my trusted kin and trusts the Familyhead. He will remind you about the roads of my journeys as I keep teaching everywhere among the many churches. Even now there are some who assert that I won't be coming back to you. But I will come quickly to you as fast as I can when the Familyhead wills it even if I don't know the time more than those who assert otherwise or those who assumed control of the church.

Paul Holds The Church Family To Account

The Homeland of God doesn't depend on my return to you or on any earthly power. What do you want? That I come to you with a paddle of blame or in loving evenness of a spiritual bond not casting blame? The whole church hears that there are sexual wrongs committed among you, and such a kind as nowhere even among the other world's people. It is said some are taking the wives of their fathers. And there you are boasting about it and not about to regret doing it! Is this practice growing among you? Now I am absent in my body but present in my spirit. I disapprove just as if I were there and as I will do once I come to you as an agent of Jesus, God's Child. When such bad actors come among you, remind yourselves of my hopes with prods to follow our Familyhead, Jesus. Remember about the Challenger, the spirit of this world, the force of the lust of humanity. It causes us be separated from God and dares our bodies to do wrong. Rescue yourselves for the coming Day of the return of the Familyhead.

Bearing Pride Only In Being In The Church Family

No good comes from being proud of your human instincts among yourselves. Don't you know it is like the smallest amount of yeast that rouses to spoil the whole batch of dough? Wipe away this pride in sexual conquest so that you may be young and innocent and without such yeast as is like our Passover bread, not bearing the leavening of peace, representing to us our murdered God's Child. Now, let us observe life as we observe the Passover, not activated by the former yeast of bad ways and sexual outrage, but without the work of such yeast in genuine sincerity and in reality.

Leaving Those Who Are Not In The Vulnerable Church Family To God's Dealing

I wrote you in another letter not to be congregating with people satisfied with their wrongdoing, but it can't be that you avoid all those who are doing wrong in this world, or those who are graspers or greedy or idol worshippers, since to avoid them you would have to leave the world. And then I wrote to you not to go mingling with them even if they were sisters or brothers bearing your family name or sexually wrongdoers or ones wanting more than their share or idol worshippers or slanderers or drunks or greedy folk or such as those you should avoid eating with. But really, what is it to me how those who are outside the church are to be considered? Nothing! You should evaluate those who are inside the church, let God do the determination about those outside. Remove a sexual violator from among you yourselves. Are any among you

so foolhardy as to risk taking your disputes for settlement by an unbeliever and not before church authorities?

The Church Family As The Source Of World Judgment

Don't you know that church members are the ones who judge the world? But if the world does the judging of you, you are exposed to those who are unworthy to judge the least important court case. Don't you know that we are the judges of people's hearts, not to mention how people should live their daily lives? There are points about everyday life which are decisive which you have knowledge of. Those who make light of those who are in churches you should not let be seated over you for judging. I tell you to do so is shameful.

Don't Resolve Internal Disputes Before Any But A Family Member

Isn't there anyone among you with enough understanding who you will appoint to resolve disputes arising between you and your friend? Also can a friend seek judgment against a friend and not have this lead to faithlessness? Already the whole church speaks of you as failures because of the lawsuits you have against each other. So listen to me! Can't you hold off from these faithless doings? Can't you avoid doing what you are about to do? For you are acting unjust and committing fraud, and this to your friends.

Family Members As World Inheritors And Who Are Not Among Them

Don't you know those who you are treating unjustly are the heirs of God's worldly inheritance. Don't act opposed to this fact. No one violating God's creation laws, nor idol worshippers, nor having sex out of family marriage, nor child abusers, nor predatory gays, nor thieves, nor graspers, nor drunks, nor slanderers, nor greedy people will share in God's Homeland. And some of you may be so categorized.

God's Approval, Regardless, To Them Vulnerable Ones Willing To Bear God's Love

But you are cleansed, and you may bear God's love, and you may feel like you are approved carrying the family name of our Familyhead, Jesus, God's Child, and this by the benefit of our God's very breath.

Living Most Beneficial To Bear God's Love-turning Your Body And Its Sex Drive Over To God

All things are okay for me to do but not everything is beneficial and I will not stoop to assert myself to do many things. Food is digested in the stomach and the stomach is in need of food. But God consumes quite differently from this. The body is not for sexual gratification but for the use of the Familyhead and the Familyhead uses a person's body. God caused the Familyhead to be raised from the dead and will so revive us into life by the same power. Don't you know that our bodies are a part of God's Child? You remove its character of being a part of God's Child's body when you commit sexual impropriety. Don't do it! Don't you know that one who joins in sexual gratification is acting only in body? God said, "They will make their two natures in the earthly form one." But one who unites his or her body with soul in the Familyhead breaths the spirit of God's breath. Fly from sexual gratifications. Everything that separates you from God is something caused from outside the body. A person who wrongs another sexually ends up being separated from God in that one's very soul. Don't you know that your body is a church floating in the breath of God's own existence and belonging to God and you don't have it to yourself.

Sex-behaviors Under Different Conditions

You were bought for an expensive price. And God keeps watch on the body which you have. Now concerning those things you wrote about, it is good for a fellow not to touch a girl. But each should take a wife for himself to satisfy the body's sexual demand and each girl should take some man to herself. A man should give marital dues to the wife and the same for the wife to her man. The woman should give over authority over her body to no one except her husband. In the same way also the man should give over authority over his body to no one except his wife. Don't turn away one from another unless by consent for a time to devote yourselves to prayer, and you may return again to the other. Don't allow the world's temptations to test you into self-indulgence. This I advise by way of suggestion, not as an order. I wish that all people could be as I am myself but each person has a calling from God, one as this and another so. I advise those who are unmarried and those who are widowed, it would be good for them if they remained as I am. But if they can't exercise self-control they should marry because it is better to marry than to be consumed with wishing for sex. To those who are married, I give a command. Let me clarify that. I don't give it. The Familyhead gives it. A woman must not separate herself or or divorce herself from her man. As for what follows, it is just me saying it, not the Familyhead. If some brother has a wife not a Christian and she agrees to live with him, don't leave her. And a woman, if she has a man who is not a Christian, and he agrees to live with her, she shouldn't leave this man. The man, not a believer, is being saved by the caring woman and the woman, not a believer, is being saved by a Christian care-giver. It used to be their child could end up with no relationship to God, but now the child lives in a state of Godly family love. Now if the nonbeliever wants to leave, let that one go. Christian brothers or sisters aren't bound in that relationship. Don't worry. God comforts you and grants you peace of mind. If you haven't tried, how could you have known, wife, if you could have rescued the man? Or how could you have known, husband, if you could have rescued the wife?

Liferole Distribution From The Familyhead, Each To Provide A Way Of Relating To God

No one but the Familyhead distributes life roles and God confirms the profession to each distributee. Act accordingly. This is what I have taught to all the churches. When someone circumsized is called to become a Christian, don't let his circumcision get in the way. To those who are called from among the ranks of non-Jews, don't let circumcision discourage them. Circumcision means nothing except as it is a reminder about God's life rules and not being circumcised means nothing.

No Lifestyle Beyond Rescue

Each one is called to have a lifestyle and being called should stay in it. Are you called to be a common field laborer? Don't let it depress you. And if you have the ability to earn free citizenship, make the better use of your new status in the Familyhead. One who is bound to work as a common laborer is freed by the Familyhead, and in the same way one who is called a free citizen is under bond to God's Child. You were purchased at such an expensive price! Never accept that you are owned by anybody.

Live As In A Family With Jesus As Familyhead

Each of you, whatever your life status, brothers and sisters, live in relationship to God. Concerning those who are not sexually active, I don't have a commission to comment from the Familyhead, but I will give an opinion that as you have been shown mercy by the Familyhead be faithful. It is a good idea to live this way considering the existing situation and it is a good idea so to stay. Have you had ties with a wife? Don't try to untie them. Have you been released from a tie to a wife? Don't seek another wife unless it has to be you should marry rather than do wrong things. It's not wrong to marry a spouse who hasn't been sexually active. Life bears such conflict from instinct demands, that I, myself, choose to abstain.

Building Sex Relationships Knowing A Death End Comes

But I do say this, sisters and brothers, the time, finally grows short before comes an endtime when those who are marriage partners won't have them any more, when those who are having to cry for the way the world's treating them won't have to cry, when those who are filled with earthly joys, won't have such particular joy, when those who are going to the grocery to buy won't have their purchases to hold onto, and when the cares of this world won't be such a weight. I wish you could all be free of sexual and worldly anxiety. An unmarried person is more attuned to the Familyhead and how to behave in con-sonence before the Familyhead. Someone married is more attuned to the world and what makes the marriage partner happy and centering on that. But an older woman or widow or unmarried girl can all of them care for the Family-head so as to be God's in their body and in their spirit. Even a woman who is married may be a care- giver to the Familyhead while householding with her man. The same applies to the older man or widower or unmarried young man.

Sexuality For Building A Godly Family And Community

Now I am telling this to you for your own good. I do not want you to be led astray by sexual temptations. Instead I say all this to help establish a stable community where people can live devoted to the Familyhead without reserva-tion. Now if someone thinks it is not right to have sex because his wife is not experienced, even when he is filled with sexual need and she is consenting, let him do as she wants. It is not wrong. Let them be truly married. But if he is firm in his heart, not wanting its trouble, he has authority to enquire and see if she evaluates the same way in her heart, to try each remaining unfettered to sex, as he does, and even when people marry between themselves it doesn't have to be sexually engaging. But overall one not marrying does better at not being consumed in sex. A woman gives herself over for her lifetime so long as her man lives. But when the man dies, she is free to pick who she wants to marry but staying united to the Familyhead. Even so, it is far better if she stays unmarried, bearing in mind the purpose for her life. And I expect the spirit of God's breath will bear her up.

Staying Away From Worship Rituals

I change the subject to the question of purchasing meat from animals slaughtered in temples of idols as part of pagan worship rituals. We know that

we all have the capacity to understand. But the process of comprehending confuses us even as our family love for each other is bonding us together. Even if some claim to know what's what, still it's not yet understood all that it is necessary to know. And if any love God, this fact gives understanding about God. Now concerning this meat from temple slaughterhouses, we know that there is no presence of God in any idol of this world and that there's no God except One.

Folk Customs Don't Matter, What Matters Is Relating To God And Our Familyhead, Jesus

It happens there are many calling on so-called gods either in Olympus or on earth, as if there could be many gods and many saviors, but we know there is only one God, the Parent of us all and we belong to this Parent, and this One give us our Familyhead, Jesus, God's Child through who's life everything is and we exist. But not in everyone is there this understanding. And some by prior custom believed in idol empowerment as they ate idol food and this understanding of theirs caused weak beliefs to wallow into error. Our food doesn't require presentment before God. We aren't worse off or better off by what we eat. But don't you see how our authority could become a stumbling block to those who are weak thinkers? For if some see you who have our belief, knowing there's nothing to idol worship, eat food dedicated to idols, they might not understand. Their faith may be shaken. To eat food dedicated to idols confuses

those whose faith is weak, and this weak one is our sister or brother for whom God's Child died. So since you're doing wrong against your brothers and sisters and wounding your consciences while you are weakening the understanding of others about God's Child, you are committing error to eat idol dedicated food. If, for this reason, food causes my sister or brother to lose understanding of faith, I would not eat any meats of any kind rather than I be the cause of a brother or sister's unbelief.

Paul's Right To Give Directions About Behavior

Am I not free? Am I not a missionary? And, Yes!, did I not see for myself Jesus, our Familyhead! If, to others, I am not a missionary, even so, I am to you. For you are the proof of my being a missionary in our Familyhead. This is my explanation to those who are questioning me. Couldn't I exercise authority about what to eat and drink? Couldn't I have the authority to have in my company a sister as wife as do the rest of the missionaries and this very world's church rulers for the Familyhead, and Peter? Or is it only me and Barnabas who do not have authority to act? What soldier ever would go to war having to pay himself? What vineyard is planted and its fruit is not eaten? What shepherd tends that one's flock but doesn't eat the cheese made from the flock's milk? Not according to the ways of people do I speak. Anyway, doesn't the law say these things? In fact, in Moses's law it is written,

"You should not muzzle an ox who is at work threshing."

Is God only concerned about a a cow? Doesn't this also say something to us all? Yes, it was written for us because there should be expectation for the plower that something will come from his plowing, and expectation for the harvester that there will be something to grow profitably. If I plant in your lives, don't I get to gather great worldly benefits from you? If others among you feel so authorized to share in what you have, can't I?

Explanation About The Problem Of Amassing Material Benefits While Ministering To Others

Even so, I cannot draw upon this right. Though I may have all the rights I could exercise, I don't want to create an obstacle to my message about God's Child. Don't you remember that the ones who work in temples eat from the temple offerings provided by those who sacrifice at that altar? Just so can't the Familyhead provide to those who are carrying out preaching about the gospels of life? But I cannot bring myself to benefit from this. Nor have I written these things so that this right comes to me. It would be better for me to want to die rather than, well, my feeling of self worth would be empty! For though I preach the gospels there's nothing in it for me to personally brag about.

Ministry As A Natural Function Like Breathing. The Reward For Doing It, Drawing Breath, Is Free And Gives Life

Instead I bring news of an emergency need and I would feel I was rendered breathless if I didn't so preach. If I go about this undertaking for free, I have a reward. What if my goal wasn't voluntary, just a matter of work ethic, what could be pay enough? This way, working free of charge, I tether myself to the gospels so that I don't need to boast of my right to benefits from the message. Being free from all ties, I can deliver myself over to serve as everybody's common laborer and I can do better and gain more. And I have become a Jew to those who are Jewish so that I can benefit Jews. To those without religious laws, I am one of them, not bound to any religious law of God except for that of God's Child, so that I can benefit them.

Ministry Brings Benefit To The Vulnerable And Life Hurt

I come to those who are tired and hungry and weakened by what they've come across in this world as one like them so that I can benefit those who suffer hurt. To all I am all they are, however life finds them. I can save their lives. And everything I accomplish comes through the hopeful message I give them, as one who may jointly share in its announcement. You know how a runner is who takes to a track and field event, how he runs, isn't it to receive a prize? That's why you run and try to overtake others. All someone has goes into competing, everything, total concentration. Same with me. I hope for all those who are subject to deathly decay that they will receive the trophy coming from running a good race. Otherwise you are deathly decay. So am I like this runner, not without a goal in mind. Otherwise I am like a boxer who punches only air. Unless I keep my body under control and keep serving others, not just preaching to others, I may not qualify this body of mine to start the race.

God's Call To The Vulnerable Is Documented In History

Don't forget, my brothers and sisters, that those who were first called to be God's family were beckoned by a cloud and they followed it across the land and through a sea. All of them became baptized by Moses in the cloud and in the sea. And all of them ate this cloud's spiritual bread and they drank from that rock which bound them together into a discipleship of the spirit. This rock was God's Child. Still God was not happy with them, even a majority of them, so they became stranded in the wilderness. These days were a warning of what was to come and was meant to temper people not to act wrong as they panted to do. Don't give yourselves over to worshiping idols as they did. As it is written,

"The people lolled in eating and drinking and stood up
only to dance."

Endtime, Second Coming, Foretelling

Don't follow this example as caused 23,000 lives to be taken in a single day. Don't question what justice comes from God's Child as they did who found themselves ravaged by snakes. Don't complain as did those who complained and found themselves destroyed by an avenging angel. These things happened as a forewarning to them. These writings are instructional for us to show us what kind of things happen in the endtimes.

Faith In Our Rescue From This Disabling World By The Familyhead Who Lets Us Handle Every Life Situation

As one who knows how to behave, look out! Don't stray! The urge to fall away can't reach only the human in you. And faith in God doesn't let you get urged beyond what you can handle and will bear you through the urging to stray from faith. Anyone feeling the bond to God will have the power to overcome temptation. So, my sisters and brothers, abandon idol worship. I say this as to those who are sensible enough to be able to think of consequences. Consider what I say to you. What is idol worship except what the idol is? And this they are sacrificing to is a mere sham and not God. I do not wish you to share in what is given to shams. You have a table bearing a cup of our Familyhead to share in and you would give yourselves over to eating with shams? Can't you become anxious for the return of your Familyhead? Do we have stronger stubbornness than God's Child?

Family Members Should Do For Others

Everything is possible but it is not to our advantage to do everything. No one should pursue his own goals but those of another. Everything that is in the meat market we could buy to eat except what we decide in our conscience shouldn't be eaten. All of it comes from the Familyhead and all its content belongs to God. If anyone, not a believer, asks you and you want to, everything set in front of you to eat can be eaten without pang of conscience. But if something is said to you like, "This is meat from an animal slaughtered at the temple as a sacrifice." you shouldn't eat it after that disclosure as a matter of conscience. I say this to those who are conscience struck. Your refusal is not for yourself but for the other.

Our Conscience As Source Of Awareness Of Our Lives In God's Story

How can I exercise free choice while acting as a matter of conscience for another? Since I share God's bounteous joy, to do otherwise would be to testify against God. Just so, whatever you eat, whatever you drink, whatever you do, do it all as a care-giver for God. Be innocents alike to Jews and Greeks and to the church of God. So do I try to be acceptable to everyone in everything not to pursue my own benefit but for everyone, so that they may be rescued. Bear in mind my example just as I bear in mind the example of God's Child. I am proud of you because you respect everything I passed on to you as tradition, and, as I have told you its value, you have seen fit to carry on God's family traditions.

Sexual Role Status Ways Of Relating To God

I want you to acknowledge that every man has God's Child's stature. The stature of a woman is relational to a man. The stature of God's Child is God. Every man loses the strength of his identity unless he prays or explains his life message as the story of a man. Every woman loses the strength of her femininity unless she prays or explains her life story in terms of her female sex physique. She is not sex-neutral while undertaking her duties as if she were a shaven man. If she cannot downplay her femininity, she should cut her hair short. And since it is out of character for a woman to either have short hair or to shave it, it is best just to downplay the femininity. A man ought not to hide his male character which marks how God thinks of him as his care- giver. A woman should seek care from a man. It is not the man who comes from a woman, but a woman who comes from a man. A man was not created from a woman, but a woman from a man. That is why a woman out to do the right thing bears a status like that of one of the angels. Even so, no woman is set apart from her husband or a man set apart from his wife in the sight of the Family-head, and as a woman is close to her man, and as a man lives for his wife, so are all relationships from God. Evaluate for yourselves these things. Is it right that women dress sexy for God when they pray? Doesn't the human condition itself teach that long hair is a matter of embarrassment to a man? If a woman has long hair, doesn't it draw attention? The fact is hair is given as a head covering. But whatever, if it may lead to arguments, we shouldn't stand on any such custom, nor should any of the churches of God.

Family-community Church Meetings Should Be Peaceful And Orderly

Now this about what you been instructed. I am not happy that things have gone from best to worst when you meet together. The first trouble I began to hear was about quarrels when you come together in your church and I could only half believe it. Then more news came saying you were stealing among yourselves so that those who are giving the appearance of being God's selected were theives. Then it was said when you were gathering together among yourselves for communion, you were really only eating supper. The Familyhead was not being remembered. Some were said to be acting rowdy during communion and even drinking the wine to get drunk. No! Don't you know you have houses where you can eat and drink? Is it really so that you have such contempt for the church of God? Isn't it shameful, these things you're doing? How can I say I am happy about you? About this, I can't take any pleasure.

The Tradition Of The Familyhead's Last Supper

I passed on to you the tradition about the Familyhead, and I entrusted it to you, how the Familyhead, Jesus, on the night he was to be betrayed, took bread and giving thanks divided it and said, "This is my body, it is for you. Do this to remember me." And as this went on, after dinner, the cup was passed with Jesus saying, "This is the cup which is the new last will and testament written in my blood. Do this, as often as you drink, to remember me." As often as you eat the bread and drink the cup, the death of the Familyhead will be proclaimed until God's Child comes again. So, anyone eating the bread and drinking the cup of the Familyhead inconsistently acts opposed to the body and blood of the Familyhead. Every person must make this connection when they eat and drink from the cup. Anyone who eats and drinks is doing wrong who doesn't contemplate the human body reference. That's why many among you have weak faith and are anxious even to your deaths. But if we make the distinction in ourselves, we cannot be condemned. And being given the power to differentiate by the Familyhead, we rise above condemnation. So, sisters and brothers, when you come together to eat among yourselves, expect this consequence. And if any is hungry, that one should eat at home so to avoid wrongdoing when you are gathered. As for the rest, I will straighten things out when I come.

God's Breathing Spirit Guides The Church Family

Concerning spirituality, brothers and sisters, I don't want you to be uninformed. Remember that you might yet be a people belonging to silent idols with your thinking led astray. Therefore I confide in you that no one talks through the spirit of God saying, "Curse Jesus!" and no one is able to say, "Jesus is Familyhead," if not through the spirit appointed by God. There is a difference in the work of God's love which is proof of the spirit. The difference appears in service and this comes from the Familyhead's urgings. This difference is active, and it is God who provides the energy for it all the time in all things. In these last days, the breath of God's spirit is given to us as a helper.

The Spirit From God's Breath Works In People In Different Ways

To a certain person God's breathing spirit gives the gift to tell a clever story. To another comes the power to understand the spirituality of the story. To a certain one, faith is given through the spirit while to another one healing gifts come through the spirit. One has the gift of industry. Another one the capacity to preach. Another is empowered to be spiritually persuasive. Another has the gift of intuition. Another can translate. The total capacity of all this draws its energy from one source and this is God's breath drawing apart and differentiating itself as it wishes. Just as the body is a unity despite its many parts, so all the parts of the body find their being in one body, and this is God's Child.

One Body With Many Members

We are one body in which each has a role. All have a role in the body. So does God's Child. We are all baptized into this one form through baptism - whether Jewish or Greek or common laborer or freedman. The body does not exist in part but in the whole thing. If a foot says, "Because I am not a hand, I am not from that thing's body," does that make it not a part of the body? Or if an ear says, "Since I am not an eye, I am not a body member," does that make it from another body? If the whole body consists of an eye, how can there be hearing? If the whole body is hearing, how can the sense of smell be explained? Now God places body members in each of our bodies as God chooses. And if they were the whole thing in one member, what kind of body would that be?

We have lots of parts, but one body. The eye can't say to the hand, "I don't have use for you," and just so the head can't say to the feet, "I don't have any use for you." It is better to think of the whole thing, all the parts of the body. Those who are weakest are still necessary. What seems the most insignificant part of the body is needed the most to be put where it is. And even our most private body parts have their appropriate uses. It is really the presentable parts of us that don't fill a work need. God has arranged the body so as to make the most useful parts to be respected most, not to cause confusion in the body but so that the body parts can bear up each's concerns one for another. If there's a sore in one part, all of them share the pain from that one part.

The Vulnerable Church And Its Vulnerable Individuals Are The Body Of God's Child

You are the body of God's Child and each an individual part of the whole. God has placed these parts together to build a church consisting of first, missionaries, second, preachers, third, teachers, next, workers, and next those who heal, help, lead, and interpret languages. Can it be possible for all to become missionaries? Can all become preachers? Can all teach? Can all be work-

ers? Can all have the gift of healing? Can all speak languages? Can all interpret? Pursue the gift that is yours to do the most.

The Primacy Of Family Love

And still, I want to point out a most special path. If I speak with persons alive or those who are beyond death, but I have no conceding love, I am a brass horn blaring out or a cymbal clashing. And if I preach and I know the answer to every theological question and I know everything else and even have faith so as to be able to remove a mountain, but I don't give myself over to love, I am nothing. And if I give pieces of bread as charity to the last penny's worth I own and if I give the clothes off my back so that I can boast how good I am, but I don't love my brothers and sisters, I am a failure. Love is patient. Love cares. It doesn't stir up jealousy, or indulge in brags, or offer any ground for arrogance. It doesn't rest on behaving acceptably, or look after its own interest at all, or lose its even temperament no matter what happens, or fail to consider the worst, or find happiness in injustice, but instead finds joy in its own expression. It endures everything, stays faithful despite everything, sees hope in everything, remains steady through everything. This love never fails. Whether preaching is heard or not, the sermons lose their punch. Whether spiritual communication happens or not, it ends. Whether knowledge comes about or not, it will be rendered out of date. We know only in bits and we preach only about life's pieces. But when comes endtime maturity, the piecemealing ends. When I was a baby, I talked as a baby, I behaved as a baby, I understood as a

baby. Then I became an adult. I passed through the stage of babyish ways. So it is now. We see through a mirror in shadows, but then face to face. Now I only know some, but then I will have knowledge beyond knowing and beyond imagining. In our earthly lifetimes, faith, hope and love keep us going, these three. But of the most importance is conceding family-building love. Follow after this goal of love. Seek after it through spirituality even more than you follow after the prophets.

Spirit Intuitions

One who speaks spiritually doesn't speak to humanity but to God. No one hears even if that one tries to explain a mystery. But when one preaches, he says to people something family and community building and encouraging and comforting. When someone speaks in spirited language, it is self- encouraging. But when one preaches, it encourages the whole church. I would like all of you to have the gift of speaking in spiritual language, but it is best to hear preaching. It is better to preach than to speak in spiritual languages unless what comes is explained so as to encourage the church. Even now, my brothers and sisters, what if I should come to you speaking a spiritual language? Would you get anything out of it if I would talk that way, either by way of explanation of how God works, or moral preaching or life teaching? Even objects can give a sound like a flute or a string instrument does, and doesn't each give off its own distinctive sound so it is known whether it's a flute or string instrument being played? If a trumpet call to arms were unrecognizable, how much preparation would there be to go to battle? You're the same about your communicating if you don't give out the meaning. How will it be known what you're saying? You will only be exhaling air. It's favorable to have so many dialects bearing the experiences of different world-speaking people and none are worthless slang. If I don't catch the meaning of the dialect, I will be considered a stranger to those who are talking it, and the one saying that is to me a stranger. So are we. When you are an advocate for the spirit wanting to establish the church in encouragement you strive to act to the most advantage. So, when someone speaks in spirited language have the message of it interpreted. If I pray in spiritual language, my spirit prays but my mind is not instructed. So what should I do? I pray in the spirit, but I will also pray so that I will be understood. I sing hymns in the spirit, but I also sing so that I be understood. The reason for this is, if the benefiting word comes in spirit, the one who has just joined into the life of the church can still say, "I have it by your rapturous revelation." Otherwise what you say won't be understood. Would you want to be fully enraptured, filled with loving compassion and care, and not have it encouraging to family and church?

Inspired Preaching For Reaching The Vulnerable

I give thanks to God that I am able to speak to all of you in spiritually co-muunicable words. In any particular church I can communicate in one of the five languages I know to speak in, so that I can teach the basics of Christianity to the countless thousands through the gift of languages. Brothers and sisters, don't be babies in your mental understanding. If you're going to act like children let it be in innocence from wrongdoing. Be attuned to endtime thinking.

In the scripture it's written that, "In strange languages and dialects and on different seashores, I will speak to other people in whatever necessary way for
them to hear me." The Familyhead says this. As for spiritual communication,
it is a Godly capacity for those that believe, but it isn't a benefit for the weak in
faith who don't understand Godly language. It only reaches the faithful ones.
What happens when the whole church comes together and multiple utterances
come upon it in spiritual language? The new members and the non-members
will report that you are crazy. But if all of you are speaking and preaching understandable words but still under the influence of the spirit, and one who is a
non-member or a potential member comes in that one is convinced by it all,
finds an answer in it all, the secret need of that one's heart appears, and sup-
plicating, that one will worship God, announcing to the world that God is truly
among you. What is this custom among you, sisters and brothers? When you
come together, each has a hymn, each has an instruction point, each has a revelation, each has a spiritual language word, each has a translation all at once?
Surrender all these things to the purpose of spirited church nurture. If someone wants to speak in spiritual language, let it be in twos, or at the most threes,
and with each one talking some, and all of it interpreted. If it can't be interpreted, keep silent about it in church, but say it individually and to God. Have
two or three speak and preach in inspiring and understandable words and the
rest of you let it sink in. And even if someone seated in the congregation gets
an insight, let him keep still about it. The reason is it can't be that everyone can
speak and preach at the same time in a way that everybody may gain the benefit
of the teaching and be inspired. The spirituality of the talking and preaching
must be subjected to the utterings. In confusion, there is no room for God and
God's peace. So it is in all the churches God cares for. The women of the
churches should not speak as do the priestesses in the pagan temples for it is
not permitted for them to talk like that and must be prohibited. So says our
scripture. If anyone wants to learn by experience what it is to be a Christian,
let it be gained from the head of household being the example of it in the home.
It is shameful for church women to speak as do the oracle-proclaiming-priest-
esses in the pagan temples. Can the story of God's life come by oracle priestesses and can it only be grasped by them? If anyone thinks to become a
preacher or wishes to be led to spiritual life, let that one understand what I
write to you because it is the demand of the Familyhead. If anyone wants to
remain ignorant, let that one stay ignorant. So my sisters and brothers, seek the
benefits of speaking and preaching under the influence of the spirit, and don't
be detoured from spiritual communication. Do everything with propriety and
in an orderly way. I want you to reach, my brothers and sisters, the gospels

which I have preached to you, and which you received, in which also you have your standing as followers of God's Child.

The Rescuing Value Of The Story Of God's Child

You have been rescued by the appearance of God's Child. Through this letter I have revealed to you how. Unless you hold fast to it, your ground of faith is lost. I have passed it down to you as I first learned it, as also it was passed down in tradition, that God's Child died on account of the gap that broke our connection to God according to the way the ancient writings predicted.

The Tradition About God's Child

God's Child was buried and arose on the third day according to the foretelling writings. He was recognized by Peter and also by his closest disciples. And also he was seen by over five thousand sisters and brothers at once. Many of them are still alive now, but some have fallen asleep. And also he was seen by James, and also by missionaries sent out to the whole world.

Jesus Appears To Paul Just As Jesus Might Have Been Preparing To Come Again

Last of all, as if he were in the process of a coming again rebirth but then held back, he appeared also to me. And I am the least of the missionaries, one not worthy to be called a missionary because I prosecuted the church of God. By the compassionate loving action of God I am who I am, and this Godly touch hasn't been emptying, but instead has caused me to work all the harder to fill myself up. I am nothing except the breakthrough of the love of God within me. Whether resulting from me or that Godly touch, I have been your pastor and so you came to believe.

The Centering Promise Of Life After Death

If God's Child preached that there was a rebirth after death, how can any among you be saying that the dead aren't reborn into new life after death? If there's no life after death, then God's Child could not now exist as he once did as an earth dweller, arose and arisen. If God's Child has no life after death, our preaching is empty and our faith is bare. We would be found to be liars before God because we would be swearing in front of God that God raised up God's Child to new life after God's Child was with us on earth. And if God's Child was not raised to new life, the dead ones, individually, are not resurrectable. Now if the dead ones aren't resurrectable, then God's Child wasn't. And if God's Child wasn't reborn into God's life, our faith is deluded. We would all still be subjected to the destroying routine of God's separated doings and also those who are asleep with God's Child would have died finally, once and for all time. If we have only the unrealized hope of a sometime life in God's Child, then we are the most crazed of people.

But now, yes really! God's Child has been reborn from the class of those who are dead, the first one of those who sleep. Now as a result, the state of death is a person's for a time but out of death one rises. As has happened from Adam's time, all people die, but now through God's Child all can return to life and each in proper turn - first God's Child and then those belonging to God's Child during an earthly return.

The Promise Of A Second Coming World Ruling Time

Then comes the endtime when this world is given over into a time of God, our Parent, and when the world's ruling principles and authority and power will be rendered null and void. It will be necessary for this world situation to continue until all contrariness to God is crushed underfoot. The last enemy to be destroyed is death. Everything must be crushed under God's foot. Can't God make all things respond to his demand? It is clear that this excepts the one acting to put all things in order. When all things submit, then the Child of God too will accede to the succession of all things to God, so that God will be the sum of all.

Jesus, The Familyhead, To Decide All Things

So what is done to those who have been baptized out of death? If all such dead do not find new life, for what were they baptized? Who among us wants to chance missing the hope of that hour? I face death every day and I swear by my pride in you that I hold to God's Child, Jesus, as our Familyhead. If I have been thrown into an arena with vicious wild animals for being a Christian, what benefit is it to me? If the dead don't gain real life, we might as well eat and drink for tomorrow we will die. Don't live such a lie. Bad companions can cause wrongdoing mind-habits to indwell. Arouse yourselves to live right and don't rebel against God along with those who avoid spiritually bonding to God. This would be a shame.

The Afterdeath Invulnerable Body

Now this is asked - how are the dead raised to new life? In what body do they dwell? This question is for a fool to question. You know the seed isn't lifeless even when it seems to be so. And after it's sown, it won't have the same form as before it's sown. As to the bare seed, it is a hopeless wish to look at it to learn what will be its final form. But God gives to it the form that God wants it to have and each of the seeds takes its own identity in a particular plant. Not all flesh is the same flesh, but some is human, some is the flesh of cows, some is the flesh of birds, some of fish. Bodies have a form within God's Homeland as well as an earthly form. God has provided for a special form in God's Homeland as well as a form to the earthly body. There is one identity given the sun, another identity given the moon, and another identity given the stars, and this star and that star differ from each other in their bright nature. Our bodies are like the seed when it is raised to real life from death. It is sown to be changed by decay and it rises to imperishability. It is sown humbly and it is raised to the level of God's care. It is sown weak and it is raised in power. It is buried as a physical body and it is raised a body borne on the spirit of God's breath. It's been written, "The first of humanity was Adam. Adam was brought to life spiritually..." On the last day, Adam will be made alive again spiritually. It's not the first form that is consciously spiritual. It is the succeeding life that is in spiritual form. The initial form of humanity is made from earthbound material. The second time a person is formed for life in God's Homeland. The stuff of earthly material of a person is earthbound and the stuff of Godly material belongs in God's Homeland. Just as we are distinguishable on earth in earthly form, then we will be distinguishable in God's Homeland.

So I say to you, brothers and sisters, that no flesh and blood has heirship in that Homeland nor does the earthly material possess the heirship of imperishablity. See, I am telling you a mystery. We will not all die but we will all be changed in form. It comes in an instant, in the blinking of an eye, at the last

608 ✝ F O L K N E W T E S T A M E N T

trumpet blast. There will sound a trumpet and those who are dead will be raised alive imperishable and in a changed state. It is necessary for the perishable to put on the clothes of imperishability and the dead to put on the clothes of immortality. Then will come the conclusion which is written, "Death, be swallowed up in victory! What happened, death, to your claim of supremacy? What happened, death, to your stick poking us?" The stick of death that pokes us is our separation from God and the condition that keeps us separated comes only from human contingencies. In God, out of God's favor there is given to us victory through our Familyhead, Jesus, God's Child. So, my beloved sisters and brothers, be firm, anchored, filled in the work of the Familyhead always, knowing that your difficult efforts for the Familyhead are never wasted.

Paul's Relief Effort For Those In Jerusalem And Church Family Concerns And Hopes

Concerning the collection for the specially needy ones, as I have directed the churches to do in Galatia so do I ask you to do. On the first day of each of your weeks set aside from your money what you can for a relief collection. Then when I may get there, I will commission deputies by letter to take it those needy in Jerusalem. If it might be more convenient and I am going, the contributions can go with me. I hope to be free to come to you when I am sent to Macedonia for I am going there and if it turns out that I stay awhile or spend the winter with you, you can help me get on my way whenever I might arrive. I don't want to just see you in passing. I want to spend some time with you if the Familyhead permits. I am staying in Ephesus until Pentecost. The opportunity here is wide open and needs satisfying even though there's opposition from many. If Timothy comes, recognize him. Give him a warm welcome. He is doing the work of the Familyhead like me. Don't treat him like he's a beggar. Help him on his way in peace so he can return to me. Expect him to come with other brothers and sisters. About Apollo, my brother, I encouraged him to go to you with the sisters and brothers. It's certainly not that he doesn't want to come but he will come when he has the chance. Be watchful, stand in the faith, be courageous, strong, do everything among you motivated by loving cares. I call you to mind, brothers and sisters. You know those who are in Stephen's house were the beginning of the Greek church and they set themselves the task of serving the ultimate needs of God's people. So also have all of you set your sights, cooperated with each and got your work done. I am happy at the coming of Stephen and Fortunatus and Akakus because they calm the ache I feel being apart from you. They give comfort to my spirit as well as yours. I appreciate them as you do. All the churches of Asia greet you. Akula and Priska wish you the very best in the Familyhead with all of those in the church membership

in their house. All the brothers and sisters wish to be remembered to you. Respond to each other in Godly fellowship. This greeting is in my hand, Paul. If anyone doesn't love the Familyhead, be damned. O God's Child, return! The accompaniment of the Familyhead's love, care, concern, gift, compassion, and hope be with you. Bear my love among all of you in Jesus, God's Child.

Renewed Correspondence And Greetings

Paul, missionary of God's Child, Jesus, through the will of God, and Timothy, a brother, to the church of God at Corinth near all the other saints in all Greece.

God's favor and peace be yours from God, our Parent, and Jesus, God's Child.

A Trinity Full Of Encouragers For The Vulnerable Church And Family

Thanks be to God, also the Parent of our Familyhead, Jesus, God's Child, the Parent of mercy and hope for comfort, the One who strengthens us to withstand all our troubles in doing those things we are called to do through an advocate who deals with these things empowered by God. Just as the concerns of God's Child welled for us, so also does our advocate for God's Child abound. If we are being set on, it provides help and escape. If we are being summoned to do something, it bears us up in encouragement and charges us up to persevere through any suffering that's a part of our task, being also our key to endurance. This ground of our hope is enmeshed in our understanding of life so that you join it in a partnership of passionate purpose to do God's will. Such is the essence of our calling.

Being In A Family Of The Life-vulnerable Doesn't Save People From Being Persecuted In This World

Don't be uninformed, my brothers and sisters, of the persecution happening in Asia which is besetting us beyond our ability to endure, as it is driving us to be desperate about our chance to stay alive. And there are those among us who have received the death sentence, which we experience bearing each other up, knowing that through God's will we will rise above this even in our deaths. The comfort of our ground of hope has blunted even this situation of constant threat of death-dealing persecution and it saves us from anxiety and fear, and it continues to rescue us. When help is brought to us from you, it is like the answer to a prayer, and our faces smile with thanks for your generosity. There is only this claim of ours, the witness of our faith and understanding that we are living a life in abundance and appreciation of God, and not depending on this world's wisdom but on comforting love reaching us. Sometimes we are not permitted to write to you or even to read scripture, or even acknowledge that we belong to God's Child. But it is our hope that until the endtime, you will remember us, so that even from time to time you will understand our situation, because we have the same claim to information as do you, that we may join you in the returning day of the Familyhead, Jesus. And in this confidence I planned to visit you as before, so you could put me up a second time, and leave off to go to Macedonia and then again to return from Macedonia by way of your town, and after enjoying your company to leave from your town to go to Judea. Did wanting this take away its doubtfulness to come to be? Was it more certain this would come to be because I, a human, wanted it as if it might be up to me to say, Yes, do it! instead of No, you can't get it done!

God's Child Says Yes To Every Request But In God's Way Of Saying Yes

Faith in God tells us that it is not up to us to say "Yes or No." For, the Child of God, Jesus, who is in us announcing what's to be done, provides no "Yes or No," not for me or Silounas or Timothy. It's always a "Yes" - what will happen will be in God's own way. All of God's promises are in the form of a "Yes." So also through God's Child is the final saying, "I approve of you," from God brought to our attention.

God's Special Approval To Them Vulnerable Joining Together To Face Persecution

So also is God the one who cements us together with you in God's Child and also decides what happens and God is also the one who approves our common purpose and insures its beneficial result through the work of the very breath of God acting through our feelings. I, a witness to God's activity, am hard-pressed with demands upon my life, but no longer able to ignore your need. I went to Corinth. It was not because I wanted to splash around my power as an approved missionary. I went out of care and concern for you. Now you are able to stand firm in your faith. I have come to this conclusion by myself. I am not going to go to you grieving. I do grieve over you and what cheer can there come from me considering I am grieving over you. And I write this letter so I may express my grief at not being able to come to you to cheer you up, still feeling that all of you are the joy of all of us. In the thick of persecution and anxiety I have written to you teary eyed. You cannot bear my grief but you bear the God implanting love and care touching that you are aware I know is full in you. That person causing trouble, that one doesn't trouble me except a little bit. I don't want you to be too hard on him. Any of you. It's right for that one to be given a court sentence to shame him in front of the whole city.

On the other side of the coin, it is best for you to forgive him and encourage his reform, not as do the rest of the population who eat up the suffering that one's been put to. So I beg you to show to this one compassion and affection. This was another reason I wrote, so that I might express my approval of you, as you are acting true in all this. And I also release from blame whoever you decide is to be forgiven for what they have done in the sight of God's Child. We cannot be in the business of letting worldly values deceive us. We should not stay ignorant of its methods. When I went to Troy to take the good news of God's Child and to open an entry path to the Familyhead, I did not have the satisfaction of finding there my brother Titus. Then after I left I went to Macedonia. In God there is a joy to me like being at the head of a triumphant parade as a follower of God's Child and it produces a sweet aura, easily recognized, about me in every place I go.

Missionarying Gives Special Identity

Because of God's Child, I have this aura, a sweet smelling perfume of favor to those who need rescuing and those who are being persecuted, to the dying, the sweet assurance that aids in their dying, to the living, in their life. And to whom is the benefit to this? I am not one of the many who sell the story of God's Child's life for profit, but differently, and as if I am distinct, I speak of God in God's Child. Must we again start off with a recital of our relationship to

each other? I don't need anything like an introductory letter to you or from you. You are the message of the letter, having it written in boldface in your hearts, knowing it and having it read in your church service before the whole population, being known by it by reputation because you are the content of God's Child being confirmed in commitment for us, having written in indelible not by black ink but through the spirit of the living God, not in a Ten Commandments like law tablet but in the tablet in the earthbound hearts.

The Vulnerable Family Relates To God Spiritually

We have no confident assurance through ourselves but we have it through the relationship of God's Child to God. We have no authority by ourselves to evaluate as among ourselves, except as we have the capacity from God, who qualifies us in a new agreement, not written down, but spiritual. The written human law penalizes and kills, but the effect of spiritually enforced law gives profit and life.

Formerly, people learned the rules of life as written in engraved stone from the ten commandments as God directed. Even so, those who are dead, these children of Israel, couldn't even look at the face of Moses to relate to him, the one who established the terms of the lifestyle because his face was obscured by a veil. Why couldn't they receive this attention more directly? Could he lead a people serving the spirit of God's breathing? No, because this former orientation was condemning. How could there be service in the spirit coming from that kind of stricture? We have so much greater a hope that I can speak out in confidence. I don't have to do as Moses did, place a veil over my face to avoid the looks of the children of Israel without which the message of God would have been impossible to be received. The message only made their hearts harder to its demands. Until the present day, a public reader of God's message has to wear a veil that stays on whenever there's a reading of the old revelation of God's demands. But in relating to God's Child, no veil is needed. And in the present day, whenever there is a reading of Moses's revelation, a veil lays upon their heart. But times changed this relationship to the Familyhead, and this veil is cast aside.

Our Familyhead In God's Homeland Reaches Us By Giving Us Spiritual Understanding

Our Familyhead is alive in the spirit and where there is the spirit of the Familyhead, there is freedom of understanding. All of us who keep the vision in mind of our God attended Familyhead as clear as the image in a mirror are changed from contact to contact as if by the work of the Familyhead's spirit. Now since we have been given the God bestowing formation how to live a serving lifestyle we can't become discouraged.

The Vulnerable Should Live Within The Story Of God's Life On Earth

We put aside shameful secrecy, not walking around knowing something hidden from others, not perjuring the story of God, but instead in the open, sharing among ourselves the truth brought before every one of God's people. And if any hide this good news, they hide it at the risk of losing it. In those, the God of the ages has blinded their unfaithful minds so that the good news can't dawn on them and bring them light, the good news being that God has come on earth concentrating God's attention on us, showing us who God is. I make no claims about myself but about Jesus, God's Child, our Familyhead. I myself am given to you to own and deal with as a piece of human property for the work of Jesus. It was God who said, "From the darkness, the light will break through." That light did break through to come into our hearts in the brilliance of knowing how God showed God's self in the face of Jesus, God's Child. I am God's investment in clay form, so that I may tell of the casting down from above of God's intention. Nothing I say comes from me. Even though I have been persecuted in every way, even so I am not restrained. Yes, I have been anxious over the future. Even so I have not despaired. Even though I have been sentenced to prison, even so I have not been abandoned. Even though I have been beaten up and knocked down, even so I cannot be destroyed.

Living In Recollection How The Death Of Jesus Gave Us Life

Always there bears before my vision the death of Jesus in body which has give life to my body. Always I am one who lives through the delivery of myself to the purpose of Jesus, so that the life of Jesus may appear in my mortal body. So, a death bears me up and brings me to you, but life comes to you as a result. I grasp for the spirit of faith about which it's written, "I believed, so I spoke. I believe, so I speak."

The Knowing That Those Who Are Vulnerable Arise After Death By The Helping Hand Of Jesus, God's Child

Since I know that Jesus, the Familyhead, arose from death also I will rise up with Jesus and I will be helped to stand up after death with Jesus. These statements are all made for your information, so that you may have the advantage of the full disclosure of the most abundant gift of the purpose of God interaction with us. So, I can't be discouraged, even if the mortal part of me gets worn out. Inside I am renewed day after day. So what if at the present time trouble bores in on me? So what if the trouble rises beyond all comparing? The full attention of eternity gives me energy, not leaving me in darkness but giving me to see what can't be otherwise seen. For I look beyond this time frame to the time beyond time that can't be seen.

Shelter From God In God's Homeland

I know that even if this earthly home of mine is wrecked, I have a shelter with God at a home not made by human hands, beyond time in God's Homeland. I yearn for this, this safe home in final reality, wishing please to be given to wear its clothes, or at least that I not find myself so vulnerable. Here I am in a body I yearn to overcome, not wanting to be released from it, but rather to find it re-dressed, so that the mortal part of it might be purged so that I can live. The one who bears us up through this process into God's similar form is God, the God who is the giver of the assurance of spiritual help to get there.

Our Familyhome Is In Realbeing With The Familyhead, Jesus

Always be confident and know that, even though we live in a body, we have the promise of a home from the Familyhead. Walk in faith, not in appearances. Be certain and content that you have a much better home out of the body to take to live in a home at the place of the Familyhead. Strive for the goal, whether or not you have a present home, to be welcomed into the Familyhead's home.

The Requirement That We Answer To Our Familyhead For Our Earthdoings

For all of us, it is necessary that we appear before the judgment bench of God's Child, who will receive each of us according to what we have done in body, whether notable or insignificant. Since I recognize the respect due the Familyhead, I try to convert people and I am being observed by God as I do so. Also I hope that you recognize you are perceived in your inner thoughts. Again, I am not present among you but I do take this opportunity to share with you this ground of relief, that you have the argument of it to present to others who do not know it in their heart. If I have taken my stand on distant ground, it is with God. If I have sound advice, it is for you. The concern over God's Child holds me, considering it as a standard, because one died for many, for all die. And for all people this one died so that those who live don't live to themselves but through God's Child beyond death to arise into a resurrected life.

Don't Think Of Family Members Like They Are Earthforms But Rather As Family With The Hope Of Lives Beyond

So from now on we don't consider anyone as flesh and bones. It's not as if we could consider God's Child as flesh and bones. And anyway, no longer could I know him that way. If anyone is in God's Child, that one is a new creation. What one was before, disappears. Yes, that one is new. All God's creation is reconciled, us included, through God's Child, who gives to us the gift of a reconciled lifestyle. This is because God was in this world. It was God's Child who was doing the reconciling for each of us not counting against them their wrongdoing and being the one who lay down his life within the story of reconciliation. For God's Child, I am an elder spokesman as God has called me to be to you. I am bonded to God's Child. You are reconciled with God. Once there was this One who did not know alienation. This One bore the weight of God's anger so that we might live in a spiritual relationship with God. As co-workers, then, let us encourage each other not to fall into the pit of receiving God's love as an empty gesture. In a decisive time I have heard from you and in a day requiring help I have been calling out to you. Be aware that now is the time for you to show proof that you are acceptable. Now is the day of rescue.

A Lifestyle For Those Who Are Approved

Don't give any offense in anything you do. Then no one can slander your lifestyle. Conform yourselves to a Godly lifestyle. Evenly accept everything: trouble, duty, emergency, sickness, imprisonment, anger, work, anxiety, hunger, despair, enlightenment, patience, care, inspiration, sincere love, honest words, using the potential God has given to you through the use of the weapons of your spiritual understanding of life received by you and pleasing to God. Likewise bear this lifestyle through proud or humiliating occasions despite slander or fame. Among liars, tell the truth, among uninformed provide revelation, among the dying show them life, among those being beaten down tell them they can't be killed, among those in constant pain cheer them, among the many poor people provide for them from your wealth, among those having nothing remember that you possess everything. My mouth gapes in wonder at what you do, Corinthians. My heart is full of concern for you. Don't let disaster overcome you. Don't let disaster strike down your lives. The prize, as I confirm it to children, is breath of life. Don't tolerate being conjoined to unbelievers. Can there be a partnership between Godly lives and those who are abandoning themselves from God's governance? Between a community of light and darkness? What agreement can there be between God's Child and Belial, the local Corinthian resident demigod? On what middlen ground can faith meet unfaithfulness? Can there be a common ground of a people of God with idol worshippers? We are a folk of God who live, as God told us to saying, "I will live in your company and I will walk with you and I will be your God and there will cling to me this folk." So, leave the crowd and be separated, says the Familyhead. Don't participate in cultic practices. "I will receive you into myself.

And I will be there for you in my Parent. You will be mine, both your sons and daughters."

The Familyhead Is In Total Control Of This World

The Familyhead, in total control, has revealed this. Since we have this promise, my loved ones, I ask you among yourselves to avoid the defilement of the flesh and spirit, so you can achieve a state of loving concern in relationship to God. Make room for this in your hearts. Don't do the wrong things. Don't cause anyone else to be doing the wrong things. Don't take advantage of anyone. I do not say this to judge you. Instead I say this as advice so that you are able to face death together and to live together. I have every confidence in you. I want every success among you. I am filled with the need to comfort you. I am filled to overflowing with concern about your troubles. Before I came to Macedonia, I couldn't relax because I was caught up in hearing about your troubles. There was quarreling on the surface and suspicions inside. But God, the one who inspires poor people, called us to be comforted through the presence of Titus, not just in his presence but also in his encouraging news in his reports about you, how you make plans, your griefs, how you concern yourselves about me, so that I am much cheered. Now if I struck a nerve in the letter, I am not sorry. Even if I had regrets about causing it, I intended that letter to cause you to feel alienated for a period of time. Now I am happy, not because you felt hurt, but because your anguish led you to reform.

The Alienation And Despair Of Those Who Are Vulnerable Leads To Rescue

Direct your alienation to God because in no one else can you despair of having a loss of connection from yourselves. And according to God's way, alienation turns into rescue free of regrets. Despair of the world works death. But this selfsame thing according to God's way of dealing with despair has worked so feverish in you, defending, indignant, fear inducing, laying you open, and eager, and disciplining. Through all this, you have stood together to be innocent in this practice. It was for this to happen that I wrote you, not just to get something corrected, nor to note the correction itself, but to remind you how what you do is done in the presense of God. This is what comforts all of us. Now after this comforting news about you, I am even more happy about the relief from Titus. Now if one among you I am proud of, it's not to be boastful, but because it reports how all of you are truly worth speaking of and the real pride of all of you is borne out in Titus. His own deep feelings are centered in you especially when he reminds us of how you are conforming to God's will, as with respect and expectation you accepted him. I am pleased to place all confidence in you. I bring to your attention, sisters and brothers, the loving concern of God coming about through gift giving in the churches of Macedonia. In all their real trouble, the swelling of their concern even out of the depth of their poverty has caused them to increase giving their wealth in a flood of generosity. Each has bound himself and herself to this concern according to capacity to witness, and of the fruits of that capacity, all acting with common purpose, even insisting on the right to contribute. The concern has forged a partnership for the relief of the conditions of them in Jerusalem. It was not as if I was realizing an ambition, but each first dedicated themselves to the Familyhead and now I am sending Titus to you following the will of God, so that as he told us to expect, he can finish up the gathering and satisfy this need.

Helping Others

Since you have plenty in everything, in faith and in reputation and in understanding and in all you strive for and in you is respect toward me, so also you can give plenty toward this undertaking of need. I do not make this a requirement for this represents an extra effort and a test of the sincerity of your commitment to the principle of family love. You realize the love toward all people of our Familyhead Jesus, God's Child, who being super-rich, became poor for us, so that we might have the benefit of the wealth of his poverty. I am telling you a purpose. It allows you to share not only with those for whom the contribution is given, but also with those who have contributed since last year. Now you have the chance to complete the project, with the same fervor in which it was hoped for, to finish with what you pledge. Now the expectation is laid out for you, contribute to the degree you decide is acceptable, not more than you have, for relief is not to cause you trouble for the sake of others, but an equalizing undertaking at this present time so that your table scraps can satisfy the needs of others. Even your leftovers given to others helps with the equalizing, as it's written, "Some don't have too much of anything. Others want for nothing." I detect compassion in the way you deal toward this situation from the way Titus has responded. Titus has accepted the call for help. He responds in excitement, voluntarily using his own resources to go to you. I am sending along another brother who has won approval among other churches, not only that, but also who has been asked for by the other churches we have visited as a joint traveler with me. He demonstrates love by helping others reach for the Familyhead and at my urging, protect him. Don't fault me for sending this extra helper of mine. I have sent along with these a brother of mine who will serve as a test of your faith commitment, one who has been a frequent visitor, and now more than ever has much need of you. About Titus, he is my partner and acting in joint work. About our brothers, they are messengers of the churches, the attended ones of God's Child. These I have named are the proof of my love for you and my pride in you which I represent before all churches. Concerning the condition of those who are saints, it's not necessary for me to write more. I know your desire which caused me to be proud of you in Macedonia how the Greeks were prepared to help a year ago and your willingness to help stirred up many more. I have sent the brothers and sisters information about my pride in you. I have bragged about you and passed along how you were getting prepared to give a donation. What if the Macedonians who might go with me found out different? Maybe you weren't prepared then to contribute making me feel ashamed of bragging about you. I shouldn't have expected the same as them to describe you and I shouldn't have such overconfidence. I considered it an emergency to call for the help of the sisters and brothers so that they might go ahead to you and they might collect in advance the promised contribution of yours. That way it would be ready as a contribution and not be left undone. And there's this, the one who plants little, only a little will that one harvest, and, the one who plants much will harvest much. The final decision comes from the heart, not out of anguish or from compulsion. God loves cheerfulness in giving.

God Supplies Help To Use For Others

God can supply every need to give you. God can supply joy even more than enough to you. In every way, always, in all things, you have what is enough for you and you have leftovers in everything to do good deeds with. As it's written, "God is generous, providing for those who are poor. God keeps on providing until the end of time." God causes seed to grow for the planter and gives bread to the hungry. God will serve as your resource and multiply the seed you plant and cause it to grow and become the point of contact between your every enterprise

and your God. God increases your plenty so that it will provide the source for generosity. Generosity generates a welcome and beneficial relationship with God. Life permits us not only to have our own provision but also to have enough for the needs of the saints. This bounty represents the excess which is provided for the many for which we thank God. Through saying "Yes!" to this habit of giving, we confirm our belief in the good news about God's Child and to those who are generous comes a partnership among themselves in every benefit of it. I say a prayer filled with longing for you to receive the love with God that settles on those who make such gifts. Have this love of God with this indescribable gift.

God's Demand For Our Lives To Be Lived Helping Others

I, Paul, write to urge you in the same quiet and simple manner as God's Child who, when he was with us face to face, seemed gentle among us, but after he went away became demanding of us. Now, since I can't be present with you to feel reliably confident, I count on whoever I can to help you make decisions as I would if I could be walking where you are. When I stayed among you physically, I did not try to impose a military bearing physically as if I were an Army officer, for the weapons of our war are not physical but rest in the power of

God to scale defenses, and tear down false reasoning, and every height of self conceit. The true weapons help people reach an understanding of God to make every idea conform to the reality of God's life on earth. I wished to be ready to respond to every challenge when your campacities seemed overcome. These concerns you saw in my face. If any acted willfully, thinking to do as they pleased because they belonged to God's Child, I got them to reckon how they weren't the only ones belonging to God's Child for so were we. If I was conceited as to want to, I could brag about my authority over you, which the Familyhead gives me for disciplining faith, but it's not for bringing you down to size or for making you ashamed. I don't want to seem to be one trying to terrify you through letters. Now, I hear my letters are considered over-demanding and too literary while in my physical person I am never this way. Do you consider me a weakling and my dialect to be of a despised people? Consider the letters and me one and the same, for as I am in all my letters, so I am when I am present in action.

I am not quick to regard people for their social standing, or treat them on the basis of their claims of privilege from others. Nor do I accept that people can set their standards on their own, or justify themselves as they choose to explain themselves. I will not try to take unlimited credit, but I acknowledge that, by way of limits, the God of jurisdiction has set you apart to me, so that I can reach out even to you. It is not so that my duty has ended now that you have completed your instruction in the good news about God's Child. Nor do I want to take advantage of some other people's work. I bear the hope toward you that you will have growth in your faith many times multiplying resulting by way of the abundant rule of faith. I also bear the hope of being a missionary in a land far away from you, not under any other persons area of influence who might already claim it. The one who takes credit can only receive credit in the name of the Familyhead. For it is not through earthly commendation that there is acceptability, but when the Familyhead gives the commendation. I want you to bear with me awhile however foolish I seem. Be patient with me. I am ambitious that you achieve God's ambitions for you. I have promised that you would stand, undefiled, pure, before God's Child. But I have a fear how, like the snake tempted Eve in her garden, your thoughts may trick you away from the plain truth from God's Child. If there's one who comes to you preaching other than the Jesus who I have preached, or bearing to you another spirit that I have not taken to you, or preached something which I have not approved, you might fall victim to it. I don't consider myself in any way to be less authoritative than the special missionaries. Even though I am a common person in the way I talk, even so I am not common in what I know, and in the full extent of it I have made it fully apparent to you.

Bear Up In Poverty If Necessary To Live The Good New Life

What have I done to separate myself from you? Haven't I borne poverty so that you may be lifted up? Why, because I wanted to preach to you the gift of the good news from God. I striped myself away from other churches accepting expense money from them to provide ministry to you. And then I stayed with you and didn't sap your financial resources or make myself a financial burden in any way. The sisters and brothers from Macedonia provided for my needs. In every way, I have kept myself from being a financial dependent and I will stay that way. There is the truth of God's Child in me so that this ground of pride cannot be silenced in the region of Greece. Why? Is it because I don't love you? God knows. What I do, I will continue to do, except that I may be deprived of the opportunity when the opportunity comes. For there are so many opportunists, those acting against the truth, those who disguise themselves as missionaries of God's Child. And it's no wonder. The devil himself disguises himself as an angel of light. So, it's not hard to swallow, that his missionaries themselves transform themselves as missionaries par excellans having their end to be according to their deeds. I say again, don't any treat me as a fool. But if you can't help it, at least give me the due of a fool, so that I can rant a little. This I say, nor do I say it in any other's behalf than the Familyhead, in foolish talk, confident as does a bragger.

Bearing Up As A Fool For God

Since many brag what they've done in their physical body, so will I brag. People learn to put up with a fool before them, being smart themselves. You learn to put up with it if someone take advantage of you, if someone eats your food, if someone takes what you have, if someone acts or says they are better than you, if someone hits you in the face. I talk in common speech since that is my way. In another way, I talk as an orator, foolishly, and I act bravely. Are they Hebrews? I am too. Are they Israelites? I am too. Are they birth-children of Abraham? I am too. Are they ministers of God's Child? I am ranting on as a fool does, I have gone beyond this. I have suffered through the hardest work, through the deepest hunger, through immeasurable sickness, through proximity to deaths. By the order of Jewish authorities, I have received five whippings of thirty-nine strokes. Three times I have been punished with a rod beating. Once I was stoned. Three times I was shipwrecked where I had to bear a night and day in the sea. I have often taken trips in dangers of floods, in dangers of robbers, in dangers from my own kind, in dangers from desperate homeless ones, in dangers in city limits, in dangers in deserted places, in dangers on the sea, in dangers from defrauders, in trouble and hardship, during frequent sleepless nights, in hunger and thirst, in frequent food deprivation, in cold and being without enough clothes. Aside from these obvious things, I have borne a burden every day - constant worry about the churches. If anyones faith is weak, then don't I try to strengthen it? If anyone speaks against God, then don't I rise up burning? If it's okay to be proud, those things of which I am proud are my vulnerabilities. God, the Parent of the Familyhead, Jesus, knows, this one being praiseworthy beyond time, because I am not lying. In Damascus, the mayor, Aretus, the son of the governor, locked the city gates of Damascus to try to arrest me, and I had to be lowered out of a window on a rope down the walls and run away to escape his hands. I should have a right to be proud of something else, although it wasn't from my doings, how I will come to see appearances and have information from beyond from the Familyhead. I know how a person through God's Child was caught up and taken beyond to a place like the third sky, beyond the earth's sky, out into the beyond, to God's Homeland about fourteen years ago, whether in body I don't know, or out of body I don't know. God knows. And I know someone's done the same as this person, whether in the body or out of body I don't know. God knows. This one was taken taken to paradise and heard words in God's language unspeakable by people.

Be Proud About Being Vulnerable Because It Gives You Rescue

I could brag more than those who are with such experiences although I don't have pride from my doings, only of having vulnerabilities. If I ever will want to be proud, I will be proud of this foolishness, for I will tell the truth. But I had better hold back, not because I reckon myself not beyond telling

about it or repeating something about myself, but because it goes beyond what I am permitted to tell. To make sure I don't get too puffed up, I have been given a sharp pointed pin in me, sent by God's oppressor, sticking me, so I can't become overly proud. On account of this, I have called upon the Familyhead three times for relief so that it might go away from me. And the Familyhead always says to me, "My loving care is enough to overcomes this frustration for its power provides the strength to bear vulnerability." So, I am happy to have the most pride in my vulnerability because it results in my reliance upon the power of God's Child and gives me to find rest. So too, I am content in times of vulnerability, during mistreatments, in dire need, in persecution, and in emergency, for the sake of God's Child for when I am most vulnerable, then I am strong. I am always foolish that way. You know that about me. I owe it to you to have this personality. Nor do I need to claim I am extra-special as a missionary. For, I am not. My missionary work was undertaken by plodding along patiently through providential happenings and in anticipation of future providential happenings and in God's empowerment. Why is it you think you are a weak link in the chain of churches, unless it's that I myself didn't depend on your financial help? Forgive me this cause of inequity. Now a third time I have made ready to come to you and I still will not burden you financially. Nor do I want something from you. Just you. Children don't owe support to their parents but the parents should provide for their children. I will spend my resources happily and I will exhaust the resources of my life for you. Is my labor of love any the less? It's okay. I don't want to be a burden on you. And, being willing to try any trick, I took advantage of every trick. Have I sent anyone to you to take advantage of you? I called upon Titus and I sent with him a brother. Titus didn't live off of your assistance either, did he? Was it not in this spirit that I went to walk with you? Are they walking in my footsteps?

Speaking For God's Child Gives Encouragement To Those Who Are Vulnerable

Do you think that all this time I was preaching to you for my own benefit? Just the opposite, I spoke for God in behalf of God's Child. All I did, my friends, was to encourage and strengthen. I don't want to be afraid somehow when I come to you in what situation I will find you, and I don't want to come off as someone you don't like. Do you want there to be quarreling, jealousy, hates, pushiness, bad- mouthings, bad-gossiping, arrogance, things upside down? After I have returned, my God may cause me to feel ashamed of you and I may have to be the agent of regret to many concerning past wrongdoings and unwillingness to change your ways from doing wrong things and sexual mistakes and engaging in damaging sex practices. There will be a third. I intend to come to visit you. From the mouth of two witnesses or three will I settle all accounts. I keep you aware of this and I quote it as I did when I came the second time and then left. It's directed to them who are habitual wrongdoers and for the benefit of all the rest of you.

Wrongdoings In The Church Family Should Be Corrected In Love

When I come the next time, I'm not holding back, otherwise, you would question whether it was God's Child speaking through me, who does not act weakly but strongly in your doings. And God's Child was crucified and vulnerable, but lives again by means of God's workings. And I am vulnerable in myself, but I will live with God's Child for the purpose of having God's workings reach you. Test yourselves. Are you living faithfully? Examine yourselves.

Live Like You Know The Story Of Jesus Overcomes Your Vulnerability

Do you recognize in yourselves that Jesus, God's Child, is in you? Otherwise you would be worthless. I hope that you understand that I am not worthless either. I pray to God to do you no harm in any way, nor that I give the appearance of doing any, nor that I do good unless for the sake of how things really are. I am glad when I have this vulnerability, so that you may be strengthened. This I pray, that you become endtimers. For this reason, I write even though I am absent so that when I am present I may not have to discipline severely in the authority which the Familyhead gives me to strengthen and not to tear down.

Finally, my friends, act joyfully! Be transformed! Be comforted! Know this too - you deserve peace and God loves this and peace will be yours. Welcome each other affectionately. All the saints greet you. The loving compassionate care of the Familyhead, Jesus, God's Child, and the family love from God joining in the work of the spirit of God's very breath be with you always.

ΠΡΟΣ ΕΦΕΣΙΟΥΣ

Salutation

1 Παῦλος ἀπόστολος Χριστοῦ Ἰησοῦ διὰ θελήματος θεοῦ τοῖς ἁγίοις τοῖς οὖσιν [ἐν Ἐφέσῳ][1] καὶ πιστοῖς ἐν Χριστῷ Ἰησοῦ, 2 χάρις ὑμῖν καὶ εἰρήνη ἀπὸ θεοῦ πατρὸς ἡμῶν καὶ κυρίου Ἰησοῦ Χριστοῦ.

Spiritual Blessings in Christ

3 Εὐλογητὸς ὁ θεὸς καὶ πατὴρ τοῦ κυρίου ἡμῶν Ἰησοῦ Χριστοῦ, ὁ εὐλογήσας ἡμᾶς ἐν πάσῃ εὐλογίᾳ πνευματικῇ ἐν τοῖς ἐπουρανίοις ἐν Χριστῷ, 4 καθὼς ἐξελέξατο ἡμᾶς ἐν αὐτῷ πρὸ καταβολῆς κόσμου εἶναι ἡμᾶς ἁγίους καὶ ἀμώμους κατενώπιον αὐτοῦ[a] ἐν ἀγάπῃ,[a] 5 προορίσας ἡμᾶς εἰς υἱοθεσίαν διὰ Ἰησοῦ Χριστοῦ εἰς αὐτόν, κατὰ τὴν εὐδοκίαν τοῦ θελήματος αὐτοῦ, 6 εἰς ἔπαινον δόξης τῆς χάριτος αὐτοῦ ἧς ἐχαρίτωσεν ἡμᾶς ἐν τῷ ἠγαπημένῳ. 7 ἐν ᾧ ἔχομεν τὴν ἀπολύτρωσιν διὰ τοῦ αἵματος αὐτοῦ, τὴν ἄφεσιν τῶν παραπτωμάτων, κατὰ τὸ πλοῦτος τῆς χάριτος αὐτοῦ[b] 8 ἧς ἐπερίσσευσεν

1 {C} ἐν Ἐφέσῳ ℵc A B³ D G K P Ψ[d] 33 81 88 104 181 326 330 436 451 614 629 630 1241 1877 1881 1962 1984 1985 2127 2492 2495 *Byz Lect* it[ar,c,d,dem] c,f,g,rl,x,z vg syr[p,h] cop[sa,bo] goth arm Ambrosiaster (Victorinus-Rome) Chrysostom Pelagius Theodore[lat] Cyril Theodoret Ps-Jerome Cassiodorus John-Damascus ∥ *omit* 𝔭[46] ℵ* B² 424c 1739 (Marcion) (Tertullian) Origen (Ephraem) mss[acc.] to Basil

a a a 4 a none, a minor: TR WH AV RV ASV RSV[mg] (NEB) (Jer) ∥ a minor, a none: BF² RV[mg] ASV[mg] (RSV) (NEB[mg]) Zür (Luth) (Seg) ∥ a none, a none: Bov
b b b 7-8 b none, b minor, b minor ∥ b minor, b none, b none: (WH) Bov BF² ∥ b minor, b none, b minor: TR AV RV ASV ∥ b minor, b none, b major: (NEB) Zür Luth (Jer) (Seg) ∥ b none, b major, b none: RSV

1 Παῦλος...θεοῦ 1 Cor 1.1; Col 1.1 3 ὁ εὐλογήσας...Χριστῷ Eph 2.6 4 ἐξελέξατο ...αὐτῷ Jn 15.16; 17.24; 2 Th 2.13 εἶναι...αὐτοῦ Eph 5.27; Col 1.22 5 εἰς υἱοθεσίαν...Χριστοῦ Jn 1.12 6 τῷ ἠγαπημένῳ Mt 3.17; Col 1.13 7 ἐν...παραπτωμάτων Col 1.14, 20 τὸ πλοῦτος...αὐτοῦ Eph 2.7

664

Opening page of Ephesians from the *Greek New Testament* that Ben Johnson used for the translation,

JAMES' ADVISORY

Advice From An Old Elder How The Sermon On The Mount Applies To Behavior

JAMES, GOD'S CHILD, dutiful to Jesus, God who come to us.

Consider all the goodly gifts of God, my sisters and brothers, when it's your lot to fall into the various trial-demanding situations of life. Keep locked up inside you the knowledge that every trial of your faith builds up the energy to patiently endure the next. Patience to survive! Have it! Work at it! Perfect it! so that you can reach the Homeland, get the whole picture of it and not lack understanding.

If any's fell short of feeling the spirit of God, all you need to do is ask for it for God's giving it in bucketfuls, not drops, and God won't insult you for asking. God just wants to give it to you.

Ask for it in faith, not doubt.

Doubt gets ahold of you inside, living in you deep, building up like sea waves that get blowed by gales, until you get as agitated as a tornado.

Don't think for a minute that a person torn up like that can be taken to the side of the Familyhead. That person is double! Gets flipflopped in every way!

Don't brag! Christians acting like brothers and sisters levels us. We're as rich as we need to be, leveled. Flowers bloom so very pretty in every field. It's from the sun rising, the warming sun, and it's shining on all the fields, perking the flowers and giving them their beauteous blooms until it goes down. Your wealth in your life journey withers away. A person that's God-loved puts up with a trial so that when you bear up in the testing of faith you can get crowned with the real life that's promised to those loving Jesus. Don't let any person say to you, "You're being tested because God's doing it." God's not able to find it inside to test. That's wrong to say.

God tests nobody.

Each of us is tempted by the same longings, driving us and catching at us. The nitty gritty is that longing seizes your gut thinking to bring out wrong wants and the wrong things fill your thinking to drive you toward death.

Don't get drove away, folks and those loving Jesus. All love giving and endtime gifts have come down to you from the Familyhead, Parent, and Giver of light. In front of this presence there's no difference in the light beams shining on us, and there's no places of darkness.

God willed, in the past and forever, for once and for all, to give a birth to us in a story of truth so that we can live in it as the vary important first dedication of God's creation.

My sisters and brothers, get to know the meaning of saintliness.

Be quick to listen, slow to speak and get mad. A mad person can't do right wisely. Shake off filth out of your mind and superimpose gentleness on impulses. Receive the story of empowerment to save your life. Then get into the story and don't be one of the only hearers led astray.

If anyone hears the story but doesn't do anything about it, this gets under the skin of the person, under the birthskin he or she sees when looking in a mirror. The person observes himself or herself but has to do a doubletake, and quick as a wink, they see they's lost the look that they's recognized by.

Look into the perfect law of freedom and continuity, not being a wonderstruck hearer but a doer of works. This is happiness, to be a doer.

Whoever thinks he or she needs to tremble while worshiping God or keep their tongues under control or fear their hearts deceive, trembles for no reason at all. Innocent and pure worship places you near to God, the Familyhead and Parent, and makes you want to visit orphans and widows in their troubles, transforms you into someone blameless as a Lamb, and separates you from the world.

Friends, don't play favorites. Have the faith worthy of the attention that comes to you from Jesus. If a person decked out in gold jewelry comes into a Godly place wearing fancy catchy duds, it's just coming in poor like the shabby dressed ones.

Show respect to the one dressed showy and say to that one, "You're sitting here so beautiful!" and to the poor one say, "Will you come and be by me, or sit by my side!" Don't point out differences in each other, or try to pick out which one's way of talking is low class. Listen, brothers and sisters and those who love Jesus, hasn't God selected the poor in this world to have the richest faith and share in the spiritual promise of a compassionate and Godly world to those wishing to love God?

Don't treat the poor as being shameful. The ones with lots of money are the ones that oppress the world and file lawsuits against people. Aren't they the ones that speak against God and try to insult you by attaching God's name to yours? Count on this! The law will bring the order of the world into perfect harmony according to the writing, "Love the things and ones near you just as you love yourselves."

If you treat one person or thing better than another, you're not witnessing to Jesus and you are breaking God's law. Whoever says they'll keep the whole law except for maybe one little thing, is guilty of breaking all of it. Now that law says, "You may not have sex outside of marriage!" and it says, "You may not take life!" So if anyone's doing these things, what's being done is violating God's law. As you talk, as you act, through the law you'll come to be able to make distinctions. A conclusion will be condemned as merciless unless it's performed in mercy. Mercy takes precedence over judgement. What benefit is there, my brothers and sisters, if your faith tells you to do something and you don't do it? Is your faith alone enough to empower you to be saved? If a brother or sister, being needy, is where you can help them out, or if they're having a time feeding themselves, and you say to them, "Go in peace," or "Keep warm," or "Hope you're eating good," you're not

providing them body needs are you? What is the benefit of having faith that says and doesn't do!

As to faith, unless it does faithful acts, death consumes it.

But will anyone say, "You can have your faith. I will just do good deeds." These show me you do have faith without having to act faithfully. Also, in my thinking, I see faith pointed out to me from the proof of it. Have faith that God's a unity. Doing good even to those acting demonic will shake the earth into faithfulness. What's to know, stupid, if you don't know that having faith without acting faithfully is just idle talk? Didn't Abraham, our ancestor, show he had faith bringing Isaac to the altar? Faith sees the need to help out with activity and the activity brings faith to completion. Also it fulfills the writing saying, "Abraham had faith in God, and he considered it to require him to act right." So are friends of God called upon.

See that you act faithfully from doing right and not only out of faith. It's like Rahab, the prostitute. Didn't she show she was doing right when she welcomed messengers as visitors and sent them out another way?

Just as you know a corpse because its life force is dead, so do you know faith without faithful activity is dead.

You will not all become preachers, friends. That's because it will be better in the future if we all do the decisionmaking.

Often, too, we all stumble.

If a person can tell the Lamb's story without missing its point, this person is mature and can guide his or herself like a horse that's headbriddled and under control. See how once we force bits into the mouths of our horses for guiding them, we give them the direction of the whole body to go. See how ships, even the biggest, being whipped by the most violent winds, are controlled by a little rudder at the whim of the pilot. So the little body part, the tongue, needs to claim much attention.

You know how just a little flame can set ablaze a great forest. Tongues flame like that. The tongue can make its own world of wrongdoing when it takes over control of the body, screwing up our whole body that way, setting on fire our behavior making a life a burning hell.

We all have under control in us a nature like wild animals, or birds, or snakes, or seafish and naturally we control this characteristic behavior inducer in our nature. But nobody can control the tongue of a person, appointed for wrongdoing, full of dart throwing death dealing. By it, we praise God, our familyhead and parent, at the same time we disparage those like us born Godly. The tongue is not anything like a fountain because from the same well gushes out both the sweet and the bitter. Friends, how can it be possible for a fig tree to bear olives or grapes, or for salt water to taste sweet? What wisdom and understanding do we have in us?

Let's let it show in how we behave and do things in fitting, faithful activity. If you have bitterness or jealousy, there's no room left in your heart for faithful deeds.

Don't brag.

Don't tell lies.

Such are not inspirations called out from your better side but muck, ill-considered and demonic.

Where folks are jealous or assaultive, there come to be riling and regretful activity.

Be thoughtful and the inspiration comes from above. It is first and foremost spiritual. Then it'll give you the spirit of peace, reasonableness, compromise, great mercy, goodheartedness, evenhandedness, and sincerity. The crop that comes from doing right is from the peace that got planted. How can you allow yourselves to fight and quarrel? Isn't it coming from this, from deepset pleasure seeking as when something is destroyed in war and we feel it in our bones? You're longing for something and you don't possess it. You even kill and you act feverish jealous, but still you can't get any satisfaction. Go ahead, even pick up a sword, start a war, you won't get what's needful in you to meet your gut demands.

Sometimes, you ask for something and you don't get it. Bad things were sought, and you keep lusting for them until you're worn clear out. Unfaithful ones! Don't you know that worldlusting is hostile to God. Even while this lusting may cause you to want to possess the whole world, God's hostility to it is really in charge. Or for that matter, do you think there's no reason for what the holy writing says, that envy inwardly drives your personality?

It is more instructive about love when it says,

"God takes away from the proud,

And gives love to those in trouble."

So act under Godly impulses. Resist the bad impulse and it will flee from you. Reach for God. God's reaching for to approach you. Wash your wrongdoing hands and you will unify your divided heart.

Patiently endure your feelings, grieve over them, be desperate for relief from them. Change your leers into sorrys and orgasm1 into grieving2. Act humble in the presence of the Familyhead and the Familyhead will lift you up.

Don't speak against each other, friends. When you speak bad of a friend, or try to judge the friend, it's speaking against the golden rule and condemning it. If you condemn on the basis of the law, you're not accomplishing the purpose of the very law you're using to judge by.

Only one is the lawgiver and judger. Only one has the power to save you or destroy you. And what power is in you to go judging the ones near you?

Now it comes to this.

Some say, either today or tomorrow we will go into the city and make our yearly visit and do our business and make the money we need. Do you really have no faith at all thinking in terms of tomorrow about the life you will have? Catch hold of air! All you ever will have is appearance! So what can you have if there's nothing but what vanishes! Instead here's guidance - Whatever the Familyhead wants, live by it and do whatever it is. For now, you brag big in your arrogance! All the bragging does for you is to make you guilty. When you know this, you can do faithful acts and not get in a wrongdoing fix.

Come now, rich people3, shriek to your souls about your sorrys to get rid of them. What's rich in you rots and your fancy duds get moth holed. Your gold and silver lose their shine, and the lustorloss has the purpose of witnessing of what's to happen to you! The elements of your body will be similar disposed as by fire. Build a storehouse filled with the wealth needed in the final days. Hear how the gain which was stole by you cries out to condemn you when you steal from the tennant farmers after they cut the crops from your fields and the disappointments of the harvesters will reach the very ears of the Familyhead over Sunday observances.

You have lived off the earth and growed fat. You have eaten your own hearts insted of communion bread on Sunday. You have condemned others. You have murdured a rightwiser when she or he offered no resistance.

Wait for the world government of the Familyhead.

You have seen the farmer holding back combining the crop until it's fully ripe while he longs for it to receive more rain, and then even more rain to come late in the season. So also do you wait. Dedicate your heart to it until the Familyhead's world government is brought about.

Don't complain, folks, because it's not judgment day. Understand that the real judge has stood once and for all time opening the endtime door. Take the example of the suffering and patient prophets who extolled the Familyhead's name. We are lucky to have the examples of them that remained so firm in faith. Remember how Jacob patiently endured. Understand that this is the goal of the Familyhead because Jesus, God who came to earth, stands for every compassion and mercy. Never swear total loyalty, folks, to anything in either the air or on earth or anywhere else. Instead affirm life's yes things and say no to the no things. That way you won't turn criminal.

If anyone has to suffer bad times, worship your way through them.

If anyone needs courage to get by, sing hymns. Do you feel too weak? Call for the elders of the church to come and let them pray over the person which has the effect of an anointing with oil in the name of the Familyhead.

And if a person prays trusting to be saved when soul weary or sick the Familyhead will raise you up. And if wrongdoing may be the doer in you, it is rendered powerless by the Familyhead.

Confess to each other the wrongs you done, and pray as agents for each other to be restored.

There is winning over strength operating when you act right. The person Elijah was like you in every way and he prayed and caused it not to rain, and it didn't rain down on the ground for a solid three years and six months. Then he prayed again and the sky give rain and the ground yielded crops nourished by it.

Folks, if any of you may end up led astray from truth, you may return to it. Let it be known that the one bringing the wrongdoer back to faith from the road of erring has saved the person's soul from death and stemmed a crowd-swelling tide of wrongdoing.

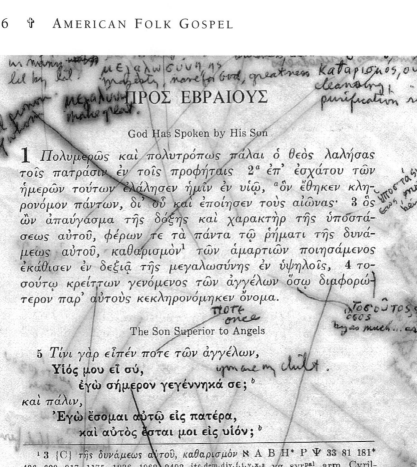

Opening page of Hebrew's Witness from the *Greek New Testament* that Ben Johnson used for the translation.

HEBREWS' TRACT

THE WITNESS OF A LETTER SHOWING JUSUS' RELATIONSHIP WITH GOD

Jesus was a Child of God and Not Like Any Former Hebrew Prophet

Wᴴɪʟᴇ Gᴏᴅ ᴛᴏʟᴅ ᴏᴜʀ ᴀɴᴄᴇꜱᴛᴏʀꜱ bits and pieces through prophets, God spoke to us in these last few years by a Child, the heir of God's total estate. God framed the span of time for him and he bears the shine of attention and character of being itself. He has taken his place -this one who upholds everything by the power of his authority and does the work of righting nonconformity at the point of full access to every dimension, having become as much different from other prophetic messengers from God as the entitlement he has inherited is more far-reaching than theirs.

To which of the prophets did God ever say,
    "You are my Child, today I have conceived you?"
Or in another reference,
    "I will be his Parent,
    and he will be my Child"?
Or when he again brings the first-born into the world, he says,
    "Have all Godly messengers fall on their knees before him."
Now of the earthly messengers - these prophets - he says,
    "Who makes his messengers winds,
    and his ministers a flame of fire."
But of the Child he says,
    "God is your throne for the span of the spans of time.
    The scepter of uprightness is the scepter of your kingdom.
    You loved justice and hated lawlessness.
    Now God, your God, has anointed you
    with the oil of approval beyond your counterparts."
And
    "You, as Familyhead, founded the earth in the beginning,
    and the cosmos are the work of your hands.
    They will perish, but you will remain.
    They will wear out like an old shirt,
    and you will dispose of them like a change of clothing.
    But you are the changeless,

and your years will never end."
Or to which of the prophets has he ever said,
"Take a ruling seat at my right hand,
till I make your enemies a footstool"?
Are they not all prophets sent into service for the sake of those who are
going to inherit salvation?

People's Responsibility

So...it is very important to grasp firmly the things we have heard to avoid
drifting into error. If the teaching preached by prophetic messengers was true,
and every deviation and disobedience results in just discipline, how shall we
escape if we disregard such a great plan as God's scheme to reconcile humanity
with the life of God?-validated to us by the Familyhead and confirmed by those
who heard him, being simultaneously attested by God by signs and wonders
and various powerful deeds and by deputizing by the Spirit according to God's
will. It wasn't to Godly prophets that God placed the responsibility for the
evolving world, but instead it has been testified somewhere,
"What is person that you remember them,
or the child of a person, that you care for them?
You lowered such temporarily of less status than a prophet,
You encircled them with attention and respect,
putting everything in subjection under their feet."
Now in putting everything in subjection to people, God left nothing outside their control. But as it is, we do not yet see everything in subjection to us.
But we see one who was lowered temporarily of less status than the Godly mes-
sengers- Jesus-crowned with attention and respect because of the suffering of
death, so that by the grace of God he might taste death for the sake of everyone.
It was fitting for Jesus, for who everything exists and by who everything
exists, in leading many children to the level of God's attention - the pilgrim
leader of their salvation! - to gain perfection through suffering. He who sancti-
fies and those who are sanctified are all from one, for which reason he is not
ashamed to call them sisters and brothers, saying,

"I will report to God that you are of the statusof my sisters and brothers.
I will sing hymns with you in the middle of thecongregation before God."
And also,

"This is how it is with me - God has given me children." This follows. Children share things in common with the parent while in the blood and flesh, and
he shared in daily events as they happened. So also, after his death he has the
strength to render meaningless the power of death, or anything contrary, and

deliver those who, in fear of death, were all of their lives bound to its slavery. It is for sure he doesn't need to help the Godly prophet messengers, but he helps the seed of Abraham. He was made like was the sisters and brothers in every respect, so that he become a merciful and faithful special preacher in the service of God, to make amends for the erros of people. He himself has suffered from human frustrations and he is able to help those who are frustrated.

Now, special brothers and sisters, chosen to join the companions from beyond in the sky of existence concentrate your thinking on Jesus, the apostle and special preacher of our religion. He was faithful to the one who created him, as was Moses in God's family. In fact he was deemed worthy of more attention than Moses, since the builder of a home has more honor than the home itself. Every house is built by someone, but the builder of everything is God. Moses was faithful for his whole realm of descendants as faithful as a chariot driver to his Master, so as to testify to the things that were later to be spoken, but God who came to us on earth is over his house as his child, whose family we are if we keep fearless and proud of the hope.

As the Spirit says,

>"Today, when you hear God's voice,
>don't harden your hearts as to start a civil war within,
>as happened on the day of frustration in the wilderness,
>where your ancestors irked me into testing their faith
>and saw my reactions for forty years.
>That's why I was provoked with this generation,
>and I said, 'They always go wandering in their hearts.
>They refuse to know my ways.'
>I swore in my frustration,
>'They shall never enter into my rest.'"

See to it, sisters and brothers, not to have in any of you an immoral, unfaithful heart, deserting the living God. Urge each other each and every day, until it becomes the theme of every today, that none of you be hardened by the deception of not witnessing for God We have a joint enterprise with God who came to us on earth if only we can keep firm to the end the standing we possess - as in the saying,

"Today when you hear God's voice,

Don't harden your hearts as to start a civil war within." Who heard and rebelled? Wasn't it all those who fled from Egypt under Moses? And who was God mad at for forty years? Wasn't it those who sinned whose bodies fell in the wilderness? And who did God swear they should never enter rest but those who were disobedient? So we see that they were unable to enter because of unfaithfulness.

Jesus as the Last Chance to Enter into God's Nest

Have us fear missing the promise of entering rest with God as happens when someone falls short of being faithful. We can hear the good news as they did, but when they heard the story, it didn't benefit them because they wasn't faithful to what they was hearing. We enter into the rest as persons of faith, as he said,

"So I swore in my anger,

'They shall never enter into my rest,'"

and yet the works of creation was intended to be finished up from the time the world was founded. God has spoken about the seventh day as follows: "And God rested on the seventh day from all his works." And again in the same place, "They shall never enter into my rest." Since then it comes about that some can enter despite disobedience, and again he sets a certain day -today-saying through David after so long a time, as was said earlier,

"Today, when you hear his voice,

don't harden your hearts."

If Jesus couldn't help folk enter into rest, he would not have spoke about the afterlife. So then, there remains a Sunday day of rest for the people of God. And the one entering into this rest is the very one who rests from his work just as God rests from God's own work.

Have us try to enter into that rest, that no one fails because they was disobedient. The story of God is living, active, and more cutting that any two-edged sword, piercing to the division of soul and spirit, of joints and marrow, and scrutinizing the desires and thoughts of the heart. And no creature can hide from him but all lie naked and vulnerable before the eyes of him before who our story stands in dialogue.

Confess Jesus as Being the Child of God

Now that we have a special preacher who has passed through the sky of existence, Jesus, the Child of God, have us hold fast to confessing this. We don't have a preacher who don't know how to sympathize with our weaknesses, but one who has been tempted the same as we without having done wrong. Have us with boldness approach the seat of grace, that we may receive mercy and find grace to help in time of need.

Our Benefit in Having the Person Jesus as Our Special Preacher

From among people, preachers are chose to act on behalf of humanity as intercessor to God. This helps when they offer gifts and make amends for error since they can empathize with the ignorant and wayward. Like their congregation, the preacher is beset with weakness, and because of this he or she is bound to offer sacrifice for his own errors as well as for those of the people. And a preacher does not seize the honor for himself, but he is called by God, just as Aaron was. So also God who come to us on earth did not glorify himself to be made a special preacher, but he was appointed by him who said to him,

> "You are my Child,
> today I have conceived you." Then God says in another place,
> "You are a preacher for the span of time,
> after the order of Melchizedek."

Jesus, in the days of his flesh, offered prayers and pleas with loud cries and tears to God who was able to save him from death, and he was heard for his piety. Although he was God's Child, he learned obedience through all he suffered and being made perfect he become a source of reconciliation for the full span of time to all who obey him, being designated by God a special preacher after the order of Melchizedek.

The Tradition of the Prophet Who Founded Jerusalem, the Earthly City of Peace

This Melchizedek, authority over Salem, preacher of the most imminent God, met Abraham returning from cutting down opposition in battle, and greeted him. Then Abraham divided up the spoils and give him one tenth because Melchizedek was the foremost among the Godly interpreters of right and wrong and the authority of Salem, a place of peace, who needed no other father or mother, nor standing by birth, nor legitimacy by being ancient in days or endlessly living. In this way, he sort of resembles God's Child who has been our preacher in the everlasting.

Consider how important he must have been for Abraham, the patriarch, to give him a tenth of the best spoils. Even today those of the children of Levi that receive the call to be preachers have a grant to take tithes from the people according to the law, that is, from their sisters and brothers, because they come out of Abraham's genitals. Those not related have give over what they come to to Abraham who was give the greeting containing peace. Without a doubt everything else is of less consequence than such a greeting. And while here it is people dying that receive the tithes, there it is by one who witness tells us He lives. One might even say that Levi himself, who receives tithes, paid tithes through Abraham, for he was still in the genitals of his ancestor when Melchizedek met him.

Now if there was perfection possible through the line of preachers from Levi where people was brought under the law, what further need would there be for another preacher to arise according to the order of Melchizedek, and not be reckoned after the order of Aaron? Well, the preacher has changed so now there is a necessary change in the law as well. The one we are referring to come from another tribe, from which no one knew how to attend the altar. It was bound to happen that our Familyhead sprung from Judah, and Moses never mentioned preachers in connection with that tribe. And it is even more abundantly evident when another preacher arises according to the likeness of Melchizedek who has become a preacher, not according to the law of mortal law but according to the power of indestructible life. It is testimony that

"You are a preacher for the span of time,
after the order of Melchizedek."

On the one hand, a former order of law is annulled because of its weakness and uselessness for the law made nothing perfect. On the other hand, a better hope is set in authority through which we draw near to God.

This wasn't nothing so much as a simple oath of alliance. Nothing like this was necessary to become preachers. Jesus was sworn in by words said to him,

"The Familyhead has decided and will not change his mind,

'You are a preacher for the spans of time,'"

- just so much better is the contract of which Jesus is the guarantor. Also while others become preachers in large numbers, because they was prevented from serving by death, Jesus has a permanent preaching assignment since it is "for the spans of time." So for all time Jesus is able to save those who approach God through him, since Jesus always lives to make intercession for them.

Such a special preacher was also fitting for us, special, innocent, undefiled, separate from the false witnesses, and exalted above the very skies of existence, who don't need, as the special preachers did, to offer sacrifices daily, first for his own failure to witness for God and then for those of the people. This Jesus done once and for all when he offered up himself. The law appoints people in their weakness as preachers, but the word establishing the alliance, coming later than the law, appoints a Child for spans of time who has been made perfect.

A New Contract Betweeen God and Folk Through Jesus

Now the chief point in what we have said is this - we have a special preacher, who took his ruling seat at the right hand of the highest authority in the skies of existence, a minister attuned to God's attention and of the true shelter which the Familyhead set up, not a human being. Every preacher is charged to make gifts and lay up sacrifices. So if Jesus was still on earth, he couldn't even be a preacher, since there already exist those who offer gifts according to the law. Such ones serve in the earthly shadow of a counterpart above the skies of existence -as Moses was instructed as he was about to complete a shelter: like he said, "See that you make everything in accordance with the engraving of the ten commandments shown you on the mountain." But now, Jesus happens to be at a place of ministry as a permanent resident that is in such a greater place and is in the middle of arranging things having enacted rules according to a better salvation promise.

If that first contract hadn't been breached, then no reason would have existed for a second. God finds fault with them when he says:

"See here, the days will come, says the Familyhead,
and I shall negotiate a new contract with the house

of Israel
and with the house of Judah,
not according to the terms I made with their fathers on
the day of my taking their hand
to lead them out of the land of Egypt.
Because they didn't live up to my contract,
I didn't care whether they paid the price says
the Familyhead.
But I will make another contract with the house of
Israel
after those days, says the Familyhead-
giving my laws into their minds,
I shall inscribe them upon their hearts,
and I shall be their God and they shall be my people.
And they will teach each fellow citizen
and each brother and sister, saying, 'Know your
Familyhead.'
They will all know me,
from the least of them to the greatest,
because I shall be merciful about their failures
and I will remember their sins no more."

In pronouncing this new contract, he superseded the first. And what is becoming obsolete and out of date is close to extinction. Also, the first contract had regulations for church services and the decoration of a holy place. The primary holy tent was outfitted with a lampstand and a table and breadboxes of the Presence. It is called the Holy Place. And behind the second curtain was a shelter, which was called the Holy of Holies, having a golden incense altar and the ark of the covenant covered all over with gold, which contained the golden urn holding the manna, and Aaron's rod that budded, and the tables of the old testament. Over this were prominent cherubim, overshadowing the mercy seat-about which we can't now describe in detail.

Being thus outfitted, the preachers enter continually into the first room of the shelter carrying out the worship services. But into the second room only the most important preacher goes once a year, never without blood sacrifice which he offers for himself and for the errors of the people.

This way God's attentive Spirit revealed something. Not everything was to be revealed about the way to God's attentions. Instead, folk was only give to go into the first phase room - which was symbollic representing how things stood at the time. Gifts and sacrifices was offered which couldn't improve the Godly

perception of the worshiper. Things was based on foods and drinks and various baptisms and diet regulations imposed until the time of change.

But God who come to us on earth having appeared as special preacher of the good things that are come, through the greater and more perfect shelter not made with hands, that is, not of this creation, and not through blood of goats and calves, but through his own blood, entered once and for all into the place of God's fixed attentions securing an eternal redemption. If there was benefit from sprinkling with the blood of innocent things - goats and bulls and the ashes of a calf - for the cleansing of a mortal, how much more shall the blood of God who came to us on earth, who through the eternal Spirit offered himself unblemished to God, clarify your Godly perception instead of doing actions with dead things for service to the living God?

Because of this he is an arbitrator of a new contract. This comes from the fact that he died to set aside the breaches under the first contract. Now folk can escape into a promise of an inheritance for the spans of time. Since it was such a contract, the death of the one who made it had to happen. A contract for an inheritance takes effect at death, since it has no force as long as the one who made it lives. It didn't have to be that the first contract was settled by human blood. Later after Moses had announced every command according to the law to all the people, he took the blood of calves and goats, with water and bloody wool and hyssop, and sprinkled the book itself and all the people, saying, "This is the blood of the contract that God prescribed for you." And in the same way he sprinkled blood on the shelter and all the liturgical vessels. And almost everything is purified with animal blood according to the law, but without the shedding of human blood there was no remission of human sins.

Jesus' Sacrifice in Terms of the Early Church

Once stand-ins of happenings in the beyond were thought to be necessary and these were to be purified by sacrifices, but the things of the beyond required better sacrifices. God who come to us on earth entered, not into a holy shelter made with hands, a counterpart of the true one, but into the sky of existence itself, to appear now in the presence of God for our sakes. Nor does he need to offer himself repeatedly as he were to enter a human holy place every year with blood not his own. If that were so, it would be necessary for him to continually suffer since the foundation of the world. But now, once and for all, at the close of the span of times, he has appeared to abolish sin through his sacrifice. And just as it is appointed for folk to die once, and after that comes judgment, so also God who came to us on earth, having been sacrificed once to bear the sins of many, will reappear a second time to those freed from sin that eagerly are awaiting him for judgment of salvation.

Since the law appeared in the shadow of the evolving good things to come and wasn't intended to give a real description of heavenly activities, it could never, by the same sacrifices continually offered year after year, perfect those who draw near. Otherwise, wouldn't they have stopped being offered, as the worshipers, rid of it once and for all, wouldn't have no more consciousness of sin? But in these sacrifices there is a reminder of sin year after year. It don't happen for the blood of bulls and goats to take away sins.

> The payoff was this. When God talks about sending Jesus into the world,
>   God says,
> "You didn't want to be provided just another sacrifice
> or offerings
> I will prepare myself a body."
> "You took no joy from burning offerings or sin offerings." "So I said,
> Yes! I am arriving,
> as it is quoted in a chapter of a book about me,
>
> 'I will do as you want, God.'"

After he referred to the above, "sacrifices and offerings" and "burnt offerings and sin offerings you didn't want nor enjoy", which are offered according to the law, then he said, "Yes, I will do as you want," He eliminates the first in order to establish the second. And by this intention, we are the sanctified through the "offering" of the "body" of Jesus God who came to us on earth once and for all.

Every preacher performs daily services and frequently offers communion which don't cut off sins. This one offered up one sacrifice for sins, good perpetually, then took his place at the right hand of God and waited for what was coming next-for his enemies to be crushed as under his feet. He completed the one sacrifice needed for all time for our sanctification. And the Godly spirit also bears witness to us, saying what has to be said´

> "This is the contract that I will make with them after those days, says the Familyhead,
> giving my laws on their hearts, I shall inscribe them upon their minds."
> "And their sins and their crimes I shall remember no more."

Now where these are remitted, there is no more need of offering for sin.

Sisters and brothers, have courage to go into the place where God's is attentive by the benefit of the blood of Jesus, and by the fresh and living way he physically tore open for us an opening through the curtain separating us from God. Having a great preacher over the house of God, have us approach Him with a true heart, in full assurance of faith, with hearts sprinkled clean from wrong understanding and bodies washed by pure water. Have us hold fast the confession of our faith without wavering, for he who promised is faithful. Have us be aware of each other, to stimulate love and good works, not deserting our congregating together, as is the habit of some, but in encouragement, and all the more so as you see the dawn drawing near.

The Price of Not Witnessing Jesus

If we don't witness Jesus deliberately after receiving the knowledge of the truth, there no longer remains a sacrifice for disloyalty, but a fearful prospect of judgment and a zealous fire ready to consume God's adversaries. Someone violating the law of Moses dies without mercy at the testimony of two or three witnesses. How much greater punishment, don't you think? will he deserved by someone who tramples underfoot the law of the Child of God and considers profane the blood of the contract by which he was sanctified, and outrageously treats the Spirit of grace? We know him who said, "Vengeance is mine. I will repay." And again, "The Familyhead will judge his family." It is serious business to fall into the hands of the living God.

Now recall the former days when, having been enlightened, you endured frequent struggle with sufferings, sometimes being made a spectacle by insults and afflictions, and sometimes becoming partners with those so treated. You sympathized with those in bonds, and you accepted with joy the plundering of your possessions, knowing that you have a better and lasting possession. Don't toss away your enthusiasm which has a great reward. You have need of endur-

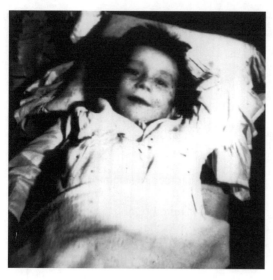

ance so that having done the will of God you may cash in what is promised.

"In a little while, a very little
  while now,
the coming one will arrive and
  not delay.
But the ones living right shall
  live by faith,
and if any shrinks back, my
  essence takes no plea-
  sure
in that one."

But we are not of those who shrink back to destruction, but those who by faith preserve their life.

Faith

Faith is an assurance of things hoped for, an evidence of things not seen. In a state of faith the elders give their witness.

By faith we perceive that the span of times was conformed with the story of God, to the end that the visible was known to be made out of that which cannot be seen.

By faith Abel offered God a more ample sacrifice than Cain, through which he was witnessed as being righteous, God bearing witness by accepting his gifts, and through this he still speaks though dead. By faith Enoch was taken up so that he never died, and he was not found because God had taken him up. Before he was taken up, it was witnessed that he had pleased God. But without faith it is impossible to please God, for it is necessary for the one who draws near to God to have faith that he exists and that the reward comes to those who seek him out. By faith Noah, being warned about the things which were still unseen, acted from out of reverence. He constructed an ark for the saving of his home. By this he lived through the sentence passed against the world and became an heir of the righteousness that comes by faith.

By faith Abraham obeyed when he was called to go out to a place that he was to receive as an inheritance. Then he left home not knowing where he was to go. By faith he traveled to the promised land even though it was in a foreign country, dwelling in tents, with Isaac and Jacob, joint heirs with him of the same promise. He looked forward to the city having foundations, whose builder and craftsperson is God. By faith Sarah herself received power to conceive when she was past the age for it because she considered God faithful to God's promise. That's how it happened that from one faithful person - now dead - were born descendants like the stars of heaven in number and as countless as the sand on the seashore.

These all died in faith, not having cashed in on the promises, but having seen and greeted them from afar, and confessed that they was strangers and pilgrims on the earth. Those who speak like that implied they was seeking out a homeland. If they had thought of the land they left behind, they would have had time to return. But now they desire a better place, that is, one in God's presence. God is not ashamed to be called their God, for he prepared for them a city.

By faith and after testing Abraham offered up Isaac, and he who had received the promises was offering up his only born child, to who it was said that 'in Isaac shall your seed be named,' having reckoned that even from the dead God is able to raise folk up. This was how he did get him back, strangely enough. By faith also Isaac gave a blessing concerning the future to Jacob and Esau. By faith Jacob, when dying, blessed each of the children of Joseph, and bowed in worship over the head of his staff. By faith Joseph, at his death, thought about the exodus of the children of Israel and gave instructions concerning his bones.

By faith Moses, after birth, was hidden for three months by his parents, because they saw the child was beautiful, and did not fear the decree of the king. By faith Moses, when grown up, refused to be called the child of Pharaoh's daughter, thinking it was better to be abused with the people of God than to have a good time enjoying the fleeting pleasures of unbelievers, accounting the reproach of God who came to us on earth greater plenty than the treasures of Egypt, for he looked forward to the reward. By faith he left Egypt behind, not fearing the anger of the king. As a person seeing the invisible, he persevered. By faith he kept the Passover and the sprinkling of blood, so the Destroyer might not touch their first-born. By faith they crossed the Red Sea like dry land, while the Egyptians, attempting the same, were drowned. By faith the walls of Jericho fell down, having been circled about for seven days. By faith Rahab the harlot did not perish with the unfaithful, having received the spies in peace.

And what more shall I say? To save time, I won't recount about Gideon, Barak, Samson, Jephthah, of David and Samuel and the prophets- who through faith conquered countries, worked for righteousness, received promises, shut the mouths of lions, quenched the power of fire, escaped the mouths of the sword, from weakness made strong, in war made mighty, put foreign armies to

flight. Women received their dead by resurrection. Others were tortured, not accepting pardon, that they might obtain a better resurrection. But others suffered mocking and scourging, or the burdens of chains and prison. They were stoned. They were burned. They were sawed in two. They died by slaughter of sword. They went about in sheepskins and goatskins, destitute, afflicted, ill-treated -of who the world is not worthy -wandering over deserts and mountains and caves and gullies of the earth.

And these all having been witnessed to through the faith did not cash in on the promise, God having forseen something better for us, that apart from us they should not be perfected.

A Life of Patient Endurance

What is the point? Well, since we are surrounded by so great a cloud of witnesses, laying aside every weight and easily ensnaring false testimony, have us run the race which lies before us with patient endurance, looking attentively to Jesus the leader and perfecter of faith, who for the joy set before him endured the cross, looking down from the shame, and has taken his ruling seat at the right hand of the throne of God. Consider him who patiently endured such hostility from liars about him, so that you not grow weary and faint-hearted. You have not yet resisted to the point of bloodshed of martyrdom, struggling against sin, and have you forgotten the exhortation which dialogues with you as children?

> "My child, do not think lightly of the Familyhead's discipline,
>   nor lose courage when punished by him.
> The Familyhead disciplines those he loves,
>   and corrects every child who he receives."

The need of discipline requires us to patiently endure. God is treating you as children. What child is there who the parent don't discipline? If you escape discipline, in which all have participated, you are abandoned from home and not children. Besides this, we have had mortal parents disciplining us and we respected them. Shall we not subject ourselves much more readily to the Parent of spirits and live? They disciplined us for a short time according to their beliefs, but God does so for our profit that we might receive our share of his attention. So what if not all discipline makes us happy but rather sorrowful. Afterward it pays back the peaceful fruit of righteousness to those trained by it.

So ... lift up the drooping hands and shaking knees, and make straight paths for your feet, so that weak knees don't cause you to get off the road of discipleship but be strengthened better.

Seek after peace with all persons and for the sanctification without which no one shall see the Familyhead, taking care that no one fail to abide in the grace of God, that "no root of bitterness spring up and cause trouble" and many become confused. What else? Don't be immoral or godless like Esau who for a single meal sold his birthright. You know that afterward, when he desired to inherit the blessing, he was rejected. Also he found no chance to change the result though he sought it with tears.

Have you not approached an untouchable thing? - a blazing fire and darkness, gloom and storm, the sound of a trumpet and a voice whose words made the hearers plead that no further word by spoken to them. Some could not bear the command that was given, "If even a beast touches the mountain, it shall be turned to stone." In fact, so terrifying was the sight that Moses said, "I am scared and shaky." But you have approached the mountain of Zion and the city of the living God, heavenly Jerusalem, where countless Godly folk are at a fair,

and to the church of the first- born enrolled in the very sky of existence, and to the God who is judge of all, and to the spirits of the just persons made perfect, and to Jesus the mediator of a new contract, and to the sprinkled blood that speaks better than the blood of Abel.

See that you don't refuse him who is speaking. If they didn't escape who refused him addressing them upon the earth, much less shall we escape if we reject him who addresses us from the place of the ultimate real place of existence. His voice shook the earth then, but now he has promised, saying, "Yet once more I will shake not only the earth but also existence." Now this phrase, "Yet once more," indicates the transformation of what is shaken might remain. How can we take this? Have us give thanks for receiving an unconquerable country, and thus offer acceptable worship to God, with reverence and awe. Our God is a consuming fire.

Have brotherly and sisterly love continue. Don't neglect hospitality to strangers for so have some folk entertained messengers from God unawares. Remember those chained in prison as though you were fellow prisoners and those who are abused since they bear the weaknesses of the flesh. Have marriage be held in honor in all circumstances, and the marriage bed be a place of innocence. God will judge the sex dealers and predators. Keep your life-style free from love of money, and be content with what you have, for God said, "I will never fail you nor abandon you." So we can confidently say,

"The Familyhead is my helper,
I will not fear.
What can a mortal person do to me?"

Remember your leaders-those who told you the story about God. Consider the result of their lives. Imitate their faith. Jesus - God who come to us on earth - is the same yesterday and today - also for the span of times. Do not get carried away with multiple and strange theologies. It is good to strengthen the heart by love, not by foods, by which the dieters gain no benefit. We have an altar from which those who serve the tent have no power to eat. The bodies of those animals whose blood is brought into the sanctuary for sin offerings are burned outside the temple grounds. So also Jesus, in order to sanctify the people by his own blood, suffered outside the temple grounds. Have us go out to him outside the camp, bearing abuse for him. Here we have no lasting city, but we seek the coming one. Through him have us offer up continually a sacrifice of praise to God, that is, the fruit of lips that confess God's name. Don't neglect good deeds and sharing for such efforts are pleasing to God.

Obey your leaders and cooperate with their enforcements. They watch over your lives as persons who will have to give account. Have them do this with joy without complaining, which would be unprofitable for you.

Keep us in your prayers. We are convinced that we have a shared understanding and wish all the best to motivate us within. I ask you the more earnestly to do this in order that I may be rejuvenated by our prayers together.

Now may the God of peace, the one who leads us out of death, the great shepherd of sheep, by an agreement spanning time and forged in blood, Yes! our Familyhead Jesus, equip you in every necessary thing to do God's will, working into your life what is pleasing before God through Jesus God who come to us on earth to who be our attention for spans of the spans of time. Amen.

I beg you, sisters and brothers, open yourselves to the message of this encoureagement even though it is written to you quickly. You should know that our brother Timothy has been sent. Through him it shall be as though I have come to see you myself quickly.

Greet all your leaders and all the saints. Those who come from Italy greet you. Peace be with you all.

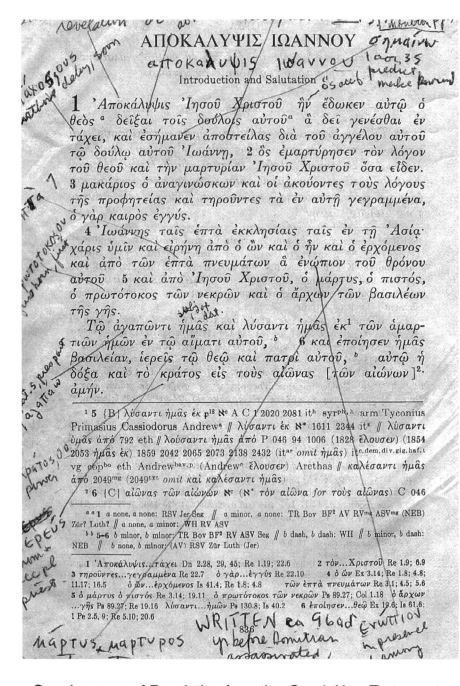

Opening page of Revelation from the *Greek New Testament*
that was used by Ben Johnson for the translation

REVELATION

A Call Upon Jesus To Destroy A Pagan Empire And Reconstitute Life[1]

An Early Christian Introduction

THIS IS A RESPONSE TO A CALL upon Jesus[2], God's child who came to us on earth, which God revealed to point out to Christians those things that have happened and will result in other happenings[3], also provided to missionaries who were being sent out to churches in the name of God's bonded one, John, who witnessed the event of God's child's coming and kept Jesus at the center of his life. God blesses the one who reads and listens to these accounts of prophesy and keeps these writings in mind...for the fullness of time is close at hand.

Introduction To John's Letter

John of Patmos, to the seven bishopric churches in Asia:

Love and peace be yours[4], in the name of Jesus, the one who is, and was, and who is coming, and from the seven icons or representations by which you present yourselves at God's locus, and from Jesus, God's child who came to

---

1. The Greek text is liberally footnoted to references not all of them synoptic gospel or prophetic scroll. This translation goes the step beyond literal translation to reintroduce the references found in the Greek text and particularly its riddles back into the text.

2. Revelation in the Greek does not state the name Jesus in its parts most contexturally clear as being original material. This was due to the setting of the time of its writing when Christians suffered persecution under pagan Roman emperors. In today's world where freedom of religion permits use of the name Jesus, the name may be safely reintroduced into the text at all appropriate places. The task is made more simple in the Greek where Jesus is refered to in shorthand as a book and a scroll, Lamb, "the right hand of God," etc. Sometimes the verb tensing gives clues that something is not of human activity. None of this helps in today's world to understand the document without expansion of the Greek writing with its Hellenistic references. My book *Revelation for Non-hellenistic Millenia* more fully describes the apparatus for recovery of the document and the specific references. I only include a few of the more arcane "riddles" as footnotes in this reading.

3. It is easy to see the theme of Revelation as close to John's understanding of the Godly purpose of Jesus's life. Jesus comes to earth "ina sothe o kosmos di autou." (to right the world by his activity). John 3.17.

4. Revelation is a "liberation document" standing for the proposition that Jesus will redeem and reform the world so that Christians - those faithful to Jesus - can live in it in love and peace. Even the impregnable Roman Empire as a pagan entity must fall since it challenges this truth. Jesus will see to it.

earth, a martyr, faithful one, first born from death, ruler of the regions of the earth. You live in Jesus's selectedness and release from your transgressions through Jesus's blood, and Jesus brings you into the hierarchy of the saved to be missionaries in service to God, Jesus's parent. In this situation there is the feel and strength of eternity. Yes!

> Look! There is one ready to come who hovers over the earth as do
>   clouds in the sky.
> And he will analyze through an all-perceiving eye.
> And whoever has wounded him,
> They will each utter mournful sounds heard by all the peoples of
>   the earth.

Yes, Yes! "I am A to Z," the Familyhead, Jesus, says, this one who is and was and who is hovering, the all powerful one.

John's Self Introduction

I am John, your brother and partner in persecution, and in citizenship, and in patient waiting for Jesus. I live on an island called Patmos through an act of God and to give witness for Jesus.

Jesus Conceived Of As Living In John's Time - A Time Of Persecution

I live spirituallly in the light of the Familyhead's coming day and I tell of

a concern filling the air around me as fully as would a horn blasting, ordering, "What you feel, write in a letter and send it to the seven churches in Ephesus, Smyrna, Pergamos, Thyatira, Sardis, Philadelphia, and Laodicea." And I reflected on this concern that was speaking within me, and after reflection, I thought of your cities. You shine in my memory as comfortingly as seven lights in the darkness of the cur-

rent Roman persecution and in the midst of the shine you all make together, I
see Jesus, our Familyhead. I remember Jesus, clearly, but today I would see his
image as needfully different. Today I see, Jesus, the child of folk, garbed in a
full foot length robe drawn together at the waist by a belt, hungering, an itinerent begger, wearing the belt to hold the few provisions that a missionary carries
with all his or her worldly possessions. Then, his head, and white hair like
white wool, as has an ageless wise elder, so snowy, and eyes as intensely attentive as if burning with fire. Also, there, feet, for walking amongst us, changed
into a material unimpairable, capable of walking over every life situation, in a
more enduring substance than flesh, as would be something brassy, as ore is
after purification in a blast furnace.

He holds in his hands stars, monuments of light in the depth of black, despairing night, and I hear his voice, as the voice of a thundershower, providing
at once nurturing rain and evidence of all the power of nature, speaking out
and his judgements are being uttered against the law of the sharp Roman
sword, and his face would appear as shining as the sun in doing so, in all its
basic radiant energy.

And when I thought of Jesus like that, I became depressed and wished
death. But then I felt as though Jesus were reaching over and taking me by the

hand so that Jesus's hand held me too, and I heard Jesus say, "Don't be depressed or anxious. I am the first and the last, and I uphold life. I was dead and, Look! I am alive in the reality of the sky of existence, the Homeland of God. And I hold the keys to the place of death, and its world of those who have died.

Now, write down your feel for the present situation, and its meaning, and what may come out of it later. I know there is perplexity why there need be these stars which I cradle in my right hand, among the seven lights in the darkness, the cities which I esteem. These stars are those martyred for God among the seven churches and the seven lights, the shine of their seven communities.

Various Messages To Comfort Churches In Cities Where Christians Are Being Persecuted

To The Church At Ephesus

Now, I, John on Patmos, address the corresponding secretary of the Ephesian church.

Jesus, the one whose Being cradles the bishopric churches in his hand, and the stars which represent their dead martyrs, Jesus, for whom we die, the one who walks in the midst of the seven precious communities shining as lights of the night in the darkness of persecution, and understands what you are going through.

I realize you are experiencing agonizing times of death-dealing by the Roman government and persecution and how you are patiently enduring, and how you can hardly endure these bad times, and what a persecution the missionaries are themselves talking about! There seems no relief. And you find the missionaries themselves sometimes to be liars. And you behave cautiously, so weighing their claims on their basis in my sponsorship and not avoiding this responsibility.

Departing from you, I left you as the foremost group of brothers and sisters in the faith. Keep this in mind before you give in and change back to act as the foremost doer of acts falling short of self-giving love.

Unless it is not to be, I am coming back to you and I will re-kindle your flame so your church won't be snuffed out.

And this is in your favor, that you have rejected the inroads of the Nikolaiton sect which also I reject. If you receive this message, listen to how its urging speaks to your community. In this there is success which I give to you to escape toward the tree of life, a shelter of atonement which is in the paradise of God.

To The Church At Smyrna

Now, I address the corresponding secretary of the Smyrna church.

Jesus, the one whose existence is the first and the last who is dead and alive, Jesus, be with you.

I realize you are afflicted and impoverished, but you are rich and still bad tales are told that you are merely Jewish imitators yourselves but you are not and theirs is a synagogue of emperor worship. Don't be afraid about what you are going to suffer. Yes, the emperor seems likely to throw some of you into prison so that you may be tested and you will have to hold to your faith the ten days given to renounce your faith before being given the death penalty as a Christian martyr. Have faith unto death and Jesus will crown you with a crown of life.

If you receive this message, listen to how its urging speaks to your church.

Jesus, the one who abides with you, offers Real Life, not requiring the steadfast to suffer a second death.

To The Church At Pergamos

Now, I address the corresponding secretary of the Pergamos church. Jesus is present with you, Jesus, the one who speaks out and whose voice is a judgement as sharp as a double-bladed Roman sword.

I realize the consequences coming from where you live, at a Roman governmental center, and you are arrested in Jesus's name, but Jesus will not renounce his confidence in you, even living where you do, where Antipas spent his days a martyr, his faithful one, who answers for you, where Satan, the Roman governor who demands Emperor worship, dwells.

Now, I have a few concerns about you, that you have there adherents of the practices of Balaam, a Baal idol worshiper, who taught Balak to teach wrong ideas to the children of Israel, eating food dedicated to idols and engaging in sex with pagan temple prostitutes. So also you have adherents of the practices of Nicholas of Antioch[5], doing the same things. Your church must reform! Otherwise Jesus may come quickly to you and Jesus will engage those adjudged to be guilty.

If you receive this message, listen to how its urging speaks to your church.

If you overcome adversity Jesus will give you to eat of the hidden manna and Jesus will give you to have the permanence of a shining rock of family membership in the afterlife and upon the rock a new name is written which no one knows except the receiver.

To The Church At Thyatira

Now, I address the corresponding secretary of the Thyatira church.

Consider that you have present with you God's child, Jesus, one having eyes as intensely attentive as if they were fiery flames and feet unstopable from tramping amidst us.

---

5. Irenaeus's references to this sect are reintroduced into this section from "Against Heresies," I 26.3 and those ideas from Clement of Alexandria, "Stromateis," 2.118 and 3.25-26.

I realize you are experiencing agonizing times of persecution, and yet you abide in churchly and family love, the posture of faith, the way you serve each other's needs, your endurance in patience until comes the endtime, and your actions regarding the poor who have greater needs than the rich. But Jesus has against you that you do not abandon the woman Jezebel, who claims for herself the status of a prophet and teaches and drives my parishiners into acts of sexual immorality and eats idol food. Now I gave her time to change, but she does not wish to be turned into a Christian from her depravities. Watch out! Jesus considers her as one sick and those committing sex acts with her and her followers die in unredeemed death. And all churches must know who Jesus is. Jesus is one who searches minds and hearts and Jesus will give to each according to the works you do.

And I say this to the rest of you in Thyatira, don't take up such teaching. Don't be such as must experience the "Hole of Hell" as the expression says. I don't charge you with any other burden, but what you have. Hold on! until I can get back to your church.

And remember Jesus, the one who completes and fulfills the work of God, even until final time enactments,

"I will give to Jesus power over people who seek a home in the skies of existence, and this one will be like a shepherd to them with a staff of iron which can break into pieces earthly forms." Jesus tells us, "As I was taken, once and for all time, to my parent, so also I will bring you to live in the life of my parent, giving as a reminder of this providential activity, the morning star, the first star of martyrdom, my own experience from crucifiction on a cross which reconciles an otherwise wasting and ruined creation."

If you receive this message, listen to how its urging speaks to your church.

To The Church At Sardis

Now, I address the corresponding secretary of the Sardis church and write.

Jesus is present with you, Jesus, one who takes notice of the seven life courses before the God of the seven bishopric churches, shining with the eternal intense white light of the stars in the night of the martyrs who have given their lives to God from each of the churches.

I realize you are experiencing agonizing times of persecution and its result is that your church is dying out. Keep continually alert and offer encouragement to the few left who are about to be martyred, for Jesus has not yet found you to be in the final hierarchical situation from which Jesus will take you before God.

Remember what you received and heard and keep it close and live to be transformed. When you least expect, Jesus will come as a thief at an unforseeable hour and Jesus will come upon you. And you have identifiable ones in Sardis who won't be dressed for the occasion, but they will nevertheless walk with Jesus in the light for they do right. You who overcome the ambiguity of your life situation will find that you are really dressed in eternal clothes and Jesus will not blot out your name from the book of life and Jesus will vouch for you before God and before every witness.

If you receive this message, listen to how its urging speaks to your church.

To The Church At Philadelphia

Now, I address the corresponding secretary of the Philadelphian church.

Jesus is with you, Jesus, who has a unique status, one who is trustworthy, who we can count on unlocking the promised door to the world rule of David's house, where God's justice prevails and people may live acceptably to God's desire for people, one who opens this way and does not close the door behind you, and at the same time, locks the door, foreclosing entry to rejecting ones and does not permit the door to life in the eternal sky of existence to open for them.

I realize you are experiencing agonizing times of Roman governmental persecution.

Jesus gives you the opportunity to enter the opening doorway to life with God. No one can close it against you even if you have only the meager strength of a human being. Only do this: Cling to the words and story of the life of Jesus, and don't renounce Jesus.

Jesus has taken the gift of the redeeming effect of communion away from the synagogue of Emperor worshipper Jews, those who are calling themselves Jews, and who are nothing but liars. Jesus will consider them for what they have become and they will be left grovelling where you are seated in the power of your steadfastness and they will know how Jesus loved you. Keep in mind the example of Jesus's patient endurance through Jewish persecution and Jesus will keep you strong in the hour of your testing until Jesus again comes down upon this whole agonized hierarchical situation to settle things upon the earth. When Jesus comes, he will come quickly. Keep the faith you have so that no one may take away your crown.

If you can live faithfully and embody the life of Jesus, you will be rendered a pillar in the church of God and you will never be rejected. Instead, Jesus will write upon it the designation, "One of God's", and designate it for delivery to Jesus's city, the new Jerusalem, which is coming down from the skies of God's existence and from God, in its new hierarchical situation.

If you receive this message, listen to how its urging speaks to your church.

To The Church At Laodicea

Now, I address the corresponding secretary of the Laodicean church.

Jesus is present with you, Jesus, the one who responds to you affirmatively, the witness providing final proof, the reliable refuge of our faith, and the one who really exists.

I realize you are experiencing agonizing times of persecution, that sometimes you are cold in rejection of Jesus and sometimes hot in enthusiasm. I would prefer you were always in a state of one spiritual temperature or the other. You are lukewarm, neither cold or hot, the temperature of vomit which is what you have done with the food of the preaching about Jesus that has been given to you. How do you defend this? By saying, I am rich? or I am super rich? or who cares? as if you can't deign to care that among you are hurting ones or needy ones or poor ones or blind ones or homeless ones!

I advise you to spend everything you have, burning your wealth in a fire if needs be, so that you may become truly rich! and thus gain eternal clothes, and then, put them on! and then, don't hide shamefully from your fellow family members in Jesus! Let the element of fire be an eye salve to permit you to see what are basic things.

I challenge and instruct so many of you as wish to bear church family membership. Bear this concern and live transformed as a family!

Think like this, that Jesus is standing outside your door, knocking. If anyone hears the sound, or recognizes the voice, and opens the door, Jesus will come in and eat with you, and you with him.

I give you the opportunity to live a life of success, to be seated with Jesus at his seat in God's sky of existence, as I also seek this victory, and as I hope to be seated with my God at the site of God's home.

If you receive this message, listen to how its urging speaks to your church.

God In God's Homeland

After preparing these messages, I felt as though a door were opening into reality, the sky of existence itself, God's home, and a primal voice as demanding as a hornblast was calling me saying, "Come here and I will show you what will happen about the present situation." It was God speaking to me just as God spoke to Moses[6] on Mt. Sinai when God gave God's people to know God participated with them in their lives, even after freeing them from the persecution they had endured from the Egyptian Pharoah. God was giving me to see how God would deal with the continuing persecution occuring in the world,

how God would fix it by reconstructing creation itself, and provide for a history[7] which would right itself.

Immediately I was given over to reflection, and Yes! there came to mind someone on an elevated seat in the sky of existence and upon the seat someone was sitting, God.[8] Yes, there was God in the place beyond earthly hierarchies where life exists in its perfection, the immortal God, the cause of life and the life of each of us, binding together the whole of history and life into a continuum and a whole, the God of goodness who gives us to participate in God's goodness and its essence, and in immortal life with God, and the hope of a conformed world which permits living lives of conformity to God's ways, in a life beyond all suffering and persecution, in a life which cannot be destroyed, God

6. aggeloi seem to me most often to refer to Godly messengers who are human beings both in Revelation and in Hebrews. I do not use the translation of angels except as adjectival in the sense of the Godly mission or nature. In fact, I reintroduce in the text who such personalities were - mainly Hebrew prophets from the Old Testament who continue to deal in the lives of Godly folk after death.

7. Revelation traces the history of persecution of Christians through time stages as "seals" as Jesus continues to engage humanity following resurrectiion into the life of God as a reforming agent.

8. This section reflects a reintroduction to the text of the discussion of God in Plato's Phaedo,l.110. The cryptic reference comes from the juxtaposition of the three stones of sard, jasper and emerald in the Greek text of Revelation. No where else in the Hellenistic writings do these three jewels so appear. Obviously the idol in the appararent reference in the Greek writing does not reflect an acceptable Christian view of God and merely acknowledges the persecution camouflaged nature of this writing.

in a place of promise confirmed to us by God's prophets that there would come a better world than the present Roman dominated one with its Emperor worship law and condemnation to death of those attempting to live lives in the life of Jesus, God who came to us in our suffering on earth.

God's Council In The Skies Of Existence

And others were present as God's folk course helpers, wearing the clothes of immortality and light, causing me to feel they had become illuminated with knowledge and innocence and they even looked victorious as would appear Olympic Games winners wearing golden wreaths upon their heads.

And from the elevated seat of authority, there, lightning and sounds and thunder which indicated the imminence of God's presence.

And there, the seven communities suffering the persecution, afire, as lights in the blackness of their persecution settings before the elevated seat, and these communities were there "out of body" before God. And at the entryway to this seat, there was a baptismal pool[9], with waters as clear as glass, which itself was as clear as crystal. And there, of the nature of God, God's very attributes, seated in authority, and in emanation, there were four living presences as of animals with eyes front and back.

And the first life presence attribute was as the strength of a lion, and the second life presence attribute was as the innocence of a calf, and the third life presence attribute had the face of a person, and the fourth life force attribute was as the authority of a winged eagle.

And these four life presences, as each of them appeared in turn, seemed to have total freedom as if having wings to fly in any direction, and each was totally aware, as if filled with eyes, all around and within, and they were taking no rest either day or night, saying,

Uniquely special,
Familyhead, God, One all powerful,
The one who Was, and Is in Being, and what Is to come.

And then these God's life presences were treated with attention and honor and thanks at their place of sitting upon the elevated seat by those who were living in the age beyond time. These conformed ones were gratefully acknowledging their existences before the One seated upon the elevated seat and

---

9. 1 Kings 7.23. Most of these kinds of references are in Rev. footnotes to annotated New Testaments. Bathing pools where baptismal kinds of washing permitted "cleaning up" before entry to King Solomon's temple.

sought and received the sponsorship of the living presences in the age beyond time and admitted that God was responsible for their positive accomplishments in life, their wreaths of victory, saying,

> Special you are, our Familyhead, and our God, to receive
> attention and honor and power
> Because you created everything and through your will, everything
> was and will come to be recreated.

Jesus In God's Council In The Skies Of Existence

And then I saw to the right of the one seated upon the elevated seat, him, Jesus, writing a book of accounts from the standpoint of the way God felt within and from those being encountered in front of the elevated seat, and it was being commented on at daily intervals.

And I heard one of those being written about cry out in a terrific plea,

"Who is favored enough to reopen this book of accountings and to erase its charges?"

And no one was able to reopen the book of accounts or rewrite it either in the realm of the sky of existence or upon the earth or into oblivion.

And they were agitated because no one could be found capable of reopening the book of the persecution accounts or rewriting it.

And one of those among the saved says to me, "Don't worry. Look, there is redemptive salvation from the very one who is writing the book, the one from the tribe of Judah, from the ancestry of David, who can reopen the book and its record of daily life accounts."

And I looked into the entity of the seated one and that one's manifestations in strength, innocence, humanity and power, and in the midst of the saved ones, and there was Jesus, standing as a Lamb who was slaughtered, endowed with authority and supervision over daily events, which represent the spiritual element of God's mission for this one onto all of the earth.

And Jesus arose, taking the book with him from the seat at the right hand of God upon the elevated seat. And while Jesus held the book, the attributes of God's living presence and those saved from every hour of earth time gratefully acknowledged Jesus, the Lamb of God. Some, who could, played happy songs on musical instruments, and others voluntarily burned incense in golden bowls, and there were others among the saved ones pledging allegiance and singing songs in renewed voices, saying,

> You are capable of taking the record of our lives
> and reconstituting the accounts in it,

because you have been wounded by life,
and purchased by God in the currency of your own
blood,
for the benefit of every tribe,
of those speaking every language,
every race,
and all those who are homeless or home-seeking
everywhere.
God has placed all these in your governance and congregation.
And they will be the ultimate gainers of the ground of Being.

And I looked and I heard the voices of many others among those saved ones among the many crowded around the elevated seat and the life presences of God and the rest of the conformed ones saved in ultimate Being and there were numbers of them in the countless thousands upon countless thousands, saying as in one exultant voice,

Appropriate it is that a Lamb, slaughtered,
receives the power and totality and wisdom and strength and
honor and attention and thanks. \

And all creation, each and every aspect of it in the sky of God's home and upon the earth and in oblivion and upon the sea and those in every one of those places I heard, began saying,

To the one seated
upon the elevated
seat and to the
Lamb,
be thanks and honor
and attention and
power in this time
beyond
imagination.

And the four living presences of God said, "Yes!" and the conformed, saved ones acknowledged them and gave them due compliments.

Jesus, Using God's Very Attributes, Conforms Creation Itself

Then I saw Jesus, the Lamb of God, undertake the first conforming act, reopening creation's genesis, and I heard one of God's attributes, the first of the four living presences of God, saying as if in an authoritative voice, "Come to be."

And I looked and there was God's strength existent in form, sent forth as a shiny, mighty horse of eternity and light and its rider was the sparker of life as an archer who bears life in a quiver for delivery by a bow and arrow and was given to wear a crown marking that one as one who would conform creation to God's way and this one went out to encounter and win over Being for Jesus.

And then creation was reopened for a second conformation to God's way and I heard the second of God's attributes, as a living presence of God, God's innocence, saying, "Come to be." And there came forth purifying fire in the form of a mighty horse and on it was sitting one who was given to take the status quo from the earth so that its aspects could be eradicated and it was given to this one a great cleaving sword.

And then creation was reopened for conformity to God's principle, justice, that is, God's desire to live with people, rightly relating, and the third of God's attributes, as a living presence of God, said, "Come to be." And I looked and there was justice in the form of black and mighty horse, and on it was sitting one who held a yoke in hand, to recast creation so that its elements would relate in love.

And I heard a voice in its course of undertaking the task of properly humanizing, saying, "I conform the value of the diversity of folk accomplishment, whether they produce wheat, three times the value of barley's measure, or olive oil or the fruit of a vinery, treating none with favoritism."

And then the fourth conforming act in creation was undertaken, and I heard the fourth of God's attribute, God's authority, as a living presence of God, saying, "Come to be." And I looked and there was a mighty horse the color of green nature and the one seated upon it was by name death and the place of death followed after this one, and this one was given authority to restore the lives of those killed by the sword, by starvation, by any other death or by a martyr's death at the hand of wild animals.

Jesus Restoring Lives In The Endtime

And then Jesus began ordering lives of the dead to be restored in a fifth period of redemptive activity and I saw lives of those reappearing emerge from Jesus's judgment seat according to this chapter in the story of God's life and according to the reputation of faithfulness their lives witnessed. And they were pleading in a loud voice saying, "How much longer, Leader, Revered and Ex-

isting One, before you restore and cleanse with your blood the region below, the earth?"

And Jesus gave to each of them clothes of light and told them to rest for a little while until there would come the fullness of time as soon as their fellow laborers, their family members, had died as they had.

Jesus Reconstitutes A Place For A New Israel

And then I saw Jesus go to work on the earth in a sixth period of redemptive activity in a panorama of restructuring of creation for the endtime like a great earthquake happening where the sun would become eclipsed as by putting on a black coat and the full moon become as blood and the stars of the sky fell into the earth, as if they were on a fig tree which shook them off under a tornado wind, and the sky became compressed as when a scroll is rolled up and every mountain and island upon the face of the earth was being recast.

And the former kings of the earth and those wealthy and those powerful and all the working folk and citizens hid themselves in caves and under mountainous rocky covers and they were swooning as they sought cover in caves and rocky hideouts, "Shelter us and hide us from the face of the one sitting upon the elevated seat and from this disrupting day of the activity of Jesus," because there had come the great day of reconstitution of the earth over them and could anyone expect to stand up while it was going on?

Then I saw four helpers of Jesus standing upon the four corners of the earth, holding on to the four winds of the earth so that no wind could blow upon the ground, nor upon the sea, nor upon forest. And I saw another helper, coming down from the east of the sun holding a marking pen to mark those who were picked to live with God, and this helper yelled with a loud voice to the four helpers who were recasting the earth and the sea saying, "Hold off re-constituting the ground and the sea and the forests until we can mark for saving the followers of our God in their ethical thinking."

And I heard the number of those Being saved, in their vast multiplicity, from each of the tribes of the children of ancient Israel:

From the tribe of Judah those matured in indefinite
multitudes were saved, as were
From the tribe of Reuben those matured in indefinite multitudes
From the tribe of Gad, those matured in indefinite multitudes,
From the tribe of Asar, those matured in indefinite multitudes
From the tribe of Nephtali, those matured in indefinite multitudes
From the tribe of Manassa, those matured in indefinite multitudes
From the tribe of Sumeon, those matured in indefinite multitudes
From the tribe of Levi, those matured in indefinite multitudes
From the tribe of Issachar, those matured in indefinite multitudes
From the tribe of Zaboulon, those matured in indefinite multitudes
From the tribe of Joseph, those matured in indefinite multitudes
From the tribe of Benjamin, those matured in indefinite multitudes.

And then I looked and Yes! there was even an additional crowd whose numbers were more than could be counted from every people and race and nationality and language standing before the elevated seat and before Jesus, the Lamb of God, dressed in clothes of light and holding in their hands palm branches and they were shouting in a triumphant voice saying,

Salvation comes from our God seated upon the elevated
seat and from Jesus, the Lamb of God.

And all of the helpers stood near the elevated seat and the apostles and patriarchs and the four living presences, the very attributes of God in God's self, and they acknowledged God and spoke affectionately to God, saying,

"Yes! We are at the place of good news
and attendedness
and wisdom
and thanksgiving
and the honor

and the power
and the strength of our God
in this time beyond time,
Yes!"

And one of the saved ones engaged me in conversation saying to me, "Do you know who these are who are dressed in light, where they come from?"

And I responded to him, "My respected friend, you are the one who knows this."

And he said to me, "These are the ancient ones who come from the great tribulations and have been given to wear their cleansed clothes and they gleam from washing in the blood of Jesus, the Lamb of God.

This is why they can stand before the elevated seat of God,
and they will attend God day and night in God's inner circle,
and the One sitting upon the elevated seat will provide shelter to them.
And they will no longer be subject to hunger,
nor thirst,
nor will the daylight fail to shine upon them,
nor the sun burn them,
And Jesus, the Lamb of God, shepherds them in the midst
of the elevation of the seat of God,
and Jesus guides them close to the lifegiving
spring of water,
And God wipes away every tear from their eyes."

Jesus, Child Of God, Will Next Destroy The Roman Empire

And then Jesus undertook a seventh act to conform the creation.

I, John, was given this understanding after my meditation had ended abruptly for about half an hour. And I saw seven trusted prophets from the days of old standing before God and they were given seven horns[10]. In my mind there came the recollection of the destruction of Jericho when seven priests blew their horns around that city for six days and on the seventh they did the same, only seven times, causing the city walls to break up and the city fall to God's chosen people.

Jesus will deal in history to cause the destruction of pagan Rome!

I have been given to see the oppressive government of Domitian, and pagan Rome itself, to be reduced similarly. Yes! An oppressor Rome, whose gov-

---

10. Seven horns caused Jericho to fall in the book of Joshua as will seven horns cause Rome (the pagan one) to fall.

ernment is fatally human, will fall as signaled by historical proofs that persecuters of God's children will fall.

But first I saw Jesus go to stand at the altar of God's justice holding out a golden bowl and Jesus took much incense, enough so that it could represent the hopes of all the saved ones joining him in front of the altar. And smoke arose from the incense combined with the hopes of the saved ones by a special operation from the hand of God. And Jesus took the incense bowl and burned it upon the flame of the altar of justice and poured it on the earth and there came the elemental sounds of thunder and voices and lightnings and earthquakes which indicated the imminence of God's presence in that situation.

The Testimony Of The Former Prophets Prophesy That Jesus Will Destroy The Oppressive Government Of Pagan Rome

Let us unseal[11] the scroll of the former prophets and see what testimony it provides.

Didn't God give Moses to deal with the persecution of the times of the Pharoah to liberate God's children?

And a first prophet, Moses of earthly life, sounded his horn and there came hail and fire down on pagan Rome, which soon became mixed with the blood of its injured residents, as the fire spread, and as it was cast at the earth. And Rome burned[12], and its trees burned and all its grass burned to signal that Jesus had begun to avenge the persecution of the saints by pagan Rome, the persecutor. And so begins the process whereby Jesus conforms the world, starting with a step to destroy pagan Rome, a just punishment rendered to a city whose government ignores God and fails to acknowledge the God-inspired teachings of Jesus, and whose idolatrous citizens, those not resting in their faith in Jesus, will be ruined, destroyed, and utterly die unredeemed deaths.

And I remembered the prophecy of Paul in 2nd Thessalonians that Jesus will be revealed to be coming by infliction of raging fire.

And Rome burns!

Didn't Aaron also deal in the fall of Egypt and the consuming fire of God? Vesuvius overflows in a spewing of lava.

---

11. The seals refer to epochs of history that Jesus will make right.

12. The burning of pagan Rome occurred in proximity to the two greatest periods of Christian persecution. The first was the great fire of Nero's time (Nero being a notable persecutor of Christians) and the second was at the time of Titus shortly before Domitian's terrible persecution of Christians. Other real events during these periods include the Vesuvius eruption burying the cities of Pompeii and Herculaneum and the great comet of 60 A.D, which are placed into their referential positions within the text as variously described.

And a second prophet, Aaron of earthly life, sounded his horn around the earth and it was as if Mt. Sinai was burning, again, as it flowed with the energy of God's frustration down into the sea, causing Roman coastal dwellers to die, and it killed off bay fish in the Ostia delta on the Tyrrhenian Sea and many of the ships of the Roman merchant fleet. And it gave us all to know that there was no strength in Rome for God's people to flee to, but only God, for trust in Rome is shame and confusion, but trust in God, and in the return of Jesus, gives rest and the knowledge that you are saved. And while God waits in patience to exalt you and smother you in mercy, and heal the wounds of the persecuted and martyrs, God pursues those of Rome that he may fall on them in judgment, and burn them in frustration. While the Christian goes with song to the mountain of God, its lava laps down in fire, illumined with lightning, joined by hail, dancing down into the Roman places, devours, scatters, tests and destroys.

The Testimony Of The Latter Prophets Prophesy Jesus Will Destroy The Oppressive Government Of Rome

Let us unseal the four scrolls of the former prophets, Jeremiah, Isaiah, Ezekiel, and the Book of the Twelve, and see what testimony they provide.

Didn't Jeremiah announce that there must be a judgment upon the nations?

I recall the prophecy in Matthew how the wise men knew that a star presaged the arrival of Jesus, God's child who came to earth.

And a third prophet, Jeremiah of earthly life, blew his horn around the earth, and there fell from the sky and into view a great inflamed comet[13], a lamp by day and night, and its intensity fell on lands with rivers and lands of oases, and the name of the starry presence was apsinthos, a bitter herb, and as it passed over, Rome's river water tasted bitter and many people died from its waters which were impure and disease causing. But to the faithful in Jesus, the Comet presaged the event of the coming of Jesus again just as the star coming from the east presaged the first entry into this world of God's child. And we await our sovereign, who will arrive in a decisive time and find us God's people, in image and claim, awaiting expectantly.

Didn't Isaiah indicate that God's children would be restored in Jerusalem?

And a fourth prophet, Isaiah, sounded his horn, and it caused the sun to disappear over Rome and the moon and a many of the stars so that there came to be an eclipse over the Roman Empire and there was neither day or night over it. The signs in the sky confirm that Jesus is coming again. The persecutions cause folk to mourn and the earth great distress and call for the Child of God's folk to come again on the clouds, in power and faze, as horn calls, so that soon the elect will be gathered up, while the Romans fall in fear and await their destruction in anxiety, for they will be given to know that where they fall they will not be gathered up or buried, but will be left as is refuse lying on the ground. And I recalled Amos's prediction that the sun would become dark and the moon turn to blood before the terrible day of the Familyhead comes.

And I saw and I heard a single eagle, God, who bears God's people as does an eagle one of its young under its wing, flying over Mesopotamia, where lived God's folk in bondage at that time. This eagle was crying shrilly, "Woe! Woe! Woe!" taking three agonizingly sad breaths, one for the destruction of each of the church's built and destroyed, built and destroyed, built and destroyed, in Jerusalem, first Solomon's, then Nehemiah and Ezra's, and then Herod the Great's. God, you see, knows the agony and feels sympathy for those among the remnant of God dwelling on earth who wander after the destruction of their church, the home of God's saved folk on earth, destroyed again and again by oppressive government, and yet gives them hope of their reunion in it.

I recalled the riddle of Ezekiel asking what were represented by plant croppings and their seeds carried by a mighty eagle to be scattered providentially in a foreign land, Mesopotamia, and the answer was given that the new plants represented God's people who must live in subjection but who would survive as a covenant people. This recollection gave me hope as my meditation continued.

13.The great comet of AD 60 as described by Tacitus.

Didn't Amos affirm the universal sovereignty of God such that they would survive every onslaught, even the destruction of Jerusalem and its church?

The Third Destruction Of Jerusalem Fulfills The Prophecy Of Jesus That There Will Be A Return After The Third Destruction

And John told us that Jesus, God's child, promised that after the third event of the destruction of the church in Jerusalem, Jesus would return and rebuild it.

And the fifth prophet's horn, Amos's, rang out. And I saw a star falling out of the sky onto the earth, Nebuchadnazzar was given to rampage in history, and he was given the lesson to teach us of the meaning of apolluon, or hell, how deeply can be mired our existence in history and smoke began escaping from the pit of that understanding and the smoke of God's presence carried out of the pit as from a raging furnace and into history until the the sun was blotted out and the air was filled with the smoke from the pit. And out of the smoke there came locusts of plaging Babylonian imperial soldiers onto the earth and authority was given to them to erase the home of God's people from the earth. Jerusalem and its church were to be conquered and destroyed. And the incense of God's presence flowed over Israel so that the grass of its earth foraged their war horses nor were destroyed any of the plants nor most trees. Only destroyed were those who held to beliefs inimical to God's ethical laws.

Israel itself, God's folk, could not be killed, but only rendered hostage with many carried off into Babylon, but there was agony among them for the five months of the seige, and the torture of them was as the sting of a scorpion when it stings a person as arrows from the seige machines called scorpions rained down upon the city and its defenders along the walls. And in those days people were coping with death and could not escape finding it and they longed to die yet death escaped from them.

And the appearance of the invading armies into Israel as locusts swarm onto a land was similar to horsemen prepared in wartime, and upon their heads there were Mesopotamian bronze helmets such as crowns of gold, and their faces were the faces of people, and they had hair as the hair of old people and their teeth were as lions, and they wore chest armor made out of iron, and the sound on the wing was as the the sound of a chariot pulled by many horses in time of war and they had tails like scorpions and and stingers and in the swish of their tails they exercized command over God's people for five months, the short time it was given the church of Jerusalem to escape Babylonian destruction, and it gave me to recall that God is not always favorable to us, does not always give us well, but rather, simply by our anthroposity, we may suffer, not because of anything we do or do not do to deserve it, all occurring in the knowledge of an inescapeable God.

Now the Jerusalem church was destroyed. Look out here comes yet a second church burning after that one!

The Testimony Of Torah (Instruction) Prophesies That Jesus Will Destroy The Oppressive Government Of Rome

Let us unseal the scrolled testimony of Torah.

Doesn't it reveal that empires will have succesive transitory days, prolonged where God's folk lose sight of their relationship to God.

And the sixth prophet, Daniel, blew his horn, to reveal another situation of persecution. And I heard a voice from the golden altar before God saying to the sixth prophet, the one who holds the horn, "Release the four spirits of the four empires: Babylonian, Median, Persian, Greek, imperial persecutors, who ruled according to their own human systems of justice. And these four empires raged cyclically for each's own hour and day and month and year, persecuting and martyring the faithful ones living during their respective empires.

And the number of the soldiers on horses was 20,000 in groups of ten thousands. I heard the number of them.

And I thought, just as the communities of God appear as representations before God in God's place, so do the empires of the successive nations. Jesus scatters God's enemies through armies empowered with God's power beyond number of troops. Jesus leads captivity captive, takes the product of wars, provides for the rebellious so that the Jesus might dwell among them, always saves and takes the issues from death, and ultimately wounds the heads of God's enemies until the redemptive period when God's people are restored to Jerusalem and the enemies of God's people are bloodied and food for dogs.

And I saw their horses in my meditation and those who were seated upon them, the might of such nations and their enforcers. And I thought, Yes! prior to the final day of judgment, God will permit the military might of successive nations to patrol the earth, giving rest to the earth from war, but as to their justice systems, Jesus, the Familyhead, says, "I remain solicitous for Jerusalem and Zion and I am very frustrated with the nations to whom I give rest because every frustration becomes further exaggerated. I will return to Jerusalem with compassion to rebuild my church there and provide it with prospertiy and I will comfort Zion and pick Jerusalem as the site of my life with humanity." And so with the Roman military. Yes, they give the world peace, but I recall Peter's prediction in his first letter to the churches that our adversary, the Romans, would prowl around as do hungry lions seeking victims to devour. And from their mouths they breath the fire and smoke and sulfur. After this came more persecutions. Many of God's faithful have been killed and martyred, from the fire and the smoke and grimy sulfur being belched out from mouths. And the strengths of their military might were complemented by the shouts from their mouths as they volley their arrows at every supposed enemy so that they hurl through the air as do venomous snakes and act against God in their own ways.

And the rest of the people, those who were not being killed in these disasters, did not repent by acts of their hands, to avoid the worship of ungodly demon people rendered into the forms of gods, and the golden idols and the silver and the bronze and the jewels and the carvings which they did not seem to be able to hear nor walk. And they did not change their ways from their murders nor from the witchcraft nor from the immorality nor from stealing.

The Testimony Of The Apostles Prophesy That Jesus Will Destroy An Oppressive Government Such As Rome

And I saw an apostle, Paul, confidently coming out of God's sky of existence dressed in a cloud, and a rainbow was upon his head, as a mark that he had come from God's home itself as a messenger as does a rainbow after a flood, and his face was like the sun and his legs were as columns of fire. And he was holding in his hand the tiniest little book, a small collection of accounts of the life of Jesus and letters he had written in the spirit of their story. And he put one of his feet on the right side of the sea and the left upon the earth. And he cried out in a great voice as if he were emitting a roar. And then he cried out and bespoke his seven thunderous epistles to the Romans, Corinthians, Galatians, Ephesians, Philippians, Colossians, and Thessalonians. And then he just preached, the seven thunderous epistles testifying with him in loud voices. And then the seven cities also encouraged others to preach in witness to the the writing, and I heard a voice from out of God's homeland saying, "You must become missionaries in this world which the thunders of the tears of daily life cry over knowing you cannot write tears. And Paul, the missionary who I recognized to be the one standing upon both the sea and the earth, was saying,

"Jesus is arousing, the one who sits at the right hand of God,
cast in the likeness of the presence of time beyond history,"

as he is becoming visible in God's homeland to those at that place and to those on the earth in designated places and seacoast dwellers and those in every commnity which has not given up its belief.

The Testimony Of John The Baptist Prophesies That Jesus Will Destroy An Oppressive Government Such As Pagan Rome (I)

And at that moment in time when his voice was heard, there came the seventh prophet, John the Baptist, who began to blow his horn of proclamation, the one which would end the mystery of God's intentionality about God's creation, as he revealed the joy of final truth to every burdened heart.

Be A Missionary In The World For Jesus So That The Roman Empire May Be Destroyed By Jesus And Jerusalem Come Again, This Time Indestructibly

And a voice which I heard coming from God's homeland again whispered to me, saying, "Go, take this writing of the story of God's life from Paul, as he proclaimed it on his missions across the seas and lands."

And I was transended out of my situation toward Paul who told me that the little book was given to me, that I, too, must become a missionary, and says to me, "Take it and flee into its gospel message about Jesus, God's child when on earth, and Jesus, now with God, acting for our salvation and redemption, and it will cause you to be soul sick, how the world treats this message, but in your mouth you will be able to taste it as honey."

And I took the little book from Paul's hand, and I consumed it and it was in my mouth of the taste of honey, but then I digested it, and it and I felt sick

to my soul, for the Roman Empire was killing those who lived in its story. And voices demanded of me to say, "God again is to be announced to peoples and homeless ones and speakers of languages and those in every jurisdiction."

And it was given to me to take up my pen and write next Ezekiel's understanding of how the suffering remnant of Israel, exiled and despairing, would be restored under the beneficent and caring rod of a shepherd, where it was written, "Go up in spirit and find the measure and extent of the church of God and the judgment altar and the where God was worshipped in it. And note the area set aside for a courtyard of the church, as in Zechariah's vision of its measureless measuring, and do not expect to find any limit to it, because God provides a place in God's presence reserved for the home-seeking peoples and races who are left for the present to be beset by persecution in gentile cities of exile.[14]

Intimitations Of The Re-established Jerusalem From Historic Returns Of Exiles To Jerusalem And The Rebuilding Of The Church

And I remembered how God caused a stirring of history and it said to me, "Here come into the whirl of my thoughts Ezra and Nehemiah, my witnesses from the second Jerusalem church, who reassembled my remnant from their foreign cities and they announced the return of Israel, coming dressed as penitents. Their government was constituted of co-leaders who appeared as two strongly spirited ones, a Davidic king and church High Priest, these of the time of Zechariah and Haggai, and reflections of the light as do those reflect who stand before the Familyhead of the earth.

They ruled Israel as ones do who are pleasing to God.

And if anyone wanted to challenge them, fire would come out of their mouth and consume their enemies. And if any will them opposition, so to them death would become their fate. These have authority to lock up the sky so that no rain may fall, as occurred through my will acting at the time fo Elijah. Such were the days of the authority which God gave to prophets and they had authority to turn waters into blood and they could strike the death with plagues as they chose."

History Proves That, Until Jesus Comes Personally To Safeguard Us From Oppressive Governments, Human Efforts To Reconstitute Jerusalem Will Fail Because We Do Not Conform Our Lives To God's Ways

So what happened then? Did Israel and God's folk remain a church-centered faith community, patterned after a Davidic ruled state, confessing a God who guides and leads out of bondage?

When the witness of Nehemiah and Ezra was ended, I saw arise the beast of God-opposed empire arising up out of its oblivion, Antiochus IV Epiphanes, its leader, and make war with God's folk and conquer them and kill them. And their corpses lie on the broad streets of the great city of Jerusalem which will

---

14. This reference derives from the "riddle of 42" in the Greek text which calls to mind Arithmoi 35.6 from the Septuaginta. The text confirms God's promise to Moses of zones of refuge in the Promised Land.

regain the label of a spiritual Sodom and little Egypt where the Familyhead of ours, Jesus, was crucified.

And Antiochus culled out God's folk and the people of the covenant and religious speakers and inheritors, rendering them corpses for three and a half years during which Antiochus IV Epiphanes held possession of Jerusalem, profaned the church and abolished religious services and the bodies were not let permitted to be buried so that the atrocities remain in memory. And the earth dwellers were so happy at this outcome among themselves and they showed it. And they passed between themselves the booty from the atrocities, so that the two re-establishers of the second church must have turned in their graves.

But after this period of carnage, the spirit of God moved to reestablish a more approved life among the people and the church was restored upon its original basis and great respect returned to those who beheld it. And they heard a great voice coming out of God's homeland saying to them, "Come to me." Jesus, yes, God's child when on earth, ministered in the form of a person to us. And those faithful martyred ones from this persecution no doubt heard the great call from God's homeland saying to them, "Come here." And they went into God's homeland in a cloud and the observed those who were God's and their enemies. And the persecuted dead see what we do not, that despite the eradication of the faithful ones to God in Jerusalem, whereby even the few remaining faithful in Israel and the fraction left and not dispersed by foreign rulers in Jerusalem are killed, that there shall be seed remaining in the diaspera and that Jerusalem will once again arise by the design of God in God's homeland. And this destruction of the second Jerusalem church left me breathing deeply. Look a third, the leveling of the Jerusalem church constructed at the time of Herod the Great by Titus in 70 A.D., came to mind too quickly!

The Testimony Of John The Baptist Prophesies That Jesus Will Destroy An Oppressive Government Such As Rome (II)

And the seventh testimony issued forth as a hornblast from the prophet John the Baptist, and there came thunderous choruses in God's home saying,

"There is coming a Godly hierarchy and our Familyhead to the rescue, God's child who comes to earth, and this hierarchy will last in time beyond time."

And the twenty four life course helpers sitting with God acknowledged God and gave God the praise saying,

"We thank you our Familyhead, God, the one who bears all
power, the one who is and was,
Who takes your control to do great things and
establishes hierarchies.
The one who stirs up the homeless ones,
And comes out of frustration
And restores time to those martyred,
And gives a rightful wage to those who toil in your
witness
And those who acknowledge you and respect your presence.
In the small things and the important things.
And the one who subdues those who claim the right to
subdue the earth."

And the church of God was opened in God's homeland and there was displayed the ark of the covenant promise in the church, and there were lightnings and shoutings and thunders and earthquakes and huge hailstones which indicated the imminence and activity of God's presence.

The Birth Of God As A Child In A Time Of Persecution

There appeared to me an ultimate sign in graphic reality as foretold by Amos to mark the time of God's presence on earth in a conception of a child.

Mother Mary, you return to our memory.

Mary, you are the one who we recall clothed as by the sun, wearing its blaze as if radiant with the love of God. You are the one who, like the moon, gave us light to abide the fears of the night. You are the one venerated by the starry presences of the universe, the twelve apostles, the ones who passed down to us the hope and faith by which we live.

And you are pregnant, reduced to crying and straining to give birth.

And there appeared in my mind another sign in graphic reality, a reptile of a man, Herod, fiery in temperament, his authority derived from the seven hills of Rome and as a reptile has a tail so did this one wield the power of Rome at this tail end of Roman authority, and on his head he wore a Roman Senatorial crown.

And, as a reptile swishes its tail in authority, so did Herod exercise his authority and destroyed many of God's children in the exercise of his power, casting them into graves. And Herod, a dragon, made a decision to destroy the baby of the woman giving birth, as would a dragon who eats children.

But a male child was born, a child who would govern all the home-seeking peoples of the world wielding an indestructible shepherd's staff, and the child was bonded to God, and to God's seat of authority.

And the mother fled into the less inhabited region of Egypt where there was a place prepared by God so that there she and her child could be provided for and fed during the days of the child's infancy, while Herod was governor.

And there arose contention in God's homeland, whereby Michael, the protector of God's people, and enforcer of the law of the spirit on earth, and his spiritual police arose to oppose the dragon emulator, Herod, and Herod kept up his war against these spirits along with his henchmen, but without the strength to succeed nor when they died was there any place for them, even yet, in all of God's homeland.

And the great dragon, Herod the Great, the old snake, called Devil and Satan, he who cheated and betrayed his entire province, was buried in the ground and his henchmen were buried after him.

And I heard David in God's homeland singing,
Now comes salvation and ecstasy and the hierarchical
time of God
And the time of authority of the one who comes to earth
as God for the contender against our brothers and
sisters is buried
There was one who contended for them in the presence of
our God day and night.
And they overcame him through the blood of the Lamb
And through the story of their own witnesses
And they did not overly value their own lives before
death.
Because of this, regard them happy, the ones in
God's homeland.
And those who reside in these places.

Take a deep breath, earth and sea,
Because the devil has been overthrown for you
Holding off his great rage.
Recognize what a short time he had!

But even after the second Herodian dragon emulator, Archelaus, understood why his predecessor Herod the Great had been cast into the ground, he decided to continue the prosecution of the woman who had born the child.

Except that God's deliverance came for flight, as on the two wings of an eagle, which were provided the woman so that she might fly into a safe desert haven where she could bring up the child there for a time and occasions and moments away from the face of the reptilian tormentor.

And this snake spit out the venom of persecution until it welled out as the waters of a river in her view so that she might have been swept away in its current. But the earth itself shouted out a warning to the woman, to keep her distance, and the earth opened its mouth and swallowed the venomous flow of orders for persecution which the Herodian tyrannizer, Archelaus, continued to order.

And the dragon-rulers have remained angry about the escape of the woman and have committed themselves to make war against the remnant belonging to her issue, Jesus, those who keep the law of God, and hold to the witness of Jesus. And one such witness, me, has been washed up on the island of the Patmos seashore of the Mediterranean Sea.

The Situation Of Imperial Blasphemy Dominating The World Which Requires Jesus To Destroy It

And as I looked out into the sea from my island of exile, the Roman Empire comes to mind which I think of as a monster emerging from its depths, the monster, Rome, having had ten emperors following Julius Caesar. I visualize each Emperor as a horn on the monster. I see Rome's seven hills as the monster's heads or capital of the empire. Each emperor claims to be perfect or divine! And upon each one of those hills are blasphemies, statues of emperors as Gods and the like.

And the monster which I saw had the combined imperial aspect of successive empires gone before with the nature of a Persian leopard, and its feet were as that of a Medean bear and mouth was as the mouth of a Babylonian lion.

And the Herodian dragons who ruled Jerusalem gave to this next monster in succession, Rome, total allegiance and received from its seat the totalitarian authority exercised.

And I thought of Gaius Caesar, Caligula, as one of the heads or emperors. We had considered him assassinated, wounded to the point of death but not so. His fatal wound is now deemed healed and he is considered God too. I remember how the entire earth was shocked at this monster.

And God's people were required to pray for their lives to the Herodian dragon who in turn owed allegiance to this monster and God's people were forced to worship the monster saying, "Who could be so glorious as Gaius and who could have the power to oppose him?"

And Gaius, the monster, had been lawgiver, speaking in thunderous words and blasphemies and authority was given him to rule that way, but only for forty two months. And he couldn't open his mouth without uttering blasphemy to God, and he tried to usurp God's name and tried to turn his residence into the site where God lived, and him being the God in the sky of existence where God lives.

And it was given to an emperor, to undertake war with God's attended ones and to be victorious over them and it was given to this monster authority over every nation and people and language group and home-seeking people.

And I remember how it was with people worshiping this monster, all of them, those who live everywhere on the earth. No! No! let not his name be written in this record of life of the Lamb from the beginning of the world.

> If any have ears, listen.
> if anyone would be an intimidator,
> the intimidation returns back.
> If someone engages in killing by a sword
> that one is killed by that sword (as Gaius
> Caesar, Caligula, was).

In this world there is need for patient endurance and the faith of the God attended ones.

And I saw another monster, Neron Caesar, Nero, coming out from the land, and he had two horns like a ram and he speaks as does a Herodian dragon. And he exercised great authority in the same manner as did Gaius before him, befouling the earth and everyone living in it so that they were in effect worshipping the first monster all over again.

And he did great deeds like bringing fire down from out of the sky to burn his own capital city in front of the whole populace, to destroy Rome. And he misleads the world about this deed and uses it undertake persecution. And he enjoys seeing torture in front of his monstrous eyes. Then he uses this event to convince the Roman citizens all over the empire of the necessity to make an

image of him, and making this worship a determinant of who shall be put to the sword and killed or live. And he has attributed to it, this statue of himself, the gift of life, so that this monstrous statute can allegedly speak, and he orders that if there are any who do not worship the monster statute they shall be killed. And he requires everybody, the little people and the powerful people, and those that are rich and those that are poor, and those that are freed and those that are slaves, that they make a mark on their right hands or their heads, and the effect is that if anyone doesn't do it, that they can't even appear in the marketplace, or purchase food there unless they have the mark of the name of the monster or the number of his name. Here is the riddle. The one who wants to confirm who the monster is, let that one add up the number equivalents from the name of the monster, and that calculation is who this person is, and the number of him is six hundred sixty six.[15]

The Saving Memory Of The Lamb Of God Who Will Destroy Rome

And then I saw another vision. There, the Lamb standing upon Mount Zion, and with him the faithful remnant who bear the name of Christians and abide in the name of their parent, which is practiced in their ethical dealings.

---

15. The famous "666." The text reintroduces Nero from the Greek riddle. Neron Caesar (Nero) is the emperor's name in the Greek transliterated into Hebrew numbers as nun (50) resh (200) vav (6) nun (50) (Neron) and qof (100) samekh (60) resh (200) Caesar,

And I heard a voice from out of God's homeland as smoothly flowing as torrents of water and as the voice of booming thunder, and the voice which I heard sounded as sweet as that of harpists who play the harp.

And they sang a new song in front of God's throne, and before God's four living presences, and before the elders, and no one has the ability to learn the words of this song unless they are a part of this remnant, bought and paid for from the merchandise of God's folk on earth. These are the ones whose lives were not given the content of homes with spouses, or are not sexually oriented, where it is possible to find refuge. These were the first purchases from among God's people, a first purchase by God and the Lamb, and there isn't anything false that my be found coming out of the throat of any of them. They are innocents.

Three Witness Against Idolatry And Emperor Worship

And I saw in my mind's eye, Nehemiah, as an angel, bearing the ageless scrolls of good news for the ones dwelling on the earth, and for all home seekers and races and language speakers and people, saying in a loud voice, "Fear God and pay attention to God who will come at God's own hour of rightwising, and worship the Maker of Being itself and earth and seas and flowing rivers."

And another, second, angel, Isaiah followed saying, "It has fallen It has fallen. Rome, the preposterous. This city forced all the world's home-seeking peoples to become drunk in frustration on the wine of its immorality." And a third angel, Jeremiah, followed after saying in a commanding voice, "If any worship a Caesar divus, a Monster, or any statue of him and act under this ethic, that one will drink from the wine of the monster claiming to be God, a wine being prepared at full strength for his or her cup of frustration. She or he will be tormented in the fire and in the divine presence before attended agents

of God and before the Lamb. And the smoke of their agony in the final eternity will rise up and they will not have relief, whether it is day or night, the ones who worship the Monster and his statues or any who deign to accept his law and ethic. Here is the need for patience for those wishing to live holy lives, those who are keeping the law of God and the faith of Jesus.

Preparatory Measures For Entry Into God's End Time Church In The Jerusalem Of The Returning Jesus

And I heard a voice from out of God's place in the sky of existence saying, "Write this down. The favored dead, those who have died into the Family-head's presence, exist at the present time. Yes, the spirit says so, because they will have been given rest from their labors, but their God sponsored activities continue on."

And I reflected and saw, Yes, a bright cloud, as the one which followed God's innocent people during the days of the Exodus, and upon a cloud seated was Moses having upon his head a golden crown, and in his hand a sharp scythe.

And Joel, as another angel, came out of the church sanctuary crying in a loud supplication to the one seated on the cloud, "Apply the scythe and harvest the crop, because the hour has come to harvest. The sappy crop of the earth has dried up." And Joel threw it down to Moses, this one seated upon the cloud upon the earth, which opened the period of harvesting the earth.

And Matthew, another angel, came out from the church in God's home-land to join this one with the sharp scythe. And Elijah, another angel came out from God's very seat of justice, this one having the duty to keep the flame of justice alive, and he called out in a loud voice to the Destroyer, with his sharp edged scythe saying, "Send down your sharp scythe and also pick the grapes from the vines of the earth because the grapes have ripened." And the Destroyer cast down upon the earth his scythe and saw to the gathering of the grapes of the earth and he thrust the produce into the winepress of God's great passion.

And the Destroyer ended the lives of those who oppressed God's people as if the Destroyer were pressing on a winepress outside a city so as to cause blood to emerge out of the winepress and those who sought to impede the liberation of God's people found history well up to destroy them as had the Red Sea[16] pressed up to drown the forces of the Pharaoh up to their horse's bridles in this sea when they presumed to reverse the tide of the Exodus.

A Baptism Of History Into God's Love

And as I contemplated, Yes, there appeared in my mind another striking and extraordinary event in God's homeland, seven angels preparing seven deliverance strokes[17] for the last times of history, because God's hurt made it time for letting go.

And I noticed how the baptismal pool into eternity in front of God's seat boiled up to a mixture of spirit and flame, and emerging were those who had won victory over the Roman persecution and from its emperors and Domitian, and they found themselves in the restored life of David's perfected Israel.

And they were singing the hymn Moses sang when God's people were delivered out of bondage, the song of delight in Jesus, the Lamb,

> How much more great and marvelous could be your activity
> Our Familyhead, God, you who control all things?
> Haven't you proved your ways to be conforming and true,
> Ruler of us who want homes?
> Can any not help respect you, our Familyhead?
> And respond when you attend to events?
> Now we owe single allegiance,
> And give praise before you,
> As ones transformed into your imminence.

And after that I saw opening up the inner place of the place allotted to witnesses to God in God's homeland, and Aaron and Moses came out as angels holding seven deliverance strokes, dressed in the shining cloth of innocence, and drawn around their waists were the belts identifying them as missionaries except that they were golden.

And God, in God's every attribute in Reality, gave these delivering angels seven cups filled to the brim with the hurt God felt in that place of time beyond time.

And this inner place in the church was filled with God's presence and energy as if it were full of smoke, and no one could enter into this church until those chosen to be the bearers had let go their deliverance into history.

---

16. The answer to the Greek text's "Red Sea" riddle is referenced in at this point. The text riddle is roughly what is like blood, in a liberation setting came to the bridles of horses, and is about 200 miles long? The answer is the Red Sea where Pharoah's horsemen following the departing Israelites found their horses awash up to their bridles when the sea closed.

17. These compare with the plagues by which the Hebrews were assisted by God in becoming liberated from the Egyptian Pharoah's persecution. The Hellenists knew of these intimately from the writings of Josephus, "Antiquities of the Jews," Chap.13.

The Pouring Out Of Cups Of God's Hurt At Creation

And I heard a great roaring voice, the church itself, saying to these cup dealing ones, "Go and pour out these seven bowls of God's hurt onto the earth."

Seven Deliverance Strokes Against The Romans To Let Christians Be

And Aaron went out and poured out a cup onto the land, and there was wielded a deliverance stroke[18] in the form of a sickness which struck the defiant ones among humanity who bore allegiance to the Roman Empire and gave praise to the statue of the Roman Emperor. The sickness spread from one place to the next until it encompassed the world. The inflicted developed severe headaches. Their eyes became red and inflamed. Their throats and tongue were bloody. They sneezed until the pain dropped down into their chests requiring them to cough, and then retch, the spasms growing more and more severe. Their skin festered into boils, ulcers, and open puss. Clothing had to be shed. Their thirst was unquenchable no matter how much water they drank. Their lives were a constant torment not permitting rest or sleep until they died, usually on the seventh or eighth day in a high fever. If they survived after, their bowels were struck causing diarrhea and death from weakness. Along the way, fingers, toes, privy parts, or eyes were lost. Memory escaped. Many died of neglect for none would try to help them because to do so would cause you to become inflicted. Their worst wound was dejection and despair on learning they had it because they knew what it meant to have it: a lingering baleful death to many but not all. Some recovered.

And then Aaron went out and poured out that one's cup onto the sea, meaning the bodies and the passions of the God opposed, and the seas became bloody as if of death's substance, and all the lives opposed to God's promise to God's people lost their heads in muddled thinking or outright died.

And then Aaron went out and poured out a cup onto the rivers, the very souls of those God opposed, and there was a deliverance stroke cast at them, and they were berated as if becoming bloody. And I heard the voice of that deliverer of the stroke against these souls saying,

> You are right, the one who is of Being itself and who
> always has been, these events are right,
> Because they are just,

---

18. This particular deliverance stroke comes from reference to Thucydides where a great sickness struck Athens during the second year of the Peloponnesian War. The riddle of elkos and plege in the Greek get us to this reference.

Now comes the manifestation of this world in the blood
of the God attentive ones and martyrs who poured out
their blood in persecutions
And their blood is given to the world to drink, The
blood of these special ones.
And I heard from the place of justice itself say,
Yes, Familyhead, God, one in total control,
These martyrs who shed their blood were ones who were
truthful and conformed through trial for you.

And then Moses went out and poured out a cup onto the sun, and the sun raged in becquerels by the douse from it, scorching humanity in its flames. And all those who bore cruel hearts toward God's people withered in the great heat, and folk hurled curses at the very name of a God who had the authority over such deliverance strokes and they did not change their ways to give God attendedness.

And then Moses went out and poured out a cup onto the Roman Emperor's seat of authority, and there came down a darkness into the palace, and the persecutors of Christians bit their tongues and they cursed the God of ultimate reality out of their feelings of pain and suffering and on account of their wounds but they did not change their ways for all these acts.

And then Moses went out and poured out a cup onto the River Euphrates, the place of all joy of the soul, and he dried up all comfort in the soul of those who persecuted Christians, so to make way for the tide of coming events from new rulers. And then I saw coming out of the mouth of the personified Roman Empire, and its emperor, and its priestly class, ignorant talk in praise of the three gods of the Capitoline triad, Jupiter, Mars and Quirinius, as lifeless frogs which are soulless, bloodless and cry out with harsh noises. The persecution of Jesus has shaken your temples as well as the whole world until now your temples must quake and fall. This triad, they are the spirits of the dead, without life in God's homeland, imagined to do miracles, who summon the governors of the whole world to make war against Christians in this great era of God the all controlling. See! Jesus comes as does a thief! Satisfied is the one who keeps the watch for this coming and keeps dressed to leave with Jesus, so he won't have to walk away naked, and be seen shamelessly undressed. And Jesus gathers them in the spirit of triumph we remember from the Song of the Judge of Israel, Deborah, who triumphed over God's enemies at Megiddo.

And then both Moses and Aaron went out and poured out their last cup into the air, And a great voice came down from the church from the seat of power saying, "Let it be." And there came lighting and shouts and thunders and earthquakes in multiples, evidencing the imminence of God in the world, so as not to have been experienced ever before by humanity upon the earth, so great were these earthquakes. And this shook the city of Rome and each of the three

tribes of Rome, Ramnes, Luceres, and Titienses, and this city of people of all of the world fell into shambles. And Rome, the greatest of all, was brought to mind before the seat of God to be given to drink of the cup of wine of God's hurt. And every heretical church and pagan temple service was dispersed. And there wasn't one of the seven hills left without damage. And huge hailstones, weighing as much as a talent, came raining down out of God's homeland upon humanity, and the God opposed cursed God on account of this deliverance stroke of the hail, which remains a record of immense consequence.

A Vision Of A Drunken, Idol Coddling Woman, Rome, Held Up By A Condemned Emperor

And one of the angels who had delivered the seven cups came and he spoke with me saying, "Come here. I want to point out to you the conviction due the great idolator seated upon the many waters, Rome, with whom the kings of the earth have pandered, and grown intoxicated over, and dwelt with on the earth in drunkenness and idolatry. And he carried me up in my imagination out into the desert. And I saw a woman seated beside a bloody emperor, bloated as with blasphemous idols, having seven heads as does the city of Rome have seven hills and ten horns representing the imperial line of emperors. And the woman was dressed in purple and scarlet and she was arrayed in gold on gold, and a rare, precious stone, with pearls, and holding a golden glass in her hand choked full of idols and in her brain an idol worshiping scheme and ethic labeling her with a secret identity, great Babylon, mother of idols and of horrors done for them on the earth. And I saw that this woman was drunk on the blood of the martyrs and on the witnesses for Jesus. And I was shocked to incredulity when I saw her. And my guide said to me, "Why are you so surprised? I will tell you the secret of this woman and the emperor who is holding her up, she who has these seven heads and ten horns. The emperor who you see used to be an emperor but is no longer one, Nero, and he is about to make his descent into oblivion and go into oblivion. Earth dwellers will wonder what became of him since his name is not written in the book of life kept from the beginning of the world, when they observe this emperor where he will be, he who was but is no longer and stands present as an idol, all of which is known to those who have an understanding of such things. The seven heads are the seven hills of Rome where the woman sits upon them. And there are seven emperors come. The five Claudians have fallen, that one, Nero, was one of them, and another one, Claudius, came after him, and when Nero left after a short reign, it was happenstance that he remained. And there is another emperor who was and is not any longer, and he, Domitian, is the eighth, but is in the line of the other seven, and is heading for the not in God's eternity.

And the ten horns which you see are ten emperors who govern what they seize but they have power as an emperor for only an hour, seizing after a prior emperor. These have a single mind set, and motivation and power, giving them the cast of an animal. These emperors will make war against the Lamb and the Lamb will defeat them, because our Familyhead, Jesus, is the ruler of the family of God's people, and the ruler over rulers, and those who are with Jesus are named by god and selected for family membership and are faithful.

And then he says to me, "The seas which you saw, on which the idol mother was sitting, these are people and crowds and ethnic races and those speaking different languages. And the ten horns which you see also are the hated idol worshipping emperors. And they will strip her and leave her naked and her flesh will be a meal, and they will even burn her down in arson. For God has given it to their hearts to do with her according to God's plan, and to execute this single plan while the gift of governance is under an emperor until Jesus, the logos, the image of God takes over finally, once and for all time. And the city which you saw is the huge city of Rome, where lives the emperor over the rulers of the earth.

A Song Of The Fall Of Rome By Isaiah, Jeremiah And Ezekiel

After these things happened, I envisioned three angels from God, Isaiah, Jeremiah, and Ezekiel, coming down out of God's homeland having a great tiding, and the earth was emblazoned by their God attendedness. And they cried out in the full strength of their voices, singing,

It falls! Mighty Rome! It falls!
Now it is an abandoned graveyard!
Now be watchful, everyone, for its stinking spirit,
and be watchful everyone for the stinking scavenger birds,
And be watchful everyone for the stink of an emperor
and his remembrance. Here the result of the wine of God's hurt over her
idols
Drink this wine, you, now homeless ones!
And you kings and governors of the earth who
took her idols with her rule!
and you merchants of the earth who grew
rich from the explosion in luxurious living!
And I heard another voice from God's homeland singing,
Get out of there, my people!
So that you won't have to share in their acts which separated them
from God.

And from these deliverance strokes!
 So that you won't have to receive their brunt! For their stupid acts
  have caused God to cleave them from God's love, even out of
  God's homeland,
 And God remembers her acts of injustice.
 Pay for her as she is worth!
 and twice the amount according to her acts! In the cup in which
  she mixes her wine, let her pour her drink out in a double
  helping!
 For so her glory deserves and her life of overabundance and
  luxury.
 Just that much pain and sorrow give her!
 Because she says, I am the Reigning Empress
 And what do I care!
 How could I ever suffer!
 So, in a single day, here come these deliverance strokes for her!
 Death and suffering and famine,
 And in a fire she will find herself consumed!
 Because there is ultimacy in the power of the
 Familyhead, God, the one who convicts her!

And they will cry out and mourn her, the kings and governors of the earth who idolize her and live in the orbit of her wealth, for how can they help but see the ashes from her burning, even taking what distance they can from the blaze, for fear that they may have to suffer also, saying,

 Too bad! Too bad!, such a magnificent city, Rome,
 And so powerful a city too!
 That in a single hour, judgment was passed on you!

And the merchants of the earth are crying out and feeling sympathy for her because their cargo can no longer be sold there, not any of the cargo of gold, or silver or precious stone, or pearls or fine linen or purple or silk or scarlet dye or any of the scented wood, or any of the ships full of ivory, or ships full of valuable lumber, or copper or iron, or marble or cinnamon, or spices or incense, or ointment, or nutmeg or frankincense, wine or olive oil or fine wheat flour or grain or cattle or sheep or horses or chariots or the bodies and souls of humanity. And the benefit from all the desires of your soul shall slip away from you and all the luxury and the radiance of your appearance shall be stripped away from you.

And no one can recover them from where they have gone.

These merchants, the ones who grew rich from her standing away from her afar because they fear they might have to share her suffering are calling out and groaning, saying,

Too bad! Too bad! Such a magnificent city, Rome,
 dressed in linen and purple and scarlet and she was
 arrayed in gold on gold, and a rare, precious stone,
 with pearl, because in a single hour so much of her
 wealth was destroyed.

And every ship captain and every one who sails any place or sails at all or so many as trade by sea routes, from far away, stand back they cry out when they see the ashes of her fire commiserating:

What can ever be like this magnificent city? And they brush off the soot from their heads and cry out bewailing and groaning, saying:

Too bad! Too bad! Such a magnificent city, Rome,
 Everyone who had a boat in the sea was made rich by her
  extravagance,
 And now in a single hour she is worthless.
 God's homeland, yes,
 And the ones who are God attended and the apostles and the
  prophets,
 You too!
 Be pleased,
 Because God has judged the crime again you committed by her.

And a powerful agent of God's hurt lifted up a stone larger than the largest millstone and threw it down into the sea, saying,

Just so violently will be you thrown down
 Rome, you great city!
 And no one will ever be able to discover you.
 And the sound of harpists and musicians
 And flutists and horn players, may never be heard in you again.
 And no worker of any line of work may any longer be found in you,
 Nor any sound of a millstone may any longer be heard in you.
 Nor the light of any lamp ever more appear in you.
 Nor the voice of a bridegroom or bride ever more be heard in you

Because So what if your merchants were the greates of earth dwellers!
Because in your magic all the home seeking peoples were
deceived,
Because in her was found the blood of the prophets and attended
ones and all of those who suffered martyrdom upon the earth.

Then I heard as if from a loud voice coming out of a large crowd in God's home, saying,
Alleluia the savior and the attender and the strength of our God tells the truth and does right and exercises God's justice. He condemns this great idolizer, Rome, wherever she misleads any on earth in her idol worshiping and he spills blood on behalf of God's followers with an avenging hand.
And so, again, let it always be said,
Alleluia for the smoke arises into the timeless air. And the twenty four folk course helpers at the throne and the four attributes of God and those who were praising God seated upon the elevated seat, continue saying,

Yes!
Alleluia, And a voice from the throne emerged saying,
Praise to our God
And all of God's helpers
and all those who respect God as one would a parent,
The least and the most.

A Choice Of Attendance At A Feast In A New Jerusalem

And I heard a sound as if it was from a tumultuous crowd, sounding as the roar of poured water, and released clapping thunder saying:

Alleluia
How comforting to know how our Familyhead rules.
Our God is the controller over everything.
Our joy and feelings of tenderness fill our lives
When we are permitted to give God every attention
God, you give us this reality,
The invitation to a marriage feast of yourself come to earth,
You invite us through those who tell the story of your earthly life
as by hornblast,
Some will not come,
Some want no feast of your companionship and go on their ways,
These deride your life, on earth and in God's homeland,

And abuse and kill the ones who bring them invitation,
And your army comes, and there is frustration on the earth, as in
  your feel for your creation,
And justice requires you take their lives and burn their cities,
But your wedding is not to be delayed, despite it all,
Your bride, this creation, has prepared herself,
Wearing the fine linen of innocence, the hand weaving of martyrs
  and missionaries and attenders to God.
You send forth new invitations, your wedding will go forth,
Your celebration of the life with the creation who wish to share
  your joy,
So now those who are in the streets, the homeless home seekers,
  those who have had no fulsome meals, whose life plates were
  empty,
Those who are bad and good,
These you invite to the celebration feast laid out with every
  sufficiency,
And all come shaking off the dust of the streets and their lives,
  except that one came only to eat and not to praise the event,
And he was removed and thrown out of the hall,
And he cursed his situation, as he departed God's homeland ,
For many are invited, but few are selected.

And God has me this to do, telling me, "Write this down." These happy
ones at the marriage feast of the Lamb call you. And he tells me.
  I tell you the truthful word of God.
  And I fell down at the feet of this one who brought me this message thinking to praise the inviter. But he says to me. "Don't you see! I am only your fellow worker and your brother and sister who keeps the witness of Jesus. I give
praise to God. The spirit of the prophets is the witness of Jesus."

Logos, The Story Of The Life Of God, Crushes Oppressive Governments And Every Opposed Life Story

And I saw the skies of existence opening, and Yes! there is a horse, coming
down as light, and the one seated upon it is Faith and Truth in bodily form.
And this one is charged to conformed the world to the story of God's life, given
to judge and wage war. The eyes of this one are as dancing flames, and it has
an authority self directed, but the name of this one is Logos, the Story of God's
Life on Earth. And behind Logos, others followed after, From among the anx-

ious ones in God's homeland, also coming after on horses of light, and wearing the white linen of the innocent.

And the story of God came forth from each breath and would a sharp sword striking down the rebellious. Logos let it be known that the new rule would be by metal rod.

And Logos was as one who treads the winepress of God's hurt from frustration over creation, on the behalf of God, the all controlling, and logos is dressed to get the job done, clothes emblazoned, Ruler over rulers, Familyhead over all other Familyheads. And I saw Ezekiel standing as if on the sun and he was crying out in a loud voice instructing all the scavenger birds of the air to gather in mid-day, "Assemble for the great feast of God. So that you may feed on the discard flesh of the ruler's feast, the flesh of Roman tribunes and officers, the flesh of the powerful ones, the flesh from the work of the horsemen on the horses of light, the flesh of those who are freed persons and from the enslaved, the small and the mighty."

The Judgment Due Oppressors Of God's Children

And I saw the Roman emperor and the governors of the earth and those legions of his trained to do his bidding engaging Logos seated on a horse of light, as we remember Judas Maccabeus, and with the troops of light cavalry, as we remember the Jewish soldiers who fought against the idolator Antiochus Epiphanes, Judas who found the Jerusalem church deserted at the command of this tyrant, its gates burned down, weeds growing in the church yards, and rebuilt it so that the worship of God could proceed, Judas who found the Jewish people reduced and forced to worship idols, and raised troops to defend the worship of God in Jerusalem. And the Roman emperor fell and so did every priest to this false god, even those trying magic by his side, and there fell also those deceived whose minds are filled with emperor worship and those who give praise to the statue of the emperor. And the emperor and his false priests were thrown while alive into a lake of fire and burning brimstone[19]. And the rest were killed by the swords of those riding upon the horses of light as the word of the story of God emerged from their mouths. And all were made the a feast to the scavenger birds who ate until they were sated. And I contemplated Peter coming down out of God's homeland holding the key of oblivion and the great chain to it in his hand. And he took Domitian, a snake of the first order,

---

19. The lake of oblivion or "fire and brimstone" is Rome at its Lake Avernus, a lake which was thought to contain fire and emitted sulphurus fumes so deadly that it killed birds flying over it. The Cumean Sibyl, a Roman pagan religious figure, dwelt near it in a grotto. It is referred to in numerous Roman mythic literature including Virgil's Aeneid Book 6, and the writings of Ovid, Lucian, Pliny and many others. In classic literature, both Odysseus and Aeneas entered into oblivion at it.

who deceives and is the child of the very idea of Anti-Godness, and he bound him for reformation into a better immortal moulding. And he cast him into the abyss and locked the gateway out and he placed a seal over him so that he could not deceive any more folk until the very end of the punishment. From time to time in history one like Domitian may seem to be released.

And then I saw seats of power and persons sitting upon them and the authority to judge was given to them, and the souls were those who had been beheaded upon their witnessing Jesus, and living for the story of God's life, and none of them were ones who had given the praise to the Roman Emperor nor his statute nor who had taken his ethic of idol worship. And they were alive and exercising their authority with God's child who had come to earth for a thousand years. The rest of the dead were not alive until the ending time of the thousand years, the time for change from the mortal to immortal, from sexual and angry, ruled by appetites and pains and pleasures, immaturity to maturity, from perishable to imperishable, from imperfect into perfect, from dead to eternal life. Each would be in the first resurrection of the dead. Death has no second hold on them, and they will be ministers of God, the God we know from the earth accounts, and they will rule with each other during this changeover period. And when the end comes of this time, deception will be released from his prison. And he will lead folk astray on every corner of the earth, the God and Magog, to gather them for war, Being of as great a number as the water drops in the sea. And he will fill the wide streets of the earth, and they will surround the encampment of the saints and the city where they are dwelling together in family love, but fire will come down from out of God's homeland and he will be consumed along with them. And the deceiver, the one who misleads them will be cast into the lake of fire and brimstone where also is Nero and the false prophet, Simon Magus, and they burn there day and night forever and forever.

The Faithful Given Entry Into The New Jerusalem

And then I conceived a great seat of light and one sitting upon it. Away from the presence of this one flee the earth and sky and no place for them offers refuge. And I saw the dead, those great and those small, standing before the seat of authority. And a book was opened, and it is the book of life. And the dead are judged from what is written in its pages according to how they acted. And the sea gave up the dead bodies in it, and the earth and Hell gave up the dead in them. And they were judged each according to their actions. And death and Hell were themselves cast into the lake of oblivion. And if anyone was not discovered to be accounted for in the book of life, that one was thrown into the place of oblivion where go those who die without accepting God, even among whole crowds who go streaming into the hereafter who have thwarted others desire to, and refused themselves, to live lives of faith and embodiment of Jesus, mothers and men, the forms with all life spent of the rich and great in life achievements, boys and girls unmarried, and young children laid out in caskets before their parents' eyes- as many disbelievers as leaves that yield their hold on boughs and fall through forests in the early frost of autumn, or as migrating birds from the open sea that darken the sky when the cold season comes and drives them overseas to distant lands. There all stand begging to be across and reach out longing hands to those living in the Family life in God.

Jerusalem

And I saw a new sky and a new earth. And the first sky and the first earth lifted away. And no longer is there a sea. And the holy city of Jerusalem, a new one, I saw, coming down out of the sky from the place God had readied it, a city calling for us and our families to come and enter as did the Jerusalem of old for our Passovers, before it was leveled by Rome, to end there in family feasting and worship of our creator and God our pilgrimage of the pangs of this life in its refuge, an event of love as when, after harried separation, a spouse with his or her beloved are united.

And I heard Jesus, as a thundering voice speaking from the seat of God's homeland, saying, "Yes, it is a shelter of God for people, and there God dwells with them, and God's folk will be there, and God, in person, will be there, and God will personally wipe away every tear from their eyes, and there will be no death any more, nor regret, nor crying, nor will there be suffering or persecution any longer, for the past will have gone away."

And God, the one seated in ultimacy said, "Yes, I am making everything new," and tells me, "Write this down, these are words to believe for they are true." And God said to me, "Let it be. I am the A to the Z, the first and the last, eternity. I will give the thirsty to drink from the spring of the water of life, a

tonic which returns the faithful to vigor and innocent vitality. It is the inheritance of any who persevere and who wish to live with me and live as my child. But to those who avoid their duty, or are unfaithful, or do horrible things, or kill, or become predators sexually, or engage in superstition, or idol worship, or all the other false things, or the rest of those things, there is the lake of oblivion, which is a second death." And Moses came to me, one of the deliverers of the cups from which the deliverance strokes were poured out upon the last days and this one talked with me saying, Come, I will show you the bride, the wife of the Lamb, the Christian church, from whom the progeny of those living in the end time are nurtured. And he carried me in my imagination away to a huge towering mountain, Mt. Sinai where God reveals God's self, and pointed out to me the holy city, Jerusalem, coming down out of God's homeland by the act of God, and bearing God's presence, a very star it looked, so cherished, and safe from oppression, where no one need feel fear, nor terror, nor strife, nor any other judgement, since God vindicates all there. There, life is placed in order by God, safeguarded by great and unscalable walls, entered into by twelve gates and upon them, twelve guardian angels, Reuben, Simeon, Levi, Judah, Issachar, Zebulun, Joseph, Benjamin, Gad, Asher, Dan, Naphtali, the children of Jacob, the founders of the twelve tribes of Israel, and guardians of the ideal life, uniting their children into one assembly, and parenting each descendant into love for one another and justice, and away from earthly desire for wealth or self-seeking, And God's family shall dwell safely there and each shall have a house and have a vocation and occupation there and they shall dwell with confidence. And the wall of the city is upheld by twelve foundation stones, and these were named for the twelve apostles of the Lamb, Simon Peter, Andrew, James, Peter's brother, and John and Philip and Bartholomew, and Matthew and Thomas and James, the son of Alphaeus, and Simon the Zealot, and Judas, the son of James, and Matthias, whose missionary activities transfigured anthropos from its human community, into the image of the Real and rule of God embodied in a diversity of every historical churches, comprising a plurality of peoples and cultural traditions, founded upon the life, death, and resurrection of Christ, created by the redemptive presence of God as Spirit, a community in which privatistic, provincial, and hierarchical modes of existence are challenged and are overcome, and in which is fragmentarily actualized at every moment a universal reconciling love that liberates from sin and death, alienation and oppression.

And as Moses talked with me, I realized the similarity of the New Jerusalem with the one prophesied by Ezekiel for the suffering remnant of Israel, exiled and despairing, who were promised it would come again and be restored under the beneficent and caring rod of a shepherd. And the city was once again the city where we had always hoped to be able to re-pilgrimage, only this time in a final, precious and indestructible existence with Jesus physically with us.[20]

And the New Jerusalem will be a better Rome[21] as well, where there is no other sovereignty except as established by God's law, with Greek in agreement with barbarian, civilian with military, all enjoying and participating in peace, prodigious and indescribable prosperity, all accouterments of power, assembled as folk, living in joy each with every needful possession and use of good things public and private, all in plentitude where there is always good fortune with happiness, persons free to worship by altars, oblations, sacrifices, persons Being priests crowned with garlands, all bright and smart cheery faces beaming with goodwill, feasts assembly, musical contests, races, revels, frolics, nightlong with harp and flutes, jollification, unrestrained holiday keeping every kind of pleasure ministered by every sense, rich with no precedence over the poor, distinguished over obscure, creditors not above debtors, nor employers above working folk, where the times give equality before God, prosperity and

---

20. The riddle of New Jerusalem gives the answer of the return of Jesus physically as a human being to once again be with us at the endtime. The parallel is between the three physical Jerusalem temples destroyed - the last of them in 70 A.D. within the memory of the ones "honing" Revelation - and the promise of Jesus that his physical body can withstand three days of destruction before his physical resurrection.

21. The answer from the riddle of the "Good Rome" is reintroduced into the text. Rome is taken from the measurements in the Greek text (something of 12,000 stadia) and then its aspects are introduced from Philo's account in Embassy 8-13 as to what the "Good Rome" is really like.

well-being, freedom from grief and fear, joy pervading households and people lasting continuously and without break.

And the New Jerusalem is a place where the apostle's successors in missionary endeavors had multiplied the population which Moses pointed out, he having measured the wall, the cities sheltering outside, at one hundred forty four cubits in human measure, and the material of the wall is jasper, and the city is pure gold in the way that glass is pure. The foundations of the city walls are all constructed of rare stone. The first foundation stone is jasper, the second, sapphire, the third, chalcedon, the fourth, emerald, the fifth, sardonyx, the sixth, sardion, the seventh, chrysolite, the eighth, beryl, the ninth, topaz, the tenth, chrysoprase, the eleventh, jacinth, the twelfth, amethyst, the stones of the twelve tribes of Israel as exemplified on the high priest's breastplate. This convinces me that the city bears the ephod of justice and that the New Jerusalem is a city where the ideal of justice prevails for all of the citizens of the endtime. Every citizen can perform the service to others in the state in which his or her nature is best adapted. All can pursue each's own dream and undertake each's own business. What one has, no one else will take. And no one is jealous of what another has. There is no deprivation of one's best, and all can have and do what is each's own to do and belongs to each's self. And the twelve gates are of twelve pearls. One after the other of the gates is made from a single pearl. All shall be given up by anyone wanting to enter. And the streets of the city are pure gold as would be transparent glass.

And I can not see any church building in it for the Familyhead, God, the all controller is the church of it and the Lamb. And the city has no use for any sun or any moon, because there is shine in it from the presence of God bringing light as God's self, and the lamp of God is the Lamb. And those who seek homes in God's light walk in it, and the rulers of the earth bear allegiance within it, and its gates are not closed daily, because there is no night there, and the gates will open to admit every one God attends to and receives among all the home seeking peoples. But there can never come into it anyone thinking that one is on a par with God or those who deny God or perjure their belief, only those whose names are written in the book of the life of the Lamb.

And Moses pointed out to me a river of living water running as clearly as crystal, borne along from the seat of God and of the Lamb. In the middle of the city's wide streets and its river at every vantage stood a tree of life of immortality giving sustenance, bearing twelve fruits, month after month bearing its fruit, and the leaves of the tree are to heal the sicknesses, anxieties and cares of its residents. And all the hurt in God will no longer suffer there. And the seat of God and of the Lamb will be there and those do service to its tasking. And they shall see God's appearance and the name of God shall identify their ethic. And there will no longer be night, nor will artificial light need to be used, nor sunlight, because the Familyhead, God, gives light to them and they arrange their lives in those rays forever and ever. And Moses said to me, "These are the words, the faith and the truth, and the Familyhead, God of the breath of the prophets, who sent God's angel to show to these followers of God what it is necessary will happen soon. And Yes, I am coming soon." Happy is the one who treasures these stories of the prophets of the former writings.

John Of Patmos Explains His Existential Situation

And I am John of Patmos, the one who heard and saw these things. And after I heard them and saw them, I fell down to praise the feet of the Godly messenger before me who had pointed out these things to me. And he said to "Don't you see? I am a simple follower like you and we among the prophets are your sisters and brothers and also those who adhere to the story of this book." To God belongs the praise. And he told me, "Do not hide these stories of the prophets in this book, for the time is near. One who does wrong, have him do wrong yet a while, and one who is a disgrace, have that one be disgraceful yet a while, but the one who does right, let that one do the things that are right yet a while, and be noticed and have them be attentive yet a while.

And then I heard the voice of Jesus, "I will come quickly and the wages I bring with me I will pay over to each as that one's acts deserve. I am Alpha and Omega, the first and the last, the beginning and the end.

The happy ones wash their clothes in readiness for their wearing under the tree of life and for their entry into the gates into the city. Outside are the dogs and the magicians and the sexually immoral and the murderers and the idol worshipers and all that kind who do wrong.

I myself Jesus sent my friends to witness to you these things for the Godly communities. I myself am the root and of David's race, and the guiding morning star. I am the beckoning future predicted by David and I become stronger to return to earth as faith builds, being more confirmed by every persecution to return to earth. And the spirit of the world and bride say, 'Come.' And the one listening says, 'I will come.' I shall have a world of my progeny with my church. And anyone who thirsts, have that one come, anyone who wishes it, receive the thirst quenching water of the gift of life, a baptism into life in the sky of existence.

I myself am witness to all these quoted statements come from the prophets of the book. And if anyone sets aside the message of this book of these prophecies, God will abandon his or her place before the tree of life from which fruit you may eat and live forever, and from the city of the attended for whom we have written this book."

He tells you, the one whose evidence you take about these things,
    "Yes I come quickly."
Oh Yes! Come, our Familyhead, Jesus.
The love of the Familyhead Jesus, be with you all.

The Birth Of God As A Child In A Time Of Persecution

There appeared to me an ultimate sign in graphic reality as foretold by Amos to mark the time of God's presence on earth in a conception of a child.

Mother Mary, you return to our memory.

Mary, you are the one who we recall clothed as by the sun, wearing its blaze as if radiant with the love of God. You are the one who, like the moon, gave us light to abide the fears of the night. You are the one venerated by the starry presences of the universe, the twelve apostles, the ones who passed down to us the hope and faith by which we live.

And you are pregnant, reduced to crying and straining to give birth.

And there appeared in my mind another sign in graphic reality, a reptile of a man, Herod, fiery in temperament, his authority derived from the seven hills of Rome and as a reptile has a tail so did this one wield the power of Rome at this tail end of Roman authority, and on his head he wore a Roman Senatorial crown.

And, as a reptile swishes its tail in authority, so did Herod exercise his authority and destroyed many of God's children in the exercise of his power, casting them into graves. And Herod, a dragon, made a decision to destroy the baby of the woman giving birth, as would a dragon who eats children.

But a male child was born, a child who would govern all the home-seeking peoples of the world wielding an indestructible shepherd's staff, and the child was bonded to God, and to God's seat of authority.

And the mother fled into the less inhabited region of Egypt where there was a place prepared by God so that there she and her child could be provided for and fed during the days of the child's infancy, while Herod was governor.

And there arose contention in God's homeland, whereby Michael, the protector of God's people, and enforcer of the law of the spirit on earth, and his spiritual police arose to oppose the dragon emulator, Herod, and Herod kept up his war against these spirits along with his henchmen, but without the strength to succeed nor when they died was there any place for them, even yet, in all of God's homeland.

And the great dragon, Herod the Great, the old snake, called Devil and Satan, he who cheated and betrayed his entire province, was buried in the ground and his henchmen were buried after him.

And I heard David in God's homeland singing,
Now comes salvation and ecstasy and the hierarchical time of God
And the time of authority of the one who comes to earth
as God for the contender against our brothers and sisters is buried
There was one who contended for them in the presence of our
    God day and night.
And they overcame him through the blood of the Lamb
And through the story of their own witnesses
And they did not overly value their own lives before death.
Because of this, regard them happy, the ones in
God's homeland.
And those who reside in these places.
Take a deep breath, earth and sea,
Because the devil has been overthrown for you
Holding off his great rage.
Recognize what a short time he had!

But even after the second Herodian dragon emulator, Archelaus, understood why his predecessor Herod the Great had been cast into the ground, he decided to continue the prosecution of the woman who had born the child.

Except that God's deliverance came for flight, as on the two wings of an eagle, which were provided the woman so that she might fly into a safe desert haven where she could bring up the child there for a time and occasions and moments away from the face of the reptilian tormentor.

And this snake spit out the venom of persecution until it welled out as the waters of a river in her view so that she might have been swept away in its current. But the earth itself shouted out a warning to the woman, to keep her distance, and the earth opened its mouth and swallowed the venomous flow of orders for persecution which the Herodian tyrannizer, Archelaus, continued to order.

And the dragon-rulers have remained angry about the escape of the woman and have committed themselves to make war against the remnant belonging to her issue, Jesus, those who keep the law of God, and hold to the witness of Jesus. And one such witness, me, has been washed up on the island of the Patmos seashore of the Mediterranean Sea.

The Situation Of Imperial Blasphemy Dominating The World Which Requires Jesus To Destroy It

And as I looked out into the sea from my island of exile, the Roman Empire comes to mind which I think of as a monster emerging from its depths, the monster, Rome, having had ten emperors following Julius Caesar. I visualize each Emperor as a horn on the monster. I see Rome's seven hills as the monster's heads or capital of the empire. Each emperor claims to be perfect or divine! And upon each one of those hills are blasphemies, statues of emperors as Gods and the like.

And the monster which I saw had the combined imperial aspect of successive empires gone before with the nature of a Persian leopard, and its feet were as that of a Medean bear and mouth was as the mouth of a Babylonian lion.

And the Herodian dragons who ruled Jerusalem gave to this next monster in succession, Rome, total allegiance and received from its seat the totalitarian authority exercised.

And I thought of Gaius Caesar, Caligula, as one of the heads or emperors. We had considered him assassinated, wounded to the point of death but not so. His fatal wound is now deemed healed and he is considered God too. I remember how the entire earth was shocked at this monster.

And God's people were required to pray for their lives to the Herodian dragon who in turn owed allegiance to this monster and God's people were forced to worship the monster saying, "Who could be so glorious as Gaius and who could have the power to oppose him?"

And Gaius, the monster, had been lawgiver, speaking in thunderous

words and blasphemies and authority was given him to rule that way, but only for forty two months. And he couldn't open his mouth without uttering blasphemy to God, and he tried to usurp God's name and tried to turn his residence into the site where God lived, and him being the God in the sky of existence where God lives.

And it was given to an emperor, to undertake war with God's attended ones and to be victorious over them and it was given to this monster authority over every nation and people and language group and home-seeking people.

And I remember how it was with people worshiping this monster, all of them, those who live everywhere on the earth. No! No! let not his name be written in this record of life of the Lamb from the beginning of the world.

If any have ears, listen.
if anyone would be an intimidator,
the intimidation returns back.
If someone engages in killing by a sword
that one is killed by that sword (as Gaius
Caesar, Caligula, was).

In this world there is need for patient endurance and the faith of the God attended ones.

And I saw another monster, Neron Caesar, Nero, coming out from the land, and he had two horns like a ram and he speaks as does a Herodian dragon. And he exercised great authority in the same manner as did Gaius before him, befouling the earth and everyone living in it so that they were in effect worshipping the first monster all over again.

And he did great deeds like bringing fire down from out of the sky to burn his own capital city in front of the whole populace, to destroy Rome. And he misleads the world about this deed and uses it undertake persecution. And he enjoys seeing torture in front of his monstrous eyes. Then he uses this event to convince the Roman citizens all over the empire of the necessity to make an image of him, and making this worship a determinant of who shall be put to the sword and killed or live. And he has attributed to it, this statue of himself, the gift of life, so that this monstrous statute can allegedly speak, and he orders that if there are any who do not worship the monster statute they shall be killed. And he requires everybody, the little people and the powerful people, and those that are rich and those that are poor, and those that are freed and those that are slaves, that they make a mark on their right hands or their heads, and the effect is that if anyone doesn't do it, that they can't even appear in the marketplace, or purchase food there unless they have the mark of the name of the monster or the number of his name. Here is the riddle. The one who wants to confirm who the monster is, let that one add up the number equivalents from the name of the monster, and that calculation is who this person is, and the number of him is six hundred sixty six.[22]

The Saving Memory Of The Lamb Of God Who Will Destroy Rome

And then I saw another vision. There, the Lamb standing upon Mount Zion, and with him the faithful remnant who bear the name of Christians and abide in the name of their parent, which is practiced in their ethical dealings.

And I heard a voice from out of God's homeland as smoothly flowing as torrents of water and as the voice of booming thunder, and the voice which I heard sounded as sweet as that of harpists who play the harp.

And they sang a new song in front of God's throne, and before God's four living presences, and before the elders, and no one has the ability to learn the words of this song unless they are a part of this remnant, bought and paid for from the merchandise of God's folk on earth. These are the ones whose lives were not given the content of homes with spouses, or are not sexually oriented, where it is possible to find refuge. These were the first purchases from among God's people, a first purchase by God and the Lamb, and there isn't anything false that my be found coming out of the throat of any of them. They are innocents.

Three Witness Against Idolatry And Emperor Worship

And I saw in my mind's eye, Nehemiah, as an angel, bearing the ageless scrolls of good news for the ones dwelling on the earth, and for all home seekers and races and language speakers and people, saying in a loud voice, "Fear God and pay attention to God who will come at God's own hour of rightwising, and worship the Maker of Being itself and earth and seas and flowing rivers."

And another, second, angel, Isaiah followed saying, "It has fallen It has fallen. Rome, the preposterous. This city forced all the world's home-seeking peoples to become drunk in frustration on the wine of its immorality." And a third angel, Jeremiah, followed after saying in a commanding voice, "If any worship a Caesar divus, a Monster, or any statue of him and act under this ethic, that one will drink from the wine of the monster claiming to be God, a wine being prepared at full strength for his or her cup of frustration. She or he will be tormented in the fire and in the divine presence before attended agents

---

22. The famous "666." The text reintroduces Nero from the Greek riddle. Neron Caesar (Nero) is the emperor's name in the Greek transliterated into Hebrew numbers as nun (50) resh (200) vav (6) nun (50) (Neron) and qof (100) samekh (60) resh (200) Caesar,

of God and before the Lamb. And the smoke of their agony in the final eternity will rise up and they will not have relief, whether it is day or night, the ones who worship the Monster and his statues or any who deign to accept his law and ethic. Here is the need for patience for those wishing to live holy lives, those who are keeping the law of God and the faith of Jesus.

Preparatory Measures For Entry Into God's End Time Church In The Jerusalem Of The Returning Jesus

And I heard a voice from out of God's place in the sky of existence saying, "Write this down. The favored dead, those who have died into the Family-head's presence, exist at the present time. Yes, the spirit says so, because they will have been given rest from their labors, but their God sponsored activities continue on."

And I reflected and saw, Yes, a bright cloud, as the one which followed God's innocent people during the days of the Exodus, and upon a cloud seated was Moses having upon his head a golden crown, and in his hand a sharp scythe.

And Joel, as another angel, came out of the church sanctuary crying in a loud supplication to the one seated on the cloud, "Apply the scythe and harvest the crop, because the hour has come to harvest. The sappy crop of the earth has dried up." And Joel threw it down to Moses, this one seated upon the cloud upon the earth, which opened the period of harvesting the earth.

And Matthew, another angel, came out from the church in God's homeland to join this one with the sharp scythe. And Elijah, another angel came out from God's very seat of justice, this one having the duty to keep the flame of justice alive, and he called out in a loud voice to the Destroyer, with his sharp edged scythe saying, "Send down your sharp scythe and also pick the grapes from the vines of the earth because the grapes have ripened." And the Destroyer cast down upon the earth his scythe and saw to the gathering of the grapes of the earth and he thrust the produce into the winepress of God's great passion.

And the Destroyer ended the lives of those who oppressed God's people as if the Destroyer were pressing on a winepress outside a city so as to cause blood to emerge out of the winepress and those who sought to impede the liberation of God's people found history well up to destroy them as had the Red Sea[23] pressed up to drown the forces of the Pharaoh up to their horse's bridles in this sea when they presumed to reverse the tide of the Exodus.

A Baptism Of History Into God's Love

And as I contemplated, Yes, there appeared in my mind another striking and extraordinary event in God's homeland, seven angels preparing seven deliverance strokes17 for the last times of history, because God's hurt made it time for letting go.

And I noticed how the baptismal pool into eternity in front of God's seat boiled up to a mixture of spirit and flame, and emerging were those who had won victory over the Roman persecution and from its emperors and Domitian, and they found themselves in the restored life of David's perfected Israel.

And they were singing the hymn Moses sang when God's people were delivered out of bondage, the song of delight in Jesus, the Lamb,

> How much more great and marvelous could be your activity
> Our Familyhead, God, you who control all things?
> Haven't you proved your ways to be conforming and true,
> Ruler of us who want homes?
> Can any not help respect you, our Familyhead?
> And respond when you attend to events?
> Now we owe single allegiance,
> And give praise before you,
> As ones transformed into your imminence.

And after that I saw opening up the inner place of the place allotted to witnesses to God in God's homeland, and Aaron and Moses came out as angels holding seven deliverance strokes, dressed in the shining cloth of innocence, and drawn around their waists were the belts identifying them as missionaries except that they were golden.

And God, in God's every attribute in Reality, gave these delivering angels seven cups filled to the brim with the hurt God felt in that place of time beyond time.

And this inner place in the church was filled with God's presence and energy as if it were full of smoke, and no one could enter into this church until those chosen to be the bearers had let go their deliverance into history.

---

23. The answer to the Greek text's "Red Sea" riddle is referenced in at this point. The text riddle is roughly what is like blood, in a liberation setting came to the bridles of horses, and is about 200 miles long? The answer isthe Red Sea where Pharoah's horsemen following the departing Israelites found their horses awash up to their bridles when the sea closed.

The Pouring Out Of Cups Of God's Hurt At Creation

And I heard a great roaring voice, the church itself, saying to these cup dealing ones, "Go and pour out these seven bowls of God's hurt onto the earth."

Seven Deliverance Strokes Against The Romans To Let Christians Be

And Aaron went out and poured out a cup onto the land, and there was wielded a deliverance stroke18 in the form of a sickness which struck the defiant ones among humanity who bore allegiance to the Roman Empire and gave praise to the statue of the Roman Emperor. The sickness spread from one place to the next until it encompassed the world. The inflicted developed severe headaches. Their eyes became red and inflamed. Their throats and tongue were bloody. They sneezed until the pain dropped down into their chests requiring them to cough, and then retch, the spasms growing more and more severe. Their skin festered into boils, ulcers, and open puss. Clothing had to be shed. Their thirst was unquenchable no matter how much water they drank. Their lives were a constant torment not permitting rest or sleep until they died, usually on the seventh or eighth day in a high fever. If they survived after, their bowels were struck causing diarrhea and death from weakness. Along the way, fingers, toes, privy parts, or eyes were lost. Memory escaped. Many died of neglect for none would try to help them because to do so would cause you to become inflicted. Their worst wound was dejection and despair on learning they had it because they knew what it meant to have it: a lingering baleful death to many but not all. Some recovered.

And then Aaron went out and poured out that one's cup onto the sea, meaning the bodies and the passions of the God opposed, and the seas became bloody as if of death's substance, and all the lives opposed to God's promise to God's people lost their heads in muddled thinking or outright died.

And then Aaron went out and poured out a cup onto the rivers, the very souls of those God opposed, and there was a deliverance stroke cast at them, and they were berated as if becoming bloody. And I heard the voice of that deliverer of the stroke against these souls saying,

> You are right, the one who is of Being itself and who always has
> been, these events are right,
> Because they are just,
> Now comes the manifestation of this world in the blood of the
> God attentive ones and martyrs who poured out their blood in
> persecutions

And their blood is given to the world to drink, The blood of these
    special ones.
And I heard from the place of justice itself say,
Yes, Familyhead, God, one in total control,
These martyrs who shed their blood were ones who were truthful
    and conformed through trial for you.

And then Moses went out and poured out a cup onto the sun, and the sun raged in becquerels by the douse from it, scorching humanity in its flames. And all those who bore cruel hearts toward God's people withered in the great heat, and folk hurled curses at the very name of a God who had the authority over such deliverance strokes and they did not change their ways to give God attendedness.

And then Moses went out and poured out a cup onto the Roman Emperor's seat of authority, and there came down a darkness into the palace, and the persecutors of Christians bit their tongues and they cursed the God of ultimate reality out of their feelings of pain and suffering and on account of their wounds but they did not change their ways for all these acts.

And then Moses went out and poured out a cup onto the River Euphrates, the place of all joy of the soul, and he dried up all comfort in the soul of those who persecuted Christians, so to make way for the tide of coming events from new rulers. And then I saw coming out of the mouth of the personified Roman Empire, and its emperor, and its priestly class, ignorant talk in praise of the three gods of the Capitoline triad, Jupiter, Mars and Quirinius, as lifeless frogs which are soulless, bloodless and cry out with harsh noises. The persecution of Jesus has shaken your temples as well as the whole world until now your temples must quake and fall. This triad, they are the spirits of the dead, without life in God's homeland, imagined to do miracles, who summon the governors of the whole world to make war against Christians in this great era of God the all controlling. See! Jesus comes as does a thief! Satisfied is the one who keeps the watch for this coming and keeps dressed to leave with Jesus, so he won't have to walk away naked, and be seen shamelessly undressed. And Jesus gathers them in the spirit of triumph we remember from the Song of the Judge of Israel, Deborah, who triumphed over God's enemies at Megiddo.

And then both Moses and Aaron went out and poured out their last cup into the air, And a great voice came down from the church from the seat of power saying, "Let it be." And there came lighting and shouts and thunders and earthquakes in multiples, evidencing the imminence of God in the world, so as not to have been experienced ever before by humanity upon the earth, so great were these earthquakes. And this shook the city of Rome and each of the three tribes of Rome, Ramnes, Luceres, and Titienses, and this city of people of all of the world fell into shambles. And Rome, the greatest of all, was brought to mind before the seat of God to be given to drink of the cup of wine of God's hurt. And every heretical church and pagan temple service was dispersed. And there wasn't one of the seven hills left without damage. And huge hailstones, weighing as much as a talent, came raining down out of God's homeland upon humanity, and the God opposed cursed God on account of this deliverance stroke of the hail, which remains a record of immense consequence.

A Vision Of A Drunken, Idol Coddling Woman, Rome, Held Up By A Condemned Emperor

And one of the angels who had delivered the seven cups came and he spoke with me saying, "Come here. I want to point out to you the conviction due the great idolator seated upon the many waters, Rome, with whom the kings of the earth have pandered, and grown intoxicated over, and dwelt with on the earth in drunkenness and idolatry. And he carried me up in my imagination out into the desert. And I saw a woman seated beside a bloody emperor, bloated as with blasphemous idols, having seven heads as does the city of Rome have seven hills and ten horns representing the imperial line of emperors. And the woman was dressed in purple and scarlet and she was arrayed in gold on gold, and a rare, precious stone, with pearls, and holding a golden glass in her hand choked full of idols and in her brain an idol worshiping scheme and ethic labeling her with a secret identity, great Babylon, mother of idols and of horrors done for them on the earth. And I saw that this woman was drunk on the blood of the martyrs and on the witnesses for Jesus. And I was shocked to incredulity when I saw her. And my guide said to me, "Why are you so surprised? I will tell you the secret of this woman and the emperor who is holding her up, she who has these seven heads and ten horns. The emperor who you see used to be an emperor but is no longer one, Nero, and he is about to make his descent into oblivion and go into oblivion. Earth dwellers will wonder what became of him since his name is not written in the book of life kept from the beginning of the world, when they observe this emperor where he will be, he who was but is no longer and stands present as an idol, all of which is known to those who have an understanding of such things. The seven heads are the seven hills of Rome where the woman sits upon them. And there are seven emperors come. The five Claudians have fallen, that one, Nero, was one of them, and another one, Claudius, came after him, and when Nero left after a short reign, it was happenstance that he remained. And there is another emperor who was and is not any longer, and he, Domitian, is the eighth, but is in the line of the other seven, and is heading for the not in God's eternity.

And the ten horns which you see are ten emperors who govern what they seize but they have power as an emperor for only an hour, seizing after a prior emperor. These have a single mind set, and motivation and power, giving them the cast of an animal. These emperors will make war against the Lamb and the Lamb will defeat them, because our Familyhead, Jesus, is the ruler of the family of God's people, and the ruler over rulers, and those who are with Jesus are named by god and selected for family membership and are faithful.

And then he says to me, "The seas which you saw, on which the idol mother was sitting, these are people and crowds and ethnic races and those speaking different languages. And the ten horns which you see also are the hated idol worshipping emperors. And they will strip her and leave her naked and her flesh will be a meal, and they will even burn her down in arson. For God has given it to their hearts to do with her according to God's plan, and to execute this single plan while the gift of governance is under an emperor until Jesus, the logos, the image of God takes over finally, once and for all time. And the city which you saw is the huge city of Rome, where lives the emperor over the rulers of the earth.

A Song Of The Fall Of Rome By Isaiah, Jeremiah And Ezekiel

After these things happened, I envisioned three angels from God, Isaiah, Jeremiah, and Ezekiel, coming down out of God's homeland having a great tiding, and the earth was emblazoned by their God attendedness. And they cried out in the full strength of their voices, singing,

It falls! Mighty Rome! It falls!
Now it is an abandoned graveyard!
Now be watchful, everyone, for its stinking spirit,
and be watchful everyone for the stinking scavenger birds,
And be watchful everyone for the stink of an emperor and his
    remembrance.
Here the result of the wine of God's hurt over her idols
Drink this wine, you, now homeless ones!
And you kings and governors of the earth who took her idols with
    her rule!
and you merchants of the earth who grew rich from the explosion
    in luxurious living!
And I heard another voice from God's homeland singing, Get out
    of there, my people!
So that you won't have to share in their acts which separated them
    from God.

And from these deliverance strokes!
So that you won't have to receive their brunt! For their stupid acts
    have caused God to cleave them
from God's love, even out of God's homeland,
And God remembers her acts of injustice. Pay for her as she is
    worth!
and twice the amount according to her acts! In the cup in which
    she mixes her wine, let her pour her
drink out in a double helping!
For so her glory deserves and her life of overabundance and
    luxury.
Just that much pain and sorrow give her!
Because she says, I am the Reigning Empress
And what do I care!
How could I ever suffer!
So, in a single day, here come these deliverance strokes for her!
Death and suffering and famine,
And in a fire she will find herself consumed!
Because there is ultimacy in the power of the
Familyhead, God, the one who convicts her!

And they will cry out and mourn her, the kings and governors of the earth
who idolize her and live in the orbit of her wealth, for how can they help but
see the ashes from her burning, even taking what distance they can from the
blaze, for fear that they may have to suffer also, saying,

Too bad! Too bad!, such a magnificent city, Rome,
  And so powerful a city too!
  That in a single hour, judgment was passed on you!

And the merchants of the earth are crying out and feeling sympathy for her
because their cargo can no longer be sold there, not any of the cargo of gold,
or silver or precious stone, or pearls or fine linen or purple or silk or scarlet dye
or any of the scented wood, or any of the ships full of ivory, or ships full of
valuable lumber, or copper or iron, or marble or cinnamon, or spices or incense, or ointment, or nutmeg or frankincense, wine or olive oil or fine wheat
flour or grain or cattle or sheep or horses or chariots or the bodies and souls of
humanity. And the benefit from all the desires of your soul shall slip away from
you and all the luxury and the radiance of your appearance shall be stripped
away from you.

And no one can recover them from where they have gone.

These merchants, the ones who grew rich from her standing away from her afar because they fear they might have to share her suffering are calling out and groaning, saying,

> Too bad! Too bad! Such a magnificent city, Rome,
> dressed in linen and purple and scarlet and she was
> arrayed in gold on gold, and a rare, precious stone,
> with pearl, because in a single hour so much of her
> wealth was destroyed.

And every ship captain and every one who sails any place or sails at all or so many as trade by sea routes, from far away, stand back they cry out when they see the ashes of her fire commiserating:

What can ever be like this magnificent city? And they brush off the soot from their heads and cry out bewailing and groaning, saying:

> Too bad! Too bad! Such a magnificent city, Rome,
> Everyone who had a boat in the sea was made rich by her
>   extravagance,
> And now in a single hour she is worthless.
> God's homeland, yes,
> And the ones who are God attended and the apostles and the
>   prophets,
> You too!
> Be pleased,
> Because God has judged the crime again you committed by her.

And a powerful agent of God's hurt lifted up a stone larger than the largest millstone and threw it down into the sea, saying,

> Just so violently will be you thrown down
> Rome, you great city!
> And no one will ever be able to discover you.
> And the sound of harpists and musicians
> And flutists and horn players, may never be heard in you again.
> And no worker of any line of work may any longer be found in
>   you,
> Nor any sound of a millstone may any longer be heard in you.
> Nor the light of any lamp ever more appear in you.

nor the voice of a bridegroom or bride ever more be heard in you
Because So what if your merchants were the greatest of earth
dwellers!
Because in your magic all the home seeking peoples were
deceived,
Because in her was found the blood of the prophets and attended
ones and all of those who suffered martyrdom upon the earth.

Then I heard as if from a loud voice coming out of a large crowd in God's home, saying,

Alleluia the savior and the attender and the strength of our God tells the truth and does right and exercises God's justice. He condemns this great idolizer, Rome, wherever she misleads any on earth in her idol worshiping and he spills blood on behalf of God's followers with an avenging hand.

And so, again, let it always be said,

Alleluia for the smoke arises into the timeless air. And the twenty four folk course helpers at the throne and the four attributes of God and those who were praising God seated upon the elevated seat, continue saying,

Yes!
Alleluia, And a voice from the throne emerged saying,
Praise to our God
And all of God's helpers
and all those who respect God as one would a parent,
The least and the most.

A Choice Of Attendance At A Feast In A New Jerusalem

And I heard a sound as if it was from a tumultuous crowd, sounding as the roar of poured water, and released clapping thunder saying:

Alleluia
How comforting to know how our Familyhead rules.
Our God is the controller over everything.
Our joy and feelings of tenderness fill our lives
When we are permitted to give God every attention
God, you give us this reality,
The invitation to a marriage feast of yourself come to earth,
You invite us through those who tell the story of your earthly life
as by hornblast,
Some will not come,

Some want no feast of your companionship and go on their ways,

These deride your life, on earth and in God's homeland,

And abuse and kill the ones who bring them invitation,

And your army comes, and there is frustration on the earth, as in
  your feel for your creation,

And justice requires you take their lives and burn their cities,

But your wedding is not to be delayed, despite it all,

Your bride, this creation, has prepared herself,

Wearing the fine linen of innocence, the hand weaving of martyrs
  and missionaries and attenders to God.

You send forth new invitations, your wedding will go forth,

Your celebration of the life with the creation who wish to share
  your joy,

So now those who are in the streets, the homeless home seekers,
  those who have had no fulsome meals, whose life plates were
  empty,

Those who are bad and good,

These you invite to the celebration feast laid o with every
  sufficiency,

And all come shaking off the dust of the streets and their lives,
  except that one came only to eat and not to praise the event,

And he was removed and thrown out of the hall,

And he cursed his situation, as he departed God's homeland ,

For many are invited, but few are selected.

And God has me this to do, telling me, "Write this down." These happy
ones at the marriage feast of the Lamb call you. And he tells me.

I tell you the truthful word of God.

And I fell down at the feet of this one who brought me this message thinking to praise the inviter. But he says to me. "Don't you see! I am only your fellow worker and your brother and sister who keeps the witness of Jesus. I give
praise to God. The spirit of the prophets is the witness of Jesus."

Logos, The Story Of The Life Of God, Crushes Oppressive Govern-
ments And Every Opposed Life Story

And I saw the skies of existence opening, and Yes! there is a horse, coming
down as light, and the one seated upon it is Faith and Truth in bodily form.
And this one is charged to conformed the world to the story of God's life, given
to judge and wage war. The eyes of this one are as dancing flames, and it has
an authority self directed, but the name of this one is Logos, the Story of God's

Life on Earth. And behind Logos, others followed after, From among the anxious ones in God's homeland, also coming after on horses of light, and wearing the white linen of the innocent.

And the story of God came forth from each breath and would a sharp sword striking down the rebellious. Logos let it be known that the new rule would be by metal rod.

And Logos was as one who treads the winepress of God's hurt from frustration over creation, on the behalf of God, the all controlling, and logos is dressed to get the job done, clothes emblazoned, Ruler over rulers, Familyhead over all other Familyheads. And I saw Ezekiel standing as if on the sun and he was crying out in a loud voice instructing all the scavenger birds of the air to gather in mid-day, "Assemble for the great feast of God. So that you may feed on the discard flesh of the ruler's feast, the flesh of Roman tribunes and officers, the flesh of the powerful ones, the flesh from the work of the horsemen on the horses of light, the flesh of those who are freed persons and from the enslaved, the small and the mighty."

The Judgment Due Oppressors Of God's Children

And I saw the Roman emperor and the governors of the earth and those legions of his trained to do his bidding engaging Logos seated on a horse of light, as we remember Judas Maccabeus, and with the troops of light cavalry, as we remember the Jewish soldiers who fought against the idolator Antiochus Epiphanes, Judas who found the Jerusalem church deserted at the command of this tyrant, its gates burned down, weeds growing in the church yards, and

rebuilt it so that the worship of God could proceed, Judas who found the Jewish people reduced and forced to worship idols, and raised troops to defend the worship of God in Jerusalem. And the Roman emperor fell and so did every priest to this false god, even those trying magic by his side, and there fell also those deceived whose minds are filled with emperor worship and those who give praise to the statue of the emperor. And the emperor and his false priests were thrown while alive into a lake of fire and burning brimstone19. And the rest were killed by the swords of those riding upon the horses of light as the word of the story of God emerged from their mouths. And all were made the a feast to the scavenger birds who ate until they were sated. And I contemplated Peter coming down out of God's homeland holding the key of oblivion and the great chain to it in his hand. And he took Domitian, a snake of the first order, who deceives and is the child of the very idea of Anti-Godness, and he bound him for reformation into a better immortal moulding. And he cast him into the abyss and locked the gateway out and he placed a seal over him so that he could not deceive any more folk until the very end of the punishment. From time to time in history one like Domitian may seem to be released.

And then I saw seats of power and persons sitting upon them and the authority to judge was given to them, and the souls were those who had been beheaded upon their witnessing Jesus, and living for the story of God's life, and none of them were ones who had given the praise to the Roman Emperor nor his statute nor who had taken his ethic of idol worship. And they were alive and exercising their authority with God's child who had come to earth for a thousand years. The rest of the dead were not alive until the ending time of the thousand years, the time for change from the mortal to immortal, from sexual and angry, ruled by appetites and pains and pleasures, immaturity to maturity, from perishable to imperishable, from imperfect into perfect, from dead to eternal life. Each would be in the first resurrection of the dead. Death has no second hold on them, and they will be ministers of God, the God we know from the earth accounts, and they will rule with each other during this changeover period. And when the end comes of this time, deception will be released from his prison. And he will lead folk astray on every corner of the earth, the God and Magog, to gather them for war, Being of as great a number as the water drops in the sea. And he will fill the wide streets of the earth, and they will surround the encampment of the saints and the city where they are dwelling together in family love, but fire will come down from out of God's homeland and he will be consumed along with them. And the deceiver, the one who misleads them will be cast into the lake of fire and brimstone where also is Nero and the false prophet, Simon Magus, and they burn there day and night forever and forever.

The Faithful Given Entry Into The New Jerusalem

And then I conceived a great seat of light and one sitting upon it. Away from the presence of this one flee the earth and sky and no place for them offers refuge. And I saw the dead, those great and those small, standing before the seat of authority. And a book was opened, and it is the book of life. And the dead are judged from what is written in its pages according to how they acted. And the sea gave up the dead bodies in it, and the earth and Hell gave up the dead in them. And they were judged each according to their actions. And death and Hell were themselves cast into the lake of oblivion. And if anyone was not discovered to be accounted for in the book of life, that one was thrown into the place of oblivion where go those who die without accepting God, even among whole crowds who go streaming into the hereafter who have thwarted others desire to, and refused themselves, to live lives of faith and embodiment of Jesus, mothers and men, the forms with all life spent of the rich and great in life achievements, boys and girls unmarried, and young children laid out in caskets before their parents' eyes- as many disbelievers as leaves that yield their hold on boughs and fall through forests in the early frost of autumn, or as migrating birds from the open sea that darken the sky when the cold season comes and drives them overseas to distant lands. There all stand begging to be across and reach out longing hands to those living in the Family life in God.

Jerusalem

And I saw a new sky and a new earth. And the first sky and the first earth lifted away. And no longer is there a sea. And the holy city of Jerusalem, a new one, I saw, coming down out of the sky from the place God had readied it, a city calling for us and our families to come and enter as did the Jerusalem of old for our Passovers, before it was leveled by Rome, to end there in family feasting and worship of our creator and God our pilgrimage of the pangs of this life in its refuge, an event of love as when, after harried separation, a spouse with his or her beloved are united.

And I heard Jesus, as a thundering voice speaking from the seat of God's homeland, saying, "Yes, it is a shelter of God for people, and there God dwells with them, and God's folk will be there, and God, in person, will be there, and God will personally wipe away every tear from their eyes, and there will be no death any more, nor regret, nor crying, nor will there be suffering or persecution any longer, for the past will have gone away."

And God, the one seated in ultimacy said, "Yes, I am making everything new," and tells me, "Write this down, these are words to believe for they are true." And God said to me, "Let it be. I am the A to the Z, the first and the last, eternity. I will give the thirsty to drink from the spring of the water of life, a tonic which returns the faithful to vigor and innocent vitality. It is the inheritance of any who persevere and who wish to live with me and live as my child. But to those who avoid their duty, or are unfaithful, or do horrible things, or kill, or become predators sexually, or engage in superstition, or idol worship, or all the other false things, or the rest of those things, there is the lake of oblivion, which is a second death." And Moses came to me, one of the deliverers of the cups from which the deliverance strokes were poured out upon the last days and this one talked with me saying, Come, I will show you the bride, the wife of the Lamb, the Christian church, from whom the progeny of those living in the end time are nurtured. And he carried me in my imagination away to a huge towering mountain, Mt. Sinai where God reveals God's self, and pointed out to me the holy city, Jerusalem, coming down out of God's homeland by the act of God, and bearing God's presence, a very star it looked, so cherished, and safe from oppression, where no one need feel fear, nor terror, nor strife, nor any other judgement, since God vindicates all there. There, life is placed in order by God, safeguarded by great and unscalable walls, entered into by twelve gates and upon them, twelve guardian angels, Reuben, Simeon, Levi, Judah, Issachar, Zebulun, Joseph, Benjamin, Gad, Asher, Dan, Naphtali, the children of Jacob, the founders of the twelve tribes of Israel, and guardians of the ideal life, uniting their children into one assembly, and parenting each descendant into love for one another and justice, and away from earthly desire for wealth or self-seeking, And God's family shall dwell safely there and each shall have a house and have a vocation and occupation there and they shall dwell with confidence. And the wall of the city is upheld by twelve foundation stones, and these were named for the twelve apostles of the Lamb, Simon Peter, Andrew, James, Peter's brother, and John and Philip and Bartholomew, and Matthew and Thomas and James, the son of Alphaeus, and Simon the Zealot, and Judas, the son of James, and Matthias,

whose missionary activities transfigured anthropos from its human community, into the image of the Real and rule of God embodied in a diversity of every historical churches, comprising a plurality of peoples and cultural traditions, founded upon the life, death, and resurrection of Christ, created by the redemptive presence of God as Spirit, a community in which privatistic, provincial, and hierarchical modes of existence are challenged and are overcome, and in which is fragmentarily actualized at every moment a universal reconciling love that liberates from sin and death, alienation and oppression.

And as Moses talked with me, I realized the similarity of the New Jerusalem with the one prophesied by Ezekiel for the suffering remnant of Israel, exiled and despairing, who were promised it would come again and be restored under the beneficent and caring rod of a shepherd. And the city was once again the city where we had always hoped to be able to re-pilgrimage, only this time in a final, precious and indestructible existence with Jesus physically with us.20

And the New Jerusalem will be a better Rome21 as well, where there is no other sovereignty except as established by God's law, with Greek in agreement with barbarian, civilian with military, all enjoying and participating in peace, prodigious and indescribable prosperity, all accouterments of power, assembled as folk, living in joy each with every needful possession and use of good things public and private, all in plentitude where there is always good fortune

with happiness, persons free to worship by altars, oblations, sacrifices, persons Being priests crowned with garlands, all bright and smart cheery faces beaming with goodwill, feasts assembly, musical contests, races, revels, frolics, night-long with harp and flutes, jollification, unrestrained holiday keeping every kind of pleasure ministered by every sense, rich with no precedence over the poor, distinguished over obscure, creditors not above debtors, nor employers above working folk, where the times give equality before God, prosperity and well-being, freedom from grief and fear, joy pervading households and people lasting continuously and without break.

And the New Jerusalem is a place where the apostle's successors in missionary endeavors had multiplied the population which Moses pointed out, he having measured the wall, the cities sheltering outside, at one hundred forty four cubits in human measure, and the material of the wall is jasper, and the city is pure gold in the way that glass is pure. The foundations of the city walls are all constructed of rare stone. The first foundation stone is jasper, the second, sapphire, the third, chalcedon, the fourth, emerald, the fifth, sardonyx, the sixth, sardion, the seventh, chrysolite, the eighth, beryl, the ninth, topaz, the tenth, chrysoprase, the eleventh, jacinth, the twelfth, amethyst, the stones of the twelve tribes of Israel as exemplified on the high priest's breastplate. This convinces me that the city bears the ephod of justice and that the New Jerusalem is a city where the ideal of justice prevails for all of the citizens of the end-time. Every citizen can perform the service to others in the state in which his or her nature is best adapted. All can pursue each's own dream and undertake each's own business. What one has, no one else will take. And no one is jealous of what another has. There is no deprivation of one's best, and all can have and do what is each's own to do and belongs to each's self. And the twelve gates are of twelve pearls. One after the other of the gates is made from a single pearl. All shall be given up by anyone wanting to enter. And the streets of the city are pure gold as would be transparent glass.

And I can not see any church building in it for the Familyhead, God, the all controller is the church of it and the Lamb. And the city has no use for any sun or any moon, because there is shine in it from the presence of God bringing light as God's self, and the lamp of God is the Lamb. And those who seek homes in God's light walk in it, and the rulers of the earth bear allegiance within it, and its gates are not closed daily, because there is no night there, and the gates will open to admit every one God attends to and receives among all the home seeking peoples. But there can never come into it anyone thinking that one is on a par with God or those who deny God or perjure their belief, only those whose names are written in the book of the life of the Lamb.

And Moses pointed out to me a river of living water running as clearly as crystal, borne along from the seat of God and of the Lamb. In the middle of the city's wide streets and its river at every vantage stood a tree of life of immortality giving sustenance, bearing twelve fruits, month after month bearing its fruit, and the leaves of the tree are to heal the sicknesses, anxieties and cares of its residents. And all the hurt in God will no longer suffer there. And the seat of God and of the Lamb will be there and those do service to its tasking. And they shall see God's appearance and the name of God shall identify their ethic. And there will no longer be night, nor will artificial light need to be used, nor sunlight, because the Familyhead, God, gives light to them and they arrange their lives in those rays forever and ever. And Moses said to me, "These are the words, the faith and the truth, and the Familyhead, God of the breath of the prophets, who sent God's angel to show to these followers of God what it is necessary will happen soon. And Yes, I am coming soon." Happy is the one who treasures these tories of the prophets of the former writings.

John Of Patmos Explains His Existential Situation

And I am John of Patmos, the one who heard and saw these things. And after I heard them and saw them, I fell down to praise the feet of the Godly messenger before me who had pointed out these things to me. And he said to "Don't you see? I am a simple follower like you and we among the prophets are your sisters and brothers and also those who adhere to the story of this book." To God belongs the praise. And he told me, "Do not hide these stories of the prophets in this book, for the time is near. One who does wrong, have him do

wrong yet a while, and one who is a disgrace, have that one be disgraceful yet a while, but the one who does right, let that one do the things that are right yet a while, and be noticed and have them be attentive yet a while.

And then I heard the voice of Jesus, "I will come quickly and the wages I bring with me I will pay over to each as that one's acts deserve. I am Alpha and Omega, the first and the last, the beginning and the end.

The happy ones wash their clothes in readiness for their wearing under the tree of life and for their entry into the gates into the city. Outside are the dogs and the magicians and the sexually immoral and the murderers and the idol worshipers and all that kind who do wrong.

I myself Jesus sent my friends to witness to you these things for the Godly communities. I myself am the root and of David's race, and the guiding morning star. I am the beckoning future predicted by David and I become stronger to return to earth as faith builds, being more confirmed by every persecution to return to earth. And the spirit of the world and bride say, `Come.' And the one listening says, `I will come.' I shall have a world of my progeny with my church. And anyone who thirsts, have that one come, anyone who wishes it, receive the thirst quenching water of the gift of life, a baptism into life in the sky of existence.

I myself am witness to all these quoted statements come from the prophets of the book. And if anyone sets aside the message of this book of these prophecies, God will abandon his or her place before the tree of life from which fruit you may eat and live forever, and from the city of the attended for whom we have written this book."

He tells you, the one whose evidence you take about these things, "Yes I come quickly."

Oh Yes! Come, our Familyhead, Jesus.

The love of the Familyhead Jesus, be with you all.

15. The famous "666." The text reintroduces Nero from the Greek riddle. Neron Caesar (Nero) is the emperor's name in the Greek transliterated into Hebrew numbers as nun (50) resh (200) vav (6) nun (50) (Neron) and qof (100) samekh (60) resh (200) Caesar, 16. The answer to the Greek text's "Red Sea" riddle is referenced in at this point. The text riddle is roughly what is like blood, in a liberation setting came to the bridles of horses, and is about 200 miles long? The answer is the Red Sea where Pharoah's horsemen following the departing Israelites found their horses awash up to their bridles when the sea closed. 17. These compare with the plagues by which the Hebrews were assisted by God in becoming liberated from the Egyptian Pharoah's persecution. The Hellenists knew of these intimately from the writings of Josephus, "Antiquities of the Jews," Chap.13. 18. This particular deliverance stroke comes from

reference to Thucydides where a great sickness struck Athens during the second year of the Peloponnesian War. The riddle of elkos and plege in the Greek get us to this reference. 19. The lake of oblivion or "fire and brimstone" is Rome at its Lake Avernus, a lake which was thought to contain fire and emitted sulphurus fumes so deadly that it killed birds flying over it. The Cumean Sibyl, a Roman pagan religious figure, dwelt near it in a grotto. It is referred to in numerous Roman mythic literature including Virgil's Aeneid Book 6, and the writings of Ovid, Lucian, Pliny and many others. In classic literature, both Odysseus and Aeneas entered into oblivion at it. 20. The riddle of New Jerusalem gives the answer of the return of Jesus physically as a human being to once again be with us at the endtime. The parallel is between the three physical Jerusalem temples destroyed - the last of them in 70 A.D. within the memory of the ones "honing" Revelation - and the promise of Jesus that his physical body can withstand three days of destruction before his physical resurrection. 21. The answer from the riddle of the "Good Rome" is reintroduced into the text. Rome is taken from the measurements in the Greek text (something of 12,000 stadia) and then its aspects are introduced from Philo's account in Embassy 8-13 as to what the "Good Rome" is really like.

Daily Spiritual Discipline

(An expanded version of Abraham Lincoln's "vestpocket devotional"
originally called *Believers Daily Treasure*. The Religious Tract Society: Londen, 1852)

January

Day 1   GOD'S LOVE. In this was manifested the love of God toward us - because God
sent God's only begotten child into the world that we might live through
Jesus. JOHN.

> *Pause, my soul, adore and wonder.*
> *Ask, "Oh, why such love to me?"*
> *Grace has put me in the number*
> *Of the Savior's family.*
> *Hallelujah! It is true!*
> *Thanks eternal God to You.*
> *Now we have a new Familyhead,*
> *Jesus, as the gospels said.*

Day 2   REDEMPTION BY THE BLOOD OF JESUS. This much you know. You were not
redeemed with corruptible things, as silver and gold - but with the precious
blood of the Familyhead, as of a lamb without blemish and without spot.
PETER.

> *Our Familyhead, when we in awesome wonder*
> *Consider all the works Your hands have made,*
> *And see the stars and hear the rolling thunder,*
> *What power to Your child You have displayed.*
> > *How great You are!*
> *Our sins and griefs on this Child were laid.*
> *Jesus meekly bore the mighty load.*
> *Our ransom price was fully paid,*
> *In crucifixion offering to God.*
> > *How great You are!*

Day 3   RENEWAL BY THE BREATHING SPIRIT OF GOD. Not by works of righteousness
which we have done, but according to God's mercy are we saved in a
washing of regeneration and renewal of the Spirit of God's own Breath. TITUS.

> *Vain is every outward rite,*
> *Unless grace be your ransom.*
> *Nothing but your life and light*
> *Can form a soul for heaven.*
> *The way is the way of the cross*
> *There's no other way than this.*
> *I shall never get sight of the gates of light*
> *If the way of the cross I miss.*

Day 4   PARTAKER OF THE DIVINE NATURE. Why are we given exceedingly great and
precious promises? We are partakers of the divine nature by escaping the
corruption that is in the world through lust. PETER.

> *Let's become like children for God.*
> *They are bought with Jesus's blood.*
> *They produce the fruits of grace*
> *In the world of righteousness.*
> > *Jesus took the children on knee*
> > *Saying, "Let them come to me."*
> *Jesus loves God's children, this I know*

> For the gospel tells me so
> Little ones to God belong,
> They are weak but God is strong.
>   Born of God, they hate all sin.
>   God's pure word remains within.

Day 5 JUSTIFIED BEFORE GOD THROUGH JESUS. By Jesus all that believe are justified from all things from which you could not be justified by the law of Moses. LUKE.

> A mighty fortress is our God,
> A bulwark never failing,
> Our present help amid the flood
> Of mortal ills prevailing.
> Did we in our own strength confide
> Our striving would be losing.
> But there is one who takes our side
> This one of God's own choosing.

Day 6 UNITED TO JESUS. I am the vine. You are the branches. Any who abides in me, and I in them, the same brings forth much fruit. Without me you can do nothing. JOHN.

> Familyhead of the vineyard, we adore
> That power and grace divine
> Which plants our wild, our barren souls,
> In Jesus the living Vine.
> Forever there may I abide,
> And from that vital root,
> Have influence spread through every branch,
> To form and feed the fruit.

Day 7 JOINT INHERITANCE WITH JESUS. If children, then heirs, heirs of God and joint-heirs with the Familyhead. Pronounce me, gracious God, your child. PAUL.

> Own me an heir divine.
> I'll pity princes on the throne
> When I can call you mine.
> Scepters and crowns unenvied rise,
> And lose their luster in my eyes.

Day 8 COMPLETION IN JESUS. For in Jesus dwells the fullness of the Godhead bodily. And you are complete in this. PAUL.

> Your saints on earth, and those above
> Join in sweet accord.
> One body all in mutual love
> And you their common Lord.
> Yes, you our body will present
> Before the Parent's face.
> Nor shall a wrinkle or a spot
> Its beauteous form disgrace.

Day 9 JESUS AS OUR ADVOCATE. If any one strays, we have an advocate with the Parent, Jesus, our Familyhead, the righteous one. JOHN.

> Look up, my soul, with cheerful eye.
>   See where the great Redeemer stands -
> Your glorious Advocate on high,

With precious incense in hand.
Jesus sweetens every humble groan,
   And recommends each broken prayer.
Recline your hope on Jesus alone,
   Whose power and love forbid despair.

Day 10 JESUS THE HOPE FOR BELIEVERS. Paul, an apostle of Jesus our Familyhead by the commandment of God our Savior and our leader, Jesus our Familyhead, which is our hope. TIMOTHY.
   Jesus, my Familyhead, look down on me.
   Who else can a lifeline throw?
   Your boundless love shall set me free
   From all my wretchedness and woe.
   Like a shepherd Jesus will guard God's children
   In open arms, Jesus carries them all day long,
   Sound God's praises, Jesus bore our sorrows,
   With love unbounded, wonderful, deep and strong.

Day 11 JESUS, THE LIFE OF THE BELIEVER. When Jesus, who is our life, shall appear then shall we also appear with Jesus in glory. PAUL.
   If my immortal Savior lives,
   Then my eternal life is sure.
   Jesus's word a firm foundation gives.
   Here let me build, and rest secure.
   Here, Oh my soul, your trust repose.
   If Jesus is forever mine
   Not death itself, that last of foes,
   Shall break a union so divine.

Day 12 JESUS, THE PEACE OF THE BELIEVER. Now in our Familyhead Jesus, you who sometime were far off are made close by the blood of Jesus. For Jesus is our peace. PAUL.
   Jesus is our peace - for by that one's blood
   Sinners are reconciled to God.
   Sweet harmony is now restored
   Humanity beloved, and God adored.
   Thus, morning guilds the sky
   And my heart awakening cries,
   Shout, suns and stars of space,
   May Jesus, the Familyhead, be praised!

Day 13 THE RIGHTEOUSNESS OF THE BELIEVER. This is the name whereby the Messiah shall be called, "The Familyhead," our righteousness. JEREMIAH.
   Savior divine, we know your name
   And in that name we trust.
   You are the Familyhead, our righteousness.
   You are Your Israel's boast.
   That spotless robe which you have wrought
   Shall clothe us all around,
   Nor by the piercing eye of God
   One blemish shall be found.

Day 14 THE TEMPLE OF THE SPIRIT. Know you not that your body is the temple of God's Breathing Spirit which is in you, which you have of God? PAUL.
   Creator Spirit! by whose aid

The world's foundations first were laid,
Come, visit every humble mind.
Come, pour your joys on human kind.
From sin and sorrow set us free
And make us temples worthy.

Day 15 SANCTIFIED BY THE SPIRIT. God has from the beginning chosen you to salvation through sanctification of God's very Breath and belief of the truth. PAUL.

Come, breathing Spirit, love divine.
Your cleansing power impart.
Each erring thought and wish refine
That wanders near my heart.
I bid farewell to the way of the world
To walk it nevermore.
Jesus says, "Come," and I seek my home
Where Jesus waits at the open door.

Day 16 UPHELD BY THE SPIRIT. God wants to grant you, according to the riches of God's glory, to be strengthened with might by the Breath of the Spirit of the inner person. PAUL.

Assisted by God's grace,
We will pursue our way,
And hope at last to reach the prize,
Secure in endless day.
Assure my conscience of her part
In the Redeemer's blood,
And bear the witness in my heart
That I am born of God.

Day 17 THE SPIRIT OF ADOPTION RECEIVED. You have not received the spirit of bondage again to fear. No, you have received the Spirit of adoption, whereby we cry, Abba, our Parent. PAUL.

Blessed assurance, Jesus is mine!
Oh, what a foretaste of glory divine!
Heir of salvation, purchase of God,
Born of God's Spirit, Washed in God's blood.
This is my story. This is my song.
Praising my Savior all the day long.
This is my story. This is my song.
Praising my Savior all the day long.

Day 18 COMFORTED BY THE SPIRIT. When the Comforter is come, whom I will send to you from the Parent, even the Spirit of truth, which proceeds from the Parent, the Spirit shall testify of me. JOHN.

In the hour of my distress,
When temptations me oppress,
And when I my sins confess -
Sweet Spirit, comfort me.
Perfect submission, then I can rest.
I and my Savior am happy and blest.
Watching and waiting, looking above
Filled with God's goodness, lost in God's love.

Day 19 SEALED BY THE SPIRIT. Grieve not the Holy Spirit of God's Breathing whereby you are sealed into the day of redemption. PAUL.

Forbid it, our Familyhead, that we
Who from your hands receive
The Spirit's power to make us free,
Should ever that Spirit grieve.
Oh keep our faith alive.
Help us to watch and pray
Lest, by our carelessness, we drive
The sacred Guest away.

Day 20 TAUGHT BY THE SPIRIT. When the Spirit comes, the Spirit of truth, the Breath of God will guide you into all truth. For the Spirit shall not speak of herself, but whatsoever she shall hear, that shall she speak. And she will show you things to come. JOHN.

Sweet peace! A glad and joyous refrain.
My debt was by Jesus paid.
My heart bears no more strain,
Nor needs other foundation laid.
Your inward teachings make me know
The mysteries of redeeming love,
The emptiness of things below,
And excellence of things above.

Day 21 FELLOW-CITIZEN WITH THE SAINTS. Now therefore you are no more strangers and foreigners, but fellow-citizens with the saints, and of the household of God. PAUL.

The kindred links of life are bright,
Yet not so bright as those
In which Jesus's favored friends unite,
And each on each repose.
Where all the hearts in union cling,
With Jesus, the center and the spring.

Day 22 LIVE A LIFE OF FAITH IN JESUS. I am crucified with Jesus. Nevertheless I live, yet not I but Jesus lives in me and the life which I now live in the flesh I live by the faith of the Child of God. PAUL.

Close to the ignominious tree,
Jesus my humbled soul would cleave
Despised and crucified with you,
With Jesus resolved to die and live.
There would I bow my suppliant knee
To join my Familyhead's family.

Day 23 LIVE A LIFE OF CONSECRATION TO GOD. I beg you therefore, brothers and sisters, by the mercies of God, that you present your bodies a living sacrifice, holy, acceptable to God, which is your reasonable duty. PAUL.

Yours, wholly yours, I want to be.
The sacrifice receive -
Made, and preserved and saved for free
To you myself I give.
If you've found in Jesus the friend you need,
If God is loving and true,
If You have found the Savior you need,
Someone else could by needing this too.

Day 24   LIVE A LIFE OF HOPE. Look for the mercy of our Familyhead, Jesus, to eternal life. JUDE.
> *Rejoice in glorious hope.*
> *Jesus, the Judge, shall come.*
> *And take God's servants up*
> *To their eternal home.*
> > *Lift up your heart. Lift you your voice.*
> > *Rejoice, Jesus bids the saints rejoice.*

Day 25   DELIVERY FROM CONDEMNATION. There is now no condemnation to those who are in the Familyhead, Jesus, who walk not after the flesh, but after the Spirit. PAUL.
> *O Love, you bottomless abyss!*
> *My sins are swallowed in your lip.*
> *Covered is my righteousness.*
> *From condemnation's grip.*
> *While Jesus's blood through earth and skies,*
> *Mercy, free boundless mercy! cries.*

Day 26   DELIVERY FROM THE POWER OF THE CHALLENGER. Since then as children are partakers of flesh and blood, Jesus also likewise took part of the same that through death Jesus might destroy the one who holds the power of death, that is, the Spirit of the Challenger. HEBREWS.
> *God leads me, Oh blessed thought!*
> *Oh words with comfort fraught!*
> *Whatever I do, wherever I be*
> *Still it's God's hand that leads me.*
> *When my task on earth is done,*
> *When by Your grace the victory's won,*
> *Even death's cold wave I will not flee*
> *Since God, through Jordan, leads me.*

Day 27   DELIVERY FROM ALL INIQUITY. Let Israel hope in the Familyhead. With the Familyhead there is plenteous redemption. And the Familyhead shall redeem Israel from all iniquities. PSALMS.
> Fixed on this ground will I remain
> Though my heart fail, and flesh decay.
> This anchor shall my soul sustain
> When earth's foundations melt away.
> > Mercy's full power I then shall prove
> > Loved with an everlasting love.

Day 28   DELIVERY FROM ALL ENEMIES. The Familyhead delivered me from my enemies. Yes, You lift me above those that rise up against me. PSALMS.
> *Foes are round us, but we stand*
> *On the borders of our land.*
> *Jesus, God's exalted Child*
> *Bids us undismayed go on.*
> *Onward then we gladly press*
> *Through this earthly wilderness.*

Day 29   ENJOYMENT OF A PRESENT SALVATION. We in time past were not a people, but we now are the people of God who had not obtained mercy, but now have obtained mercy. PETER.
> *When I survey the wondrous cross,*

On which the Prince of glory died,
My richest gain I count but loss,
And pour contempt on all my pride.
Were the whole realm of nature mine,
That were a present far too small.
Love so amazing, so divine,
Demands my soul, my life, my all.

Day 30   PRESERVATION UNTO ETERNAL SALVATION. We are kept by the power of God through faith to salvation ready to be revealed the last time. PETER.

Jesus call us over the tumult
Of our life's wild restless sea.
Day by day the sweet voice sounds,
Saying, "Christian, follow me."
Jesus calls us. By Your mercies
Savior may we hear Your call?
Give our hearts to Your obedience,
Serve and love You best of all.

Day 31   A PILGRIM TO GOD'S HOMELAND. Now they desire a better country, that is, God's Homeland where God is not ashamed to be called God for God has prepared for them a city. HEBREWS.

It's true, we are but strangers
And sojourners below.
Countless snares and dangers
Surround the path we go.
Though painful and distressing,
Yet there's a rest above,
And onward we are pressing
To reach that land of love.

February

Day 1   SUPREME LOVE TO GOD. Familyhead, Sir, what shall I do to inherit eternal life? - And Jesus answered saying, "You shall love the Familyhead, your God, with all your heart and with all your soul, and with all your strength, and with all your mind." LUKE.

In the cross of Jesus I glory,
Towering over the wrecks of time.
All the light of sacred story,
Gathers around Jesus's head sublime.
When the woes of life overtake me,
Hopes deceive and fears annoy,
Never shall the cross forsake me,
Lo! it glows with peace and joy.

Day 2   GRATITUDE TO GOD. And one of the ten lepers, when he saw that he was healed, turned back and with a loud voice praised God. LUKE.

It's midnight. On Olive's brow,
The star is dimmed that lately shone.
It's midnight in the garden now.
The suffering Savior prays alone.
It's midnight and from all removed
The Savior wrestles alone with fears.

> *Even the disciple whom He loved*
> *Heeds not the Teacher's grief and tears.*
> *It's midnight and for others' guilt,*
> *The Familyhead of humanity weeps in blood.*
> *Yet Jesus is not forsaken by God.*

Day 3   OBEDIENCE TO GOD. You were the servants of sin, but you have obeyed from the heart that form of doctrine which was delivered to you. Being then made free from sin, you became the servants of righteousness. PAUL.

> *Love is the fountain whence*
> *All true obedience flows.*
> *The Follower serves the God of love*
> *And loves the God that knows.*
> *Where are trials and temptations?*
> *Where is trouble anywhere?*
> *We can never be discouraged*
> *Taking all to God in prayer.*

Day 4   SUBMISSION TO GOD. We have had parents in the flesh who corrected us, and we gave them reverence. Shall we not much rather be in subjection to the Parent of Spirits, and live? HEBREWS.

> *Oh, let my trembling soul be still,*
> *While darkness veils this mortal eye*
> *And wait your wisdom, your holy will*
> *Wrapped yet in tears and mystery.*
> *I cannot, my Familyhead, your purpose see,*
> *Yet all is well, since You rule me.*

Day 5   FAITH IN JESUS. Whosoever believes that Jesus is the Familyhead is born of God. JOHN.

> *My Familyhead, I believe your word.*
> *I wish to have my soul renewed.*
> *I mourn for sin, and trust the Word*
> *To have it pardoned and subdued.*
> *O may your grace its power display.*
> *Let guilt and death no longer reign.*
> *Save me in your appointed way.*
> *Nor let my humble faith be vain.*

Day 6   LOVE TO JESUS. The one who loves father or mother more than me is not worthy of me. He or she that loves son or daughter more than me is not worthy of me. MATTHEW.

> *Who do I have on earth below?*
> *You, and only you, I see.*
> *Who have I in the Homeland but you?*
> *You are all in all to me.*
> *Be crowned with many crowns!*
> *Lamb upon a throne!*
> *Hark! How the heavenly anthem drowns*
> *All music but its own.*

Day 7   SELF-DENIAL FOR JESUS. If any person will come after me, let that one deny the self and take up the cross daily and follow me. LUKE.

> *Take up your cross, let not its weight*
> *Fill your weak spirit with alarm.*

> *My strength shall bear your spirit up,*
> *And brace your heart, and never your arm.*
> *Take up your cross, and follow me.*
> *Nor think till death to lay it down.*
> *For only the one who bears the cross*
> *May hope to wear the glorious crown.*

DAY 8   CONFESSION OF JESUS. Whoever shall confess that Jesus is the Child of God, God dwells in them, and they follow God. JOHN.

> *This is my Parent's world*
> *And to my listening ears,*
> *All nature sings and round me rights*
> *The music of the spheres.*
> *This is my Parent's world.*
> *Oh, let me never forget*
> *That thought the wrong seems often so strong,*
> *God is the ruler yet.*

Day 9   DEVOTEDNESS TO JESUS. For whether we live, we live to the Familyhead. And whether we die, we die to the Familyhead. Whether we live therefore, or die, we are the Familyhead's. PAUL.

> *My soul and all its powers,*
> *Yours, wholly yours, shall be.*
> *All, all my happy hours*
> *I consecrate in me.*
> *Whatever I have, whatever I am*
> *Shall magnify my Savior's name.*

Day 10   IMITATION OF JESUS. For I have given you an example that you should do as I have done to you. JOHN.

> *Your fair example may I trace,*
> *To teach me what I must pursue.*
> *Make me, by your transforming grace,*
> *My Savior, daily more like you.*
> *Sun of our life, Your quickening ray*
> *Sheds on our path the glow of day.*
> *Star of our hope, Your softened light*
> *Cheers the long watches of the night.*

Day 11   JESUS IS PRECIOUS. Behold, I lay in Zion a chief corner stone, elect, precious: and anyone who believes on Jesus shall not be confounded. To you therefore who believe Jesus is precious. PETER.

> *Jesus, in your transporting name*
> > *What glories meet our eyes!*
> *You are the angel's sweetest them,*
> > *The wonder of the skies.*
> *Oh, may our willing hearts confess*
> > *Your sweet, your gentle sway.*
> *Glad captives of your matchless grace,*
> > *Your righteous rule obey.*

Day 12   POSSESSION OF THE SPIRIT OF THE FAMILYHEAD. You are not in the flesh, but in the Spirit. If so let it be that the Spirit of God's breathing dwell in you. Now if anyone has not the Spirit of Jesus, none of this is owned. PAUL.

> *The Spirit of Abraham Lincoln*

Urges praises to God's name
Who was and is and is to be
And still remains the same!
The Spirit flows free
High surging where it will
In our patriarch's work God spoke of old
And speaks to America still.
God gives eternal life
Implanted in the soul.
God's love will be our strength and stay
While coming ages roll.

Day 13 LED BY THE SPIRIT. For as many as are led by the Spirit of God, they are the children of God. PAUL.

Lead us to holiness - the road
That we must take to dwell with God.
Lead us to Jesus - the living way,
Nor let us from God's pasture stray.
Lead us to God - our final rest
In God's enjoyment to be blest.
Lead us to the Homeland - the seat of bliss
Where pleasure in perfection is.

Day 14 CONVICTION OF SIN. There is no soundness in flesh because of your anger. Neither is there any rest in my bones because of my sin. For my iniquities are gone over my head. As a heavy burden they are too heavy for me. PSALMS.

O, you that hear the prayer of faith,
Will you not save my soul from death,
My soul that rests on you?
I have no refuge of my own,
But fly to what my Familyhead has done
And suffered once for me.

Day 15 REPENTANCE FOR STRAYING. Godly sorrow works repentance to salvation not to be repented of. But the sorrow of the world works death. PAUL.

My lips with shame my sins confess
Against your law, against your grace.
Help! Should your judgments grow severe,
I am condemned, but you are clear.
Author of our new creation,
Let us all Your influence prove.
Make our souls Your habitation
Shed abroad the Savior's love.

Day 16 HATRED TO SIN. Whosoever is born of God does not commit sin. That one's seed remains within. This one cannot sin, because re-born to God. JOHN.

Oh! give me, Familyhead, the tender heart
That trembles at the approach of sin.
A Godly fear of sin impart,
Implant and root it deep within.
On you alone my hope relies.
Beneath the cross I fall.
My Familyhead, my life, my sacrifice,
My Savior, and my all.

Day 17   MORTIFICATION OF SIN. Those who are Jesus's have crucified the flesh with the affections and lusts. PAUL.
> *Great God, assist me through the fight.*
> *Make me triumphant in your might.*
> *You the depressed heart can raise -*
> *The victory mine and mine the praise.*
> *Breathing Spirit, keep us pure.*
> *Grant us Your strength when sins allure.*
> *Our bodies are Your temple, Lord.*
> *Be in thought and act adored.*

Day 18   SELF-RIGHTEOUSNESS RENOUNCED. Yes, doubtless and I count all things but loss for the excellency of the knowledge of Jesus, my Familyhead for whom I have suffered the loss of all things, and do count them but refuse, that I may win Jesus. PAUL.
> *Lord of all being, throned afar,*
> *Your glory flames from sun and star.*
> *Center and soul of every sphere,*
> *Yet to each loving heart how near!*
> *Lord of all life, below, above,*
> *Whose light is truth, whose warmth is love.*
> *Before Your ever-blazing throne,*
> *We ask no luster of our own.*

Day 19   THE WORLD OVERCOME BY FAITH. Whosoever is born of God overcomes the world. This is the victory that overcomes the world, even our faith. JOHN.
> *It is faith that conquers earth and hell*
> > *By a celestial power.*
> *This is the grace that shall prevail*
> > *In the decisive hour.*
> *Hear Jesus, you deaf. God's praise, you dumb.*
> > *Your loosened tongues employ.*
> *You blind, behold the Savior comes,*
> > *And leap, you lame for joy.*

Day 20   NON-CONFORMITY TO THE WORLD. Love not the world, neither the things that are in the world. If any persons loves the world, the love of the Parent is not in them. JOHN.
> *Why should our poor enjoyments here*
> *Be thought so pleasant and so dear*
> *And tempt our hearts astray?*
> *Our brightest joys are fading fast.*
> *The longest life will soon be past.*
> *And if we go to the Homeland at last,*
> *Don't we wish to stay?*

Day 21   SPIRITUAL MINDEDNESS. Those who are after the flesh do mind the things of the flesh, but those who are after the Spirit do the things of the Spirit. PAUL.
> *In heavenly love abiding,*
> *No change my heart shall fear,*
> *And safe is such confiding,*
> *For nothing changes here.*
> *Green pastures are before me,*
> *Which yet I have not seen.*

> *Bright skies will soon be over me,*
> *Where darkest clouds have been.*

Day 22 HOMELAND MINDEDNESS. Our conversation is in God's Homeland from where we look for the Savior, the Familyhead, Jesus. PAUL.
> *Beyond the bounds of time and space*
> *Look forward to that Homeland place,*
> *The saints's secure abode.*
> *On faith's strong eagle pinion rise*
> *And force your passage to the skies.*
> *Strong in the strength of God.*

Day 23 CONSTRAINED BY LOVE. The love of Jesus constrains us because we thus judge that if one died for all, then were all dead, and that Jesus died for all that those who live should not thereafter live to themselves but to Jesus who died for them and rose again. PAUL.
> *Be all my heart, be all my days,*
> *Devoted to your single praise.*
> *And let my glad obedience prove*
> *How much I owe, how much I love.*
> *Jesus, our divine Companion,*
> *By Your lowly humble birth,*
> *You have come to join the workers*
> *Burden-bearers of the earth.*

Day 24 LOVE OF THE TRUTH. We are of God. The one that knows God hears us. The one that is not of God does not hear us. Thereby we know the Spirit of truth and the Spirit of error. JOHN.
> *Order my footsteps by your word,*
> *And make my heart sincere.*
> *Let sin have no dominion, God,*
> *And keep my conscience clear.*
> *When any turn from Zion's way,*
> *(Alas! what numbers do!)*
> *I think I hear my Savior say,*
> *Will you forsake me too?*

Day 25 PERSEVERANCE IN THE TRUTH. They went out from us, but they were not of us. If they had been of us, they would no doubt have continued with us. But they went out that they might be made manifest that they were not all of us. JOHN.
> *Work for the night is coming.*
> *Work through the morning hours.*
> *Work while the dew is sparkling.*
> *Work midst the springing flowers.*
> *Work when the day grows brighter.*
> *Work in the glowing sun.*
> *Work for the night is coming.*
> *Work till the truth is won.*

Day 26 LOVE OF THE GOSPEL. I love your commandments above gold. Yes, above fine gold. PSALMS.
> *Your testimonies are wonderful.*
> *Therefore does my soul keep them.*
> *Here mines of knowledge, love and joy*

> *Are opened to our sight.*
> *Your purest gold without alloy,*
> *And gems divinely bright.*

Day 27   LOVE TO ENEMIES. Love you your enemies and do good, and lend, hoping for nothing in return. Your reward shall be great. You shall be the children of the Highest. God is kind unto the unthankful and to the evil. LUKE.

> *Oh Jesus I have promised.*
> *To serve You till the end.*
> *Be forever near me*
> *My Master and my Friend.*
> *I will not fear the battle*
> *If You are by my side.*
> *Nor wander from the pathway*
> *If You will be my guide.*

Day 28   LOVE TO BROTHERS AND SISTERS. Beloved, let us love one another. Love is of God. Everyone that loves is born of God and knows God. JOHN.

> *Just as I am without one plea*
> *But that Your blood was shed for me.*
> *And that You bid me come to Thee*
> *Oh, Jesus, my Familyhead, I come.*
> *Just as I am and waiting not*
> *To rid my soul of one dark blot.*
> *To You whose blood can cleanse each spot,*
> *O Lamb, of God, I come. I come.*

Day 29   **(Leap Year)**

THE WITNESS OF CONSCIENCE. Hereby we know that we are of the truth and shall assure our hearts before Jesus. Beloved, if our hearts don't condemn us, then we have confidence in God. JOHN.

> *How happy are the new-born race*
> *Partakers of adopting grace!*
> *How pure the bliss they share!*
> *Hid from the world and all its eyes,*
> *Within their hearts the blessing lies*
> *And conscience feels it there.*

MARCH

Day 1   GOD, THE BELIEVER'S SUN AND SHIELD. The Familyhead, God, is a sun and shield. The Familyhead will give grace and glory. No good thing will God withhold from them that walk uprightly. PSALMS.

> *If you are my shield and my sun,*
> *The night is not darkly blue.*
> *Fast as my moments roll on,*
> *They bring me but nearer to you.*
> *My Familyhead, let your grace surround me still,*
> *And like a bulwark prove,*
> *To guard my soul from every ill,*
> *Secured by sovereign love.*

Day 2   GOD, THE PORTION OF THE BELIEVER. God is the strength of my heart, and my portion forever. PSALMS.

> Jesus's boundless grace shall all my need supply
> When streams of creature-comfort cease to flow.
> Should God some inferior good deny,
> It's but a greater blessing to bestow.
> I am coming home. Jesus I am coming home today.
> I have found there's joy in you alone.
> From the path of sin I turn away.
> Nevermore to stray, Jesus, I am coming home.

Day 3   GOD, THE REFUGE OF THE BELIEVER. God is our refuge and strength, a very present help in trouble. Therefore will not we fear, though the earth be removed, and though the mountains be carried into the midst of the sea. PSALMS.

> God is our refuge in distress,
> A present help when dangers press.
> In God undaunted I'll confide,
> Though earth were from her center tossed,
> And mountains in the ocean lost,
> Torn piece-meal by the roaring tide.

Day 4   GOD THE GUIDE OF THE BELIEVER. This God is our God forever and ever. God will be our guide even to death. PSALMS.

> Free from the law, Oh happy condition.
> Jesus has bled and now there's remission.
> Cursed by the law and bruised by the fall
> Grace has redeemed us once and for all.
> Now we are free - there's no condemnation.
> Jesus provides a perfect salvation.
> "Come to me." Oh hear the sweet call.
> Jesus saves us once and for all.

Day 5   GOD, THE GLORY OF THE BELIEVER. You, Familyhead, are a shield for me - my glory and the lifter of my head. PSALMS.

> Must Jesus bear the cross alone,
>   And all the world go free?
> No there's a cross for everyone
>   And there's a cross for me.
> How happy are the saints above,
>   Who once went sorrowing here!
> But now they taste unmingled love
>   And joy without a tear.
> The consecrated cross I'll bear
>   Till death shall set me free,
> And then go home my crown to wear,
>   For there's a cross for me.

Day 6   ALL BLESSINGS THROUGH JESUS. All things are yours, whether Paul, or Apollos, or Cephas, or the world, or life, or death, or things present, or things to come. All are yours and you are Jesus's and Jesus is God's. PAUL.

> I love to tell the story of unseen things above.
> Of Jesus now in glory, of Jesus in God's love.
> I love to tell the story because I know it's true.

It satisfies my longings as nothing else can do.
I love to tell the story for those who know it best
Seem hungering and thirsting to hear it like the rest.
And when in scenes of glory, I sing the new, new song,
It will be the same old story that I have loved so long.

Day 7   ALL BLESSINGS IN JESUS. Blessed be the Parent of our Familyhead, Jesus, who has blessed us with all spiritual blessings in the place of the Homeland of Jesus. PAUL.

> *Oh, the rich depths of love divine!*
> *Of bliss a boundless store!*
> *Dear Savior, let me call you mine,*
> *I cannot wish for more.*
> *Let Jesus's assurance be mine*
> *I nothing want beside.*
> *My soul shall at the fountain live*
> *When all the streams are dried.*

Day 8   PARDON THROUGH JESUS. (It is) Jesus in whom we have redemption through blood, even the forgiveness of sin. PAUL.

> *O Lamb of God, your precious blood*
> *Shall never lose its power*
> *Till all the ransomed church of God*
> *Is saved, to sin no more.*
> *Ever since, by faith, I saw the stream*
> *Your flowing wounds supply,*
> *Redeeming love has been my theme,*
> *And shall be till I die.*

Day 9   JUSTIFICATION THROUGH JESUS. (You are) justified freely by the grace of Jesus through the redemption that is in Jesus, the Familyhead. PAUL.

> *No other righteousness do we need own.*
> *No ransom but Jesus's blood alone.*
> *While on the Parent's name we call*
> *Our faith pleads Jesus as all in all.*

Day 10   RECONCILIATION THROUGH JESUS.   If, when we were enemies, were reconciled to God by the death of God's Child, much more, being reconciled, we shall be saved by that life. PAUL.

> *Let us love, and sing, and wonder.*
> *Let us praise the Savior's name.*
> *Jesus hushed the law's loud thunder.*
> *Jesus quenched Mount Sinai's flame.*
> > *Jesus washed us with blood.*
> > *Jesus brought us nigh to God.*

Day 11   ADOPTION THROUGH JESUS. As many as receive Jesus, to them were given the power to become the children of God, even to those that believe on the name of Jesus. JOHN.

> *Let others boast their ancient line*
> > *In long succession great.*
> *In the proud list, let heroes shine*
> > *And Presidents swell their state.*
> *Descended from the Ruler of Kings*
> > *Each saint a nobler title sings.*

Day 12 REST IN JESUS. Come to me, all you that labor and are heavily laden and I will give you rest. MATTHEW.
> Sowing in the morning. Sowing seeds of kindness.
> Sowing in the noontide and the dewy eve.
> Waiting for the harvest and the time of reaping,
> We shall come rejoicing bringing in the sheaves.
> Sowing in the sunshine. Sowing in the shadows.
> Fearing neither clouds nor winter's chilling breeze.
> By and by the harvest and the labor ended.
> We shall come rejoicing bringing in the sheaves.
> Going forth with weeping, sowing for the Master,
> Through the loss sustained our Spirit often grieves.
> When our weeping is over, God will bid us welcome.
> We will go rejoicing bringing in the sheaves.

Day 13 SAFETY IN JESUS. I give to them eternal life and they shall never perish. Neither shall any person pluck them out of my hand. JOHN.
> "Unnumbered years of bliss
> I to my sheep will give.
> And while my throne unshaken stands
> Shall all my chosen live."
> Enough, my gracious Familyhead,
> Let faith triumphant cry.
> My heart can on this promise live,
> Can with this promise die.

Day 14 STRENGTH THROUGH JESUS. I can do all things through Jesus who strengthens me. PAUL.
> Do not wait until some deed of greatness you can do.
> Do not wait to shed your light afar.
> To the many duties ever near you now be true.
> Brighten the corner where you are.
> Just above are clouded skies that you may help to clear.
> Let not narrow self your way debar.
> Though into one heart alone may fall your song of cheer
> Brighten the corner where you are.
> Here for all your talent you may surely find a need.
> Here reflect the Bright and Morning Star.
> Even from your humble hand the bread of life may feed.
> Brighten the corner where you are.

Day 15 SPIRITUAL FREEDOM THROUGH JESUS. If the Child shall make you free, you shall be free indeed. JOHN.
> Sweet is the freedom Jesus bestows
>   With which the people of God are free.
> It's a liberty no mortal knows
>   Till they the great salvation see.
> Now "Children of God," Oh glorious calling
>   Surely God's grace
> Will keep us from falling,
>   Passing from life to peace.

Day 16   CONSOLATION THROUGH JESUS. Now our Familyhead, Jesus, and God, even our Parent, who loved us has given us everlasting consolation and good hope through grace. PAUL.

> Softly and tenderly Jesus is calling,
> Calling for you and for me.
> See on the portals waiting and watching,
> Watching for you and for me.
> Why should we tarry when Jesus is pleading,
> Pleading for you and for me.
> Why should we linger and heed not the mercies,
> Mercies for you and for me.

Day 17   PEACE WITH GOD THROUGH JESUS. Being justified by faith, we have peace with God through our Familyhead, Jesus. PAUL.

> Onward Christian soldiers, marching as to war
> With the cross of Jesus going on before.
> Jesus the faithful Savior leads against the foe.
> Forward into battle see God's banners go.
> Like a might army moves the Church of God.
> Friends we are treading where the saints have trod.
> We are not divided. All one body we.
> One in hope and doctrine. One in charity.
> Powers and nations may perish. Races rise and wain.
> But the Church of Jesus constant will remain.
> Hell can never against the Church prevail.
> We have God's own promise which can never fail.

Day 18   ACCESS TO GOD THROUGH JESUS. In (Jesus) we have boldness and access with confidence by that faith. PAUL.

> Come boldly to the throne of grace,
>   Where Jesus kindly pleads.
> Our's cannot be a desperate case
>   When Jesus intercedes.
> No fiery vengeance now,
>   Nor burning wrath comes down,
> If justice calls for sinners' blood
>   The Savior sheds God's own.

Day 19   VICTORY THROUGH JESUS. Thanks be to God who gives us the victory through our Familyhead, Jesus. PAUL.

> Thus strong in the Redeemer's strength
> Sin, death and hell we trample down,
> Fight the good fight and win at length,
> Through mercy, an eternal crown.
> You may have wandered far away.
> Do not risk another day.
> Do not turn from God your face
> But today accept God's grace.

Day 20   INDWELLING OF THE SPIRIT. Don't you know that you are the temple of God and that the Spirit of God dwells in you? PAUL.

> Think what Spirit dwells within you.
> Think what Parent's smiles are yours.
> Think that Jesus died to win you.

> *Child of the Homeland, prepare to soar.*
> *Ring the bells! There is joy today.*
> *Souls return from the wild.*
> *Jesus meets them on their way.*
> *Each is reborn as ransomed child.*

Day 21 INTERCESSION OF THE SPIRIT. The Spirit also helps our infirmities. We know not what we should pray for as we ought. But the Spirit itself makes intercession for us with groanings which cannot be uttered. PAUL.

> *Let pure devotions fervor's rise.*
> *Let every hilly feeling glow.*
> *Oh, let the rapture of the skies*
> *Kindle in our cold hearts below.*
> > *Come, vivifying Spirit, come,*
> *And make our hearts your constant home.*
> *Now, the winter is past.*
> *The rain is over and gone.*
> *The flowers appear on the earth.*
> > *The time of singing of birds is come.*

Day 22 SANCTIFICATION BY THE SPIRIT. (You are the) Elect according to the foreknowledge of God, the Parent, through sanctification of the Spirit, to obedience and sprinkling of the blood of Jesus. PETER.

> *Can anything beneath a power divine*
> *The stubborn will subdue?*
> *It's yours, eternal Spirit, yours*
> *To form our hearts anew.*
> *It's yours the passions to recall,*
> *And upwards bid them rise.*
> *And make the scales of error fall*
> *From reason's darkened eyes.*

Day 23 THE FRUITS OF THE SPIRIT. The fruit of the Spirit is love, joy, peace, long-suffering, gentleness, goodness, faith, meekness, temperance. Against such there is no law. PAUL.

> *The glory of the Spring, how sweet!*
> *The newborn life, how glad!*
> *What joy the happy earth to greet*
> *In Springtime raiment clad!*
> *Divine Renewer, You we bless,*
> *For Your great love and power.*
> *And thank You for the loveliness*
> *Expressed in leaf and flower.*

Day 24 INHERITANCE AMONG THE SANCTIFIED. Sisters and brothers, I commend you to God and to the word of God's grace which is able to build you up and to give you an inheritance among all those who are sanctified. LUKE.

> *From earth we shall quickly remove,*
> *And mount to our native abode.*
> *The house of our Parent above,*
> *The palace of angels and God.*
> *Come to Jesus, confession make.*
> *Trust in Jesus day by day.*
> *Come to Jesus pardon take.*

Let Jesus keep you all the way.

Day 25   INCREASE OF GRACE. The righteous shall flourish like the palm tree. Such a one shall grow like a cedar in Lebanon. They shall still bring forth fruit in old age. They shall be fat and flourishing. PSALMS.

> *Our Familyhead, one thing we want,*
> *More holiness grant.*
> *For more of your mind and your image we pant*
> > *While onward we move*
> > *To Canaan above,*
> *Come, fill us with holiness, fill us with love.*

Day 26   PERSEVERING GRACE. The righteous shall hold on their way, and those that have clean hands shall be stronger and stronger. JOB.

> *The righteous, blessed with light divine,*
> *Shall prosper on their way*
> *Brighter and brighter still shall shine,*
> *To glory's perfect day.*

Day 27   CONFIDENCE IN PRAYER. This is the confidence that we have in Jesus, that if we ask anything according to the will of Jesus, it shall be heard. JOHN.

> *The one who for humanity their Surety stood,*
> *And poured on earth precious blood,*
> *Pursues in God's Homeland the mighty plan*
> *The Savior and the friend of humans.*
> *With boldness, therefore, at the throne,*
> *Let us make all our sorrows known*
> *And ask the aid of God's power*
> *To help us in the evil hour.*

Day 28   PRESERVATION IN TROUBLE. In the time of trouble I shall be hid in God's pavilion. In the secret of God's tabernacle shall I be hid. The Familyhead shall set me upon a rock. PSALMS.

> *When I can trust my all with God*
> *In trial's fearful hour -*
> *Bow, all resigned, beneath God's rod,*
> *And bless the sparing power,*
> *A joy springs up amid distress,*
> *A fountain in the wilderness.*

Day 29   ALL THINGS WORK TOGETHER FOR GOOD. We know that all things work together for good to those that love God, to those who are the called according to God's purpose.

> *God will keep God's own anointed.*
> *Nothing shall harm them - none condemn.*
> *All their trials are appointed.*
> *All must work for good to them.*
> > *All shall help them*
> > *To their Homeland diadem.*

Day 30   PEACE OF MIND. You will keep the Familyhead in perfect peace whose mind is stayed on you, because this one will trust in you. ISAIAH.

> *Savior, on earth I covet not*
> *That every woe should cease.*
> *Only, if trouble be my lot,*
> *In you let me have Your peace.*

> *With warmth new life and strength upspring*
> *And plants are new life given.*
> *And let all nature's song to ring*
> *Throughout the earth and heaven.*

Day 31 PEACE IN DEATH. Mark the perfect person and behold the upright. The end of such a person is peace. PSALMS.

> *How blessed the righteous when such dies*
> *When sinks a weary soul to rest!*
> *How mildly beam the closing eyes!*
> *How gently heaves the expiring breast!*
> *Life's labor done, as sinks the clay.*
> *Light from its load the spirit flies.*
> *While God's Homeland and earth combine to say,*
> *"How blessed the righteous when such dies."*

APRIL

Day 1 GOOD WORKS TO BE DONE. These things I will that you affirm constantly, that those who have believed in God might be careful to maintain good works. TITUS.

> *Whatever is noble, pure, refined,*
> *Just, generous, amiable, and kind -*
> *That may my constant thoughts pursue,*
> *That may I love and practice too.*
> *Now the conquerors bring their palms*
> *To the Lamb amidst the throne,*
> *And proclaim in joyful psalms,*
> *Victory through God's cross alone.*

Day 2 GOOD WORKS TO BE DONE TO THE GLORY OF GOD. Whether therefore you eat, or drink, or whatever you do, do all to the glory of God. PAUL.

> *Through Jesus the Just,*
> *Our needs are give.*
> *And we in your goodness trust,*
> *And to your honor live.*
> *To do God's will*
> *Was Jesus's employment and delight*
> *Humility and holy zeal*
> *Shone through divinely bright.*

Day 3 GOOD WORKS TO BE DONE AFTER THE EXAMPLE OF JESUS. One that claims to abide in Jesus ought also so to walk, even as Jesus walked. JOHN.

> *I'll love You in life, I will love You in death.*
> *And praise You as long as You give me breath.*
> *And when the death-dew lies cold on my brow,*
> *If ever I loved you, my Jesus it's now.*
> *In mansions of glory and endless delight,*
> *I'll ever adore You in the Homeland so bright.*
> *I'll sign with the glittering crown on my brow*
> *If ever I loved You, my Jesus it's now.*

Day 4 GOOD WORKS TO BE DONE THROUGH THE GRACE OF JESUS. Now the God of peace make you perfect in every good work to do God's will, working in you that which is pleasing in God's sight, through Jesus our Familyhead to whom be glory for ever and ever. HEBREWS.

> Then shall we do, with pure delight,
> Whatever is pleasing in Your sight
> As vessels of Your richest grace
> Look only to your approving face.
> To You and Your co-equal Child raise
>   The everlasting praise.

Day 5   GOOD WORKS TO BE DONE IN THE NAME OF JESUS. Whatever you do in word or deed, do all in the name of the Familyhead, Jesus, giving thanks to God and our Parent through Jesus. PAUL.

> Whatever I say or do
> Your glory be my aim.
> My offerings all be offered through
> Your ever blessed name.
> Then I'll take a starry crown
> Where the gates swing outward never
> At Jesus's feet I'll lay burden down
> And reign with Jesus forever.

Day 6   IMPROVEMENT OF TIME. Know the time, that now it is high time to awake out of sleep. Now is our salvation nearer than when we believed. PAUL.

> Just a few more days to be filled with praise
> And to tell the old, old story.
> Then when twilight falls and my Savior calls
> I shall go to Jesus in glory.
> The time is short, but who can tell
> How short one's time below may be?
> Today on earth a soul may dwell
> Tomorrow in eternity.

Day 7   IMPROVEMENT OF PRIVILEGES. On good ground are those who, through an honest heart, have heard the word, keep it, and bring forth fruit with patience. LUKE.

> I own not the riches of silver or gold
> Nor the glittering jewels of time,
> But I am content with stories of old,
> For the wealth of God's Homeland is mine.
> Parent of mercies, we have need
> Of Your preparing grace.
> Let the same hand that gives the seed
> Provide a fruitful growing place.

Day 8   IMPROVEMENT OF OPPORTUNITIES. Whatever your hand finds to do, do it with your might. There is no work, nor device, nor knowledge, nor wisdom in the grave where you go. ECCLESIASTES.

> Whatever our hands shall find to do
> Today may we with zeal pursue.
> Seize fleeting moments as they fly,
> And live as we would wish to die.
> God's Spirit is guiding our pilgrimage here,
> God's love-beams from heaven shall shine,
> Through all of life's shadows till God appear

to give us the joys divine.

Day 9 SPIRITUAL DILIGENCE. This one thing I do, forgetting those things which are behind, and reaching forth to those things which are before, I press toward the mark for the prize of the high calling of God in our Familyhead, Jesus. PAUL.

> *A scrip on my back and a staff in my hand*
> *I march on in haste through an enemy's land.*
> *The road may be rough, but cannot be long.*
> *So I'll smooth it with hope and I'll cheer it with song.*

Day 10 ENTIRE CONSECRATION. Neither yield you your members as instruments of unrighteousness to sin, but yield yourselves to God, as those that are alive from the dead, and your members as instruments of righteousness to God. PAUL.

> *Yield to the Familyhead with simple heart*
> *All that you have in every part.*
> *Renounce all strength, but strength divine,*
> *And know God's peace shall then be mine.*
> *No pleasures of Egypt shall draw me away*
> *From the love that comes to me divine.*
> *A legion of angels will carry me home*
> *For no tomb can my spirit confine.*

Day 11 OPEN PROFESSION OF JESUS. Whosoever shall confess me before humanity, that one will I confess also before my Parent who is in the true Homeland. MATTHEW.

> *Should I to gain the world's applause,*
> *Or to escape its harmless frown,*
> *Refuse to countenance Your cause*
> *And make Your people's lot my own*
> > *What shame would fill me in that day*
> > *When You Your glory shall display!*

Day 12 EVIL APPEARANCES TO BE AVOIDED. Abstain from all appearance of evil. PAUL.

> *Our Savior by God's Homeland birth*
> *Calls us to holiness on earth,*
> *Bids us our former follies hate*
> *And from the wicked separate.*
> *We must have holy hearts and hands*
> *And feet that go where God commands.*
> *A holy will to keep God's ways*
> *And holy lips to speak God's praise.*

Day 13 DILIGENCE IN KEEPING THE HEART. Keep your heart with all diligence. Out of it are the issues of life. PROVERBS.

> *What a joy it will be when I wake to see*
> > *God for whom my heart is burning.*
> *Nevermore to sigh. Nevermore to die.*
> > *For that day my heart is yearning.*
> *Your business it is to keep your heart*
> > *Each passion under control.*
> *Nobly ambitious well to rule*
> > *The empire of your soul.*

Day 14   SEARCH THE GOSPELS. Search the gospels. In them you can accept you have
eternal life and they testify of me. JOHN.
> Familyhead, Your teaching grace impart
> That we may not read in vain.
> Write Your precepts on our heart
> Make the truths and doctrine plain.
>> Let the message of Your love
>> Guide us to Your rest above.

Day 15   SECRET PRAYER. You, when you pray, enter into a closet and when you have
shut the door, pray to the Parent in secret. The Parent who sees in secret
places shall reward you openly. MATTHEW.
> Far from the paths of humanity, to You
>> I solemnly retire.
> To see You, who does in secret see,
>> And grant my heart's desire.
> Jesus, Lover of my soul,
>> Let me to your bosom fly,
> While the nearer waters roll,
>> While the tempest still is high.

Day 16   THANKSGIVING. In everything give thanks. This is the will of God in our
Familyhead Jesus concerning you. PAUL.
> When I draw this fleeting breath,
> When my eyes shall close in death,
> When I rise to worlds unknown,
> And behold You on Your throne,
> Plenteous grace with You is found
> For your healing streams abound.

Day 17   MEDITATION. God's delight is in the law of the Familyhead and in that law
God mediates day and night. PSALMS.
> I love in solitude to shed
> The penitential tear
> And all God's promises to plead
> When none but God is near.
> I love to think on mercies past,
> And future good implore.
> And all my cares and sorrows cast
> On God who I adore.

Day 18   SELF-EXAMINATION. Examine yourselves, whether you be in the faith. Prove
your own selves. PAUL.
> At evening to myself I say,
> My soul, what have you gleaned today?
> Your labors how bestowed?
> What have you rightly said or done?
> What grace attained or knowledge won,
> In following after God?

Day 19   IN PROSPERITY BE HUMBLE. For I say, through the grace given to me, to every
man that is among you, not to think yourself more highly that you ought to
think. PAUL.
> Familyhead, if You Your grace impart,
> Poor in spirit, meek in heart,

> *I shall as my Savior be*
> *Rooted in humility.*
> > *Pleased with all that God provides*
> > *Weaned from all the world besides.*

Day 20 IN ADVERSITY TO TRUST GOD. Who is among you who fears the Familyhead, that obeys the voice of God's servant, that walks in darkness and has no light? Let such a one trust in the name of the Familyhead, and stay upon God. ISAIAH.

> *If Providence our comforts shroud,*
> *And dark distresses lower,*
> *Hope paints its rainbow on the cloud*
> *And grace shines through the shower.*
> *Praise to God, immortal praise*
> *For the love that crowns our days.*
> *Bounteous Source of every joy,*
> *Let Your praise our tongues employ.*

Day 21 SELF-GOVERNMENT. One who is slow to anger is better than the mighty, one that rules the spirit within than one who takes a city. PROVERBS.

> *Happy the one whose cautious steps*
> *Still keep the golden mean,*
> *Whose life by gospel rules well formed*
> *Declares a conscience clean.*
> *I hang my helpless soul on the cross*
> *Leave, Oh leave me not alone,*
> *Still support and comfort me*
> *Other refuge have I none.*

Day 22 SELF-DENIAL. All things are lawful for me, but all things are not expedient. All things are lawful for me, but not all things edify. PAUL.

> *Familyhead, ever let me freely yield*
> *What most I prize to be.*
> *Who never has a good withheld*
> *Or can withhold from me.*
> *Your favor all my journey through*
> *You are engage to grant.*
> *What else I want, or think I do*
> *It's better still to want.*

Day 23 CONTENTMENT. Be content with such things as you have. Jesus has said, "I will never leave you, nor forsake you." HEBREWS.

> *Since God has said, "I'll never depart,"*
> > *I'll bind God's promise to my heart*
> *Rejoicing in Jesus's care.*
> *This shall support me while here I live*
> *And, when in glory I arrive,*
> *Will praise God for it there.*

Day 24 PATIENCE. You have need of patience, that, after you have done the will of God, you may receive the promise. HEBREWS.

> *I would submit to all Your will*
> *For You are good and wise.*
> *Let every anxious thought be still,*
> *Nor one faint murmur rise.*

Your love can cheer the darksome gloom,
And bid me wait serene
Till hopes and joys immortal bloom
And brighten all the scene.

Day 25 MEEKNESS. Walk worthy of the vocation wherewith you are called, with all lowliness and meekness, with long suffering, forbearing one another in love. PAUL.

Meekness, humility and love
Through all Your conduct pours.
Oh, may my whole deportment prove
A copy, Jesus, of Yours.
Let the water and the blood
From your wounded side which poured
Be of sin the double cure
Save from wrath and make me pure.

Day 26 TEMPERANCE. Take heed to yourselves, lest at any time your hearts be overcharged with surfeiting, and drunkenness, and cares of this like, and so that day come upon you unawares. LUKE.

The world employs its various snares
Of hopes and pleasures, pains and cares,
And chained to earth I lie.
When shall my fettered powers be free,
And leave these seats of vanity,
And upward learn to fly?

Day 27 GRAVITY AND SINCERITY. In all things show yourselves a pattern of good works, in doctrine showing uncorruptness, gravity, sincerity. TITUS.

Pure may I be, averse to sin,
Just, holy, merciful, and true.
And let Your image formed within,
Shine out in all I speak or do.
Soon will a glorious dawn of peace
Break to our longing eyes.
Song of a mighty victory
Shall reach clear through the skies.

Day 28 WATCHFULNESS. Blessed are those servants, who the Familyhead - upon the return - shall find watching. Verily I say to you, that Jesus shall be gird and give them to sit down to eat and will come forth and serve them. LUKE.

Arm me with jealous care,
As in Your sight to live.
And Oh, Your servant, God, prepare,
A strict account to give.
Help me to watch and pray,
And on Yourself rely.
Assured if I my trust betray
I shall forever die.

Day 29 DILIGENCE IN WORLDLY CALLING. Study to be quiet, and to do your own business, and to work with your own hands as we commanded you. PAUL.

I must go home by way of the cross.
There is no other way but this.
I shall never get sight of the Gates of Light

If the way of the cross I miss.
Amid hourly cares, may love present
Its incense to Your throne.
And while the world our hands employs,
Our hearts be Yours alone.

Day 30 EMINENT HOLINESS: THE DESIRE OF THE BELIEVER. It is not as though I had already attained perfection or were already perfect. I simply follow after Jesus so that I may apprehend that for which I am apprehended by Jesus, the Familyhead. PAUL.

Not through a strategy of folk
Or carnal weapons may
The gates of sin be battered down
And evil swept away.
Oh, for a closer walk with God,
A calm and Homeland frame,
A light to shine upon the road
That leads me to the Lamb!

MAY

Day 1 SHOW FORTH THE PRAISES OF GOD. You are a chosen generation, a royal priesthood, a holy nation, a peculiar people. Show forth the praises of Jesus who has called you out of darkness into marvellous light. PETER.

This is my Parent's world and to my listening ears
All nature sings
And round me rings
The music of the spheres.
This is my Parent's world. The birds their carols raise,
The morning light,
The lily white,
Declare their maker's praise.

Day 2 DEPART FROM ALL INIQUITY. Let everyone that names the Name of the Familyhead depart from iniquity. TIMOTHY.

Faith must obey the Parent's will,
As well as trust God's grace.
A pardoning God is jealous still
For God's own holiness.
Not by your words alone,
But by your actions show
How much from Jesus you have received,
How much to Jesus you owe.

Day 3 STEADFASTNESS IN THE FAITH. Stand fast in the liberty wherewith the Familyhead has made us free, and be not entangled again with the yoke of bondage. PAUL.

From Egypt lately freed
By the Redeemer's face,
A rough and thorny path we tread
In hopes to see God's face.
The flesh dislikes the way,
But faith approves it well.
This only leads to endless day,

All others lead to hell.

Day 4   ZEAL IN DEFENCE OF THE GOSPEL. I exhort you that you should earnestly contend for the faith which was once delivered to the saints. JUDE.

> *In the conquests of your might,*
> *May I loyally delight.*
> *In your ever-spreading reign,*
> *Triumph as my greatest gain.*
> *Make me conscious by this sign,*
> *Gracious Savior, You are mine.*

Day 5   ZEAL FOR GOOD WORKS. Let us consider one another to provoke to love and to good works. HEBREWS.

> *All hail the power of Jesus's name,*
> *Let angels prostrate bend,*
> *Bring forth the royal diadem,*
> *And crown Your Familyhead.*
> *Crown Jesus, you morning stars of light,*
> *Which light the earthly bed,*
> *Hail the strength of Israel's might*
> *And crown Your Familyhead.*

Day 6   ZEAL FOR DIVINE WORSHIP.   Not forsaking the assembling of ourselves together, as the manner of some is, ut exhorting one another, and so much the more as you see the day approaching. HEBREWS.

> *Awake, my soul, awake, my love*
> *The Savior's love pursue*
> *In works which all the saints above*
> *And angels cannot do.*
> *Then I will find a place,*
> *Within the churches of your grace*
> *Till God command my last remove,*
> *To dwell in churches made above!*

Day 7   CONCERN FOR THE PEACE OF THE CHURCH.   Be perfect, be of good comfort, be of one mind, live in peace and the God of love and peace shall be with you. PAUL.

> *Make us of one heart and mind,*
> *Courteous, pitiful, and kind in blend*
> *Lowly, meek in thought and word,*
> *Altogether like our Familyhead.*
> *All must be kept near the cross,*
> *There a precious fountain,*
> *Frees to all a precious stream*
> *Flowing from Calvary's mountain.*

Day 8   CONCERN FOR THE PROSPERITY OF THE CHURCH.   Peace be within your walls and prosperity within for your palaces. PSALMS.

> *For our dear brother's and sister's sake*
> *Zion, we wish you peace.*
> *Prosper, oh! prosper long.*
> *And may your children increase.*
> > *We seek your good, we love the road*
> > *Which leads us to God's blessed abode.*

Day 9 MUTUAL LOVE. Walk in love, as Jesus also has loved us, and has given up life for us an offering and a sacrifice to God for a sweet-smelling savor. PAUL.

> Through the mist of years, I can seem to see
> The church of my childhood days.
> And its memories sweet, so with joy replete,
> Shall live in my heart always.
> Yes, on memory's page, I can see again,
> The church by the side of the road,
> And wherever, I roam, it is guiding me home,
> The church by the side of the road.

Day 10 MUTUAL SUBJECTION. All of you be subject one to another. Be clothed in humility. God resists the proud and gives grace to the humble. PETER.

> Our Familyhead, forever at Your side
> May my place and portion be.
> Strip me of the robe of pride.
> Clothe me with humility.
> Among the saints on earth
> Let mutual love be found,
> Heirs of the same inheritance,
> With mutual blessings crowned.

Day 11 MUTUAL HONOR. Let nothing be done through strife or vanity. In lowliness of mind let each esteem other better than themselves. PAUL.

> Oh, let each esteem a sister or brother
>   Better than one's self to be.
> Let each prefer another,
>   Full of love, from envy free.
> Happy are we,
>   When we all agree.

Day 12 MUTUAL FORBEARANCE. Forbearing one another, and forgiving one another, if anyone has a quarrel against any, even as Jesus forgave you, so also do you. PAUL.

> May we each with each agree,
>   Through Your uniting grace.
> Our gift shall Yours accepted be,
>   Our life be love and praise.
> Make us by Your transforming grace
>   Great Savior, daily more like You.
> Your fair example may we trace
>   To teach us what is good and true.

Day 13 MUTUAL CANDOR. Judge not, that you be not judged. Why gape upon a splinter that is in your friend's eye, but consider not the beam that is in your own eye? MATTHEW.

> Holy, Holy, Holy, Our Familyhead Almighty!
> Early in the morning, our song shall rise to thee!
> Holy, Holy, Holy, Merciful and Mighty,
> God in Three Persons, blessed Trinity.
> Holy, Holy Holy, Though the darkness hides You,
> Though the eye of sinful folks, Your glory may not see,
> Only You are holy. There are none beside You,
> God in Three Persons, blessed Trinity.

Day 14 MUTUAL FORGIVENESS. Be kind one to another, tenderhearted, forgiving one another, even as God for the sake of Jesus has forgiven you. PAUL.

> Is the Familyhead divided? What can part
> The members from the Head?
> Oh, surely those be one in heart
> For whom the Savior bled.
> Live for Jesus a life that is true,
> Striving to please God in all that you do.
> Yielding allegiance, glad-hearted and free,
> This is the pathway of blessing for me.

Day 15 MUTUAL ADMONITION. I myself am persuaded of you, my brothers and sisters, that you are also full of goodness, filled with all knowledge, able also to admonish one another. PAUL.

> Bonds of everlasting love
> Draw our souls in union,
> To our Parent's house above,
> To the saints' communion.
> There may our hopes ascend.
> There may all our labors end.

Day 16 MUTUAL CONSOLATION AND EDIFICATION. Comfort yourselves together and edify one another, even as also you do. PAUL.

> While we journey, let us
> Help each other on the road.
> Foes on every side beset us.
> Snares through all the way are strewed.
> It behooves us
> Each to bear another's load.

Day 17 MUTUAL INTERCESSION. Pray for one another. - The effectual fervent prayer of a righteous person avails much. JAMES.

> Blessed assurance, Jesus is mine!
> Oh, what a fortaste of glory divine!
> Heir of salvation, purchase of God,
> Born of God's Spirit, washed in God's blood.
> Perfect submission, perfect delight.
> Visions of rapture now burst on my sight!
> Angels descending, bring from above,
> Echoes of mercy, whispers of love.
> Perfect submission, all is at rest.
> I in my Savior am happy and blest.
> Watching and waiting, looking above,
> Filled with God's goodness, lost in God's love.

Day 18 UNITY OF SENTIMENT. What we have already attained, let us walk by the same rule. Let us mind the same thing. PAUL.

> Before our Parent's throne
> We pour our ardent prayers.
> Our fears, our hopes, our aims are one -
> Our comforts and our cares.
> Bound of one Familyhead, by common vow
> In one great enterprise,
> One faith, one hope, one center now

> *One common home, the skies.*

Day 19 UNITY OF JUDGMENT. I beg you, sisters and brother, by the name of our Familyhead, Jesus, that you all speak the same thing. Let there also be no divisions among you. Be perfectly jointed together in the same mind and in the same judgment. PAUL.

> *Jesus, subdue our selfish will,*
> *Each to each our tempers suit.*
> *By your modulating skill,*
> *Heart to heart, as lute to lute.*

Day 20 UNITED PRAYER. Where two or three are gathered together in my name, there am I in the midst of them. MATTHEW.

> *There's a garden where Jesus is waiting,*
> *A place that is wondrously fair.*
> *For it glows with the light of God's presence,*
> *It's the beautiful garden of prayer.*
> > *There says the Savior, will I be*
> > *Amidst the little company.*
> *Where two or three with sweet amen,*
> *Obedient to Godly ways*
> *Meet to recount God's acts of grace*
> *And offer solemn prayer and praise,*
> > *There says the Savior, will I be*
> > *Amidst the little company.*

Day 21 UNITED PRAISE. Teach and admonish one another in psalms and hymns and spiritual songs, singing with grace in your hearts to the Familyhead. PAUL.

> *My hope is built on nothing less*
> *Than Jesus's blood and righteousness.*
> *I dare not trust the sweetest frame,*
> *But wholly lean on Jesus's name.*
> *When darkness veils Jesus's lovely face,*
> *I rest on God's unchanging grace.*
> *When all around my soul gives way,*
> *Jesus then is all my hope and stay.*
> *On Jesus, the solid Rock, I stand.*
> *All other ground is sinking sand.*

Day 22 PIOUS CONVERSATION. Let no corrupt communication proceed out of your mouth, but that which is good to the use of edifying, that it may minister grace to the hearers. PAUL.

> *Wherever two or three*
> *Meet, a Christian company,*
> *Grant us Savior to meet with you*
> *Gracious Familyhead hear!*
> *When with friends beloved we stray,*
> *Talking down the closing day,*
> *Savior, meet us on the way,*
> *Gracious Savior hear!*

Day 23 COMPASSION FOR THE WEAK. We that are strong ought to bear the infirmities of the weak, and not to please ourselves. PAUL.

> *When weaker Christians we despise,*
> *We do the great Redeemer wrong*

> *For God, the gracious and the wise,*
> *Receives the feeble with the strong.*
> *Teach us, though in a world of sin,*
> *God's Homeland employment to begin.*
> *To sing our great Redeemer's praise*
> *And love God's name and learn such ways.*

Day 24 COMPASSION FOR THE AFFLICTED. Remember those that are in bonds, as bound with them, and those who suffer adversity, as being yourselves also in the body. HEBREWS.

> *With pity let my breast overflow,*
> *When I behold another's woe,*
> *And bear a sympathizing part,*
> *Whenever I meet a wounded heart.*
> *Awake, my charity, and feed*
> *The hungry soul, and clothe the poor.*
> *In God's Homeland are none in need*
> *There all these duties are no more.*

Day 25 COMPASSION FOR THE POOR. As we have therefore opportunity, let us do good to all people, especially those who are of the household of faith. PAUL.

> *Be not dismayed whatever betide,*
> *Beneath God's wings of love abide.*
> *Through days of toil when the heart does fail,*
> *When dangers fierce your path assail,*
> *All you may need God will provide.*
> *Nothing you ask will be denied.*
> *No matter what may be the test,*
> *Lean, weary one, upon Jesus's breast.*

Day 26 COMPASSION TO THOSE WHO HAVE ERRED. Sisters and brothers, if a person is overtaken in a fault, you who are spiritual, restore such a one in the spirit of meekness, considering yourself, lest you also be tempted. PAUL.

> *Familyhead, we would strive, and hope and wait,*
> *The offending still to reinstate.*
> *And when a broken heart we view,*
> *Our Christian friendship quick renew.*
> *In the gladness of the morning,*
> *In the sunshine, in the air,*
> *In God's compassion for all people,*
> *God's presence is everywhere.*

Day 27 FREEDOM FROM SLANDER. Speak no evil one of another, sisters and brothers. One speaking evil of sister and brother, and judges such sister and brother, speaks evil of the law and judges the law. If you judged the law, you are not a doer of the law, but a judge. JAMES.

> *Love is a pure and Homeland flame,*
> *And much regards a friendly name.*
> *It hopes all things, and believes,*
> *Nor easily a charge receives.*
> *Your name, Jesus, is my delight.*
> *It's manna to my hungry soul.*
> *It is a never failing light*
> *That marks the reef and rocky shoal.*

Day 28 ESTEEM FOR THE MINISTRY.   We beg you to know those who labor among you, and are over you in the Familyhead, and admonish you, and to esteem them very highly in love for their work's sake. PAUL.

> How beautiful are their feet,
> Who stand on Zion's hill,
> Who bring salvation on their tongues,
> And words of peace reveal!
> With power, Our Familyhead, defend
> Those who we now to you commend.
> Your faithful messengers secure,
> And help them to the end endure.

Day 29 PRAYER FOR THE MINISTRY. Praying always with all prayer and supplication in the Spirit; - and for me, that utterance may be given to me, that I may open my mouth boldly, to make known the mystery of the gospel. PAUL.

> How sweet amid earth's wild alarms,
> To hear of the everlasting arms,
> To know God's caring day by day,
> Who does not turn our prayer away.
> God hears one plea and sends relief.
> God gives us solace from our grief.
> God gives us ministry like shower down
> And thus our lives with blessing crown.

Day 30 UNBELIEF SHOULD BE GUARDED AGAINST. Take heed, sisters and brothers, lest there be in any of you an evil heart of unbelief, in departing from the living God. HEBREWS.

> The story of You is my delight.
> It's manna to my hungry soul.
> It's a never-failing light,
> That marks the reef and rocky shoal.
> It guards me from the tempter's snare,
> And counsels wiser than a friend.
> It comforts grief and lightens care.
> It's yield of riches has no end.

Day 31 CAUTION AGAINST APOSTASY. Look diligently, lest any person fail of the grace of God, lest any root of bitterness springing up trouble you, and thereby many be defiled. HEBREWS.

> What bright exchange, what treasure can be planned
> For the lost birthright of a hope in God's Homeland?
> If lost, the gem which empires could not buy,
> What yet remains? - a dark eternity.
> How often, deceived by self and pride,
> Has my weak heart been turned aside.
> And Jonah-like, has fled to sea,
> Till you have looked again on me!

JUNE

Day 1 BELIEVERS ARE THE SALT OF THE EARTH. You are the salt of the earth. But if the salt has lost its savor, how can it be salt? It is simply good for nothing except to be cast out and to be stamped under people's feet. MATTHEW.

> *Strive with studious care to find*
> *Some good your hands can do.*
> *Some way to serve and bless humanity*
> *Console the heart, avoid sin's vanity*
> *And open comforts new.*

Day 2   BELIEVERS ARE THE LIGHT OF THE WORLD. You are the light of the world. MATTHEW.

> *Walk in the light - and yours shall be*
> *A path, though stormy, bright;*
> *For God in love shall dwell with you*
> *And God alone is light!*

Day 3   THE UNIVERSAL RULE OF EQUITY. All things whatsoever you would that man would do to you, do you even so to them. This is the law and the prophets. MATTHEW.

> *Blessed Redeemer, how divine,*
> *How righteous does this rule apply*
> *To do all people just the same*
> *As we expect or wish from them.*
> *How blessed would every nation prove*
> *Thus ruled by equity and love!*
> *All would be friends without a fore,*
> *And form a paradise below.*

Day 4   TO GLORIFY GOD BY HOLY CONDUCT. I beg you as strangers and pilgrims, abstain from fleshly lusts, which war against the soul. Have your conversation honestly among the Gentiles. PETER.

> *Oh, Love, that will not let me go.*
> *I rest my weary soul in Thee.*
> *I give You back the life I owe*
> *That in Your ocean depths its flow*
>   *May richer, fuller be.*
> *O cross that lifts up my head,*
> *I dare not ask to fly from thee.*
> *I lay in dust life's glory dead,*
> *And from the ground there blossoms red*
>   *Life that shall endless be.*

Day 5   ABOUNDING IN THE WORK OF JESUS. My beloved sisters and brothers, be steadfast, unmovable, always abounding in the work of the Familyhead, for so you will know that your work is not in vain. PAUL.

> *Sow in the morn your seed,*
>   *At evening hold not your hand*
> *To doubt and fear give you no heed*
>   *Broadcast it round the land.*
> *The day of the Familyhead is breaking!*
>   *See the flowering from afar.*
> *Children from the graves are waking.*
>   *Hailing the bright morning star.*

Day 6   DECISION OF CHARACTER. No person can serve two employers. Either one will be hated and one loved or the other way around. You cannot serve God and a god of this world. MATTHEW.

> *Not a broken, brief obedience*

Does the boss of the Homeland demand.
God requires our whole allegiance,
Words and deeds, and heart and hand.
  God will hold divided sway
  With no deity of clay.

Day 7   HOLY EXAMPLE. Let your light so shine before folk that they may see your good works and glorify your Parent in God's Homeland. MATTHEW.
So let our lips and lives express
The holy gospel we profess.
So let our works and virtues shine
To prove the doctrine all divine.
In the world you've failed to find
Aught of peace for troubled mind.
Come to Jesus and believe.
Peace of mind you will receive.

Day 8   LIVE IN PEACE WITH ALL FOLK. If it is possible, as much as lies in you, live peaceably with all people. PAUL.
Oh! grant us, Jesus, to feel and own
The power of love divine.
The blood which does for sin atone,
The grace which makes You mine.
If you are happy and praise fills your heart,
Trust God to carry you through.
When the Familyhead give you love and care,
You also have things you must do.

Day 9   LOVE TO OUR NEIGHBOR. If you fulfil the royal law according to the gospel, to love your neighbor as yourself, you do well. JAMES.
Love lays its own advantage by
To seek its neighbor's good.
So God's own Child came down to die
And bought our lives with blood.
Love is the grace that keeps its power
In all the realms above.
There faith and hope are known no more
But saints forever love.

Day 10   SEEK THE EDIFICATION OF OUR NEIGHBOR. Let every one of us please our neighbor for the sake of good edification. PAUL.
May I from every act abstain,
That hurts or gives another pain.
Still may I feel my heart accede
To be a friend to all in need.
God's purpose is that we should bear
God's image now on earth,
And by our peaceful lives declare
Our new and Godly birth.

Day 11   LOVE TO ALL PEOPLE. May the Familyhead give you to increase and abound in love one toward another, and toward all people, even as we do toward you. PAUL.
When morning gilds the skies, my heart awaking cries,
Let Jesus, Our Familyhead, be praised!

> *Alike at work and prayer to Jesus I repair*
> *Let Jesus, Our Familyhead, be praised!*
> *Let earth's wide circle round in joyful notes resound,*
> *Let Jesus, the Familyhead, be praised!*
> *Let air and sea and sky from depths to height reply*
> *Let Jesus, the Familyhead, be praised!*

Day 12   SEEK THE SALVATION OF OTHERS. One who converts a sinner from the error of a sin shall save a soul from death, and shall hide a multitude of sins. JAMES.
> *My God, I feel the mournful scene.*
> *My bowels yearn over dying folk.*
> *And how I wish I could reclaim*
> *The ones who hell has daily poke.*
> *May love, that shining grace*
> *Over all my powers preside,*
> *Direct my thoughts, suggest my words*
> *And every action guide.*

Day 13   GIVE DUE HONOR TO ALL FOLK. Tender to all their dues. Give tribute to one to whom tribute is due, custom to custom, fear to fear, honor to honor. PAUL.
> *Our sovereign with your favor bless.*
> *Establish Your throne in righteousness.*
> *Let wisdom hold the helm,*
> *The counsels of our senate guide,*
> *Let justice in our courts preside.*
> *Rule and bless this realm.*

Day 14   CONSISTENCY. Be blameless and harmless, children of God, without rebuke, in the midst of a crooked and perverse nation, among whom you shine as lights in the world. PAUL.
> *That wisdom, Jesus, on us bestow*
> *From every evil to depart,*
> *To stop the mouth of every foe*
> *While upright both in life and heart.*
> *The proof of Godly fear we give,*
> *And show them how the Christians live.*

Day 15   CIRCUMSPECTION. See then that you walk circumspectly, not as fools, but as wise. Redeeming the time because the days are evil. PAUL.
> *Let every flying hour confess*
> *I gain the gospel fresh renown,*
> *And when my life and labors cease,*
> *May I possess the promised crown.*
> *Gratefully sing God's power and love,*
> *Our shield and defender, the Ancient of days,*
> *Pavilioned in splendor*
> *And girdled with praise.*

Day 16   DISCRETION. A good person shows favor, and lends so as to guide personal affairs with discretion. PSALMS.
> *Believers love what God commands*
> *And in those ways delight.*
> *Their gracious words and holy hands*
> *Show that faith is right.*
> *They converse with God above.*

> *Their labors bless humanity.*
> *Their works of mercy, peace and love*
> *Show Jesus as God wished to be.*

Day 17 MODERATION. Let your moderation be known to all people. The Familyhead is at hand. PAUL.

> *We'll look on all the toys below*
> *With such disdain as angels do.*
> *And wait the call that bids us rise*
> *To mansions promised in the skies.*
> *I take, Oh cross, your shadow*
> *For my abiding place.*
> *I ask no other sunshine*
> *Than the sunshine of God's face.*

Day 18 FORBEARANCE. Dearly beloved, avenge not yourselves but rather give place to wrath. This is the case: "Vengeance is mine. I will repay." So says the Familyhead. PAUL.

> *May I feel beneath my wrongs*
> *That vengeance to Jesus belongs,*
> *Nor worse payback dare*
> *Than the meek revenge of prayer.*
> *Much forgiven, may I learn,*
> *Love for hatred to return.*

Day 19 INDUSTRY. Let a person labor, wor**king w**ith hands the things which are good, that each may be given all that is needed. PAUL.

> *Somebody knows when you're tempted.*
> *Somebody knows when you're weak.*
> *Somebody knows when you've fallen.*
> *Somebody knows what you seek.*
> *Somebody loves you when weary.*
> *Somebody cares that you're blue.*
> *Somebody wants your friendship.*
> *The fact is that Jesus loves you.*

Day 20 INTEGRITY. Walk honestly toward those that are outside the circle, that you may lack in nothing. PAUL.

> *Come let us search our ways, and try*
> *Have they been just and right,*
> *Is the great rule of equity*
> *Our practice and delight?*
> *In all we sell, in all we buy,*
> *Is justice our design?*
> *Do we remember God is nigh,*
> *And fear the Wrath Divine?*

Day 21 FIDELITY. One who is faithful in that which is least is faithful also in much and the one that is unjust in the least is unjust also in much. LUKE.

> *Your gifts are only then enjoyed*
> *When used as talents lent,*
> *Those talents only well employed*
> *When in God's service spent.*
> *To you my very life I owe.*
> *From you do all my comforts flow.*

> *And every blessing which I need*
> *Must from Your bounteous hand proceed.*

Day 22   TRUTH AND SINCERITY. Wherefore, put away lying, speak every person the truth with a neighbor, for we are members one of another. PAUL.

> *I have a friend who abides in my heart.*
> *I cannot live from God's presence apart.*
> *Never a foe that God's eye cannot see.*
> *Never a moment that God forgets me.*
> *God will the vilest of sinners forgive.*
> *No heart so dead but God's touch can make free.*
> *There is a home at the end of life's way.*
> *Where in God's presence I'll gratefully stay.*

Day 23   GENTLENESS AND MEEKNESS. Speak evil of no person, nor be brawlers, but gentle, showing all meekness to all humanity. TITUS.

> *Let those who bear the Christian name*
> *Their holy vows fulfil.*
> *Your saints, the followers of the Lamb*
> *Are folk of honor still.*
> *Blessed are the folk of peaceful life*
> *Who quench the fires of growing strife.*
> *They shall be called the heirs of bliss,*
> *The Children of God, the Children of peace.*

Day 24   BENEVOLENCE. Pure religion and undefiled before God and the Parent is this - to visit the orphans and bereaved widows and widowers in their affliction and to keep one unspotted from the world. JAMES.

> *The poor are always with us here.*
> *It's our great Parent's plan*
> *That mutual wants and mutual care*
> *Should bind us hand in hand.*
> *Parent of eternal grace,*
> *Glorify Yourself in me.*
> *Meekly beaming in my face,*
> *May the world Your image see.*

Day 25   OVERCOME EVIL WITH GOOD. If your enemy hungers, feed them. If they thirst, give them to drink. In so doing you shall heap coals of fire on their heads. Be not overcome of evil, but overcome evil with good. PAUL AND PROVERBS. (The hostility of folk to each other gets realized and burned out that way.)

> *Artists melt the sullen ore of lead*
> *With heaping coals of fire upon its head.*
> *In the kind warmth the metal learns to glow,*
> *And loose from dross the silver runs below.*
> *So refine me with the story of Jesus.*
> *Make its image my heart's every word.*
> *Tell me the story most precious,*
> *Sweetest that ever was heard.*

Day 26   PERSEVERANCE IN DOING GOOD. Let us not be weary in well- doing. In due season we shall reap if we faint not. PAUL.

> *Meek pilgrim Zionward, if you*
> *Have put your hand into the stew.*

> *Oh, look not back nor droop dismayed*
> *At thought of victory delayed.*
> *Doubt not that you, in season due,*
> *Shall own the gracious promise true.*
> *You shall share your glorious lot,*
> *When doing well has wearied not.*

Day 27 SUBMISSION TO AUTHORITY. Put those in mind to be subject to principalities and powers, to obey magistrates, to be ready to every good work. TITUS.

> *Jesus, you have bid Your people pray*
> *For all that bear the sovereign sway,*
> *Who as Your servants reign,*
> *Rulers and governors, and powers -*
> *Behold in faith we pray for ours*
> *Nor let us plead in vain.*

Day 28 UNIVERSAL HOLINESS THE BELIEVER'S AIM. Whatever things are true, whatever things are honest, whatever things are just, whatever things are pure, whatever things are lovely, whatever things are of good report, if there be any virtue, and if there be any praise, think on these things. PAUL.

> *The church's one foundation is Jesus, our Familyhead.*
> *She is God's new creation, in the cup and the bread.*
> *From heaven, God came and sought her to be a holy bride.*
> *With God's own blood God bought her, and for her he died.*
> *Elect from every nation, yet one over all the earth,*
> *Her charter is salvation, one God, one faith, one birth.*
> *One holy name she blesses, partakes one holy food.*
> *And to God's rest she presses, to rest in grace endued.*

Day 29 BELIEVER'S HUMBLE CONFESSION. So likewise you, when you have done all those things which are commanded of you, say, "We are unprofitable servants. We have done that which was our duty to do." LUKE.

> *Finish Your new creation.*
> *Pure and spotless as at birth.*
> *Let us see Your great salvation,*
> *Perfectly restored on earth.*
> *My present triumphs, and my past*
> *Are yours, and must be to the last.*
> *If the crown of life I wear,*
> *Your hand alone must place it there.*

Day 30 THE GREAT MOTIVE TO ALL DUTY. You are not your own. You are bought with a price. Therefore glorify God in your body and in your spirit, which are God's. PAUL.

> *God of our Parents, whose almighty hand*
> *Leads forth in beauty all the starry band*
> *Of shining worlds in splendor through the skies,*
> *Our grateful songs before Your throne arise.*
> *Refresh Your people on their toilsome way.*
> *Lead us from night to never-ending day.*
> *Fill all our lives with love and grace divine.*
> *And glory, laud and praise be ever thine.*

JULY

Day 1   JOY IN GOD. Let all those who put their trust in You rejoice. Let them ever shout for joy, because You defend them. Let those also that love Your name be joyful in You. PSALMS.

> *Oh, Savior from the mountainside,*
> *Make haste to heal these hearts of pain,*
> *Among the restless throngs abide*
> *O tread the city's streets again.*
> *Till all shall learn compassion's might,*
> *Following where your feet have trod,*
> *Till glorious from your realm of light*
> *Shall come the city of our God.*
> *There no temptation can abide*
> *Nor any detraction of clan or race,*
> *Where cross the crowded ways of life*
> *We'll hear your voice of grace.*

Day 2   JOY IN JESUS. We are the circumcision, those who worship God in the spirit, and rejoice in Jesus, the Familyhead, and have no confidence in the flesh. PAUL.

> *When with God's smiles my soul is blessed*
> *No cares nor crosses can destroy my peace,*
> *If I possess God all I want is reached,*
> *Enjoying all things a person can possess.*
> *The opening Homeland of God shines*
> > *With beams of sacred bliss,*
> *When Jesus shows a heart to mine*
> > *And whispers, "Love is this."*

Day 3   JOY IN THE SPIRIT OF GOD'S BREATH. God's Homeland is not meat or drink, but righteousness and peace and joy in the Spirit of God's Breath. PAUL.

> *Spirit Breath, dispel our sadness*
> *Pierce the cloud of sinful night.*
> *Come, You, source of joy and gladness*
> *Breathe Your life and shed Your light.*
> *Blessed are the souls that hear and know*
> *The gospel's joyful sound.*
> *Peace shall attend the path they go*
> *And light their steps surround.*

Day 4   THE GOSPEL AS A SOURCE OF PATRIOTISM. Blessed are the people who know the joyful sound. They shall walk, O Familyhead, in the light of Your countenance. PSALMS.

> *My country is of thee, sweet land of liberty,*
> *Of You I sing.*
> > *Land where my parents died,*
> > *Land of the pilgrims' pride,*
> *From every mountainside, let freedom ring.*
> *Our parent's God, to thee, author of liberty,*
> *Of You I sing.*
> > *Long may our land be bright,*
> > *With freedom's holy light,*
> *Protect us by Your might, Great God, our King.*

Day 5   THE ATONEMENT A SOURCE OF JOY. We joy in God through our Familyhead, Jesus, by whom we have now received the atonement. PAUL.
> There is a fountain filled with blood,
> Drawn from Immanuel's veins.
> And sinners plunged beneath that flood
> Lose all their guilty strains.
> The dying thief rejoiced to see
> That fountain on his sentencing day,
> And here may I though vile as he,
> Wash all my sins away.

Day 6   THE SCRIPTURES A SOURCE OF JOY. Your words were found, and I did eat them. Your word was to me the joy and rejoicing of my heart. I am called by Your name, O Familyhead, God of hosts. JEREMIAH.
> Oh, may these Homeland pages be
>   My ever dear delight.
> And still new beauties may I see
>   And still increasing light.
> We will love both friend and foe
>   In all our strife
> And preach your word wherever we go,
>   By kindly words and virtuous life.

Day 7   THE SABBATH A SOURCE OF JOY. This is the day which the Familyhead has made. We will rejoice and be glad in it. PSALMS.
> Often as this peaceful day revolves,
> I raise my thoughts from earthly things,
> And bear them to my Homeland loves
> On faith and hope's celestial wings.
>   Till the last gleam of life decay,
>   In one eternal Sabbath day.

Day 8   FAITH A SOURCE OF JOY. Love one whom you have not seen, in whom - though now you have seen not, yet believing, - you can rejoice with joy unspeakable and full of glory. PETER.
> A bleeding Savior seen by faith,
>   A sense of pardoning love.
> A hope that triumphs over death,
>   Gives joys like those above.
> Stand in Jesus's strength alone
>   The arm of flesh will fail.
> Dare not trust your own.
>   But God's arm will prevail.

Day 9   PARDON A SOURCE OF JOY. Blessed is one whose transgression is forgiven, whose sin is covered. Blessed is the one to whom the Familyhead imputes no iniquity and in whose spirit there is no guile. PSALMS.
> The Savior smiles! o'er my blessed soul
> New tides of hope tumultuous roll.
> Earth has a joy unknown in heaven,
> The new-born peace of sin forgiven,
> Tears of such pure and deep delight,
> You angels! never dimmed your sight.

Day 10 HOPE OF GLORY A SOURCE OF JOY. Through Jesus, we have access by faith into this grace wherein we stand and rejoice in hope of the glory of God. PAUL.

> By faith to Pisgah's top I fly,
> And there delighted stand
> To view beneath a cloudless sky,
> The spacious promised land.
> The Familyhead of all the vast domain
> Has promised it to me -
> The length and breadth of all the plain,
> As far as faith can see.

Day 11 GODLY FEAR A SOURCE OF JOY. Blessed is everyone who fears the Familyhead, that walks in God's ways. For You shall eat the labor of your hands. Happy shall You be, and it shall be well with you. PSALMS.

> Brightly beams our Parent's mercy
> From God's lighthouse evermore.
> But to us, God gives the keeping
> Of the lights along the shore.
> Dark the night of sin has settled
> Loud the angry billow roar,
> Eager eyes are watching, longing,
> For the lights upon the shore.
> Trim your feeble lamp, my friend
> Some poor one seabound is tempest tossed,
> Trying now to make the harbor,
> In the darkness may be lost.
> Let the lower lights be burning!
> Send a gleam across the wave!
> Some poor fainting struggling person
> You may rescue, you may save!

Day 12 OBEDIENCE A SOURCE OF JOY. I will delight myself in Your commandments which I have loved. PSALMS.

> Happy, beyond description, the one
> Who fears and loves our God -
> Who hears the threats with holy awe
> And trembles at God's rod.
> Then shall my heart have inward joy
> And keep my face from shame
> When all Your statues I obey
> And honor all Your name.

Day 13 COMMUNION WITH GOD A SOURCE OF JOY. There are many who say, "Who will show us any good?" Our Familyhead, lift us up to the light of Your countenance. You have put gladness in my heart, more than in the time that their corn and their wine increased. PSALMS.

> God, what is life unless spent with you
> In humble praise and prayer?
> How long or short my life may be
> I feel no anxious care.
>> Though life depart, my joys shall last
>> When life and all its joys are past.

Day 14 COMMUNION OF SAINTS A SOURCE OF JOY. My goodness extends not *to You, but to the saints that are in the earth, and to the excellent, in whom is all my delight.* PSALMS.

> It it's sweet to mingle where
> Followers meet for fervent prayer,
> If it's sweet with them to raise
> Songs of holy joy and praise,
> Passing sweet that state must be
> Where they meet eternally.

Day 15 PRAYER A SOURCE OF JOY. Even those will I bring to my holy mountain, and make them joyful in my house of prayer. ISAIAH.

> Prayer makes the darkened cloud withdraw.
> Prayer climbs the ladder Jacob saw.
> Gives exercise to faith and love.
> Brings every blessing from above.
> Salvation! Oh! the joyful sound!
> It's pleasure to our ears.
> A sovereign balm for every wound,
> A cordial for our fears.

Day 16 SALVATION, A SOURCE OF JOY. We will rejoice in Your salvation, and in the name of our God we will set up our banners. PSALMS.

> God's tomorrow is a day of gladness
> And its joys shall never fade,
> No more weeping, mo more sadness
> No more fuss to make afraid.
> God's tomorrow is a day of glory.
> We shall wear the crown of life
> Sung through countless year's love's old story
> Free forever from all strife.

Day 17 EARLY PIETY A SOURCE OF JOY. O satisfy us early with Your mercy, that we may rejoice and glad in all our days. PSALMS.

> Grace is a plant, wherever it grows,
> Of pure and Godly root,
> But fairest in the young it shows,
> And yields the sweetest fruit.
> The marvelous grace of our Familyhead!
> Grace that exceeds our sin and our guilt.
> Yonder on Calvary's mountain overhead
> There's where the blood of the Lamb was spilt.

Day 18 A GOOD CONSCIENCE A SOURCE OF JOY. Our rejoicing is this, the testimony of our conscience, that in simplicity and Godly sincerity, not with fleshly wisdom, but by the grace of God, we have had our conversation in the world. PAUL.

> O happy soul, that lives on high,
> While we lie grovelling here,
> Whose hopes are fixed above the sky
> And faith forbids the fear.
> The conscience cleaned from all the sins,
> Love, peace and joy combine
> To form a life whose holy springs

Are hidden and divine.

Day 19 BENEVOLENCE A SOURCE OF JOY. Remember the words of the Familyhead,
Jesus, how it was said, "It is more blessed to give than to receive." LUKE.
> *Blessed is the one whose heart expands*
> *At melting pity's call,*
> *And the rich blessing of whose hands*
> *Like Homeland manna fall.*
> *Marvelous, infinite, marchless grace*
> *Freely bestowed in all who believe.*
> *Charity gives you to see God's face*
> *Will you this moment God's grace receive?*

Day 20 TRIBULATION A SOURCE OF JOY. We glory in tribulation, knowing that
tribulation works patience, and patience, experience, and experience, hope.
> *Then let us wait the appointed day,*
> > *Nor call this world our home.*
> *To pilgrims in a foreign land*
> > *Afflictions needs must come.*
> *Who rules the world, overrules their end,*
> > *And destines them for good.*
> *And bears the saints to realms of rest,*
> > *On winds as mighty as a flood.*

Day 21 TEMPORAL BLESSINGS SOURCES OF JOY. You shall eat in plenty, and be
satisfied, and praise the name of the Familyhead, your God, that has dealt
wondrously with you. My people shall never be ashamed. JOEL.
> *Your bounty gilds the path of life*
> *With every cheering ray,*
> *And oft restrains the rising tear,*
> *Or wipes that tear away.*
> *Dark is the stain we cannot hide.*
> *What can avail to wash it away?*
> *Look, there is flowing a crimson tide.*
> *Whiter that snow, you may be today!*

Day 22 THE DIVINE BLESSING. The blessing of the Familyhead, it makes one rich,
and God adds no sorrow with it. PROVERBS.
> *Better than life itself your love,*
> *Dearer than all beside to me*
> *For whom have I in heaven above,*
> *Or what on earth, but God's charity?*
> *Everyone ought to know God's kindness.*
> *Oh! how tenderly God deals with humans.*
> *Though your sin-sick soul is dark with blindness*
> *God can make you see the light again.*

Day 23 THE DIVINE PROTECTION, A SOURCE OF JOY. Because You have been my
help, therefore in the shadow of Your wings will I rejoice. PSALMS.
> *There is never a day so dreary.*
> *There is never a night so long, so long.*
> *But the soul that is trusting Jesus,*
> *Will somewhere find a song, a song.*
> *Since you have been my help,*
> *To You my spirit flies, it flies.*

> *And on the watchful providence*
> *My cheerful hope relies, relies.*

Day 24 DIVINE ACCEPTANCE, A SOURCE OF JOY. Go your way, ear your bread with joy, and drink your wine with a merry heart. God now accepts your work. ECCLESIASTES.

> *While I see Your love to me,*
> *Every object teems with joy.*
> *Here, oh may I walk with you*
> *Then Your presence die!*
> *Let me but Yourself possess,*
> *Total sum of happiness.*
> *Real bliss I then shall prove -*
> *The Homeland below and the Homeland above.*

Day 25 JOY FOLLOWING SORROW. Weeping may endure for a night but joy comes in the morning. PSALMS.

> *When comforts are declining,*
> *God grants the soul again,*
> *A season of clear shining,*
> *To cheer it after rain.*
> *Have a faith that can never be shaken,*
> *A faith that lays hold upon Jesus,*
> *And from your heart it can't be taken*
> *The crucifixion scene for us.*

Day 26 JOY, THE DUTY OF THE BELIEVER. Be glad in the Familyhead, and rejoice, you righteous ones. Shout for joy, all you that are upright in heart. PSALMS.

> *Let those refuse to sing*
> *Who never knew the Familyhead.*
> *But children of the Homeland King*
> *Should joys their lives attend.*
> *Remember, God is holding me,*
> *Safely, firmly, enfolding me.*
> *By God's grace I am made free.*
> *God's saving power is Jesus who died for me.*

Day 27 JOY TO BE SOUGHT THROUGH JESUS. Before now, I have asked nothing in my own name. Ask and you shall receive, that your joy may be full. JOHN.

> *Dark and cheerless is the morn,*
> *Unaccompanied by You.*
> *Joyless is the day's return*
> *Till Your mercy's beams we see.*
> *Day-spring from on high, be near -*
> *Day-star in our hearts appear.*

Day 28 BELIEVER'S JOY IS SATISFYING. Blessed is the one whom You choose, and cause to approach to Yourself, that one may dwell in Your courts. We shall be satisfied with the goodness of Your house, even Your holy temple. PSALMS.

> *My faith looks you to You,*
> *Lamb of Calvary, Love mature.*
> *Now hear me when I pray,*
> *Take all my sin away,*
> *O let me every day be wholly yours.*
> *May Your rich grace impart*

Strength to my fainting heart,
As you died for me,
Oh may the faith in me,
Pure warm and changeless be, a living fire.

Day 29 BELIEVER'S JOY IS ABIDING. These things have I spoken to you, that my joy might remain in you and that your joy might be full. JOHN.

These are the joys which satisfy,
And sanctify the mind,
Which made the spirit mount on high
And leave the world behind.
Are you not mine, my living God?
And can my hope, my comfort die?
I fix on Your everlasting word -
The word that built the earth and sky.

Day 30 THE BELIEVER HAS JOY IN DEATH. Familyhead, now let You Your servant depart in peace, according to Your word. Mine eyes have seen Your salvation. LUKE.

When you have numbered all our years,
And stand, at length, on Jordan's brink.
Though the flesh fail with mortal fears,
Oh! let not then the spirit sink.
But strong in faith, and hope, and love,
Plunge through the stream to rise above.

Day 31 GOD'S HOMELAND, THE CONSUMMATION OF JOY. Well done. You are a good and faithful servant. You have been faith over a few things. I will put you in charge over many things. Enter into the joys of the Familyhead. MATTHEW.

Soldier of Jesus, well done!
Praise be your new employ.
While eternal ages run
Rest in your Savior's joy.
When life's dark maze is tread
Be You my guide.
When griefs around me spread
Stay by my side.

AUGUST

Day 1 BELIEVER FOREWARNED OF SORROW. These things I have spoken to you, that in me you might have peace. In the world you shall have tribulation but be of good cheer, I have overcome the World. JOHN.

In summer fields are grasses green
Which ripple like the seas,
And glowers as thick as stars at night
And butterflies and bees.
While overhead the robin sings,
Upsoars the tireless lark
And mouse and mole thread through the earth
In burrows cool and dark.

Day 2 SOURCES OF SORROW - LOSS OF DIVINE FAVOR. Restore to me the joy of Your salvation and uphold me with Your free Spirit. PSALMS.

Ah, why, by passing clouds oppressed,
Should vexing thoughts distract your breast?
Turn, turn to God, in every pain.
Who never suppliant sought in vain.
The path of sorrow, and that path alone,
Leads to the land where sorrow is unknown.
No traveller ever reached that blessed abode,
Who found not thorns and briars in one's road.

Day 3   SOURCES OF SORROW - INDWELLING SIN. I see another law in my members, warring against the law of my mind, and bringing me into captivity to the law of sin which is in my members. PAUL.
Nature may raise her fleshly strife,
Resistant to the Homeland life.
But grace omnipotent at length
Shall arm the saint with saving strength.
The hour the sharp war with aids attend,
And one's last conflict sweetly end.

Day 4   SOURCES OF SORROW - A DECEITFUL HEART. The heart is deceitful above all things, and desperately wicked. Who can know it? JEREMIAH.
With flowing tears, Oh God, I confess
   My folly and unsteadfastness.
When shall this heart more do
   The grace that comes to rest in you?
Give us the faith of our parents!
   In spite of dungeon, fire and sword,
Oh how our hearts beat high with joy
   Whenever we hear that glorious word.
Faith of our parents, holy faith!
   We shall be true to You till death!

Day 5   SOURCES OF SORROW - INGRATITUDE OF THE UNGODLY. They who render evil for good are my adversaries I follow the things that are good. Don't forsake me my Familyhead. Oh my God, be not far from me. PSALMS.
If wounded love my ego swell
Deceived by those I prized too well,
God will pitying aid bestow
Who knew the earth of bitter woe
At once betrayed, denied, or fled
By those who shared God's daily bread.

Day 6   SOURCES OF SORROW - REPROACH OF THE WORLD. Let us for forth therefore to God outside the camp, bearing God's reproach. HEBREWS.
If on my face, for Your dear name,
Shame and reproach shall be,
I'll hail reproach, and welcome shame,
If you remember me.
Humanity may trouble and distress me,
Driving me to Your breast.
Life with trials hard may press me,
God's Homeland will bring me rest.

Day 7   SOURCES OF SORROW - PERSECUTION. Though I walk in the middle of trouble, You will revive me. You will stretch forth Your hand against the wrath of my enemies and you Your right hand will save me. PSALMS.

> *Stand up, stand up for Jesus,*
> *You, soldiers of the cross,*
> *Lift high the royal banner*
> *It must not suffer loss.*
> *From victory unto victory*
> *So armored as God leads*
> *Till every evil is vanquished*
> *And Jesus is our Familyhead indeed.*

Day 8   SOURCES OF SORROW - EARTHLY LOSSES AND BEREAVEMENTS. Naked I came out of my mother's womb and naked shall be my end. The Familyhead gave and the Familyhead has taken away. Blessed be the name of the Familyhead. JOB.

> *Oh! blessed be the hand that gave,*
> *Still blessed when it takes.*
> *Blessed be the one who smites to save*
> *Who heals the heart one breaks. Perfect and true*
> *are all God's ways*
> *Whom the Homeland adores and earth obeys.*

Day 9   SOURCES OF SORROW - THE FAILURE TO WITNESS BY OTHERS. Rivers of water run down my eyes, because they do not keep Your law. PSALMS.

> *I sorrow for the mental night*
>   *In which humanity around me lie.*
> *Almighty Parent, by Your might,*
>   *Arouse them from their lethargy.*
> *To God who made all things that be*
>   *Yet nothing made the same,*
> *Lift up heart, lift up song,*
>   *And glorify God's name.*

Day 10   SOURCES OF SORROW - THE NUMBER OF THE WICKED. Broad is the way that leads to destruction and many are there which go in because straight is the gate and narrow is the way which leads to life and few are there that find it. MATTHEW. [QUOTING A SAYING OF JESUS]

> *Oh my God! When I in awesome wonder*
> *Consider all the worlds Your hands have made.*
> *I see the stars. I hear the rolling thunder.*
> *Your power throughout the universe displayed.*
> *Then sings my song, my Savior God to You.*
> *How great You are! How great You are!*
> *How great You are! How great You are!*

Day 11   SORROW CHOSEN RATHER THAN SIN. Moses, when he was come to years, refused to be called the child of Pharaoh's daughter, choosing rather to suffer affliction with the people of God, than to enjoy the pleasures of sin for a season.

> *It is not for me to be seeking my bliss,*
>   *And building my hopes in a region like this.*
> *I look for a city which hands have not piled.*
>   *I pant for a country by sin undefiled.*

> *I need Your presence every hour.*
> *What but your glance can spoil the tempter's power?*
> *Who but Yourself can my guide and stay be?*
> *All changes except You in everything I see.*

Day 12 BELIEVER'S CONFIDENCE IN TROUBLE. Although the fig tree shall not blossom, neither shall fruit bend the vines. The labor of the olive shall fail, and the fields shall yield no food. The flock shall be cut off from the fold, and there shall be no herd in the stalls. Yet I will rejoice in the Familyhead. I will joy in the God of my salvation. HABAKUK.

> *Although my wealth and comfort's lost*
> *My blooming hopes cut off I see.*
> *Yet, will I in my Savior trust*
> *Whose matchless grace can reach to me.*
> *Calm on the listening ear of night,*
> *Come God's Homeland's melodious strains*
> *"Peace on earth. Good will to folk!"*
> *Over America's mantled plains.*

Day 13 BELIEVER'S COMFORT IN TROUBLE. This is my comfort in my affliction. Your Word has strengthened me. PSALMS.
Thus trusting in Your word, I tread

> *The narrow path of duty one.*
> *What though some cherished joys are fled?*
> *What though some flattering dreams are gone?*
> *Yet purer brighter joys remain.*
> *Why should my spirit then complain?*

Day 14 JESUS AS AN EXAMPLE TO THE AFFLICTED. Even so were you called - because Jesus also suffered for us, leaving us an example, that you should follow the same steps. PETER.

> *Lead, Kindly Light, amid the encircling gloom.*
> *The night is dark, and I am far from home.*
> *Keep my feet. I do not ask to see*
> *The distant scene - one step enough for me.*
> *So long Your power has blessed me, sure it still*
> *Will lead me on, over field, barren and hill.*
> *The night is gone and angel faces smile*
> *Where I have longed to be but lost awhile.*

Day 15 THE MATRIARCHS AND PATRIARCHS - EXAMPLES TO THE AFFLICTED. So seeing we also are compassed about with so great a cloud of witnesses, let us lay aside every weight, and the sin which confronts us, and let us run with patience the race that is set before us. HEBREWS.

> *Once they were mourning here below,*
> *And wet their couch with tears.*
> *They wrestled hard, as we do now,*
> *With sins, and doubts, and fears.*
> *Our ancestors claim our praise*
> *For God's own pattern stands,*
> *While the long cloud of witnesses*
> *Show the same path to God's Homeland.*

Day 16 THE PROPHETS - EXAMPLES TO THE AFFLICTED. Take, my sisters and brothers, the prophets, who have spoken in the name of the Familyhead, for an example of suffering affliction and of patience. JAMES.

> And shall we not aspire
> Like them our course to run?
> The crown if we would wear
> The cross must first be borne.
> Divinely taught, they showed the way.
> First to believe, and then obey.

Day 17 BENEFITS OF AFFLICTION - SELF-ABASEMENT. Surely, after that I was instructed. I was stricken upon my thigh. I was ashamed, yes, even confounded because I bear the reproach of my youth. JEREMIAH.

> *Dumb at Your feet I lie,*
> *For You have brought me low.*
> *Remove Your judgments, lest I die.*
> *I faint beneath Your blow.*
> *What though afflictions pierced my heart!*
> *I bless the hand that caused the smart.*
> *It taught my tears awhile to flow,*
> *But saved me from eternal woe.*

Day 18 BENEFITS OF AFFLICTION - CONTRITION FOR SIN. I will go and return to my place, till they acknowledge their offense, and seek my face. In their affliction they will seek me early. HOSEA.

> *Tell me the old, old story of unseen things above,*
> *Of Jesus alive in glory, Of Jesus's love,*
> *Tell me the story simply as to a little child*
> *For I am weak and weary and helpless and defiled.*
> *Tell me the story softly in earnest tones and grave.*
> *Remember I'm the sinner who Jesus came to save.*
> *Tell me the story always when in trouble I be.*
> *I need to know that always God will remember me.*

Day 19 BENEFITS OF AFFLICTION - PATIENCE. The trying of your faith works patience. But let patience have her perfect work, that you may be perfect and entire, wanting nothing. JAMES.

> *Through waves, and clouds and storms,*
> *God gently clears Your way.*
> *Wait God's time - the darkest night*
> *Shall end in brightest day.*
> *To the heart truly humbled by woe,*
> *The anointing of joy shall balm.*
> *To the tears that from penitence flow,*
> *The peace of the New Jerusalem.*

Day 20 BENEFITS OF AFFLICTION - HUMILITY. If I am wicked, woe to me. And if am righteous, yet will I not lift my head. I am full of confusion. Therefore assess my affliction. JOB.

> *Say them over again to me,*
> *Wonderful words of life.*
> *Let me more of their beauty see,*
> *Wonderful words of life.*
> *Sweetly echoes the gospel call.*

> *Offering pardon and peace to all.*
> *Words of life and beauty,*
> *Teach me faith and duty,*
> > *Beautify words, wonderful words,*
> > *Wonderful words of life.*

Day 21 BENEFITS OF AFFLICTION - SUBMISSION. I was dumb. I opened not my mouth. You did it. PSALMS.
> *Take all, great God, I will not grieve,*
> *But still will wish that I had still to give.*
> *I hear Your voice. You bid me quit*
> *My paradise. I bless, and do submit.*
> *I will not murmur at Your word.*
> *Nor beg Your angel to sheath up sword.*

Day 22 BENEFITS OF AFFLICTION - HOPE. Why are you cast down, Oh my soul? And why are you disquieted in me? Hope in God. I will praise God for the help of God's own countenance. PSALMS.
> *I have found a friend in Jesus, everything to me,*
> *The fairest of ten thousand to my soul.*
> *The Lily of the Valley, in Jesus alone I see*
> *All I need to cleanse and fully make me whole.*
> *Yes, the Lily of the Valley, in sorrow my comfort,*
> *In trouble my stay. The bright and morning star and*
> *the fairest of ten thousand to my soul.*

Day 23 BENEFITS OF AFFLICTION - HOLINESS. Now no chastening for the present seems to be joyous, but grievous. Nevertheless afterward it yields the peaceable fruit of righteousness to those who are exercised thereby. HEBREWS.
> *What Child is this who laid to rest*
> *On Mary's lap is sleeping?*
> *Who angels greet with anthems sweet,*
> *While shepherds watch are keeping?*
> *This is Jesus, our Familyhead.*
> *The Magi reach them starward led.*
> *Haste to bring laud*
> *This Child of Mary and God.*

Day 24 BENEFITS OF AFFLICTION - TRIALS OF OUR SINCERITY. God knows the way that I take. When God has tried me, I shall come forth as gold. JOB.
> *Though sorrows rise, and dangers roll*
> *In waves of darkness over my soul,*
> *Though friends are false, and love decays,*
> *And few and evil are my days -*
> *Yet even in nature's utmost ill,*
> *I love You, God, I love you still.*

Day 25 BENEFITS OF AFFLICTION - BRINGS SIN TO REMEMBRANCE. If they are bound in fetters, and restrained in cords of affliction, then God shows them their work and their transgressions that they have exceeded. JOB.
> *My former hopes are fled.*
> > *My terror now begins.*
> *I feel that I am dead*
> > *In trespass and in sins.*

Day 26   BENEFITS OF AFFLICTION - LEADS TO PRAYER. O remember not against us former iniquities. Let Your tender mercies speedily prevent us. We are brought very low. PSALMS.

> What a friend we have in Jesus,
> All our sins and griefs to bear,
> What a privilege to carry everything to God in prayer!
> Oh, what peace we often forfeit,
> Oh, what needless pain we bear,
> All because we do not carry everything to God in prayer!
> Have we trials and temptations?
> Is there trouble anywhere?
> We should never be discouraged, Our Savior is our care!
> Do your friends despise and hate you?
> In strong arms Jesus will bear.
> Jesus knows our every problem. You will find a solace
> there!

Day 27   BENEFITS OF AFFLICTION - BRINGS US BACK TO GOD. I will hedge up Your way with thorns, and make a wall, that she shall not find her paths. Then she will say, "I will go and return to my first husband. Then it was better with me than now." HOSEA.

> Long unafflicted, undismayed
> In pleasure's path secure I strayed.
> You made me feel Your chastening rod,
> And straight I turned to God.
> Where can we flee for aid
> When tempted, desolate, dismayed?
> Or how the hosts of hell defeat
> Had suffering saints no mercy-seat?

Day 28   BENEFITS OF AFFLICTION - EXERCISES OUR FAITH. You are in heaviness through manifold temptations. The trial of Your faith, being much more precious than of gold that perishes, though it is tried with fire, might be found to praise and honor and glory at the appearance of our Familyhead, Jesus. PETER.

> Beneath of the cross of Jesus I have to take my stand,
> The shadow of a mighty rock within a weary land.
> A home within the wilderness, a rest upon the way,
> From the burning noontide heat, and burden of each day.
> Upon that cross of Jesus my eye at times can see
> The very dying form of One who suffered there for me.
> And from my heart with tears two wonders I confess:
> The wonders of redeeming love and my unworthiness.

Day 29   BENEFITS OF AFFLICTION - TEACHES OUR FRAILTY. My age is departed, and is removed from me as a shepherd's tent. My life has been cut off like a weavers thread, just as God will cut me off with pining sickness. ISAIAH.

> Jesus, let me know my end,
> My days, how brief their date,
> That I may timely comprehend
> How frail my best estate.
> Dark are the ways of Providence
> While those who love You groan.

> *Your reasons lie concealed from sense,*
> *Mysterious and unknown.*

Day 30   BENEFITS OF AFFLICTION - REMIND US OF FORMER MERCIES. We had the sentence of death in ourselves that we should not trust in ourselves, but in God who raises the dead, who delivers us from so great a death, and does deliver, in whom we trust that God will yet deliver us. PAUL.

> *God's love in times past forbids me to think*
> *God will leave me in a trouble to sink.*
> *Each sweet Ebenezer I have in review*
> *Confirms God's good pleasure to help me quite through.*
> *All trials and sorrows of Christians prepare*
> *For the rest that remains above.*
> *On earth tribulation awaits one, but there*
> *The smile of unchangeable love.*

Day 31   AFFLICTION SUCCEEDED BY GLORY. Our light affliction which is but for a moment works for us a far more exceeding and eternal weight of glory. PAUL.

> *According to Your gracious story, in meek humility,*
> *This will I do, my dying Jesus, I will remember thee.*
> *Your body, broken for my sake, my bread from heaven shall be*
> *Your testament I will take, and thus remember thee.*
> *When to the cross, I turn my eyes. And rest on Calvary,*
> *O Lamb of God, my sacrifice, I must remember thee.*

SEPTEMBER

Day 1   TEMPTATIONS PERMITTED BY GOD. The Familyhead said to the Challenger, "Look. All that Job has is in Your power. Only upon himself put not forth your hand." JOB.

> *Still Your integrity holds fast*
> *The tempter's counsel spurn.*
> *Hope against hope, and God at last*
> *Will for Your help return.*
> *My crimes, though great do not surpass*
> *The power and glory of Your grace.*
> *Oh! Wash my soul from every sin*
> *And make my guilty conscience clean.*

Day 2   GOD DOES NOT TEMPT TO UNWITNESS. Let no one say when tempted, "I am tempted by God." God cannot be tempted with evil. Neither does God tempt any one. Even so everyone is tempted when drawn away by thoughts of lust and enticed. JAMES.

> *Abide with me! Fast fall the eventide.*
> *The darkness deepens, Jesus with me abide.*
> *When other helpers fail and comforts flee*
> *Help of the helpless, Oh abide with me!*
> *Hold the cross before my closing eyes.*
> *Shine through the gloom and point me to the skies.*
> *God's morning breaks and earth's vain shadows flee.*
> *In death as life, Jesus, abide with me.*

Day 3   TEMPTATIONS - FROM THE CHALLENGER. (Beware) Lest the Challenger should get an advantage of us. We are not ignorant of the Challenger's devices. PAUL.

> To rule by hate and vengeance is not our practice here.
> If a person's repentant, they're saved by love not fear.
> If one is lost a loving hand shows them with joy our happy
> land. Here peace and mercy govern.
> By love alone we live.

Day 4   TEMPTATIONS - FROM A DEPRAVED NATURE. I find then a law, that, when I would do good, evil is present in me. PAUL.
> Oh, who can free my troubled mind
> From sin's oppressive load?
> O wretched one! how shall I find
> Acceptance with my God.
> My soul with transport turns to You,
> To You my Savior turns.
> Cleansed by the blood, and saved by grace,
> My Soul No Longer Mourns.

Day 5   TEMPTATIONS - FROM THE LOVE OF RICHES. Those who want to be rich fall into temptation and a snare, and into many foolish and hurtful lusts which drown folk in destruction and perdition. TIMOTHY.
> Oh, lay not up upon this earth
> Your hopes, your joys, your treasure. Here sorrow
> clouds the pilgrim's path,
> And blights each opening pleasure.
> All, all below must fade and die,
> The dearest hopes we cherish,
> Scenes touched with brightest radiancy,
> Are all decreed to perish.

Day 6   TEMPTATIONS - FROM THE FEAR OF FOLK. The fear of humanity brings a snare but anyone who puts trust in the Familyhead shall be safe. PROVERBS.
> The taunts and frowns of folk of earth
> What are they all to me!
> Oh, they are things of little worth,
> Weighed with one smile to me.
> You bore a sorrow deeper far
> Than all these stingless trifles are.

Day 7   TEMPTATION TO NEGLECT GOOD WORKS. You did run well. How were you hindered that you did not obey the truth? PAUL.
> Jerusalem, my happy home.
> My soul still pants for you.
> When shall my labors have an end
> In joy, and peace, and truth?
> When shall the everlasting doors
> The saints receive?
> Join with angel powers,
> In glorious joy to live?
> Far from a world of grief and sin,
> Let us with God eternally shut in.

Day 8   TEMPTATION TO PROVOKE HISTORY. Are you so foolish? Having begun in the Spirit, are you now made perfect in the flesh? PAUL.
> Any who try to be -
> Without authority try to be -

Like God who is alone
And needs no earthly home -
Yes, any who try to be
Like God are downthrown
Into destruction whether me,
My nation, or period of history
Like my own.Go, you that rest upon the law,

Day 9 TEMPTATION TO FORMALITY IN RELIGION. Be watchful, and strengthen the things which remain that are ready to die. I have not found your works perfect before God. REVELATION.
God is a Spirit just and wise.
God sees our inmost mind.
In vain to God's Homeland we raise our cries
And leave our souls behind.
Let us praise God with immortal praise,
For the love that crowns our days.

Day 10 TEMPTATION TO SLOTHFULNESS IN RELIGION. Nevertheless, I have something against you. You left Your first love. Remember therefore from where you have fallen, and repent, and do the first works. REVELATION.
I need the influence of Your grace
To speed me in the way,
Lest I should loiter in my pace,
Or turn my feet astray.
Better that we had never known
The way to God's Homeland through saving grace
Than basely in our lives disown,
And slight and mock You to Your face.

Day 11 TEMPTATION TO SELF-INDULGENCE. I keep within my body and bring it into subjection let that by any means when I have preached to others, I myself should be a castaway. PAUL.
When the statutes I forsake,
When my graces I deplore,
When my covenant I break
Jesus, then remember Yours.
Check my wanderings
By a look of love divine.

Day 12 TEMPTATION TO TRIFLE WITH SIN. Shall we continue in sin, that grace may abound? God forbid. How shall we, who are dead to sin, live any longer in it? PAUL.
Shall we go on to sin,
Because Your grace abounds?
Or crucify the Familyhead again
And open all God's wounds?
We will be slaves no more,
Since Jesus has made us free,
Has nailed our tyrants to the cross
And bought our liberty.

Day 13   TEMPTATION TO SPIRITUAL PRIDE. For who makes you to differ another? And what have you that you did not receive? Now if you didn't receive it, why do you glory as if you hadn't received it? PAUL.

> *Often have I turned my eyes within,*
> *And brought to mind some latent sin,*
> *But pride, the vice I most detest*
> *Still lurks securely in my breast.*
> *Their feet are in a slippery place.*
> *Their riches swift as shadows fly.*
> *Their honors end in deep disgrace.*
> *In mirth they live, in anguish die.*

Day 14   TEMPTATION TO ENVY THE WICKED. As for me, my feet were almost gone. My steps had almost slipped. I was envious at the foolish when I saw the prosperity of the wicked. PSALMS.

> *Beneath the form of outward rite,*
> *Your supper God is spread,*
> *In every quiet upper room,*
> *Where fainting souls are fed.*
> *The bread is always consecrate*
> *That fried divides with friend.*
> *Each act of true community*
> *Repeats the act again.*

Day 15   TEMPTATION TO MISTRUST PROVIDENCE. If God so clothes the grass of the field which is there today and tomorrow is cast into an oven, will he not much more clothe you, Oh you of little faith? MATTHEW.

> *I know not what may soon betide*
> *Or how my wants shall be supplied,*
>   *But Jesus knows, and will provide.*
> *When creature comforts fade and die,*
> *Worldlings may weep - but why should I?*
>   *Jesus still lives, and still is nigh?*

Day 16   TEMPTATION TO DESPAIR. I sink in deep mire, where there is no standing. I am come into deep waters where the floods overflow me. I am weary of my crying. My throat is dried. My eyes fail while I wait for my God. PSALMS.

> *Prostrate before Your mercy-seat,*
> *I cannot if I would despair.*
> *None ever perished at Your feet*
> *And I would lie forever there.*
> *Savior, Your dying love,*
> *You freely gave though not due.*
> *Kindnesses are foreshadows of*
> *The nothing I withhold from You.*

Day 17   TEMPTATION HUMBLES THE BELIEVER. So that I should not be exalted above measure through the abundance of the revelations, there was given to me a thorn in the flesh, the messenger of the Challenger to buffet me, so that I should not know exaltation above measure. PAUL.

> *What though a thorn my bosom bears,*
> *And varied are the wants and cares,*
> *That mark my checkered way!*
> *My God has said, in whom I live*

> *"My grace is yours, and strength I give*
> *According to your day."*

Day 18   TEMPTATION TO BE RESISTED. For we wrestle not against flesh and blood, but against principalities, against powers, against the rulers of the darkness of this world, against spiritual wickedness in high places. PAUL.

> *O Master let me walk with You*
> *In lowly paths of service true.*
> *Help me the dutiful strain to bear*
> *That gives me to live a life of care.*
> *Then from strength to strength go on!*
> *Wrestle, and fight, and pray!*
> *Tread all the powers of darkness down!*
> *Win the well-fought day!*

Day 19   TEMPTATION TO BE AVOIDED. Do not enter the path of the wicked and go not in the way of evil person. Avoid it, pass not by it, turn from it, and pass away. PROVERBS.

> *A wicked world and wicked heart*
> *With the Challenger are combined.*
> *Each acts a too successful part*
> *In harassing my mind.*
> *But fighting in my Savior's strength,*
> *Though mighty are my foes,*
> *I shall a conqueror be at length*
> *Over all that can oppose.*

Day 20   TEMPTATION AVOIDED BY WATCHFULNESS AND PRAYER. Watch and pray so that you do not enter into temptation. MATTHEW.

> *Go to dark Gethsemane,*
> *You that feel the tempter's power.*
> *Your Redeemer's conflict see,*
> *Watch with God one bitter hour.*
> *Turn not from Jesus's grieves away*
> *Learn of Jesus's love to pray.*

Day 21   TEMPTATION OVERCOME BY FAITH. Above all, take the shield of faith through which you will be able to quench all the fiery darts of the wicked. PAUL.

> *Let faith exert its conquering power,*
> *Say in Your tempted, trembling hour,*
> *"My God, my Parent, save Your child!"*
> *It's heard - and all your fears are nil.*
> *The Godly warrior - see such stand*
> *In the whole armor of God?*
> *The Spirit's sword is in the hand*
> *And feet with gospel shod.*

Day 22   BELIEVER ARMED AGAINST TEMPTATION. Take to you the whole armor of God, that you may be able to withstand in the evil day, and having done all, to stand. PAUL.

> *Out of plenty summer pours,*
> *Autumn's rich overflowing stores.*
> *Flocks that whiten all the plain,*
> *Yellow sheaves of ripened grain.*
> *As the prospering Hand has blessed*

May we give You of our best.
And in thanks of bounteous joy
Let Your praise our tongues employ.

Day 23   PRESERVATION FROM TEMPTATION. Because you have kept the word of my patience, I also will keep you from the hour of temptation. REVELATION.
Thus preserved from the Challenger's wiles,
Safe from dangers, free from fears,
May I live upon Your smiles
Till the promised hour appears
     When the Children of God shall prove
     All their Parent's boundless love.

Day 24   PRESERVATION IN TEMPTATION. Blessed is the one who endures temptation. When this one is tried, the reward shall be the crown of life which the Familyhead has promised to those that love God. JAMES.
When anything shall tempt my soul to stray
From God's Homeland's wisdom's narrow way
To shun the precept's holy light
Or quit my hold on Jesus's might,
May the one who felt temptation's power
Still guard me in that dangerous hour.

Day 25   DELIVERANCE FROM TEMPTATION. The Familyhead knows how to deliver the Godly out of temptations. PETER.
What though fierce and strong temptations
Press around you on the way,
And your sinful inclinations
Often cause you great dismay!
Look to Jesus.
You through God shall gain the day!

Day 26   THE FAMILYHEAD, THE STRENGTH OF THE TEMPTED. My grace is sufficient for you. My strength is made perfect in weakness. PAUL.
Why should I fear the darkest hour,
Or tremble at the tempter's power!
     Jesus vouchsafes to be my tower.
Though hot the fight, why quit the field?
Why must I either fear or yield,
     Since Jesus is my mighty shield.
Touched with a sympathy within,
     Jesus knows our feeble frame.
Jesus knows what sore temptations mean
     For Jesus felt the same.

Day 27   JESUS'S SYMPATHY WITH THE TEMPTED. In that Jesus has suffered being tempted, Jesus is able to succor those that are tempted. HEBREWS.
In haunts of wretchedness and need
On shadowed thresholds fraught with fears
From paths where hide the lures of greed
We catch the vision of Your tears.
From tender childhood's helplessness,
From human grief and burdened toil,
From famished souls, from sorrow's view,
Your heart has never known recoil.

Day 28 JESUS'S INTERCESSION FOR THE TEMPTED. The Familyhead said, "Simon, Simon, look, The Challenger has a desire to have you so that he may sift you as wheat, but I have prayed for you, that your faith does not fail." LUKE. [QUOTING A SAYING OF JESUS]

> *Though faint my prayers, and cold my love,*
> *My steadfast hope shall not remove,*
> *While Jesus intercedes above.*
> *Against me earth and hell combine.*
> *But on my side is power Divine.*
> *Jesus is all, and Jesus is mine.*

Day 29 THE FAMILYHEAD'S PRAYER FOR THE TEMPTED. Lead us not into temptation, but deliver us from evil. MATTHEW. [QUOTING A PRAYER TAUGHT BY JESUS]

> *Protect us in the dangerous hour*
> *And from the wily tempter's power.*
> *Familyhead, make our spirits true,*
> *And if temptation should assail*
> *May mighty grace over all prevail*
> *And lead our hearts to You.*

Day 30 FREEDOM FROM TEMPTATION IN GOD'S HOMELAND. To one who overcomes, will I grant to sit with me in my throne, even as I also overcame, and am set down with my Parent on God's throne. REVELATION.

> *Though temptations now attend you,*
> *And you tread the thorny road.*
> *God's right hand shall still defend you.*
> *Soon Jesus will take you home to God.*
> *   Full deliverance -*
> *You shall have in God's Homeland above.*

OCTOBER

Day 1 DUTY OF RETROSPECTION. You shall remember all the way which the Familyhead, your God, led you these forty years in the wilderness, to humble you, and to prove you, to know what was in your heart, whether you would keep God's commandments. DEUTERONOMY.

> *Thus far the Familyhead has led me on,*
> *And made God's truth and mercy known.*
> *While I tread this desert land,*
> *God's Spirit is searching my own.*
> *So lift you your heads, mighty gates.*
> *Behold the glorious ruler waits.*
> *The Sovereign one is drawing near,*
> *The Savior of the world is here.*

Day 2 OF THE DIVINE HELP. Then Samuel took a stone, and set it between Mizpeh and Shen, and called the name of it Ebenezer, saying, "Up to now, the Familyhead has helped us."

> *Here I raise my Ebenezer,*
> *Here, by your help, I'm come,*
> *And I hope, by Your good pleasure*
> *Safely to arrive at Jerusalem.*
> *So come, our Savior, enter in,*

Let new and nobler life begin!
Your Breathing Spirit guide us on,
Until the glorious crown be won!

Day 3   OF THE DIVINE GUIDANCE. Who am I, Oh God? And what is my house that you have brought me here? And this was yet a small thing in Your sight, Oh My Familyhead God. SAMUEL.

Rendered safe by God's protection,
I shall pass the watery waste.
Trusting to God's wise direction,
I shall gain the port at last.
And with wonder,
Think on toils and dangers past.

Day 4   OF THE DIVINE FAITHFULNESS. You have dealt well with your servant, Oh God, according to Your word. PSALMS.

Since first the maze of life I trod,
Have You not hedged about my way?
My worldly vain designs withstood,
And robbed my passions of their prey?
Three times happy loss to sue,
My happiness is alone in you.

Day 5   OF THE DIVINE FORBEARANCE. It is by the Familyhead's mercies that we are not consumed because God's compassions don't fail. They are new every morning. Great is Your faithfulness. LAMENTATIONS.

Lift up to God the voice of praise,
Whose goodness, passing thought,
Loads every minute as it flies
With benefits unsought.
And fulfill we now the great commission
To heal the sick and preach the word,
Let us not neglect our mission
And the gospel go unheard.

Day 6   OF DIVINE MERCY. God has not dealt with us after our sins. God has not rewarded us according to our iniquities. PSALMS.

God has with a piteous eye
Looked upon our misery.
Let us then with gladsome mind,
Praise our God for God is kind.
God's mercies shall endure,
Ever faithful, ever sure.

Day 7   OF DIVINE COUNSEL AND INSTRUCTION. I will bless the Familyhead who has given me counsel. My reins also instruct me in the night seasons. PSALMS.

Sure the Familyhead has brought me,
By watchful tender care.
Sure, it's God has taught me
How to seek God's face in prayer.
After so much mercy past
Will God give me up at last?

Day 8   OF DIVINE PROMISES FULFILLED. You know in all your hearts and in all your souls, that not one thing has failed of all the good things which the

Familyhead, your God, spoke concerning you. All are come to pass to you, and not one thing has failed. JOSHUA.

> *In all my ways Your hand I own.*
> *Your ruling providence I know.*
> *Assist me still my course to run,*
> *And direct to you to go.*
> *Proclaim to every people, tongue, and nation,*
> *That God is love.*
> *God stooped to save a lost creation*
> *By sending a Child from above.*

Day 9 OF UNNUMBERED BLESSINGS. Many, O Familyhead my God, are Your wonderful works which you have done, and Your thoughts which are to us us-ward. They cannot be reckoned up in order to You. If I would declare and speak of them, they are more than can be numbered. PSALMS.

> *I've got peace like a river -*
> *A river through my soul.*
> *I've got joy like a fountain -*
> *A fountain in my soul.*
> *I've got love like an ocean -*
> *An ocean in my soul.*

Day 10 OF EARLY PIOUS INSTRUCTION. Continue in the things which you have learned and have been assured of, knowing of whom you have learned them. TIMOTHY.

> *Jesus, have You made me know Your ways?*
> *Conduct me in Your fear.*
> *Grant me such supplies of grace*
> *That I may persevere.*
> *For mercies countless as the sand*
> *Which daily I receive*
> *From Jesus, my Redeemer's hand*
> *My soul, what more to need?*

Day 11 OF THE NATURAL STATE. You who were sometimes alienated and enemies in your minds by wicked works, yet now has God reconciled. PAUL.

> *Plagued in a gulf of dark despair,*
> *We wretched sinners lay*
> *Without one cheerful beam of hope*
> *Or spark of glimmering day.*
> *Then came the Almighty King*
> *Our Parent glorious*
> *Over all victorious,*
> *Whose praises we sing.*

Day 12 OF THE LACK OF WITNESS FOR GOD IN HIS LIFE. How many are my iniquities and transgressions? Make me to know my failures to witness God. JOB.

> *My past transgressions pain me.*
> *Jesus, cleanse my heart within.*
> *Evermore restrain me*
> *From the presumptuousness of sin.*
> *So let my whole behavior,*
> *Thoughts, words, and actions prove,*
> *Oh God, my strength and Savior*

Acceptable to You.

Day 13 OF PAST UNPROFITABLENESS. For when you were the servants of sin, you were free from righteousness. What fruit had you then in those things that now cause you shame? PAUL.

> *Familyhead, I confess my numerous faults.*
> *How great my guilt has been!*
> *How foolish and vain were all my thoughts!*
> *All my life was sin!*
> *But now my faith looks up to the cross,*
> *There you took all my guilt away,*
> *And made my life no loss,*
> *But changed my night to day.*

Day 14 OF THE SEASON OF CONVERSION. Giving thanks to the Parent, who has made us meet to be partakers of the inheritance of the saints in light, who has delivered us from the power of darkness, and has translated us into the Homeland of the Child. PAUL.

> *Since the dear hour that brought me to Your foot*
> *And cut up all my follies by the root,*
> *I never trusted in an arm but Yours,*
> *Nor hoped but in Your righteousness outpoured.*
> *Cast at Your glorious feet, my only plea.*
> *This is what dependence means to me.*

Day 15 OF SPIRITUAL DELIVERANCE. Great is Your mercy toward me. You have delivered my soul from the lowest despair. PSALMS.

> *God pardoned my transgressions,*
> *Bade all my sorrows cease.*
> *And, in God's rich compassions,*
> *Restored my soul to peace.*
> *Have done with lesser thoughts,*
> *And serve with heart and soul.*
> *This life for you is bought*
> *Upon the cross, behold!*

Day 16 OF SPIRITUAL ENJOYMENTS. I sat down under God's shadow with great delight, and God's fruit was sweet to my taste. God brought me to the banqueting house and the banner over me was love. SONG OF SOLOMON.

> *Kindly God brought me to the place*
> *Where stands the banquet of God's grace.*
> *God saw me faint, and over my head*
> *The banner of God's love was spread.*
> *Live for Jesus a life that is true.*
> *Strive to please God in all that you do.*
> *Yield your allegiance glad hearted and free*
> *This is the pathway of blessing for me.*

Day 17 OF SUPPORT IN AFFLICTION. Unless Your law has been my delight, I would then have perished in my affliction. PSALMS.

> *God of my life, how good, how wise,*
> *Your judgments to my soul have been!*
> *They were but blessings in disguise,*
> *The painful remedies of sin.*
> *How different now Your ways appear,*

Most merciful, when most severe!

Day 18 OF ANSWERS TO PRAYER. I love the Familyhead because God heard my voice and my supplications. Because God has inclined an ear to me, therefore will I call upon God as long as I live. PSALMS.

> *"Are you able," said the Master,*
> *"To be crucified with Me?"*
> *"Yes," the sturdy dreamers answered,*
> *"To the death for we are free!"*
> *"Yes, we are able. Our spirits are stirred!*
> *Remould them, make them, like You, divine."*
> *"You are able," said the Good Shepherd,*
> *"Love and loyalty make you mine."*

Day 19 OF DELIVERANCE FROM ADVERSITY. I will be glad and rejoice in Your mercy. You have considered my trouble. You have known my soul in adversity. PSALMS.

> *Oh, magnify the Familyhead with me.*
> *Come, join God's name to bless.*
> *To God did I in trouble flee.*
> *God saved me from distress.*
> *Oh, let God then your refuge be,*
> *Nor shall you fail success.*

Day 20 OF DELIVERANCE FROM DANGER. You drew near in the day that I called upon You. You said, "Fear not." Oh, my Familyhead, You have pleaded the causes of my soul. You have redeemed my life. LAMENTATIONS.

> *Be all my added life employed*
> *Your image in my soul imbue.*
> *Fill with Yourself the might void.*
> *Enlarge my heart to compass You.*
> *Did ever trouble yet befall,*
> *And God refuse to hear Your call?*
> *And has God not every promise passed*
> *That You shall overcome at last?*

Day 21 OF DELIVERANCE FROM DEATH. Oh, my Familyhead, You have brought up my soul from the grave. You have kept me alive so that I should not go down to the pit. PSALMS.

> *Sunset and evening star,*
> *And one clear call for me.*
> *And may there be no moaning*
> *When I put out to sea.*
> *Twilight and evening bell,*
> *And after that the dark.*
> *And may there be no sadness of farewell,*
> *When I at last embark.*
> *For though the bourne of time and place*
> *The floods may bear me far,*
> *I expect to see my Pilot,*
> *When I have crossed the bar.*

Day 22 OF THE VANITY OF HUMAN LIFE. And Jacob said to Pharaoh, The days of the years of my pilgrimage are one hundred and thirty years. Few and evil have been the days of the years of my life. GENESIS.

This life's a dream, an empty show
But the bright world to which we go
Has joys substantial and sincere.
When can I awake and find me there?
Life now appears as a hallowed wraith,
It speaks! "Oh, you of little faith."
It is a form, the voice divine,
That fears for every heart, and mine.

Day 23 OF DEPARTED FRIENDS. I would not have you to be ignorant, brothers and sisters, concerning those who are asleep. Don't sorrow as do those without hope. We believe that Jesus died and rose again, even so those also who sleep in Jesus will God bring with Jesus. PAUL.

Though loved and lost, not ours the pang of those
Whose earth-born grief no heavenly balsam knows.
We would not call their spirits from their home
Where sin assails them not, and sorrow cannot come,
Where all their labors and trials are over,
And they are safe on that beautiful shore,
    So close to the Familyhead I adore.

Day 24 AGED BELIEVER'S RETROSPECT. Oh, God, You have taught me from my youth and before now I have declared Your wondrous works. Now also when I am old and greyheaded, Oh God, do not forsake me. PSALMS.

Still have my life new wonders seen
Repeated every year.
Behold, my days which yet remain,
I trust them to Your care.
    Friends are dead which I loved long ago,
    Joy like a river around them flows.
    Soon I will see a smile from the Familyhead I know.

Day 25 RETROSPECTION SHOULD LEAD TO GRATITUDE. What shall I render to the Familyhead for all God's benefits toward me? I will take the cup of salvation and call upon the name of the Familyhead. PSALMS.

When all Your mercies, Oh my God,
My rising soul surveys,
Transported with the view I'm lost
In wonder, love and praise.
Some bright morning, some glad morning,
When the sun is shining in the eternal sky,
That bright morning, that glad morning,
We shall see God's Harvester by and by.

Day 26 RETROSPECTION SHOULD LEAD TO SELF-EXAMINATION. I have considered the days of old, the years of ancient times. I call to remembrance my song in the night. I commune with my own heart. My spirit makes diligent search. PSALMS.

More about Jesus I would know.
More of God's saving fullness see.
More of God's grace to other's show.
More of God's love who died for me.
Help me, Oh my Familyhead, to try my heart,
To search with strictest care,
And all my thoughts, and words and ways

> *With the Gospel to compare.*

Day 27 RETROSPECTION SHOULD LEAD TO SELF-ABASEMENT. And Jacob said, "I am not worthy of the least of all Your mercies, and of all the truth, which You have showed to Your servant." GENESIS.

> *Unworthy, my Familyhead, of all*
> *Your mercies though we be,*
> *Yet for the greatest we may call.*
> *The greatest are most free.*
> *Your great lightning breaks our days.*
> *The earth trembles and sees*
> *The mountains melt at your ways*
> *And fire before you flees.*

Day 28 RETROSPECT SHOULD LEAD TO REPENTANCE. Surely it is right to be said to God, "I have borne chastisement. I will not offend any more. That which I see not teach me. If I have done iniquity, I will do it no more." JOB.

> *In thought, in will, in word and deed*
> *What evils I have piled,*
> *Against the God of grace and love*
> *God's Spirit and God's Child!*
> *Blessed Jesus, in You is refuge,*
> *Safety for my trembling soul,*
> *Power to lift my head when drooping*
> *Midst the angry billows' roll.*

Day 29 RETROSPECTION SHOULD LEAD TO AMENDMENT OF LIFE. I thought on my ways, and turned my feet to Your testimonies. I made haste, and never delayed to keep Your commandments. PSALMS.

> *You are my portion, Oh my God,*
> *As soon as I know Your way.*
> *My heart makes haste to obey Your word,*
> *And suffer no delay.*
> *Lead on Your cloud of presence,*
> *That leads us to our home,*
> *Through this life's wilderness*
> *Our lonely feet roam.*

Day 30 RETROSPECTION SHOULD LEAD TO CONFIDENCE IN GOD. Return to Your rest, Oh my soul. The Familyhead has dealt bountifully with You. You have delivered my soul from death, my eyes from tears, and my feet from falling. PSALMS.

> *The Familyhead loves those who hate evil*
> *And seek to live upright.*
> *No shame can set to bedevil*
> *One who lives a Godly life.*
> *For this, when future sorrows rise,*
> *To God will I direct my cries.*
> *For this, through all my future days,*
> *Adore God's name, and sing God's praise.*

Day 31 RETROSPECTION SHOULD LEAD TO BELIEF IN MIRACLES. Miracles are signs pointing to the presence of divine power in nature and history and they are in no way negations of natural laws. PAUL TILLICH.

> *Joy, You Goddess fair. immortal*

> *Attribute of God's Love,*
> *Mad with rapture, to the portal*
> *Of Your holy fame we come!*
> *Fashions laws, indeed, may sever,*
> *But Your magic joins again.*
> *All humanity are brothers and sisters ever*
> *Beneath Your mild and gentle reign.*

NOVEMBER

Day 1   BELIEVERS CONFIDENCE IN GOD. My times are in Your hand. Make Your face to shine upon Your servant. Save me for Your mercies' sake. PSALMS.
> *My times are in Your hand.*
> *My God, I wish them there.*
> *My life, my friends, my soul, I leave*
> *Entirely in Your care.*
> > *Under the blood my sin to atone*
> > *I have peace and my guilt is gone.*

Day 2   OF FUTURE SUPPORT. Trust in the Familyhead, and do good. So shall You dwell in the land and truthfully you shall be fed. PSALMS.
> *The birds outside the barn are fed*
> *From them let us learn to trust for our bread.*
> *God's saints what is fitting shall never be denied.*
> *So long as It's written, "The Familyhead will*
> > *provide."*
> *Jesus reigns wherever shines the sun,*
> *For God's love is spread from shore to shore,*
> *Wherever the sun's journey's run,*
> *Until moons shall wax and wane no more.*

Day 3   OF DELIVERANCE FROM TROUBLE. You, who have showed me great and sore troubles, shall anger and quicken me again, and shall bring me up again from the depths of the earth. PSALMS.
> *From every piercing sorrow*
> *That heaves our breast today,*
> *Or threatens us tomorrow,*
> *Hope turns our eyes away*
> *On wings of faith ascending*
> *To see the land of light,*
> *And feel our sorrows ending*
> *In infinite delight.*

Day 4   OF BEING KEPT BY JESUS. I know whom I have believed, and am persuaded that Jesus is able to keep that which I have committed against that day. TIMOTHY.
> *Beneath God's smiles my heart has lived*
> *And part of heaven possessed,*
> *I thank God for the grace received*
> *And trust God for the rest.*
> *This is the hope that shall sustain me*
> *Till life's pilgrimage be past.*
> *Fears may vex, and troubles pain me.*
> *I shall reach my home at last.*

Day 5 OF COMPLETION OF THE WORK OF GRACE. I am confident of this very thing - that God who began a good work in you will perform it until the day of Jesus, the Familyhead. PAUL.

> *Fairest Jesus, ruler of all nations,*
> *O You who are of God, come down.*
> *You will I cherish in celebration*
> *My soul's glory, joy and crown.*
> *Fair are your pastures and woodlands*
> *Robed in the blooming garb of Spring.*
> *Fairer though is your Hand*
> *Which makes our souls to sing.*

Day 6 OF THE TRIUMPHS OF THE GOSPEL. God's name shall endure forever. God's name shall be continued as long as the sun and humanity shall be blessed in God. All nations shall call God blessed. PSALMS.

> *God will complete the work begun,*
> *God will God's own defend.*
> *God will give me strength my course to run*
> *And love me to the end.*
> *Our Familyhead, let the thought of that bright day*
> *Kindle our hopes, and warm our love.*
> *Cheer us while here on earth we pray,*
> *And crown our songs in Your Homeland above.*

Day 7 OF THE END OF GOD'S WARFARE. The time of my departure is at hand. I have fought a good fight. I have finished my course. I have kept the faith. TIMOTHY.

> *Oh, most delightful hour by folk*
> *Experienced here below,*
> *The hour that terminates life's poke*
> *Of conflict and of woe!*
> *We view the cross of our Savior's love*
> *Where Jesus died to set me free,*
> *And now the Savior with God's love*
> *Has pled the sinner's perfect plea.*

Day 8 OF VICTORY OVER THE CHALLENGER. The God of peace shall bruise the Challenger under your feet shortly. PAUL.

> *Now let my soul arise,*
> *And tread the tempter down.*
> *My Captain leads me forth*
> *To conquest and a crown.*
> *A feeble saint shall win the day,*
> *Though death and hell obstruct the way.*

Day 9 OF VICTORY OVER FAILURE TO WITNESS. Oh, wretched person that I am! Who shall deliver me from the body of this death? I thank God, through Jesus, the Familyhead. PAUL.

> *Now to the God of victory,*
> *Immortal thanks be paid,*
> *Who makes us conquerors while we die,*
> *Through Jesus our living Head.*
> *Jesus showed a loving heart*
> *That felt my deepest woe,*

> *And in my sorrows bears the part*
> *That none can bear below.*

Day 10   OF VICTORY OVER THE GRAVE. God will redeem my soul from the power of the grave. God shall receive me. PSALMS.

> *Jesus's is the name I love to hear,*
> *And recommend its worth,*
> *It is the music of my ears*
> *The sweetest name on earth.*
> *Through the name, till trumpet sound,*
> *Ages of silence I shall lie.*
> *Then from my earthly cell rebound,*
> *Glorious with Jesus in immortality.*

Day 11   OF THE CERTAINTY OF DEATH. When a few years are come, then I shall go the way where I shall not return. JOB.

> *Jesus walked alone the lonesome valley.*
> *Jesus walked it all alone.*
> *Jesus walked it alone for me*
> *Now I retrace its route home.*
> *Welcome, sweet hour of full discharge,*
> *That sets my longing soul at large,*
> *Unbinds my chains, breaks up my cell,*
> *And give me with God to dwell.*

Day 12   OF SUPPORT IN THE HOUR OF DEATH. Yes, though I walk through the valley of the shadow of death, I will fear no evil. You are with me. Your rod and Your staff they comfort me. PSALMS.

> *When the vale of death appears*
> *(Faint and cold this mortal clay.)*
> *Kind Forerunner, soothe my fears,*
> *Light me through the darksome way.*
> *Break the shadows!*
> *Usher in eternal day!*

Day 13   OF THE END OF THE WORLD. The day of the Familyhead will come as a thief in the night. Then the skies shall pass away with a great noise and the atoms shall melt with fervent heat. The earth also and the works that are within shall be burned up. PETER.

> *It's midnight and on Olive's brow*
> *The star is dimmed that lately shone.*
> *It's midnight in the garden now*
> *The suffering Savior prays alone.*
> *It's midnight and for others guilt*
> *The Life of Sorrow weeps in blood.*
> *Yet Jesus was not in anguish knealt*
> *Forsaken by Our God.*
> *It's midnight and from Homeland plains*
> *Is bourne a song that angels know.*
> *Unheard by mortals are the strains*
> *That gently sooth the Savior's woes.*

Day 14   OF THE JOYFUL RESURRECTION. I know that my Redeemer lives. I know that this one will stand at the last day upon the earth. Though after my skin worms destroy this body, yet in my flesh shall I see God. JOB.

> *Though worms may waste this withering clay,*
> *When flesh and spirit sever,*
> *My soul shall see eternal day*
> *And dwell with God forever.*
> *Be watchful! it comes - the day of wonder!*
> *Louder chorals shake the skies.*
> *Hell's gates are burst asunder.*
> *See the new born myriads rise!*

Day 15 OF THE COMING OF JESUS TO JUDGMENT. Look! Jesus comes on clouds. Every eye shall see Jesus and they also who pierced his mortal body. All the families of the earth shall wail because of him. REVELATION.
> *Great God! What do I see and hear!*
> *The end of things created.*
> *The Judge of humanity appears*
> *On clouds of glory seated.*
> *The trumpet sound. The graves restore*
> *The dead which they contained before.*
> *Prepare, my soul, to meet Jesus.*

Day 16 OF MEETING THE JUDGE. We must all appear before the judgment seat of Jesus. Everyone must receive the things done in her or his body, according to that which has been done, whether good or bad. PAUL.
> *Oh! on that day, that wrathful day,*
> *When humanity to judgment wakes from clay.*
> *Our Familyhead, be the trembling sinner's stay*
> *Though skies and earth shall pass away.*
> *When life is over and daylight is passed,*
> *In the Homeland's harbor my anchor is cast.*
> *When I see Jesus, my Savior at last,*
> *Then that will be sunrise for me.*

Day 17 OF ENTIRE ACQUITTAL. Who shall lay anything to the charge of God's elect? It is God that justifies. Who is God that condemns? It is Jesus that died. Yes, rather, it is Jesus risen again who is even now at the right hand of God who also makes intercession for us. PAUL.
> *Fear not the drum's earth-rending sound.*
> *Dread not the day of doom.*
> *Jesus is to be the Judge.*
> *The Savior's is the Courtroom.*
> *Justice is the murmur of the dove*
> *Against all challenge to take flight -*
> *Like the vigor of a wind of love*
> *A flame no wrong can fight.*

Day 18 OF PARTICIPATION IN THE JUDGMENT. Don't you know that the saints shall judge the world? PAUL.
> *See the Judge, our nature wearing,*
> *Clothed in majesty divine.*
> *You who long for God's appearing,*
> *Then shall say, "This God is mine."*
> *Gracious Savior,*
> *Own us in that day of Yours.*

Day 19   OF BEING PRESENTED FAULTLESS. To the one that is able to keep you from falling, and to present you faultless before the presence of God's glory with exceeding joy. JUDE.

> *What transport then shall fill my heart,*
> *When You my worthless name will own,*
> *When I shall see you as You are*
> *And know as I myself am known.*
> *When comes to the weary, blessed release,*
> *When upward we pass to God's Homeland of peace,*
> *When free from the woes that on earth we bear,*
> *We'll say, "Good-night" here, but "Good Morning" there.*

Day 20   OF AN INCORRUPTIBLE BODY. So when this corruptible shall have put on incorruption, and this mortal shall have put on immortality, then shall be brought to pass the saying that is written, "Death is swallowed up in victory!" PAUL.

> *Where then your triumph, Grave?*
> *And where your sting?*
> *O sullen Death?*
> *What terror do you bring?*
> *We burst your iron band, and soar on high -*
> *Glory to Jesus the Familyhead who brings us victory!*

Day 21   OF A GLORIOUS BODY. Who shall change our vile body, that it may be fashioned like God's glorious body, according to the working whereby God is able even to subdue all things unto God's self. PAUL.

> *My flesh shall slumber in the ground*
> *Till the last trumpet's joyful sound,*
> *Then burst the chains, with sweet surprise*
> *And in my Savior's image rise.*
> *Thus, Jesus, your servants will gather,*
> *Standing in Your risen power,*
> *Ready to worship in love together*
> *Knowing love is yours in every hour.*

Day 22   OF BEING WITH JESUS. To me to live is Jesus and to die is gain. I am in a strait between the two, having a desire to depart and to be with Jesus which is far better. PAUL.

> *It's best! It's infinitely best*
> *To go where storms never come,*
> *Where saints and angels, ever blessed,*
> *Dwell, and enjoy their heavenly home.*
> *Blessed be the tie that binds*
> *Our hearts in Christian love,*
> *That fellowship of kindred minds*
> *Is like to that above.*

Day 23   OF BEING EVER WITH JESUS. Then we who are alive and remain shall be caught up together with those in the clouds, to meet the Familyhead in the air, and so shall we ever be with the Familyhead. PAUL.

> *Jesus eye to eye we there shall see.*
> *Our face like God's shall shine.*
> *Oh, what a glorious company,*
> *When saints and angels join!*

> *Oh, who can tell what joy shall beam*
> *On all the ransomed race,*
> *When they shall join the hallowed strains*
> *And see the Savior's face.*

Day 24   OF REIGNING WITH JESUS. It is a faithful saying - If we are dead with Jesus, we shall also live Jesus. If we suffer, we shall also reign with Jesus. TIMOTHY.
> *Every upward may we move,*
> *Wafted on the wings of love,*
> *Looking when our Familyhead shall come,*
> *Longing, gasping after home!*
> *There may we with You remain*
> *Partners of Yours in endless reign.*

Day 25   OF BEING LIKE JESUS. Beloved, now are we the children of God, and it does not yet appear what we shall be. But we know that, when Jesus shall appear, we shall be likewise. We shall see Jesus in reality. JOHN.
> *On a hill far away stood an old rugged cross,*
> *The emblem of suffering and shame.*
> *And I love that old cross where the dearest and best,*
> *For a world of lost sinners was slain.*
> *Oh, that old rugged cross, so despised by the world,*
> *Has a wondrous attraction for me,*
> *For the dear Lamb of God left glory above*
> *To bear it to dark Calvary.*
> *To the old rugged cross, I will ever be true,*
> *It's shame and reproach gladly bear,*
> *Then God will call me one day to God's home far away*
> *Where God's glory forever I'll share.*

Day 26   OF GOD'S HOMELAND'S HABITATION. We know that if our earthly house of this tabernacle were dissolved, we have a building of God, a house not made with hands, eternal in God's Homeland. PAUL.
> *There is a home for weary souls,*
> *In sin and sorrow's pang,*
> *When tossed on life's tempestuous shoals*
> *Where storms arise, and ocean rolls,*
> *It's found above - in God's Homeland.*

Day 27   OF PERFECTION OF KNOWLEDGE IN GOD'S HOMELAND. Now we see through a glass darkly. But then face to face. Now I know in part. Then shall I know even as also I am known. PAUL.
> *As through a glass I dimly see*
> *The wonders of Your love.*
> *How little do I know of You,*
> *Or of the joys above?*
> *It's but in part I know Your will -*
> *I bless You for the sight -*
> *When will Your love the rest reveal*
> *In glory's clearer light?*

Day 28   OF A CROWN OF RIGHTEOUSNESS. Henceforth there is laid up for me a crown of righteousness, which the Familyhead, the righteous Judge, shall give me at that day. TIMOTHY.
> *God has laid up in the Homeland for me*

A crown that cannot fade.
The righteous Judge, in that great day,
Shall place it on my head.
Yet with these prospects full in sight,
I'll wait the signal for my flight.
While the service of You I pursue
I find God's Homeland in all I do.

Day 29 OF REUNION WITH GLORIFIED SPIRITS. What is our hope, or joy, or crown of rejoicing? Aren't even you in the presence of our Familyhead, Jesus, at God's coming? PAUL.

We soon shall joint the throng,
Their pleasures we shall share,
And sing the everlasting song
With all the ransomed there.
  Hallelujah!
We are on our way to God.

Day 30 BELIEVER'S ANTICIPATIONS - A CALL TO HOLINESS. Wherefore, beloved, seeing that you look for such things, be diligent that you may be found with Jesus in peace, without spot, and blameless. PETER.

The saints in God's presence receive
Their great and eternal bed.
With Jesus in God's Homeland they live.
They reign in the smile of the Familyhead.
This Familyhead was birthed in a cow's stall
With wise folk, and shepherds and all,
But high from God's Homeland a star did fall
The promise of salvation it did recall

DECEMBER

Day 1 FINAL BLESSEDNESS OF THE BELIEVER. Now being made free from sin, and become servants to God, you have your fruit to holiness, and the end everlasting life. For the wages of sin are death but the gift of God is eternal life through Jesus, our Familyhead. PAUL.

From You, my God, my joys shall rise
And run eternal rounds
Beyond the limits of the skies
And all created bounds.
You have redeemed our souls with blood
Have set the prisoners loose,
Have made us Presidents and Ministers to God,
And we shall reign with you.

Day 2 ETERNAL LIFE THE PURCHASE OF JESUS. Neither the blood of goats and calves, but by God's own blood, Jesus entered in once into the holy place, having obtained eternal redemption for us. HEBREWS.

Pardon and peace to dying folk
And endless life are give
By the rich blood that Jesus shed
Our souls are off to live.
Savior, draw my to Your side.
Songs of praises I would sing.

There would I in peace abide.
Praise and glorify my King.

Day 3 ETERNAL LIFE SECURED BY THE SPIRIT. The Spirit of God's Breathing promises the earnest money of our inheritance until the redemption of the purchased possession into the praise of God's glory. PAUL.

Do You not dwell in all the saints
And seal us to the Homeland?
When will you banish my complaints
About my earth-time errand?
Jesus, like a rose, bloom within my heart
So my life abroad
The beauties of Your truth impart
And the sweet fragrance of God.

Day 4 GOD'S HOMELAND - THE DESIRE OF THE SAINTS. While we are at home in the body, we are absent form the Familyhead. We are confident and willing rather to be absent form the body and to be present with Jesus. PAUL.

In the bright city I would dwell,
With that blessed church the Savior praise
And safe, redeemed from death and hell
Sit at God's feet through endless days.
Take the name of Jesus with you,
Child of sorrow and of woe!
It will joy and comfort give you,
Take it then wherever you go.

Day 5 GOD'S HOMELAND A REST. There remains a rest to the people of God. HEBREWS.

Oh! were shall rest be found
Rest for the weary soul?
Where vain the ocean-depths to sound
Or pierce to either pole.
Beyond this vale of tears,
There is a life above,
Unmeasured by the flight of years -
And all that life is love.

Day 6 GOD'S HOMELAND COMPARED TO A MARRIAGE SUPPER. Write, blessed are those who are called to the marriage supper of the Lamb. REVELATION.

"Worthy the Lamb!" aloud they cry,
"That brought us here to God."
In ceaseless hymns of praise they shout
The merits of God's blood.
Oh then shall the veil be removed
And round me Your brightness be poured.
I shall meet God whom absent I loved.
I shall see God whom unseen I adored!

Day 7 GOD'S HOMELAND, AN INHERITANCE. Jesus is the mediator of the new testament, that by means of death, for the redemption of the transgressions that were under the first testament, those that are called might receive the promise of eternal inheritance. HEBREWS.

There is my house and portion fair
My treasure and my heart are there

> *And my abiding home.*
> *For me my older siblings stay*
> *And angels beckon me away,*
> *But Jesus bids me come.*

Day 8   GOD'S HOMELAND AS A PLACE. I appoint to you a place of habitation, as my Parent has appointed one to me, that you may eat and drink at my table in my place. LUKE. [QUOTING A SAYING OF JESUS]

> *Clad in raiment pure and white,*
> *Victor-palms in every hand*
> *Through their great Redeemer's might*
> *More than conquerors they stand.*
> *Oh God! Oh Good beyond compare!*
> *If all Your meaner works are fair*
> *How glorious must that place of habitation view*
> *Where the redeemed shall dwell with you.*

Day 9   GOD'S HOMELAND IS PREPARED MANSIONS. In my Parent's house are many mansion. If it were not so, I would have told you. I go to prepare a place for you. JOHN. [QUOTING JESUS]

> *High yonder realms of light,*
> *Far above these lower skies,*
> *Fair and exquisitely bright,*
> *God's Homeland's unfading mansions rise.*
> *Glad within these blessed abodes,*
> *Dwell the enraptured saints above,*
> *Where no anxious care corrodes*
> *Happy in Immanuel's love.*

Day 10   GOD'S HOMELAND COMPARED TO PARADISE. Jesus said to him, "In truth I am telling you today you shall be with me in paradise." LUKE.

> *There is a land of pure delight,*
> *Where saints immortal reign,*
> *Infinite day excludes the night,*
> *And pleasures banish pain.*
> *There everlasting spring abides,*
> *And never-withering flowers.*
> *Death, like a narrow sea, divides*
> *This Homeland hand from ours.*

Day 11   GOD'S HOMELAND AS A STATE OF HOLINESS. There is no way anything defiled can enter into it, or anything that works abomination, or makes a lie. Those enter in who are in the Lamb's book of life. REVELATION.

> *Oh glorious hour! Oh blessed abode!*
> *I shall be near and like my God.*
> *And flesh and sin no more control*
> *The sacred pleasures of the soul.*
> *I'll trust the dear Parent who know what's best.*
> *I will be satisfied there.*
> *In yonder home there is a rest.*
> *Yes, I will be satisfied there.*

Day 12   GOD'S HOMELAND, A STATE OF HAPPINESS. You will show me the part of life. In your presence is fulness of joy. At the right hand there are pleasures forevermore. PSALMS.

The soul, from sin forever free,
Shall mourn its power no more.
But clothed in spotless purity
Redeeming love adore.
Love, in an ever-deepening tide,
Over all the plains above
Spreads, like a sea immensely wide --
For God is Love.

Day 13   GOD'S HOMELAND AS A STATE OF SERVICE. They serve God day and night in God's temple. The one that sits on the throne shall dwell among them. REVELATION.

And swift to do God's high behest
Each spirit wings its flight.
And virtue glows on every breast,
A gem of purest light.
I am happy in the service of the King.
I have peace that nothing else can bring.
Through the sunshine and shadow I can sing
For to his guiding hand I cling.

Day 14   NO SORROW IN GOD'S HOMELAND. God shall wipe away all tears from their eyes, and there shall be no more death, neither sorrow, nor crying, nor shall there be any more pain. The former things are passed away. REVELATION.

Joy and gladness banish sighs.
Perfect love dispels their fears.
And forever from their eyes
God shall wipe away all tears.
Earthly pleasures vainly call me.
God has broken every fetter.
Nothing worldly shall enthrall me
For my soul prefers God better.

Day 15   NO CURSE IN GOD'S HOMELAND. There shall be no more curse, but the throne of God and the Lamb shall be in it. REVELATION.

When we shall Jesus in glory meet,
Our utmost joys shall be complete.
When landed on that Homeland shore
Death and the curse shall be no more.
Nor needed is the shining moon,
Nor even the sun's bright ray.
Glory from the sacred throne
Spreads everlasting day.

Day 16   NO NIGHT IN GOD'S HOMELAND. There shall be no night there and they need no candle, nor light of the sun. The Familyhead, God, gives them light and they shall reign forever and ever. REVELATION.

Guide me, O You Great Jehovah,
Pilgrim through this barren land.
I am weak, but You are mighty,
Hold me with Your powerful hand.
Open now the crystal fountain,
Whence the healing waters flow.
Let the fiery cloudy pillar
Lead me all my life through.

> *When I tread the verge of Jordan,*
> *Bid my anxious fears subside.*
> *Bear me through the swelling current*
> *Lead me safe on Canaan's side.*

Day 17 NO DEATH IN GOD'S HOMELAND. They who shall be accounted worthy to obtain that world, and the resurrection from the dead, neither marry nor are given in marriage. Neither can they die anymore. They are equal to angels. LUKE.

> *There pain and sickness never come,*
> *And grief no more complains.*
> *Health triumphs in immortal bloom,*
> *And endless pleasure reigns.*
> *While the day is dying in the west,*
> *Wait and worship while the God of night*
> *Is touching the earth with rest*
> *And setting the evening lamps alight.*

Day 18 PRAISES OF GOD'S HOMELAND. They sang a new song, saying, "You were slain, and have redeemed us to God by Your blood out of every family, and tongue, and people and nation. REVELATION.

> *Hark! hark! the voice of ceaseless praise*
> *Around Jehovah's throne.*
> *Songs of celestial joy they raise,*
> *To mortal lips unknown.*
> *There's within my heart a melody*
> *Jesus whispers sweet and low,*
> *"Fear not for I am with you*
> *In all life's ebb and flow."*

Day 19 SOCIETY OF GOD'S HOMELAND. These are those who came out of great tribulation and have washed their robes and made them white in the blood of the Lamb. Therefore they are before the throne of God. REVELATION.

> *Our Familyhead came down to earth*
> *And was a baby born,*
> *And angel choirs sang with heavenly mirth*
> *On that fair Christmas morn.*
> *Let us, in love, with them unite*
> *And celebrate with the wind wild*
> *The birthday of the world's Delight,*
> *Our glorious Savior Child.*

Day 20 SAINTS WILL BE WITH GOD. God will dwell with them, and they shall be God's people, and God shall be with them and be their God. REVELATION.

> *I hear the bells for Christmas Day,*
> *Their old, familiar carols play,*
> *And wild and sweet, the words recall*
> *Peace on earth, good will to all.*
> *And ringing, singing on its way*
> *The world revolves from night to day*
> *A voice, a chime, a chant, a call,*
> *For peace on earth, good will to all.*

Day 21 SAINTS SHALL BE WITH JESUS. Parent, I will that they also, whom You have given me, be with me where I am. Let them behold my glory. JOHN. [QUOTING JESUS]

> *Oh, little town of Bethlehem,*
> *How still we see you lie*
> *Above the deep and dreamless sleep,*
> *The silent stars go by.*
> *Yet in your dark streets shine,*
> *The everlasting light,*
> *The hopes and fears of all the years*
> *Are met in you tonight.*
> *For Jesus was born of Mary*
> *And gathered all above,*
> *While mortals sleep, the angels keep*
> *Their watch of wondering love.*

Day 22 SAINTS SHALL INHERIT ALL THINGS. The one that overcomes shall inherit all things. I will be this one's God and this one will be my child. REVELATION.

> *Oh come, Oh come, Immanuel,*
> *And ransom captive Israel*
> *That mourns in lonely exile here*
> *Until the Child of God appear.*
> *Oh come, Desire of nations,*
> *Bind all peoples in one heart and mind.*
> *Bid envy, strife and quarrels cease.*
> *Fill the whole world with Homeland peace.*

Day 23 SAINTS SHALL BE PERFECT. You are come to the general assembly and church of the first-born which is written of as God's Homeland, and to God the Judge of all, and to the spirits of just persons made perfect. HEBREWS.

> *A life in God's Homeland! Oh what is this?*
> *The sum of all that faith believed -*
> *Fullness of joy, and perfect bliss*
> *Unseen - unfathomed - unconceived.*
> *In Bethlehem, how a rose prepares to bloom.*
> *From tender stem comes this rose I have in mind.*
> *The rose is God's love aright.*
> *Through Mary we behold the King of humankind.*

Day 24 SAINTS SHALL BE GLORIOUS IN APPEARANCE. Then shall the righteous shine forth as the sun in the Homeland of their Parent. MATTHEW.

> The Lamb is their light and their sun.
> Lo, by reflection they shine.
> With Jesus ineffably one,
> And bright in effulgence divine.
> Silent night, holy night,
> All is calm, all is bright.
> With the angels let us sing
> Alleluia to our King.

Day 25 GOD'S DAY OF CHILD BEARING. Oh Immanuel, our Ruler, and giver of the law, the people await your coming. Come and save us, O Familyhead. Oh morning star, you are the splendor of eternal life. You are the dawning sun,

the Sun of justice. Come and lead us out of the prison house the captives
who sit in darkness and in the shadow of death. ISAIAH.

> *Oh Morning Star, how fair and bright*
> *You shine with God's truth and light,*
> > *Aglow with grace and mercy.*
> *Come, shine on us, Oh heaven's sun,*
> *Our hearts to serve you Only.*
> *In Your one body let us be*
> *As living branches in a tree,*
> > *Your mercy warms and cheers us.*
> *Draw us near, rich in blessing,*
> *Rule with might with all possessing.*

Day 26 SAINTS SHALL BE PRESIDENTS AND MINISTERS TO GOD. You have made us to
our God Presidents and Ministers and we shall reign on the earth. REVELATION.

> *It came upon the midnight clear*
> *That glorious song of old*
> *From angels bending near the earth*
> *To touch their harps of gold.*
> *"Peace on the earth, good will to all,*
> *From God the All-gracious power."*
> *And now the days recall God's grace*
> *In the Child of a single hour.*

Day 27 JOYS OF GOD'S HOMELAND ARE SURE. Oh how great is Your goodness which
You have laid up for those who respect You. Look what you have built for
them that trust in You before the children of humanity. PSALMS.

> *Oh come all you faithful,*
> *Joyful and triumphant,*
> *Come to Bethlehem! Come and Behold the Child.*
> *Yes, God we greet You,*
> *Born this happy morning.*
> *Jesus in you we greet God's own flesh reconciled.*

Day 28 JOYS OF GOD'S HOMELAND ARE ABUNDANT. The Lamb who is in the middle
of the throne shall feed them and shall lead them to living fountains of
water. REVELATION.

> *Christians awake! Salute the happy morn,*
> *When the Savior of the world was born.*
> *Rise to adore the mystery of love*
> *Which hosts of angels chanted from above.*
> *God spoke and straightway the celestial choir*
> *In hymns of joy unknown before conspire.*
> *The praises of redeeming love they sang.*
> *And God's Homeland with alleluias rang.*

Day 29 JOYS OF GOD'S HOMELAND ARE SATISFYING. I will behold Your face in
righteousness. I shall be satisfied when I awake with Your likeness. PSALMS.

> *Once for us a Child was born,*
> *Joy and gladness bringing.*
> *Long ago on Christmas morn,*
> *Both God and folk were singing.*
> *Come you all and praise with sport*
> *The Child of God's own glory.*

The meaning of life we now report
In this Special Child's story.

Day 30 JOYS OF GOD'S HOMELAND ARE ETERNAL. The one that overs will I make a pillar in the temple of my God. This one shall no more out. REVELATION.
Ring out, wild bells, to the wild sky,
The flying cloud, the frosty light.
The year is dying in the night.
Ring out wild bells and let it die.
Ring out the old, ring in the new.
Ring happy bells across the snow.
Ring out all darkness where cold winds blow.
Ring in the Jesus that we knew.

Day 31 BELIEVERS TO WAIT FOR GOD'S HOMELAND. Blessed is one who waits, and comes to the thousand three hundred and five and thirty days. But go you your way till the end be. For you shall rest and stand in your lot at the end of the days. DANIEL.
Once again to its close comes a year full of days.
Joyful we sing of Your bountiful ways.
For the peace of our land, for abundance and cheer
Parent we thank You for life this past year.
Now a new year will dawn and its days are unknown.
Jesus be our guide, we shall not be alone.
May the Spirit of truth in our living appear.
Parent be with you throughout this new year.

A SPECIAL DAY WHENEVER IT MAY FALL

Easter RESURRECTION AND LIFE. We know that Jesus, being raised from the dead, will never die again. Death no longer has dominion. The death Jesus died, Jesus died to earthly grip, once for all, but the life Jesus lives, Jesus lives to God. So you also can consider yourselves dead to earthly grip and alive to God in our Familyhead, Jesus. PAUL.
Jesus, our Familyhead, has risen today.
All creations joins to say, Alleluia!
Raise your joys and triumphs high,
Ours the cross, the grave, the skies, Alleluia!
Soar we now where Jesus led.
Following our exalted Head, Alleluia!
Made like Jesus, so we rise,
Ours the cross, the grave, the skies, Alleluia!

THE ELDER ON THE AMERICAN FRONTIER

As American settlers moved within the continent from the coastal regions, settlements appeared in the valleys and ridges of Appalachia and into the lands beyond. It was a time of new beginnings and an opportunity to shake off the interminable quarrels and corruptions of former places of habitation. A new society required building carved out of a great wilderness of forest, plain, mountain and desert. Characteristic attitudes and values began to appear. Among these were absolute values such as the love of freedom, a respect for the individual, a pragmatic approach to problems, suspicion of intellectuals and a democratic spirit that was tolerant of the moral values of others.

The frontier elder untrained by monarchical church structures began to appear in the churches of this land of new opportunity. Such persons did not fear following the precepts or practices called for by the Witnesses to the life of Jesus. They dreamed of the union of all believers and the unity of the church everywhere, the conversion of the world to God's Child and the hope that soon would come the millennial age. The congregations in the wilderness neighborhoods elected such elders and they took upon themselves the special ministry of teaching, ruling, guarding, shepherding and leading in worship. Deacons managed the material and financial concerns of the church.

Elders ruled their congregations and took responsibility for points of Christian teaching and even behavior. One elder wrote the following: Bro. _____: We can't hire Bro. _____ to preach for us. Some of the members wants him, but we won't have no man what parts his hair in the middle. Very truly, _____-. Elders were known to rise to their feet during the courses of sermons to challenge the preacher on teachings. Many preachers developed a repertoire of a few sermons and after preaching them moved on to another congregation. Eventually, the educational level of the memberships of frontier churches grew and more educated preachers were needed. Thus began the opening of the colleges of America which generally preceded the founding of the current great public universities.

As the wealth of the Americas grew, the level of tolerance of others increased. Through immigration from abroad and through movements of peoples from farms and small towns to cities, America became a great melting pot of people of diverse ethnic and cultural backgrounds enjoying the savory richness of pluralism of life within the view of God's Child. Now the little one-room churches, or rather "neighborhood meeting houses," became more elaborate structures with carpets, choirs, organs, stained glass windows, pulpits, beautiful communion tables, candles, orders of worship, gowns for the minister and choir, Sunday school rooms, fellowship halls, steeples, bell towers, and locations on the most prominent streets of the town or city.

Now the elders of the churches take a more limited role leaving the leadership of the churches to the more democratically elected church boards under the leadership of settled preachers who preach polished sermons, lend dignity to formal orders of worship, lead meaningful marriage and funeral services, counsel the troubled in a wise and skillful way and represent the churches in the communities. It remains the elders however who generally preside over the Communion tables and invoke the Spirit of God's Breathing to enter the church congregation's place of worship.